Russian Wondertales

THE COMPLETE RUSSIAN FOLKTALE

❀ ❀ ❀

This splendid multivolume work will acquaint readers with a rich folktale tradition that has not been easily accessible or well known in the West.

In the first volume of the series, *An Introduction to the Russian Folktale*, Jack V. Haney discusses the origin, structure, and language of folktales; the "discovery" and collection of folktales; Russian tale-tellers and their audiences; the relationship of folktales to ritual life; and the major folktale types.

Compared to other European traditions, the East Slavs have an extremely large number of tale types. Using the Russian version of the Aarne-Thompson index to folktale types, and drawing on both archival and written sources dating back to the early sixteenth century, Haney has collected examples of the full range of Russian animal tales, wondertales, legends, and tales about everyday life. These tales are translated in the volumes of *The Complete Russian Folktale*.

THE·COMPLETE·RUSSIAN·FOLKTALE

Russian Wondertales

II. Tales of Magic and the Supernatural

Edited and Translated
with an
Introduction by
Jack V. Haney

M.E. Sharpe
Armonk, New York
London, England

Library of Congress Cataloging-in-Publication Data

The complete Russian folktale / Jack V. Haney.
p.   cm.
Includes bibliographical references.
Contents: v. 1. An introduction to the Russian folktale / by Jack V. Haney;
v. 2. Russian animal tales / edited by Jack V. Haney;
v. 3. Russian Wondertales I: Tales of Heroes and Villains / edited by Jack V. Haney;
v. 4. Russian Wondertales II: Tales of Magic and the Supernatural /
edited by Jack V. Haney
ISBN 1-56324-489-6 (v. 1 : alk. paper) — ISBN 1-56324-490-X (v. 2 : alk. paper)
ISBN 1-56324-491-8 (v. 3 : alk. paper) — ISBN 1-56324-492-6 (v. 4 : alk. paper)
1. Tales—Russia. 2. Russia (Federation)
I. Haney, Jack V.,   1940–   .
GR202.C645   1998
398.2'0947   dc21
98-30059

CIP

BM (c)   10   9   8   7   6   5   4   3   2   1

CONTENTS

v

CONTENTS ❂ vii

PREFACE

Volumes 3 and 4 of *The Complete Russian Folktale* are devoted to wondertales. Volume 1, *An Introduction to the Russian Folktale*, and Volume 2, *Russian Animal Tales*, appeared in 1999. Subsequent volumes will feature Russian legends, anecdotes, and tales of everyday life.

The aim of Volumes 3 and 4 is to present to the English-reading public at least one example of every type of wondertale known to have existed in the vast Russian folktale corpus.

I have received assistance from many friends and colleagues in the preparation of this volume. I am especially indebted to the Interlibrary Borrowing Division of the Henry Suzzallo Library of the University of Washington for locating and obtaining many rare collections of tales; to Dr. Michael Biggins of the library for his assistance in obtaining microform copies of tales from Russia; to A.A. Nikiforov of St. Petersburg, Russia, for permission to use materials from the archives of his late father, A.I. Nikiforov; to Aleksandr Finchenko and Tatiana Bogomazova of TASK, and especially to my friend Aleksandr Bobrov of the Russian Academy of Sciences, St. Petersburg. I also owe much to the enthusiasm and encouragement of many students at the University of Washington over the past quarter-century, some of whom provided early drafts of tales included in this volume. Again my wife, Barbara, has been extremely helpful in more ways than I can mention, and my son Andrew served too many times as my technical advisor when the word processor did not want to do what I thought it ought. They deserve my special gratitude.

TECHNICAL NOTE

Several tale-numbering systems are used in these volumes. This brief explanation is offered for the convenience of readers who are not already familiar with these conventions.

The tales that are translated in the successive volumes of *The Complete Russian Folktale* are numbered sequentially.

When making reference to a type of tale in general and not some specific rendition of it, I will cite an Aarne–Thompson (A–T) type number. This number is given in its Russian (SUS) version. Sometimes the tale-type number may be followed by a subscript, a Latin letter, and/or asterisks, indicating a particular variant or subclassification.

Reference to a specific rendition of a tale is to the printed collection (e.g., Onchukov 110). The tales collected by Afanas´ev have been published in a number of editions, but the tale number is always the same regardless of edition. Thus, Afanas´ev 363 invariably refers to "The Vampire." When a tale appears without an identifying number in a collection, reference is made to the pages in the edition (e.g., Korol´kova, p. 152, "Fenist the Bright Falcon," or Sokolov 1932:147–50, "How the Landlord Gave Birth to a Calf ").

When referring to a book or article in the text, I give the title in English; in the bibliography I cite the language of the original. The transliteration system used here is the Library of Congress system, with some simplifications to enhance readability. Variant spellings of some common names will be encountered in the forms used in the original texts. Thus, Koshchei, Kashchei, and Kashshei.

GLOSSARY

Ataman	headman, leader, especially in Southwest Russia and Ukraine
Batiushka	Father, used of Tsar and Priest
Bogatyr	warrior, especially in the epics (byliny)
Bylina	heroic epic
Chervonets	probably ten rubles
Dead and living waters	The former ends "chaos" and brings form, while the latter provides the life force.
Devichnik	pre-nuptial social occasion for bride and friends, equivalent to a shower
Esaul	Cossack captain
Grivennik	ten-kopeck coin
Gubernia	a large administrative unit in tsarist Russia
Gusli	traditional musical instrument resembling a small harp
Hegumen	head of an Orthodox monastery
Idolishche	giant, villain, hostile warrior, pagan warrior, in tales or heroic epics, in #151, a serpent
Kalin Bridge	the locus of fights between hero and villains, especially in A–T 300 and 301 tales
Kasha	porridge often made of buckwheat, staple of peasant life
Kokoshnik	headdress of North Russian married woman
Kupala	St. John's Eve
Kvass	slightly alcoholic brew made from stale rye bread
Lapti	bast boots or shoes
Leshii	forest spirit
Lubok	chapbook; a booklet made from bast, stripped from the inner bark of the lime tree
Makhorka	coarse tobacco, twisted

Matushka	priest's wife
Mizinets	little finger or toe. Amputated in ancient times in initiatory rites
Pertsovka	vodka flavored with hot peppers
Poezd	train; here, a Wedding Train, or procession
Pood	weight equivalent to thirty-three pounds
Postel'nichii	guardian of the nuptial chamber (chamberlain)
Sarafan	pinafore dress of peasant women
Sazhen'	length equivalent to 2.13 meters
Shchi	cabbage soup
Shirinka	embroidered towel or covering; part of a trousseau
Skazochnik	teller of folktales
Skomorokh	a jester, purveyor of pre-Christian lore, entertainer in Muscovite Russia
Skomoroshina	a text preserved in what is thought to be the style of the skomorokhs
Starosta	commune leader; a mayor
Station	postal station where horses were changed, meals served, and beds provided
Svad'ba	the peasant wedding, reflecting many pre-Christian customs and beliefs
Taiga	the vast forest zone of northern Russia and Siberia
Venchanie	the crowning or wreathing—a Christian wedding rite conducted by the priest
Venik	small bundle of dried leaves and branches used to "tease" the skin in the baths
Verst	length equivalent to 3,500 feet
Vodianoi	undersea or underwater spirit or deity
Volshebnaia skazka	wondertale
Wine/Vodka	used interchangeably in the tales for vodka
Wreathing	*see* Venchanie
Yurt	the round felt hut of the Mongols, a ger

INTRODUCTION

"Is maith sceal go dti sceal eile."
(A tale is good until another is told.)

Tales like those included in *The Complete Russian Folktale* under the rubric wondertales are popularly referred to in English as "fairy" tales, following the archaic use of the word *faerie*, which meant "enchanted." Certainly, there were never many fairies in the tales, although a number do involve some very peculiar characters as well as enchantments of various sorts. English scholars of the English tales still use the term fairy tale occasionally. Katharine Briggs, for example, justified her usage as being rooted in English tradition and let it go at that. The senior American student of the folktale, Stith Thompson, generally avoided the term in his influential *The Folktale*, referring instead to Tales of Magic, which are subsumed in his classificatory system under Ordinary Folktales, a concept he claims is covered by the German *Märchen*. If Thompson is consistent in distinguishing Tales of Magic, Animal Tales, and the many other sorts of folktales, other Americans are not. Jack Zipes's translations of the Grimms' tales were published as *The Complete Fairy Tales of the Brothers Grimm*, even though many of the tales in the collection are generally classified as animal tales, legends, or jokes, and not fairy tales.

In the volumes comprising *The Complete Russian Folktale* consistency has been maintained as far as possible. All the tales translated for the various volumes are folktales. They were thus told, and not composed in written form (which is not to say that some of them were not derived from written sources). They were oral, traditional, and popular. We do know who actually told some of the tales, as this information was sometimes recorded for preservation along with the tale itself. Occasionally we know that a tale has been incorporated into the Russian oral tradition from some other tradition, but in most cases we do not know by whom, or when, or how, a given tale was first told. This does not really matter. In pre-modern Russia a painting was never signed, all music before that time is anonymous (although we can guess), and only a very few literary texts are identified by author—and such attributions are often mere conjecture or wishful thinking on the part of subsequent readers. Even the architects of the great cathedrals are phantoms save in a few exceptional cases when an eyewitness recorded the name of the master builder. What distinguishes the folktales from these other types of anonymous artistic endeavor is that they have been preserved in the oral tradition, with all the vagaries implied by that. One can never know who first told a tale, and, indeed, the notion of authorship is generally regarded as irrelevant. In the Russian tradition tales are usually referred to by their collector's name: Sokolova, Afanas'ev, Onchukov. Occasionally, one will find reference to a tale told by a particular narrator: Korol'kova, Vinokurova, Novopol'tsev.

Aside from the most general categorization, folktale, four terms are used in English to classify the material collected here. In addition to the unfortunate "fairy tale," other terms are "tale of enchantment," "wondertale," and "tale of transformation." "Fairy tale" is not an appropriate term for the Russian tales in this grouping. Whatever a fairy is in folklore, it is not met in the Russian tradition.

"Tale of enchantment" probably comes closest to the Russian term, *volshebnaia skazka*. It is quite true that many of the Russian tales involve magic spells of various sorts, but by no means all do. The first great compiler of Russian folktales, A.N. Afanas'ev, intuitively ordered his many tales so that these tales came together after the animal tales, but he nonetheless gave them no special classification. Twentieth-century Russian editors and compilers almost universally use the term *volshebnaia skazka*, although popular editions are not so consistent.

The leading twentieth-century Russian scholar of the folktale, V.Ia. Propp, referred to the *volshebnaia skazka*, while at the same time arguing that the essential feature of the genre was a transformation that takes place in the tale. These transformations are of great interest. Russian scholars have established a large number of binary pairs, opposites, to which ancient Russian societies gave value, either positive or negative. The task in these folktales is for the hero/heroine to obey the rules of the world in which he/she finds himself/herself, thus obtaining the power to transform certain negative "baggage" into its positive opposite. Defeating a villain, gaining a wife, acquiring wealth, discovering privileged information, or undergoing the physical alterations that change a youth into an adult constitute some of these transformations. The binary pairs also provide the storyteller with structuring elements that serve as a shorthand between him and his savvy audience, for whom the tales are scarcely unfamiliar. Certain activities are associated with the hut in the forest; other activities always take place at the tsar's palace. It is because of this system of binary opposites, which seems to be part of the linguistic and psychological makeup of the Slavs from pre-historic times, that heroes and heroines invariably succeed against the greatest of odds. However, almost without exception, they return to society as changed individuals: transformation is the key to their success.

Finally there is the term "wondertale." It is certainly not as accurate as "tale of transformation" to describe what takes place in these tales, but it would seem to encompass something of the notions of enchantment and otherworldliness that most readers associate with the tales. I have therefore elected to use the term wondertales for these tales as it appears to be the most neutral of the four terms. Which tales are included here and in what order depends on their actual classification.

Classification

For nearly a century there has been a convention much used by folklorists to classify folktales. This system, which was inspired by the pioneering work on folktales of A.N. Afanas'ev, was first worked out by the Finnish scholar Antti Aarne, and then expanded and modified by an American, Stith Thompson. This Aarne–Thompson system (A–T) seeks to classify all folktales on the basis of perceived similarity of structure and coincidence of motifs. The system assigns numbers 1–300 to the animal tales (see Vol. 2 of *The Complete Russian Folktale*). A–T numbers 300–750 comprise the wondertales (of necessity they extend here over two volumes, Vol. 3 and Vol. 4). Legendary tales are classified 750–849, novellistic tales 859–999, tales about deceived or outwitted devils 1000–1199, and then anecdotes and jokes conclude the system, 1200–2400. (These will be covered in future volumes.)

The contemporary standard Russian index to the folktale, the *Comparative Index of Types. The East Slavic Folktale* (Barag et al. 1979), known by its Russian abbreviation SUS, catalogues only two hundred twenty-five types of wondertale, but some of these also have variants that are so different from the basic types as to warrant separate numbers, if the overall system had room for that. *The Complete Russian Folktale* includes two hundred fifty wondertales, reflecting some new additions to the SUS catalogue and a few tale types duplicated for reasons given in the commentaries. The commentaries will also indicate a number of tales not attested in any tradition other than Russian. It is to be noted that a Western index to tale types will not necessarily list all the types known in the Russian tradition. Unfortunately, no up-to-date composite index for the world's tales exists.

Within the category of folktales known as wondertales there are a number of subdivisions. The tales in the first three subdivisions (ranging over A–T numbers 300–499) may be thematically characterized as tales about heroes and villains. These appear in Volume 3 of *The Complete Russian Folktale.*

Tales numbered 300–399 in the A–T system feature supernatural adversaries such as serpents, ogres, giants, Death, or the Slavic prince of darkness, Koshchei. This is by far the most popular type of wondertale in the Russian tradition, as regards both the number of types and the number of recordings.

Tale types 400–459 are concerned with enchanted relatives, especially spouses. Here one will encounter tales about maidens released from otherworldly forms, the lovely story of Fenis the Bright Falcon, and maidens doomed to marry serpents, crayfish, or worms.

Tale types 460–499 are characterized by a strange, outlandish, most often otherworldly task that is set for the hero or heroine. One group of tales in this category, 480 and related forms, features stepsisters, one of whom the stepmother seeks to destroy but who returns unharmed and enriched while the stepmother's own ill-mannered child is destroyed. In a very fine version of this tale the test for manners involves sharing a meager meal with a mouse and then encountering a bear in wedding dances or a raucous round of blindman's bluff. The audience knows, if the modern English reader does not, that when the girl leaps from a bench into a pinafore (*sarafan*), she is performing a part of a pre-nuptial ritual still practiced in Russia. Even today in parts of Russia and Belarus, newlyweds may be referred to as bears. As for the game, it is still encountered at weddings in Russia (see Vol. 1:117).

In Volume 4 the emphasis shifts to magic, with four subdivisions of tale types (A–T nos. 500 to 750).

Tale types 500–559 are united by there being a helper whose assistance enables the hero to succeed where he otherwise might have failed. In the Russian tales dwarves are common helpers, but so are many animals, including the horse and the wolf. The Russian version of the well-known European story of Cinderella falls into this group, even if the helper is in fact a fish!

Quite closely related to the tales where a helper is of paramount importance are tales where the hero needs, or needs to acquire, a magic agent (560–649). Not infrequently these magic agents are phallic in nature, emphasizing the initiatory origins of many of the wondertales. Common among the agents are rings, sacks or bags, a fife for herding rabbits, a magic fiddle or flute, or various fruits.

Although there is a miscellaneous "catch-all" category (700–749), the final true grouping of wondertales (650–699) features the possession of magic powers or know-how. Ivan the Bear's Son simply does not know his own strength; several tales deal with hypnosis; a youth runs metaphorically not like a deer but having been actually transformed into one, or into a hare or a bird, as is appropriate. A boy interprets dreams; a maiden asks riddles; a poor peasant can understand the language of the animals and birds.

The A–T classification system would be a true work of genius if not for several drawbacks. The chief of these, and one that is universally agreed, is that very few actual renditions of tales consist of merely the one *sujet*, the one simple plot. One example of just such a simple tale is "Alionushka and Her Little Brother," A–T 450, in an early nineteenth-century version preserved by I.A. Khudiakov.[1]

From his first wife this peasant had these two children and once he undertook to marry again. He got married. And then his wife said, "Take your children away, wherever you like!"

So he agreed to take them off. He took them into the forest. "Go wherever you like, my children," he said, "and collect berries while I chop some wood." Then he made this wooden thing [that sounded like wood being chopped when the wind blew], and the children picked and picked their berries and they listened and listened. "No," they said, "our father is still chopping wood over there." It got late and they started calling him. They called and called, but they didn't find him. Their father had ridden off long ago, he had left them.

The sister took her brother by the hand and started leading him down the road. As they were going down the road, he said, "I want a drink!"

She said to him, "You can't drink from the wagon ruts (in the road where the wheels go) or else you'll become a wheel!"

So they walked on. They saw some goat hoof prints. "Sister, sister! I really want to drink!"

"Don't drink, brother, or you'll become a goat." But he drank his fill: he had really wanted that drink! And he became a goat. They went along together.

Some gentlemen were coming along the road. "Beautiful maiden! Where did you catch that goat?"

She said, "This is my brother." She told them all about it. So these gentlemen put her in their carriage with them and they put the goat on the running board. One of them brought her to his home and she was such a beauty that he married her. And then he went away somewhere.

But the servants took stones and put them in her pinafore and threw her in the pond. And one of the servants, a young girl, had a similar face, and she dressed in her clothing and pretended to be his wife. The master came back and she behaved around him as if she were his wife. And she prompted him to slaughter the goat because the servants were afraid the goat would tell everything. But the master wouldn't agree.

So the goat came and said, "Master, master! Let me go down to the pond to get a drink, to wash my guts!" And he let him go. So off he went and he shouted, "Alionushka, little sister! Come out to me, talk to me! They are sharpening their steel knives, they want to slaughter me, the goat."

"Oh, my brother Ivanushka! I can't come out to you. Fierce serpents are sucking at my breasts, a burning stone drags me to the bottom!" So then he went off home. And the next time he asked, he went to the pond again. And the third time, too. The master noticed it and went after him and heard it all. He dragged Alionushka out of the pond, and he tied the other girl to a horse's tail and ordered her scattered over the steppe.

Only a few Russian wondertales can be classified so simply, although none is as complicated as "The Fox and the Wolf" (tale no. 1 in Volume 2), which actually consists of eight A–T types strung together to constitute one tale. The Russian tradition does know, however, wondertales that have as many as four types: 302 + 554 + 518 + 552A. For example, the popular tale Maria Morevna begins with the death of Koshchei, followed by an episode where the young man spares the lives of various animals who help him fulfill some difficult tasks, after which some devils or other world spirits are defeated, and finally the hero's three brothers-in-law (all birds) rescue him from his last brush with death. Russian authorities classify this tale under the 552A category for reasons that are not necessarily clear. In a tale featuring a combination of several tale types, either one arbitrarily selects one type to identify the entire tale and ignores what the Russians call the "contaminants," or one might catalogue the tale under each of the four rubrics, which will make the system very unwieldy. For the most part I have selected one type to identify the tale, while also indicating the contaminants.

The Structure of the Wondertales

Anyone who has the opportunity to listen to an expert teller of folktales is soon aware of the structure of tales and the importance that structure has for the narration. Even very small children will quickly comprehend that structure and be able to replicate it. A.I. Nikiforov found that in the Russian North children as young as eight or nine could tell their own wondertales perfectly well although they were illiterate (Nikiforov 1961).

Two types of structure are important for the discussion here: structures that are part of the Russian oral tradition but not part of a given tale's syntax; and the wondertale's syntax as such.

Many observers have noted that the language of folklore as inherited from the ancient oral tradition contains much that is remembered, learned from a previous generation or another performer and then incorporated into an artist's own language and performance. Outside its specific context the language of the wondertales becomes cliché ridden. In the English tradition, "Once upon a time, in a far-off land" is just such an opening formula and is a cliché, as is the traditional "And they lived happily ever after." So, too, are such phrases as "the big, bad wolf" or "the deep, dark forest." The Russian tradition knows its own elaborate formulae, including "In the thrice-nine tsardom, in the thrice-ten land, there lived and dwelt a tsar," or the humorous ending formula to many a folktale concluding with a wedding: "I was there; I drank mead and beer; it ran through my moustaches and none got into my mouth." Originally this was not a very subtle hint that the narrator would like a drink for his efforts. In more modern times with women increasingly telling wondertales in Russia, their repetition of the formula shows the power of the tradition and suggests that the female narrator was more concerned about following it than about the literal meaning of what she was saying!

In between these epithetical beginnings and endings one finds the stock characters of the wondertales: wicked stepmothers and witches, handsome tsareviches and beautiful tsarevnas, crystal bridges, deep woods or forests, and the three-, six-, nine-, or even twelve-headed serpent just waiting for the hero to lop off those heads. In the Russian tradition whole utterances are connected with these stereotypical figures. There is a formula that will gain Ivan Tsarevich or Ivan the Peasant's Son access to the witch's hut, and it will be found in tales from the White Sea to the Lower Volga.

It is worth pointing out that these formulae are generally associated with situations in the tales and not with particular tale types. The reader will soon recognize them as he or she moves through the collections, and it will soon become clear that they are a major structuring device for the narrator as well as for the audience, eager to understand the course of events in the tale. Two tales in this collection, told by a mother and daughter, illustrate this clearly. They show the constant features within the tradition as well as the innovation that can take place. Reference is to tales 305 and 306. Tale no. 305 was told before 1915 to Mark Azadovskii by the fabled narrator Natal′ia Osipovna Vinokurova, an impoverished peasant from a tiny village on the Kulenga River, not far from Verkholensk, Yakutia. Tale no. 306 was recorded by L. Suprun from Raisa Egorovna Shemetova, the daughter of this same Vinokurova. Moreover, the two women tell the same tale, Siberian versions of a tale well known in the English-speaking world as "Prince Ivan and the Firebird" or "Ivan Tsarevich and the Gray Wolf."[2]

Vinokurova's tale bears evidence of *lubok* (chapbook) influence, as does Shemetova's, but apparently nothing is known of the exact source. Vinokurova's tale was first published in 1926; Shemetova's tales were published in 1974, posthumously. There is no question that Shemetova learned most if not all of her tales from her mother, but the published literature tells nothing more of the actual circumstances under which that took place.

The tale itself is not particularly common in the European Russian oral tradition. It is more frequently recorded in Siberia and is known in Ukrainian and Belarusian. Of the two versions included here, that of the mother (no. 305) is less artistically told. The episode of the middle brother's standing watch over the golden apple tree through the night is largely omitted, and it is not an error, for the narrator says, "In short, the same thing happened with Mitia." Her tale is noteworthy for the attention she pays to the psychological and physical states of the characters in the tale; they are much more than just the traditional figures in tales. Oddly enough, she seems very much attracted to the tsar, who is so distraught that he has given up eating and drinking on account of the theft of the apples. Shemetova's version is extremely similar. She does, it is true, fill in some parts of her mother's narrative that she may have felt were too sparse, restoring the second brother's vigil, for instance. Her true originality lies in the tale's ending, however, and here she creates something that I think is quite unique in Russian wondertales. The gray wolf has just delivered Ivan Tsarevich to his father's court and disappeared. Ivan Tsarevich appears at the court and is recognized by Elena the Beautiful, who pronounces him her future groom. But then Ivan Tsarevich holds up the wedding until his "dear guest" arrives, and that dear guest is none other than the gray wolf. The ending is drawn out by Shemetova's having the tsarevich beg his father to behave politely toward this guest when he arrives.

The gray wolf's arrival is spectacular: "They saw a troika of horses flying up, and a gold carriage. All the guests went out to welcome him. And in the golden carriage sat the gray wolf. The guests were frightened. 'Oh, what sort of guest is that?'" Of course, there are thousands of versions of the Russian wondertales, but this is the only one I have encountered where the hero's helper, the gray wolf, is an honored guest at his wedding! The function of the episode seems clear enough: to delay the conclusion of the tale and provide an element of surprise for the audience.

Any reader of wondertales will quickly note the propensity of wondertales to triplification. Tsarevich Ivan may be asked to herd Baba Yaga's horses three times. The unnamed girl of "The Swan-Geese" encounters three potential helpers. Serpents have heads in multiples of three. There are three places action may take place: in the forest, in the thrice-ten land, at the tsar's court. This fixation on threes is very characteristic of the Indo-European tradition as a whole and is deeply imbedded in the languages, mythologies, and social structures of all those peoples. What the tripling means is less certain. In the wondertales tripling plays at least four roles. It clearly is intended to protract the tale for the general pleasure of the audience. There is evidence from among the Russians that in the twentieth century a longer, more convoluted tale was prized more than the simple, straightforward one. Furthermore, within the oral tradition in general this kind of repetition permitted the teller of the tales to gather his thoughts. He had no notes of any kind and there were severe limits on his freedom to extemporize. At the same time, the triple repetition assured that the audience would grasp the meaning of the narrative. Finally, I suspect that favorite parts were repeated for the sheer joy of it, the jingles, rhymes, and songs especially.

The formal structural study of the Russian folktale, specifically the wondertales, is associated with Vladimir Propp, whose *Morphology of the Folktale* first appeared in 1928. Rarely has a scholarly book written by a Russian had such an impact on the rest of the world, an impact that goes beyond the study of the folktale to find applications in the study of Shakespeare or the French novel.

Despite its title, Propp's book is about the wondertales, and among wondertales he looks only at some of those in the three-volume edition of Afanas'ev. The originality of Propp's approach lies in his use of what he termed functions, and what are here called predicatives, to analyze a tale. Propp points out that there are a limited number of actions take place but those actions can be performed by a variety of actors in different tales. Only those predicatives that are connected to the hero of the tale are relevant to his study. Propp then argued that the predicatives invariably occur in the same order, and thus all Russian wondertales are of the same type. Variations in the tales come from there being different actors and different combinations of predicatives.

Propp identified thirty-one predicatives and only seven classes of actors in the wondertale.[3] The fact that many of the predicatives are found only in conjunction with one or another of the actors further limits the structural possibilities of the tale. Indeed, several of Propp's successors have argued that the original system consists largely of binary pairs that can be combined, thus reducing the number of possible functions nearly by half. Thus, there is no Russian tale where the pursuit of the hero is not followed by his rescue. A difficult task is invariably followed by its resolution by the hero. Propp's system can best be understood by applying it to an actual tale, in this case "The Swan Geese," no. 267 in this volume.

In Propp's notation this tale "reads"

$$A^1\ B^4\ C \Uparrow \quad \left\{ \begin{matrix} D^1\ E^1\ F^1 \\ d^7\ e^7\ f^9 \end{matrix} \right\} \quad G^4\ K^1 \Downarrow Pr^1\ Rs\ ^4_3$$

Which may be interpreted as: A^1 a kidnapping takes place, followed by an announcement of the misfortune in various forms, B^4. Then someone "consents" to Counteraction, C. The upward-pointing arrow means a departure. The sequence $D^1E^1F^1$ represents a testing sequence of the donor, whose main function is to provide the magic agent to the would-be hero who can pass the test, but in this tale the little girl fails the test three times and only at $d^7e^7f^9$ with the encounter with the hedgehog does she succeed. G^4 indicates that the route somewhere, in this tale to the hut of Baba Yaga, is shown to the hero. The K^1 means that the misfortune (the kidnapping) was liquidated by force or cunning. The downward arrow says there is a return, and the Pr, a Pursuit through the air, followed by a Rs, a rescue accompanied by concealment. This is among the simplest of tales, consisting of just one misfortune and its liquidation ($A^1 \sim K^1$). (I have ignored the initial part of the tale as it does little to show the overall structure.) (Propp 1969:86–89)

Many tales contain multiple misfortunes; three or four are not uncommon. The point is that each negative predicative is at some point neutralized by its opposite: a pursuit is followed by a rescue, something lost or stolen is followed by something found or recovered, and so to the end. The wondertales thus are defined by their binary structure, or what V.Ia. Propp has called "wondertale balance."

From the hero's departure in search of a bride or fortune to his return, he has either one or three encounters, and each of these consists of a series of predicatives that make up a test. In the fullest case, the hero will first encounter the wicked witch, Baba Yaga, who lives in the thrice-nine tsardom in her unforgettable little hut on cock's legs. The hero will be tested for his ability to follow instructions and/or demonstrate his command of social manners. He will pass all the tests, and after having been fed, given something to drink, and "steamed" in the bathhouse, he will typically be given some item that will enable him to succeed on his next testing ground. The exception will be when this single episode completes the tale. In "The Swan-Geese" what is lacking just at the beginning is the little boy, who has been kidnapped by the birds. The girl's testing along the way allows her to rescue her little brother, liquidating the lack, in Propp's terms, and to return home just in time for her reward: a bun from her parents or grandparents, in some versions of the tale. In many tales, however, there will be two further encounters (never just one more; the wondertale's balance does not permit that). In such tales the central episode involves the struggle with the villain, any sort of villain. The hero is invariably victorious, but he is never successful of his own accord. He will always need to make use of the magic agent he received from his tester in the first encounter. And if that encounter was in fact a test of manners and learning, the central test is one of arms. He must prove himself the fittest to mate with the tsarevna, for that is what the classical wondertales are about. Not all of these contests with the villain are tests of physical superiority. Some of them involve outwitting the enemy, often employing techniques that have little to do with the good manners or deportment our hero displayed at the hut of Baba Yaga.

But what if the hero defeats the ogre only to discover that the tsarevna not only does not wish to be rescued but that she is bent on mutilating him or even killing him? Russian tradition knows many such young ladies. Their peculiar behavior is to be explained only in conjunction with the final test, one that typically takes place "back at the palace" and concerns the recognition of the true tsarevich and the unmasking of any possible false heroes. When this test has been performed, there is little left to do: the hero weds the tsarevna, the tsar dies, and he is succeeded by the hero. The reluctance of the daughter is bound up in her knowledge that her marriage to the hero will lead to the death of her father.

There are many variants of this basic structure of the thirty-one predicatives clustered around one or three testing episodes; but, his detractors notwithstanding, Propp's system has done a great deal to shed light on the wondertales from many different points of view. I have selected a few new approaches that are based on Propp's work, namely those by Holbek, Meletinskii, and Bremond.

Among the critics, the Danish scholar Bengt Holbek has been one of the most positive, arguing that Propp's original analysis remains essentially valid even today (Holbek 1987; 1989). In general his concerns really need not detain us here, but his own work may be regarded as a continuation of Propp's thought to its next logical level. Holbek's approach is to combine Propp's analysis with the paradigmatic approach of the Canadian Elli Köngäs Maranda, which is based on three sets of binary oppositions (Maranda and Maranda 1971). These are sex, age, and social position, seen as oppositions between male and female, younger and older, low-born and high-born. From just these three sets of oppositions Köngäs Maranda proposed to define all the characters of the wondertales, and Holbek's research supports that contention.

The Köngäs Maranda argument differs from Propp's notably in that the Russian scholar defined his seven spheres of influence by reference to the predicatives he saw underlying the structure of the tale. Köngäs-Maranda's scheme is based on semantic notions. Holbek does a masterful job of employing these paradigmatic distinctions to define the roles of the actors in the wondertales. He notes that in tales where the hero is masculine, which can be defined as those where the impetus to action comes from a male character, the lead characters, as Holbek sees them, will inevitably be a low-born young male and a high-born young female, or LYM and HYF. The parents of a low-born male (LAM and LAF) will fill the tale role of donor. When the combination is LYM + LAF or LYF + LAM, then the relationship between the two tends to be friendly, although there may be sexual overtones. When both the young person and the parent are of the same sex, the relationship is usually hostile. When the tale deals with high-born parents (HAM and HAF), they are the guardians of their children (HYM and HYF), and they are frequently hostile toward low-born interlopers. Some tale types are identified precisely by the relationships among these eight character types.

Yet another way of looking at the structure of the wondertales was proposed by E.M. Meletinskii (1969). Meletinskii established that four criteria were sufficient to distinguish most wondertale types: the Object (a female, a magic agent, or none at all—if the hero is a victim or exile); the opposition Selfless or Selfish with regard to the hero; a "normal" family situation or one in which the hero is persecuted, perhaps by older brothers or a stepmother; and finally the mythological or non-mythological nature of the crucial testing sequence. The dragon-slaying types (A–T 300–303) are characterized by the quest for a female by a selfless hero from an unhappy family and a mythological test in the middle of the tale. They differ therefore from tales like "Tsarevich Ivan, the Firebird, and the Gray Wolf," only in that the object of the second group is not a female human being but a bird (the marriage to a princess is generally a reward for the hero's success). If there is no object sought and if the hero is selfish, the family an unhappy one, and a mythological world the nexus for the central test, then the stories are A–T 311, 312, 314, 327, stories featuring children in the clutches of cannibals and witches.

Meletinskii's proposal was to use his system to study the structure of all the wondertales. He thought that his formula (any particular combination of the four criteria mentioned here) might lead to a different understanding of the dynamics of the wondertale, but he himself never carried the study beyond the initial stages presented in his postscript to the 1969 edition of Propp's *Morphology of the Folktale* (Propp 1969:134–62). A fuller study of the tales along the lines proposed by Meletinskii might lead in the direction of recovering some of the basic myths that gave rise to the wondertales some centuries ago.

In 1977 the French folklorist Claude Bremond proposed quite a different approach to the structure of the wondertale, or fairy tale as he calls it. Bremond presented an "ethical model" holding that wondertales, with the "optimistic requirement of a happy ending" (1977:49), were structured such that deterioration leads to improvement in condition, merit to reward, and unworthiness to punishment. Thus the plight of the victim leads to an improvement in status; the villain is eventually punished while the hero receives his reward. Although Bremond's scheme appears to be applicable to the French tales, such a simplification of the materials in the Russian tradition runs the risk of obscuring the corpus of tales themselves.

There are no doubt other attempts to describe the structure of the wondertales, but the above have been the most widely accepted. It is worth noting that, despite its faults, the system proposed by Vladimir Propp is still widely recognized as valid.

The Age of Wondertales

No one contends that folktales are a modern phenomenon in human society. On the other hand, it is extremely difficult to prove that a given tale is of any great antiquity unless, of course, there is a written record of it. The evidence is strong that Aesop's fables are more than two thousand years old, and the Sanskrit *Panchatantra* is of similar antiquity. There is no evidence that wondertales are of such great antiquity. At this point it is important to stress that wondertales are not myths. They feature real people who, with assistance from a mysterious otherworld figure, perform quite outlandish actions, but these actions and the people who perform them are not part of any religious or mythic system. By and large the people who tell wondertales and their audience know full well that they are fictive. But the subject matter of the wondertales is extremely similar to that of the ancient myths of heroes who rescue maidens from dragons or other monsters; the plots are similar. The structures are similar, too. Writing his *Historical Roots of the Wondertale* (1946), Vladimir Propp was aware that the materials that make up the wondertales are in many instances extremely ancient and found throughout the entire world, but he was careful to refer to the "roots" of the wondertales without suggesting that the Russian wondertales were particularly old.

A major effort to answer the question was undertaken in 1989 by the European Folktale Society, which held a conference in Wilhelmsbad on the theme "How Old Are Our Folktales?" (see Oberfeld 1990). Rainer Wehse (1990) described efforts to date the tales to five thousand years ago through identification of elements of the tales with elements from archaic cultures, ancient rituals, and ancient beliefs. Many of these are in fact the common property of all human beings, but it seems that their significance within a culture may have altered enormously over such immense periods of time just as the actual elements may change.

Nevertheless, it can scarcely be denied that materials from prehistoric times are imbedded in the wondertales. Scholars such as Pierre Saintyves (1923) and Vladimir Propp (1946) amassed an enormous amount of material to prove this.[4] Although Propp's work appeared later, it seems that, probably because he was working in Stalinist Russia, he did not have access to much West European work, and he was forced to approach Saintyves from the ideologically approved position of his day. Propp's book is a logical continuation of his *Morphology of the Folktale*. In that book, which is to be read "action by action," the wondertale's structure is seen to reflect a young man's adventures after he departs from his parents' home (Propp ignored wondertales about young girls with one or two exceptions). He is tested three times before his reintegration into society takes place: at the little hut in the forest presided over by Baba Yaga, where his mental awareness is proved; either deep in the forest or beyond the thrice-nine tsardom in the thrice-ten tsardom of death, where his physical prowess is established; and finally at the court, where his sexual maturity is tested. Propp knew that the wondertales dealt with the preparations of a young man about sixteen years of age for a rite or rites of passage into manhood, in Russian a combination of puberty and initiation rites, and he also knew that many of those rites were still alive in one form or another in mid–twentieth-century Russia. They had been carefully described by the Russian ethnographers, some of whom had been Propp's teachers and others his colleagues and contemporaries.

It is too often assumed that by puberty only physical puberty is meant. With regard to the Russian wondertales, it is clear that the physical aspects of the process are of little consequence. As van Gennep pointed out nearly a century ago, this is the case with a great many societies, but, nevertheless, there has long been a tendency to confuse the physical attainment of puberty with initiation rites.[5] In the Russian experience the ritualistic moments in the wondertales may not only reflect rites contemporary to the telling of the tales; they also reflect rites of infancy and childhood. Thus, in the wondertale the hero may receive a new name. This is perhaps analogous to his receiving a new name at eight days old, and then a second in his teenage years, the pattern in many Russian villages even today.

Propp did not date the formation of the wondertales; that has been done by E.A. Tudorovskaia (1965) in a most interesting way. Tudorovskaia noted that the Russian wondertale knows but four kinds of hero and that each occurs in a distinct social milieu. The first of these she terms the archaic. These tales feature a total lack of conflict among humans. The hero acts for his human society as a whole in his struggle against the forces of nature as personified by such figures as Morozko (Frost), Vodianoi (Water spirit or god), or Baba Yaga, the Russian witch who was also guardian of the forest and its animals. Such stories as "Morozko" (A–T 480*B) and "About the Sea Tsar and Vasilisa the Most Wise" (A–T 313) clearly illustrate the type. Closely related are tales where the hero must obtain something of communal value, such as fire, from a hostile force, usually a witch. Perhaps the hero is sent into the dangerous forest to obtain fire and on the way he or she will encounter natural phenomena personified by men riding on horses of various colors. Alternatively, the hero must guard some precious object from an enemy intent on stealing it—in the tale "The Witch and the Sun's Sister," that very same fire (A–T 313J*). Typically in tales of the archaic type the hero does not actually fight his opponent. Rather, he flees, relying on trickery to succeed against the hostile forces of the natural world. The archaic tales are often set in the forest or some other untamed space, and not in the city. Some of them emphasize ancient rituals that are thought to have gone out of practice before the beginning of the Tatar–Mongol invasions of the thirteenth century. Thus, A–T 502 (see tale no. 281 in Vol. 4, "A Prince and His Uncle") describes the relationship between a young prince and his "uncle" or foster parent. This is not to say that vestiges of the practice of mentoring did not survive, but it was evidently highly institutionalized among the court nobles in ancient Russia.

The second group of tales features a hero in physical combat with a monster—a gigantic serpent with multiple heads, or the skeletal Koshchei, or perhaps an enemy known by name only and with little or no physical description. In these tales the hero tends to act alone and in his own interests. There is little sense of any social background unless one considers that the hero is often forced to right a wrong done to him. Tales such as "Tsarevich Ivan, the Firebird, and the Gray Wolf" (A–T 550) are good examples of this type. This second type of wondertale is often set at the royal court, where there is a tsar and the hero is most frequently a tsarevich. In none of the tales is there a grand prince or even duke (*[velikii] kniaz'*), the title used by the rulers of Kievan and Muscovite Rus to 1547. In that year Ivan IV (the Terrible) became the first tsar of the Russians. Tudorovskaia certainly does not suggest that all these wondertales were composed in the sixteenth century, but this does appear a likely time to begin looking for them, especially when one considers that it was precisely in the sixteenth century that the Christianization of the Russian peasantry reached its greatest intensity and this might have provided some impetus for the creation of different kinds of tales.

Family conflict dominates the third type of wondertales, according to Tudorovskaia. She argues that such tales could not appear in societies organized along clan lines. In these tales a single member of a family, most frequently a young girl, is persecuted by other members of the group, most frequently a stepmother. Many of the tales of the 480 type fit here, especially those dealing with the persecution of the "good" girl and the punishment of the "bad" or naughty stepsister.

The most recent wondertales, which comprise the fourth category, are very much about social conflict. In these tales the hero, often a soldier or a peasant, is socially inferior to the heroine. His opponent may well be an evil tsar, or perhaps a haughty tsarevna. The hero's task is made more difficult by the intervention of a supernatural force on the side of the opponent. The latter often ends up siding with the hero, however, tipping the balance in his favor. Within this group of tales Tudorovskaia would place those featuring a hero sent out to perform a task involving a class or social conflict, such as a farm laborer sent out to collect the rents from devils. Frequently the hero is an audacious young man with a handicap. He may be stupid, he may not be able to speak, he may be the third son in a society in which everything is inherited by the first son. The tasks set this young man may be the same as those given the tsarevich, but the world in which he operates is a more complex one. There may be social tensions, although there are no distinct social classes as a rule. This is the kind of world and the kind of hero that appeared in Muscovy in the second half of the seventeenth century, with high adventure and high jinks, the Russian picaresque, where a low-born young man could gamble with his life, win, and prosper.

A variant in this fourth and final stage in the development of the wondertales is focused on tradesmen or other gainfully occupied men. Occasionally these are merchants, or, more accurately, the sons of merchants. More frequently we find soldiers. The soldiers are no longer young; they have been away from their wives for a long time, and here we find a curious fact: they have just completed their term of service in the army, set by Catherine II at twenty-five years. Often their wives have taken other lovers and the plot centers on the soldier's attempts to win back his bride. Sometimes, however, the soldier deserts, is caught and beaten. He runs away again, to another land, one of milk and honey—or, more likely, strong drink.

As Tudorovskaia and others have noted, this fourth kind of tale stands closest to the novella and to the short story, which were to develop in Russia only from the later seventeenth century.

In conclusion, there is no direct evidence of the age of most Russian wondertales, but it is not too much to state that, although their roots may go very deeply into the past, the tales are products of later times. And in the end, a tale is only as old as its particular telling.

The Question of Analogues

The application of Vladimir Propp's structural morphology to folktales around the world established that wondertales are not found in every human culture. They have been found, however, from India and Iran in the east to Ireland and Iceland in the west. Was the distribution of the phenomenon of the wondertales to be explained by their having a common point of origin, by diffusion, or by some creative impulse embedded in the national psyches of many peoples? The existence of similar motifs among cultures geographically distant from each other might easily be explained, but the appearance of tales so structurally similar as to be indistinguishable is more difficult. In the nineteenth century many scholars in Europe and in Russia as well were convinced that the wondertales were all part of their Indo-European heritage, and indeed it cannot be denied that all languages descendant from ancient Indo-European today possess wondertales of a remarkable similarity. Yet the wondertales themselves, as I have pointed out above, cannot be said to be so very old, suggesting that the Indo-European theory is in need of adjustment.

One who rejected the theory of the Indo-Europeanists was the German scholar Theodor Benfey. Writing about the *Panchatantra* in 1859, Benfey insisted that the European folktale was overwhelmingly derived from India and Indian tradition and that it had fanned out from India through the Near East to Europe and from the Indian heartland eastward throughout Asia. The borrowing across linguistic lines was accomplished by traders and merchants, perhaps soldiers and even slaves, and took place over hundreds of years. In Russia such views were unattractive to those who saw the tales as products of a great Slavic past with a moral and spiritual authority far outshining anything to be found beyond Slavdom's borders. But for half a century or more Benfey's views were extremely prominent in West European thinking.

Early Russian folklorists were attracted to the writings of Wilhelm Grimm and his followers. As early as 1819 Grimm attempted to lay out his theory of the folktale, admitting the possibility of borrowing across national lines while at the same time arguing for the necessity of there being something deep within human cultures that produces time and time again similar narratives. All in all, Grimm advanced arguments that find many adherents even today, albeit in very different form. He argued for the existence of a large body of tales possessed by peoples of Indo-European origin and he also argued that folktales, particularly the wondertales, were in fact derived from discarded myths.

Looking back over the literature devoted to the folktale in the nineteenth century, one is tempted to regard Grimm's statements as among the sanest. Unfortunately, his notion that folktales were the product of diseased myths was particularly productive throughout European universities. Scholars of the "mythological school" found that the folktales, and by that they usually meant the wondertales, were really about astronomical, meteorological, and geographical phenomena dating back to ancient times when men feared and revered thunder, the sun, winds, and rain as gods and goddesses. The most prominent Russian "mythologist" was Aleksandr Afanas'ev, who as collector and compiler of the three-volume *Popular Russian Tales* may be regarded as Russia's equivalent to the Grimm brothers, while as compiler, editor, and author of *Poetic Views of the Slavs on Nature* he was the Russians' Sir James Frazer of *The Golden Bough* (Afanas'ev 1984; 1994). Afanas'ev's views and those associated with the "mythological school" are no longer regarded seriously but this is not to say that there is no relationship between myths of various kinds and some folktales.

An important trend in wondertale scholarship was inaugurated by the Belgian scholar Arnold van Gennep in 1922. Van Gennep was fascinated by the obvious relationship between rituals and the highly ritualized wondertales. Postulating the universality of certain rituals, which he termed rites of passage, van Gennep suspected that many of the analogous passages in wondertales could be explained by their derivation from rites of similar form, structure, and content. The relationship among concepts such as myth and ritual, tale and custom, is still discussed today, not least by Russian scholars.[6]

The problem of analogues and the interpretation of the tales inspired the psychological or psychoanalytical approaches to the folktale, also dating from the nineteenth century. Both Sigmund Freud and C.J. Jung employed wondertales in everything from dream analysis to the study of trauma. In recent times their work has continued in studies by Marie-Louise von Franz, Joseph Campbell, and Bruno Bettelheim, a number of which directly relate to the wondertale.[7]

Perhaps the best that one can say about the problem of the analogues is that there is no tidy solution. Unquestionably some of the plots of the wondertales are extremely ancient and may well derive from an Indo-European past. Others are obviously borrowed, either in ancient times or more recently, from travelers and traders who have visited Russia over many centuries. Yet others seem to have developed out of earlier versions and have come to reflect changes in the social milieu that told them and preserved them.

The Narrator and the Tale's Function

Although the evidence is inconclusive, it appears that in Russia it was the *skomorokhi* (discussed in Vol. 1) who carried the ancient pre-Christian beliefs through the centuries, and one of their vehicles was the wondertale. Certainly until the very end of the eighteenth century wondertales were mostly related by men; indeed, women as narrators of wondertales became common only in the twentieth century. The reasons for this are associated with the function of the tales and the original audience. The evidence suggests that in pre-modern times the tales were told primarily to older boys and young men in all-male audiences. Often these might be the fishing or hunting parties in the far north that lasted for weeks at a time. They were also told at weddings, during the winter holiday period after St. Nicholas's Day (6 December), or at various feasts. A fact connected to the association of the wondertales with magic and especially magic spells is the complete avoidance of the tales at certain times of the year, particularly in spring and summer, or before sundown. As I pointed out in Volume 1 (pp. 40–41), in pre-revolutionary Russia it was not uncommon for the gentry or landowners to employ professional tellers of tales, and several of the tsaritsas maintained them at court through the eighteenth century.

It seems likely that narrators of tales were trained by masters of the art. In the nineteenth and twentieth centuries much of this training took place at home, with women gradually taking over more and more of the narration. In this century parents and especially grandparents were the sources for tales. As a result the didactic elements in the wondertales were replaced by tales that were socially ambiguous, and thus telling the tales could become a public event.

Some of the storytellers were regarded as virtual magicians and their tales as magic. A number of tales make direct reference to this special regard with which stories and story telling were held, even in the twentieth century. One tale collected by Iurii and Boris Sokolov (Sokolovy 102) from the Belozersk (White Lake) region far north of Moscow[8] combines the ritualistic search for fire with a visit to a solitary old man wearing a fox fur trimmed with marten. The first two brothers fail because they cannot tell a story. In the excerpt below, from the tale "Fact and Fiction," the third one, Ivan Durachok (the Fool), succeeds and wins the old man's strange garments and strips of his hide to make a strap and a clasp. He returns to his father and brothers, who are lost in the woods, with the fire.

> The third son was Ivan Durachok, the Fool. "You go round there, Vania, and find out why they [the two older brothers] are so long."
>
> Ivan found the little hut. He went in and there sat the old man in his fox fur with the marten collar. He asked him for some fire: "Grandfather, give me some fire," he said.
>
> "I'll give you some fire if you can tell me fact and fiction, but if you don't do that, I'll cut a strap from your back and a clasp from your ass."
>
> "And if I tell you fact and fiction, grandfather, then I'll take your fox fur, cut a strap from your back, and a clasp from your ass.
>
> "Listen then. A father was walking with his three sons in the forest. They lost their way and could not find their way out to any dwellings. The father sent one of his sons to climb up a spruce tree to look for fire or some dwellings. He saw a little fire and set out after it. Now we are rich folk, we have lots of money. And we live well and we've got lots of money saved up. We've heard that overseas flies are expensive but cows are cheap. So I caught up a bag full of flies and set off overseas. I sold all the flies there and bought myself some cows. I herded them back to the sea. But the sea hadn't frozen. There was no way for me to herd the cows over it, but if I

tried to get them to swim, they'd drown. So I took and cut off a pine whorl and shoved it up a cow's ass. I turned it around in there and pulled out a lump of fat on it. I threw it into the sea along with a lot more. So then the sea got hard with the fat and I herded the cows across. There was just the bull left behind. I felt sorry for the bull so I went back over the sea, where I had been. A wind came up. It carried all the fat away. There was no way to drive that bull across. I grabbed hold of the bull by the tail and twisted it right around. Then I flung the bull and it flew right over the sea, and I didn't let go of the tail so I flew across behind him! So I herded the cows home because it was time to feed them. It was haying time. I cut the hay field and it was time to take it in. I made some oat kasha and spread it over the field. Then some ravens flew up and some hawks and began to eat the kasha. They took it to this one spot and with their talons brought all the hay into a stack.

"Then I went after the hay. I harnessed my horse, and loaded up the hay, and set off for home. My cart got stuck in a stream bed. I sent the horse on, but it couldn't budge it. So then I whipped the horse and cut it right in two! I took and skinned this horse, cut the hide into straps, tied one end to the cart and the other I dragged home. It reached to the threshing floor. I tied the other end to the threshing floor and set the threshing barn alight. As the threshing barn burned, the horsehide strap began to shrink and it pulled the cart toward the threshing floor. But then I sensed that the gods in heaven had no boots and I needed to sew them some. So I slaughtered all the cows, skinned them, and cut them out. I made myself a ladder and set off for heaven. I made a little hole and climbed out in heaven. I sewed boots for all the gods and I sewed some boots for all the minor gods. They gave me masses of money for it. So I set off back home. I came to the little hole but the ladder was gone and there was no way for me to get back down. A peasant was burning oats and his threshing floor had no sides to it. So the chaff was being carried right to me. I started grabbing this chaff to braid a rope. I twisted this rope together and let it down through the hole, but it didn't quite reach earth. A wind came up and carried some sand. I grabbed some of the sand and wove it into the rope. Then I grabbed hold of the sand and let down the rope. It reached to the ground and I started letting myself down by the rope. While I had hold of the chaff rope, it held me, but when I started going down with the sand rope, it broke and I fell into a swamp. I sank right into the muck. And then a duck came and she wove a nest right on my head, but then a wolf chanced by, intending to eat up the eggs. He ate an egg and then he started scratching his ass on my teeth. I knew that he'd come to eat the last egg. I stretched and stretched my arms out of the mud. The wolf came to eat the last egg, and when he'd eaten it, he started scratching his ass on my teeth. I grabbed him by the tail and yanked. The wolf leapt up in fright and dragged me out of the muck. I fell down on my knees and he took off running, I don't know where. So now, take off your fur coat, old man. I told you fact and fiction."

He took the fur coat off the old man, cut out a strap from his back and from his ass a clasp. Then he took some fire and set off to his father.

It is obvious that this tale is told in the manner of the medieval *skomoroshina*. The story is meant to be regarded as comic nonsense but it contains some deeply archaic materials that, in this case, have to do with the attitude of the Russian audience toward the tales themselves. The old man living alone in the woods, dressed in this strange garb of fox fur trimmed with marten, is the keeper of fire and apparently of other secrets as well. Many of the versions surviving in the Russian corpus feature the telling of stories in the woods in return for magic fire or a magic horse. A high percentage of these are wondertales. The final episode where the wolf pulls the lad out of a swamp is reminiscent of a very ancient theme. This "Cosmogonic Dive," as Mircea Eliade called it (1972:76–130), is known throughout most of the world. In many of the European versions a god forces an angel (or devil) to dive from heaven to the bottom of the sea and fetch up mud or earth from which the god proposes to create the earth. In the Russian variants a duck features prominently, sometimes even preceding the god and the devil in the story, although in other versions serving as the devil himself.

In A–T 552A the magic horse races away from the Russian witch:

Then he whinnied, stamped his legs and set off to catch up to Ivan Tsarevich. She got into her mortar and chased after him with her pestle. The horse got there first. "Well, Ivan Tsarevich, a rumor is spreading throughout the land that Yega Yegishna is after you. Wave your kerchief."

He waved the kerchief and a fiery river appeared. He managed to get away. "Now, where, Ivan Tsarevich? What is our destination?"

"We are headed for the ocean-sea. In the sea and in the ocean there is an oak, and beneath that oak is a trunk, and in the trunk is a hare, and in the hare a duck, and in the duck an egg. We must obtain that egg."

By the time he had managed to say all that, they had appeared there. The good horse tore out the oak and Ivan Tsarevich broke open the trunk. But the longears ran away into the forest. Suddenly out of nowhere appeared the bear—she had caught the hare and she brought it to him. So he killed the hare and took out the duck. He slaughtered the duck and took out the egg. He started rinsing it in the sea, but it slipped away. So the pike brought it back to him.

He wrapped it in his kerchief and said, "Now, take me to such and such a place."

He hadn't had time to turn about when he was there. Maria Marevna, the Princess with the Pouch, met him. There was no point in their talking at length, so they got on the horse and rode away. Kashshei the Immortal came flying after them.

"Where is Maria Marevna, the Princess with the Pouch?"

"Ivan Tsarevich has carried her away."

"Oh, those sons of bitches, those brothers-in-law have brought him to life. Go and ask my good horse when I need to set off to catch up to them."

His good horse said, "Quickly, get on and we'll see what we can do."

They chased after them, and [Ivan's] horse said, "Well, Ivan Tsarevich, only a little time remains. Kashshei the Immortal is nearby. It is time to hoist the egg."

As Kashshei came nearer, Ivan Tsarevich raised the egg, and Kashshei began to die. One brother horse said to the other, "Wait, stop!" But Ivan Tsarevich took the egg, got up, and crushed it. Kashshei fell from his horse. So Ivan Tsarevich burned him, scattered the ashes, he all went up in smoke, and our tale resolved itself with that.

This tale is an interesting variant of the Sokolovs' tale, but in this instance the "hero" of the story within the story falls from heaven into a swamp or pit of mud and he is stuck there. A duck comes along and builds her nest on top of his head. When a wolf steals the duck eggs, the hero manages to grab onto the wolf's tail and the wolf frees him from the swamp. The abrupt ending to this story suggests that there was a continuation, but other versions of the story are equally incomplete. Suffice it to say that in both stories there are echoes of a Slavic creation myth that involves a cosmic egg laid by a diving duck. That some of these wondertales contain equally ancient mythic materials in the guise of "mere stories" can scarcely be doubted.

The attitude of the narrator to his wondertales is not always easy to know. Certainly most of the twentieth-century tale tellers were unwilling to argue for the veracity of all aspects of their tales, but caveats were recorded. Some said that although incidents related in the tales were unlikely, nonetheless they had been told the tales by their grandparents, and "why would the old folks start fibbing?" (see Vol. 1:5–6). There is a sense in which the wondertales repeat the old verities, however. The girl will be tested for her kindness and thoughtfulness, and her ability to follow the traditional patterns of life. Her adversaries are all from the men's world, including the witch Baba Yaga and her lecherous male relatives. The hero must be willing to leave the comforts of home and mother and venture into the woods where he will be tested. He must dare to succeed, must remain alert and awake, and rely only on what he has earned the right to use. For the young men and women who succeed, the rewards are great. For the girls there is usually the wealth that becomes her dowry and thus her means to marriage. For the boy there is recognition as a man and status in the community (either as a married man or a landowner, or both). Both boys and girls will experience their being part of the natural world, which is not without its terrors, but they will find the whole series of encounters a necessary part of growing up.

In reading the Russian wondertales one soon becomes aware of the differences an accomplished narrator makes. In some wondertales there is a poetic diction, a grand manner of delivery, while in others the narrator seems keen to finish and go on to something else. Several tales are truncated. Either the narrator has forgotten the tale—for any number of reasons—or perhaps the narration has been interrupted by something from outside, such as a knock at the door!

The Actors in the Russian Wondertale

There are only a few classes of actors in the Russian wondertales. The only one who is absolutely essential is the hero or heroine, for the wondertale is utterly hero-centric. As Propp demonstrated in his work of 1928, and as others have reiterated, all actions in the wondertales take place in relation to the hero (Meletinskii et al. 1969:115–18). Frequently the hero will share much of the central act of the tale with an anti-hero, or, as Propp terms him, a false hero. In stories with a male hero one often encounters two older brothers who serve as the foil to the hero. Alternatively, a false hero might use a disguise and present himself as the hero at court, only to be unmasked in the nick of time. One of the more common tales, classified as A–T 480, features a heroine. In these, the heroine is the innocent young daughter of a widower who remarries. The stepmother seeks to destroy the girl while showering favors on her own, thoroughly spoiled, daughter. In these tales, the second girl is a polar opposite to the heroine, and, although she is confronted with all the same tests, she fails them miserably.

Because of his frequent appearance in the most popular wondertales, one might regard the tsarevich as the typical hero. He is certainly not the only hero, however. One encounters soldiers, fishermen and hunters, merchants' sons and peasants' sons, the sons of destitute widows, and the much-loved fool who prefers to occupy his time lying on the great Russian stove, swatting flies. There are some tales where the hero is juxtaposed to a cruel stepmother with magical powers. Social background is not the determining factor in these Russian wondertales. What these heroes all share is the quality of being underdogs. Each one must struggle through to win the rewards for success given at the end. The tsarevich's royal background is not necessarily an aid to him in his struggle with the nine-headed serpent. Nor is he the only hero who must confront a serpent or other fierce beast. Whether physically incapacitated or lazy, most of the heroes encounter such dangers and all of them succeed.

The number of tales featuring heroines is limited in the Russian tradition. My list numbers only twenty-six types versus about two hundred with heroes.[9] Nearly all of these heroine-centered tales are set in a broken family, most typically a daughter and her father, and a stepmother and her daughter. Alternatively, one encounters a number of stories with the theme of incest. A boy is "ordered" to marry his sister, or a father or uncle seems destined to marry the daughter or niece. Some of these stories tend toward the gruesome but in the end the heroine of course receives her reward. Often that is a dowry, a necessary prelude to marriage in old Russia, but sometimes she actually marries at the conclusion of the tale.

There is also the heroine who corresponds to the well-known maidens of western wondertales such as Rose Red, Snow White, or Sleeping Beauty. Although the narrator often builds the story around these attractive figures, analysis shows that the heroines really do very little in the tales to direct their own destiny. They serve primarily as the object of the hero's quest. In the Russian wondertales there are fewer such maidens than in the western wondertales and their characters are less vividly drawn, the narrative focus being on the young man. But still, Elena the Beautiful or Most Wise, Vasilisa the Beautiful or Most Wise, and Nastasia of the Golden Tresses are Russian maidens who fall into this heroine group. A maid such as Cinderella is different in that she is in dire need of rescue by the hero, but nonetheless she is in fact nothing more than the prince's object.

It is not necessary for there to be a villain in Russian wondertales. Indeed, one can be sure of encountering an honest-to-goodness villain only in tales with three testing sequences of the hero. The villain will always appear in the second test. Nor is there invariably only one villain or one kind of villain. Some villains are mythological figures embodying the terrifying forces of the natural world: frost and whirlwinds, for instance. Because of their roles as progenitors and potential mates, bears appear in the role, especially in tales featuring heroines. Wolves, oddly, do not. Their role in the wondertales is quite different.

Two villains stand out: the serpent and Koshchei the Deathless. The serpent was described by an informant (an eyewitness, no doubt) from Saratov: "He is black, with the girth of a barrel. He's two *sazhens* [four and a half meters] long, with an enormous human head. He sits on a curled-up tail and talks in a human voice but you can't understand him" (Vlasova 1995:153).

This serpent occasionally breathes fire, but certainly his most notable feature in the wondertales is his multiple heads—3, 6, 9, or even 12. The hero dispatches these in multiples of three and with consummate ease. Often he burns the corpse (as he will burn the skins of maidens transformed into swans by an evil force, or as his own frog skin will be burned to free him from a spell). Fire as a purgative is highly regarded by the Slavs and this explains its association with a number of rituals as well as its appearance in verbal texts (see above, "Fact and Fiction").

Serpents come in two varieties—male and female. If the serpent (not a dragon) is in pursuit of a tsarevna or princesses for amorous reasons, the hero will confront a male serpent. But occasionally the serpent protects a brood of little serpents, and the hero is in conflict with a female serpent. Here he often compromises and does not kill the serpent. The males are always killed, although not necessarily immediately.

The serpent is not without defenses. He or she threatens to devour the hero or pound him into the ground! It should be noted that neither of these catastrophes has ever taken place in a Russian wondertale.

The wondertales are associated with water (lakes or rivers) and with mountains, which appear in the tales just as they are in the heroic epics or *byliny*. They clearly fly but there is no mention of wings. Some of them have patronymics, usually Gorynich, which suggests fire, but they are not prominently fire-breathing serpents. Some serpents have sisters. These turn out to pursue the hero after he has killed the villain, thus retarding the narrative.

The hero has two potent weapons: his sword and his horse. With the sword he slices off the serpent's heads. His horse not only tramples little serpents, he also alerts the hero if he should fall asleep in the thrice-ten land of the dead, which is the abode of the serpent. Of course, the horse is also the most common vehicle to and from that ultimate testing ground. (Though not the only one: the wolf is a vehicle for the hero in a few stories, and there is one Siberian story in which the hero is transported across an enormous body of water by a beaver!)

Koshchei the Deathless is a more complicated figure. It is clear from the stories in which he figures as villain that he is a skeleton, that he flies, or perhaps he rides a flying horse that has only three legs, that he kidnaps women, and that the secret of his mortality is to be found "in a certain place [where] there stands an oak, and beneath the oak is a casket; in the casket is a hare, in the hare is a duck, in the duck is an egg, and in the egg is [my] death" (Afanas'ev 156; A–T 302_1 + 301). So on the one hand Koshchei is said to be a skeleton, but "without death," or *Bessmertnyi*, while at the same time his mortality is contained in a duck's egg. This peculiarity may in fact reflect widespread Russian, and Slavic in general, beliefs in the separate existence of the soul, beliefs that continue to the present time. The fact that, historically speaking, the image is derived from a pre-Christian creation myth and some equally ancient myths about a god of the underworld (*koshchiuny*) does not explain the figure of Koshchei in Russian wondertales.[10] Like the serpent, Koshchei is a composite villain, Death with some Russian twists.

The most familiar of the Russian otherworld figures is certainly the witch, Baba Yaga. Actually, there are a number of variants to her name. In the north she is commonly known as Yegibishna. Russian folklorists have identified her with an ancient goddess of death, while Propp argued that she was distantly related to the ancient Hindu mistress of the forest. She lives in a tiny hut on cock's legs deep in the thrice-nine forest. This hut is capable of turning around. The witch is a frightening apparition. She has one skeletal leg and the other is made of excrement. She is blind and lies on her cot or on the ninth brick of her stove with her long, pointed nose stuck in the ceiling. She propels herself through the air riding in a mortar with a pestle tucked between her legs and with her broom she sweeps away her traces. Like her English counterpart she has an acute sense of smell. At the approach of Ivan or Masha she will shriek "Phoo! Phoo! Phoo! It reeks of a Russian one!"

Masha and any little children are definitely in a dangerous situation. Many of the A–T 480 tales are replete with dismembered girls and small children, barrels of their blood and severed heads. Ivan, however, may well be frightened by Baba Yaga, but she does nothing more than threaten him. She is absolutely essential for the success of his quest, and, whether she likes it or not, she will end up aiding him. She is in fact the guardian to the thrice-ten kingdom, the kingdom of the dead, or the underworld. Thus, she presides over the youth's initiation into manhood, which is seen as a journey to the land of the dead and back.

There is another denizen of the forest who will guide the hero on his way. This is the Old Man, probably identical to the Leshii or forest spirit. His function in the tale is to give the raw youth instruction. In one Olonets tale the youth's father clearly states it. "I thought it over and then decided to give him [the youth] to grandfather Leshii to be taught." The Leshii is also clearly in charge of the forest and the creatures who live there. Sometimes he is accompanied by a pack of wolves. One story from the Vologda district tells of a Leshii who would occasionally drop into a wayside tavern, drink a bucket of vodka, and then continue on driving his pack of wolves down the forest track (Pomerantseva 1975:29). There are many references to the Leshii's substituting for the devil (or vice versa) in such curses as "May the forest spirit [lesnoi] take you!"

The Leshii appears in a number of forms. Sometimes he is a giant with stars for his eyes and as he walks he causes the wind to blow. But he can also be dwarf size, the size of a mushroom as one tale has it. One curious reference suggests that he is capable of inverse perspective: at a distance he is huge but up close he is small! He is always a hairy creature and sometimes his hair and beard are even "forest green." Another text insists that he is covered over with moss.

The Leshii is a shape-shifter, appearing as various birds of the forest, even a calf, and, most significantly, a bear, who, like the Leshii, is also regarded as the "tsar of the forest." Sometimes the Leshii is said to be married and even to have children. Of his wife it is said that she is a "fallen" maiden or a cursed woman, and his children are invariably cursed. Often they are the peasant children who have been stolen. One story tells of a village woman who is forced to attend the Leshii's wife during childbirth.

The Leshii lives in or near the forest, but sometimes he inhabits the swamps, while other times he has an enormous palace. He and his comrades, the serpents and beasts who live in the forest, celebrate 27 September as their festival day, and peasants traditionally avoided venturing into the forests on that day for fear of meeting them. Encounters with the Leshii are not thought to be fatal to the peasant, however. The Leshii are more likely to frighten human beings, or to cause them to lose their way. Fortunately, there are some sure ways to drive them away: prayer alternating with the "mother curse," and the application of salt and fire (Vlasova 1995:203–13).

The members of the older generation, the hero's or heroine's parents, play an important role in the wondertale, but it is invariably passive. As parents they often make an admonition to their son and then promptly die. The son is thus given impetus to depart on his quest. Sometimes when the tsar is the father and he is perplexed by a problem, he will send off his son or sons on a quest. This type of tale is unusual in that the hero will actually return to his ancestral home for the reward he then receives from a living father. In the majority of Russian tales the hero does not return to his own home but rather to that of the princess he rescues.

The social status of the parents makes little difference to the outcome of the tale. The hero is bound to succeed. Nor does marital status play any role. It appears that in cases where the aged parents are poor, they die almost simultaneously, and this is the case with the royal figures as well. In a large number of tales the hero's mother is a widow, and it is the hero's desire to alleviate the household's poverty that propels the hero into action. Mention has already been made of tales where a widower and his kind and beautiful daughter find themselves in a household with a nasty widow and her boorish daughter. In absolutely all such tales the kind daughter of the widower will succeed in her tasks and win rich rewards, while the boorish daughter of the widow fails at all tasks and is penalized, sometimes even with death.

If the hero encounters a parental figure at the end of the tale who is not in fact his own father, then this figure will always be the father of the bride and bestower of rewards on the successful hero.

This brief overview does not exhaust the personae of the wondertale by any means. One will meet such figures as "Nikto," equivalent to the unseen "Mr. Nobody" who hides keys, steals hot cookies while mother isn't looking, or perhaps drops a dish. Russian mythology knows the Domovoi or household spirit and Mr. Nikto is perhaps a mild, much reduced in stature, relative of that ubiquitous spirit, who is very much alive in Russia even today. A number of giants come to the aid of the hero: Storm Warrior (Buria-bogatyr´), Young Man of Steel (Bulat). And there is the nasty dwarf: the Thumb-Sized Man with the beard long enough to trip him up at just the right moment. The remarkable thing about the characters in the Russian wondertales is how little variation one encounters among the hundreds of tales from such a vast area.

What the Wondertales Might Mean

One should be wary of any attempt to characterize the Russian wondertales as a whole, but I would like to suggest that there are essentially three types, each with its own possible interpretation. In general, the meaning of each type is derived from its traditional function in the peasant society. Sometimes it is only certain particular features of a tale that allow us to classify it within an overall type and thus understand its meaning. For example, there is no question that all the tales belonging to the type A–T 480 are related by structure, but within that group one must differentiate between the ages of the female protagonists and the likely outcome of the story to arrive at a probable interpretation.

The first group of wondertales is small, consisting of tales that structurally resemble the classical wondertales with one major difference: the central characters are children and they undergo no transformation, without which the wondertale is really incomplete. These children's tales are perhaps best named *cautionary* tales. The outstanding example in this collection is A–T 480A*, "The Swan-Geese," no. 117, or "The Little Boy at the Witch's," no. 118. As in most wondertales, the story begins with an admonition given by the elders to the children. The little girl is to watch her little brother and guard him from harm. In wondertales the admonition is given only to be disregarded, and she is easily distracted and the little brother is soon carried away to the house of the evil witch. His guilty sister sets out to rescue him. Her arrogance makes it difficult for her to answer the riddles set her along the way and only a good deed permits her to find brother Ivashka. The return is more successful as she now answers the questions. But she returns no different than she was when she set off to right her failure to look after her little brother. The point of such tales seems twofold: to teach obedience and to warn against premature ventures into the woods.

In the second group of wondertales the chief actor in the tale is a girl of marriageable age. These tales provide information about the ritual life of young women in Old Russia: many of them deal with aspects of the peasant wedding, but certainly not all of them. Recall that in A–T 480A* (The Swan-Geese), the little girl is disobedient and pays for it dearly until she learns to respect the rules of the "natural world." Her punishment, however, is hardly of an enduring sort when compared to that of the older girls in group two. A related tale, A–T 480B* (Vasilisa the Beautiful), depicts a household where the fire has gone out and the teenage daughter, Vasilisa, is sent to fetch "new" fire, a ritual activity usually performed on the first of September. In the forest she encounters three horsemen, one dressed in white on a white horse, one dressed in red on a red horse, and one dressed in dark brown on a dark brown horse. Each warns Vasilisa not to persist in going to "the lout" (in some versions, Baba Yaga). She continues on and is ghoulishly murdered and eaten.

In the 480 category there are many tales in Russian in which there are a pair of stepsisters. In these tales only one of the pair is successful. They all feature the stepmother or mother sending two girls into the forest and a testing sequence that is the equivalent of the young boy's first test. His second (fight with the serpent, beast, or champion) and third (recognition as marriage partner) would be inappropriate for a young girl. Abandoned in the forest, the girls may be tested in their ability to make porridge, their kindness to a mouse, and their ability to play games with a bear (see Vol. 1:58–59). Failure to win will cost the girl her life. If she wins, she will have a successful wedding. Indeed, the girl often returns to her father and stepmother with a casket of gold, as fitting a dowry as could be imagined. (As for the bear, in many parts of Russia the bride and groom were actually known as the he-bear and she-bear.) Alternatively, the "nice" girl may be forced to descend into the underworld to fetch a lost object, frequently her spindle or something else associated with "women's work." In any case, she will be tested in several ways and then she will invariably receive a fine reward, often a chest of gold or money. She will eventually find her way back home, to the consternation of the stepmother. The latter will inevitably be envious of the rewards her stepdaughter has obtained and thus she will send her own daughter on the same quest. But the stepmother's daughter is rude and disobedient and she fails at every task. She may be eaten by a bear, burned by fire, or simply sent home in disgrace, but she receives no reward. Her well-behaved and mature stepsister may now marry, while the disgraced daughter never does. A clearer contrast could not be made.

And what of the stepmother? Her presence in so many wondertales can hardly be explained from the actual frequency with which stepmothers were encountered in the peasant life of Russia of any era. Nor, of course, are all stepmothers "wicked"! Indeed, the figure of the wicked stepmother is restricted in Russian folk tradition to the character of a very few wondertale types. Jacqueline Schechtman, who knew nothing of the Russian tales, recognized that the stepmother of the West European wondertale has nothing at all to do with real stepmothers (1993:xviii), but then she went on to find the archetypal "wicked" stepmother in feminine figures of loss and bereavement, especially loss of beauty that comes with aging. She sees the relationship between the "stepmother" and the "stepdaughter" in terms of sexual rivalry and economic instability between mother and natural daughter, with husband and father providing the point of the rivalry.

There is, I believe, another candidate who fits the paradigm of the wondertale stepmother: the mother-in-law. There is little doubt that well into the nineteenth century the bride's mother-in-law played a dominant and dominating role in her life. From the time when the future mother-in-law examined the prospective bride for her physical wholeness and haggled over the dowry, the mother-in-law made the decisions. If all went well and the weddings (church and traditional) took place, then the bride was expected to join her husband's mother's household. Here she would be treated as a very junior member of the kitchen staff, abused by her mother-in-law in far too many instances, and by her sisters-in-law as well. That was not her only concern. She had constantly to be alert for the predatory advances of her father-in-law, brothers-in-law, and uncles. This is attested to by many folktales and folk songs. If the wicked stepmother of the wondertale were in fact to represent the mother-in-law, then the message of these four hundred eighty tales becomes clear: obey the rules you encounter upon leaving your mother's house and you will enjoy success in your new life. Insist on following the rules of your traditional household and you are bound to fail in your new surroundings.

It is not surprising that flight or disappearance is a major concern in tales where girls are the chief actors. This is a theme also met in lyrical songs. It is usually connected with incest, which is a theme unknown in tales with masculine heroes. Three male figures are encountered: the girl's father, her uncle, and her brother. In her attempts to avoid "marriage" to the forbidden relative, the girl often disappears into the underworld. This then triggers the quest of the true hero. A good example is tale no. 177, "Prince Danila Govorila," A–T 327A. In some of these strange and unsettling tales the girl is unable to avoid marriage to the relative, even though she undertakes to disappear in some very ingenious ways. The meaning of the stories could not, in any case, be expressed more clearly.

Many of the western wondertales have undergone a shift in narrative focus from the hero to the beautiful but utterly incapable (and usually supine) maiden, and the English reader can be excused from failing to recognize the Russian analogues to familiar stories. The Russian equivalents of the popular Western wondertales are all here. "Cinderella" (Zamarashka, Zolushka) is 510A, "Snow White" is 709, "Beauty and the Beast" is 425C, and so on. Naturally, only the type is the same; the actual tale will vary in significant ways.

Although Russian wondertales do not end "and they lived happily ever after," as so many in the English tradition do, marriage is the goal of both the tales focusing on a teenaged girl and those focusing on a teenaged boy. There is ample evidence from the nineteenth and twentieth centuries that in the Russian village the process of growing up was regulated by social custom and ritual as far as possible. V.Ia. Propp could have found all the evidence right in the Russian countryside in support of his theory that the wondertales were derived from rituals, particularly those relating to puberty and marriage. This is therefore an appropriate moment to discuss the wedding rite or *svad'ba* as it took place in the nineteenth century, as aspects of it elucidate so many of the Russian wondertales in both groups two and three.

Although in the Muscovite period peasant weddings tended to be arranged affairs, as, of course, were those of the nobility and the court, in more modern times the boy and girl had considerable say in the final decision. Prior to actual courtship both young men and young women socialized primarily within groups of the same sex, groups in which the age ranged from early puberty to marriage. The older boys, especially, were charged with mentoring the younger boys in matters of social deportment. Social mixing of the sexes took place at holidays and on ritual occasions (Bernshtam 1998; Eremina 1991; Morozov 1998).

In nearly all regions of Russia females married earlier than males, often by three or four years. The peasant wedding was conducted over a rather long period of time, from several weeks to several months. When a young man and young woman decided to marry, female representatives from either side (the two mothers and typically two aunts) began the courtship rituals. The groom's party visited the prospective bride to ascertain the suitability of the bride—her physical health and economic well-being. As a result of this an agreement was drawn up and signed. The dowry was the major element in this. The date of the wedding was also agreed. This was not so difficult.

There were in fact few periods in the year when custom and the church allowed marriages. The period after St. Nicholas (6 December) was the most popular, but Shrovetide, Trinity, and All Saints days, Midsummer (Kupala, on 24 June), and St. Peter's (29 June) were also frequently chosen. Weddings during periods of church fasts or when there was heavy field work to be done were prohibited either by canon law or by local custom.

Once the date had been chosen, the bride began to prepare her trousseau and the groom to organize the *poezd* or train that would enact the major portions of the three-day ceremony. The girls gathered together to embroider the *shirinka*, hand towels or cloth, and to complete the *sarafan* and head dress that were obligatory in any wedding.

The groom's father usually provided horses for the *svad'ba*, the number depending on his economic status and the size of the wedding. The groom, now known as "young prince" or jocularly as "bear cub," would ride one horse, his best man a second, and there would be horses for his younger brothers, including cousins, and best friends. All this merry band was a survival from ancient days of bride stealing, but also a reflection of royal weddings.

Three days before the wedding, the "young princess" or "female bear cub" retired behind a curtain in her hut, dressed in sack cloth. From then until the beginning of the wedding she was considered to be dead, or in the underworld, undergoing the transformation from maiden to bride-to-be. She became a *nevesta*, unknown because dead. Her family and any guests referred to her in the past tense, and her girl friends sang the sad lamentations characteristic of the funeral.

The men appeared at a given time to "demand" the bedframe, and finally they all trooped into the bride's hut to purchase the bride, which they did for a pittance, and then there followed some ribaldry and play, usually involving the bride's youngest brother. The bedstead was taken to the groom's house, where in most cases he and the bride would begin their married life under the watchful eyes of his mother. There the groom's female relatives arranged the nuptial chamber. When all was ready, the room was sealed by the chamberlain (*postel'nichii*), often the groom's maternal uncle.

On the wedding day the young prince and his best man rode on their horses accompanied by a sleigh—regardless of the weather or season—to the bride's house. The sleigh figures in the earliest descriptions of weddings and funerals, from tenth- and eleventh-century sources. It was considered the ideal vehicle for rites of passage, which the wedding surely was. The bride, dressed in her best, with red, yellow, and green predominating, and accompanied by her own best man, and the groom rode to the church where they were married in the rite known as the *venchanie* or wreathing. There is evidence that this church ritual was performed at the insistence of the church and secular authorities and that the peasant youth regarded only the *svad'ba* as necessary.

For the rest of the day of the wedding the young prince and princess were feted, first at his house then at hers, dancing, eating, and drinking with friends and relatives alike. Finally, in the evening, the couple was led to the bed chamber, where the wedding was consummated and that fact announced to one and all.

The second day featured the ritual baths of both groom and bride, but separately. On this occasion it was customary for the groom to give presents to the bride, usually utensils associated either with the bath or with the kitchen and commonly of copper.

Finally, on the third day, both families feasted together and by the end of the day the wedding was over. With its mixture of modern and archaic elements, and with the rituals of the funeral thoroughly combined with those of the wedding, the Russian *svad'ba* was an extraordinary affair, one that in some places is still being performed at the beginning of the twenty-first century.[11]

The third group of wondertales, the most numerous, contains tales where the chief actor is a young man who is a bachelor or an older man who has been away from home for many (twenty-five) years in service to the tsar. When one compares the beginnings of the wondertales with their ends, one discovers that in most cases a traditional family situation has been disrupted, or soon will be disrupted, either by death or by some other loss. In the end an "unexpected" young man will have emerged to claim a bride, a tsar's throne and thus status, or riches. The beginning and the end are linked by the quest of that young man.

He sets off down a narrow path with no idea of his ultimate destination. In the course of his journey he will venture into a strange forest, often termed the "thrice-nine tsardom," cross some formidable barrier into the thrice-ten tsardom of Death, and eventually return to human society, although rarely to the one he left. There are, of course, many variations.

In "Maria Morevna" he merely sets off to visit his three married sisters and quite out of the blue he meets and marries a bride from the otherworld whose injunctions he cannot at first obey, thus setting the scene for his own journeys to the thrice-nine and then thrice-ten tsardoms. He loses his bride to Koshchei the Deathless on account of his own inability to carry out orders, and so must visit the forest of Baba Yaga in search of a mighty warhorse that will enable him to outwit Koshchei and rescue his wife, Maria Morevna. He has some highly suspect dealings with a number of animals before he arrives at the witch's hut. These turn out to be his helpers in performing the task Baba Yaga sets him, which is to herd her mares for three days. Although she hinders Ivan Tsarevich in every way, the mares are herded, and he takes the promised horse, in reality a mangy colt, and sets off for the thrice-ten tsardom. He flies, over a fiery river on the little colt, who has now become a warhorse, leaving the witch to plunge into the flames and perish, at least for the remainder of this tale. In this instance he manages to defeat Koshchei the Deathless, even destroy him, and he and his otherworldly wife return, but to no recognizable location.

As in "Maria Morevna," there will be either one or three points in the third group of wondertales in which the hero is tested. At the witch's hut he is given myriad strange tasks to perform and equally strange questions or riddles to answer to test his sociability and his knowledge of the social "catechism." In the thrice-ten tsardom his strength and virility are tested, either in battle with the villain or in overcoming the reluctance of the maiden to give herself to him. Finally, at the court of a prospective father-in-law, he proves his suitability to be the tsar's heir. In the overwhelming majority of cases he will then quickly marry and accept society's obligations.

The purpose of the testing sequences is clearly to prepare the young man for integration into the society as a fully qualified adult. The lessons he is supposed to learn in the woods, as it were, are vigilance, courage, devotion, acceptance of his surroundings, willingness to take advice, the importance of cooperation, and altruism. None need fail and in fact none does fail, from lazybones on the stove, to a lad crippled since birth, to the son of some unlikely half-human and half-animal union. But noting these obvious features of the wondertale raises another question: is this the interpretation given the tales by the nineteenth-century peasants who enjoyed them in their natural setting? It is one thing for scholars or psychologists to decide the meaning of the tales but quite another to attribute that meaning to the tellers of tales and their audiences. I doubt very much that Russian peasants ever believed that young men went out slaying dragons. I am quite sure that Russian peasants knew very well that Baba Yaga was not a denizen of the Russian forest, much less of the Russian steppe, which is not to state that she did not play a role in some long-lost rite. If Koshchei is in some sense to be derived from an ancient pre-Christian religious system, his figure is reduced in the tales to a figure representing death and evil but there is certainly nothing of the negative divinity he might once have been. The Russian peasant seems to have accepted almost without question what the more sophisticated reader of the tales finds doubtful, uncertain, preposterous, and even irritatingly naive. This is not to say that he failed to find meaning in the tales. I am convinced that he found deep moral significance in them, something that goes deeper than the mere surface meaning attributed to him by scholars who have never experienced the totality of peasant life. Perhaps, in assuming a certain naivety on the part of the Russian peasant, the Western reader has failed to find the truth: that the truth and the pleasure of the Russian wondertale are in the understanding.

Notes

1. Khudiakov 21, recorded in Mishino, Zaraisk District. Cf. tale no. 251 in Vol. 3.
2. The title "Prince Ivan and the Firebird" is closely associated with the ballet by

Igor Stravinsky, but Ida Zeitlin's version (1926) is "Ivan Tsarevitch and the Gray Wolf." Afanas´ev's version combines them: "Ivan Tsarevich, the Firebird, and the Gray Wolf."

3. For a listing of the thirty-one functions see Propp 1990:149–55.

4. Saintyves's books are readily available in French. That of Propp is available in the original Russian (1946, reprint 1986) and in translations into German, Italian, Spanish, and French.

5. Van Gennep (1960:10–11) subdivides the rites of passage into rites of separation, transition rites, and rites of incorporation.

6. The translator of Grimms' folktales and several studies on the West European tradition, Jack Zipes, has offered a neo-Marxist (or perhaps a Marx-without-Engels) interpretation of the wondertale ringing with class warfare but shunning historical analysis that might take him beyond the peoples who in one way or another were affected by the Italian Renaissance. His provocative study *Fairy Tale as Myth. Myth as Fairy Tale* (1994) considers the impact the West European tales have had on American culture and includes a long, vitriolic, and highly amusing dissection (pp. 96–118) of Robert Bly's 1990 bestseller *Iron John: A Book About Men*. The reader will find herein the Russian equivalent of "Iron John" as tale no. 281, "A Prince and His Uncle." In general, had the Slavic analogues of this tale been known to Bly and Zipes, they might have seen that interpretations of the tale other than either of theirs are suggested.

7. See, for instance, Marie-Louise von Franz, *Interpretation of Fairytales* (1982), and *Shadow and Evil in Fairytales* (1980); Joseph Campbell, *The Hero with a Thousand Faces* (1949); and Bruno Bettelheim, *The Uses of Enchantment* (1989). Certainly the most interesting recent work on the Russian wondertales using the theories of Freud is that by Andreas R.B. Johns. See his Ph.D. dissertation, "Baba Iaga, the Ambiguous Mother of the Russian Folktale," and related article, "Baba Iaga and the Russian Mother" (Johns 1996; 1998).

8. Narrated by Dmitrii Kirillovich Sirotkin, about sixty, from the village of Rogovskaia.

9. A–T types with females as heroes (including some not covered in this volume): 313C, 313E*, 403, 403A*, 480*B, 480*C, 480*, 480A*, 480A**, 480B*, 480C**, 510A, 510B, 510B*, 511, 706, 709, 712, 875, 875E*, 875*, 875**, 883A, 883A*, 883A*, 883A***, 883A****, 883B.

10. Note the modern Russian *koshchunstvo* = blasphemy.

11. For a depiction of the sixteenth-century wedding see Kolesov 1985.

Bibliography

Aarne, Antti, and Stith Thompson. 1987. *The Types of the Folktale*. 2nd. ed. Helsinki.

Afanas´ev, A.N. 1984. *Narodnye russkie skazki*. Moscow.

———. 1994. *Poeticheskie vozzreniia slavian na prirodu*. Moscow.

Azadovskii, Mark. 1994. *A Siberian Tale Teller*, trans. James R. Dow. Austin.

Barag, L.G.; I.P. Berezovskii; K.P. Kabashnikov; and N.V. Novikov. 1979. *Sravnitel´nyi ukazatel´ siuzhetov. Vostochnoslavianskaia skazka*. Leningrad.

Bergt. 1987. *Interpretation of Fairy Tales. Danish Folklore in a European Perspective*. Folklore Fellows Communication No. 239. Helsinki.

Bernshtam, T.A. 1998. *Molodezh´ v obriadovoi zhizni russkoi obshchiny XIX– nachala XX v.* Leningrad.

Bettelheim, Bruno. 1989. *The Uses of Enchantment: The Meaning and Importance of Fairy Tales*. New York.

Bremond, Claude. 1977. "The Morphology of the French Fairy Tale: The Ethical Model." Pp. 49–76 in *Patterns in Oral Literature*, eds. Heda Jason and Dimitri Segal. The Hague–Paris.

Campbell, Joseph. 1949. *The Hero with a Thousand Faces*. New York.

Eliade, Mircea. 1972. *Zalmoxis, the Vanishing God*. Chicago.

Eremina, V.I. 1991. *Ritual i fol'klor*. Leningrad.

Holbek, Bengt. 1987. *Interpretation of Fairy Tales. Danish Folklore in a European Perspective*. Folklore Fellows Communication No. 239. Helsinki.

———. 1989. "The Language of Fairy Tales." In *Nordic Folklore. Recent Studies*, eds. Reimund Kvideland and Henning K. Sehmsdorf. Bloomington.

Johns, Andreas R.B. 1996. "Baba Iaga, the Ambiguous Mother of the Russian Folktale." Ph.D. dissertation. University of California.

———. 1998. "Baba Iaga and the Russian Mother." *Slavic and East European Journal* 42, no. 1: 21–36.

Khudiakov, I.A. 1964. *Velikorusskie skazki v zapisiakh I.A.Khudiakova*, eds. V.G. Bazanov and O.B. Alekseeva. Moscow–Leningrad.

Kolesov, V.V. 1985. "Chin svadebnyi." In *Pamiatniki literatury drevnei Rusi, serediny XVI veka*. Moscow.

Kostiukhin, E.A. 1997. "Skazki, kotorye plokho konchaiutsia," *Zhivaia starina*, 4(16), pp. 15–18.

Maranda, Elli Köngäs, and Pierre Maranda. 1971. *Structural Models in Folklore and Transformational Essays*. The Hague.

Meletinskii, E.M. 1958. *Geroi volshebnoi skazki*. Moscow.

———. 1969. "Strukturno-tipologicheskoe izuchenie skazki." Pp. 134–66 in Propp 1969.

Meletinskii, E.M.; S.Iu Nekliukov; E.S. Novik; and D.M. Segal. 1969. "Problemy strukturnogo opisaniia volshebnoi skazki." *Trudy po znakovym sistemam*. Vol. 4, pp. 86–136. Tartu.

Morozov, I.A. 1998. *Zhenit' ba dobra molodtsa*. Moscow.

Nikiforov, A.I. 1961. *Severnorusskie skazki v zapisiakh A.I. Nikiforova*. Moscow–Leningrad.

———. 1975. "Towards a Morphological Study of the Folktale." Pp. 155–63 in Oinas and Sudakoff 1975.

Oberfeld, Charlotte, ed. 1990. *Wie alt sind unsere Märchen?* Veröffentlichungen der Europäischen Märchengesellschaft. Vol. 14. Marburg.

Oinas, Felix, and Stephen Sudakoff. 1975. *The Study of Russian Folklore*. The Hague–Paris.

Pomerantseva, E.V. 1975. *Mifologicheskie personazhi v russkom fol'klore*. Moscow.

Propp, V.Ia. 1946. *Istoricheskie korni volshebnoi skazki*. Leningrad (reprint, 1986).

———. 1969. *Morfologiia skazki*, 2nd ed. Moscow.

———. 1990. *Morphology of the Folktale*. 2nd ed. Austin–London.

Saintyves, Pierre. 1924. *Les contes de Perrault et les récits parallels. Leur origins (costumes primitives et liturgies populaires)*. Paris.

Schechtman, Jacqueline. 1993. *The Stepmother in Fairytales: Bereavement and the Feminine Shadow*. Boston.

Tudorovskaia, E.A. 1965. "O klassifikatsii volshebnykh skazok." *Sovetskaia etnografiia*, no. 2: 57–66.

van Gennep, Arnold. 1960. *The Rites of Passage.* Chicago.

Vlasova, M. 1995. *Novaia abevega russkikh sueverii.* St. Petersburg.

von Franz, Marie-Louise. 1980. *Shadow and Evil in Fairytales.* Dallas.

————. 1982. *Interpretation of Fairytales.* Dallas.

Wehse, Rainer. 1990. "Uralt? Theorien zum Alter des Märchens." In Oberfeld 1990.

Zeitlin, Ida. 1926. *Skazki. Tales and Legends of Old Russia.* New York.

Zelenin, D.K. 1997. *Velikorusskie skazki permskoi gubernii.* St. Petersburg.

Zipes, Jack. 1988. *The Complete Fairy Tales of the Brothers Grimm.* 2 vols. New York.

————. 1994. *Fairy Tale as Myth. Myth as Fairy Tale.* Lexington, KY.

Russian
Wondertales

279. Give Up What You Don't Know Is at Home

A man was walking along and he wanted a drink. He bent over a puddle and at that very moment a devil grabbed him by the beard and wouldn't let go. "Let me go," shouted the man.

"I won't let you go! Only if you give up what you don't know is at home, what you're not aware of, then I'll let you go," answered the devil.

The man thought and thought: what didn't he know at home? Well then, he spat and agreed. He came home and his wife greeted him with joy and told him a son had been born. So then the man confessed everything to her, but for a long time she wouldn't be calmed down: "Oh, you old devil, just look what you've done!"

The devil came to collect what he had won. They begged him, they pleaded with him to leave them their child. But no way! Then he offered the condition that they would have to guess his name and then he would leave them the baby. He gave them the period of a week. So they went to witches and they went to magicians. The week passed and they hadn't found it out.

Once the old man was clearing a wood and suddenly saw that very same devil jump out into a clearing, and he started to hop and mutter: "Oh, I am Trapeza Pilemneiavich, and the old woman's son will be mine!"

The man came running and shouting: "Old woman, old woman, quickly write it down, he is Trapeza Pilemneiavich."

Soon after the devil came and, well, who has found out the name? The old folks began guessing it: "Maybe it's Ivan, or perhaps Trofim. Or maybe Trapeza Pilemneiavich?"

And that did the devil in. "A compact is dearer than money!"

A–T 500

280. The Lazy Spinner

This daughter was idle when it came to spinning. So once this tsaritsa was riding by and she heard the quarrel inside the hut. She came and asked, "Why are you beating your daughter?"

"You see, she's so untiring with her spinning that I can't cure her of it."

"Come, my dear, with me. I have spinning enough for you, two store-rooms-full or more. You shall spin a fine wonderful thread and then I shall accept you for my son." And she took her away.

3

And so they brought her there and the very first day she didn't begin a single thing. The tsaritsa came to her and asked, "Why, my dear, have you not begun anything?"

"I didn't start anything because I am homesick for my homeland."

So she stroked her head on that account. She did nothing the second day either and no one questioned her about it. Then three strange old aunties came and said, "You will invite us to your wedding and we will spin for you two storerooms of flax, and we shall make a fine, wonderful thread.

So on that third day they set to work and they spun. And the tsaritsa came and was amazed. The whole thing was finished, it was all spun.

So then the wedding began. And the aunties came to the wedding and to the royal feast, and they made themselves comfortable at the table. One of them had a long nose, and another had a fat finger, and the third had a thick foot. And the young man asked her, "Why, auntie, do you have such a long nose?"

And she replied, "Because I pull the spindle, and I prop myself up with my nose, that's why."

So he asked the second, "Why, auntie, do you have such a fat finger?"

"I twist the thread."

And he asked the third, "Why, auntie, do you have such a thick foot?"

"Because I turn the spinning wheel with it."

He took fright. "Well, you, my wife, don't spin, or you will have just such a long nose and fat finger and thick foot." But that was all because she wouldn't spin.

A–T 501

281. A Prince and His "Uncle"

There lived and dwelt this king, and he had an adolescent son. The prince was excellent in every way: handsome and well mannered, he caused his father no pain, for the king was tormented by greed, by a desire to squeeze even more profits and increase his quit rents a little. Once he saw an old man with sables and martens and beavers and foxes. "Halt, old man! Where are you from?"

"By birth I'm from such-and-such a village, father, but now I'm serving the forest spirit [leshii]."

"And how do you catch these beasts?"

"Well, the forest spirit sets out snares and the beast is stupid and gets caught."

"Now, listen, old man! I shall supply you with wine and give you some money, then will you show me where to put out these snares?" The old man was tempted and showed him. The king immediately ordered the forest spirit caught and fettered to an iron post, and then he put out the snares in his own forest preserves.

So the forest spirit sat there at the iron post and looked in a window because that post was standing in a garden. The prince came out with some women and nannies and with some trusty servant girls to walk about the garden. He walked by the post and the forest spirit shouted at him: "Oh princely child! Release me! I shall be of service to you."

"But how should I release you?"

"Go to your mother and tell her this: 'Dear Mother of mine, look for some lice on my head!' Then you lay your head on her knees and she will start searching around on your head. You seize the moment to pull the key out of your mother's pocket and then let me free!" So that's what the prince did. He pulled the key out of his mother's pocket and ran into the garden, then he made himself an arrow, placed it on a taut bow, and let it go far, far away, and then he shouted to the women and nannies to go fetch the arrow. The women and nannies all ran away and at that moment the prince unlocked the iron post and freed the forest spirit.

The forest spirit set off to tear up the royal snares! The king saw that he wasn't snaring any more beasts, he got angry and attacked his wife; why had she given out the key and let the forest spirit loose? And then he called his boyars, his generals, and his councilors so that they might judge: should her head be removed on the block or should she be sent into exile? Things were bad for the prince. He pitied his own mother and so he admitted to his father that it was his fault. "It was this way and that way and that's how it happened." The king was sorely aggrieved and what should he do with his son? He could not execute him, so it was decided to send him out into the four corners of the world to the four winds of the summer, to all the winter blizzards, to all the autumn whirlwinds. They gave him a pack and an old "uncle" as a servant.

So the prince and his "uncle" went out into the open steppe. They walked near or far, high or low, and then they saw a well. The prince said to the "uncle": "Go get some water!"

"I won't do it!" answered the "uncle."

They went on further, they walked and walked, and there was another well. "Go fetch some water! I feel like a drink," the prince asked the "uncle" a second time.

"I won't go," said the "uncle."

So on and on they walked, and then they encountered a third well and the "uncle" again would not go, so the prince went after the water himself. He let himself down into the well and the "uncle" banged the top onto it and said, "I won't let you out. You be the servant and I'll be the prince." There was nothing to be done so the prince agreed and gave him a note to that effect in his own blood. Then they exchanged clothes and set off further.

So they came to another country. They went to the tsar in his palace, the "uncle" in front, and the prince behind him. The "uncle" began living at that tsar's as a guest, and he ate and drank with him at the same table. He said to him: "Your royal highness! Take my servant into the kitchen, at least." So they took the prince into the kitchen and made him fetch wood and scour the pots and pans. A little time passed and the prince had learned to prepare food better than the tsar's cooks. His lordship found out about this, befriended him, and began giving him gold. The cooks were offended by this and they began seeking a way to be rid of him.

Once the prince made a pie and put it in the oven, and the cooks got hold of some poison, took it and put it in the pie. The tsar sat down to eat and they handed him the pie. The tsar was about to take his knife to it when the chief cook ran in: "Your highness! Please don't eat it!" And he said a lot of nasty things against the prince.

The tsar did not spare even his favorite dog. He cut off a piece of pie and threw it onto the ground. The dog ate it and died right then and there. The king summoned the prince and shouted at him in a loud voice: "How did you dare to prepare a pie for me with poison in it? I order you to be executed immediately!"

"I know nothing, your highness, I know nothing of it at all!" the prince answered. "It is obvious that your cooks were offended when you favored me, they have brought me down on purpose." The tsar forgave him and ordered him to be his groom.

The prince led the horses off to be watered. On the way he encountered the forest spirit. "Greetings, royal son! Come visit me!"

"I'm afraid the horses would run away."

"Never mind, come on!" Then a hut appeared on the spot. The forest spirit had three daughters. He asked the first one: "And what will we reward the king's son with for having freed me from the iron post?"

The daughter said: "Give him the self-setting tablecloth." The prince left the forest spirit with the gift and looked: all the horses were there. He spread the cloth: "Whatever you want, you just ask for it—food and drinks!"

The next day he herded the tsar's horses to water and the forest spirit again appeared: "Come visit me!" He brought him and asked his second daughter: "And what will we reward the king's son with?"

"I will give him a mirror: whatever you like you can see in this mirror."

On the third day the forest spirit again encountered the prince, took him into his home, and asked the youngest daughter: "And what will we reward the king's son with?"

"I will give him a fife. Just press it to your lips and musicians and singers will immediately appear." So the king's son began to live happily. He ate and drank well, he knew and found out about everything, and music resounded the whole day long. What could be better? And the horses?! It was a miracle purely and simply: they were happy and handsome and quick off the mark.

The tsar began to boast to his favorite daughter how the lord had sent him this fabulous groom. But the beautiful tsarevna had long since taken notice herself of the groom—why should a beautiful maiden not note a handsome lad! The tsarevna became curious. Why were the new groom's horses faster and more stately than those of the others? "I think I'll just go into his chambers," she thought, "and take a look at how he's living, poor fellow." Well it's a well-known fact: what a woman wants to do she does. She awaited a time when the prince had herded the horses out to be watered, then she went into his chambers and stole a glance in his mirror. Immediately she understood everything, and she carried away with her his self-setting tablecloth, his mirror, and the fife.

At that very moment a misfortune struck the tsar. The seven-headed monster Idolishche attacked his kingdom and demanded a tsarevna for his wife. "And if they won't give her to me, I'll take her by force!" he said, and he arrayed his troops, which were thousands upon thousands. It looked bad for the tsar. He sent a clarion call throughout the entire tsardom, he summoned the princes and the bogatyrs. Whoever should defeat Idolishche of the Seven Heads would receive half the kingdom and in addition a daughter in marriage. So the princes and the bogatyrs gathered and rode off to do battle against Idolishche, and "uncle" set off together with the tsar's army. And our groom mounted his gray mare and dragged along behind all the rest.

He rode along and then he met up with the forest spirit. "Where are you going, royal son?"

"To fight."

"You won't go far on that nag! And a groom at that! Come pay me a visit!"

He brought him into his hut and poured him a glass of vodka. The prince drank it. "Do you feel much strength in yourself now?" asked the forest spirit.

"If I had a cudgel of fifty poods [a ton], I'd throw it up into the air and let it fall on my head and I wouldn't even feel the blow!"

He gave him another glass to drink. "And now do you have much strength?"

"Why, if I had a cudgel of a hundred poods, I could throw it beyond the clouds!"

So he poured him a third glass. "And now how's your strength?"

"Why, if you could place a column from the earth to heaven, I could turn over the entire universe!" The forest spirit filtrated some vodka from another tap and gave it to the prince. The prince drank it and his strength was diminished to one-seventh.

Afterward the forest spirit led him onto the porch and whistled a hero's whistle. Out of nowhere there came running a jet-black horse and the earth shook and flames came from its nostrils and smoke poured out of its ears in a column and sparks showered from under its hooves. It ran up to the porch and fell on its knees. "Now there's a horse for you!" He also gave him a fighting cudgel and a silk lash. The prince rode out on his jet-black horse against the hostile force. He looked and there was his "uncle" who had climbed up in a birch and was sitting there shaking from fear. The prince lashed him a time or two with his lash and flew off at the enemy force. He slashed down many of the foe with his sword, still more he trampled with his horse, and he carried off all seven heads of Idolishche.

And the tsarevna saw the whole thing. She couldn't wait to look in the mirror to see how it would turn out. So she immediately rode out and asked the prince: "With what do you order us to show our gratitude?"

"Kiss me, beautiful maiden!" The tsarevna was not embarrassed, she pressed him to her ardent heart and kissed him loudly and soundly so that the entire army might hear.

The prince struck his horse—and was off! He returned home and sat in his misery as if he had never been at the battle. But his "uncle" was boasting to everyone, saying to them all: "It was I who defeated Idolishche."

The tsar greeted him with great honor and betrothed him to his daughter and gave a great feast. Only the tsarevna was no fool, suddenly right out of the blue she had a headache, her heart burned. What will happen, what is to be done for the promised son-in-law? "Father," he says to the tsar, "give me a ship and I will go for medicines for my bride. Only let that groom go with me. You see, I've really grown very used to him. . . ." The tsar listened to him, gave him the ship and the groom.

So they set off, near or far away they sailed, and the "uncle" ordered a sack sewn. And he put the groom in it and threw it into the water. The princess looked in the mirror and saw the misfortune! She got into her carriage and rushed to the sea, but the forest spirit was already sitting there, knitting a net. "Little man, help me in my great sorrow, an evil "uncle" is drowning the prince!"

"Allow me, beautiful maiden, the net is already ready. Stretch out your white hands to it!" So the princess let the net out into the deep sea and she hauled in the prince and took him with her. And at home she told her father the whole story.

So now there was a happy little feast and then a little wedding. The tsar didn't need to brew any mead or distill fine wines—there was plenty! And "uncle" bought up various supplies and went back. He came into the palace and they seized him right there. He pleaded, but it was too late. They shot him in a flash at the gates. The prince's wedding was happy. All the taverns and public houses were opened for a whole week to all the people for free. And I was there, and drank mead and wine, it flowed over my moustache, but none got into my mouth.

A–T 502

282. The Hunter and the Princess

There was this hunter, a merchant's son. He went out hunting. In this oak tree he had a bed. Beneath the oak someone had tied a princess. Perhaps it was cutthroats, perhaps robbers who wanted to cut off her head. But he shouted down from the oak that they should sell her to him. "How much will you give?"

"I have only three hundred, but I'll give that to you." So he climbed down and gave them the money; then they handed the princess over to him. But then they thought it over and decided they should kidnap both of them, so they returned. They hid in the roots of that tree. The tree had been upturned by the wind and they hid under the roots. But they didn't find them anywhere.

Now a peasant and his wife were going to a christening. They asked them whether they would take them to the village, and they did so.

They came to their own house and for three full days she didn't say a thing. He thought she was mute. On the third day she started to speak, and she told him that she was the daughter of a king.

Then they got ready, his uncles, to go to other lands trading. She sewed a hand towel. The uncles took to trade what didn't exist in Russia, and then this hand towel. So they went there and the uncles brought there what didn't exist in Russia, and this hand towel. And on this hand towel was embroidered who her rescuer was, who had saved her, that the godmother had been sought, but robbers, or perhaps cutthroats, had wanted to cut off her head, but he had ransomed her for three hundred. Then they had got married. "Receive my husband's godfather as if he were my husband. I humbly beg and ask that someone reward him."

He rewarded him. He gave him a ship with splendid goods. They came home. The godfather cheated the uncles. None of those goods that he had been given was there.

They prepared to pay a visit to her father. And they went to her father. Once more she sewed a hand towel for her dear father, and on it was written that the bearer of the towel was the one who had rescued her and that he was now her husband. So then this general, or prince, who wanted to marry her, wrote a letter asking her to come there, and he sent a telegram asking her husband to dine with him without her.

She guessed it and wouldn't go, but her husband's mother said to her, "What sort of wife will you be for your husband if you don't obey?" She went overland and he went by sea on ships. When she got there, her husband wasn't there yet. And that prince started going on at her, trying to get married to her. As they were feasting, her husband came. He was unhappy with affairs and scolded his mother for sending his wife there. They got ready to go after his wife.

He set off. When he arrived, there was this piper there, playing on his bagpipe. Her husband bought the pipes from him. Then he went to a feast at the king's with the pipes. And there his wife recognized him. He was dressed in beggar's clothing, very poor. She began asking the prince, "Don't you think that piper plays extremely well? I am going to invite him into my chambers." So she took him into her chambers and they feasted. She gave the prince much cognac to drink and he fell asleep. Then they went and got into their car and rode away. They came home and began living there. She never went back to her father's. And that is all.

A–T 506B

283. Serezha, the Merchant's Son

There were three brothers. One, the oldest, died, and he left behind a son named Serezha. Gradually he and his mother used up all his father's capital; his father had possessed shops and ships. Over time the ships rotted in the harbor. Serezha then started to work, hauling rubbish away to a dump and making bricks. And so it was that one time he found an icon in the refuse dump. The icon was besmeared, all dirty. You couldn't see the face of God at all. He brought it home and said to his mother, "Here, Mother, I found this icon, but I don't know what's written on it."

His mother was a religious old woman. She washed the icon and the face of St. Nikolai appeared She placed the icon in the icon corner and prayed to God. She kept on praying. And Serezha kept on working. He'd sometimes make twenty kopecks, sometimes thirty in a day. And that's what they lived on.

His uncles, his father's two brothers, had shops and lived well. (But Serezha and his mother had already used up his father's capital.) So then. Once an old man came to him, and he looked like St. Nikolai. He said, "Granny, can I spend the night here?"

She said, "Of course, you can spend the night. But we live poorly, I have nothing to eat, nothing to feed you with."

He responded, "God will give us the day, God will give us our food." That's how the old man responded.

So fine. Evening fell. Serezha came home from work and his mother said, "Did you buy a little bread for us?"

"No, I didn't buy anything at all."

"What will we have for supper then?"

And then the old man replied, "Granny, look well around you. Perhaps on a shelf there's a little meat lying, or some bread, or something else."

"No, there's nothing. Yesterday I searched but I found nothing. There's nothing to eat."

"Go and have a look anyway. That was yesterday's business. Maybe you didn't look very well."

So the old woman, Serezha's mother, heeded him. She went, lit a splinter, and looked. And there lay some meat, and a good hunk of bread. An onion too, and even cabbage. Everything! "And you said there was nothing there. You just didn't look very well."

So they lit some candles and started cooking supper. When they had finished supper, they went to bed. In the morning Serezha hopped out of bed and drank some tea, and then he set off once more to work. And the old man on the bench just lay there, all the while repeating, "God will give us the day, God will give us our food."

The old woman repeated that there was nothing to eat, and he said, "No granny, that's old business. Maybe there's a loaf lying about on that shelf." The old woman heeded him and went to see, and in fact there was a loaf, and some meat, and a bit of onion. And so that's how they lived.

Serezha even forgot that he had to buy bread, hoping that his mother would find something to eat. One wonderful time Serezha came and said, "Do you know what, mama? My uncles are getting ready to go to another country on ships. They have got together a lot of furs: sables, fox, and squirrel. All sorts of furs."

And his mother said, "Serezha, your uncles are rich but you and I have nothing. Somehow we are going to go on living. What's the point of trying to keep up with your uncles! They have shops and furs and everything. They can go abroad—everywhere for goods."

The old man sat there, and he said, "Well, granny, did your husband have a ship or did he not?"

"He had one," she said, "But it rotted. It was anchored in the harbor for several years and then it sank."

Just then Serezha came in for dinner. He said to him, "Serezha, do you know where your father's ship sank?"

"Yes, I know. I never saw it because I was just a child, but I know where it stood at anchor. Mother showed me where it sank."

"Let's go there," he said. "Let's take a look; perhaps we can raise it."

"Grandfather, how could we raise it? It's been ten years since it sank in that harbor."

"Let's go anyway."

So they went there, of course, to the harbor. Serezha said, "This is where father's ship was anchored, and that's where it sank."

"You go off to work now, Serezha, and I'll stay here a little longer."

So while Serezha went off to work, the old man raised the ship (you see, it was St. Nikolai, and whatever he says comes to pass).

He raised the ship and in an instant it was beautifully fitted out, all the engines, everything just like on the line. So that's fine. Grandfather came up and said, "Well, granny, you've got a fine ship there. It's a waste to have it in the water so many years. I raised it. Now that ship's just like new. Now it's ready to go out to sea."

Then Serezha came and grandfather said, "Well, Serezha, let's go have a look at your ship. It's a ship unlike any that your uncles have."

Serezha trusted the old man. They went to the harbor and looked: the ship stood there, steaming away, all fitted out, with all the engines shining and hooting. "Now, Serezha, you make up a sign that says the ship is yours. Write 'Serezha Petrov.'"

So he wrote it and so after four or five days had passed, Serezha said, "Do you know, grandfather, my uncles are going abroad on their ships? They take furs there: sable, foxes, and squirrels. And they bring goods back."

The old man responded: "Serezha, let's go abroad, too. We have a fine ship!"

Serezha said, "Of course, grandfather, we'll go abroad, and, yes, we have a fine ship, but we don't have any furs at all."

"Do you know what? We can take on bricks, a few thousand. And we'll buy some lime."

"And just where will we get the lime?"

"Where will we get lime? We'll run around to Maksimikho to Shadurskii. They deal in lime. We'll buy three or four tons. I'll give you the money. And we'll go together. Abroad lime is expensive and so are bricks. Furs don't play any role in this at all."

Serezha paid attention to the old man. Now the old man gave him some money. "Go to Maloe Uro now and buy some bricks, four or five thousand.

They'll carry them on horses for you to Lake Baikal." The old man gave him the money, as much as he needed he gave him. Then Serezha ran off to Maloe Uro, bought five or six thousand bricks, and hired drivers to haul them. He bought three or four tons of lime in Maksimikho and they loaded everything onto the ship. Then Serezha said, "Do you know, grandfather, my uncles left five or six days ago. We are late!"

"Don't worry! Don't hurry! We'll catch up to them and even pass them. Our ship is better than theirs. They are going to travel ten to fifteen days to get abroad, but we'll get there in five."

Serezha's father had a fiddle and Serezha had wanted to learn to play it for a long time. He was then sixteen years old. Grandfather asked him, "Well, Serezha, do you have a desire to learn to play the fiddle?"

"My father was a well-known player. Why should I not learn?"

"And would you like to be a really good player?"

"Of course, that would be very desirable, grandfather."

"Then you go into that hut mornings before the sun rises and play. The sun will roll around, and in the evening you play. And thus you'll learn to play. I sense a great talent in you; you will also be a well-known player."

Serezha obeyed the old man. In the morning he would jump up early, run quickly to the hut, and start playing on the fiddle. Late in the evening he would also play. And so he learned how. Once he came to the old man and said, "Grandfather, I've started to play a little."

"Well, then, play for me."

Serezha started playing and everything all around started dancing: the glasses and goblets on the table—everything. "Oh, what a fine player you are! There are none such on earth!" the old man said.

Serezha rejoiced that he had become a fiddler such as grandfather had never encountered before. In the evening he got together with his friends. "Heh, you guys! I play the fiddle really well now."

And his friends responded, "Ah, cut it out! You're just playing with us! Who wants to listen to you?"

"No, guys, come on and I'll play for you. I have this grandfather living with me, and he taught me how to play. And when I play, the glasses, goblets, and tables start in dancing."

The friends got together out of curiosity. He took up his fiddle, and when he started playing, even the guys started dancing! "Heh, Serezha, you have learned to play the fiddle really well!"

"You see, I have this grandfather living with me, and he taught me to play. Early in the morning and late at night I'd play in this hut, and that's how I learned to play. If you want to learn, go there and you'll also be able to play. (He had already become a well-known fiddler.) And thus it was that they loaded everything onto the ship.

And then granny said, "Now that you are going away, what am I going to live on? You could spend a month, or two, or three abroad."

And the old man replied, "Oh, granny, don't be sad. God gives the day and God gives our food. You just go on with things and look at the shelves. You'll have enough for dinner and for supper."

And that's how it was as granny said farewell to them. They boarded the boat and set off. They went for a day, a second, and a third. They caught up to the ships of his uncles. They caught up, passed them, and went on ahead. His uncles looked. What could that be? A ship had sailed past with the identification marker on it, "Serezha Petrov." The uncles were astonished. "Where did they get that ship? Why, his father's ship has been rotting in the harbor a long time, and yet they went flying by."

So then they arrived abroad and docked their ships. They spent a day, two, then three before the uncles appeared. Serezha quickly got into his dinghy and went to his uncles. "Good health to you!"

"And good health to you! How did you get here?"

"Well, this grandfather came to me and spent about two weeks with us, and then he raised father's ship. So then we set off abroad just like you."

"And what did you bring?" his uncles asked.

"We collected some lime—about three or four tons—and several thousand bricks."

"Oh, you fools! And the old man is a fool! He's driven you out of your mind. You've brought bricks and lime abroad. Don't you think they have that rubbish here?"

So then the uncles got ready to go to the tsar to ask permission to sell their furs in his country and buy up goods to take back. Serezha listened to them. "I'll go too, uncles."

"Where will you go? We are taking valuable gifts for the tsar. One is a sable coat and the other is a sable muffler for the tsaritsa. What will you take with you?"

"Oh, I'll have something to take."

So he went back to his ship and said to grandfather, "Grandfather, my uncles are going to the tsar to ask permission to sell their furs and buy up goods in his country. One uncle is taking a sable coat for him, and the other a sable muffler for the tsaritsa. What can I take?"

"Here! I'll wrap half a brick up for you and a piece of lime."

"Grandfather, if I take those to the tsar, they'll shoot me straight away."

"No, the tsar will first receive you and only afterward will he invite your uncles. He'll give you a stool and say, "Sit down, young lad, you will be my honored guest."

So grandfather wrapped the lime up in a newspaper for him, and the half brick, and Serezha set off behind his uncles. They wouldn't take him.

"Where are you going and what are you taking?"

"I'm going to see the tsar; my grandfather told me to go with you."

Well, they came before the tsar and asked permission to see him. The tsar permitted them to approach and they went in. One uncle gave him the sable coat as a gift, and the other, of course, gave him the sable muffler made from the most expensive Barguz sables.

The tsar accepted the gifts. Then the uncles looked at Serezha to see what he would give. Serezha unwrapped the newspapers and handed him the half brick. It had turned into gold. The tsar accepted it with joy. Then he opened the second newspaper. There was a chunk of diamond! Everything in the royal chamber was lit up. His uncles were amazed. "Where did he get that, where did he steal that diamond and that gold? They lived in poverty, they ate whatever came along."

The tsar was overjoyed as he accepted the diamond, and he said, "So, young lad, come and sit down." (He asked Serezha first and then his uncles.)

They said, "Your imperial highness, we have come from abroad to sell our goods, our furs, and to collect some goods from you."

"Please," the tsar said, "I permit you. But with one condition: that each of you is to sleep in the church alone for one night."

They were surprised. What did this mean? For what reason? But he said nothing more.

This tsar had a daughter who was about eighteen years old, and this daughter was an enchantress.

When she was dying, she had said, "Oh my parents, do not bury me, but make me a crystal coffin and place it in the church. And then for three years send me one man each night to amuse me. All this time I won't die and then after three years bury me. This order is a strict one; fulfill it."

So the uncles said farewell to the tsar and went to their own quarters. They dropped in to see some rich foreign merchants and said to them, "We were just with the tsar and asked permission to sell our goods and buy his. The tsar gave his permission but said that each of us had to spend a night in the church alone."

"That's an obstacle for you."

"But what does it mean?"

"Well, he had this daughter and she was an enchantress. As she was dying, she said, 'Papa and Mama, don't bury me but make a crystal coffin for me, put me in it, and place the coffin in the church. And every night send a single person to watch over me and amuse me. After three years you can bury me.' More than a year passed, and every night they send someone there. They lead him into the church in the evening and in the morning he is not to be found. They open the church and she is lying in her coffin just as she was placed, but the man is gone. And so many people have disappeared now. Whether she devours them or what—it just isn't known."

So it was an obstacle for his uncles. What was to be done? Should they turn the ships back and flee to their own country? But the tsar had given an order and it must be obeyed. They, the two brothers, discussed the matter between themselves and said, "We'll hire Serezha for the first night. Let him get lost. That will be no big misfortune. And if he is lost, we'll turn our ships around and be gone. We'll run away, or else we won't stay alive. People are convinced that all those young men were really there but in the morning when they open up the church, they're gone. Where do they get to?"

So they went onto their ship, took counsel, and decided to hire Serezha. They shouted from their ship, "Serezha, come here!"

He got into his dinghy. "What is it, uncle?"

"Do you know what, Serezha? We are going to hire you," said one uncle. "We are going to hire you to stand watch tonight. How much will you require? A hundred or two hundred rubles? We'll give it all to you."

He said, "I don't know, uncle. I need to talk about it with my grandfather. I'll do as grandfather tells me." He went back to his ship and said, "Grandfather, my uncles want to hire me to stand watch. One uncle, the elder, would give me a hundred rubles or two."

His uncle said, "No, Serezha, we don't need their money. We have some gold, and half a ship full of diamonds. But if your uncle will give you his ship and all the furs, then you go. And if he won't, then don't go."

So Serezha got back in his dinghy and went back to his uncles. He said, "Well, now, uncles, I'll agree to be hired, but only if you give me one of these ships. I don't need any money. We have plenty of gold and lots of diamonds."

The uncles talked about it. They didn't want to give up the ship, but to go and stand watch was just terrifying. So then they decided to give up the ship. "If he remains alive," said the second brother, "tomorrow I'll go and stand watch. If Serezha remains alive."

But Serezha said, "Give me the ship." He took the ship, took command of it, and sailed it up next to his own. So then he and his grandfather had two ships.

But now evening was coming. Serezha had to go stand watch for his uncle. "Now you go and report that you are coming to stand watch for your uncle. The tsar won't mind at all—as long as somebody comes," said grandfather. Grandfather gave Serezha a torch. "Here's this torch for you. When you come into the church, make a circle all around. And here's a book for you (Serezha could read). You read this book. At midnight she will fly out of the coffin, this royal daughter will. She'll fly out and then fly around the church because she absolutely has to devour a man. She'll fly up to that circle you marked and then she'll leap back, but don't you pay any attention to her: just read and read. And when the cocks crow, she will fall into the coffin and lie there again just as before. In the morning they'll come and the tsar and all his courtiers will open the door, knowing that you aren't there, and the tsar will ask, 'Young lad, what kind of things happened to you?' And you just say, 'None at all! I went into the church quietly, and that's the way I am going to go out.' No matter how much the tsar is astonished, don't you say anything. Then in the morning come back on board the ship to me."

Very fine. Grandfather gave him the book and the torch. "For the time being, hide all this in your pocket, and when they have led you into the church, light the torch. They'll lock up the church, and the tsar will take the key. He won't give it to the guards because they might take pity and let you out for the night and back inside in the morning. Maybe for gold or diamonds you could bribe the guards."

So the tsar took the keys himself, so that there was no deception. Then Serezha was led into the church. He made the circle, lit the lamp, and began reading. They locked the church and the tsar took the key.

At midnight she flew out and then flew around the church. She had to find him and eat him. She flew up to the line, but it threw her back. She screamed, and she wailed. Serezha read and read. He did just as grandfather had told him. Even though fear had overcome him, he carried out grandfather's instructions precisely.

At daybreak the tsar and his courtiers came. They thought that the young lad would no longer be among the living: so many young men had died. They opened the church and there was the young lad, still alive. He walked out.

"Well, young lad, what has been happening to you?"

"Nothing at all."

"How's that? Something has been going on. Perhaps something frightened you, something appeared to you?"

"Nothing at all, your imperial highness! I went in quietly and that's how I am coming out."

The tsar could learn nothing at all.

So Serezha went back on board his ship, and he told his grandfather everything that had happened to him. And that's fine. The next day it was time for the second uncle to go stand watch. "What should I do? Serezha managed to stay alive. Shall I go? But I am afraid. You stayed alive, brother, but maybe I'll perish. Let's hire Serezha again. They've already got one of our ships. Maybe this time they'll take money instead."

So once more he called Serezha onto his ship. "Well, Serezha, you stood watch one night?"

"That's right; I did."

"If you'll stand watch for me, I'll hire you. How much will you take? Three hundred or five hundred—even a thousand rubles I'll give you. And I'll give you furs, the most valuable sable furs. Just say you'll do it!"

"I don't know; I'll have to ask grandfather."

So he came and said, "Well, grandfather, my second uncle wants to hire me to stand watch."

He said, "But we don't need any money, and we don't need those furs either. So you take the second ship. That way we'll have three ships, and they won't have a single one. We can leave them on a sandbar, in the shallows, and let them live there."

So Serezha got back into his dinghy and went off.

"So uncle, I am willing to be hired, but you'll have to give me your second ship. I don't need any money, nor furs, nor gold, nor silver—nothing at all. We have enough of what we need, even more."

"Have you gone out of your mind, Serezha? We would be left without a ship, and you would have all three."

"Well, that's your business. If you want to, accept my conditions; if not, go and stand watch yourself."

So the uncles were here and there. They talked, they argued, and then they decided to give him the ship. And so they transferred everything into their dinghy on the sandbar, in the shallows, just like here in Ust'e. They lit a bonfire and started cooking potatoes.

And then Serezha sailed that ship alongside his, and he and grandfather had three ships. So then evening fell and grandfather said, "Well, Serezha, I'll give you this torch. And this time mark off two circles. And I'll give you this second book, and you read it. The royal daughter is especially hungry today, and she's going to yowl and shout in all sorts of voices, and from out of her mouth flames and fire are going to come, but don't you be afraid. She won't eat you. In case she manages to fly over that first circle, she still won't get over the second. And you read and read. And then no matter what happenings there are in there, don't you tell the tsar. Just be quiet. Go in and come out quietly. Don't say a thing to the tsar," the grandfather said to Serezha.

Evening approached and Serezha went to the tsar. "Well, your imperial highness, I have come to stand watch for my second uncle. For some reason they won't do it."

"Very well. Go, young lad, and watch for your uncle."

So they led him into the church again and locked it up. "What's going on?" thought the tsar. "Such a young lad, only sixteen years old, and he stays alive. She has eaten hundreds of men, but this one is alive." He was utterly astonished.

They locked him in, of course. And the tsar took the keys with him. At midnight she flew out of the coffin and started flying in the church, howling, and shouting in various voices. She wanted to eat him up, but she couldn't. She flew across one line, but she couldn't cross the other. No matter how much she howled and shouted, she could do nothing. And even though Serezha was alive, and fear had seized him, he kept on reading and reading. He was fulfilling his grandfather's orders.

The cocks crowed, she fell into the coffin, and again all became quiet and peaceful. Then the entire royal court came and they opened the doors. There was the young lad, just as he had been. The tsar asked, "Young lad, what sort of happenings have taken place in there, tell us!"

"There were none at all, your imperial highness."

So then he came back to his ship and told grandfather about everything that had taken place. And grandfather said to him, "Now, Serezha, tonight will be the third night. And you will have to stand watch for yourself. But that's no big thing. You stood watch for your uncles, and you can easily do it for yourself." So that's fine. His uncles were over on the sandbar cooking potatoes. And Serezha had three ships standing near the shore. (He and the old man were managing them.)

Evening came and grandfather said, "I'll give you this torch and you make three circles. She'll fly across the first, then the second, but she won't fly across the third. Today she'll have been hungry for three full days. She'll howl and she'll shout in various voices. She needs to gobble you up, but she won't gobble you up. You just keep reading this third book. And when the cocks start crowing, she'll fall into the coffin and be quiet and peaceful. And then they'll come and open the door and the tsar will ask you, 'Young lad, what sort of things happened to you in there?' And you say, 'There were none at all. I went in quietly and peacefully and that's the way I'll come out.' And no matter how much the tsar tries, he'll get nothing out of you. You do just as I say."

They led him into the church. He drew the three circles. At midnight she flew out and shouted even more loudly, and she howled in various voices. She needed to gobble him up. She flew around and she shouted. She flew over the first circle, then the second. But whenever she tried to fly over the third, she was thrown back. No matter how much fear overcame Serezha, he fulfilled grandfather's instructions: he kept on reading and nothing more. When the cocks crowed, she fell into the coffin and all was quiet and peaceful.

So they came and opened the doors, and the young lad came out. He came out just as he was when he went in. The tsar said, "Young lad, what sorts of things happened to you in there?"

"Nothing at all."

"That cannot be. Something must have appeared in there, frightened you—there's that corpse lying there in the coffin! Something knocked, jangled!"

"There was nothing, your imperial highness. I went in there quietly and peacefully, and that's how I came out." The tsar got nowhere.

So Serezha went back to his ship and said to his grandfather, "Well, I've stood watch for my uncles and for myself. We have the right to sell gold and diamonds now, and furs and everything."

"No, young lad," said grandfather, "Don't you and I already have everything? We have all we need—and we can sell the furs in our own land. We don't need the goods when we have so much gold and diamonds. We don't need anything more. Let's get our ships in order and leave here."

Serezha obeyed his grandfather. Whatever he said was what would be.

So they got ready to sail home, to their own country. Suddenly in the evening a messenger appeared before them.

The tsar had sent this messenger to say, "Here at the shore are these ships and on them is a young lad, Serezha. He stood watch for me three nights in the church, and I need him right now. There is something I must talk over with him."

The adjutant appeared there on the shore and asked, "Is there a young lad on that ship? His name is Serezha Petrov. The tsar demands his presence."

Serezha got ready. Grandfather allowed him to go to the tsar. He went. "So then, young lad, you stood watch for me one night, then two, and then three. I am astonished by that and that I could get you to say nothing about it. How much will you take to stand watch for me just one more night?" (The tsar suspected "He knows something.")

"I don't know, your imperial highness. I'll talk it over with my grandfather. Whatever grandfather advises I'll come and tell you."

So he went and told grandfather. "So you see, grandfather, the tsar is summoning me to come and stand watch one more night. And he promises me whatever I need. He will meet all conditions."

Grandfather answered, "No, Serezha, we don't need anything. Tell the tsar just this one thing: 'Your imperial highness, if I get your daughter out of that church alive, and she agrees to enter into a legal marriage with me, there must be no obstacles from your side. With that condition I'll agree to stay there one more night.'"

So Serezha got ready and went to the tsar. "Your imperial highness, I don't need anything at all! Neither gold nor silver. But if on the fourth night I get your daughter out of the church alive, and if she agrees to enter into a legal marriage with me, there must be no obstacles from your side. And if she doesn't want to, then I'll take nothing for it. I'll stand watch for nothing."

The tsar responded, "Please, please. I certainly won't have anything against that."

"Although she has been lying in that coffin in the church a long time, on this fourth night I shall bring her alive out of there."

The tsar agreed and Serezha went back to the ship. Grandfather said, "I'll give you this torch, and you draw four circles. She will fly. The first circle she'll fly over, and the second, and third. She'll fly up to the fourth circle and stop. When the cocks begin to crow, she'll go no further. I'll give you this little gold cross. You put it around her neck and then she won't gobble you up (I know everything!). Don't be afraid. Then take her by the hand and lead her out of the church. When they come to open the doors, you both pound on them and shout together, 'Open up!'

"So then the entire royal court will be frightened. "What is that? Last evening we put but one person in the church and now there are two voices." The tsar will be amazed."

Grandfather told him everything and then Serezha left. Evening was approaching. "I've come to stand watch, your imperial highness, for the fourth night." They let him into the church and locked it.

All night long no one could sleep: not the tsar, nor the tsaritsa, nor the court, nor the generals, nor the admirals, nor the princes. None slept. They were all expecting some big event to take place.

In the church the youth drew four circles, took the book, and began to read. As soon as the cocks crowed, she flew out, howled, and shouted. She had already flown across three of the circles but Serezha just went on reading. Then she came up to the fourth circle and the cocks crowed. But she didn't fall into the coffin. Now was the moment, it occurred to Serezha, to put the little cross on her. He took the cross out of his pocket and put it on her neck. Then he took her by the hand and wondered, "Will she gobble me up—or not? Not!"

As soon as it was light, the royal court was standing by the church, right at the doors. They were all waiting for some big events to take place. "Open up!" It was two voices, one feminine and the other masculine. So they opened the doors and there it was! He led the tsar's daughter out of the church. And she was just as she had been before.

So that's fine. And Serezha went back to his ship, and the daughter went to her father's. All the court got together and they drank and caroused. The daughter had been lying in the coffin for a year and a half dead, but now she had come to life. The young lad had come from somewhere far away, from abroad, and he had brought her to life.

That's fine. Then the tsar spoke, "Do you know what, daughter? You lay in that crystal coffin for a year or a year and a half, and then some lad from abroad came and on the fourth night he led you out alive. I would have given him many fine things but he wouldn't take anything, he wouldn't agree to anything. He just said that if 'your daughter wants to enter into a legal marriage with me, you must put up no obstacles to our marriage. But if she doesn't, that's your affair.' He would have nothing, but he did stand watch."

His daughter said, "All right, father, we'll have a party this evening and invite him. If I find him to my liking, I'll get married to him. If he isn't to my liking—he takes nothing, you say."

So that's how it was that the tsar gave a party, and he sent his adjutant to Serezha. "Here, Serezha, the tsar demands that you come to the party."

Serezha answered, "Grandfather, we'll go together."

Grandfather replied, "No, I'm too old for that. I'm an old man and there's nothing for me to do there. I'll remain here on the ships. Your uncles could try some shenanigans. Envy could get the best of them. We've got all three ships, and they're sitting there in the sand cooking potatoes."

Serezha took his fiddle. (He had his father's fiddle there on the ship.) "I'll go to the tsar's party and maybe I'll even play there." And so he went. And all sorts of important people were gathered there—princes, generals, and admirals. And Serezha appeared. And they all drank a good deal there, and Serezha said, "Your imperial highness, permit me to play. Even though you have every sort of music here, I would like to play for you."

"Of course. Please do!" The tsar gave his consent.

Serezha took his fiddle and started playing, and all were immediately brought under his spell. The princes and important people, the tsar and tsaritsa, the bride—all began dancing, and the tables and chairs started speaking.

The tsar's daughter fell in love with him. He was such an outstanding musician. She'd never met such a musician in her life. She said, "Well, papa, I want to enter into a legal marriage with this young man. But besides that I don't want to get married in this tsardom. Everybody would consider us brother and sister here, so we'll go to another country to be married."

And so she agreed. So fine. Then they announced and had a wedding. They celebrated for three days. Then Serezha got ready to go with his bride to his own country. The tsar said farewell to them, as did all his court. They boarded their ship and sailed away. And the uncles shouted, "Serezha, take us back to our homeland. What are we supposed to do here? How else would we get back home?"

He asked his grandfather. "Grandfather, do you give permission to take them or not? My uncles are begging."

"Oh, let's take them. We'll put them on the third boat. Let them sit there, and our ship will go ahead first."

So they set off. They traveled for a long time or a short time, but then grandfather said, "Do you know what, Serezha? You and I raised your father's boat together, didn't we?"

"We did it together."

And we bought the goods, and the lime, and bricks together, didn't we?"

"We bought them together."

"And we turned all that into gold and diamonds?"

"Yes."

"And I taught you to play the fiddle?"

"You did."

"And you and I obtained the royal daughter together?"

"Together."

"Then let's divide her in half."

"How should we divide her in half, grandfather?"

"What do you mean? We'll take her and chop her in two."

"No, grandfather. You had better take two ships and I just one, but leave the tsar's daughter to me so that she will remain alive."

"No, I don't agree," grandfather said.

"Well, you are in charge. There is nothing I can do."

So grandfather took a dagger and cut her into two halves. He cut her open, and all sorts of insects came tumbling out. Grandfather started washing her, rinsing her, and putting everything together again. He sprinkled her with the living water and everything grew together, and then she came back to life. Then grandfather said, "Wait. I'm getting off the boat and going to my own country."

"Where are you going?"

"I'm going to my homeland, where I came from."

"No, come to our town. My mother is waiting for me there," Serezha answered.

"No, I've done all that I can. Now you go and live on your good fortune. You have a fine bride now, but if we hadn't cut her open and cleaned her, she would have eaten you some time. Now she will be a faithful wife to you until old age."

No matter how much Serezha tried to persuade grandfather, grandfather would not agree. He got in the dinghy, Serezha rowed him to the shore, and then he disappeared wherever his nose might take him. Serezha boarded his ship again and said to the tsar's daughter, "Now there are just the two of us alone."

And she said, "We will be bored. Let's put your uncles on this first ship. It will be more cheerful as we go."

Serezha obeyed her. But grandfather had never told him that his uncles would be enemies forever.

"Well, uncles, come and board our ship."

So they boarded the ship and set off, and the uncles agreed among themselves that Serezha was the very least of people, just a crumb. He had earned ten or fifteen kopecks a day and they were rich although they had become nobodies. He had taken the tsar's daughter, he had three ships, and they would be going back home naked. They decided to destroy him!

Fine. They talked between themselves and then—bang—they threw him into the water as the ship was moving at maximum speed. Then they said to her, "Whom did you marry? I have a son," one of them said, "and he's ten times better than Serezha. We will take you there and marry you to him, but you are not to tell anybody that we drowned Serezha. If you do, then we'll straightaway finish you off, too, and we'll take all the ships."

She started praying, crossing herself, and begging, "Let me live and I'll agree. I'll marry Kolia if Serezha has already perished."

But Serezha swam and swam in Lake Baikal. He chanced on a board from an old ship, grabbed hold of it, and soon the wind had carried him to the shore.

They came back to their own land, and Serezha's mother learned that the uncles had returned. She went and asked them, "You didn't see Serezha and grandfather there, did you?"

"What are you talking about? Some old fool tricked your Serezha. Their ship was old. In the middle of Baikal it fell apart in the wind and they were drowned, they're dead."

The old woman started weeping and lamenting. "The Lord brought that old man. He deceived my son and killed him, buried him. I am left alone, all alone, in my old age."

The rich uncles had arrived, and one of them said, "Well, Nikolai, we have courted a bride for you in another country. The tsar's daughter ought to be pleasing to your eye!" So then they had the wedding and married the couple.

About a year passed and the tsar said in a year on such and such a date of such and such a month they would go to visit. Meanwhile, Serezha was feeding himself on the shores with berries and cedar seeds, but he was losing weight. He was losing touch completely, and he had been lost in the taiga for a year already. His mother kept lamenting his loss and crying that Serezha was lost for no reason at all. But grandfather didn't come at all.

So then the tsar came from the other country to visit his son-in-law. And on the eve of that very day Serezha appeared back in his home town. He had been wandering for an entire year.

He knocked at the door and his mother asked, "Who's that?"

"It's me, mama."

"Oh Lord, that's Serezha's voice."

She opened the door. "Where have you come from?"

"Oh, I've just come from somewhere. I'm not going to talk about it to you, mother." He was in tatters, hungry, and starved. "Now, mama, let me eat my fill, drink my fill, and go to sleep."

His mother replied, "Do you know, Serezha, tomorrow there will be a feast. Our Kolia is getting married. His father brought him a bride from abroad. The tsar has come to visit."

Serezha listened to all this attentively. "Well, mama, I'll crawl into the cellar and don't you let on that I have come home. If you say anything, they will surely burn us and there'll only be ashes left. Don't say anything at all until tomorrow. It's as if I haven't been here and won't be either."

So fine. His mother listened to all this and agreed. Serezha ate his fill, drank his fill, and went into the cellar to sleep.

In the morning merchants from the town made the announcement: "Today there will be a party because his lordship the emperor from the other country has come to visit."

So fine. But the fiddle was still on the ship. In the morning his mother said to him, "Today is the tsar's party. Many people are going to attend, many rich folk."

When the party began, Serezha put on an old suit and went. He came in and stood in the kitchen. He had changed in appearance, he was very underweight.

When he had been married to the tsar's daughter, they had exchanged rings. On her ring was her name and surname. She had given this ring to Serezha and he had given his to her. When Serezha had drowned, he had her ring on his hand. And that ring was still there even now. When he had been thrown on the lake shore on that board, the ring was there.

So then. The musicians were playing. Serezha stood in the kitchen. The musicians played and played on, and then they sat down to have a bite to eat.

Serezha went up and said, "Musicians, you have been playing and the people have been enjoying themselves. Permit me to play in your place for a little."

So they said, "Please, please, young lad. Go and play."

He took the fiddle from one of them and started playing, and all began dancing. The tables, the chairs, everything was dancing. It immediately occurred to his bride that "This is the way it was at my wedding with Serezha; when they were saying goodbye, my husband Serezha played like that. In his memory I'll offer that musician and fiddler a glass of vodka." (It was all in her memory. But she didn't like this other husband and somehow or other she'd had to get married to him in order just to remain alive.) So now the tsar's daughter poured out a goblet of vodka and said, "People, hand this glass of vodka to that fiddler who was playing just now."

The glass went along from hand to hand. "Who was playing?"

"I was." They gave it too him and he, of course, drank it down, leaving only a little wine in the glass. Then he took the ring, dropped it into the glass, and said, "Hand this goblet to the tsarevna."

People took it in hand and covered over the ring. They passed it along and she took the glass. "What's this? He didn't drink all the vodka? And a golden ring! What does that mean?" She took the ring in her hands and there were her name, her surname, and her father's name. "Why, this is the ring I had when I got married to Serezha! How could it get here? But it's my ring."

If Serezha had perished, then the ring ought to have perished with him. How did it turn up here? Is this some sort of miracle? Could Serezha possibly be alive?

Then she said, "Ladies and gentlemen! Let that man pass through, the one who was just now playing on the fiddle and to whom I gave the glass of vodka."

The crowd parted and Serezha approached. He had changed enormously in the past year: he was very much thinner and his face had altered; he had aged. She said, "Serezha, that isn't you, perhaps, is it?"

He said, "It is."

"And how are you still alive?"

"Here's how: When they threw me into the water, I came upon a board. I got up onto it and the wind quickly carried me to the shore. For a year I survived in the taiga on berries, cedar seeds—on anything I chanced upon—and I got back to my own country after that year. A whole year passed!"

She embraced him and they kissed and caressed, and then she said to the tsar, "Papa, this is my intended groom, the one I originally married. That other one is not my husband. They are barbarians!"

"What do you mean?"

"This is what. When those uncles were on the third ship, I said to Serezha, 'Let's invite your uncles onto this ship.' So we went and invited them, and grandfather got off the ship and hid from us. Serezha took him to the shore in his dinghy and he just disappeared. So it appeared that with his uncles we would all have a happier time. But those barbarians threw my husband Serezha into the water and drowned him, and they made me eat sand and give a promise to say nothing to anyone about it. They forced me to get married to this other man, but this one is the intended one."

So then the tsar flew into a rage and shouted angrily: "What is this? They must be shot, these uncles, for their deed, and all their capital must be transferred to Serezha."

So later Serezha became ruler and his grandfather disappeared and never came back, but his uncles were killed; they shot them. And with that this tale is at an end.

A–T 507B

284. The Serpent and the Fisherman

Two fishermen lived as neighbors. They caught fish in the sea, sold them, but then when there were no more fish, they still had to live. Well, their wives said to them, "Go and hire yourselves out as laborers."

They heeded their wives and set off to seek work. They walked for a day, and then another, and then a third. They got bored with walking, but there was still no work. They sought and they sought but they still found nothing. Then they came to this one town, spent the night, and went away. They were walking through the steppe, it was a hot day, and they felt like a drink. They saw a stream. They went up to it, drank their fill, and went on further. It was already after noon by the sun. They were tired and wanted to eat.

"I am tired, I can't go on any further," said one of them. "Let's rest."

The other answered him, "Well, you rest and I'll go to that town and ask for some bread." So one of the fishermen went into the town to ask and the other remained there. He saw a stone and sat down on it. Now underneath that stone a serpent was lying. And he was squeezing it. He sat there and heard somebody talking beneath the stone.

"Let me out, fisherman."

The man took pity on the serpent. He got up and lifted up the stone and the serpent crawled out and wrapped right around his neck. It wanted to bite him, but he asked, "What's the matter with you, serpent? People repay good with good, but you want to repay good with evil. Don't bite me."

So then the serpent crawled down onto the earth and said, "Let's go, peasant†, and we'll ask whomever we meet how they repay good."

So the peasant agreed and they went off together. They went along and they met a bull. The fisherman asked, "Tell us, with what do people repay good?"

The bull replied, "People repay good with evil. I plow the ground for my master and sow it all and haul water. But the time will come and my master will slaughter me, cook my meat, remove my skin, stretch it, and walk on me."

So the serpent said, "So now, fisherman, let me bite you."

"No, serpent, let's go on further."

So they walked along and they met a horse. The fisherman asked, "Tell us, horse, with what do people repay good? The serpent and I have been quarreling. I say that people repay good with good but the serpent says that people repay good with evil."

The horse listened and then answered, "For twenty years I have worked for my master and I have become old. He doesn't feed me now and threatens to slaughter me and skin me. No, people repay good with evil."

---

†Enserfed fishermen were also called peasants.

The serpent said, "Did you hear what that horse said? Let's go and I'll bite you now."

"No, serpent, we'll ask for the third time."

So they went along and they met a donkey. They asked him, "Tell us, donkey, with what do people repay good?"

And the donkey replied, "They repay good with evil."

So then the fisherman said, "Now you can bite me."

But the serpent answered him, "I believe you, fisherman. I will pay good for your good." And so the serpent led him back to that same stone, crawled beneath it, and gave the peasant a little gold, and then he instructed him: "Come to me every time you need some money."

So the fisherman took the gold and went away. And with that gold he began to live, and he quit working. The fisherman spent all that gold and went to the serpent and the serpent gave him some more money. And he spent this money and for the third time he went to the serpent. And the serpent gave him some money. The fisherman set off, thinking, "Why does the serpent give me so little?"

So then he spent this money and he went to the serpent. He was going along and he thought to himself, "Why does the serpent give me so little? I'll go to it and kill it and take all the money. Then I'll have a lot of gold and live well." He decided that but the serpent heard his thoughts. The fisherman came to the serpent and the serpent bit him. And the fisherman died.

A–T 507C*

285. The Soldier Warrior

A soldier served in the service for twenty-five years; he served out his twenty-five without a single red mark. But he got no release to go home. Once he was standing on guard duty and he thought and thought and said "I think I'll run for it!" And off he went.

He went out of town and up to a forest and then through the forest. Suddenly he saw a deer. He went after the deer—he wanted to kill it. But the deer wouldn't let him come close and yet wouldn't get far away from him. The soldier kept on going after him. He came into a forest that was overgrown with moss. In the middle of the forest stood a palace and the palace was overgrown with moss. Near the gates stood a rider and he, too, was covered with moss. The deer ran up and right into the courtyard.

The rider spoke: "Soldier, do not kill the deer, what's it done to you?

Better come with me and you read a book. I will give you more!" The soldier agreed. This rider brought him into the palace, gave him the book, and the soldier remained there reading while the rider went away.

He sat at the table and read. Suddenly the doors flew open and in came his father. "Oh, son, you ran away from the tsar but you haven't yet approached your own house. Abandon everything and let's go home. You have a wife and children." The soldier didn't look at him but just kept on with what he was doing—he read.

His father went away and his mother came. "Oh, my son, just look! You ran away from the tsar but you haven't yet approached your own house. Let's go home." The soldier didn't even look at her. His mother started crying and went away.

Then his wife came with the children. "What is this, husband? You ran away from the tsar but you haven't even approached your own house. Look! You have children!" But the soldier didn't even look at her. So then she took a child, raised it higher than her head, and threw it on the floor. She went away leaving the child there on the floor, dead.

The soldier paid no attention to any of this. Suddenly a fiery serpent fell on the book from up above. The soldier grabbed a lance and pierced the serpent. Then he himself fell back and went to sleep.

In the morning he woke up and heard a fearful racket. He looked: instead of being in a hut overgrown with moss, he was lying in a golden palace. He looked out the window and there was an enormous capital city. He went out into the courtyard. Near the gates was the rider and there was a general of the watch. His clothing was shining with gold. Then the general said, "Thank you, soldier, for rescuing our town. It had been enchanted." (That was when his mother and father had visited him. The devil had come to him to try to make him go away.) So then the rider brought him a little bag of gold for his work.

The soldier went away into the city and rented an apartment, and began living there. He lived there a month, then two or three, and finally the host said to him, "Well, serviceman, you have been living all this time with me and you haven't paid for your quarters. God see you on your way out of here!" So the soldier brought him his little bag of gold, poured out a small pile, and gave it to the landlord. The landlord was delighted with such a lodger.

One splendid morning the soldier set off to take a walk in the town. And there in the town were three warriors who had been killed. They kept asking for someone to bury them. No matter how often they buried them—they would bury them today and tomorrow they would come back up and ask for someone to bury them again. Then the tsar said, "Whoever succeeds in finally burying these warriors will receive a big reward."

That soldier immediately agreed to bury them. He bought forty barrels of wine, called all the town together, and even people from the outskirts. When they had buried these warriors, the soldier rolled out all the barrels of wine and ordered all to drink as much as he could. When they were all drunk, the soldier ordered some of them to roar, others to sing songs, some to dance, and others to fight. Then they made such a noise that nobody could make out anything. And the warriors didn't like this at all. A day passed, then a week, a month passed but the warriors didn't come out and thus they were properly buried.

Then the tsar made the soldier distinguished throughout the town: no one anywhere for any reason was allowed to detain him no matter where he went or what he did.

Once he asked his host, "Can I go into the town to take a walk?"

"But of course, soldier. Why, who doesn't know you?! Doesn't the tsar know you, and all the gentlemen? All the town respects you."

So the soldier went through the town and he went out of the town and he went up to a big lake and there he saw three warriors coming over the lake. One was on a chestnut, one on a black, and the third on a gray. They were the same three he had buried. The soldier was terrified and fell flat over on his back.

Then one of the warriors got down from his horse and went up to the soldier and said, "Don't be afraid of us, little soldier, because you buried us so well, I am going to give you a chestnut hair from my horse. And whichever warrior approaches your city, just throw this hair from your pocket and a giant chestnut horse will appear before you. Mount it and you will defeat any warrior."

Then another warrior gave him a black hair, and the third gave him a gray hair, and they all said the same things. The soldier came back home to his apartment.

After a few days a warrior rode up to the town and asked to marry the tsar's daughter. "If you will not give her to me," he said, "I will kill all your warriors, burn down your city, and take you into captivity, and I will take your daughter away as my wife anyway."

The soldier heard this, went out into the street, took the chestnut hair out of his pocket and threw it, and then said, "Behind me is a colored gown, before me a fine steed!" And in front of him there appeared such a chestnut horse as to hurt the eyes!

The soldier mounted the horse and rode off through the town. The horse kicked up clods of earth the size of rising loaves. When they were riding by the tsar's palace at a slow trot, a clod flew right into the wall and shook the very wall. The tsar said "Oh my Lord, who are these warriors marching out against me? Servant, go and find out whom they are going to serve: are they for me or are they not Russians?!"

The servant went out and shouted, "Whom are you going to serve, our tsar or one not Russian?"

The soldier answered, "I am going to serve the one that is strongest of all." The servant told that to the tsar, and the tsar was sorrowful because he didn't have any strong warriors.

The soldier rode up to the unknown warrior, who said to him, "Let's fight!"

The soldier answered, "Who are you, some drunken drunkard just out of a tavern? Let's fight! Let's each ride back a half verst and then we shall see who takes whom." When they had clashed together, the soldier's horse reared up and he pierced the unknown warrior to the ground with his hoof and trampled him in the mud.

The soldier returned to his apartment, left his horse in the courtyard, untethered, and the horse remained there as if rooted, not moving from that spot.

The next day a new warrior came up to the city. Then the soldier went out into the street, threw the black hair out of his pocket, and there appeared before him an enormous black horse. He got on the horse and rode off. The horse started running, tossing up clods of earth over the good path. He also defeated the second warrior.

And then the third warrior approached. And he defeated the third one, on his gray horse. Then he returned home, back to the city, and as he rode, clods of earth flew out toward a low-lying little hut. And then when he was riding by the palace, a clod flew out right at a wall and knocked out the window frames. Then the tsar said, "Very likely that warrior is serving me because he has already defeated those three warriors. But who he is, this I do not know. Servant, go and see in which direction he is riding." So the servant went out beyond the gates and set out after the warrior. The warrior rode to his own quarters, stabled his horse alongside the other horses and went into his hut. The servant saw this but he didn't dare go into the hut. He was afraid of the horses. He returned to the tsar and described to him what he had seen.

The tsar got ready and went off himself to visit this distinguished warrior. He came to his quarters and said, "Oh, soldier, are you the one who has conquered so many warriors and rescued me from captivity?"

"I am, your majesty."

Then the tsar took him by the hand and led him to his palace. When he had entertained the soldier, he spoke to him: "I should like to have such a powerful and mighty stepson as you. If you agree, then after a certain time I will give over all my tsardom to you." The soldier agreed with pleasure and he married the tsar's daughter. And after a certain time he received the tsar's throne as well.

A–T 508

286. The Gratitude of a Corpse

There was this old man in Saint Petersburg whose surname was Nimeniaev, and he had just the one son, whose name was Vasilii. So fine. This Nimeniaev lived several years and then he died, and Vasilii was left there at eighteen with his mother. But there was an enormous amount of capital left them by the father. Shops and huge department stores. So one splendid day this Vasilii decided to go to a store and trade there with the clerks in the store. And he heard the sacred singing in Million Street as they were carrying out someone recently deceased. He looked at the people who were carrying the corpse and saw that some were beating the coffin of the deceased with clubs. So he stopped some of these men and asked them what they were doing and why they were doing it. These gentlemen answered that he had been in debt to these men and that therefore these men were seeing him to his grave. He said to the men, "Stop this. Don't touch the deceased. Come into my shop and I will pay you what he owed."

People paid attention to this and a few men went into Vasilii's store, and there Vasilii paid them what they were owed, and the entire public was very satisfied.

Later, on another splendid day, Vasilii was again in the shop and he felt like going into the cellar for a drink. He went there and in the cellar sat a village peasant in a gray kaftan waiting for a handout. "Well, Vasia, hire me on as a worker."

Vasia answered, "All right, come along."

Vasia went home to eat dinner, and he ordered the man to come two hours later (he had been drinking before dinner). After two hours that village peasant came to Vasia, made his presence known, and Vasia's mother let him in. So fine. So they sat down to dinner and the peasant asked for a quarter of a jug of vodka, and then he demanded a goblet, and he drank the whole goblet full. So fine. So he drank that quarter over dinner. They finished dinner and this worker asked, "Well, Vasia, do you have a horse for me? I want to do your deliveries for you." Vasia answered that in his stables he had three horses and that he could choose any one. So that worker went into the stable. Two of the horses he didn't like at all, but the third horse was fine and he liked it. It was a young horse. He mounted up but the shaft arch bent and wouldn't carry him. "Vasia, it would be better if you gave me a hundred rubles so that I could buy a horse and cart." One that would carry him and pull the cart. So fine. That peasant started delivering every sort of good from the stores to the shops, and he didn't even require help from his co-workers in loading it. After some time, one splendid time, he gave Vasia some advice: "Let's go hunting; we'll get provisions for several months." And so he and the best worker, Ivan, got on that Finnish cart. He said a warm farewell to his mother, and off they went. And they went out hunting along the postal route, and they traveled for several versts, and a dark, autumn night came over them. So fine. They let the horse graze on a green meadow, built a small fire, warmed themselves, and ate well. Suddenly there was this shriek in the tree. It was a huge parrot-bird. Vasia the merchant's son strung his bow, pulled it tight, and sent a steel arrow to bring down the parrot-bird. But the parrot-bird didn't fall from the tree. It dropped some iron keys. Vasia hid these keys. "These keys we will need, but we certainly don't need you."

Day broke, and they came on into Saratov district where they sold the cart and horse and bought a small steamship. They boarded the steamship and sailed off to a foreign land. They came to this foreign king and he had a daughter, Nastasia, who was very fine. Vasilii asked the worker Ivan to go and arrange his marriage to Nastasia. But the foreign king wouldn't agree, even though Vasilii was much attracted to Nastasia. The emperor and lord demanded to see the groom and the courtier. "Now then, courtier Ivan, is he your son or no relation?"

Vasilii answered, "He is my clerk, and I am his faithful servant." So the lord emperor said, "Build me a church in three days."

Vania built the church, but after one day it was only higher than the windows. After the second it was up to the ceiling. On the third day they put on the roof.

Ivan the worker appeared before the lord, and said, "Please accept your completed cathedral!" The lord came and saw that the church was finished, so he immediately betrothed his daughter to Vasilii. When the church was consecrated, they were married. Then in three days the lord ordered twelve ships loaded with trade goods, and he sent Ivan, Vasilii, and Nastasia out to sea. They had favorable winds and pleasant weather and soon arrived at their place and his mama. Mama met them with tears. They unloaded the twelve ships for a week before they were empty. And then the worker asked Vasilii to "please settle up with me." And he did. But that worker had kept a secret from Vasilii. Now he told him that he was that very person they had been carrying in the coffin. "And you paid off my debts, and I have served you faithfully and truly." So Vasia stayed with his mama and young wife to live in the house of the Nemeniaevs, and it is said they lived well and properly, and with all pleasures.

A–T 508*

287. The Golden Slipper

There lived and dwelt this old man with this old woman. The old man and the old woman had two daughters. Once the old man rode into town and there he bought one sister a little fish and the other sister a little fish, too. The older daughter ate her fish but the younger one went to the well and said, "Oh, Little Mother Fish, shall I eat you or not?"

"Don't eat me," said the little fish; "let me go into the water; I will be of use to you." She let the little fish go in the well and went home. The old woman really disliked her younger daughter. She dressed her sister in the very best clothing and went with her to the liturgy in the church, but she left the younger one at home with two measures of rye and ordered her to clean all the chaff out of it before she came back from church.

The girl went after some water and sat down by the well, crying. The little fish swam up to the surface and asked her, "What are you crying about, beautiful maiden?"

"How should I not cry?" the beautiful maiden answered. "Mother dressed my sister in the very best clothing and went away with her to the liturgy, and she left me at home and ordered me to clean all the chaff out of two measures of rye before she comes back from church!"

The little fish said, "Don't cry. Go and get dressed, and go to church; the rye will be cleaned." She got dressed and went to the liturgy. Her mother didn't recognize her. The liturgy was ending and the girl came home. Her mother also came home and asked, "Well, you little fool, did you clean the chaff out of the rye?"

"I cleaned it all," she answered.

"There was such a beautiful maiden at liturgy!" her mother said. "The priest couldn't chant or read—he just kept looking at her. And you, fool, just look at yourself, how you go around."

"Even though I wasn't there, I know," said the maiden.

"How could you know?" her mother said.

The next time the mother dressed the older sister in the very best clothing and set off with her to liturgy. She left the younger daughter three measures of grain and said, "While I am praying to God, you get the chaff out of that grain."

So then she went to liturgy and the daughter went for some water from the well. She sat by the well and wept. The little fish swam up to the surface and asked, "Why are you weeping, beautiful maiden?"

"How should I not weep? My mother dressed my sister in the very best clothing and went with her to liturgy, and she left me at home and ordered me to clean the chaff out of three measures of grain before she comes home from church."

The little fish said, "Don't cry! Go home and get dressed, then go after her to church; the grain will be cleaned!"

She got dressed and went to church and began praying to God. The priest couldn't chant or read—he just kept looking at her. The liturgy was finishing. There happened to be at that liturgy a tsarevich from some distant place. Our beautiful maiden was most attractive to him. He wanted to find out who she was. He threw some pitch under one of her slippers. The slipper got stuck and she went home. "I'll marry whomever's slipper this is!" The slipper was all stitched in gold.

So then the old woman came home. "Oh, what a beautiful maiden there was there!" she said. "The priest couldn't chant or read—he just kept looking at her, and you, fool, just look at yourself: you're a ragamuffin!"

So after that the tsarevich sought the maiden who had lost her slipper through all the districts, but he couldn't find anyone whom the slipper fit. He came to the old woman and asked her, "Show me your maiden. Perhaps the slipper will fit her."

"My daughter would soil that slipper," the old woman answered. The beautiful maiden came out and the tsarevich tried the slipper on her foot. It fit her perfectly. He married her and they began to live and prosper and acquired wealth. I was there, I drank beer. It flowed over my lips but none got into my mouth. They gave me a blue kaftan, but a crow flew by shouting, "Blue kaftan, blue kaftan!" I thought it was saying "Off with the kaftan," so I took off the kaftan. Then they gave me a top hat and started putting it down over my neck. Then they gave me some red slippers, and the crow came flying and shouted, "Red slippers, red slippers!" I thought it was saying, "Stolen slippers," so I took them and tossed them.†

A–T 510A

288. The Hunchback

There lived and dwelt this old man and old woman. They had just the one daughter. Then the old woman died and the old man married another woman, an evil stepmother. The evil stepmother did not like the daughter and began trying to drive her out. She took all her belongings, putting a bundle in front and a bundle in back. And so she set off like a dirty, old woman. So then she walked near or far and she came into a village and there she tried to find a position as a laborer. They offered her a hundred rubles but she wouldn't take it. She just wanted a dress sewn that would be like the sun in the heav-

---

†See Volume I, p.42

ens. The master agreed and hired her, and he agreed to make her such a dress with a sun in the heavens on it. But then she lived a year at that master's and then she went away. So then she went to another village. And she went to a rich peasant and asked that a dress be sewn like the moon in the heavens. And that master agreed. She lived there a year and he sewed her the dress and then she left. She went to a third peasant who agreed to sew her a dress like the stars in the heavens. And then she went on from him with her bundles, her packs, and she came to the tsar to be hired as a laborer. "What can you possibly do, you hunchback?"

"I can do anything." She agreed and he hired her for a year. He set aside a hundred rubles for her.

Now that tsar had a son, Ivan Tsarevich. Whenever he would go to church services, she would come up to sweep the back room. And so he said, "Hunchback, give me my boots."

And she would carry his boots to him, saying "If only this boot were on my foot!" And he would take the boot in his hands and give her head a poke with it and say, "Oh, my Hunchback! How could you keep this boot on your foot?" But then while he was away at church, she would finish airing the room and go off to church after him, wearing the dress with the stars in the heavens. And all the baptized folk would look at her and say, "Oh, what a beauty she is!" And Ivan Tsarevich couldn't even pray for staring at her.

So finally he couldn't stand it any more and he sent someone to ask "Which town are you from, miss?"

She answered, "I'm from not far away, where they poke you in the head with boots." But that Ivan Tsarevich was very slow-witted. She went off home from the church ahead of him, took off her bundles, and removed her dress. When Ivan Tsarevich came from the church, he explained to his parents how "a certain miss had been in the church and all the baptized folk were amazed by her. She was such a beauty and her clothing was such that there has never been better on earth. I sent someone to ask who she was and so forth and she said that she was from a place where they beat you about the head with boots. I am going to go now and search for this city." He rode and rode, looking for the maiden, but he couldn't find her.

The next day he again went to the church service and she went to sweep out his room. He said, "Hunchback, hand me my fur cap."

She took it and put it on her head: "Oh, if only I had a fur cap to wear on my head!"

So then he took it and popped her on the head with it. "Oh you, hunchbacked devil, how would you hold a cap on?" And so he went off to church. She finished the sweeping and her other work, put on her dress in the hall, the one like the moon in the heavens, and she was even more beautiful as she

set off for church. The people looked at her even more than before: there
was no way they could pray to God as they kept on looking at her. Where did
such a beauty come from?

Ivan Tsarevich stood there. He stood there until he could stand it no more.
He sent a servant to find out. The servant asked and she answered, "I'm from
a nearby town where they hit you on the head with caps."

The liturgy was finished and she went home, removed her dress, and put on
her bundles again. Ivan Tsarevich came home and told about "the beautiful girl
in church and all the baptized folk were amazed and distracted from their prayers."
He said he would go search out her town. So his father gave him permission to
go. He rode and rode through the night, but he couldn't find the town and returned home empty-handed. She came on the third day and started sweeping.
He said, "Hand me that mirror hanging on the wall, Hunchback!"

She took the mirror from the wall and said, "If only I had such a mirror of
my own."

"Oh, you hunchbacked devil! Why would you want to spend time looking
at yourself in a mirror?" Then he took the mirror and cracked her on the head
with it before setting off for church.

Again she finished sweeping, finished the housework, and went to change
into the dress that was like the sun in the heavens, the most beautiful dress of
all. She arrived at the church. The priest discontinued the liturgy as there was
such a bright light shining in the church when you looked at her. The servant
asked, "From which town are you?"

"I'm from a nearby town where they beat you about the head with mirrors."
So there was no further service and she came home and removed the dress.

Ivan Tsarevich thought it all over and concluded, "Well then, she's from a
nearby town." Then he thought about it, he thought about hitting her with his
boot on her head, and popping her with his cap, and so maybe there was
something here! He came home from church and went down on his knees
before his mother. "Bless my marriage to the hunchbacked girl! She's the
one God has destined for me!"

But at first his mother and father wouldn't give their blessing. But he
stood up, took her right hand, and, first kissing it, placed his ring on her. "Be
the one chosen for me by God!"

Then she later said to him, "Permit me to go out for a few minutes."
So she took her bundles off to a barn and put on the dress like the stars in
the heavens. He took her by the right hand, kissed her sugary sweet lips,
they organized the wedding, and were married. And they began living
and prospering.

A–T 510B

289. The Golden Lantern

It is unknown where and when there lived a certain tsar. His wife, the tsaritsa, died and left him with an eligible daughter. The tsar was still young and handsome and he decided to marry another. But however much he traveled, however much he looked, however much he examined beautiful maidens, he did not find a single one who in both appearance and speech reminded him of his beloved late wife. He grieved, the poor tsar was downcast. He didn't want to remain a widower, but there was no bride to his taste. The tsar looked and looked at his daughter and fell into even deeper despair. "Oh," he thought, "if I could just find someone like my daughter! She is so like my late wife, no portrait would be needed!" He thought and pondered, did the tsar, and he decided to marry his daughter, he decided and gave the order that his daughter prepare for the marriage wreath.

The poor tsarevna, when she learned about it, begged and implored her father: "Do not destroy me, my own dear father!" What next! The tsar wouldn't even hear of it. "Alright," the tsarevna finally said to her father. "Let it be so, I will marry you, but just make it so that by tomorrow there is a big lake or sea around our palace and that on this lake or sea are both big and little ships, royal and noble, and free merchants, and brave brigands, and all these boats and ships must dock at our porch and give us gold for their right to passage."

The tsar's daughter woke up in the morning and looked: all was ready. All around the big royal palace stood a big lake or sea, and about it sailed all sorts of ships with white sails, and they came right up to the porch and docked, and for the right to transport their goods they gave gold. This amusement had cost the tsar dearly.

"Very good," said the tsar's daughter to her father, "So be it, I shall marry you if by tomorrow you make a huge golden lantern such that this lantern shines all over our lake or sea so that the ships from far away can see it and come up to our royal porch to sell the most expensive goods to us."

The tsar's daughter woke up in the morning and looked: All was in readiness: next to the high royal porch on the very shore of the lake or sea there stood an expensive gold lantern, shining of its very self, it illuminated everything around. The ships saw it, and sailed right up to the royal porch, and for their passage they paid the tsar in pure gold, and from it they paved a path for their goods for the third time. The tsar was himself amazed at his amusement, he did not just hope to marry his daughter, he was waiting impatiently for the end of all the fuss before permitting them to go beneath the wedding crown. He bought up so many of all kinds of the most expensive goods for his daughter such that, it seemed, he had given out all the money from his treasury for them.

"Very good," said the tsar's daughter to her father, "So be it, I shall marry you if by tomorrow you can prepare me the most expensive dowry ever and that dowry must be able to fit inside one tiny little chest."

In the morning the royal daughter woke up and looked: all was ready: there stood a little chest before her—you could tuck it under your arm—and it was filled to the brim with every sort of rare goods. And everything was fitted in it and packed so cleverly. You could cover the whole palace with all those goods. All the things were outstanding, of unlimited quality, they had been bought by the tsar the day before. There was nothing that wasn't lying there in that clever chest: there were expensive bed coverings and a cot, and a troika of horses, and every little toy to bring joy to the royal daughter.

"Well," said the royal daughter to her father, "Now, father, I am ready to be your wife, let the wedding be this evening. Only permit me, my lord, to go to the grave of my dead mother. I shall go and call out to her and ask her blessing, and then you will lead me beneath the wedding wreath with you."

So the royal daughter went to her mother's grave to take her leave and the tsar in his joy began organizing the feast and party. He summoned everyone to appear before him at the palace. The tsars and lords gathered, and merchants and brave bandits, too. All came by ocean-sea sailing to the tsar. The tsar thought of buying up all the goods from the merchants for the feast so that there would be plenty at the feast, but they told him that his royal treasury was already empty. The money had been spent on important works, like building the ocean or sea, the golden lantern, and the most had gone on the little chest for his daughter.

So the tsar came to the church for the wreath—such a fine lad that all the guests crowded round him and their eyes were dimmed by his beauty. The tsar stood in the church and awaited his bride. He waited for an hour, a second, and more, and still there was no tsarevna. "Well," he thought angrily, "this is not the time for wasting in saying farewell to a dead mother, it's the time for getting married."

Suddenly a royal messenger came into the church and said, "Such and such, your royal highness, wherever we've gone, wherever we've looked, we can't find your daughter anywhere."

The tsar went out of the church and was going home. They looked everywhere, rummaged everywhere, shook everything up, moved everything from place to place ten times. The tsar himself searched, the guests searched, but the tsarevna bride was not to be found, it was as if she'd dissolved in water!

"No," said the tsar, "there's no place else for her to hide here, it's all surrounded by water. Some disaster must have taken place. As she left her mother for the church as unfortunate as can be, she must have thrown herself into the sea." But no one, neither friends, nor servants, nor the tsar himself guessed to look into the golden lantern. And the tsar's daughter had crawled into it soon after dawn and just stayed there.

So the tsar didn't get married to his daughter. After all those preparations he began living poorly. He would eat only two dishes, very few ships came sailing in to him, and as a result the royal treasury did not grow.

Once a rich merchant came from distant lands sailing up to the royal palace and he saw at the tsar's all kinds of exotic things, but especially the golden lantern. He noted that the tsar was living in great poverty, suffering great need in all things, there was nothing to sell him, and he could buy nothing from him, and so he began trying to trade with the tsar for the gold lantern. "Sell it," he says, "and I'll give you really good money for it."

The tsar was pleased at the prospect. The gold lantern had for a long time been standing around in his way and to no good purpose. He hadn't known what to do with it so he sold it to the merchant.

The merchant put it in an obvious place on his ship and set sail to trade in other lands. He sailed into a different tsardom, unpacked and set up a big tent, and in the tent he placed the golden lantern and he began trading and taking profits. But in the morning wherever the merchant looked, he was missing many expensive goods, and he was also missing a lot of money, and the merchant, as is known, did everything by careful reckoning. Where could it all be going? The merchant simply couldn't fathom it. It seemed that everything was tightly locked up. So the merchant noticed the loss from his tent once, then he noticed it a second time, and so he put a strong guard around the tent at night, but nothing helped. In the morning he went into his tent and looked: it was practically empty. Even more goods were missing and all the gold was stolen. "Oh," the merchant thought, "I must have come to a bandits' land. I can't trade here, these people are really adroit thieves, I'll be left without even my shirt!"

So the merchant began carrying what goods he still had back onto his ship so that he could go trading in another land when suddenly he saw something: a young prince went into his tent. The prince bought up a great many goods of all sorts, gave him even more money than was necessary, and asked the merchant, "You won't sell your golden lantern, will you?"

"Why not sell it?" the merchant responded. "We have nothing cherished around here." And he sold it.

The golden lantern turned up in the chambers of the young tsarevich, standing in a visible place. Now this tsarevich had a disagreeable bride. The tsar was intending to force him to marry her. Once the tsarevich was riding off hunting and he gave an order to his bride: "If you want to please me, tidy up my room nicely while I'm gone." He came back from the hunt and looked: Everything in his chamber was changed around, everything was in its place, and it was a pleasure to look at it. There were silks and carpets, everything, goodness knows from where. The tsarevich looked at his bed and said to his bride: "You have done a splendid job of fluffing up my featherbed and shaking out the pillow."

The bride said to him: "I've fussed around you so much that my arms are worn out. I've ordered my dowry sent to your rooms."

The next time the prince went off hunting he gave an order to his bride: "If you wish to please me, prepare a fine meal for me." He came back from the hunt and looked: on the table in his rooms was a rich meal. There were wines and every sort of pastry—to eat and drink it would be a pleasure. The tsarevich was amazed.

His bride said to him: "I baked everything, cooked everything, I got my father's own wines for you. I'm tired from the baking, trying to please you."

"Tomorrow we shall go to the church to be married," the tsarevich said, "only by morning make a fine silk carpet for my feet so that we'll have something to stand on beneath the wreaths, and a fine silk kerchief, so that we'll have something to hold onto in the church."

In the morning the tsarevich got up earlier than usual and looked—amazing! The little door of his golden lantern seemed to be opening of itself, and the tsar's daughter stepped down out of the lantern onto the floor, all covered in silver and gold, her neck entwined in expensive coins, and her face was just like your sun! The tsarevna went up to the table, opened her little chest, got out of it a silk carpet and handkerchief, put them on the table, and was just about to go and hide in the lantern when the tsarevich grabbed her by the hand: "Now you won't get away from me, my dear!" he said to her.

"Oh, tsarevich," the royal daughter begged him, "don't touch me, let me sleep one last night in this golden lantern, and then I will be yours forever."

The tsarevich let the tsarevna go and she locked herself in the golden lantern.

In the morning the tsar and tsaritsa came into the tsarevich's chambers, and all the best men and matchmakers, to see the bride's work together and to make ready to go to the church. The tsar and tsaritsa began to praise the bride's work, the best men to criticize it openly as if it were shoddy and crooked and made ever so badly.

"Well, now, tsarevich," said the bride's parents. "Come here, now it's your turn—to praise it and admire it, she is such a skilled worker at it."

"Very good," said the tsarevich, "now I will show all of you the skilled worker who could make all this and much else too."

Then the little door of the golden lantern opened of itself, and from the lantern in all her beauty the royal daughter appeared. She opened her little chest and began showering all the guests with all kinds of expensive goods.

She tossed to the tsar and tsaritsa some very dear cloth, to the best men she poured out rare wines, and she showered the bride's matchmakers with all kinds of gold coins.

All were amazed, and then frightened, and they quickly took themselves out of the room because they were horribly afraid that she would throw them all out on their heads too. The tsar's daughter remained with the tsarevich in the room alone, but the bottom still couldn't be seen in her little chest: everything just kept coming out and coming out! Soon the room was overflowing from floor to ceiling with every sort of good, with gold and silver, so that they were really crowded.

The tsar's daughter became the tsarevich's bride. He got married to her and received the rich little chest as her dowry. And for however long the tsarevich lived with his wife after that, he was still amazed that the little chest never ever became empty to the very bottom.

The tsarevich placed the golden lantern a little higher up, on his palace roof. And it is still shining there, it lights up the whole tsardom, and it warms all the people. The earth is fertile from its warmth: there's rye and wheat and all that's good began to be born of it. So that's where you and I should live and make our fortune, do away with need and misery!

A–T 510B*

290. Burenushka the Little Red Cow

In no certain tsardom, in no certain land, there lived and dwelt a tsar with his tsaritsa, and they had a single daughter, Tsarevna Maria. When the tsaritsa died, the tsar took another wife, Iagishna. This Iagishna gave birth to two daughters: one had two eyes, but the other had three eyes. The stepmother didn't like Tsarevna Maria and she sent her out to herd the little red cow and she gave her just a dry crust of bread.

The tsarevna set off into the steppe, and she bowed to the little red cow's right leg, and then she ate and drank her fill, and then she got herself all pretty and spent the whole day walking after the little red cow just like a landlord's wife. The day passed and again she bowed to the right leg, removed her pretty clothes, and came home, bringing back the crust of bread, which she placed upon the table. "How's that bitch keeping alive?" wondered Iagishna. The next day she gave Tsarevna Maria the same old crust of bread, but she sent her older daughter out with her. "Watch carefully and find out what Maria Tsarevna is finding to eat."

They came into the steppe and Maria Tsarevna said, "Let me look for lice on your head." She started looking while at the same time mumbling, "Sleep, sleep, sister! Sleep, sleep, my very own! Sleep, sleep little eye! Sleep, sleep, the other one, too." The sister went fast asleep and Maria Tsarevna got up, went up to the little red cow, and bowed to her right leg. Then she ate and drank, dressed herself up, and walked around all day like a landlord's wife. Evening came; Maria Tsarevna changed clothes and said, "Get up, sister, get up, my dear. Let's go home."

"Oh, no," said the sister sorrowfully. "I've slept all day and seen nothing; mother will scold me now."

They came home and her mother asked her, "What did Maria Tsarevna drink? What did she eat?"

"I didn't see anything." Iagishna cursed her and in the morning she sent her three-eyed daughter out. "Go and watch what that bitch eats and drinks." So the maidens came into the steppe to herd the little red cow. Tsarevna Maria said, "Sister, let me search for lice on your head."

"Go right ahead, sister, go ahead, my dear." Maria Tsarevna began looking and mumbling, "Sleep, sleep, sister! Sleep, sleep, my very own! Sleep, sleep little eye! Sleep, the other one too!" But she forgot the third eye and that third eye watched and watched what Maria Tsarevna was doing. She ran up to the little red cow, bowed to the right leg, drank and ate her fill, and got dressed in fine clothes. When the sun began to set, she again bowed to the right leg and changed her clothes and then woke up the three-eyed one: "Wake up sister, wake up, my dear! Let's go home."

So Maria Tsarevna came home, and she put the dry crust of bread on the table.

Her mother asked her daughter, "What did she drink and eat?" The three-eyed daughter told her everything. Iagishna demanded, "Old man, slaughter the little red cow." The old man slaughtered the cow and Maria Tsarevna begged him to give her the lower intestine at least. The old man give her the lower intestine. She took it and planted it on the gatepost, and a willow bush grew up with all sorts of beautiful berries flourishing, and on it various kinds of little birds sat and sang the songs both of tsars and peasants.

Ivan Tsarevich heard about Maria Tsarevna and he came to her stepmother. He put a platter on the table and said, "Whichever maiden can pick me a full platter of berries I will marry." Iagishna sent her elder daughter to pick berries, but the little birds wouldn't let her come close. When she tried, they tried to peck out her eyes. So then she sent her second daughter, but they wouldn't let her come close either. Finally she let Maria Tsarevna go. Maria Tsarevna took the platter and set off to pick the berries. She picked and the tiny birds added twice or three times as many to the platter. She came back and put the platter on the table, and then she bowed to the tsarevich. Then came a happy feast and the wedding as Ivan Tsarevich took Maria Tsarevna for himself and they began to live and prosper, and acquired wealth.

Whether they lived for a long time or a short time, Maria Tsarevna gave birth to a son. She wanted to visit her father. She went to visit him with her husband. Her stepmother turned her into a goose and she arranged for Ivan Tsarevich to marry her older daughter. Then Ivan Tsarevich went back home.

An old man who was his tutor got up early in the morning, washed himself white as snow, took the infant into his arms, and went out into the steppe to a little bush. Some geese were flying, gray geese were flying. "Oh, geese, gray geese! Where have you seen the mother of this infant?"

"In the next flock," they answered.

Another flock came flying. "Oh geese, gray geese! Where have you seen the mother of this infant?"

The mother of the infant flew down to earth, removed her skin and put on another, took the infant into her arms and began feeding it at her breasts, crying, "Today I shall feed you, tomorrow I shall feed you, but day after tomorrow I shall fly away beyond the dark forests, beyond the high mountains."

The old man set off home. The little lad slept until morning without waking while the substitute wife scolded the old man for going off into the steppe and for having nearly starved her son. In the morning the old man once more got up early, washed himself as white as snow, and went with the child into the steppe and Ivan Tsarevich got up, set off unseen after the old man, and climbed into the bush.

Some geese were flying, gray geese were flying. "Oh, geese, gray geese! Where have you seen the mother of this infant?"

"In the next flock."

Another flock came flying. "Oh geese, gray geese! Where have you seen the mother of this infant?"

The infant's mother leapt to the ground, pulled off her skin, pulled off another, threw it on the bush, and began feeding the infant at her breast. As she was saying farewell to him, she said, "Tomorrow I will fly away beyond the dark forests, over the high mountains!"

She gave the infant back to the old man. "What is that awful smell?" she said. She was about to put her skins back on. She reached for them but they were not to be found. Ivan Tsarevich had burned them. He grabbed Maria Tsarevna and she turned into a frog, then into a lizard and every sort of reptile, and then afterward into a spindle. Ivan Tsarevich broke the spindle in two, threw the top of it over his head and the bottom in front of him, and then she appeared as a beautiful young woman.

They set off home together. Iagishna's daughter shrieked and yelled, "The destroyer is coming, the murderess is coming!"

Ivan Tsarevich summoned the princes and boyars and asked them, "With which wife do you want me to live?"

They said, "With the first."

"Well, gentlemen, I'll live with whichever wife first leaps to the top of the gates." Iagishna's daughter went right up to the top of the gates, but Maria Tsarevich grasped it tightly and did not climb up. So Ivan Tsarevich took his rifle and shot the false wife, and lived with Maria Tsarevna as before, happily and prosperously.

A–T 511 + 403

291. The Bogatyr Warriors

In a certain tsardom, in a certain country, there lived and dwelt a peasant and his wife. They had a son Ivashka. And when he was pretty grown up, they sent him off to learn to write. So he started studying and he also started playing with the lads outside. Whoever he grabbed hold of by the arm, off came the arm, whoever by the head, off came the head. Everyone became angry with Ivashka and they sent him away out of town.

He walked along the road, the way. And he saw a man tearing oak trees out by the roots. "Good health, Oak Man! What are you doing?"

"I am tearing out oaks."

"Be my sworn brother and come along with me."

"Alright, let's go."

And so they set off. They walked along the road, the way, and they saw a man shooting with a bow and arrow. They asked him, "What are you aiming at?"

"I am aiming at the forehead of a fly over some versts."

"Be our sworn brother, come with us."

So he set off with them. They walked along the road, the way and they saw a man sitting with his head bandaged. "Why is your head bandaged?"

"My hair is tied up because if I let it down, there will be a frost."

"Be our sworn brother, come with us."

So he set off with them. They went on a little further and they saw a man sitting in a tree holding one nostril and blowing air out the other. "What are you blowing?"

"There's a mill standing there, more than a thousand versts away. I blow and it turns."

"Come on," they said, "be our sworn brother."

So they go on further and they see a man sitting and listening. "What are you listening for?"

"I'm listening to the grass grow."

"Be our sworn brother."

So all seven of them went off together then, and they came to another tsardom. And in this tsardom the tsar had announced that "the tsar's daughter will run to the well for water and if anyone can out-race her, he shall receive her in marriage. But if anyone makes the attempt and fails to out-race her, off with his head."

So Ivashka went to the tsar and said, "Is it possible for someone to run in my stead?"

"That's possible, but if he doesn't out-race her, it's off with your head. So Ivashka let loose a runner with wooden legs, and the runner flew faster than an arrow and he flew right up to a well and he took some water in a tankard and started running back, but at the halfway point on the road he put the tankard down and lay down to sleep. The tsarevna still hadn't run the first half of the way. She ran up to the runner, took his tankard with the water, and left her own empty one. Then she ran off home with his tankard and the runner kept on sleeping.

At this very time Ivashka and the other bogatyrs were standing in the tower. They saw that the runner was still sleeping and that the tsarevna was close to the city. So then the one who had been aiming to hit the fly in the forehead from several versts took an arrow and shot it right into the runner's coat and he woke up, jumped up, grabbed the tankard, and like an arrow flew to the well, took some water and got back before the tsarevna.

But the tsar didn't want to marry his daughter to Ivashka. He ordered the bogatyrs to come and dine in an iron room. They came, he gave them dinner, and then he locked them up there. And then underneath the floor he started a fire. He wanted to burn them up. The very legs of the chairs were about to burn when the peasant with the tied-up hair took his hair and let it go. Immediately everything froze. Even the food was covered with ice. So there was a frost up above and down below there was a fire, and they didn't burn, nor did they freeze. But anyway, the tsar thought that they had all burned up and he ordered the doors opened. They opened the doors and there they were, unharmed.

The tsar was astonished but the tsar was still sad about giving his daughter in marriage to a simple peasant. So he said to him, "Take gold instead of the tsarevna! I will give you as much gold as a single person can carry away." Ivashka agreed and ordered that there be brought from the entire tsardom canvas for the tailors to sew together. And they sewed up an enormous sack. They poured the tsar's gold in but it didn't fill the sack. They brought gold from throughout the tsardom but that didn't fill it either. Then Dubynia, the oakman, took the sack and raised it up and started carrying it off. Ivashka and all the other sworn brothers went with him and they went out of the town. They went far away.

Then the tsar began to feel sorry about losing his gold and he sent an army after the bogatyrs. The bogatyrs didn't know anything about, they went on quietly. Only the one who could listen to the grass grow put his ear to the earth and said, "We'll have to get in boats and sail away from them!" So they got into boats and sailed off. The tsar's army also got into boats and started sailing out after them, to catch up to them. Then the one who could turn a windmill at a thousand versts, aimed one of his nostrils at the tsar's fleet and the other at their own sails, and did he blow! . . . It knocked the tsar's fleet back and they immediately sailed up to the other shore.

They went out on the shore and went up to their city and there they saw an army, a mighty force. There was no way they could pass by it into their own city. So they had a council. "How should we get into our city?"

Dubynia said, "Let the one who blew away the tsar's fleet now blow half the walls and I'll defeat half the enemy force and from the city the people can defeat the other half." And that's what they did. They defeated the mighty army and started to live and prosper in their own city.

A–T 513A

292. The Airship

A certain young man married and he took a beautiful wife. The tsar was riding through the village and she looked out the window. The tsar found her pleasing. The tsar said, "I shall take your wife away from here."

The young man said, "I married her, I love her. How will you take her?"

"Well," the tsar said, "if you can get me an airship, then I won't take her."

He thought, "How can I get an airship?" He fell into deep thought.

His wife said, "What are you thinking about?"

"Well, the tsar has ordered me to get an airship, but where shall I obtain one?"

She said, "The morning is wiser than the evening, don't worry."

In the morning they got up and she gave him a sort of stick. "Take this stick and go into the forest. There you will find a thick, thick tree with a hollow. Knock on this tree with this stick three times and an airship will appear before you. When you ride on this airship, pick up whomever you see."

He rode and saw a peasant carrying a bundle of straw. "Get in, let's go." So now there were two of them riding along. A peasant was carrying a load of wood. "Where are you carrying that?"

"To sell at the bazaar."

"Get in, let's go." And on they go. A peasant was carrying three loaves of bread. He asked, "Why are you carrying so much bread?"

"To eat."

"Can you really eat three loaves at a go?"

"For me that's nothing. I can swallow them in one gulp." So then there were four of them riding along.

They looked and saw a peasant standing on one leg with the other folded over his shoulder. "Why are you going about on one leg?"

"If I let go of that leg, I'll step off three versts at one go."

"Get in." And now there were five of them riding. They saw a peasant shooting at something. He asked, "At whom are you shooting?"

"A hare started up three versts away." They took him in.

They rode on further. Another one was listening with his ear to the ground. "What do you hear?"

"I hear what's going on in the world." And on they go. Someone was walking beside the sea. "Why are you walking here beside the sea?"

"I want a drink."

"Don't you really see the water that's in that sea?"

"But if I swallow, the sea will dry up."

"Get in and let's go." There were now eight of them riding along. They came to the tsar.

"Here, I present you with the airship."

"Oh, just great, but now a foreign land has declared war on us. If you destroy it with your gang, then I won't take your wife."

The young man thought hard. How could they destroy the enemy with only eight? Perhaps a million were marching toward them. His comrades asked him, "Why are you thinking so hard?"

"Well, the sovereign has ordered a foreign army destroyed."

The one who had been carrying the wood said, "Help me throw away this wood." They threw away the wood and from it an entire army rose up. And in three days they had defeated that other country.

Then the tsar said, "I shall now treat you for having beaten them. I shall roast forty oxen so that you eight may eat."

The young man was pensive, "How could eight men eat forty oxen?" But the one who had been carrying the bread said, "Roast them, I'll eat them alone." So he sat down and ate all those oxen himself.

Then the tsar said, "Now drink up forty casks of wine and if you don't drink them, then I'll take your wife away anyway."

The one who had been walking by the sea said, "Let them put the casks up, I'll drink them all."

Then the tsar said, "Catch me a white hare alive, and if you don't I'll take your wife."

The young man fell into thought: how was he to catch a hare alive? The one who had been standing on one leg put his leg down and started running. He caught the hare, lay down by the bridge, and lay there sleeping. Only a half an hour remained until the time would run out. Where was he? The one who listened to the ground lay down on the ground. "I will find out where he is. Aha, he's lying three versts away, by a bridge."

The one who was a hunter shot in that direction. The bullet hopped by and woke up the man who brought the hare. The tsar then said, "Now I shall honor you," and he sent them to the bathhouse. But he told his servants to heat the bathhouse up to boiling, then to lock it and burn them. Three hours passed. The tsar sent his servants. "Go and dig them out, they've burned in the bathhouse." The servants opened the bathhouse and saw them all sitting and talking, and the water in the cauldrons was getting cold.

A–T 513B + 465

293. Uncle Toropyga the Hustler

There lived and dwelt this tsar and he had this son, Ivan Tsarevich, and he had this uncle Toropyga the Hustler. And Ivan Tsarevich got married to Maria the Wise. And she had a stepmother, a really nasty one. So Ivan Tsarevich and Maria the Wise were sleeping and a bird of prophecy came flying to them and said, "Ivan Tsarevich is asleep and Maria the Wise is asleep and they do not know misfortune, but the stepmother has sent them a change of horses, and when they mount them, they will die and whoever hears this and tells them shall be petrified up to the knee. Toropyga the Hustler heard it, but said nothing, and when the stepmother sent the horses, he killed them. Ivan Tsarevich was furious but there was nothing to be done.

The next night the same bird of prophecy came flying to them and prophesied: "Ivan Tsarevich is asleep and Maria the Wise is asleep, and they do not know misfortune but the stepmother is sending them a change of clothing and if they put it on, they will die, and whoever hears this and tells them shall be petrified up to the waist. Toropyga the Hustler heard everything, but he said nothing, and when the stepmother sent the clothing, he burned it in the stove. Ivan Tsarevich was once more furious, but that was all.

The third night the bird of prophecy came flying once more and she prophesied: "Ivan Tsarevich sleeps and Maria the Wise sleeps and they do not know that in the night their very stepmother shall come crawling to them as a fierce serpent and devour them, and whoever hears this and tells them shall be completely petrified. Toropyga the Hustler heard this, took his saber, and went and stood in the bedroom in the night. The serpent came crawling up and he started hacking at it, and he hacked it up, but he accidently hit Ivan Tsarevich and cut off his arm.

When Ivan Tsarevich woke up, he saw that there was blood on the floor and that his arm was cut off, and there was Toropyga the Hustler with his saber. Ivan Tsarevich said to him, "Well, now I see that you killed the horses and you burned up the clothing and you tried to kill us. Tell me, why did you do this?"

Toropyga the Hustler started telling him. "The first night," he said, "the bird of prophesy came and prophesied: 'The wicked stepmother will send a change of horses and when they mount them, they will die. And whoever hears this and tells them will be petrified to the knee.'" And Toropyga the Hustler was petrified up to the knee. "The second night," he said, "the bird of prophecy came flying once more and said, 'The wicked stepmother will send a change of clothing, and when they put it on, they will die. And whoever hears this and tells them will be petrified up to the waist.'"

And Toropyga the Hustler was petrified up to the waist. "The third night," he said, "the bird of prophesy once more came flying up and said, 'Ivan Tsarevich is asleep and Maria the Wise is asleep, and they don't know the misfortune that in the night that same stepmother will come as a fierce serpent and devour them. And whoever hears this and tells them, will be entirely petrified.'" And Toropyga the Hustler was completely petrified. Ivan Tsarevich had found out how much Uncle Toropyga the Hustler had loved them and he started weeping and he ordered him placed in a coffin in the church.

Then a son was born to Ivan Tsarevich and when he was three years old they went to the church and they said to him, "Here lies our uncle Toropyga the Hustler; kiss him, for three times he saved us from death, but he himself was petrified. The tsarevich was trying to kiss but he fell and broke his fingernail and his blood dropped onto Toropyga the Hustler and he came to life. And they began living and prospering and becoming wealthy.

A–T 516

294. The Sorcerer Child

There lived and dwelt this tsar and he had a son and a daughter. Well, he got old and he said to his son, "Dearest son! I will soon die. You must rule as I have ruled. When you decide to get married, here is a ring. Use it to select your bride. And if you do not select according to this ring, then do not marry."

When he had buried his father, the son set off to search for a bride for himself and he traveled around the whole world. But he could not find a bride. When he had come home, he threw the ring on the table. He went away and when his sister was tidying up the room, she saw the ring.

"Tell me, what is this, brother? You have never hidden anything from me but you have been hiding this. With whom were you engaged with this ring?"

"No one, father gave me the ring." She put it and it fit her hand like a glove. Her brother said, "Well, sister, you must be my bride."

"How is that possible?" she said, "how can a brother marry a sister?"

"Apparently, our father foresaw this." He began to press her. "Be my wife."

But she kept resisting. She said, "If this is how it is, brother, build me a house on the shore of the sea, and I will live there a while, and then I will marry you."

So they built the house and she set off to live there, and she took just one maiden with her. She lived there for a while and she saw a fisherman catching fish in the sea. She called him to her, "Listen, fisherman, do you have such and such a fish?" He gave her the fish. She sent the maid with the fish to her brother. The girl took the fish to her brother and said that he should get ready for the wedding. And she (the tsarevna) at that time rode away with the fisherman beyond the sea.

She came to the other side of the sea and gave the fisherman a significant sum of money for carrying her across and for not telling anybody about it. Then she set off to wander through the empty land. She wandered in the steppes for a long time. Then she came to an enormous forest. She lived in that forest for a lot of time and fed herself on forest fruits, and she walked and tore all her clothes. And her dwelling was a hollow, an empty tree. And she lived there for quite some time and she didn't see anybody in that forest.

Suddenly one time she came out of her hollow and saw a woman collecting mushrooms in the forest. She took fright and went away back into her hollow. The woman noticed, went up to her and said, "If you are an old man, let you be my brother; if an old woman, then my sister. If you are a young man, then be my son, if a young woman, then be my daughter. Come out!"

She answered, "I cannot come out, I am completely naked. Bring me a dress!"

Now the old woman was a forester in the forest. She ran into a hut and said, "Old man, old man! God has given me a treasure, but I don't know what: a son or a daughter." The old man immediately gave her a dress and some food and sent off. They brought the dress. She dressed, ate, and set off with the old woman.

They brought her to their home and she lived in that house for some time. The old man and the old woman began speaking to her about marrying their son. She resisted, and she finally grew tired of them. She asked them, "Where is your son?"

"He has been herding swine these eighteen years."

She said, "Bring him to me then." She thought to herself, "Better to marry a swineherd than my own brother." They brought him, the herder, and moss had grown completely all over him. She cut it off and shaved it with her own hands. She rode into the town, bought him German dress, and various books. She started teaching him and she taught him how to speak several languages. "Now I can marry your son." The old man was so happy, as was the old woman. They married them in the village.

They lived together, the man and the woman, for a certain time, a year or two, and then a son was born to them. At that time somebody came to them from the village and invited them to a wedding. She stayed at home: with a nursing child you can't go visiting. He set off for the wedding and she stayed at home and thought, "I should take a look at what they are doing there. It's fine if my husband doesn't get drunk, but if he is drinking I'll go away, I won't live with him." So she put on beggar's clothing and set off for the village. She saw where the wedding was so she went up to the window and asked for some alms. An old woman caught sight of her and invited her into the house. They got some dinner for her and when she had eaten, there was a sudden heavy downpour of rain. She couldn't go home. She saw her husband sitting there in the company of a priest and since he was observing the law to the priest, the priest could say nothing against him. Because of the rain she stayed the night there at the wedding.

Now her nursing child was lying there in his cradle and thinking to himself, "Why am I lying like this? I'll just go away, I'll go and find out about my uncle's health." So he got out of the cradle, threw himself against the floor, and became a fox. He ran off to his uncle. He ran up to the sea—the sea became dry. He ran up to the palace as his uncle was riding up from hunting and they caught sight of the fox. They rushed after it, ran right through the town and up to the sea. The sea once more became dry. The tsar galloped across with his dogs but the hunters remained on the other side because the sea had already become as it was before. The fox ran into a thicket and the dogs ran after it and the tsar after it, too. The tsar rode up and saw that his dogs were all torn up. And it was getting dark. He thought to himself, "Where shall I go now?" He rode and rode about the thicket, but he couldn't find where he was. Then he saw a little fire. He thought, "If that's where robbers live, it would be better to die at the hands of humans than to be eaten here in the woods by wild beasts."

He rode up to a hut. The gates were open. He thought to himself, "I haven't come to a very good house." He rode into the courtyard and tied up his horse. And he set off for the hut. He went into the hut, prayed to God, and said, "Good health, lord and master!"

A voice answered him from the cradle. "Good health, uncle!"

Once more he looked all around and said, "Good health, lord and master!" And the voice from the cradle answered him, "Good health, uncle." He sat down and started thinking about it.

"What are you thinking about, uncle? Your horse is tired—you should have fed it."

"Alright, I'll feed it."

"Take those keys on the wall there," the voice said, "open the stable, and in the stable are oats and hay." So he went to open the stable and give it some food, and the child hopped out of the cradle, caught a hen who was wandering around the yard, butchered her, plucked her, put half of her into a soup and fried the other half. His uncle led his horse off, came in again, and sat down and began thinking. "What are you thinking about, uncle? Probably, you feel like having something to eat."

"That would be fine, lord master, to eat something now."

"Take this," the voice said. "On the table there is a cup, a spoon, and a knife, and take the soup from the stove." He opened the stove and saw the soup bubbling in there. He tried the stove, but it was cold. He ate the soup. The child said to him, "Now, uncle, in the cupboard take that fried chicken." So he opened the cupboard and saw a chicken in the frying pan. He ate, prayed to God, thanked him, sat down and fell into thought.

"What are you thinking about, uncle? Perhaps you want to sleep?"

"It would be good, my lord master, to sleep a little now."

"Lie down here," he said, "in my mother's bed."

He lay down to sleep and thought to himself, "Tomorrow I will get up earlier and go away."

Early in the morning he got up and went to the gates. The gates were not locked but they would not open. He went back inside the hut, started thinking, and sat down. "Well, uncle, have you become pensive or do you wish to ride away?"

"It would be a good thing, lord master, to ride away now."

"Take me with you, uncle."

"And where should I take you?"

"Mama's fur coat is lying over there," he said, "take it, cut out the sleeves, put me in one sleeve, and tie me to your saddle."

"Well, I'll take him along for company," he said. So he cut off one sleeve, put him in it, tied him, and attached him to his saddle. He set off. The gates were open for him. He rode up to the sea. The sea was covered with ice. He rode out to the middle and thought, "Why should I take him with me?" He untied him and threw him down. Then he began to drown. "Oh, lord master, I am drowning," he said.

"Take me with you, uncle," he said. He took him and once more the sea was covered with ice.

They came to the tsardom. A ball had been summoned. They were all talking at the ball about why the tsar didn't get married. He said there was no bride. One [guest] said that "in such and such a tsardom there is a bride." And another [guest] said that "Elena the Most Beautiful was beyond the thrice-nine land in the thrice-ten tsardom. Only it was difficult to get her because she was such a mighty sorceress."

The little boy was sitting on the floor and he said, "Uncle, do you want me to fetch her?"

"Be so kind, lord master."

He immediately asked for some paper and with a pencil he sketched a twelve-cornered ship and said, "Do you have such masters here who can make just such a ship?"

They answered, "No."

The tsar took the sketch out onto the porch. And there the boy's master was already waiting. "What sort of person are you?"

"I am a master."

"Have the ship ready by the right time."

When the ship was ready, he ordered a hundred barrels of wine prepared, a hundred ladles and a hundred buckets and a hundred soldiers. When everything was readied, he said, "Well, uncle, now you can reward me with a rank, otherwise these soldiers will not obey me!" So he gave him the rank of colonel. He got all ready and said, "Well, uncle, expect me in a year! Today is Saturday, expect me on a Saturday!" He boarded the ship and set off: "Drink, soldiers, as much as you like!"

They sailed for a while and then he said to the soldier on watch: "Look, don't you see something?"

The soldier said, "A mountain is visible and on that mountain there stands a city and in the city is a golden palace."

"Sail for the city!"

When they had sailed up to the city, they fired a shot with the cannon, and Elena the Most Beautiful said to her father, "Who is that ignoramus who has

THE SORCERER CHILD ● 55

dared to come here without my permission and to stand there at anchor? Send someone to find out." So the tsar sent his chief minister to find out who had come, from which tsardom, and where he was going.

The little boy said to his soldiers, "Whoever comes will ask whose ship this is. Send them to the cabin to make their inquiries."

The minister came and asked the soldiers, "Whose ship is this?"

And they answered him, "Go and ask the master in the cabin." When he came into the cabin he saw standing in front of him a little man. He asked him coarsely, "Whose ship is this?"

And he [the little boy] said, "This is my ship."

"How is it that you, such a good for nothing, could own such a ship?" He immediately shouted at his soldiers, "Drive him away by the neck!" They drove him out by the neck and he went to the tsar and said, "They drove me out of there by the neck."

The tsar said, "Where don't they abuse fools?! Apparently, you must have addressed him very coarsely."

The tsar sent his lord chamberlain, "Interrogate him. Whose ship is it, where is it going? But deal with them politely and invite him [the little boy] to me."

So the commander said to the soldiers, "When somebody comes here, show him honor. He will ask whose ship this is. Send him to the cabin." So he came and the soldiers showed him honor. He asked, "Whose ship is this?" and they sent him to the cabin. He entered the cabin, asked the little boy from which tsardom he had come and where he was going.

The little boy answered, "I am from such and such a tsardom and we are going somewhere."

"Our tsar asks you to come to him."

"My respects to your tsar. Tell him that I shall come."

He said, "They have sent horses for you."

"No, I have my own," he said. When the lord chamberlain had gone away, he got all ready and went out onto the deck and shouted for the horses. They immediately gave him a carriage and four. He got in and set off.

The tsar greeted him and began questioning him. "What tsardom are you from and where are you going?" He told him that he was "from such and such a tsardom, that they were going somewhere, to some other tsardom."

Dinner was prepared and they dined. He (the little boy) asked them to come to the ship. "Very good," they said, "we shall come."

"And how many of you will be coming?" The tsar began counting and said it would be twelve men. He (the little boy) set off again for his ship and prepared twelve places and wrote on each "tsar," "tsaritsa," and so forth. Then twelve carriages arrived and they got out and all bowed. He (the little boy) came right out and gave the coachmen some money. "Go, sing and have fun! At such and such an hour come for your lords." Only the tsarevna noted that beneath each place was a name. "What a proper man," she said. He gave his guests so much to drink that they went to sleep as they sat there. Then he shouted for his soldiers. The soldiers came in. "Carry them to the shore, by rank." But he ordered them to leave the tsarevna there and he ordered them to hoist the anchor.

He gave instructions to one soldier: "Whatever may appear before you— beasts or some sort of serpent," he was not to be afraid but not let it in the door. They went off. Suddenly Elena the Most Beautiful woke up and saw that she was not at home. She threw herself upon the floor and became a beast, she turned herself into various beasts, then she became a serpent. The soldier on watch took no fright, nor did he let her pass. She became a maiden again. The commander came in to her again and they engaged each other in various conversations. Then the commander went out and she turned back into beasts but she saw that it did her no good and she stopped that. And so they arrived back at their tsardom.

The tsar welcomed them with much joy. He organized a ball. There was a wedding right away. They married them. "Well, uncle," he said, "when you go to bed, she will pretend that she is not well, so here is a three-pood stick. Hit her with it three times. And if you don't hit her, then you won't see me anymore." So the tsar went to bed and she said to him that she was unwell. He took the three-pood stick and hit her—nothing at all. He hit her again— she died. He took fright and was very sorry for her. He immediately ordered them to dig a grave, and they dug the grave and lined it with marble stones. They took a golden coffin and buried her. The tsar was deprived both of her and of that little boy.

The little boy went away and he came to a village. He dug himself into a haystack, into the straw. A peasant came for some straw and began taking it with a pitchfork. The little boy said to him, "Uncle, you are going to stab me!"

The peasant got frightened, and once more tried to take some straw with his pitchfork. "Uncle, you are going to stab me!"

He opened up the stack right away and saw the boy and he was so glad because he had no children. He asked him, "Will you come and be a son to me?"

"If you desire, I will with pleasure." The peasant threw the straw away with joy and carried the little boy into the hut and said, "Wife, God has given me a son!" So they began to look after him, and the peasant went to the town to buy him some presents.

He came back from town and he brought the presents. "Well, isn't there anything new?" That's what the little boy asked.

"Here is what is new: the tsar has raised a column of enormous size and covered all over with pure lacquer. Whoever climbs this column will receive two hundred thousand rubles."

The little boy said to him, "Well, is that something you desire?"

"How could one not desire it? That's very pleasant."

So the little boy right away took a rope, tied knots throughout it and said to him, "Go into town and untie one knot. Grab onto the column and climb up a little, [and go on doing this]." He saddled up his horse and went into town and came up to the column. He untied a knot and climbed up the column. He climbed up the column, untying all the knots, and from the top he climbed back down. He took the money and wanted to leave. The guards stopped him and started questioning him: who was he and was he doing this by himself or had someone taught him how? He said that he was a peasant from such and such a village. "I am by myself, no one taught me to do this." They didn't believe him and put him in prison. He sat there for a long time and they questioned him but he didn't want to say who had taught him. The tsar ordered that he be hanged if he would not admit the truth. They led him out to be hanged and he said, "Should I perish on account of a little boy?"

The tsar began questioning him: "What sort of little boy is this?"

He said, "I found him in the straw."

"And where is he now?"

"He's in the village."

The tsar ordered that his carriage be fitted out immediately and he set off with the peasant for the village. They came to the village and went straight to the hut of this peasant. The tsar went into the hut and saw the little boy sitting there. "Oh, good health to you, lord master!"

"Good health, uncle!" answered the little boy.

"Why did you run away and come here?"

"Why did you not obey me?"

"Come back with me!"

"If it please you, with pleasure, but you must obey me!" The tsar rewarded the peasant and took the little boy with him.

They came into the town. Some time passed and they he said, "Well, uncle, is your wife alive?"

"No," he said, "I buried her."

"And where did you bury her?"

"In the cemetery," he said.

"No, she's not there."

"No, she is there, I buried her myself." So they went to make sure and they opened the grave and then they opened the coffin. The coffin was empty!

"Well, I told you, uncle, that your wife would go away."

"Lord master, can you get her back?"

"It's possible. Order them to fit out that ship for me with two hundred barrels of wine, two hundred buckets, two hundred ladles, and two hundred soldiers, only such soldiers as know how to fly."

"But can one find such soldiers? I don't have a single soldier who knows how to fly."

"No, you have many who do. Gather your army together." So they gathered the army together and they went to watch. He went up to one soldier and said, "Fly!" The soldier rose up and started flying. And so he chose out several such soldiers and then he said to them, "Choose your comrades so that there will be two hundred men." Then he ordered them to report to the ship and he said farewell to his uncle, saying, "I will come back in two years, you and the tsaritsa wait for me!" Then they went for some time over the sea and he said to the soldier on watch: "Look, don't you see anything?"

"Besides the heaven and the sea, there is nothing to be seen."

So once more they went on for a long time. And he again ordered the soldier on watch to look. The watchman looked and said, "There on an island beneath the very clouds a house is scarcely visible."

"Sail for that island."

They sailed up to the island. And he said, "Listen, soldiers, when I start playing the fife, be ready to fly. When I start playing a second time, fly. When I start playing the third time, strike at the first person you meet."

So he turned himself into a bird, flew off to the island, arrived, and perched on the well. A cook came out after some water and started to let down the bucket. He [the little boy] said, "Don't beat me, uncle!"

The cook was frightened. "Who is that there?" he said.

"I am a man," he said, "pull me out and I will give you a fistful of gold."

"Well, grab onto the bucket!" he said. And the cook pulled him out of the well. He (the little boy) gave him a fistful of gold.

"Take me, uncle, and put me down on the stove. I'm frozen!" The cook took him, brought him into the scullery and put him down on the stove.

On that island Elena the Most Beautiful herself lived. For servants she had only the cook and a man. She ate at eleven o'clock in the morning and at eleven in the evening. The cook lay down to sleep and said to the little boy, "Here is a watch. When this hand gets up to this place, wake me up." The little boy, pretending he didn't understand, began pointing at various places, did the cook mean here or was it here. Finally the cook taught him that when the hand got to a certain place, he was to awaken him. It got to be ten o'clock but the boy didn't wake up the cook. He prepared the food himself most beautifully and at eleven o'clock he woke them up. The cook and the man jumped up, frightened. It was time to carry in the food but the food wasn't ready. They started scolding the little boy for not having awakened them earlier. The cook started looking at the food and he saw that everything was ready. He tested it. It was so tasty, so well prepared. He'd never prepared anything like it before.

They set the table and brought the food out. The tsaritsa tried it and asked, "Who prepared the food?" (She had never tasted such food in her whole life. It was very tastefully prepared.)

The man answered, "The cook prepared it."

"Summon the cook!" He came and she asked him, "Did you prepare this food?"

"I did," he said.

"Be sure that by evening even better food is prepared." They took everything away, they themselves ate, and then they fed the little boy.

They lay down to sleep and again they ordered the little boy to wake them up at ten o'clock. Once more he prepared all the food and woke them at eleven o'clock. They were frightened and thought that they were late. The cook saw that the food was ready. He tasted it and it was very well prepared. The man gave the tsaritsa the food. Once more she asked him, "Who prepared this food?"

"The cook did."

"Call the cook to me."

"Listen, did you prepare the food?"

"I did," he said.

"Make it tomorrow even better prepared." So again they lay down to sleep and ordered the little boy to wake them up at ten o'clock. Once more the little boy prepared everything himself and woke them up at eleven o'clock. Again the man began serving the tsaritsa her food. She asked him, "Who prepared this food?"

The man said, "The cook prepared it."

"Call the cook. Did you prepare the food?"

"I did," he said.

"You are lying, it wasn't you. Speak the truth or I shall hang you."

"Call him here," he said.

The little boy came and bowed to the tsaritsa. "So it is you," she said, "I'll hang you immediately."

"Have mercy," he said, "what are you hanging me for?"

The tsaritsa wrote a letter and sent it to her father asking him to come with his entire court immediately. The tsar came, they had a council about what to do with the little boy. They determined to hang him.

They erected the gallows and next to the gallows they put a bench with three steps. They ordered that he be brought to the gallows. When he came to the first step, he said, "Let me play my fife." The tsar let him. He mounted the second step and said, "Let me play it a second time."

The tsaritsa said, "No, papa, don't let him play any more!"

"Have mercy on me, why shouldn't I play?" he said, "they are just about to put the noose on my neck." The tsar let him play a second time. He played and then got on the third step. "Permit me," he said, "to play for the last time." The tsaritsa begged her father not to let him.

"It's nothing," he said, "let him play." So he started playing his fife the third time and the soldiers began striking the first one they met.

"Look, tsar," he said, "my hens have begun pecking at your wheat." The tsar looked around and saw that only his daughter remained. The little boy went and put the noose on the tsar. He got off the gallows, took the tsaritsa, and set off for the ship.

They went for a long time and then they came home. The tsar greeted them with honor and glory and they were married once more. The little boy said, "Listen, uncle, when you lie down to sleep, hit her with this three-pood stick three times, or else you will never see me or her again."

When evening was finished, all the guests departed and the young ones went off to bed. She began pretending: "I am sick, send for the doctor." He struck her once, then a second time, and she became as if dead. He struck her the third time and she came alive and started begging for his forgiveness. And so they lived just fine for quite some time.

The tsaritsa said to her husband, "Why do you call that little boy 'master'? What kind of master is he?"

The tsar went to the little boy and said, "Listen, from now on I am not going to call you 'master.'"

"Be so kind, why are you alarmed?"

"And you must not call me uncle."

"No, I am obliged to call you uncle."

"Why is that so?"

"Because I am the son of your sister."

"And where does my sister live?"

"She lives in some forest." The tsar immediately ordered his horse saddled. He took the little boy with him and set off for the forest. They came to the hut. The tsar went into the hut, saw his sister and was overjoyed. He took her to his palace together with her husband, and the old man and woman. They began living and prospering and doing well. I was there. I drank mead and beer, it ran down my moustaches but none got into my mouth.

A–T 516**

295. The Peasant's Son Ivanushka

In a certain tsardom in a certain country on the shores of a deep blue sea there lived an old man with his old woman. They had this young son Ivanushka. So Ivanushka grew up. The old ones thought and thought for a long time about which trade to have their son taught. They didn't want him to be a simple peasant. Finally they decided to give him to a master tailor to be an apprentice. Ivanushka spent a week there and went home.

The old folks grieved and grieved and then gave him over to a silversmith. Ivanushka spent a week with the master and again came home. The old people were even sadder and this time they decided to give him to a goldsmith. So Ivanushka lived a week with the master and on the final day of the week Ivanushka poured a duck with her ducklings out of gold. The master saw the duck and ducklings and was amazed at the work. He said to Ivanushka, "For us to teach those who know how is just a waste. Here is a hundred rubles for yourself. Now go home."

So Ivanushka came home. Once more the old folks grieved. The old woman said to the old man, "Old man, tomorrow you must go to the sea for some water and take Ivanushka with you. Frighten him that you will throw him in the sea if he doesn't study."

The next day, as soon as it was light, the old man woke his son up and went with him to the sea to get some water. So they drove up to the sea. The old man got a bucket of water and then said, "Well, Ivanushka, let's bathe." Ivanushka didn't have a chance to throw off his clothes when the old man grabbed him from the rear and shouted, "Oh, you lazybones, will you study? Otherwise, I will throw you into the sea."

Ivanushka suddenly slipped out of his father's hands, threw himself into the sea, and started swimming. The old man was frightened and started shouting with a loud voice, "Ivanushka, my son, where are you going? I was only joking, that damned old woman put me up to it."

"Farewell, father!" Ivanushka answered. "You could not hold me in your hands and now you can't hold on to me at all." And Ivanushka disappeared in the waves of the sea.

The old man cried for a while, then he picked up his son's clothes. Out of the pocket of his ripped coat dropped the hundred ruble note. The old man was astonished. He picked up the money and wept even more. "Oh, old woman, you are the guilty one, if only I hadn't listened to you, our son would be with us. He spent a week there and earned a hundred rubles." And the old man set off home alone. He came home and told the old woman what had happened.

The old woman started weeping, "Where are you, my Ivanushka? Are you alive or have you drowned?"

Just then a king was sailing over the sea in a ship. He was searching for a bride to court. Passing by a certain island, the king saw through his telescope some living object on it—it was neither beast nor man. The king said to his servants, "Oh servants, faithful servants, go to that island and see who is on it. If it is a beast, kill it. If it is a man, bring him here." So the servants set off to the island and there they saw this naked man. They took him and brought him to the ship. The king ordered them to dress and feed the man. In the morning the king said, "My servants, faithful servants! Will I be able to handle my self-cutting sword and can I cut with it?"

The servants giggled and answered, "Well, you are the educated fool if you don't know how to cut!".

But Ivanushka answered, "You will be able to handle the self-cutting sword, but it is not for you to cut with it."

The king grew angry and ordered Ivanushka to be quiet. Then he asked his servants once more, "Servants, my faithful servants! Can I handle my bow and arrow and can I shoot with it?"

The servants giggled and answered, "Oh you are the educated fool if you can't shoot!"

But once more Ivanushka said, "You can handle the bow and arrow, but it is not for you to shoot with them."

The king got madder than ever and ordered Ivanushka to shut up and this time he asked, "Oh servants, my faithful servants! Will my pitch-black horse submit to me? Will I be able to ride him?"

The servants again giggled and said, "Oh, you are an educated fool if you cannot ride."

But Ivanushka again spoke up. "The pitch-black horse will submit to you, but it is not for you to ride him." The king got angry and ordered them to throw Ivanushka into the water.

The ship went fast, but Ivanushka swam still faster. The king understood what sort of person Ivanushka was and he ordered his servants to pull him out of the water.

Soon the ship sailed to the land where the beautiful maiden and possible bride lived. The king, the father of the bride, announced that he would give his daughter to the person who could lift his daughter's dowry. Out came two mighty warriors carrying a self-cutting sword so big that goose pimples crawled along the skin of the king who would be groom. The guest looked at the king-groom and the king-father said, "Well, my amicable son-in-law to be, take the dowry." The king-groom tried to take the sword, but he could not lift it.

So Ivanushka went up to the mighty warriors, grabbed the self-cutting sword from their hands, struck them with it on their warrior heads, and their heads rolled right up to the feet of the king. The guests were astonished at the strength and agility of Ivanushka. The king-father's face turned dark. He waved a white kerchief. Four warriors brought out the bow and arrow. To the tip of the arrow a fifth warrior was tied. Once more goose pimples crawled all over the king-groom's body. He was about to try the bow and arrow but he couldn't hold it in his arms. So Ivanushka took the bow out of the warriors' arms with one hand and with the other he pulled back the bow string. The arrow, along with the warrior, flew away beyond the clouds. The guests were astonished and the king-father fell into thought. For the third time he waved the white kerchief. They led the pitch-black horse out of the stables. Six warriors could scarcely hold him. The king-groom turned white from fright. He could not even approach the horse. Like an arrow Ivanushka flew to the horse. No one had a chance to grasp what was going on before Ivanushka had mounted the horse. The horse soared up with him beneath the clouds. Ivanushka took out three iron rods and he struck and struck until he broke them. The horse descended a little. Ivanushka took out three bronze rods and he struck and struck until he broke them. The horse came back to earth. The horse stood there, meek and mild. The guests shouted for joy, but the king-father grew angry.

The beautiful maiden and bride was sitting next to the window and she saw everything. She was very attracted to Ivanushka. She led Ivanushka up to the king her father and said, "Here, father, is my chosen one."

The king-father did not want to give his daughter to a common person, but there was nothing to be done. He could not go against his own words. Soon they played out the wedding. There was a feast for the whole world. Ivanushka's mother and father were at the feast.

A–T 517*

296. The Moon and the Star

In a certain tsardom, in a certain land, there lived and dwelt a tsar, and he had no children. So they asked God to give them a child for their comfort. After a little while her Ladyship conceived and they rejoiced. Soon a daughter was born and they gave her the name Luna, or Moon. Oh, how happy the Lord was! He wrote out orders to all the courtiers that they were to teach her. And then in a little while her Ladyship conceived again, and they were just as happy that God had given them this gift. Another daughter was born to them, and they gave her the name Zvezda, or Star. They were such beauties. The mind simply cannot comprehend it! Indescribable beauty. And these beauties grew and all came to gaze upon them, to admire them. When they were twelve years of age, they had a birthday celebration for the daughters, and the tsar gave a most wonderful ball. They came from all the towns and all the districts to congratulate them, and everyone wanted to look upon their beauty. They went walking in the garden, leaving mama and papa at home. Suddenly, a whirlwind appeared, swept up both sisters, and carried them off. All the guests shouted and made a most unusual noise. "What is it? What is it?" "Oh, father tsar! Your children!" And he fell into a faint.

All the senators immediately sent out their soldiers to look for them. Perhaps they had fallen down somewhere. They searched and searched, but they couldn't find them anywhere. They looked, they gazed into unusual mirrors, perhaps they were to be seen there? No, nothing. They asked the wizards, they searched one day, then two, three, a week and more. Finally a month passed, but nothing. They looked in the forests, but they didn't find them. "Perhaps they have fallen into the sea?" someone said.

A year passed and then another. Finally after several years her Ladyship conceived again, and she gave birth to Ivan Tsarevich. Ivan Tsarevich grew not by the days but by the hours, and he was so clever and smart. But her Ladyship kept crying, crying without consolation for her daughters Luna and Zvezda. In came Ivan Tsarevich. "Dear mama, why are you crying?"

"Oh, it's nothing."

"Mother, my dear, tell me!"

"Oh, my friend, Vanechka, before you I had these two daughters."

"Where are they?"

So she told him, and then she said, "And there's been no sight or sound of them."

"Mama, let me go and look for my sisters."

"No," she said, "Don't go. You can't find them. We have lost our daughters, and we would lose you, too."

But he kept on asking, and his father found out, and implored him not to go, and then he summoned his ministers. "Now, my lord senators, my son day and night cries, wanting to go look for his sisters."

The senators said, "Why not bless him for this if he has such a strong desire?"

"How can I when he is so young? What sort of rumors are they that led him to this?" He was very angry with her Ladyship. "Why did they inspire him this way?"

They thought and thought, and then they blessed him. "I would go," he said, "without all else except your blessing." Then he set off. "Mama, don't cry, don't grieve, I will find my sisters!" He walked for a week and then a second through the forest and suddenly he saw two huge forest spirits, fighting.

"Oh, Ivan Tsarevich, you must judge between us, please." These forest spirits had three objects: a tablecloth that set itself, boots that walked by themselves, and a cap that made its wearer invisible.

Ivan Tsarevich said, "Go and run a verst. Whoever wins will get two of the objects, and the loser will get the third." So they ran, first one and then the other leading.

They finished and returned. Ivan Tsarevich put on the invisible cap and was nowhere to be seen. "Oh, where is Ivan Tsarevich? Where is he gone?" They ran around him, but they couldn't see him. They looked for about three hours; then they cried before rushing off into the forest to look for him.

But Ivan Tsarevich removed the cap, put on the speedy self-walking boots and marched off, doing five versts as if it were nothing at all. Then he felt like something to eat. He said, "Well, self-setting tablecloth! Spread yourself." Suddenly every sort of food appeared, all kinds of drinks. Some peasants came along the road. He called them, "Peasants, please, come here. Sit down, please." They sat down and ate and drank their fill. Ivan Tsarevich thought, "Thank God, I have everything!" The peasants were astonished, thanked him, and left.

He went on and entered a deep forest. There stood a little hut that could turn on cock's legs. "Little hut, little hut! Stand with your rear to the forest and your front to me." It turned. He went into the hut and there was Baba Yaga, that old witch.

"Now that a Russian spirit has come into full view," she said. "What business are you trying to do, or are you fleeing some business?"

"My two sisters have disappeared. You don't know, you haven't heard where they are, have you?

"I know your sisters. The spirits have taken them away and you'll not get them back. Some sort of powerful whirlwinds, magic ones. There's no way you can approach. Your sister Luna is in a silver palace, and Zvezda is in a gold one. But you won't find them. It's far, far away.

"No," he said, "I'll go."

"Then off you go! My sister's there. Here's a ball for you. Wherever this ball rolls, you follow it and you'll come to my sister." He thanked her and the ball set off rolling. He went, too, and for about a week he went toward her sister. He got there. She was even angrier and nastier.

"I am angry, clever, wise, and my third sister is even nastier. Here is a kerchief. Give it to her as a gift from me. Then she will receive you."

So he set off after the little ball again. When he arrived, he gave her the kerchief as a gift from her sister. "Well, what is your business here?"

"I am looking for my sisters," he said. "You wouldn't know where my sisters are, would you?"

"Luna is with the first whirlwind, but there is a stone wall and twelve men day and night. They won't let you through. There's nothing to be said about the second whirlwind. He's very nasty." So they said farewell, and he set off.

He approached that palace. The stone wall was the highest. There was no possible way one could scale it, and twelve men stood there day and night. He went up and asked whether they would let him in, but they certainly wouldn't agree to that. He put on his invisible cap and flew right over the wall. He saw the sentries as he walked about the courtyard. "Well, it's as if we'd agreed; this is a spirit testing us," they said.

Ivan Tsarevich went into the palace and entered a room, but there was nobody there. He went into a second, then a third, and finally he went into a fifth room where on a couch his sister was resting. It was Luna, and what a beauty she was! She lay there resting in the deepest sleep. "Oh, my dear sister, wake up! Wake up! Papa and mama have sent their regards."

"I have no brothers."

He told her and she rejoiced, but she was frightened. She cried and cried from joy. "Oh," she said, "soon Whirlwind will come flying in and he will tear you into tiny little bits!"

"I'm not afraid of anybody on earth," he said.

"But he's so nasty." Ivan Tsarevich showed her his invisible cap and that calmed her.

Suddenly Whirlwind arrived, and Ivan Tsarevich put that invisible cap on: he couldn't be seen.

"So, Luna, it smells here of a Russian's spirit; probably your brother has come."

"I have no brothers."

Then Whirlwind rushed about looking, looking everywhere, in the closets and trunks, but he couldn't find him anywhere. "Probably your brother has come!"

"But if he had come, what would you do?"

"Nothing."

"Ivan Tsarevich, show yourself!" He took off his invisible cap.

Whirlwind saw him and said, "I am clever, but he is wiser than I. How did you get here?"

"My blood caused me to search, and therefore I found her." Then his sister quickly ran out to bring something to eat. "Don't bother," he said. "I'll feed you myself. Tablecloth, spread yourself!" And there appeared many sorts of foods and drinks.

Whirlwind ate and praised it: "Oh, in Russia you have such foods and drinks."

Ivan Tsarevich stayed there about two weeks. "I told you, sister, that I would carry you away."

"You can't. He'll catch up to you and kill you. You had better go to Zvezda. A maiden tsaritsa lives there with great power over these spirits."

So Ivan Tsarevich said goodbye and went off to his other sister, Zvezda.

He came to a palace surrounded by a high, high wall. Twelve men stood guard and let no one into the palace. Zvezda's husband was Whirlwind, Lord of all Whirlwinds, the most suffocating of them all. The guards would not let Ivan Tsarevich in, so he put on his invisible cap and walked through. They said, "Now he's walking about the courtyard; a spirit must be amusing us!"

Ivan Tsarevich went into the first room, but there was no one there; then into a second, a third, but in the fifth was his sister, Zvezda, even more beautiful. She was sound asleep. "Dearest sister! Wake up, wake up! I am your brother, bringing greetings from your mama and papa."

"No, I have no brothers," she said. He told her everything and she was happy, so very happy. Then she said to him, "I have this fierce Whirlwind, and he will tear you into pieces."

"Don't be alarmed. He won't see me." He showed her his invisible cap.

Whirlwind flew in. "Oh," he said, "Your brother has come, Zvezda."

"I don't have any brothers."

"No, it smells of a Russian soul here; he's come; show him to me."

"But you'll tear him to pieces."

"Oh, my God, I wouldn't tear him to pieces."

So Ivan Tsarevich removed his invisible cap and visited them for some time. Then he said to Zvezda, "I will carry you away from here."

"No, Whirlwind will catch us. But in this country there is a maiden tsar and she has great power over these spirits. She wishes to see you."

So Ivan Tsarevich spent about two more weeks with his sister, then he said farewell, and rode away.

Then he went to the maiden tsar. She was delighted to see him. And what a beauty she was, that maiden tsar! "Oh, Ivan Tsarevich, how did God manage to bring you here?"

"Blood brought me here," he said. "Fulfill my wish: would it not be possible to rescue my sisters? I will marry you, if you do."

So she said, "Good. I have this twelve-headed serpent who has been chained up for twelve years. I'll let him loose and he will defeat Whirlwind." They talked a little while and then she said, "Well, Ivan Tsarevich, let's go to the serpent." So they went there, and she asked the serpent, "Can you defeat those two spirits, those Whirlwinds?"

"I can, only give me a month to eat as much beef and drink as much beer as I want," he said. So they let the serpent go and gave him a beef every day to eat and a whole cauldron of beer. The serpent grew stronger and stronger. A month passed and then the serpent took his weapons and flew off. "Wait," he said. He flew to the spirits. They flew at each other and fought and fought. They knocked off ten of his heads but he fought back with fire and claws. He killed them, threw their corpses into the sea, and brought their heads back to the maiden tsar.

Ivan Tsarevich and the maiden tsar rode through the steppe and welcomed the serpent with joy. Then they went to Zvezda. "Dear sister! Look what the maiden tsar has done for us!" They rejoiced and made merry. Then they gave the serpent his freedom to eat and drink what he wished. The serpent was so happy, so happy that he kept his freedom. And then he grew out another twelve heads, because, you see, the serpent was a spirit. They feasted with Zvezda for about a week.

"Probably Luna is wondering why she hasn't seen her spirit anywhere."

Ivan Tsarevich said, "Well, sister, get ready and let's go."

"I've nothing to ready."

So she went out onto the porch, murmured a spell, and rolled an egg on a saucer. "Oh, my house, come into this egg on this golden saucer! Flying carpet! Fly to me!" she said. The flying carpet appeared and all three of them flew to Luna.

When they arrived, he said, "Well, dear sister, we have to get ready!" So she went out onto her porch, murmured a spell, and rolled an egg over a silver saucer. Her house rolled into the silver egg. They got on the flying carpet and flew to their own country. They flew like birds. Then went out into the garden and rolled an egg and palaces appeared from them. They sent someone to the tsar saying, "Two palaces have just appeared in the garden." The tsar went out and learned of it all. There was such joy. They organized a ball and Ivan Tsarevich was married and the tsar gave him his tsardom. They began living and prospering, and they live even now.

A–T 518 + 301A

297. The Footless Warrior and the Blind Warrior

In a certain tsardom, in a certain country, there lived and dwelt a terrifying tsar who was famous throughout all lands, and frightening to all kings and princes. This tsar decided to get married and he issued a decree to all cities and villages: "Whoever finds me a bride more beautiful than the sun, brighter than the moon, and whiter than snow shall be rewarded with uncounted wealth." News of this went out throughout the entire tsardom, and all, from young to old, talked about it, and discussed it, but no one would take it upon himself to look for such a beauty.

Not far from the tsar's palace there stood a large brewery. For some reason some workers were gathered there and a conversation started up about the amount of money one would receive from the tsar and where one might find such a bride. "Well, brothers," said one peasant by the name of Nikita Koltoma, "other than me there's nobody who can find a bride for the tsar. And if I undertake it, I'll find her for sure."

"You're a fool to boast like that! How in hell will you do it? There are well-born folk, rich even. We're no match for them, and they've tucked their tails in already. You'd never even dream of such a thing, let alone when you're awake."

"Just as you wish, but I shall trust in myself. I said I'd find her, and I'll find her."

"Oh Nikita, don't boast! You know yourself that our tsar is terrifying. For empty boasting he will order you executed."

"I dare say he won't execute me but reward me with money."

Right away they reported these words to the tsar himself. The tsar was overjoyed and ordered Nikita brought before his very own person. Soldiers came running up and grabbed Nikita Koltoma, and they dragged him into the palace. His friends shouted out after him, "Well, brother, did you come to an agreement? And you think you can make jokes with the tsar! Oh, well, go now to your punishment."

So they led Nikita into the grand chambers and the terrible tsar spoke to him, "Well Nikita, have you been boasting that you can find a bride for me more beautiful than the son, brighter than the moon, and whiter than the snow?"

"I can, your majesty."

"Very good, brother. If you serve me properly, I will reward you with uncountable wealth and make you my first minister. But if you have lied, then my sword and your head from your shoulders!"

"I am pleased to try, your majesty! Permit me to go out looking for a month." The tsar agreed to this and gave Nikita an open letter with his signature so that in all the taverns and saloons he would be treated to all drinks and foods without paying.

So then Nikita Koltoma set out to go about the capital. No matter which tavern he dropped in to, he had only to show the open letter and they would immediately bring him everything that his soul might desire. He walked around for a day, then two and three, then he walked for a week and then a second and third. Finally the time was up. It was time to appear before the tsar. Nikita said farewell to his friends and went to the palace and asked the tsar to gather twelve young men who were height for height, hair for hair, and voice for voice the same, and also thirteen white linen tents with golden designs.

The tsar had everything at the ready. In an instant the youths were brought together and the tents made. "Well, your highness," said Nikita, "Now we'll get ready and ride off after your bride." So they saddled their fine horses, tied on the tents, and after that they attended a prayer service for travelers, said their farewells to the city residents, mounted their horses and galloped off, leaving a pillar of dust in their wake.

They rode one day, then a second and a third, and there in the open steppe stood a smithy. Nikita said, "You ride on with the grace of God, but I'll just drop in at the smithy and smoke a pipe." He entered the smithy and inside there were fifteen smiths forging iron, pounding it with their sledge hammers. "God aid you, brothers!"

"Thanks, good man!"

"Make me a fifteen-pood rod!"

"We aren't against making it, but who will be able to handle so much iron? Fifteen poods is no joke."

"It's nothing, brothers. You beat it with your sledges and I'll handle it." So the smiths set to work and they forged an iron rod of fifteen poods. Nikita took it and went outside, threw it up in the air about fifteen sazhens, and stretched out his hand. The iron rod fell onto his hand, but it couldn't withstand his warrior's strength and broke in two. Nikita Koltoma paid the smiths for their efforts, threw them the broken rod, and rode away.

He caught up to his comrades. They rode on for three more days and there in the steppe stood another smithy. "You ride on ahead and they'll forge me a twenty-five pood iron rod, they'll pound it out with their sledges."

He went into the smithy where twenty-five smiths were forging iron, pounding with their sledges. "God aid you, brothers!"

"Thank you, good man."

"Make me a rod of twenty-five poods."

"It's no big deal to make such a rod, but where's the mighty man who could handle so much iron?"

"I can handle it myself." So he took the twenty-five pood of iron, heated it until it was red hot, and then he began turning it over and over on the anvil while the smiths struck it with the sledges. They made a rod of twenty-five poods. Nikita took that iron rod, went out into the steppe, threw it up about twenty-five sazhens, and held out his hand. The rod struck his warrior's hand and broke in two. "No, it's no good," Nikita said. Then he paid for the work, got on his horse, and rode away. He caught up to his comrades.

They rode for a day, then a second and a third, and again there stood in the open steppe a smithy. Nikita said to his comrades, "You ride on ahead, and I'll drop in to the smithy—just to smoke a pipe." He entered the smithy and there were fifty smiths torturing this old man. The gray-haired old man was lying on the anvil, and ten men were holding him by the beard with their pincers, while forty others were battering him on his sides with their sledges. "Brothers, have mercy!" the old man shouted as loud as he could. "Release my soul to repent."

"God aid you, brothers," said Nikita.

"Thank you, good man," the smiths answered.

"Why are you torturing the old man?"

"This is why: he owes each one of us a ruble but he won't give us the money. Why should we not beat him?"

"Oh, the poor unfortunate," thought Nikita. "He's getting such a punishment just for fifty rubles." So then he said to the smiths, "Listen, brothers, I'll settle for him. Let the old man go free."

"As you wish, my good man, to us it's all the same from whom we get it, as long as the money is there."

So Nikita Koltoma took out fifty rubles. The smiths took the money and they no sooner had let the old man loose from their iron pincers than he simply disappeared from sight! Nikita looked: "Where did he go?"

"That's that! Now you just look for him," said the smiths. "Why, he's a wizard." So Nikita ordered them to forge an iron rod of fifty poods. He took it, threw it up in the air fifty sazhens high, and held out his hand. The rod withstood its fall onto his hand and didn't break "This one will do," said Nikita, and he rode off to catch up to his comrades.

Suddenly he heard a voice behind him: "Nikita Koltoma, wait!" He looked over his shoulder and saw that same little old man running along, the one he'd ransomed from the torture. "Thank you, good man," said the old man, "for saving me from that cruel torture. For thirty years I'd been suffering that misfortune. Here's a present to remember me by: take it. It will prove useful." And he gave him an invisible cap. "When you put it on your head, no one will be able to see you." Nikita took the invisible cap, thanked the old man, and galloped on. He caught up to his comrades and they set off together.

Whether long or short, near or far, they rode up to a certain palace. This palace was encircled by a high iron palisade. The young men couldn't enter the courtyard on horseback or on foot. Then the terrible tsar said, "Well, brother Nikita, there's no place else for us to go."

And Nikita Koltoma answered, "What do you mean, there's no place to go, your highness? I will search throughout the entire universe and find you a bride. This palisade is no barrier. . . . Well, lads, let's break it down and make the gates into a broad courtyard."

The young men all got off their horses and set about the palisade, but whatever they did, they couldn't smash it down. The palisade stood there, it would not be pulled down. So then Nikita said, "Hey, brothers, you are just fiddling about there; I simply can't rely on you! I'll have to do it by myself." So he jumped down from his horse, approached the palisade, grabbed hold of the grating with his hands, twisted it once, and then he brought the whole palisade to the ground. The terrible tsar came riding out and the young men rode into the broad courtyard and there in a green field they set up their white linen tents with gold designs. They ate whatever God provided, lay down, and then on account of their exhaustion they fell into a deep sleep. Every one of them had a tent except for Nikita Koltoma. So he sought out three holey bast mats, made himself a lean-to, and lay down on the bare earth, but he didn't go to sleep: he waited to see what would happen.

At first light in the morning Tsarevna Elena the Beautiful woke up in her chambers, looked out her beautifully framed windows and saw on the green field the thirteen white linen tents with their embroidered gold flowers and in front of them all stood a lean-to made of just bast mats. "What is this?" thought the tsarevna. "Where have all these guests come from?" She looked and the iron palisading was all broken. Elena the Beautiful became furious and summoned her most mighty warrior and she ordered him, "Get on your horse immediately and ride out to those tents and all those who have disobeyed our orders put to death, toss their corpses beyond the palisade, and deliver their tents to me."

The most mighty warrior saddled his good warhorse, put on his war armor, and set out against the uninvited guests. Nikita Koltoma saw him and asked, "Who's that coming this way?"

"What sort of ignoramus are you to ask?"

Nikita did not like these words so he jumped out of his lean-to, grabbed the warrior by the foot and dragged him from his horse onto the damp earth. He raised an iron rod weighing fifty poods, gave him just a single blow, and then said, "Go back to your tsarevna now and tell her that she hasn't long to be so haughty, that she need not waste her troops, and that she will get married to our tsar."

When Elena the Beautiful heard these brazen words, she immediately became alarmed and she summoned all her mighty warriors and ordered them, "My trusted servants! Collect together an innumerable army and destroy those white linen tents and slaughter those uninvited guests so that not even dust remains of them." The mighty warriors didn't think long about it but collected an innumerable army mounted on their warhorses and rushed off toward the white linen tents with their gold designs.

When they had just drawn even with the bast lean-to, Nikita Koltoma leapt out in front of them, took his iron rod of fifty poods and began swinging it in various directions. In a short time he had beaten the entire army and all those mighty warriors, leaving just one warrior among the living. "Ride back," he said, "to your tsarevna Elena the Beautiful and tell her that she shouldn't waste any more troops. She won't frighten us with troops. Just now I have fought you alone. What will happen with your tsardom when my comrades wake up? We will leave no stone upon stone and scatter you all throughout the steppe."

So the warrior returned to the tsarevna and told her that her army was defeated and that there weren't sufficient forces to overcome these valiant knights. Elena the Beautiful sent a message to the terrible tsar, inviting him to her palace, and then she ordered a highly tempered arrow fashioned. She herself went out to meet her guests amiably and with honor. The tsarevna approached him and behind her were fifty men carrying bows and arrows. Nikita Koltoma saw the war bows and immediately guessed that they were intending to entertain them with the arrow, so he put on his invisible cap, leapt up, drew his bow, and sent the arrow into the tsarevna's chambers, and in so doing he knocked down the whole upper story of the palace! There was nothing else to be done. Elena the Beautiful took the terrible tsar by the hand and led him into the white stone chambers, sat him down at the oaken tables with their pressed tablecloths. They began eating and drinking, and rejoicing. And the chambers were beautifully furnished—you could travel round the whole world and never find anything like them.

After dinner Nikita said to the terrible tsar, "Does your royal highness find this bride pleasing? Or shall we go riding after another?"

"No, Nikita, there's no need to go off riding in vain. There's no better in the whole wide world."

"Well, then, get married. She's in your hands now. But watch out, your highness, don't let down your guard. For the first three nights she will test your strength. She'll put her hand on you and begin to crush you firmly, hard. There's no way you will be able to endure it. So then leave the room quickly and I will come in your place and tame her in short order." So they prepared the wedding, but tsars don't have to brew the mead or distill the vodka—everything's already done. They played out the wedding and then the terrible tsar and Elena went off to take their rest.

He lay down on the soft bed and pretended that he wanted to sleep. Elena the Beautiful put her hand on his chest and asked him, "Is my hand heavy?"

"Well, it's just as heavy as a feather on water," the terrible tsar replied, but in fact he could hardly breathe, so much was she crushing his chest. "Wait a moment, Elena the Beautiful. I forgot to give the orders for tomorrow. I'll just run and do it." And he left the bedroom. Nikita was standing at the door. "Well, brother, you got it just right: she nearly suffocated me."

"Never mind, your highness. Wait here and I'll go do my thing," said Nikita and he went off to the tsarevna, lay down in the bed, and started snoring.

Elena the Beautiful thought that the terrible tsar had returned and so she placed her hand on him and pressed and pressed, but to no avail! She put both hands on him to press more than ever before. . . . Then Nikita Koltoma grabbed her as if he were in his sleep and threw her onto the ground with such force that the whole chamber shook! The tsarevna picked herself up, lay down quietly, and fell asleep. So then Nikita got up and went out to the tsar. He said, "Now go quickly and nothing will happen until tomorrow night." So with the help of Nikita Koltoma the terrible tsar got through the first three nights and began living with his tsarevna Elena the Beautiful as a husband and wife ought to.

Sooner or later Elena the Beautiful found out that the terrible tsar had taken her by trickery, that his strength wasn't so great, and that people were laughing at her. They were saying that Nikita had slept with the tsarevna for those three nights! She became absolutely furious and in her heart she hid a desire for revenge. The tsar decided to ride to his own tsardom and he said to Elena the Beautiful, "We've lived here enough; it's time to go home. Get ready for the journey." And they decided to go by sea. They loaded a ship with many various precious things, boarded, and set off over the sea. They sailed for a day and then another, and finally a third. The tsar was happy, he couldn't have been more pleased that he was bringing his tsarevna who was more beautiful than the sun, brighter than the moon, whiter than snow. But Elena the Beautiful kept thinking thoughts of how to pay him back for the insult. Just then Nikita Koltoma was overcome by drowsiness and he went to sleep for a full twelve days and nights. When Elena the Beautiful saw that Nikita was sleeping the sleep of the warrior, she summoned her faithful servants and ordered them to chop off his legs at the knees, then put him in a sloop and send him off into the open sea. They chopped off sleepy Nikita's legs at the knees in front of her very eyes, put him in the sloop, and sent him off to sea. On the thirteenth full day poor Nikita woke up and looked: all around there was water, but he was lying there without any legs, and there was no trace of the ship at all.

Meanwhile, the ship sailed on and on and into the harbor. Cannons roared, all the citizens came running, and the merchants and the boyars, and they met the tsar with bread and salt, and they congratulated him on his legal marriage. The tsar began feasting and summoning guests, and he never gave a thought to Nikita. But he didn't have long for rejoicing. Elena the Beautiful soon deprived him of his tsardom and took over the rule of everything, and then she sent him out to herd swine. Even that wasn't enough for the tsarevna's heart. She ordered them to search everywhere in all lands for any relatives of Nikita Koltoma that might survive. If any were found, they were to be brought to the palace. So the messengers galloped off and began searching everywhere and they found a true brother of Nikita, a Timofei Koltoma. They seized him and brought him to the court.

The tsarevna ordered his eyes put out and then his exile from the city. So at that very moment, they pierced Timofei's eyes, led him out of the city, and abandoned him in the open steppe.

The blind man dragged himself about by touch. He walked and walked and came to the sea shore. He took a step or two and then he felt water beneath his feet. He stopped and stood in one place, afraid to go either forward or backward. Suddenly the sloop carrying Nikita came up to the shore and Nikita saw the man. He was overjoyed and spoke to him, "Well, good man! Help me step out onto the land."

And the blind man replied, "I would be glad to be of aid to you, but I am without eyes. I can see nothing."

"Where are you from and what is your name?"

"I am Timofei Koltoma, and the new tsaritsa, Elena the Beautiful, pierced my eyes and chased me out of her tsardom."

"Oh, then you are my own brother. I am Nikita Koltoma! Come here, Timosha, and on the right side there is a tall oak growing. Uproot this oak, drag it here, and throw it from the shore into the water. Then I'll be able to crawl out along it to you."

So then Timofei Koltoma turned to the right, took several steps, felt the tall old oak, grabbed it round with both of his hands and pulled it out by the roots. He pulled it up and threw it into the water. The tree lay with one end on the ground and the other alongside the sloop. Nikita crawled out onto the shore some how, exchanged kisses with his brother, and said, "Now how is the terrible tsar living now?"

"Oh, brother," Timofei Koltoma answered, "Our terrible tsar is in a great misfortune now. He herds swine in the fields, and every day he receives a pound of bread, a pitcher of water, and three strokes on the back." After that they began talking about how they were going to live and feed themselves.

Nikita said, "Listen to my suggestion, brother! You carry me because I have no legs and I'll sit on your back and tell you in which direction to go."

"Very well, let's do it your way. Although we are both crippled, the two of us can act together like one healthy one."

So Nikita Koltoma got on his brother's neck and pointed out the way to him. Timofei walked and walked and came to a deep forest. In this forest stood the hut of Baba Yaga. The brothers entered the hut, but there wasn't a soul there. "Well, brother," said Nikita, "feel along the stove. Perhaps there's something there?"

Timofei climbed up on the stove and dragged down all sorts of things to eat. He placed them on the table and they both began to stow it away. They were so hungry that they ate everything up. Then Nikita began looking around the hut. On the windowsill he spied a small whistle. He took it and put it to his lips and began whistling. He looked and what a marvelous sight! His blind brother was dancing, the hut was dancing, and the table and the benches and the dishes—everything was dancing! The pots started smashing themselves to smithereens even! "Enough, Nikita, stop playing around!" the blind man begged, "I have no more strength for this." So Nikita stopped whistling and everything immediately became quiet.

Suddenly the door opened and in came Baba Yaga. She shouted in a loud voice, "Oh, you homeless tramps! Up to now not a bird has flown by, nor a beast run by, and then you two break in, eat all my food, and break the pots to bits. I'll fix the two of you and fine, too."

Nikita answered, "Quiet, you old whore! We know how to deal with you, too. Now, brother Timokha, you hold the witch tightly." So Timofei grabbed Baba Yaga with his arms as tightly as he could, and Nikita got hold of her braids, and they started yanking her about the hut.

"Fathers, don't beat me," Baba Yaga pleaded, "I shall be of service to you. Whatever you want, I'll get it for you."

"Alright, old thing. Tell us, can you get the healing and living waters for us? If you get them, I'll let you go alive, but if you don't, then you'll face a cruel death."

Baba Yaga agreed and brought them to two springs. "Here is the healing water, and this other is the living water." Nikita Koltoma ladled out some of the healing water and poured it on himself, and he grew two legs. His legs were completely healthy but they didn't move. So then he ladled out some of the living water and moistened his legs and he could control them. The same thing happened with Timofei Koltoma. He rubbed the eye sockets with the healing water and eyes appeared, completely well but he still could see nothing. So he rubbed them with the living water and he could see better than before. The brothers thanked the old woman and let her go off home, and then they went off to rescue the terrible tsar from his misfortune and catastrophe.

They came into the capital city and saw the terrible tsar herding swine right in front of the very palace. Nikita Koltoma played on the little whistle and the swineherd and his swine began to dance. Elena the Beautiful saw them out the window and became angry. She ordered them to bring a bundle of whips to whip the herder and the musician. The guard came running, seized them, and brought them into the palace to be "treated with the whips." Nikita Koltoma came into the palace to Elena the Beautiful but he didn't want to detain her long. He grabbed her by her white hands and said, "Do you recognize me, Elena the Beautiful? I am Nikita Koltoma. Now then, terrible tsar, she is in your power. Do with her what you wish." So the terrible tsar ordered her shot, and he made Nikita his prime minister, and he always honored him and listened to him in everything.

A–T 519

298. Sivko-Burko

There lived and dwelt an old man, and he had three sons. The third was Ivan the Fool, who did nothing but sit on the stove in a corner and sniffle. The father was dying and he said, "Children, when I die, you are to take turns coming to my grave to sleep for three nights." Then he died. They buried the old man and then night fell. It was time for the oldest brother to go spend the night on the grave, but he—whether he was lazy or afraid—said to his little brother, "Ivan the Fool! You go to our father's grave and sleep there instead of me. You don't do anything anyway."

So Ivan the Fool got ready and went to the grave. He lay down and at midnight the grave suddenly opened, the old man came out, and he asked, "Who are you? Are you my oldest son?"

"No, father, I am Ivan the Fool."

The old man recognized him and asked, "Why didn't my oldest son come?"

"He sent me, father."

"Well, that's your good fortune." The old man whistled and shouted in a warrior's voice: "Sivko-Burko, Magic Black Steed!" Sivko ran and the earth shook, sparks flew out of his eyes, and from his nostrils a pillar of smoke! "Here's a good warhorse for you, my son. And you, horse, serve him as you have served me." When the old man had finished saying that, he lay down in his grave.

Ivan the Fool stroked and petted his Sivko and then released him. He himself went home.

At home his brothers asked him, "Well, Ivan the Fool, did you spend the night well?"

"Very well, brothers."

The second night came and the middle brother also didn't want to spend the night on the grave. He said, "Ivan the Fool! Go to the grave of our father and spend the night there instead of me."

Ivan the Fool without saying a word got ready and went off to the grave. He lay down and waited for midnight. At midnight the grave opened and his father came. He asked, "You, are you my middle son?"

"No," said Ivan the Fool. "It's me again, father." The old man shouted with his warrior's voice, he whistled with a young man's whistle: "Sivko-Burko, Magic Black Steed!" Burko ran and the earth shook, flames came out of his eyes, and from his nostrils a pillar of smoke. "Well, Burko, as you have served me, now serve my son. Now be gone!" And Burko ran away. The old man lay down in his grave, and Ivan the Fool went home.

Again his brothers asked him, "How did you sleep, Ivan the Fool?"

"Very well, brothers!" The third night it was Ivan's turn. He could scarcely wait. He got ready and set off. He lay down on the grave and at midnight the old man came out again. He already knew it was Ivan the Fool. He shouted with the warrior's voice and whistled with a young man's whistle. "Sivko-Burko, Magic Black Steed!" The black steed ran and the earth shook, from his eyes flames burst, and from his nostrils a pillar of smoke. "Well, Black Steed! As you have served me, now serve my son." When the old man had said this, he said farewell to Ivan the Fool, and lay down in his grave. Ivan the Fool stroked his black steed, looked him over, and released him. Then he went home.

Again his brothers asked him, "How did you spend the night, Ivan the Fool?"

"Very well, brothers."

They went on living. Two of the brothers worked, but Ivan the Fool did nothing. Suddenly the tsar sent out a proclamation: he would marry his daughter to the person who could tear down the tsarevna's portrait from high up on the house. The brothers got ready to watch someone try to tear down the portrait. Ivan the Fool sat on the stove behind the chimney and begged, "Brothers, give me a horse and I'll go and have a look, too."

His brothers ridiculed him: "You sit there, Fool, on the stove. Why should you go? Just to make people laugh?" But Ivan the Fool would not be denied. His brothers couldn't put him off. "All right, Fool, you take that three-legged mare there."

So they all rode off. Ivan the Fool rode with them into the open steppe, into the wide expanses. He got down from his little mare, killed her, skinned her, and hung the skin on the corral. He just threw the flesh away. Then he whistled with a young man's whistle and shouted with a warrior's cry: "Sivko-Burko, Magic Black Steed!" Sivko ran and the earth shook, out of his eyes flames burst, and from his nostrils came a pillar of smoke. Ivan the Fool climbed in one ear and ate and drank his fill, then he climbed out the other, dressed and became a handsome young man, such that his brothers would not recognize him. He got on Sivko and went to tear down the portrait.

There was a huge crowd of people. When they saw the young man, they all started staring. Ivan the Fool started his horse with a wave. His horse leapt but missed the portrait by three logs. They had all seen from where he came, but no one saw him go away. He released his horse and went home, back to the stove. Soon his brothers came back and told their wives, "Well, wives, there was this young man there whom no one had ever seen before. He only missed taking the portrait by three logs. We saw where he came from but we don't know where he went. He'll probably come again."

Ivan the Fool sat on the stove and said, "Brothers, wasn't I there?"

"How in the devil could you be there? Sit, fool, on the stove and wipe your nose."

Time passed. Another proclamation from the tsar. Again the brothers got ready to go and Ivan the Fool said, "Brothers, give me some horse or other."

They answered, "Sit there, you fool, stay at home. You'd just ruin another horse." But they couldn't put him off, so they gave him another lame mare. Ivan the Fool dispatched her, too. He killed her, hung up her skin on the corral, and threw away the flesh. Then he whistled with a young man's whistle and shouted with a warrior's cry.

"Sivko-Burko, Magic Black Steed!" Burko ran and the earth shook, from his nose flames burst, and from his nostrils a pillar of smoke. Ivan the Fool climbed in the right ear and dressed, and then he climbed out the left. He had become a handsome young man. He leapt onto his horse and rode off. This time he was only two logs short of the portrait. They all saw where he came from but no one saw where he went. He released Burko and walked home. He sat down on the stove, waiting for his brothers.

His brothers came and said, "Women, that same young man came again. He only missed the portrait by two logs."

Ivan the Fool said to them, "Brothers, wasn't I there?"

"Sit there, fool! You might as well have been with the devil."

Not long after this there was another proclamation from the tsar. The brothers got ready, and Ivan the Fool asked, "Give me, brothers, some sort of horse. I'll go and have a look too."

"You sit at home, fool. Why should we waste a horse on you?"

But they couldn't deny him. They argued and argued and then they gave him a poor old mare. They rode off. Ivan the Fool went off, killed her, and threw away the flesh. Then he whistled with his young man's whistle and shouted with a warrior's cry: "Sivko-Burko, Magic Black Steed!" The black steed ran and the earth shook, and from its eyes flames burst, and from its nostrils a pillar of smoke. Ivan the Fool went in one ear and ate and drank his fill, then he climbed out the other and was dressed as a young man. He got on his horse and set off. When they got to the tsar's apartments, he tore down the portrait and bunting around it. They saw where he came from but they didn't see where he went. He released his black steed and went home.

He sat down on the stove and waited for his brothers. His brothers came and said, "Well, mistresses, that same young man jumped so high today that he tore down the portrait."

Ivan the Fool was sitting behind the chimney and he spoke up, "Brothers, wasn't I there?"

"Go on sitting there, you fool. You might as well have been with the devil."

After a little time the tsar held a ball and he summoned all the boyars, voevodas, princes, councilors, senators, merchants, traders, and peasants. And Ivan's brothers went. Ivan wasn't left behind. He went and sat there behind the chimney on the stove, watching, and with his mouth open. The tsarevna greeted her guests, bringing beer to each of them and wondering whether one of them wouldn't wipe his brow with that bunting. That would be her groom. But no one did. And she didn't see Ivan the Fool on the stove.

The guests all left. The next day the tsar held another ball, but again they couldn't find the one with the cloth. On the third day the tsarevna was once again offering beer to the guests. She had served them all, but no one had wiped himself with the cloth. "My intended one is just not here!" she thought to herself. Then she glanced behind the chimney and saw Ivan the Fool. He was dressed poorly, he was covered in soot, his hair was unkempt. She poured him a glass of beer and his brothers watched, thinking, "the tsarevna is offering beer to that fool!" Ivan the Fool drank some of the beer and wiped himself with the cloth. The tsarevna rejoiced and took him by the hand. She led him to her father and said, "Father, this is my intended!"

The brothers felt as if they had been stabbed in the heart with a knife. "What is the tsarevna doing? Has she gone mad? She's made that fool her intended groom."

Conversations were short. There was a happy feast and then the wedding. Our Ivan is no longer Ivan the Fool; now he is Ivan the Tsar's son-in-law. He got ready, he bathed, and he became that young man such that people couldn't recognize him. Thus, the brothers found out what it means to go to the grave of one's father.

A–T 530

299. The Pig with the Golden Bristles

There lived and dwelt this tsar, and he had a daughter, Incomparable Beauty, and you can't tell about her in a tale or describe her with a pen. The tsar made an announcement throughout all the towns that whoever should kiss the tsarevna through twelve panes of glass, should, regardless of his birth, have the tsarevna as his bride and receive half the tsardom. Now in this tsardom there lived a merchant who had three sons. Two—the oldest and the middle— were intelligent, but the third was a fool. The two oldest sons said, "Father, we are going to win the tsarevna!"

"Go with God," the merchant said.

They took for themselves the very best horses and got ready for the journey, the trip, and the fool also made preparations. "Why are you going, fool?" the brothers said, "Where would you kiss the tsarevna?" and they laughed hysterically at him.

So off they rode, and the fool dragged along behind them on a mangy, poor old nag. He rode out into the steppe and shouted in a loud voice, "Heh, Sivka-Burka, Magical Steed! Stand before me as a leaf before the grass." Suddenly out of nowhere there appeared an outstanding steed. As it ran, the earth shook. The fool climbed in one ear and out the other and became a handsome young man such has never been seen nor heard of. He got on the horse and rode to the tsar's court. There he let fly and he broke six panes of glass. Everybody gasped and shouted, "Who is he?" or "Hold him!" or "Catch him!" But by then all trace had gone. He rode off into the steppe, climbed in one ear and out the other of his horse, and became once more the fool. He got on his nag and rode home. Then he sat down on the stove. When his brothers returned, they told the story.

"There was this young man, father, and he broke through six panes of glass at once."

And from the stove the fool shouted, "Brothers, oh brothers! Wasn't that me you saw?"

"What are you on about, you fool? Should you love the tsarevna? You aren't even worth her fingernails."

The next day the brothers once more got ready to ride to the tsar's court, and the fool also made his preparations. "What for, fool?" the brothers laughed. "Didn't you get enough the last time?"

The fool rode out on his mangy, poor old horse into the steppe again and shouted in a loud voice, "Heh, Sivka-Burka, Magical Steed! Stand before me as a leaf before the grass." The horse ran, the earth shook. Once more he climbed into one ear and out the other, and he became a handsome young man such has never been seen nor heard of.

He flew off to the tsar's court where he broke all twelve panes of glass and kissed the tsarevna, Incomparable Beauty, and she put a stamp right in the middle of his forehead. Everybody gasped and shouted, "Who is that?" "Catch him, hold him!" But all trace of him was long gone. He rode off alone into the steppe, once more climbed into one ear of his horse and then out the other, and thus became the same fool he had been before. He came home, tied up his forehead with a rag, pretending that he had a headache, and lay down on the stove.

His brothers returned and told the story, "Oh, father, there was this young man, and he broke through all twelve panes at once and kissed the tsarevich."

And from the stove the fool responded, "Brothers, dear brothers! Wasn't that me you saw?"

"What do you mean, you fool!"

All this time the tsarevna was wondering who her husband was to be. She came to the tsar and said, "Let me gather all the tsareviches and princes, nobles and merchants, and all the peasants to a feast, a council, and find out who kissed me." The tsar permitted it. So all the baptized world came together. The tsarevna herself made the rounds, treating all to wine and looking carefully to see who might have a mark on the forehead. She went around to all, and at the end she brought some wine to the fool. "What's that you're hiding with that bandage?" the tsarevna asked.

"Oh, it's nothing. My head aches," answered the fool.

"Well, untie it."

So the fool untied his head and the tsarevna recognized the mark—and fainted. The tsar said, "It's too late as we've given our word: that's how it must be. You shall be his bride."

So the fool and the tsarevna were married. She wept most bitterly, and the other two tsarevnas, her sisters, who got married to tsareviches, laughed at her. "You got married to a fool!"

Once the tsar summoned his sons-in-law, and he said to them, "My most amicable sons-in-law! I have heard that in a certain tsardom, in a certain land, there is a marvelous creature: a pig with golden bristles. Could you not obtain one? Try!" So the two clever sons-in-law saddled the very best horses there were, mounted them, and rode away. "Well," the tsar said to the fool, "You go, too."

So the fool took the very worst horse there was in the stables and set off after the tsareviches. He rode out into the open steppe and shouted in a loud voice, "Heh, Sivka-Burka, Magical Steed! Stand before me like the leaf before the grass." Out of nowhere there appeared a wonderful horse. When he snorted, he pawed the earth with a hoof. The fool climbed in one ear and out the other. When he jumped out, there stood before him two young men and they asked him, "What do you want? What do you desire?"

"That there should be a tent set up with a bed in it, and near it a pig grazing with golden bristles."

It all appeared within a minute. The tent was set up, a bed was in the tent, on the bed the fool was stretched out, and such a handsome young man that no one could recognize him! And in a nearby meadow a pig with golden bristles was grazing. The other sons-in-law rode and rode but they never saw a pig with golden bristles and they had to return home. They rode up to the tent and there they saw the marvelous creature. "Oh, there's a pig with golden bristles strolling around here! Let's go and whatever it takes, we'll give. We'll buy the pig with golden bristles and please our father-in-law."

They rode up to the tent and exchanged greetings. The fool asked them, "Where are you going? What are you looking for?"

"Won't you sell us your pig with the golden bristles? We've been looking for one for such a long time."

"No, it's not for sale. I need it for myself."

"Take whatever you want, only sell it to us." They offered a thousand for the pig, and even two, then three thousand and more.

But the fool wouldn't agree. "I wouldn't take even a hundred thousand."

"Oh, please, give it to us. Take what you want."

"Well, if it's so much needed by you, I'll give it to you, and I won't take much for it. Just the mizinets or little toe from your foot."

They thought and thought about it, but then they took off their boots and cut off a little toe. The fool took the toes and hid them on himself, and then he gave them the pig with the golden bristles.

The brothers-in-law came riding home, bringing with them the pig with the golden bristles. The tsar was overjoyed and didn't know how to address them, where to seat them at the table, or what to treat them to. "You didn't see the fool anywhere?" the tsar asked them.

"We didn't see hide nor hair of him, nor did we hear him at all."

But the fool climbed in one of his horse's ears and out the other, and now he was the same fool as before. He killed his nag, skinned her, and put the skin on himself. Then he caught some magpies, ravens, daws, and sparrows, pinned them inside his skin, and set off home. He came into the court and let all the birds go. They flew around to various places and broke out all the windows. Tsarevna Incomparable Beauty broke out into tears when she saw this, while her sisters laughed at her. "Our husbands have brought the pig with the golden bristles, but your fool, just look at him, your fool is dressed as an utter imbecile."

The tsar shouted at the fool, "You ignoramus!"

Another time the tsar summoned his sons-in-law and said to them, "My amicable sons-in-law! I have heard that in such and such a tsardom, in such a land, there is this marvelous creature: A deer with golden antlers and a golden tail. Could you not obtain it for me somehow?"

"We could, your royal highness." So the two clever sons-in-law saddled up the best horses that there were and set off.

"Well," said the tsar to the fool, "you had better go, too."

So the fool took the worst nag there was in the stables and rode out after the clever sons-in-law. He rode into the steppe, shouted in a loud voice, "Heh Sivka-Burka, Magical Steed! Stand before me like a leaf before grass." Out of nowhere there appeared a wonderful steed. When he snorted, he pawed the earth with a hoof. So the fool climbed in one ear and out the other, and then out of somewhere there leapt two young men. They asked him, "What do you want, what do you desire?"

"That there be a tent set up here, with a bed in the tent, and nearby be grazing a deer with golden antlers and a golden tail." And in just one minute the tent was set up, there was a bed inside it, on that bed the fool was stretched out, and so handsome he was that you wouldn't recognize him! And in a nearby meadow grazed a deer with golden antlers and a golden tail.

The clever sons-in-law rode and rode but they never saw such a deer and were returning home. They rode up to the tent and saw the marvelous creature. "There's where that deer with the golden horns and golden tail is grazing! Let's go! Whatever it takes, we'll give for it. We'll buy the deer and please our father-in-law."

They rode up and exchanged greetings. The fool asked them, "Where are you going? What are you looking for?"

"Won't you sell us that deer with the golden horns and golden tail?"

"No, it's not for sale. I need it myself."

"Take whatever you want for it," and they would give a thousand, two, or three thousand, even more. The fool didn't want to hear of it; he wouldn't take the money.

"If you need my deer so much, then I'll just take something of little value for it: the finger from one hand." They thought and thought about, but then they agreed. They removed their gloves and cut off the mizinets from one hand. The fool hid the fingers on himself and gave them the deer.

The sons-in-law came home, bringing the golden-horned and golden-tailed deer; the tsar was overjoyed. He didn't know how to address them, where to seat them at the table, or what to treat them to. "You didn't see the fool, did you?" asked the tsar.

"We didn't see hide nor hair of him, nor did we hear him at all." But the fool climbed in one ear of his horse and out the other and became just the same fool as he had been. Then he killed his mare, skinned her, and put the skin on himself. He caught all sorts of daws and crows, and magpies and sparrows, and he pinned them in the skin around himself, and he went home. He came into the courtyard and let the birds go in various directions.

His wife, the tsarevna, wept and her sisters laughed at her. "Our husbands brought home the deer with the golden horns and golden tail, and your fool— just look what he's done."

The tsar shouted at the fool, "You are an ignoramus." and then he gave half his tsardom to the clever sons-in-law.

For the third time the tsar summoned his sons-in-law and said, "Well, my amicable sons-in-law, I will give you all my tsardom if you can obtain for me the golden-maned and golden-tailed horse, which I have heard is in a certain tsardom, in a certain land." So the two clever sons-in-law saddled the very finest horses there were, just as before, and rode off on the highway and byway. The tsar sent the fool, too. "Well? You go, too."

So the fool took the very worst nag from the stables, got on her, and rode out after the clever ones. He rode out into the steppe and shouted with a very loud voice, "Sivka-Burka, Magical Steed! Stand before me like a leaf before the grass." Out of somewhere the marvelous horse appeared. It snorted and pawed at the ground with its hoof. So then he climbed in one ear and out the other and became such a handsome young man that you wouldn't have recognized him. And then out of nowhere there appeared two young men who asked him, "What do you want? What do you desire?"

"That a tent should stand here, and in the tent a bed, and nearby a golden-maned and golden-tailed horse should graze."

Immediately a tent was set up and in the tent was a bed and on the bed lay stretched out the fool, while nearby in the meadow there grazed the golden-maned and golden-tailed horse. The clever sons-in-law rode and rode but nowhere did they see a golden-maned and golden-tailed horse. They were returning home and then they rode up to the tent and saw the miraculous creature. "So that's where the golden-maned and golden-tailed horse roams and grazes. Let's go and give whatever it takes, and we'll purchase that golden-maned and golden-tailed horse."

The fool said, "Where are you going? What are you looking for?"

"Sell us that golden-maned and golden-tailed horse."

"No, he's not for sale. I need him myself."

"Whatever you want, we'll give you, but sell him to us." And they offered for the horse, a thousand, then two, three, and even more.

"I won't take even a hundred thousand," said the fool. "But if the horse is so necessary for you, I'll give him to you and take nothing much of value. Let me cut a strip off your back the size of a strap." They thought and thought, they turned it over and over. They really wanted the horse, but they felt sorry for themselves. Finally they decided. They stripped off their clothes, removing their shirts, and the fool cut a strip the size of a strap from their backs. He hid the strips on himself and gave them the horse.

The son-in-law came home and brought forth the golden-maned and golden-tailed horse. The tsar was overjoyed and didn't know how to address them, or where to seat them at the table, and what to treat them with. But he gave them the other half of his tsardom. And once more the fool climbed in one ear of his horse and out the other, and thus became what he had been before. Then he killed his old nag, skinned her, and put the skin on himself. He caught daws, magpies, crows, and sparrows, and pinned them up in the skin. He went into the courtyard and let the birds go on all sides. They flew off in all directions and broke nearly all the windows. The tsarevna, his wife, wept, and her sisters laughed at her. "Our husbands have brought home the horse with the golden mane and the golden tail, and your fool, just look at him, what an imbecile he is!"

The tsar shouted at the fool, "What an ignoramus! I shall have you shot."

And then the fool asked, "What are you going to reward me with?"

"And why should I reward you, you fool?"

"If the truth be known, I was the one who acquired for you the pig with the golden bristles, the deer with the golden horns, and the horse with the golden mane and tail."

"How can you prove that?" asked the tsar.

The fool said, "Order my brothers-in-law to take off their boots." The sons-in-law began protesting; they didn't want to remove their boots.

"Take off your boots," the tsar insisted. "There's no harm in that." So they took off their boots and the tsar noticed that the mizinets was missing from one of their feet.

"Here they are," said the fool. "Now order them to take off their gloves." They took off their gloves, and there was no mizinets on one hand. "Here they are," said the fool. "Now order them to take off their shirts." The tsar saw that the truth was coming out, and he ordered them to undress. They removed their shirts and the tsar saw on each of them a strip of skin had been cut out the size of a strap, about a finger or two wide. "Here are the strips!" said the fool, and then he told how it had all happened. The tsar didn't know how to treat him or reward him. He gave him the entire tsardom, and the other sons-in-law who had deceived him—he ordered them shot. The fool went out into the steppe, and shouted in a loud voice, "Heh you, Sivka-Burka, Magical Steed! Stand before me like a leaf before the grass." The horse ran, the ground shook. The fool climbed in one ear and out the other, became a young man and handsome too, returned home and began living happily and prosperously with his tsarevna.

A–T 530A

300. Little Lost Son

There lived an old man with an old woman. They had no children. They were old and extremely poor and there was a severe famine. They had nothing to eat. The old woman went to the millstones, ground all her flour, and she baked a little man out of dough. She took it, the dough man, out of the oven and saw before her a little old man. He asked her to feed him. The old woman took a roll, broke it up, and gave half to the little old man. The little old man took the roll and suddenly disappeared. They searched everywhere for him, but no way could they find him. They looked in the courtyard, in bushes, and suddenly they saw a nest, and in it were twelve little eggs. The old man said, "Let's take them."

But the old woman said, "No, that's not right." But anyway they decided to do it and took them home with them. The old woman put them on the bed and she herself went away. Later she came and instead of twelve little eggs she saw twelve boys. The old man and old woman were frightened—twelve children in such a famine, how would they feed them? They must be baptized, godparents have to be chosen, and as they watched, the boys grew before their very eyes, by the minute, and all were clad.

They went to look for godparents. Everyone was interested in seeing the boys. Even some from rich families became godparents. Then they drove the boys to the church, where a priest baptized them. They baptized eleven but the twelfth disappeared. They searched and searched but he was nowhere. The old man and old woman began to grieve because the twelfth was the most handsome. When they came out of the church, one of the servants looked behind the altar and there stood the boy behind the altar. What name should they give him? They gave him the name "Lost Son" because he had disappeared but not really disappeared.

They celebrated the christenings and all the guests dispersed. In a day the children were already adults. They began to work. The old people were satisfied; now they lived well. The sons cut much hay and put it in stacks. One morning the old man went to look at the stacks. He looked and noted that one wasn't there! He came and said to his sons, "Children, your hay, someone has eaten your labor."

The children decided to guard it. One each night. They eldest son fell asleep and woke up and saw that another stack of hay was gone. And so it went every night. Finally it was the youngest son's turn. First, Lost Son went to the blacksmith and ordered a twenty-pood stick of iron. When it was ready, he threw it into the sky, it fell on his palm and bent. He ordered another pood added. He also took a teazel with him and set off to guard. He sat down in the field and put the teazel between his legs. If he should fall asleep, it would strike him in the forehead and wake him up. At midnight he saw that a storm had arisen and a mare and twelve colts had flown up through the air. All fell from the air and onto the last haystack. He was most clever, leapt on the mare, and began to beat her with his stick. She lifted him into the air but he still wouldn't leave her. She said to him: "Don't beat me. I will go back down onto earth, let me go and you can take my twelve colts. Take the first by the mane and all the rest will go of themselves behind you."

And that is what he did. He came home and everyone looked at him. He gave each brother a colt and said, "I'll take the one left over." And the one that remained was the most pathetic of all.

Now they were all rich. The old ones said to them, "You are now men, now where will we find twelve sisters for brides?" They began to ask whether anyone had heard of twelve unwed sisters. Someone said that beyond the thrice-nine lands lived Baba Rágana, a witch, and that she had twelve beautiful daughters. So they decided to go there.

As they were getting ready for the road, they fed the horses. Suddenly Lost Son heard a human voice from his horse: "You go a day later than your brothers." Lost Son obeyed. He said he was ill and remained home. And he spent the whole day there. Then he got on his little horse, rose up into the air, and flew off through the air. He saw a big meadow and there his brothers' horses were pastured. "You put me behind a bush and not with the others," his little horse said. And that's what he did. The horse then said to him: "When we get there, there will be large iron gates, no one will open them. So I shall ride up, hit them with a hoof, and they will open for us. In the stables tie me to the rotten windowframe." And that's what he did.

They were well met, treated well, they drank, and they even danced. The little horse said to Lost Son: "They will put you to sleep with the daughters in the same room, but on one side the twelve maidens will sleep and on the other—you. Move the beds because above you a self-cutting sword will be placed and above the daughters self-playing geese. You change the beds around. On a signal from the geese the sword will start hacking, Once you've changed them, the geese will start playing, and you get away quickly. Take some of that herb, sprinkle it in the mortar in which Baba Rágana will be sleeping, she won't wake up.

After the feast the guests lay down to sleep. The brothers soon fell asleep. Only the youngest managed to exchange the bed so that the geese started playing and the self-chopping sword hacked all the daughters. Lost Son woke up his brothers, and they began to ride off. As they rode, they came into a large forest and met a decrepit old woman. The youngest son stopped and asked the old lady what was distressing her.

"You are tired. Let me give you a ride."

She answered, "How should I, an old person, ride on a horse?! For your kindness take this little ball and brush and red kerchief. As you ride behind the little ball, throw the brush behind you and a forest will grow up. If you throw the red kerchief, a fire will appear behind you. That's how to save yourself from the witch."

They rode on and saw a witch warming herself. She nearly caught up to them. But then a forest arose before her because of the brush. She gnawed at it. She gnawed through the forest and started catching up. He threw the kerchief and through the flaming lake she did not pick her way.

The little ball brought them to a large city, to the palace of a king. They wanted to seek work from him. The king looked at them all, and they pleased him. He said to them: "Come and serve me as soldiers."

The king liked Lost Son best of all. "You shall instruct your brothers."

But the brothers were not pleased that the very youngest of them should be head over them. They decided: "Let us tell the king to have our brother bring him the self-playing gusli."

The king summoned Lost Son to him. "Bring the gusli and I'll thank you. If you don't, I'll execute you."

Lost Son was full of woe. He went to his horse and began to complain. "That's just half the trouble. There's more to come," said the horse. "Mount up and let's fly. Take some of that herb with you. On the sixth corner at the gates is a passage, sprinkle the witch with the herb and she will fall asleep. Ask the geese with whom they want to live and they will say they want to live with you."

And that is what he did. He sprinkled some of the herb and asked the gusli whom they wanted to serve. The geese said, "We would rather serve you!" He brought them and gave them to the king, who was overjoyed. But the geese would obey only Lost Son. They played beautifully and the king thanked him.

Lost Son found out what his brothers had done and began to discipline them. They once more started thinking up things. Some said, "Let him bring the self-cutting sword a second time and he won't come back, he'll perish."

The king summoned him and said, "Bring me the self-cutting sword. If you bring it, I'll thank you. If not, I'll execute you."

The little horse said, "That's still no woe, the woe is still to come." They set off. He selected some herbs, found the passage in the corner, sprinkled the herbs on the witch, asked the self-cutting sword whom it wished to serve, and brought it to the king. The king was very satisfied and rewarded him by making him a regimental commander. He began "mustering" his brothers still more. And they were thinking about how to escape from him. They found an old woman who hinted to them that the witch still had a thirteenth daughter who sailed the sea in a little house but the little house could not come onto the shore. [They told the king that] he should go and fetch this daughter, who was an indescribable beauty.

The king summoned Lost Son and ordered him to bring her. The horse said, "Now this is woe, real woe, but we shall try all the same. Let us go, but let us drop in on your old parents because they have nothing to eat." They rode to his parents and he told them about his woe. They wept, pitying him.

The little horse said, "Kill me, bury me in the ground, and sow wheat on the spot. When this wheat grows up, you grind thirteen barrels. Twelve barrels are for your parents and the thirteenth leave by my headstone." Lost Son killed the little horse and sowed the wheat. In three days the wheat had grown up. He took the wheat and ground thirteen barrels. Twelve he gave to his parents but the thirteenth he put alongside the little horse's head.

On the third day the little horse suddenly snorted. Lost Son went out of his house and saw his little horse, more beautiful than before. He was overjoyed, embraced the little horse and kissed it. The horse said, "Now don't be sad, mount up on me, and let's fly." They flew for a long time. They came down near the sea. They saw far from shore a little house sailing. A girl came out onto the porch, so beautiful that he immediately lost his head. The horse said, "Kill me again. When you have killed me, cut open my stomach, take out the guts and throw them in the ocean. A lobster will grab hold of them. Pull it out and that will be the king of the lobsters. Don't let him go; just ask for the key to that little house. When they bring you the key, go a little further away. A crow will fly up and peck at me, and you have to catch her. Then you will ask her for the living water. When she brings it, don't believe her. Tear off her leg and rub it, if it grows back it's the living water. Then you can heal me."

So he did just that. He dragged out the lobster king, it called all the lobsters together and he commanded them to search for the key, but they couldn't find it. The king asked, "Have you all come?" But the lobsters replied, "Nedoluga the Lame has stayed behind." The king ordered them to bring him. They dragged him in and he said, "I have the key."

Lost Son took the key and hid it. The crow flew up and began to peck at the little horse. He sneaked up on her and caught that crow. He began to torture her, to ask for some living water. The crows brought some water. Lost Son tore off her leg and rubbed it with the water, but it didn't grow back. He tortured the crow some more and the second time the leg grew back.

He then rubbed his little horse and the horse came alive and became even more beautiful. It walked up to the shore, knocked with its little leg, the circle came unchained and let the little house sail up to the shore.

When it had come to the shore, "she" saw him and fell mindlessly in love with him. She said, "Who are you, how have you rescued me? I have been here forever."

Lost Son said, "I saved you not for myself but for the king."

She said, "I'll go with you and don't be sad, for you shall be my husband." They soon flew back. The king was happy, he fell in love with her and lost his head. They rode up and he wanted to take her by the hands.

She said, "You are old," she said, "you must become young once more. Here is young Lost Son. I want to make you like him, to make you young." The king became frightened and then she decided to kill Lost Son. She killed him, chopped him up into pieces, and cooked him in milk. He popped out even more beautiful and younger than he had been earlier. Well, the king was convinced. They killed him—and that's all, because he was bad, and all the people were now happy. So she married Lost Son and said," People, are you agreed that we should be your guardians?" The people agreed and the brothers became frightened. But Lost Son forgave them everything. After the wedding they brought his parents and all were content, everything was very good for them all.

A–T 531

301. Know-Nothing

The tale begins from the dusky gray, from the chestnut, from the magic roan. In the sea in the ocean on an island, on Buian, there stands a roasted bull with a sharpened garlic in his butt. If you slice that bull from the one side, from the other just dip in and eat.

There lived and dwelt this merchant and he had a son. So then his son began to grow up and trade in the shops, but the merchant's first wife died and he got married to a second. Several months passed and the merchant got ready to travel to foreign lands. He loaded his ships with goods and ordered his son to keep good watch on the house and conduct the trade as was proper. The merchant's son asked his father, "Father! Before you go away, seek my fortune."

"Oh, my dear son!" the old man answered, "Where should I find it?"

"It would not take long to find my fortune. When you get up tomorrow morning, go out the gates and the first thing you meet, buy it and give it to me."

"Very well, my son."

The next morning the father got up very early; he went out the gates, and the first thing he met was a peasant pulling a mangy, feeble colt along to the dogs for food. Well, the merchant started trading for it and finally bought it for a silver ruble. He led the colt into the yard and tied it up in the stables. The merchant's son asked, "Well, father, did you find my fortune?"

"Whether I found it, I don't know, but it's really bad."

"Then that's just what I need. Whatever fortune the good lord sent me is exactly what I'll possess."

The father set off with his goods for foreign lands, and the son remained sitting in the shop and taking care of the trade. And he had this habit: whenever he would go to the shop and then home and back, he would always drop by to see his little colt. But the stepmother hated her stepson and started looking out for a sorceress who might destroy him. She found this old witch who gave her a potion and directed her to place it beneath the threshold at the very moment when the stepson would be coming home.

Returning from his shop, the merchant's son dropped into the stables and saw his colt standing in tears up to his ankles. He slapped him on his flanks and asked, "Why are you crying, my dear horse, won't you tell about it?"

The colt answered, "Oh, Ivan the Merchant's Son, my dear master! How should I not cry? The stepmother wishes to destroy you. You have a dog. As you are about to go into the house, let the dog go ahead of you, and you will see what would have happened." The merchant's son obeyed. As soon as the dog crossed over the threshold, it was torn into tiny little bits.

Ivan the merchant's son gave no sign to his stepmother that he knew about her evil intent. The next day he set off for the shop, and the stepmother to the sorceress. The old woman made her another potion and ordered her to put it in a drink. In the evening on his way home, the merchant's son dropped into the stables, and again the colt was standing up to its ankles in tears. He slapped it on the flanks and said, "Why, my good horse, are you crying and yet telling me nothing about it?"

"How should I not cry, how should I not weep? I hear of a great misfortune. Your stepmother wants to destroy you utterly. Watch out. When you go into the pantry and sit down at the table, the stepmother will bring you a drink in a glass. Don't drink it but pour it out a window and you will see what happens outside the window." Ivan the merchant's son did just that. As soon as he had thrown out the drink, it began tearing up the earth. But he didn't say anything to the stepmother.

On the third day he went once more to the shop, and the stepmother again went to the sorceress. The old woman gave her a magic shirt. In the evening, on his way from the shop, he stopped in to see his colt. His good horse was standing there up to his ankles in tears. He struck him on the flanks, and said, "Why, my good horse, are you crying and why have you told me nothing about it?"

"Why should I not cry? The stepmother wants to destroy you utterly. Listen now to what I say: when you come home, your stepmother will send you to the bathhouse and she'll send a clean shirt to you with a boy. Don't try that shirt on. Put it on the boy instead. What happens next you'll soon see."

So the merchant's son came into the parlor, the stepmother came out and said to him, "Wouldn't you like to go steam yourself? Our bathhouse is ready."

"Very good," said Ivan, and he set off for the bathhouse. A little later the boy brought the shirt. As soon as the merchant's son had put it on the boy, the boy closed his eyes and fell dead on the platform. When he took the shirt off him and threw it in the fire, the boy came back to life, but the stove fell to pieces.

The stepmother saw that nothing had happened. She rushed back to the old sorceress and begged her, she pleaded for her to destroy the stepson. The old woman said, "While his horse is alive, there is nothing I can do! But you pretend to be ill, and when your husband comes home, tell him this: 'I saw in a dream that we have to kill our colt, get its gall, and smear me with that gall, and then my sickness will pass by!' "

The time came for her husband to return, and the son got ready to welcome him. "Greetings, my son!" said the father. "Is everything alright in the house?"

"Everything's well except that stepmother is ill." The merchant unloaded his goods and went into the house where his wife was lying in bed and moaning. "I'll get well," she said, "only if my dream is fulfilled."

The merchant immediately agreed and summoned his son. "Well, my son, I wish to slaughter your horse. Your mother is ill and we need to cure her."

Ivan the merchant's son wept bitterly. "Oh father, You wish to take away my last fortune." Having said this, he went to the stables.

The colt saw him and began speaking, "Oh my dear master! I have kept you from three deaths; you must save me from just the one. Beg your father to let you go for a ride on me just one last time. We'll go riding out into the open steppe with your best friends."

The son begged permission from his father to go for one last ride on his horse, and his father gave him permission. Ivan the merchant's son mounted his horse, galloped into the open steppe, enjoyed himself with his friends and comrades, and then he wrote his father this note: "Cure my stepmother with a horsewhip with a dozen tails; and other than that there's not a thing that will cure her." He sent the note with one of his trusted comrades and set off traveling in distant lands.

The merchant read the note and started curing his wife with the horsewhip with a dozen tails, and soon the woman was completely healed!

So the merchant's son rode through the open steppe, and through the vast expanses, and then he saw a herd of cattle. His good horse said to him, "Ivan the merchant's son! Let me go in freedom, but pluck three hairs out of my tail. When you are in need of me, just burn one of these hairs and I will immediately appear before you, like a leaf before the grass. And you, young lad, go now and join those herders. Buy a single bull from them and butcher it. Dress yourself in the bull's skin, put its bladder on your head, and wherever you are, no matter what they ask you, always give the same answer, 'I don't know.' " So Ivan the merchant's son let his horse go free, dressed himself in the bull's skin, put the bladder on his head, and set off for the seacoast. A ship was traveling over the deep blue sea and the sailors saw this strange marvel—neither beast nor man, with a bladder on its head, and covered all over with hair. They approached the shore in a little boat and began asking, trying to figure it out. But Ivan the merchant's son gave them one and the same answer, "I don't know."

"If that's the case, then let you be 'Know-Nothing.' "

So the sailors took him with them onto the ship and they sailed off to their own kingdom. Whether for a long time or a short time they sailed to their capital city and they went to their king with presents and told him about Know-Nothing. The king ordered them to bring this marvel before his own bright eyes. So they brought Know-Nothing into the palace, and all the people came running together to take a look at such a strange sight. The king began interrogating him: "What sort of man are you?"

"I know nothing."

"From what land are you?"

"I know nothing."

"What is your tribe or your clan?"

"I know nothing." The king spat and sent Know-Nothing into the garden. Let him serve as a scarecrow to keep the birds from the apple trees! But he ordered that he be fed from his own royal kitchens.

This king had three daughters. The older two were beautiful, but the youngest was even better! Not long afterward an Arabian prince began courting the youngest princess. He wrote to the king with a threat. "If you won't give her to me of your own free will, I'll take her by force."

This was not at all to the king's liking and he answered the Arab prince, "Go ahead and begin a war. Let the will of God prevail!" So then the prince collected an innumerable host from the entire reaches of his country. Know-Nothing cast off his skin, removed the bladder, went out into the open steppe, burned a single hair, and shouted in a loud voice, with a warrior's whistle. Out of nowhere his wondrous horse appeared. As the horse ran, the earth shook. "Greetings, young man! Why do you need me so soon?"

"It's time to go to war." So Know-Nothing got on his good horse, and the horse asked him, "How high should I carry you? At half the height of trees or completely over the top of the forest?"

"Carry me over the top of the forest." The horse rose from the ground and flew off toward the enemy force.

Know-Nothing galloped toward the enemy. From one enemy he grabbed his fighting sword, and from another he tore off his gold helmet and put it on himself. He was protected by a visor and began fighting the Arabian force. Wherever he turned, heads would fly—it was just like mowing hay.

From the city ramparts the king and princesses watched and were amazed. "Oh, what a mighty hero that is! Where did he come from? Could that be St. George the Brave come to our aid?" They hadn't the slightest notion it was that very Know-Nothing who scared off crows in the garden. Know-Nothing slaughtered many troops, though not so much slaughtered as trampled them under by means of his horse. There were only left alive the Arabian prince himself and about ten men to serve him—on the journey back.

After this great defeat Know-Nothing rode up to the city wall and said, "Your royal highness! Is my service not pleasing to you?" The king thanked him and invited him to be his guest, but Know-Nothing didn't listen to him. He galloped away into the open steppe, released his horse, and returned home, where he put on his bladder and skin and began to walk through the garden, frightening off the crows, just as before.

Neither a little nor a lot of time passed and the Arabian prince again wrote to the king. "If you won't give me your youngest daughter to marry, I'll burn your entire kingdom down and take her captive!"

The king thought this most unseemly. He wrote in answer that he was waiting for him with an army. The Arabian prince gathered a force larger than the previous one. He searched throughout his entire kingdom and placed three mighty warriors at his army's head. Know-Nothing found out about this, threw off his skin, removed his bladder, summoned his good horse, and galloped off to the battle. One of the warriors rode out against him. They approached each other, exchanged greetings, and struck at each other with their lances. The warrior struck Know-Nothing with such force that he hung on with but one stirrup. Then he righted himself and flew at him as a young man should. He took off the warrior's head, grabbed it by the hair and threw it up in the air. "And that's how all your heads are going to fly!" The second warrior rode out and the same thing happened to him. The third rode out. Know-Nothing fought with him for an entire hour. The warrior cut his hand and blood appeared, but Know-Nothing took off his head and threw it up in the air. Then the entire Arabian army shuddered and fled in all directions.

At that time the king and the princesses were standing on the city wall. The youngest princess saw that the brave warrior's hand was dripping with blood. She took a kerchief from her neck and wrapped the wound herself, and the king summoned him to be his guest. "I shall come," said Know-Nothing, "but not just now." He galloped away into the open steppe, released his horse, dressed again in his skin and put the bladder on his head, and then once more he began walking in the garden, frightening off the crows.

There passed not a lot and not a little time, and the king had agreed to marry his two older daughters to excellent tsareviches, and he sponsored a large celebration. The guests went into the garden to stroll, and they saw Know-Nothing and asked, "What sort of monster is that?" The king answered, "That is Know-Nothing, he lives here with me as a scarecrow. He frightens the birds away from the apple trees." But the youngest daughter looked at Know-Nothing's hand and noticed her kerchief. She turned red but didn't say a word. Since then, after that time, she began walking in the garden more often, and she observed Know-Nothing. She forgot about even thinking of feasts and parties. "Where are you always going, my daughter?" her father asked her.

"Oh, father. No matter how many years I've lived here, how many times I've walked in the garden, I've never seen such a charming little bird as I've just seen there." And she begged her father to bless her marriage to Know-Nothing. But no matter how much her father tried to dissuade her, she insisted. "If you don't marry me to him," she said, "I'll remain a maiden forever; I won't marry anyone at all." So her father agreed and they were married.

After that the Arabian prince wrote him for a third time, asking that the youngest daughter be married to him. "And if not, I'll burn your entire country and take her by force."

The king responded, "My daughter is married. If you like, you can come and see for yourself." The Arabian prince came and saw the monster to whom the splendid princess was married and he decided to kill Know-Nothing. He called him out to a duel unto death. Know-Nothing threw off his skin, took the bladder off his head, summoned his fine horse, and rode out such a fine young man as can't be told of in a tale or described with a pen. They met in the open steppe, the vast expanse. The battle didn't last for long. Ivan Know-Nothing was no monster. He was a mighty and splendid warrior and he was made the heir to the throne. So Ivan the merchant's son and his princess lived and dwelt happily, and prospered, and he brought his father to live with them, and he executed the stepmother.

A–T 532

302. The Cuckoo Helpmate

There lived and dwelt this tsar and tsaritsa. They had twelve sons but not a single daughter. The tsar very much longed for a daughter. So then the tsaritsa got with child. And the tsar set off for distant cities. He said, "If you give birth to a daughter, hang a spindle and spinning wheel by the gates. But if you have a son, hang out a bow and arrow."

Then the tsaritsa gave birth to a daughter, she had a daughter. And she hung the spindle and spinning wheel by the gates. But there was this girl there, called Chernavka. She was supposed to have been married to the tsar. So out of spite she took the spindle and spinning wheel and threw them away, and she hung up a bow and arrow. The tsar saw it and thought it meant the tsaritsa had given birth to another son, and he was angry and went away to distant lands to rule. So the tsaritsa had to bring up the daughter by herself. She brought her up until she was grown. The daughter greatly longed for her father. But the maid Chernavka said, "Who ever saw or heard of it that a daughter didn't know her father? I'll take her to the tsar."

So the tsaritsa let her go. They loaded a sleigh. The tsarevna got in the sleigh with Chernavka on the bumper. And they set off. So they were riding along and Chernavka said, "Who ever saw or heard of it that a daughter went to her father all dirty? Tsarevna, get out and wash your feet."

But a cuckoo in a tree said:

> —*Cuckoo, Natashenka!*
> *Don't get out of the sleigh,*
> *Don't wash your feet!*

And the tsarevna said, "My feet are clean." So they rode on. And then there was this little lake.

"Who ever saw or heard that a tsarevna went to her father all dirty? Tsarevna, get out and wash your hands." But the cuckoo said:

> —*Cuckoo, Natashenka!*
> *Don't get out of the sleigh,*
> *Don't wash your hands!*

And the tsarevna said, "My hands are clean."

They rode on, and then Chernavka said, "Who ever saw or heard that a tsarevna went to a tsar dirty? Get out of the sleigh and wash your face." But the cuckoo said:

> —*Cuckoo, Natashenka!*
> *Don't get out of the sleigh,*
> *Don't wash your face!*

And then the tsarevna said, "My face is clean."

And Chernavka said, "Oh, you are so lazy and so dirty that I can't take you to the tsar." So then the tsarevna got down from the sleigh. Then

Chernavka threw her onto the ground, took everything off her, all her clothes.
And she dressed herself in them. She got into the sleigh, and told the tsarevna
to look after herself. She came to the tsar. "I am your daughter, tsar. The
maiden Chernavka deceived you and hung up the bow and arrow. But I was
the one who was born."

The tsar was overjoyed. He sat her down at a table; he dressed her well.
But he sent his real daughter Natasha out to a garbage dump to herd cows.
She was herding them and singing:

> *Oh, Oh my little cuckoo!*
> *Oh, Oh my little talking one!*
> *Go and tell my mother*
> *That her daughter's herding cows,*
> *That Chernavka's eating pies with the tsar.*

A shepherd heard this and went to the tsar. "Oh tsar, that is Chernavka
rather than your daughter sitting there. Your daughter is herding."

The tsar became angry and sent the shepherd away. And the next day the
tsarevna was still herding cows: "Eat and drink, my father's cows!" Then
she wept:

> *Oh, Oh my little cuckoo!*
> *Oh, Oh my little talking one!*
> *Go and tell my mother*
> *That her daughter's herding cows,*
> *That Chernavka's eating pies with the tsar.*

A coachman heard her and came to the tsar. "This isn't your daughter,
tsar. Your daughter is herding cows at the garbage dump."

The tsar became angry and sent the coachman away. But then he started
thinking about it. "I have the most trusted servants; I ought to look into this."
The next day he went out himself. The tsarevna was at the garbage dump,
weeping:

> *Oh, Oh my little cuckoo!*
> *Oh, Oh my little talking one!*
> *Go and tell my mother*
> *That her daughter's herding cows,*
> *That Chernavka's eating pies with the tsar.*

And then the cuckoo began to coo back to her:

—*Cuckoo, Natashenka*
I tried to teach you:
Don't climb out of the sleigh,
Don't wash your face.
The maid Chernavka
Threw you onto the earth,
Took off your clothes,
Climbed out the sleigh,
Came to the tsar as his daughter,
And you, the tsar's daughter,
She chased off to the garbage dump.

Then the tsar jumped up and greeted her. He had Chernavka shot on the gates. And he and the tsarevna went back to the tsaritsa. There were also twelve young men, twelve good breadwinners. They began living well. Perhaps they're all still alive.

A–T 533

303. Dirty Face

This merchant had a young daughter. She didn't have a woe in the world. Then she said, "What is woe in the world? I think I'll go and find out what woe in the world really is." So she selected some clothing for herself, and lots of money, and all sorts of provisions—whatever she might need. Then she went out onto the highway. And there stood a pillar, and on the pillar was an inscription that read: "If you go in this direction you'll find riches; if in the second direction, you'll have plenty to eat; if in the third direction, you'll find woe." So she chose the third way. She went through the forest, through swamps, and she ripped her clothing up, and she ate all the food she had with her, her provisions, and she had nothing left at all. She had some money, but there was nowhere to buy anything. But anyway the Lord brought her through and she came out into a clearing where there stood a house. She knocked on the door, but there was no answer. She sat there almost until sundown and then she went up to the back porch and looked, and the door opened. She went into the house. A chest of drawers was standing there. She looked in the chest of drawers and there was some women's clothing, and also some men's. So here every sort of provision was prepared for her. She could eat something—everything. In the light she saw a book lying there—a psalter. Then she said, "I'll go along into the hall" (this was from the entrance). She went into the hall and there stood a coffin with iron bands. There was a man in the coffin, and on it was the inscription: "If only someone will read the psalter over me for three years and if it be a male of my age, he will be my brother. If an older man, then my father. If it be a woman who reads and who is my age, then she shall be my wife, and if she is older, then she will be my sister."

Then in the morning she prayed to God and took the psalter to read. She read it for one year and not a single bird came by, so she read it a second year. . . . Two women were leading a dirty girl to sell her in the town. She asked them, "Where are you going?"

"We are going to town," they said.

"And for what good reason?"

"We are taking this dirty-faced girl to sell her."

"Sell her to me in my boredom. I am so alone here!"

"Please, go ahead and buy her!" they said.

"Would I have to pay a lot for her?"

"Oh, and how much would you give for her?"

"Maybe I'd give you a ruble."

"You can give us thirty rubles, miss." So she took out the money, handed it over to them, and prepared a bath for the girl. She washed her, and dressed her as was appropriate.

So then the young lady had been reading the psalter book for two and a half years now, and she was worn out by it. She said, "I'll lie down, I'll just lie down. I just don't care. I am exhausted. You, dirty face, go out for a walk. Only don't touch this book lying here." She lay down, of course, and rested, and then she went to sleep for just about half a year. She was exhausted after the year and a half. But she had taken precaution to wake up. That's how interested she was in what would happen!

So then the dirty-faced maiden walked and walked. She tried to wake up the mistress, but she wouldn't get up. So she took the book, opened it up, and started tearing pages out of it (because she was illiterate). She tore them out and threw them around. She got up to the very last page and then she tore it out. The iron bands snapped and the coffin opened. A body rose up in it. Then it spoke: "Well, was it you who read the psalter over me?"

"Yes," she said, "it was me."

"So it was really you?"

"Yes, it was me."

Then he asked her for the third time, "Was that you who read?"

"Yes," she said. But this time her mistress got up, although she was silent.

"Well, if it was you, then you must be my bride," he said. "But who is that there?"

"That is my servant!"

"Well, if that is your servant, then ask her how I should thank her."

So the dirty-faced girl came and asked, "What do you need? My groom wants to thank you, so what trinket would you like?"

"Why thank me? I don't need anything at all. I need only three dolls and three plates, and three forks, three knives, and three spoons."

Of course, she prepared something for them to eat and gave them dinner. Then she arranged her dolls around the kitchen workbench, and she placed the knives, forks, and plates out, too. This was the ruler's son on whom a witch had cast her spell (there used to be these wizards in olden times!). She thought for a little time: "Why is it that I don't need anything? I need three dolls, three plates, three knives, three forks, and three spoons! I should have taken a little money for some occasion."

Then having thought and pondered all this, she got up from the table and ran into the kitchen to see what could be done with the dolls. And she told the dolls, "You, little dolls, eat and hear my woe. I went out to find woe. I came out onto the highway, and there stood a pillar, and on the pillar was an inscription that read (but go on eating, dolls, hear my woe): 'If you go in this direction you'll find riches; if in the second direction, you'll know no hunger; if in the third direction, you'll find woe.' (But eat, my dolls, and listen to my woe.) So in fact I went through the forest and the swamps, and I tore all my clothes. I had money, but there was no place to buy anything. I could have starved (but you, my dolls, keep on eating and listen to my woe). I came to a clearing and there stood a house. (You eat, my dolls, and listen to my woe.) I sat there from morning until evening and thought. I wondered what would happen to me— only God alone could know! So then I went up to it, but the doors were all locked. (Eat, my dolls, and listen to my woe.) So I went into the house, and there stood a chest of drawers, and in it hung some clothing, both men's and women's. Of course, I had something to eat, and I rested. (And you, my dolls, eat and listen to my woe.) So then I went down and into a hall. I came into the hall and there stood a coffin with iron bands. (Now you eat, my dolls, and listen to my woe.) There was an inscription on the coffin. I read the inscription, which said that whoever read the psalter for three years over the corpse should be rewarded. (But you eat, my dolls, and listen to my woe.) I read the psalter over it a year. Then these two women were leading this girl with the dirty face to sell her. (But you, dolls, eat and listen to my woe.) They brought her up to me. I asked them, 'Where is God taking you?'

"'Mistress, we are going to sell this dirty-faced girl.'

"'Perhaps you will sell her to me?'

"'If you want to buy her, buy her!' (But you, dolls, eat and hear my woe.)

"'How much are you asking?'

"'Thirty rubles.' (And you, my dolls, eat and listen to my woe.)

"So I paid thirty rubles, and I prepared a bath, and I washed away her village filth, clothed her, and gave her shoes. (You, my dolls, eat and listen to my woe.) Then I read the psalter a year over this corpse, and then two and a half years, before I became exhausted and I lay down to rest. I said, 'Don't take up this book, don't handle it at all.' (You, dolls, eat, and listen to my woe.) After I had slept much or a little time, she took the book and handled it, and she tore out the pages and threw them on the ground. (But you, dolls, eat and listen to my woe.) She got to the last page and ripped it out, too. (And you, dolls, eat and listen to my woe.) Then the iron bands broke, the coffin lid rose up, and the body got up. 'Oh, how soundly I have slept!' he said. 'Yes,' she said, 'you have really slept soundly.'

"He said, 'Why are you sitting there on the divan so silently, mistress?' (But you, dolls, eat and listen to my woe.) Then the body asked, 'Are you the one who read the psalter over me?' 'Yes,' she said. And he asked her three times, and she answered, 'Yes, it was me.' (But you eat, dolls, and listen to my woe.)"

So then the tsar's son came in to her in the kitchen. "So, was it you, then, who read the psalter?"

"It certainly was." And he asked her three times.

"Then you shall be my bride. And you, dirty face, acted improperly. I shall tie you to a horse's tail and let you go into the steppe so that your bones will never be seen in this world again. You can't act according to the rules, you went against the law."

A–T 533**

304. Bukhtan Bukhtanovich

In a certain tsardom, in a certain land, there had lived and dwelt a certain Bukhtan Bukhtanovich. And in the middle of a field this Bukhtan Bukhtanovich had built a stove on pillars. He lay on the stove in cockroach milk halfway up his elbow. A fox came to him and said, "Bukhtan Bukhtanovich, if you like, I'll marry you to the tsar's daughter."

"What do you mean, Foxy?"

"Do you have any money at all?"

"Yes, I have some. I have a five-kopeck coin."

"Hand it over!" So then the fox went off and exchanged the coin for smaller coins—one and one and a half and two kopeck coins—and then she went to the tsar and said, "Oh, Tsar and free man! Give me a quart measure to measure Bukhtan Bukhtanovich's money."

He said, "Take it!"

So the fox brought it home and the money, a kopeck, she stuck behind the hoop on the measure and brought it back to the tsar and said, "Oh, Tsar and free man, the quart measure is too small. Give me the full half measure to measure all Bukhtan Bukhtanovich's money." The tsar told her to take it.

She took it, brought it home, and stuck a coin, a kopeck, behind the measure hoop and took it back to the tsar. "Tsar and free man, the half measure is too small. Give me the full measure."

"Take the full measure." She took it, brought it home, and put the rest of the coins behind the iron hoop around the measure. Then she took it back to the tsar. The tsar asked, "Well, foxy, did you measure it?"

The fox said, "All of it. But now, tsar and free man, I have come to you with a good piece of business. Marry your daughter to Bukhtan Bukhtanovich."

"Very good, just show me the groom."

She ran home. "Bukhtan Bukhtanovich! Do you have some sort of clothes? Put them on." Bukhtan Bukhtanovich got dressed and set off with the fox to see the tsar. They were walking along single file and they had to cross over a plank, and it was filthy! The fox shoved him and Bukhtan Bukhtanovich pitched into the mud. She came running up to him, "What happened, what happened, Bukhtan Bukhtanovich?" But she had got him muddy all over. "Wait here, Bukhtan Bukhtanovich! I'll run to the tsar."

The fox ran to the tsar and said, "Oh Tsar and free man! Bukhtan Bukhtanovich and I were going along over a plank bridge, and it was really filthy. We weren't being very careful and he fell off. Now Bukhtan Bukhtanovich is all filthy and he can't very well come into town that way. Would you have any everyday clothing for him?"

"Here, take this."

Off ran the fox. And she came running back. "Bukhtan Bukhtanovich, change your clothes and let's go." So they came to the tsar. The tsar already had everything ready on the table. Bukhtan Bukhtanovich didn't look anywhere but at himself—he'd never seen such clothing in his life.

The tsar winked at the fox. "Say, Foxy, why does Bukhtan Bukhtanovich look at nothing except himself?"

"Oh, Tsar and free man, it seems that he's embarrassed to be dressed in such clothing. Bukhtan Bukhtanovich has never worn old clothes since he was born. Oh, Tsar, give him the clothing that you wear for Easter." Then she went and whispered to Bukhtan Bukhtanovich: "Don't keep looking at yourself." Bukhtan Bukhtanovich immediately started staring just at a chair. It was a gilt chair.

The tsar whispered to the fox, "Now why does Bukhtan Bukhtanovich look at nothing but that chair?"

"Oh, Tsar and free man, it's just that they have lots of chairs like that in the bathhouse." The tsar tossed the chair behind a door. The fox whispered to Bukhtan Bukhtanovich, "Don't look at just one thing—look here and there!" So then they started talking about the good business at hand, the courtship.

So then they played out the wedding—could it take long at the tsar's? There was no beer to be brewed, no wine to be made, everything was ready. They loaded up three ships for Bukhtan Bukhtanovich, and then they set off home on those ships. As they were sailing home, Bukhtan Bukhtanovich was sailing with his wife, but the fox was running along the shore. Bukhtan Bukhtanovich caught sight of his stove and shouted, "Foxy, foxy! That's my stove over there!"

"Be quiet, Bukhtan Bukhtanovich. Aren't you ashamed?" So Bukhtan Bukhtanovich sailed on and the fox ran ahead along the shore. She ran on and up onto a hill, and on that hill there stood a really huge stone house and with it an enormous tsardom. In the hut there was no one at all. She ran into the palace and in the main corner there lay all stretched out a serpent, Zmei Zmeevich. On the chimney pipe there sat perched the raven Voron Voronovich, and on the throne was the cock, Kokot Kokotovich. The fox said, "Why are you all sitting here? The tsar is coming with fire, the tsaritsa with lightning, and they will light and burn up all of you."

"Foxy, where should we all go?"

"Cock, you go into that barrel." Then the fox sealed the barrel. "Raven, you get into the mortar." And then she sealed up the mortar. And the serpent curled up in the straw and she carried it outside. The ships docked. The fox ordered them all to be brought to the water, and the servants immediately threw them all into the water.

Bukhtan Bukhtanovich moved all his household into that house, and there he lived and dwelt, and he prospered, and he ruled, and there he ended his days.

A–T 545B

305. Ivan Tsarevich, the Gray Wolf, and Elena the Most Beautiful

There lived and dwelt Prince Enislav Andreich. And he had three sons: Kolia, Mitia, and Vania, who was youngest of all. So then all these children grew up to be big and they needed to be married. And he had a splendid garden. Saints alive, what a splendid garden it was! But then someone started thieving, started stealing his precious apples. And thus the prince very much regretted spending the labor on the garden, which was still being raided. No guards seemed to be able to catch the thief. So the tsar stopped drinking and eating, and was really grieving over it. And his children also stopped playing.

"Dear papa, why have you become so sad? Dear papa, we had better pursue the thief, but please don't grieve so."

Their father rejoiced that the children promised to guard the garden. This is what the oldest son promised:

"Papa, today it will be my turn. I will go and stand watch in the garden."

So Kolia went out to stand watch in the garden. From evening on he walked and walked around, but he saw no one. He sat down on the soft grass, put his head down, and went to sleep. In the morning his father sent a messenger to summon him back. "Well, did you see anything good out there? Can't you bring some joy to me with something? Did you see the thief perhaps?"

"No, my dear father and parent. I didn't sleep all night, I didn't take my eyes off the tree, and I saw no one."

The tsar thought deeply about this.

In short, the same thing happened with Mitia. He responded with the same experience. And he also had slept all night. And now it was the youngest son's turn to go into the garden. Ivan Tsarevich, the youngest son, set off to stand watch in his father's garden. He was even afraid to sit down, let alone lie down. When he got sleepy, he washed himself with dew from the grass, but he didn't lie down—he kept watch over the garden.

Halfway through the night, or so it seemed to him, something suddenly lit up the garden. It got lighter and lighter in the garden, and then he saw the firebird fly in and perch on the golden apple tree. So Vania quietly stole up and then crawled to the tree stealthily and grabbed the bird by the tail. The bird was powerful and tore away, leaving just a single feather in his hand.

So the youngest son came back to his father, without any messengers, and his father asked him, "Well, my dear Vania, did you perhaps see any of the thieves?"

"Well, my dear father, I didn't manage to catch him quite, but I did find out who is devastating your garden. Father, it isn't an old woman and it isn't an old man. Here, father, I brought a remembrance of the thief for you: it's the firebird."

The tsar rejoiced; all his sadness and grief disappeared. From then on he ate and drank, and he knew no sadness, and the garden ceased being raided. But then one splendid day the tsar had this premonition about this firebird.

"Now, my dear sons, you ought to catch a good horse for yourselves and go out riding, look around the territory, and see whether you can come upon that firebird."

The children thanked their father and set off on the road and way, all three of them. So then the youngest son, rode whether for a long or short time, and he came to a crossroads. On a pillar there was an inscription. Ivan Tsarevich read the inscription: "Whoever goes to the right shall die.

Whoever goes along the middle way will have his horse stolen, and then a gray wolf will devour it. If you go to the left you will yourself be hungry and cold."

So Ivan Tsarevich stood there for a whole hour, thinking. "Which road should I decide to take? I guess I'll take the middle road, even though my horse will be eaten by a gray wolf."

So he went off down the middle road and then out of nowhere a gray wolf was running alongside. "Well, Ivan Tsarevich, get off your good horse. There's no point in fussing about it: you read the inscription on the pillar."

So Ivan Tsarevich was forced to dismount his good horse and then in front of his very eyes the gray wolf tore him into tiny pieces. Ivan Tsarevich was deeply saddened by this and he set off on foot. Sooner or longer, or shorter, he walked until he was tired. He wasn't used to walking on foot and he sat down on the soft grass. He sat there sadly thinking: "What am I going to do now?"

Then suddenly out of nowhere the gray wolf came running up to him. "Well now, Ivan Tsarevich, why are you sitting here feeling so sad?"

"How should I not feel sadness when I've been left without my good horse?"

"Where were you going on your good horse? Tell me the whole truth!" So then he told him everything in detail. "Oh, phooey! You would never have found the firebird in all your lifetime on your good horse! That's why I tore your horse up into bits. I will serve you in faith and truth. You'd have ridden for three years on your good horse to get to the firebird, but I'll get you there in just three hours," the wolf said. "I won't abandon you, Ivan Tsarevich, I will serve you in faith and in truth. Get on my back and hang on tightly."

Well, quicker to say, he ran up to the fortress where the firebird was sitting. "Now, Ivan Tsarevich, listen to the instructions I have for you. Hear me, and don't forget. There's that very high fortress. You get into that fortress and the firebird will be sitting there. This is an excellent time—the sentries are all asleep. But hear me: don't take the cage."

So Ivan Tsarevich climbed into the fortress, and took the firebird, and to his good fortune the sentries were asleep. He took the firebird and then he gazed at the cage. His heart caught fire. "Oh, that's purest gold! Why should I not take it too?"

So he forgot the wolf's instructions. As soon as he touched the cage, a noise resounded: strings were strummed, drums beaten, and all the courtiers jumped into action. They caught Ivan Tsarevich right there. They brought him before Tsar Afron for questioning.

"Who are you and where are you from?"

"I am Ivan Tsarevich."

"Oh, how embarrassing. A tsar's son and he's come thieving. What stupid things to do! Like a simple peasant."

"But your bird was flying into our garden."

"Since I know your father, you should have come to me and asked me in good conscience, and I'd have given you the bird out of respect for your father. But now I'll send out bad reports about you to all the towns and all the Moscows. Although you could do me a favor and I would forgive you. In such and such a town in such and such a land there is a Tsar Kusman with a golden-maned horse. Bring me the horse and I'll give you the firebird and its cage. (Now he's sending him off to be a thief.)

Ivan Tsarevich was very sad as he went to the gray wolf. "I told you not to touch that cage. Why didn't you listen to my orders? Oh well, get on my back." They went up to the fortress where the golden-maned horse was stabled, to Prince Kusman. They rode right up to it. "Well, crawl into the fortress while all the court is asleep. But watch out: don't touch the bridle."

So he entered the fortress and he caught the golden-maned horse. Then Ivan Tsarevich spied the bridle and it was all decorated in diamonds. Oh, how fine it would be to walk that horse in it! He had no sooner touched the bridle when a sound went throughout the fortress. It carried right to the prince, and all the court woke up. They brought Ivan Tsarevich in for questioning.

"Who are you and where are you from?"

"I am Ivan Tsarevich."

"Oh what stupid things you've got yourself into, Ivan Tsarevich! Horse stealing—not even a simple peasant would agree to do that. Well, maybe I can forgive you. Prince Dalmat has this Elena the Beautiful. You bring her to me. I'll give you the horse and the bridle too."

So Ivan Tsarevich was very sad. He set off back to the gray wolf. "Oh, Ivan Tsarevich, you didn't heed my instructions. You make so much trouble for me, the gray wolf, and you just mess everything up."

"Oh, forgive me, forgive me, gray wolf. For God's sake!"

"Alright, you are forgiven. Get on my back. In for a penny, in for the pound!"

They made their way to that prince, that Dalmat. They went up to the Prince Dalmat's fortress and into his garden. And there was no one in the garden but Elena the Beautiful with her nannies and her mummies, who were all strolling around.

"I don't think I'll let you into that garden," said the gray wolf. "I'd better go myself. You had better go on back and somewhere I'll catch up to you."

So Ivan Tsarevich set off back and the gray wolf went into the fortress and into the garden. He wouldn't let the tsarevich go with him. The gray wolf sat down behind a bush and watched. Elena the Beautiful came out with her maids to stroll in the garden. The gray wolf watched her. And then, when she had wandered a little to one side of her nannies, the gray wolf grabbed Elena the Beautiful and threw her onto his back. He caught up with Ivan Tsarevich and Ivan Tsarevich was overjoyed that the gray wolf and Elena the Beautiful had caught up with him.

"Well, get on, Ivan Tsarevich, you act as if there's no one pursuing us."

But Ivan Tsarevich thought to himself. "Why should I part with such a beautiful maiden? Why should I exchange her for a horse?"

The gray wolf asked him, "Why are you so sorrowful now, Ivan Tsarevich?"

"Why should I not be sad, gray wolf? How can I part with such a treasure?"

The gray wolf answered, "But I won't abandon you, I won't be parted from such beauty!"

So they went back to Prince Kusman because they had to deliver Elena the Beautiful to him and he had to take the horse.

"So now, Ivan Tsarevich, we'll hide Elena the Beautiful here somewhere, and I'll turn inside out and then become an Elena the Beautiful, and you can take me and we'll obtain the horse."

So the gray wolf turned round and round and turned into an exact Elena the Beautiful. Ivan Tsarevich led him in and Prince Kusman was overjoyed that they had brought Elena the Beautiful to him. He took her and gave the horse with its bridle to Ivan Tsarevich, and he also thanked him.

So Ivan Tsarevich led the golden-maned horse with its bridle out and he and Elena the Beautiful got on it and set off. They rode for a long time or a short time.

"What are you thinking about, Ivan Tsarevich?"

"I'm just thinking how sad it will be to part with this treasure, this golden-maned horse. But what would Elena the Beautiful and I ride on?"

"Don't be sad. I'll help you."

So they came to Prince Afron. The gray wolf said, "This time I'll turn myself into a golden-maned horse, and you hide this horse with Elena the Beautiful, and take me to Afron."

So Ivan Tsarevich led him to Prince Afron. When the prince had received the golden-maned horse, he thanked him and gave him the cage together with the firebird. So then he and Elena the Beautiful got on the golden-maned horse together with the firebird and they set off down the road.

They rode for a long or a short time. Then the gray wolf caught up to them.

"So, Ivan Tsarevich, let's say farewell now. You are just about to ride up to the borders of your own land."

So Ivan Tsarevich got off his horse and bowed three times to the earth before the gray wolf. He thanked the gray one with deep respect. And the gray wolf said, "Don't be so quick to say farewell; I'll still be of use to you."

But he thought to himself, "How can you still be of use to me? All my desires have been fulfilled."

They were not far from his homeland. It occurred to him to rest. He set up his tent and they lay down to rest. Ivan Tsarevich fell soundly asleep. Then his brothers rode up to him. They had been riding around different lands looking for the firebird. They made one firm decision: "Let us kill our brother and all his treasures will be ours. Otherwise, if we go to our father, we will have nothing, and he will have the firebird, the golden-maned horse, and Elena the Beautiful."

So having decided this, they killed their brother and tore him into bits. Then they got on the fine horse, took the firebird, and set Elena the Beautiful on the horse. They threatened her, "Don't you say anything to anyone at home!"

Out of nowhere the gray wolf came running to the bits and pieces they had torn up. And some ravens were flying overhead. The gray wolf caught a little raven. "Send this little raven of yours! Let him fetch the living and the dead waters. And if you don't send him, I'll destroy your entire family of ravens!"

So the raven flew away. And the gray wolf started putting together all the pieces of Ivan Tsarevich. The raven flew back with the living and dead water. When the gray wolf sprinkled Ivan Tsarevich with this water, he once more became alive.

"How could I have slept so long?"

"You slept very well," said the gray wolf. "You were completely torn to bits. If I hadn't come along, you'd have remained like that forever. Your own dear brothers did you in and then took away all your treasures. Well, get on my back."

So Ivan Tsarevich got on the wolf's back and they caught up with his brothers and took away his treasures. The gray wolf put Ivan Tsarevich on the golden-maned horse with all his treasures and then he asked Ivan Tsarevich, "Well, shall I devour your brothers, tear them to bits, or will you forgive them?"

"Oh, gray wolf! I will forgive them, but will you also forgive them?"

So he thanked the gray wolf and they parted forever. And Ivan Tsarevich rode off home to his father.

His father was overjoyed when he welcomed Ivan Tsarevich, and they had a great feast, and there was much merrymaking, and then a wedding. And Ivan Tsarevich and Elena the Beautiful were married. He became tsar when the tsar gave him his tsardom for his services.

A–T 550

306. Ivan Tsarevich and the Gray Wolf

So now then.

In a certain tsardom there lived this tsar Enislav Andreich. And he had three sons. The oldest son was Mitia, the middle son was Kolia, and the very youngest was Vania, Ivan Tsarevich. This tsar had a really splendid garden. And in the garden grew golden apples. For about twenty years the gardener here had been Arkhipovich. And this was the only such garden in the entire tsardom. The golden apples hung there openly. And then one time this Arkhipovich came and counted the apples—and one was missing! He went to the tsar and reported it: "Oh tsar and father, it's like this you see, I am missing one apple; someone has stolen one of the golden apples."

"Oh, go and count them better!"

But no matter how Arkhipovich counted the apples, one apple was missing. It was just as it had been in the morning, one apple simply wasn't there. Time passed very slowly. The tsar put Arkhipovich into prison and he ordered another to stand guard. But that other guard was also losing apples, you see.

Now this was too much for the tsar, it was most unpleasant. His guards, his sentries, they couldn't find a single thief, as it were.

The tsar went to bed, he was sick in his conscience, from shame: they were stealing apples in his garden and he didn't know who was doing it. So then his sons were wandering in the garden and talking among themselves. "Let's keep watch on the garden ourselves, brothers, one of us each night, and perhaps we will catch sight of the thief."

So they went to the tsar, "Dear papa, we want to keep watch in the garden each for a night." Their father permitted it.

The first night Mitia went to watch over the garden. He walked, he wandered, but there was no one there and he was getting wet from the dew. So then at midnight a heavy sleep came over Mitia. He lay down beneath a linden tree and fell fast asleep. In the morning he woke up and counted—one more apple was missing. He went to his father. "Dear papa, I didn't sleep all night long, I didn't even squeeze my eyes together for a moment, but an apple is gone."

So then the second night Kolia went to keep watch. So Kolia came and from evening he would walk a little, then wander around a little. All was good, there was no one there. Of course, the sentries were standing there. But then shortly after midnight sleep came on this Kolia, a heavy sleep and he couldn't fight it. He lay down in the same place, beneath the linden, and slept. In the morning he jumped up, counted and counted, but an apple was missing. He came to his papa: "Dear papa, all night I didn't sleep, I didn't even squeeze my eyes together for a moment, but an apple is gone. One more is lost."

All right then. The third night came. So it was time for the little son to go. And Vania went out to watch the garden. So Vania walked and strolled, and all was well, and he wouldn't sleep. But just after midnight the same heavy sleep came over Vania and he couldn't struggle against it. He stripped off all his clothes, rolled around in the grass, and washed himself in the dew. And this made him a little more cheerful. Again he walked and strolled through the garden. He walked and walked, and he thought about it's soon going to be dawn. And then dawn began to show light over the mountains. It became lighter and lighter. But why should dawn be coming so very early? Suddenly the firebird landed in the garden and began to pick over the golden apples, to peck at them. Aha, the thief! So that's who was coming into the garden! Ivan Tsarevich crept up beneath the tree and grabbed her firmly by the tail. The bird struggled and as she was big, she tore away and flew off. But Ivan Tsarevich was left with the tail, with a feather in his hands.

"Oh fly away, tailless one! But I have this souvenir to bring to papa!" Then Ivan Tsarevich waited for dawn, and when it came, he ran to his father shouting. "Oh, dear papa, I brought you this souvenir from the thief. That's who has been stealing our apples. It's the firebird who's been coming here."

"So you've discovered the thief and now you will bring him to me. Wherever you have to go, find the firebird for me."

The three brothers got ready and rode off. They rode on the highways and byways. They rode and they rode and they rode. Vania said to them, "Why are we all going along the same road, brothers? It would be better to take different roads. You go there, and I'll go here, and the third will go that way, and we'll find the firebird much sooner."

So the other brothers went off together and Ivan went his own way from them. He went along his own road. He rode and rode and here was a marker, and there a border, and then there was this inscription: "Who goes to the left goes to Katerina and a goose-down bed." "Why do I need a goose-down bed?" he asked himself. "I sleep on those at home." Then, "Who goes to the right will not survive, and whoever goes straight on—his horse will be eaten by the gray wolf."

Vania stood there for some time, thinking. "If I go straight on, then the gray wolf will eat my horse, and that's better than not to be alive at all."

So he set off along the straight road, looking here and there, but there was no gray wolf. He rode and rode and then he saw a gray wolf loping along, with a long tail. Ivan Tsarevich jumped down from his horse and handed him over. "Well, good gray wolf! Here's my horse."

"Oh, Ivan Tsarevich, how kind you are. I always have to take horses in combat, and you have just handed him over." So the wolf devoured the horse and then disappeared, he ran away.

Ivan Tsarevich remained alone. He walked a little, then sat down for a time. There wasn't anything else to do, he was so far away. Then he saw the gray wolf running toward him. "Now he'll want to devour me," thought Ivan. "Well," said Ivan Tsarevich, "You've probably come after me next."

"Of course not. You gave me your horse with such grace that I am going to help you. Where are you going and why?"

"Here and there, and this is why." So then he told him how the firebird was stealing golden apples from the garden and how papa had sent him out to search for her.

"Well, climb on my back," said the wolf. "I'll help you."

So Ivan Tsarevich got on the gray wolf's back, and he carried him off just as if he were on a swan's back. "I know where the firebird is," he said, "I know everything. We have to go to a foreign city."

So the gray wolf ran with him there, wherever was necessary. And he said to Ivan Tsarevich: "I'll stay here beneath this linden tree and you go and steal the firebird. Slip through the fence right here, the sentries are asleep again. Only take the firebird without the cage. Take her and run away quickly."

So Ivan Tsarevich climbed through the fence where the gray wolf had told him. And in truth, the sentries were asleep. He took the firebird, but the cage was like on fire, it was so beautifully decorated. Oh, what a cage! "Why not take the firebird to papa in that cage? Well, he touched it and drums started drumming! The sentries jumped up and seized Ivan Tsarevich and led him before the tsar.

"So now then, we have caught a thief who was carrying the firebird." The tsar began questioning him and interrogating him. "Whose son are you? Where are you from?"

"I'm from such and such a town, and I'm the son of tsar so and so."

"The son of Enislav Andreich, you mean to say. But he's my friend, is Enislav Andreich. But who are you? Have you been let loose to go thieving? Have you no conscience? You should have come here and asked, and I would have given you the firebird. So, now then, let's exchange one piece of luck with another. In such and such a city a certain tsar has a golden-maned horse, a warhorse. Since you are a thief, steal him and bring him to me. Then I'll give you the firebird."

So what did Vania do? He hung his head and went to the gray wolf. "And so it's like this and like that."

"I already knew all that," said the wolf. "Well, get on my back and let's go."

And off they went to steal the horse. They came to this foreign town and the wolf said, "I'll stay here. You go by that path over there. The sentries are asleep. Take the horse but without its bridle. Hold it by your belt and lead it here."

So Ivan crept up to the horse. Oh, what a fine warhorse! His mane shone like fire. And the bridle! It was as if it was covered with sparkling beads. "Oh, I can't leave that bridle behind!" He touched it and they caught Ivan Tsarevich together with the horse.

They brought him before the tsar. "Now then, we've caught this thief."

And the tsar began to interrogate him. "Where are you from and from what city? Whose son are you?"

"I am the son of so and so."

"Oh, he's an acquaintance of mine, your father is. But how have you come to this? To go thieving? Are you not ashamed? Had you come here and had you asked me, I would have given it to your papa. So, now then, let's exchange one piece of luck with another. In a certain city at the court of this tsar is Elena the Beautiful. You steal her for me and bring her here, and I'll give you the horse together with the bridle. (The tsar was a bachelor, and young.)

So then what? Ivan Tsarevich set off for the gray wolf, very sad. "This and this, this and that."

"But I already knew that when you were gone so long, they had caught you. Oh well, get on my back and I'll help you."

So once more they set off for a strange city. They came to where Elena the Beautiful was. He said, did the gray wolf, "You stay here beneath the linden and I'll go and steal Elena the Beautiful." Now in the city where Elena the Beautiful was it was terribly hot. She often walked in the garden, strolling about before the sun rose as it was so hot. The gray wolf stole into the garden, beneath a linden, hid himself, and sat there. Along came Elena the Beautiful with her nanny and with her mamma, walking into the garden. When they were in the garden, they went their separate ways—one this way, and one another, and they were all walking and strolling. Then the gray wolf leapt out, threw Elena the Beautiful onto his back, went through the fence, and carried her off.

The nanny fell into a faint. She lay there until she came to and then she went off to the tsar. "So here's what happened: a gray wolf dragged Elena the Beautiful away."

And where were they now? Ivan Tsarevich and the gray wolf were taking Elena the Beautiful away. Far away. Ivan Tsarevich was holding Elena the Beautiful. He was also holding onto the wolf by his ears. So they were carrying her off, and she had lost consciousness. Later she regained consciousness. "Well," she thought, "I seem to have landed myself in a good spot. Floating along on a wolf is like being on a swan." And so he took her to the city where they were supposed to, where they were supposed to exchange Elena the Beautiful for the warhorse.

Oh, how sorry Ivan Tsarevich was, for Elena the Beautiful was so fair! But he had to exchange her for the horse. "All right," said the gray wolf, "you are sorry for the bride. Of course, you are. Never mind. I'll change my shape. I'll become exactly like Elena the Beautiful. You take me and exchange me for the horse."

So the gray wolf became like a Elena the Beautiful. Ivan didn't know which was which, which one he was to lead away. "Let's go, lead me," said the wolf. And they left Elena beneath a linden tree.

So he brought her in and the tsar met him. They brought in Elena the Beautiful! They beat the drums. So Ivan Tsarevich handed Elena the Beautiful over to the tsar and the tsar led out the horse together with the bridle. Ivan Tsarevich and the horse came back to Elena the Beautiful beneath the linden. The tsar said, "We must quickly marry Elena the Beautiful." And then they moved quickly to arrange the wedding. When the wedding was over, they sat down with the guests. The house was full of guests. And then Elena the Beautiful turned back into the gray wolf and rushed away.

"Oh, my dear!" shouted the guests. "What has happened? Elena has turned into a gray wolf! What can this be?"

The wolf ran back to Ivan Tsarevich. "Get on my back and hold tightly." Now they had to change the horse for the firebird. This time the wolf turned into the horse. They led him to the tsar, the horse I mean. How they greeted him! He brought out the firebird and its cage when he received the horse. The horse was his.

"Let's go!" said the groom. "Let's go for a ride in the steppe! The tsar is on his warhorse, his warhorse with the golden mane. We've got to go out for a ride."

And so they went out into the steppe. They rode everywhere with the tsar on his horse. But then it happened that he carried the tsar into a swamp. He brought him into the swamp and threw him into the brambles. Then he turned into a wolf again and ran away. And those others?! They saw him turn into a wolf! How could that be?

So then he ran, of course, to Elena the Beautiful and Ivan Tsarevich. "Now it's time for us to part." He said goodbye to them and ran away. Not far from his own town Ivan Tsarevich stopped in a little meadow and set up a little tent to rest in. He let the horse with the golden mane graze, and both the firebird and Elena the Beautiful were there with him. They were all having a very pleasant rest.

His brothers came riding by. What sort of weird wonder was this? All around everything was burning with this bright light, and there were the firebird and the horse with the golden mane. They came closer and saw that their brother was there together with the beautiful Elena, resting very pleasantly.

So they went and chopped him up. Then they told Elena the Beautiful that she was to say that they had found her and the firebird. They cut him up into three pieces and they took Elena the Beautiful together with the firebird and the horse with the golden mane. They set off and left Ivan there, all chopped up.

So we'll let them ride off home.

Then ravens began to fly over Ivan, for a day or two, and the gray wolf recognized that Ivan was not alive, so he came running and there were the ravens flying. So he caught a baby raven. "I'll destroy your entire generation if you don't do me a big favor."

The mother raven said, "Don't do that. Don't do anything to my little raven and I'll ransom him."

"Here's the ransom: you go and bring a flagon of each of the living and the dead waters."

"I'll bring them. Here, tie two little bags on me and I'll be back in three hours."

The raven flew away and the wolf put Ivan Tsarevich together as he was supposed to be. Then he splashed him with the dead water first and afterward with the living water, and Ivan Tsarevich stood up. "Oh, how long I've been asleep!"

He saw that there was nobody around him except the gray wolf standing there in front of him.

"Yes," said the wolf, "If it hadn't been for me, you'd have slept even longer. You'd have slept forever. And that's that. So now, Ivan Tsarevich, I knew all this, but I was offended because you didn't invite me to your wedding. But now that hurt has passed by. Get on me and I'll carry you home quickly."

So the gray wolf carried him home and then he disappeared. Ivan Tsarevich went in and his brothers and Elena the Beautiful were already there. Elena the Beautiful recognized him immediately. "Where have you come from, Ivan Tsarevich? You shall be my groom!"

So fine. They would have a wedding.

Vania went out into the forest and shouted, "Dear gray wolf! You must come to my wedding!"

All the guests arrived, and the tsar said, "It's time to go to the wedding."

"No, dear papa," answered Ivan Tsarevich. "I am awaiting my dear guest."

"And who is this dear guest?"

"He'll be here soon. And you, dear papa, must welcome him a little more politely."

Then they saw a troika of horses flying up, and a gold carriage. All the guests went out to welcome him. And in the golden carriage sat the gray wolf. The guests were frightened.

"Oh, what sort of guest is that?"

Vania just asked them, "Don't be afraid of him, he won't hurt you at all."

Elena the Beautiful and Ivan Tsarevich kissed him and embraced him, and all the guests looked on, astonished.

Then they were married. And they rode in that carriage, they celebrated. And the wolf gave them the troika of horses together with the gold carriage, and he said, "Do you know, Ivan Tsarevich, now I'm going to devour your brothers."

Ivan felt sorry for them. He said, "No, don't eat them."

"They had no pity on you; they hacked you into pieces," said the wolf. And that's what had happened; they had hacked him up. But Ivan Tsarevich had pity on them and he didn't let the wolf eat them up.

A–T 550

307. The Rejuvenating Apples

There was a poor peasant who had three sons. The oldest had already turned twenty. The parents had become old, and they felt like becoming young, like getting hold of some rejuvenating apples. The father sent the eldest son, who got ready to go:

"Well, father, bless me as I'm off to show myself, to see people!"

"Well, my child, off you go, and God be with you!"

The father and mother blessed him, mother got some provisions together for the journey, and our Egor set off on his journey, on the long road. This son came to a road junction. There were three roads: one to the right, one straight on, and one to the left, and at the junction of the roads there was written: "If you go by the right, it's to die; if you go straight, it's to prison; if you go by the left, you'll find nothing." Well, he had no longing to be killed. . . . Our Egor thought and thought, and set off along the left road.

For a long while, for a short while, soon he encountered a little house that was no little house, but simply a palace surrounded by paling, a fence, and gates. They took him in, he steamed in the bathhouse. The mistress was young. Whether she was a tsaritsa there or a grand duchess is your business, but let's say the tsaritsa had ordered the bathhouse heated. They washed him, fed him, and gave him sweet wine to drink. Then she tricked him: "Now, please, onto the cot!" He plopped down and plunged into a pit.

Whether a year or perhaps two passed in time, no news, and the old man kept withering away, and he sent his second son. Whether long or short, soon the tale is told, not so soon the deed is done. So he rode, and rode up to the same junction. He thought and thought and then he chose the same, he rode out along the same road. And the same thing happened. They gave him something to drink, fed him, and let him steam in the bathhouse. They gave him sweet wine, and then the tsaritsa tricked him: "Now, please, onto the cot!" He plopped onto the bed and rolled off beneath a mountain.

Next came Ivan's turn. "Go, Ivanushko, search for your brothers, and see whether you can't find some such apples, only three apples are needed." So that was that. Ivanushko did not protest, he was glad to be riding out. Our Ivanushko went by the road, the path, and a hare hopped out to meet him. Ivanushko removed his bow from behind his back, arrow to bow, intending to shoot the hare. But the hare said to him in a human voice: "Don't shoot, Ivanushko, I'll be of use to you!" So that was that. Our Ivanushko didn't shoot. "Off you run," he said, "If you're of use, fine; if you're of no use, it's also alright."

He went further by the road, the path. Near or far, low or high, a bear happened to meet him. Ivan wanted to shoot him, but the bear spoke with a human voice. "Don't shoot, Ivanushko, I'll be of use to you."

So then our Ivan came out to the blue sea. And there on the sand beside the sea lay a pike, its mouth gaping, it was intending to die. "Oh, Ivanushko, peasant's son, throw me back into the sea; I'll be of use to you."

Well, Ivanushko threw the pike into the sea, and set off further. He came up to a hut on cock's legs, with a rooster's head. "Hut, little hut! Turn with your rear to the woods, with your front to me, so that I, a youth, might come in and then leave." The hut turned. Ivan the Peasant's Son entered the hut, and in that hut was an old woman.

"Phoo, phoo, it smells of a Russian soul! Whose ever are you, young lad, where would you be from?"

"And you, granny, first give your guest a drink, feed him, and put him to sleep. Then ask." So granny heated up the bathhouse and steamed our Ivan, then put him to bed, and began to question him.

"So now, granny, and now so. . . . I am Ivan the Peasant's Son. I have set out to seek my brothers and to look for some apples for my father in order to rejuvenate him."

"Oh, Ivanushko, Ivanushko! You will have to endure much misfortune. Well, sleep on. Morning is wiser than evening." In the morning the granny gave him a drink, fed him, and outfitted him for the road. "Here's a little ball," she says, "Wherever the little ball rolls, you follow after it!"

So Ivan set out after the ball. The ball rolled and Ivan went on and came to the junction where his brothers had been. Our Ivan thought a great deal and set off where it was written: "Go to the right and you'll find death." And he came into a town. He stopped at an old granny's who lived alone on the edge of town and he saw how the people all go around sad, and he asked the old granny, the one who lives alone on the edge of town, "Why is it so sad in your town? The people go about so sad and despondent."

"Oh, don't speak of it, my child. Each day," she says, "we pay a tribute. A serpent takes a maiden, a beautiful maiden, and tonight it is the turn of the tsar's daughter. Therefore, my child, we have such mourning. And the tsar says 'Whoever saves my daughter . . .' and to that one he promises half the kingdom and his daughter in marriage."

Our Ivan ate and listened to the granny, then set off for the palace, to the tsar. "Forge me," he said, "three cudgels of ten, fifteen, and twenty poods." Well, at the tsar's a deed is soon done, smiths forged him the first cudgel. Our Ivan took that cudgel, his arms didn't even feel its weight. "And now forge me one of fifteen poods." They forged him a cudgel of fifteen poods. "Oh, this one's just fine. Now forge one of twenty and one of twenty-five poods." They were added to his others. He inquired where they took away the girls, went there earlier, and hid among the bushes. The time came, they brought the girl and left her on shore alone. But our Ivan didn't show himself, he sat. The morning star appeared, a serpent of three heads flies up, smoke pours from its nostrils, fire flies from its ears.

"Phoo, phoo, breakfast is ready!"

Our Ivan jumps out. "Won't you choke on that breakfast?"

"Ooh, a second for starters!" The serpent shouted. It flew at our Ivan, but Ivan was there with his cudgel, the fifteen-pood one. They fought and fought, he chopped off one head and planted his cudgel in the ground. Grasp, grab, but his arms couldn't reach the second cudgel, and the serpent was overcoming Ivan. Suddenly, out of nowhere, the hare came dragging the cudgel to within arm's reach. Again they fought and fought, he chopped off the second head and shoved the second cudgel into the ground. His hands couldn't reach the third and the serpent was overcoming him. Well now, the hare has little strength, and out of nowhere came the bear. The bear dragged the third cudgel to him, and Ivan overcame the serpent. But the tsarevna was barely alive. He went up to that tsarevna and kissed her sugary lips. "Well, let's go to your father. What is promised we'll let him deliver."

They rode, they came to town. The tsar was joyful, delighted, with a happy little feast for the wedding. They played out the wedding, entertained everyone. But Ivan kept thinking just one thing, that he had to ride back to the junction, to take the second road. He left his young bride there and set off alone. He came again to the junction. He thought and thought: "Where to now?" He set off where it was written: "Go straight and you'll land in jail." He walked and walked and walked—near or far, low or high—he came up to a little hut on a cock's legs, with a rooster's head.

"Little hut, little hut, turn with your rear to the forest, with your front to me so that I, a good lad, can go in and come out again."

The little hut turned. Ivan the Peasant's Son went in and in that hut sat an old woman. "Phoo, phoo, phoo," she said, "it smells of a Russian soul. Whose are you, good lad, and where would you be from?"

"And you, granny, first of all, give a guest a drink, feed him, put him to bed, and then you ask."

Well, granny heated up the bathhouse, steamed our Ivan the Peasant's Son, put him to bed and then began to question him. "This is this, granny, and that is that. I am Ivan, the son of a peasant, and I've come to search for my brothers, and for apples for my father to rejuvenate him. I went to the right and found a wife, but now I don't know where to go."

"Sleep," she said, "morning is wiser than the evening." In the morning the old woman directed him: "Go and come to a tower. Don't go close, don't show yourself, and when night falls, you'll get through the paling." And she gave him an amulet. "Put this on that paling and then you'll see how to go in and come out."

So our Ivan set out further on his journey. He came to the town. He looked from afar, he couldn't walk round it, ride round, or jump over it. He waited for darkest night. He approached the paling, hung the amulet on the paling, stretched and pulled, and at that spot a passageway was formed. And granny had instructed him: "When you come back, don't forget to take it back."

He made his way to the passage. And you won't believe the plants there: apples trees, pears, and plums, like in the garden of Paradise. Ivan walked about the garden, and saw three apple trees. He picked one apple from each tree and then went back by the same path and road. He removed the amulet from the paling and the hole was gone, the gates were gone.

So he came back to the junction. "Well, now I'll go by this road, by the left." He came to a tower, the beauty there gave him a drink, fed him, and led him to a bed to sleep, she wanted to put him down. He grabbed her by her white hand and thrust her head onto the bed, and the mistress of the bed rolled ahead, underground. He dragged back the bed, and there was a pit. And you could hear the mistress shouting: "Ivan the Peasant's Son, don't destroy us! Take those keys there and unlock the door!"

He collected the keys and opened the door in the cellar, and there were more or less twenty people and his two brothers among them. He led them out, Ivan set them free. "Well, what shall you do with the mistress? Now it's up to you."

"Hack off her head!"

"Hack it off, chop it off, and send her house up in smoke." That's what they did. Then they all departed, each on his own way.

"Well, brothers, you go with me now." They came to the junction. Now which way? They can't go home. And he says nothing of the apples. "So let's go that way," he said, "to the tsar's. My wife is there." The tsar entertained them, equipped them for the road, as many goods as they could grasp, and they went home to their father and mother. They put a wedding together, it isn't said whether mother and father were rejuvenated or not. Probably they became young on account of the apples. And that's all.

My speech wasn't, as they say, like pouring out melted butter—one word from another, but now it has all come out. So much about tsar and serpent, and what of the hero? Ivan the Russian peasant comes out smelling like a rose!

A–T 551 + 300A

308. The Three Sons-in-Law

Not in an unknown tsardom, not in an unknown land, but in fact in the one in which we live, there lived and dwelt this ruler. And the ruler had three daughters and one son. They called him Ivan Tsarevich. When the ruler was dying, he instructed his son, "Dearest son, listen and you will know to whom you are to marry my daughters, your sisters."

"I am listening, papa."

Suddenly a storm came up, with the most terrible earthquakes. An eagle flew up, struck itself against the earth, turned into a young man, and went into the palace. "Good health, Ivan Tsarevich!"

"Come in, young man. Why has God brought you here?"

"I heard that you have an eligible bride. Do you wish to marry off your oldest sister?"

"I'd like to know to whom I'm marrying her."

"In three years you'll find out."

The tsar hardly had time to brew the beer and distill the wine. They were married and off to bed!

In the morning Ivan Tsarevich got up to congratulate the newlyweds, to see how they were. "So that's it. I somehow didn't think that the eagle would carry off my sister! Now how will I marry off my middle sister?"

A terrible storm arose and there was an earthquake, and up flew a falcon. It struck itself against the earth, became a young man, and went into the palace. "I wish you good health, Ivan Tsarevich. I have heard that you have a sister and I wish to take her in marriage."

"I'd like to know to whom I am giving her."

"You'll find out in three years."

Well, the tsar hardly had time to brew the beer and distill the wine. They were marred and off to bed! In the morning Ivan Tsarevich got up, but the falcon had carried off his middle sister. And soon he had given the third to a raven.

Three years passed, and Ivan Tsarevich remembered that he needed to visit his sisters, to search them out. So he set off to search for them. He saw a woman warrior approaching, Maria Tsarevna, the Princess with the Pouch. They rode together to do battle, but then they agreed to conditions: "If I knock you off your horse, you will live in my tsardom; if you knock me off mine, I'll live in yours."

So they rode at each other, she came out first. At her attack he didn't move on his horse. When he knocked her off her horse, she fell, and his horse stepped onto her breast. Then she got up and they became acquainted. She said to him, "First let's go to my tsardom as I need to put things in order there."

So when they arrived, she paid visits to her regiments. She left him with the keys to twelve rooms, but to a thirteenth there was no key. It was tied with a little string and sealed. He walked and walked. "What was this? He could walk through all the rooms except that one. He went there and saw Kashshei† the Immortal hanging on twelve chains.

"Why are you here?"

"I was sewing your wife some slippers and I tricked her. She put me in here and desires to starve me to death. Oh, Ivan Tsarevich, bring me a glass of water, give me a drink. You will live two lifetimes."

He drank a glass of water and flexed his muscles—three chains flew off him. "No, Ivan Tsarevich, bring me a second glass of water, and you'll live three lifetimes." He drank. When he flexed himself, the rest of the chains flew off and off flew Kashshei the Immortal.

He went out on the upper balcony and saw all the regiments in mourning. He asked why this was so, why the soldiers were in mourning. "Because you let Kashshei the Immortal free. He has carried away Maria Tsarevna, the Princess with the Pouch."

"Beyond how many towns and how many lands?"

"What does it matter? Whoever goes there loses his head."

But he rode off to look for her. First he went to his sisters. He came out on a fine little porch. He whistled and shouted a command: "Sivka-Burka, magic

---

†Also known in the tradition as Koshchei or Kashchei.

horse. Stand before me like a leaf before the grass." And Sivka came running, Mother Moist Earth trembled, fire came out of its backside, from its nostrils a pillar of smoke, coals flying from its ears. He began putting on the saddle blankets, and on top of the blankets a Circassian saddle. "I shall stand like steel, sit in my Circassian saddle, and whip my horse's sides." His horse became angry, flew right off the earth, higher even than the forest, but lower than the clouds it went.

He rode near or far, low or high, then there stood a palace in the steppe. His sister sat on the balcony and she shouted out to him. She met her brother and kissed his sweet lips, she led him to the table, laid with a tablecloth. Mead drinks were ready.

"Well, my dear brother, drink, feast, be merry. But soon my kind husband and your kind brother will come flying here. We shall have to hide you or he'll eat you."

Her husband came flying up, threw himself on the ground, and became a good young man. He entered the palace. "Good health, kind wife. Who is visiting you? Unseen and unheard, but Russian bones have come by themselves!"

"You have flown by way of Russian towns and through Siberian lands, and you have picked up that Russian scent, you can safely say."

"No, tell me who is here. It's your brother and my kind brother-in-law. And I know where he's going."

So Ivan Tsarevich came out and they celebrated and they drank and they made merry. They spent the night. And then he set off to visit the second sister. Again, a palace stood in the steppe. His sister sat on the balcony. She caught sight of him and shouted. She met her brother, kissed his sweet lips, led him to the table, laid with a tablecloth, with mead drinks. "Well, my own dear brother! Drink, feast, and be merry. Soon my kind husband and your kind brother-in-law will arrive. We shall have to hide you or he'll eat you."

Her husband came, threw himself upon the ground, became a good young man, and entered the palace. "Good health, kind wife! Who is visiting you? Unseen and unheard, but Russian bones have come by themselves!"

"Oh, that's because you have flown by way of Russian towns and through Siberian lands, and you have picked up that Russian scent, you can safely say."

"Tell me who is here. It's your brother, my kind brother-in-law. And I know where he is going."

He came out, they drank and they made merry. They spent the night and in the morning he set off for the third sister.

Once more a palace stood in the steppe. His sister was sitting on the balcony. She caught sight of him and shouted. She met her brother. She kissed his sweet lips, led him to the table, laid with a tablecloth and with mead drinks. "Well, dear brother, drink, feast, and be merry. Soon my kind husband and your kind brother-in-law will arrive. We will have to hide you or he'll eat you."

Her husband arrived, threw himself upon the ground, turned himself into a good young man, and entered the palace. "Unseen and unheard, but Russian bones have come by themselves. Tell me who is visiting you?"

"Oh, you have been flying through Russian towns and Siberian lands, and you have picked up that Russian scent."

"I know who it is. It is your own brother, my kind brother-in-law. And I know where he is going." So he came out and they drank, feasted, made merry. Then he spent the night with his youngest sister. He was ready to go on when his two brothers-in-law, the eagle and the falcon, came. "Leave us something to look for you with."

To the oldest he left a sword. "If I should be ill, this sword will become dull, and if I should die, it will blacken." He gave the falcon a ring in the same way: "If I should be ill, this ring with become dull, and if I should die, it will blacken." To the third he gave half a glass of water. "If I should be ill, it will be full, but if I die, it will turn to blood."

Then he rode off. When he had arrived at Kashshei the Immortal's, there were lions standing at the gates of the palace. Maria Tsarevna met him. She shouted, "Nannies, mummies, servants! Take those lions a chunk of meat so they won't walk on the steps."

She gave the lions the chunks and then set off with him. "Well," he thought, "I'll carry you away."

Kashshei the Immortal came flying home and he asked his servants where Maria Tsarevna was. "Ivan Tsarevich has carried her off," they said.

"Go and ask my good horse when we need to set off in pursuit."

The horse said, "Do your plowing, plant your grain, brew the beer, bake the pies, and we'll still catch up to them halfway there."

So Kashshei the Immortal drank a barrel of wine, nibbled on half a beef, slept such that the ground shook. All this passed, then he set out in pursuit. They caught up to them on the road, he took Maria Tsarevna, and said to Ivan Tsarevich, "Here's one glass of water, Ivan Tsarevich, and you still have two lives to live."

But he went after her again in the same tracks. And the same thing happened. The horse told him to wait, but they caught up to them. Kashshei took a little barrel with him, opened it, and put Ivan Tsarevich in it. Then he let it go out to sea.

Soon the eagle flew to the falcon. The brothers-in-law were becoming uneasy. "What's happening with you?"

"The ring has started to blacken."

They flew to the youngest one. "What's happening with you?"

"There is blood in the glass."

They flew off looking for him, through the mountains and valleys, over the broad steppes, the forests and the seas. Then they saw a little barrel floating in the sea. The eagle made the falcon pick it up. "Fly up higher, then go down and pick up that little barrel. Let it down so that it breaks open and we'll see what's in it."

The falcon said, "No, eagle, you are stronger. You lift it and knock it open."

The eagle soared above him, then lifted up the little barrel, and put it down. When they had broken it open, Ivan Tsarevich lay inside. The eagle said, "I'll put him together again. Falcon, you fly for the living water, and you, raven, for the dead water."

When he had barely managed to put Ivan together again, they brought the water. The eagle got him all together and then sprinkled him with the dead, then the living waters. He said, "Come ride with us."

"No, I must search for her. Although I'm now on foot, I'll go."

"But here's what you have to ask. Let Maria Marevna ask Kashshei how to fly across fiery rivers and how he got his horse from Yega Yegishna,†and let her ask him where his death is to be found."

So once more he came to the palace of Maria Marevna. She met him, she rejoiced, and she hid him. Kashshei came flying in, drank a barrel of wine, nibbled on half a beef. Having eaten and drunk, he lay down to sleep. She sat down on the bed beside him.

"Oh, my dear friend, now that you have stolen Ivan Tsarevich from me, tell me: where is your death?"

"My death is in the horns of a bull." She made them bring that bull in and she decorated its horns with precious stones, and she wept, sitting beside it. Kashshei saw it. "Oh, you woman, foolish woman! A woman's hair is long, but her wit is short. Here is where my death is: in the sea, in the ocean, there stands an oak, and beneath the oak is a trunk, and in the trunk is a hare, and in the hare is a duck, and in the duck is an egg, and there is my death."

"Oh, my dear friend, now I am calm. And where did you acquire your horse?"

"I acquired this horse from Yega Yegishna. She has his brother who is much more lively than mine. You would have to be clever to get him."

"What did you have to do to get your horse?"

"I had to herd twelve mares and these mares are her daughters. Finally, it's hard to get away from her."

"And how did you get away from her?"

"I have this kerchief. I wave it and out comes a fiery river. She can't cross the fiery river. Then you also have to count poppy seeds."

---

†Also Baba Yaga, the Russian witch.

"Are there many?"

"Three zillion forty thousand poppy seeds in all."

Then she said, "Is that all there is to tell about it?"

"That's all."

"Then sleep, my friend."

He fell asleep, and as he slept, the earth shook. She took his kerchief and gave it to Ivan Tsarevich.

"Go to Yega Yegishna, most cunning of all, with one skeletal leg." She baked him some tasty snacks to have along the way. As he walked, he ate them, and finally he sat down hungry. He was sitting beside a path and he saw a bear. He aimed at her to shoot her for food.

"Don't shoot me, Ivan Tsarevich, I'll be useful to you in the future. Sit on that old rotten log. Gnaw it and you'll be satisfied.

He sat down and gnawed it, and his hunger was somewhat eased. He went through the steppe and he saw some wasps with their honeycombs. He wanted to eat some honey, but a wasp said to him, "Don't ruin me, Ivan Tsarevich. Swallow some spit instead and you'll be satisfied. Then in the future I'll be of use to you."

He walked on, he walked along the sea, and there lay a pike. He decided to eat it. "Don't eat me. Push me back into the sea with your foot. I'll be useful to you later on."

He walked along, and he came to a palace surrounded by pickets, and on every picket was a head.

Only one picket was without a head. "Well," he said, "there'll be no getting by that for this good lad either! One picket without a head means that will be my own unruly one!"

So then he came to a hut in which the Yegishna was lying, most cunning of all, she of the skeletal leg, with one leg in one corner and the other in the other corner. She raised her head and asked, "Where are you going, young man, Ivan Tsarevich?"

"So, you old whore. You haven't fed me or given me a drink and yet you question me."

She raised her head, opened the cellar, got on her knees, and got some cake. She wet it with a little cabbage soup and fed him. But then she went back to asking him questions, where was he going?

"I have heard, Yega Yegishna, that you have a warhorse."

"I have much work: herding my mares and counting poppy seeds."

In the morning she got up and fed him, and then she drove out the twelve mares. The mares tore off for the forest. They simply raised their tails and were gone. He went over to the hemp barn, wove himself a knout, put it beneath his head, and went to sleep. There was nothing more to be done as the mares had gone away.

He slept very soundly until the bear came running to him and slapped him on a cheek. "Get up, Ivan Tsarevich. Take charge of the mares now for your service to me." So she led them to him and he controlled them with his knout so that they could scarcely run. He herded them into the yard and Yega Yegishna came out.

"For shame, for shame, Ivan Tsarevich! You didn't feed them but let them roam more than usual."

She gave him something to eat and then she went and took three brass rods, three iron rods, and three lead rods. While he was eating, she went into the yard, and he listened to everything. She was lambasting them. "Oh, you so and sos! Don't you know that your mother hasn't eaten Russian flesh in such a long time? And you couldn't even run away from him."

"But there was no way for us to run away in the forest. There were beasts everywhere tormenting us." The next day they were herded out again. Once more they raised their tails and disappeared into the forest. And he went up to the hemp and lay down to sleep. When it was time to go home, a wasp flew up and bit him on the cheek.

"Ivan Tsarevich, get up! That's for your service to us." So he led them back, he herded them. And he fed them better than the day before. He herded them home. "For shame, for shame, Ivan Tsarevich! Yesterday you fed them well, but today still better, such that they are scarcely alive."

So then he said, "I myself have had enough of roaming."

But she went and got three iron rods, three brass rods, and three lead rods. And she began letting them have it, "Oh, you so-and-sos! You know I haven't eaten Russian flesh for so long, and you couldn't run away from him."

The next day he herded them out again. And again they raised their tails and disappeared into the sea. He went to the hemp and lay down to sleep. Then the sea became agitated and the pike hit him in the forehead with its tail. "Get up, Ivan Tsarevich! Take this for your service to me." The pike led the mares to him and he let them have it with the knout more than before. They were hardly alive as he drove them home. He drove them into the yard and Yega Yegishna came out.

"Well, Ivan Tsarevich, you are no herder! You are killing my mares."

But he drove them in, and she gave him something to eat, and then she took three iron rods and three rods of brass and three lead rods, and did she let them have it! "Oh, you so and sos! Don't you know that your mother has not eaten Russian flesh for a long time? Why couldn't you run away from him? Alright. Ivan Tsarevich, you have one more task. Now you must count these poppy seeds, and then you may take a horse for your work. But he's a poor horse; he's in the root cellar."

He took the poppy seeds and tossed them from hand to hand. "Three zillion forty thousand."

"You guessed it." Then at night she curried her mares, just as smooth as silk, and then she led out that warhorse. "Choose any one," she said.

He took the warhorse and led it off. But it was frightening to mount it. "Well," it said, "let me go, Ivan Tsarevich. I'll roam for three dawns and three dusks."

So Ivan Tsarevich set off on foot. When the horse had finished roaming, he ran up and said, "Let me go back, Ivan Tsarevich, to my old mistress. When I arrive, she'll be overjoyed. And when she is so happy, she'll put my warhorse armor on me and tie me to a white oak pillar with a silver ring. Then she'll sit down with her daughters to drink tea and I'll break loose and run away."

He came running up to her and whinnied. The mistress was overjoyed, made her daughters bring out the warrior's saddle and all the warrior's armor. Then she tied him to a white oak pillar with a silver ring. They all sat down to drink tea and admire him. "So, Ivan Tsarevich, it was never for you to possess my horse."

Then the horse whinnied, stamped his legs, and set off to catch up to Ivan Tsarevich. She got into her mortar and chased after him with her pestle. The horse got there first. "Well, Ivan Tsarevich, a rumor is spreading throughout the land that Yega Yegishna is after you. Wave your kerchief."

He waved the kerchief and a fiery river appeared. He managed to get away. "Now, where, Ivan Tsarevich? What is our destination?"

"We are headed for the ocean-sea. In the sea and in the ocean there is an oak, and beneath that oak is a trunk, and in the trunk is a hare, and in the hare a duck, and in the duck an egg. We must obtain that egg."

By the time he had managed to say all that, they had appeared there. The good horse tore out the oak and Ivan Tsarevich broke open the trunk. But the long ears ran away into the forest. Suddenly out of nowhere appeared the bear— she had caught it and she brought it to him. So he killed the hare and took out the duck. He slaughtered the duck and took out the egg. He started rinsing it in the sea, but it slipped away. So the pike brought it back to him.

He wrapped it in his kerchief and said, "Now, take me to such and such a place."

He hadn't had time to turn about when he was there. Maria Marevna, the Princess with the Pouch, met him. There was no point in their talking at length, so they got on the horse and rode away. Kashshei the Immortal came flying after them.

"Where is Maria Marevna, the Princess with the Pouch?"

"Ivan Tsarevich has carried her away."

"Oh, those sons of bitches, those brothers-in-law have brought him to life. Go and ask my good horse when I need to set off to catch up to them."

His good horse said, "Quickly, get on and we'll see what we can do."

They chased after them, and the horse said, "Well, Ivan Tsareavich, only a little time remains. Kashshei the Immortal is nearby. It is time to hoist the egg."

As Kashshei came nearer, Ivan Tsarevich raised the egg, and Kashshei began to die. One brother horse said to the other, "Wait, stop!" But Ivan Tsarevich took the egg, got up, and crushed it. Kashshei fell from his horse. So Ivan Tsarevich burned him, scattered the ashes, it all went up in smoke, and our tale resolved itself with that.

A–T 552 + 302

309. About a Raven

There lived an old man and an old woman. The old man and old woman had three daughters. The old man said to his eldest daughter: "Go fetch some water so the old woman can mix up some pancakes. I've a hankering after pancakes!" The daughter went to the well; a raven flew up, grabbed her, and dragged her away. Then the old man sent his second daughter and she was hauled away by the moon. Finally he sent the third daughter. And the sun dragged her away. The old man waited and waited, but no daughters appeared! He went after the water himself.

He went up to the well and the raven flew by and said, "Well, old man, come visit me!" (This means he has married the daughter he dragged away.) He led the old man home and said, "Wife, heat up the bath!" His wife heated up the bath and he and the raven went into the bathhouse. The raven threw off his raven wings and became a man.

Then they went home. They ate and began lying down to sleep. The raven flew onto a rafter, took his wife, spread out one wing and with the other covered her (and that was all—those were the bed and blankets).

The next day the old man got up, went out of the hut and the moon stood by the gates and called, "Father, honor me with a visit!" So he went to the moon's. The moon's wife heated up the bath, and he and the old man went into the bathhouse. When they had come home, the moon forgot and left his trousers here. He came home and said, "Wife, go to the bathhouse."

"But it's dark there."

"Oh, I'll shine there." He put a fist up in the window and asked, "Is it light now?"

"It's light, it's light!" So the old man slept overnight at the moon's house.

On the third day he went to the sun. And the sun said, "Wife, bake up some pancakes!"

"But there's no wood, nothing to heat the stove with."

"I'll lie down beside the dough-rising trough and you pour the pancakes on me and bake them off. They'll bake just fine." And they ate.

The old man went home and began to work through this whole story. He lay down beside the rising trough and told the old woman to pour and take the pancakes off the stove. The old woman poured and poured, but nothing cooked. She flipped the cakes and the pancake rounds stuck to the old man.

Then he went to the bathhouse. When he got there, he sat on a beam and called the old woman in to go to sleep. "Won't we fall down?"

"But I saw our son-in-law sleep like that and he didn't pitch off!" When the old woman climbed onto the rafter and tried to lie down, she fell onto a crossbeam and there she was killed.

A–T 552B

310. Ivan Tsarevich and the Raven

Once upon a time a sparrow and a mouse became acquainted. They even started dragging grains in together for the winter. They piled up a whole lot. And then autumn came. They thought, "We've dragged and dragged in grain but we'll still need to live apart." They came to an agreement to divide everything. So they divided and divided, but one grain remained left over. The mouse said to the sparrow, "You bite off a half of the grain."

The sparrow answered, "I have no teeth so you bite it."

The mouse said, "I've got an inflamed tooth. I might swallow it whole." But the mouse bit it, she bit it and swallowed it. The sparrow was offended.

So up flew a raven. Among the birds he's considered the prince. He asked, "What's going on here?"

And the sparrow said to him, "I have a request for you. We dragged all the grain in together, then we started dividing it, and one grain was left over. The mouse bit and bit on it, and ate it." So the raven came down to judge the mouse. "We must take two grains away from you and give them to the sparrow." The mouse was offended, but the sparrow was pleased that he had won the case.

The raven was flying, but no matter how much he flew, he couldn't find a snag. There was just steppe. And wherever he soared, the mouse was following him. The raven finally had to perch on a pile. The raven fell soundly asleep and the mouse started plucking his wings. He plucked them bare. When the raven woke up, he flapped and flapped his wings, but there was nothing there. He thought, "Can it be that the mouse plucked my feathers?" So the raven walked around and then he staggered up to a birch tree. Somehow he climbed up into it.

Just then Ivan Tsarevich was out hunting. He hadn't met a soul and he thought, "If only I chanced to meet even a raven!" Then suddenly he saw something black in a birch tree. He aimed at it, but a voice said, "Ivan Tsarevich, don't shoot me." He thought, "What is that? There's not a man around and yet that was a voice." Once more Ivan Tsarevich aimed, and the raven said to him, "Don't shoot me. I'll be of use to you." For a third time Ivan Tsarevich aimed, and the raven said, "Take me with you, bring me down from this birch. I am Prince of the birds, but I can turn into a man. Take me and feed me for three years. I've gotten hitched to the wrong sleigh. I judged a mouse and she plucked all my wing feathers out."

Ivan Tsarevich took him down and carried him off. He brought him home and explained it all to his wife. She said, "What are you going to feed that bird with?" And they had to have rare birds, wild fowl, to feed the raven.

Ivan Tsarevich fed him for a year. Then the raven said, "Well, I'll try my wings now." He spread them and started flying. Then he came back. "No, I can't fly to my sisters yet." The tsarevich fed him for another year. Again the raven flew away and then back again. "Feed me for one more year and I'll pay you a hundred times over for it." So Ivan Tsarevich fed him for a third year. The raven flew away. He was gone for a long time, then he came and perched. "Get on me, Ivan Tsarevich, we will fly to my sisters and they will repay you." So Ivan Tsarevich got on him and they flew away.

They flew across the steppe. Then they had to fly over the sea. The raven flew out from under Ivan Tsarevich and he started falling down. Then the raven flew under him again and raised him up higher than before. Then he flew out from under Ivan Tsarevich again. When he started to fall, the raven flew under him again and raised him still higher. Then for a third time he flew out from under him and again flew under him.

When they had flown over the sea, the raven stopped on the shore to rest. "Well, Ivan Tsarevich, I've paid you back now. The first time you aimed at me, I was frightened; then the second time you aimed at me, I was more frightened; and then the third time, I was most frightened of all. Now you have been frightened."

And so they flew to his sisters. The oldest sister asked him, "Where did you endure all this, dear brother?"

The raven answered, "I put up with it. I stuck my nose in somebody else's business. I judged a mouse and she plucked all my wing feathers out. Ivan Tsarevich fed me for three years. We need to pay him back for this."

The sister asked him, "What do you need, Ivan Tsarevich?" (The raven had told him not to take anything; just ask for a casket of gold.) So Ivan Tsarevich answered, "I need only a casket of gold." She said, "I pity my brother, but I'm sorry for the casket of gold even more!"

So then they flew to the middle sister. She greeted them with tears and joy. She asked, "Where did you endure all this, dear brother?" The raven answered, "I endured it because I stuck my nose in somebody else's business. I judged a mouse. She plucked my wing feathers. Then Ivan Tsarevich fed me for three years. Now we have to pay him back." The sister asked, "What do you need, Ivan Tsarevich?" Ivan Tsarevich responded, "I need a casket of gold." Oh," she said, "I'm sorry for my brother, but I'm even more sorry for that casket of gold."

Ivan Tsarevich was very sad. They rode away—I don't know where. The raven said, "Well, Ivan Tsarevich, let's go to my youngest sister. She was really my most favorite."

She met them anxiously and asked, "Where did you endure all this, dear brother?" The raven answered, "Oh, I've endured everything because I stuck my nose in somebody else's business. I judged a mouse, and she plucked all my wing feathers out. For three years Ivan Tsarevich fed me. We need to pay him back for this."

The sister asked, "What do you need, Ivan Tsarevich?"

"I need," he said, "only a casket of gold."

She said, "Oh, I'm sorry for that casket of gold, but for my brother even more." She gave him the casket of gold. The raven said, "Now we are even. I'll see you on your way. But, Ivan Tsarevich, you can open this half of the gold casket, but you must not open this other half until you get home." They said farewell. Then the tsarevich uttered a command and out jumped twelve young men from the casket. They picked him up and carried him over the sea.

They flew on. Then they saw an enormous field. Ivan thought he would rest there. He thought, "I'll just go into this one half of the coffin." When he opened it, he saw a palace building standing there, and all sorts of livestock came tumbling out of the casket. He was quite beside himself: "What am I ever going to do with all these animals?"

An ancient wizard claimed this land. He said, "Ivan Tsarevich, why have you let all those animals loose here? Round them up!" But Ivan Tsarevich didn't know what to do. "I'll gather them for you if only you'll sign for me what has come to you from home."

"What do you mean?"

"Cut off that nameless finger and sign in blood that you will give me what has arrived for you at home."

So he signed it and the wizard took the letter, gathered up the livestock, and the young men carried Ivan Tsarevich home. When he got home, a son and a daughter had been born to him. They called the son Ivan also.

So then Ivan Tsarevich, the father, opened the casket, and there was a palace. But he was sad. The children grew and he watched them but was near tears. And his wife kept asking him, "Vania, why do you cry when you look at the children?" But he wouldn't tell her.

When the children had grown to about fifteen years of age, they said, "Papa, we are going away. Something is calling us."

He said to them, "Where are you going?"

They said, "It's a little too depressing here." The children went away in the night. They searched for them, but they couldn't be found.

The children walked for a long time through the steppe, then through the forest. They saw a little hut standing in the forest. They were overjoyed. They approached it and entered. There was nobody there. Then they saw bread on the shelf and a soup made of fowl. They ate and lay down exhausted, and then they fell asleep.

Here there lived an old man—a hunter, with his dog. He came home and saw the children lying there. He asked, "Who's that sleeping in my little house? If it's a boy, let him be my son. If it's a girl, then let her be my daughter."

They said, "There are a boy and a girl here!"

"So, you will be my children."

The boy started going out with the old man hunting. But the wizard started paying close attention to the girl. When she would go out for water, the wizard would beckon her across the river, and she would go into his hut while the others were out hunting.

The old hunter died. His son, the boy, buried him and then started going hunting. Before his death the old man had instructed his dog: "Serve him as you have served me!"

The wizard kept visiting the girl, trying to convince her to destroy her brother. "I have great power," he said to her. "When he comes back from hunting, I'll kidnap him."

The lad came back with the dog. He saw this huge Tatar sitting there. He rushed at the boy, but the dog got him by the throat. The boy chased the wizard away and he asked where he had come from. The girl said, "I don't know where he came from."

The next day the boy went out hunting again. When he came home, the wizard once more threw himself at the boy, but the dog wouldn't let him close. Once more the boy chased him out. The third day the boy came back from hunting and the wizard was sitting there again. The boy shot him, hacked him into pieces, and threw him out the window. He went off hunting, but the wizard reappeared. He had this magic tooth, you see.

Now the boy began to be afraid of him, and he said to his sister, "I can't do anything."

He went away hunting, and the wizard said to the girl, "You must start wasting away as of this night, and he must bring you some down from a raven's nest. There the ravens will peck him to death."

The next day the girl pretended to be ill, and she asked her brother, "Bring me some down from a raven's nest."

So the boy set off and he saw a raven there. He said, "Help me in my misfortune, give me some down from your nest."

The raven's children wanted to attack him, but the raven wouldn't let him. "No, this person came here not of his own free will." The raven took one little raven chick and said, "Here, Ivan Tsarevich, take one of my little children."

The boy came home and the wizard was sitting there again. The dog and the raven roughed him up. The next day the wizard appeared again and said to the girl, "Send him to the warrior-eagle."

So she once again "fell ill," and she asked her brother to bring some down from an eagle's nest. The boy went there and the little eaglets rushed at him. The eagle said to them, "Don't touch him; this person came here not of his own free will." He then said to the boy, "Here is a little warrior-eaglet. Let him serve you as you served me." The boy came home, and once more the wizard was sitting there. Once more the dog, the raven and the eaglet roughed him up.

The next day the wizard said to the girl, "This time send him to the wolf. He won't come back from there." Once more she "fell ill" and asked him to bring her some fur from a wolf.

So off he went. He came to the wolf and the little wolves rushed at him. But the wolf said to him, "Don't eat him; he didn't come here of his own free will." And he gave the boy a little wolf. "Here, Ivan Tsarevich, here's a little wolf-warrior. Let him serve you as you served me."

The boy came home and the wizard was sitting there. The dog, the raven, the eagle, and the little warrior-wolf tore him to bits.

Once more the wizard came to the girl and said she must send her brother to a bear. No way would bear cubs let him go. The girl once more "fell ill" and asked her brother to bring her some bear fur. He set off. The little bear cubs rushed at him, but the bear said, "Don't touch him, this person came here not of his own free will." He gave the boy a bear cub. The boy came back and once more they hacked the wizard to pieces.

The next day the wizard said to the girl, "If we've been unsuccessful, this time send him to where there's a mill on twelve pillars. From the furthest stones let him bring back some pebbles for beads." She sent her brother away. So Ivan got up to the furthest stone, and there was this spring, and it locked all twelve doors at once. He stayed there. Then the raven carried him out. When the wizard saw that, he said to the sister, "Heat the bath and let him wash himself well."

So Ivan went to the bathhouse very sad. He washed and washed, and then the raven came flying and said, "Ivan Tsarevich, wash more quietly; his magic force has already come through some doors."

In came the wizard and asked, "Have you washed?"

"Not yet."

When the wizard had gone away, the raven flew up. "Ivan Tsarevich, wash more quietly; the magic force has already come through the three doors." Ivan Tsarevich washed. And in a little while all that force tore into the bathhouse. It seized the wizard and tore him up. Then Ivan Tsarevich dragged him into the bathhouse and burned down the bathhouse.

But the wizard had earlier told the girl that he had a fire-proof tooth. You could scatter his ashes and he would come back to life. "You can scatter the ashes, but then you must find that tooth in order to do me in."

Once more Ivan Tsarevich and that force went out hunting. The girl noticed everything, how Ivan Tsarevich kept scattering the ashes. She found the tooth. Ivan Tsarevich lay down to sleep and his sister pretended to search about his head. He knelt down with his head on her knees and soon started snoring. Previously that wizard had said to her, "Stick that tooth in his ear. He'll die and I'll come to life." That's what the girl did.

"Well," said the wizard, "You and I'll live together." He stabbed Ivan Tsarevich in the side and sent him out to sea.

But the magical force was sleeping. It slept for twelve full days and then looked for Ivan Tsarevich. The dog sniffed in the direction of the sea. Then the force said, "Well, raven and eagle, go find out where he is."

The raven and the eagle flew off. They saw a barrel that had washed up onto an island. The eagle and raven flew back and said, "We've found him." They dragged the barrel onto the shore and there lay Ivan Tsarevich. On the barrel was written, "Whoever pulls out this tooth will die." It was necessary to pull out the tooth and dip your nose in the sea. You had to get that tooth. That was no job for the bear or the wolf. And the eagle's nose was hook-shaped. The raven would have to do it. So they dragged Ivan Tsarevich onto the beach and the raven calmly pulled the tooth out of Ivan Tsarevich's ear and then dipped his nose in the sea. He saved him and was himself saved.

So they threw the tooth away and went back to the hut where they boarded up all the shutters and then they burned his sister and the wizard. Ivan Tsarevich went to his father. He was already old. The whole business was explained and both father and mother were happy. They put on a feast. And I was there. I drank mead and beer, but it ran through my moustache, and none got into my mouth.

A–T 553

311. Anastasia the Beautiful and Ivan the Russian Warrior

There lived and dwelt this tsar, and this tsar had three daughters, and there was Ivan, a Russian warrior. The father was dying and he instructed his son: "Oh, my beloved son! I will die and matchmakers will come to you. Give your sisters to the first who asks!"

"Yes, father!" So then the father died, that tsar passed away, and they buried the tsar, and then some matchmakers came to court the oldest sister. No one knew where they were from and they said, "Ivan, Russian Warrior! Give your sister to us for this marriage. If you do not give her willingly, we shall take her by force!" There was nothing to be done; according to his father's instructions he gave her away. They sat her [in the sleigh] and took her away, but no one knows where they took her.

After a certain time they came courting the second one, the middle one. Again they said, "Ivan, Russian Warrior! Give your sister to us for this marriage. If you do not give her willingly, we shall take her by force!" There was nothing to be done; according to his father's instructions he gave her away. They sat her [in the sleigh] and took her away, but no one knows where they took her.

After a little time they came for the youngest sister. "Ivan the Russian Warrior! Give your sister to us for this marriage. If you do not give her willingly, we shall take her by force!" There was nothing to be done; according to his father's instructions he gave her away. They sat her [in the sleigh] and took her away, but no one knows where they took her.

After a certain time Ivan the Russian Warrior became lonely. "I shall go up to my borders and inspect my army," he said. So he got ready and rode off. He rode for a day, then another. He came to the first border and all his forces were defeated on this first boundary. Ivan the Russian Warrior sighed bitterly. He shouted out in his loud warrior's voice, "Is there any man in this army, this force, who is alive?"

And one living head replied to him, "There is, Ivan Russian Warrior, just one living man."

And he asked him, "Who has defeated this army, this force?"

And the one living man answered him, "This army and great force was defeated by Maria Marevna, the beautiful princess, and she defeated it with her right leg alone."

"And where did she go?"

"She went to another boundary."

So he went to another boundary. He rode up to this boundary and saw that all his force had been defeated. Ivan the Russian Warrior bitterly sighed. "Who is this warrior? What have I done to him? There have been no rumors, I've sent no letters, and yet he has defeated my entire force?" Ivan the Russian Warrior shouted with his loud voice, "Is there any man in this army or force who is alive?"

And one living head replied to him, "There is, Ivan Russian Warrior, there is one man alive." He asked him, "Who has defeated this army and force?"

"This army and force were defeated by Maria Marevna, the beautiful princess, with her left hand!"

"Where did she go?"

"She went to our third boundary."

Ivan the Russian Warrior hurried, he rode to the third boundary. All his forces at the third boundary had been defeated. Ivan the Russian Warrior wept bitterly, he pitied his forces. He shouted in his loud voice, "Is there in this great defeated army or force a living person?"

"There is, Ivan the Russian Warrior, one living head."

He asked, "Who has defeated this great army and force?"

"Maria Marevna, the beautiful princess, and she did it with just her right leg."

"And where did she go?"

"She went over there, into the green fields." Ivan the Russian Warrior rode off into the green fields.

He came into the green fields and saw that a tent had been set up. A horse was tied to the tent and it paced with spring wheat scattered for its food. He went and put his own horse to the feed of the other horse. He then entered the tent himself. He entered and saw Maria Marevna, the beautiful princess, lying there asleep. Ivan the Russian Warrior became highly incensed. He drew his sharp sword, wanting to cutting her head from her shoulders. But he thought to himself, "What sort of warrior, what sort of fighting man would I be! To kill someone sleeping is like killing the dead!" So he up and lay down to sleep too and he fell fast asleep.

Maria Marevna, the beautiful princess, woke up and said, "What ignoramus has come here to me? He has come without papers and without my permission into my white tent, he has moved my horse away from his own fodder and let his own in there instead." She grew livid with anger, drew her sharp sword, and wanted to cut his head from his shoulders, but then she thought, "To kill the sleeping is like killing the dead! What sort of fighter am I! He came here before I did, he could have killed me but he didn't."

So she began to arouse Ivan the Russian Warrior. "Get up, Ivan, Russian Warrior. Wake up, not on account of my waking you, but for your own salvation." So Ivan the Russian Warrior woke up from his sleep and he was enraged with a bitter fury. Maria Marevna said to him, "What an ignoramus you are! You rode right into my white tent without my permission, you moved my horse off his fodder and let your own in there."

Ivan Tsarevich answered, "And what an ignoramus you are, what a warrior! You fight and conquer, but you do everything like a robber; you sent no letters, no parcels, and as for the fight, you opened fire and never told me anything at all about it!" They taunted each other with their anger and pride and then they got angry themselves, and were heated with fury, and they started parting. They rode apart for three versts and then they rode at each other and struck each other. Ivan the Russian Warrior struck Maria Marevna and knocked her into the ground up to her ankles. Again they rode apart. They rode four versts apart, came at each other and struck with their lances. Ivan the Russian Warrior once more struck Maria Marevna up to the waist. Maria Marevna again struck her horse and again flew up as if she had never been there. Again they rode apart for five versts and they incited each other. Ivan the Russian Warrior struck her with such pride and knocked her clean off her horse and into the ground up to her very shoulders. He drew his sharp sword and wanted to remove her head from the shoulders.

But Maria Marevna repented all to Ivan the Russian Warrior: "Do not beat me, Ivan the Russian Warrior! I am not Maria Marevna, the beautiful princess, I am Anastasia the Beautiful." Ivan the Russian Warrior was delighted at that. He cast off his former enmity, drew her out of the ground, and she removed her warrior's clothing and was dressed in a woman's gown. "Well, Ivan the Russian Warrior, let us ride to my tsardom!" So they came to her tsardom, he married Anastasia the Beautiful and they began to live together, and to prosper.

Anastasia the Beautiful gave him all the keys to the tsardom, let him look at all the jewels, let him go throughout the entire tsardom, but she forbade him go into just one room. Ivan the Russian Warrior went everywhere, he looked at all the jewels. All the commoners and all the generals, everybody paid their respects to him. He went everywhere and looked at everything, only he had not been in this one room where she had forbidden him to go.

He said, "Why won't she let me go into this one room? Let's go in!" The room was locked behind twelve doors with twelve chains. He went in and began opening them. He unlocked the last door, opened it, and saw Koshchei the Deathless in the fire, in a kettle, boiling in pitch. Ivan the Russian Warrior was about to draw his bow as he wanted to kill Koshchei with an arrow, but Koshchei gave a start and then began to fly. "Oh, thank you Ivan the Russian Warrior, for freeing me from this bondage. I have been sitting here for fifteen years on account of the beauty of Anastasia the Beautiful." (She had jailed him there on account of her beauty, by deceit so to speak.) He flew off and found Anastasia, he seized her and carried her off.

Ivan the Russian Warrior was left with nothing, and he thought to himself, "I got her because of my wisdom but I lost her because of a lack of it." He lived there for a month without her and he was lonesome. "I shall go and fetch back my Anastasia the Beautiful."

He got ready and set off. The generals and the counts tried to stop him. "Where are you going? Koshchei the Deathless will kill you."

"There cannot be seven deaths, nor will you escape even one," he said.

So the generals gave him the troops. "Take with you as many as you like."

"No, better to die alone than that we should all perish." So he set off on his journey alone.

He rode for a day, he rode the next, he rode for the third, then a week, and a month, and perhaps even more. A tale is soon told, but the deed is not so soon done. He rode into a forest, and in that forest stood an enormous palace. Near the palace stood three oaks and of such enormity as to give one fright. He came up to the palace and asked to be let in to spend the night. Suddenly his oldest sister appeared. She recognized her brother and started crying bitterly. "Where are you going, brother? Will your journey take you far?"

"Oh sister, just feed me after my journey, give me something to drink, and then ask me; I am still hungry!" So she led him into her palace, she gave him something to drink, she fed him, and then she began asking him, "Where are you going, where will your journey take you?"

"I am going to fetch back my Anastasia the Beautiful."

"Oh, Ivan," she said, "a Russian warrior got her with wisdom and without that wisdom he lost her. My husband is more powerful than you. He chased after her, but could not win her back. Better don't go, brother, he will kill you."

"Oh, sister, there cannot be seven deaths, nor will you escape even one!" And he lay down to sleep.

Her husband, tsar raven, came flying in. Such an explosion from the air, from the force of it, that it was as if some storm had got up. From the air alone the three oaks bent to the earth. Her husband, tsar raven, flew up. He immediately asked, "Why does it smell of a Russian here?"

"My brother has come!!"

"And where is he?"

"He is sleeping."

So the tsar raven immediately woke him up, sat him down at the table, and began talking with him, and he asked him, "Where are you going, will your journey take you far?"

"I am going to fetch back my Anastasia the Beautiful!"

"Oh brother, what you got with wisdom you lost without it. I advise you, it would be better to go back home."

"What?" he said, "there cannot be seven deaths, nor will you escape even one! We all have to die sometime." They finished eating and lay down to sleep. In the morning they got up and drank their tea. Ivan the Russian Warrior took something to eat and set off on his journey once more.

His brother-in-law and sister saw him on his way. "Well," they said, "Go then. If you have some misfortune, I will come to your aid." So they took their leave and he rode off down the road and way.

He rode for a day, for two, a week, and a month, all just as before. Once more he came into a forest. In this forest stood a palace even better than the other one and there were six oaks standing around it. He rode up to the palace, knocked, and asked to be let in to spend the night. Suddenly out came his middle sister. She began weeping bitterly, greeted him and asked him, "Where are you going, brother? Where will your journey take you?"

"Sister, first you give me a drink, then you feed me, and only then ask. I want to drink and eat!"

So she led him into the palace, sat him down, got something together for him to eat and she fed him, she gave him something to drink, and then she started questioning Ivan the Russian Warrior, "Where are you going, where will your journey take you?"

"I am going to fetch back Anastasia the Beautiful."

"Oh brother, what you got with wisdom, you lost without it. My husband, the falcon tsar, is much stronger than you. He chased after her, but he could not get her away."

"Oh sister, there cannot be seven deaths, nor will you escape even one!" And he lay down to sleep.

He had just got to sleep when there was this explosion. (It was like an explosion—the oaks were all forced to the ground by the air.) Tsar falcon came flying in. He immediately asked, "Why does it smell of a Russian here?"

"My brother has come!"

"Where is he?"

"He went to sleep." So immediately that tsar falcon woke him up and sat him down with him, and they began to eat and drink and they began talking about the way they lived. "Where, brother, are you going, where is your journey taking you?"

"I am going to fetch back Anastasia the Beautiful."

"Oh brother, what you gained with wisdom, you lost without wisdom! I advise you, you would be better to go home."

"Brother, there cannot be seven deaths, nor can you escape even one." They lay down to sleep. In the morning they got up, they drank their fill of tea, and had a bite to eat, and then they said goodbye to Ivan the Russian Warrior. The falcon tsar said, "Off you go, Ivan the Russian Warrior! If you have any misfortune, we shall aid you." They said their farewells and he set off on his road and way.

He rode for a day, two, three, a week, and a month. Again he came to a forest. There stood an enormous palace in the forest and near the palace stood twelve enormous oaks. Ivan the Russian Warrior rode up to the palace and asked to be let in to spend the night. Out came his youngest sister, she recognized him and started crying bitterly. Then she began asking him, "Where are you going, brother, and where will your journey take you?"

He said to her, "First you must feed me, give me something to drink, and then you may ask me. I want to eat and drink."

So she led him into the palace, fed him, gave him something to drink, and then she started asking him, "Where are you going, brother, and where will your journey take you?"

"I am going to fetch back my Anastasia the Beautiful."

"Oh, brother, what you gained with wisdom, you lost without wisdom. My husband is stronger than you. He chased after her but could not get her back."

"Well, sister, there cannot be seven deaths, nor can you escape even one." And he lay down to sleep.

Suddenly the eagle tsar flew up, and there was such an explosion! From the air, from that alone, all twelve oaks disappeared into the earth. He flew up and asked, "Why, does it smell of a Russian one here?"

"Yes," she said, "my brother has come!"

"Where is he?"

"He lay down to sleep."

So the eagle tsar immediately woke him up, brought him to the table, they began to talk, and he began to ask him, "Where are you going, my brother? Where will your journey take you?"

"I am going to fetch my Anastasia the Beautiful!"

"Oh, brother, what you got with wisdom, you lost without wisdom. I advise you: it would be better to go home!"

"But there cannot be seven deaths, nor can you escape even one." So they went off and went to sleep. In the morning Ivan the Russian Warrior had a bite to eat and set off on his way. They said farewell to him. "No matter what the misfortune, we will help you!" And he set off down the road and way.

He rode for a day, another, and a week, and a month, and then he rode up to an enormous palace where his Anastasia the Beautiful lived. He went into the palace and there sat his Anastasia the Beautiful just as if she had been tortured. She saw Ivan the Russian Warrior and started weeping bitterly. "Oh," she said, "Ivan the Russian Warrior! What you gained with wisdom, you lost without wisdom. You have come here in vain, Ivan the Russian Warrior! Koshchei will kill you and it will be bad for me!"

"What should be done? Seven deaths there cannot be, nor can you escape even one. It would be better for you and me to die together." He spent the night with her, she fed him, and gave him drinks. The next day he got ready to leave and he rode off with Anastasia the Beautiful.

They had no sooner left than an ill spirit (in the form of a dove, it served Koshchei the Deathless) flew out from beneath the stove and flew off after Koshchei. "Koshchei, why are you drinking and carousing and you don't even know what is going on at home? Ivan the Russian Warrior has carried off Anastasia the Beautiful."

"How did he get here? By what fates indeed?"

The ill spirit replied to him, "I don't know anything about that!"

Koshchei the Deathless went up to his horse right away. "Well, good horse! We have been playing, carousing, and we don't know what is going on at home? Ivan the Russian Warrior has carried off Anastasia the Beautiful."

The horse replied "What is this? Why, we can drink for three full days, carouse, bake pies, and still catch up to them!" The three days and nights passed and they baked the soft pies. Ivan the Russian Warrior and Anastasia the Beautiful were probably about three hundred versts away from them.

So Koshchei the Deathless mounted his horse and caught up and he took away Anastasia the Beautiful, and Koshchei the Deathless said, "Well, Ivan the Russian Warrior! Because you once helped me out of a disastrous situation, I will forgive you and let you live. But in the future, do not come back here." So he got on his three-legged horse, took Anastasia the Beautiful, and rode off to his own country. He brought her to that country and put her back in his castle.

Ivan Tsarevich stayed right at the same place and thought to himself, "How is it to be, how am I not to get back Anastasia the Beautiful? I shall go and fetch her even if he wants to kill me. Why, seven deaths there cannot be, nor can you escape even one."

Again he set off. And once more he came to Anastasia the Beautiful. She saw him and started crying bitterly. "Why did you come here, Ivan the Russian Warrior? Koshchei will kill you!"

"Oh well, I'll have to die sometime anyway." The next day they got ready and then rode off on their journey.

That little dove flew off again and it flew right to Koshchei the Deathless. "Oh, you Koshchei the Deathless! You drink and carouse and you know nothing of what goes on with your own lands! Ivan the Russian Warrior has carried off Anastasia the Beautiful!"

So Koshchei the Deathless went right up to his three-legged horse, "Well, horse of mine! We drink here, we carouse, but we don't know what is going on with our own land. Ivan the Russian Warrior has carried off Anastasia the Beautiful!"

"Well, what of it? We can drink for three days and nights, we can eat, we can bake pies and eat them, and still we will catch up to them!" So Koshchei the Deathless mounted his horse and right away he caught up to Ivan the Russian Warrior and Anastasia the Beautiful, and he hacked him into little pieces, and he took her and rode off to his own country. And Anastasia the Beautiful cried bitterly because Koshchei the Deathless had destroyed Ivan the Russian Warrior.

After a little time (and it was summertime), the raven tsar sensed something and he said, "Something smells of our very own blood. I will have to fly over to my falcon brother and ask him whether my brother eagle is alive." He flew to his falcon brother. And his falcon brother was alive. "Well, brother falcon, do you not smell something wrong with our very own blood?"

"I do smell it. Is our brother eagle alive? Let us fly over to him and find out about him." So they flew over to brother eagle and brother eagle was alive. "Well, brother, isn't something wrong with our very own blood?"

"I sense it too," he said. "Is our brother-in-law alive? Let us fly over and find out!" So they flew like the wind, they flew to their brother-in-law. Their brother-in-law had been chopped into tiny bits. Brother falcon, the junior of them, immediately flew after the living and the dead waters. He flew quickly, there and back in three days.

He brought the waters and they sprinkled him with the living and dead water and from the dead his body grew together and from the living water he came alive. And suddenly he was again Ivan the Russian Warrior. "Ah," he said, "what a long time I slept!"

"You would have slept an eternity, had it not been for us. It would be better, brother, to turn back or Koshchei the Deathless will kill you again."

"What are you saying, brothers?! Seven deaths there cannot be, nor can you avoid even one. I shall go to fetch her again!!"

"If you go, ask Anastasia the Beautiful to find out from him where he got his horse. Otherwise, you won't manage to do anything." He thanked his brothers, said farewell to them, and set off home.

He came to the tsardom of Koshchei the Deathless. He came to Anastasia the Beautiful. She was astonished: how was this possible? She saw that it was Ivan the Russian Warrior, but she had been thinking that Koshchei the Deathless had long since destroyed him. She couldn't believe it and thought that Koshchei the Deathless had turned himself into his image. But he greeted her. She wept tearfully from her joy. "Is that you I see, Ivan Tsarevich?"

"Yes, ma'am," he said.

"That cannot be. You are Koshchei the Deathless, you have turned yourself into Ivan the Russian Warrior, haven't you?"

"No, I am Ivan the Russian Warrior, my brothers-in-law resurrected me. And you, when Koshchei the Deathless flies here, ask him where he got his horse. And hide me someplace. Otherwise, I won't be able to do anything." So she fed him, and gave him something to drink, and she hid him in her clothes closet.

Koshchei the Deathless came flying in to her and he said, "What is this? It smells of a living Russian here."

"You have been flying all over Rus and you have picked up some of that Russian smell. There has been nobody here with me at all. My husband will not come because you chopped him into tiny bits."

"How could he possibly live? I told him not to come here another time. He wanted to laugh at me, and I cannot stand laughter!"

"Oh, my dear Koshchei the Deathless! Where did you get your horse?"

"Are you thinking that your husband can get one?"

"How is my husband supposed to get one when you chopped him up? Very likely the ravens have already scattered his bones."

"There is," he said, "a certain mare who roams beyond the sea and twelve wolf packs follow her. And for one hour only is she pregnant. And a tulip tree stands there and she runs beneath that tree and just like the wind she lies down and gives birth in a single minute and then she runs away again. And now the wolves: the twelve wolf packs run up to tear apart the foal. But none of them can get it!" Koshchei the Deathless spent the night with Anastasia the Beautiful, he said farewell and flew away again.

Anastasia the Beautiful came to her Ivan the Russian Warrior and let him out of the clothes closet. He began to question her about this and that. And she started telling him everything. "There is," she said, "such a one [a horse]. But there is no way to get it. The wolves will tear you apart. Beyond the sea there roams this mare, and twelve wolf packs follow her and for just one hour she is pregnant. And there is a tulip tree growing there. She runs underneath this tree and immediately the twelve wolf packs come running up to devour the colt. You won't get it, you would be better off to go on home."

"No, my dearest, I shall go and get it. I cannot live without you." So Ivan the Russian Warrior said goodbye and set off.

He walked for a day, for a second and a third, for a week and a month, and for half a year. He walked and walked and he came to a forest. He had already eaten all the provisions that he had in his sack. And he was terribly hungry. He walked around, looking for something. But there was nothing to eat. He saw some bees in a hollow tree and climbed into the hollow, hoping to get some honey to fill up on it. But the queen bee said to him, "Don't eat anything, Ivan the Russian Warrior! In time I shall be of use to you." He would just agitate the nest, if he took the honey, and the hive would be destroyed. So Ivan the Russian Warrior didn't take anything to eat, he took out his penknife, cut a piece of bast, then sucked some nectar, and with that he nourished himself.

He came up to the sea and there was no way to get across it, nor was there anything for him to eat there. He saw a burrow in a knoll there and thought to himself, "I'm going to perish all the same!" He climbed into the burrow and saw some beaver kits there.

He dragged a young beaver out of the burrow and took out his penknife. He was going to kill the beaver and eat it. But the old beaver ran up and said, "Don't eat him, Ivan the Russian Warrior! I shall be of good use to you. I know why you have come here and without me you won't accomplish a thing!" There was nothing else to do, he had to endure it, he let the beaver go.

The old beaver said to him, "Get on my back and I will take you across the sea!" So Ivan the Russian Warrior got on the beaver and he went across the sea and they crossed it and he got off the beaver. The beaver said, "Well, Ivan the Russian Warrior, you go up to that tulip tree and climb up in it. The mare will run up at midnight and in one minute she will foal. You instantly jump out of the tree, take the foal in your coat flaps and run here quickly to me. Otherwise the wolves will come running and they will devour you and me and the foal." So he went to the tree, and climbed up in it. Night came, it was twelve o'clock. Suddenly, like a flash of lightning, the mare came running up, threw herself upon the earth, lay there, and in one minute she foaled. Then she jumped up and ran away. He quickly jumped down from the tree, took the little foal in his coat flaps, and ran off with him toward the sea. He ran to the sea, sat on the beaver's back, and the beaver started carrying him away.

The beaver had just started carrying him off, when the twelve wolf packs came rushing after them. They rushed into the sea to swim and they were catching up. Ivan the Russian Warrior got frightened. "Oh, Mother bee, you wanted to be of assistance to me but you have deceived me!" Suddenly out of nowhere these bees appeared, a host and multitude of them! And they began stinging the wolves right in their eyes. The wolves didn't know where to run and some swam and some drowned. And the beaver brought Ivan the Russian Warrior across the sea.

Ivan the Russian Warrior thanked the beaver. The beaver was very satisfied with this and offered Ivan the Russian Warrior any beaver he wanted. But Ivan the Russian Warrior thanked him once more. It was not quite dawn and Ivan the Russian Warrior set off with his foal. But Ivan the Russian Warrior went up to the bee and thanked her for her kindness to him. The bee answered, "Now eat as much honey as you like, and feed your horse." So Ivan the Russian Warrior ate and he fed his horse and he thanked the bee. So he took and stripped some bast and made a bridle for his horse because he was so heavy to carry: he was growing fast.

So he led him on and they went for some time and he saw a church standing in the forest all covered over with moss. Since he was tired from his journey and God had given him everything he had desired, he went into God's church to pray and to let the colt rest. He went into God's church and there stood a deacon. Ivan the Russian Warrior stood and prayed. Suddenly the colt began to neigh in a loud voice such that the entire church shook. Ivan the Russian Warrior was frightened. "Has some misfortune occurred to my colt?"

So he suddenly went out of God's church and the colt said to him, "Ivan the Russian Warrior, mount up on me! What we need to do we are going to! And order me how to ride: higher than the roaming clouds or lower than the standing forests?"

Ivan the Russian Warrior was astonished and from his joy he did not know what to do so he gave him his free will. "Go ahead and do as you know best!" So that colt rose up higher than the roaming clouds and flew like lightning and he flew to the tsardom of Koshchei the Deathless and went up to Anastasia the Beautiful. She was extremely happy and kissed him. He hurried her to get ready to go but she said to him, "Don't be so timid, Ivan the Russian Warrior! Don't hurry, let's get ready what we need for the journey, take the precious jewels." So they got ready, they collected everything together that they needed, and on the third day they set off.

The little dove flew out from beneath the stove once more and flew to Koshchei the Deathless. "Well, Koshchei the Deathless, you are drinking and carousing and you don't even know what is going on in your own lands! Ivan the Russian Warrior has carried off Anastasia the Beautiful."

"Oh what a nimble one he is! We will drink for three days and eat and then we shall catch up to him. But this time I won't chop him up that way!" So Koshchei came up to his three-legged horse. "Well, three-legged horse! We are drinking here, eating here, and we know nothing of what is happening in our own lands. Ivan the Russian Warrior has once more taken away Anastasia the Beautiful."

"Oh, Koshchei the Deathless, this time there is nothing for us to do."

"Why not? Or don't you want to serve me?"

"I shall serve you, but we still won't be able to do anything." Koshchei got on his horse and caught up to Ivan the Russian Warrior.

His horse said to Ivan the Russian Warrior: "Ivan the Russian Warrior, Koshchei is chasing after us, get down and I shall destroy your Koshchei alone." Ivan the Russian Warrior dismounted. His horse said to his brother, "Well, my three-legged brother! Rise up on high and knock down Koshchei the Deathless and we shall kill him. Otherwise I shall kill you both!" The three-legged horse reared up and knocked Koshchei the Deathless down and they built a fire and burned his corpse and with a broom they scattered his ashes. Ivan the Russian Warrior sat Anastasia the Beautiful on his three-legged horse and they rode off thus to his own tsardom. They stopped off at his brothers', thanked them, and then rode into their own country. There everyone rejoiced and they had a ball. They began living and prospering.

A–T 554

312. Where the Bears Came From

One splendid morning the old woman said to the old man: "Chop some firewood, or else there'll be nothing to stoke the stove with. We haven't a stick of wood left."

The old man took his axe, went off into the woods and there he saw a linden tree. It was enormous and beautiful. The old man took aim and he was about to chop it up for firewood when the linden tree spoke in a human voice: "Don't cut me, I'll do anything, I'll ransom myself."

The old man answered, "But we haven't a stick of firewood."

"Go home, old man . . . ," the linden tree said to the old man.

So the old man went home and there was a huge woodpile stacked up, the old man had never seen one like it. The old woman was amazed that the old man had been so quick. "Just look at what I've chopped."

"There's plenty of wood, but there's no grain."

So the old man went off to ask for some of the linden tree. He took his axe, came up to the linden tree, aimed, and got ready to chop. Once more the linden tree spoke to him: "What do you need, old man? I'll ransom myself with whatever you want."

"We've got no grain," the old man answered.

"Very well," said the linden tree, "go home."

The old man came home and the old woman's kitchen was filled with grain, the granaries were filled, there was no room to move. So then the old woman said: "Well, we've got lots of grain now, but we've got no money. Maybe you'd go ask the linden tree for some money."

Once more the old man went to the linden tree, took his axe, took aim. "Don't chop me, old man," said the linden tree. "I'll ransom myself at any price you like, only what do you desire?"

"We have a lot of firewood, plenty of grain, but the old woman and I have no money. You wouldn't give us some money, would you?"

"Run home," the linden tree said. "You shall have money."

The old man came back and the old woman was sitting there counting the money. The old man and woman lived richly, with lots of money and grain, but they didn't sleep nights, they were uneasy about somebody stealing the money. The old woman said: "Run around to the linden tree, old man, and make it so that people are afraid of us."

The old man set off for the linden tree, aimed with his axe, but the linden tree spoke up: "Don't chop me, old man, I'll ransom myself at any price, whatever you desire."

The old man said, "We have grain, and firewood, and money, but we are afraid that somebody will rob us. Make it so that people are afraid of us."

"Run home, old man, and all will be fulfilled."

The old man came home and opened the door, but he tripped and fell and became a big black bear, and he snorted and shook his head. The old woman got scared and started running. She stumbled on the threshold and became a cinnamon bear. And since then people have been afraid of them. And that's how bears got started.

A–T 555

313. The Greedy Old Woman

There lived and dwelt this old man with his old woman. Since their youth they had never had any children born to them, and now in old age they no longer sought them. The sadness of old age had come and there was no one to feed or offer a drink to them. The old man said to the old woman, "Old woman, let us pray to God even more fervently. For our prayers perhaps God will grant some money for our support."

The old woman was sitting on the stove, gnawing a string from her linen roll. She struck her spindle against the stove and said to him, "Oh, you are an old fool! Do you really think God gives money to people? You might just give it to him! You would be better off saying 'Old woman, go to that witch

Shosha.' She is so cunning in everything, she will tell and show you where to get a gold hoard. Then we'll live without a care until death."

The old man groaned, scratched his gray head and said, "You are the clever one, old woman, you do as you know best. Just don't kill your old man off with hunger."

So the old woman got ready and went off to the witch Shosha. She came to this Shosha, bowed deeply and said such and such, my lady, we are old now, we want to eat and drink, we can't work anymore, our strength is all gone. A child in old age is for feeding you. We will die and there will be none to remember us. Help us, oh lady, two old ones. Where and how can we find a gold hoard?" The witch looked out from under her heavy brow, blew three times backward, and said to the old woman, "Permit me, old woman, on account of your old age and the dignity of your old man, I will help you. Now then, take this root and go away from me, go away by the road and way, go for a day and a night toward the northern land. There dark night will overcome you, go on, and you will come to a river. You will see a mill, now go up on the dam and throw this root into the mill pond as hard as you can. Then once more come by the road and way, but don't look back, and only say, 'Grandfather Water Spirit, send me the gold werewolf!' Then this black cat will come rushing at you, it will come between your feet. You pet it on the head. You will fall, this is good, it will fall apart and then gather up the gold treasure, and now look and do not forget me."

So the old woman went off with the root. She went along as instructed and as it is written. She came to the dam, she threw the root, she was coming back. The night was dark, as dark as pitch. The old woman went along intoning, "Grandfather Water Spirit, send me the gold werewolf." The mill pond rustled, the water splashed, the wind on all sides howled with the dark forest. The old woman felt a damp cold come over her, she was shaking as with a fever, but she kept on intoning it. Then a black cat came rushing between her feet and the old woman petted it on its head. The cat shrieked and howled with an infant's voice and said, "Old woman, old woman, why have you killed me, a tiny, innocent baby?"

The old woman shivered even more fiercely than before, but between her legs the gold fell out and rang. The stars and the moon began shining brightly behind the clouds and the old woman's eyes, looking at the gold, jumped out. She started gathering the gold up in a bag. The old woman brought the money home and said to the old man, "Well, you old fool, now we can live without need and everyone will bow to us."

But it seemed little to the old woman. "I think I'll go back to the witch. Perhaps she will give me another root. I'll get some more money." So she went to Shosha and said to her, "My lady, give me another root, I used that one up to no purpose. I got frightened and didn't get the money." Shosha looked at the old woman out from under her brow, but she gave her a root anyway. The old woman set off again. She went as instructed, as it is written. And she brought some money to the old man, "Father, you old fool, we shall be merchants! We shall start trading!"

But again it seemed to the old woman too little and she went off to the witch and bowed to her and said, "Again I have come to you, my lady, because I did not obtain the gold treasure, give me one more root." The witch looked at her from under her brow, but she gave her a root anyway. The old woman went to the mill, threw the enchanted root in the pond, and went back to the old man again, and she said, "Father, you old fool, we will buy youth with this money, we shall start living all over again." But the money seemed too little to the old woman. Again she went to the witch. She came and bowed to her and said, "My lady, give me a root, I didn't obtain the treasure." Shosha looked at her from beneath her brow, but nonetheless gave her a root. The old woman came to the mill pond and she threw the root into the water. The water rustled more than before and the deep forest groaned, a whirlwind began to whistle, lightning flashed, and thunder rolled. The old woman walked back, intoning the same. A gray cat came between her legs and the old woman petted it. The cat laughed right out at the deep forest and flashed like lightning. Thunder struck and from the cat, which burst into flames, a fiery river flowed and swallowed up the old woman. She didn't even cry out. That very night the old woman's hut and her golden treasure burnt down and her old man went right out of his mind.

A–T 555*

314. The Tsarevna Who Would Not Laugh

Just think on it! How great is God's world! People live in it rich and poor and for all of them there is plenty of room, and the Lord watches over and judges them all. The wealthy live and celebrate and the wretched live and they labor: to each his own fate!

In the royal palace, in the princess's mansion, in a high chamber, a tsarevna who would not smile sat and displayed herself to all. What a life she had! What freedom! What luxury! She had much of everything, everything that her heart could desire. But she never, ever smiled, she never laughed, it was as if her heart had never taken joy in anything at all.

Her father and the tsar looked upon his pitiable daughter bitterly. He opened his royal palace to one and all, to anyone who desired to be his guest. "Let them try to amuse this tsarevna who will not smile," he said. "Whoever succeeds shall be her husband." He had scarcely stated this when the people began to crowd around the royal gates. They came from all directions, there were tsareviches and princes, boyars and noblemen, officers and commoners. The feasting began, they began pouring the meads, but still the tsarevna did not laugh.

At the other end of town in his little corner sat an honest workman. In the mornings he cleaned up the yard, in the evenings he tended the cattle, he was constantly occupied with his labors. His master was a rich but just man, and he did not stint his pay. When the year ended, he put a bag of money on the table. "Take as much as you want!" he said, then he went through the door and left. The workman went up to the table and thought: "How can I not sin before God by taking anything extra for my labors?" He took just one coin, squeezed it tightly in his fist, and thought to go have a drink. He bent over the well and his coin dropped away into it and sank to the bottom.

The poor man was left with absolutely nothing. Any other would have wept in his place, would have been remorseful and folded his arms with vexation. Not he. "God gives, the lord knows to whom to give it. Some he rewards with money but from others he takes it all away. Obviously, I have not tried hard enough, I have labored too little, and so now I shall try even harder!" So he went once more back to work, and everything that came into his hands was as if on fire!

He finished his term, another year passed, and his master put a bag of money on the table: "Take whatever your soul desires!" and then he was through the doors and away. The workman once more thought about how not to offend God, about taking any extra for his labors. He took a coin and went off for a drink. He accidentally let the coin slip from his hands and into the well it went and sank. So he started working even more assiduously. He didn't sleep at nights, nor did he eat his fill during the days. You could see, too. For some people the grain dried up and turned yellow, but his master's kept on filling. Some folks' cattle would get tangled up, but the master's went smartly through the streets. Some had to drag their horses downhill, while his couldn't be held with the reins. The master understood whom he had to thank. When the period of the contract finished, when the third year had passed, he put a pile of money on the table. "Now, my workman, take as much as your soul desires; it is your labor, therefore your money." And then he went away.

The workman took just one coin and then he went to the well to have a drink. He looked: his newest coin was still there and the other two were floating on the surface. He picked them up, having guessed that God had rewarded him for his services. He was overjoyed and thought, "It is time for me to take a look at the wide world, to get acquainted with people!" He thought a little and then he set off wherever his eyes should lead him.

He was walking though a field when a mouse came running up to him, "Smith, dear cousin! Give me a coin and I will be of use to you!" He gave the mouse a coin. He was going through the forest when a beetle crawled up to him, "Smith, dear cousin! Give me a coin and I will be of use to you!" He gave the beetle a coin. He started swimming over a river and he met a cat-fish. "Smith, dear cousin! Give me a coin and I shall be of use to you." So he did not refuse the catfish and gave him his last coin.

Then he came into the city and there were so many people, so many house-holds. He looked around, he turned around in all directions, but he didn't know where to go. In front of him stood the royal palace, all decorated with gold and silver, and at the window the tsarevna who would not laugh sat looking right him. Where could go? Everything clouded over in his head, a dream came over him;, and he fell headfirst right into the mud. Suddenly out of nowhere the catfish with its great big moustache was there, followed by the little old beetle and the mouse. They all came running. They looked after him, they caressed him. The little mouse took off his clothes, the beetle cleaned his boots, and the catfish chased away the flies. The princess who would not laugh watched all these doings intently and then she broke out laughing.

"Who has amused my daughter?" asked the tsar.

One said, "I," and another said "I," but "No!" said the tsarevna who would not laugh. "It was that man over there," and she pointed to the workman. They brought him into the palace immediately and the workman appeared before the tsar and as a handsome young man! The tsar kept his royal word. What he had promised, that he now gave. I say, didn't that workman just dream all of this? They say that "No, this is the whole truth of the matter." I guess we have to believe it.

A–T 559

315. The Magic Ring

In a certain tsardom, in a certain state, there lived and dwelt an old man with his old woman, and they had a son, Martynka. The old man had spent all his life hunting. He had killed beasts and birds and by this means he had nour-ished himself and fed his family. But the time came and the old man fell ill and died. Martynka and his mother were left behind. They wept and grieved, but there was nothing to be done: you cannot bring back the dead. They managed for about a week and they ate up all the grain that they had in storage. The old woman saw that there was nothing left to eat and that it was necessary to obtain some money. You see, the old man had left them two hundred rubles. She really did not want to start on the piggy bank, but no matter how firm she was, she would have to start just not to die of hunger. She counted out a hundred rubles and said to her son, "Well, Martynka, here are a hundred ruble notes. Go ask our neighbor for a horse and ride into the town to buy some grain; then somehow we'll manage to get through the winter and in the spring we'll look for work."

Martynka asked for a cart and horse and set off for the town. He rode by the butcher shops—noise, quarreling, and a crowd of people. What was this? The butchers had caught a hunting dog, tied it to a stake, and they were beating it with sticks. The dog was jerking, howling and growling. . . . Martynka ran up to the butchers and asked them, "Brothers, why are you beating this poor dog so unmercifully?"

"How could we not beat him, the cursed thing," answered the butchers, "when he has spoiled an entire side of beef!"

"Enough, brothers. Don't beat him. It would be better to sell him to me!"

"Alright, buy him then," said one peasant, joking. "Give us a hundred rubles." Martynka pulled the hundred out from next to his chest, gave it to the butchers, untied the dog, and took it with him. The dog began to fuss about him, and wag his tail. He knew, it seems, who had saved him from death.

So Martynka came home and his mother immediately began asking him, "What did you buy, my son?"

"I bought myself our first good fortune."

"What are you fibbing about? What good fortune?"

"Here it is, Zhurka!" and he showed her the dog.

"And you didn't buy anything else?"

"If there had been any money left, maybe I would have bought something, but the whole hundred went on the dog."

The old woman started cursing him out. "We have nothing at all to eat! I've collected the last scrapings from the bin and baked this flat cake, and tomorrow we won't have even that."

The next day the old woman pulled out another hundred rubles, gave it to Martynka and instructed him: "Now, my son, ride into town and buy some bread and don't be wasting our money."

So Martynka came into the town and began walking among the streets, just looking around. He caught sight of a certain nasty little boy. The boy had caught a cat and fixed a rope to its neck and was dragging it toward the river. "Wait," Martynka shouted, "Where are you dragging that Vaska?"

"I'm going to drown him, the fiend!"

"For what crime?"

"He pulled a pie off the table."

"Don't drown him, sell him to me instead."

"Alright then, buy him. Give me a hundred rubles."

Martynka didn't take long to think it over. He reached in next to his chest and pulled out the money and gave it to the boy, and he put the tomcat in a sack and carried it home. "What have you bought, my son?" asked his old woman.

"A tomcat, Vaska."

"And you've bought nothing else?"

"If there had been any money left, maybe I would have bought something else."

"Oh, what a fool you are!" the old woman shouted at him. "Leave this house at once, go and seek some bread for yourself among other people."

So Martynka set off for the next village to search for work. He went along the road and behind him Zhurka and Vaska came running. Along the way he met a priest. "Where are you going, my light?"

"I am going to hire myself out as a laborer."

"Come to my place. Only I just take workers without contract. Whoever serves me for three years I shall not harm." Martynka agreed and for three summers and three winters he worked for the priest tirelessly. The time came to be paid and his master called him, "Well, Martynka, go and take what you have earned for your service." He led him to a barn, pointed to two full bags, and said, "Take whichever one you wish!"

Martynka looked. In one of the bags there was silver, but in the other there was sand, and so he got to thinking, "This business has been prepared for some good reason. Maybe all my labors will be in vain, but I'll try it, I'll take the sand and see what comes of it." So he said to his master, "Father, I choose for myself the bag with the fine sand."

"Well, my light, that is your choice. Take it if you are squeamish about the silver."

Martynka slung the bag onto his back and set off to search for another position. He walked and walked and wandered deep into a dark, dense forest. In the middle of the forest was a glade and in the glade a fire was burning. In the fire a maiden was sitting, such a beauty as you can't imagine or dream of, only in a tale could she be told of. The beautiful maiden said, "Martyn, the widow's son, if you want to obtain good fortune for yourself, save me. Sprinkle the flames with that sand you have been working for three years to get."

"And truly," thought Martynka, "why should I drag this burden around with me. It would be better to be of aid to a person. It is no great wealth, just sand, and there is lots of that everywhere." He took off the bag, untied it, and began sprinkling it on the fire. The fire immediately went out, the beautiful maiden threw herself to the ground, and turned into a serpent, which leapt onto the good lad's chest and wrapped itself around his neck in a ring. Martynka took fright. "Don't be afraid!" the serpent proclaimed. "Go now beyond the thrice-nine land into the thrice-ten realm, into the underground tsardom. That is where my father rules. When you come to his court, he will give you much gold and silver and precious stones. Don't take anything, just ask him for a little ring for your little finger. That won't be just an ordinary ring: if you move it from one hand to the other, twelve lads will immediately appear, and whatever they are ordered to do, they will do it in one night."

So the young man set off on the way, the road. Whether it was near or far, whether quickly or shortly, he came to the thrice-ten tsardom and saw an enormous stone. The serpent jumped down from his neck there, threw herself against the damp earth, and became as before a beautiful maiden. "Walk behind me!" the beautiful maiden said, and led him beneath the stone. They walked for a long time by an underground passageway when suddenly a light began to appear, and it got lighter and lighter. They came out into a broad steppe beneath a clear sky. In that field a splendid castle had been built and in that castle lived the father of the beautiful maiden, the tsar of that underground land.

The travelers went into the white stone palace and the tsar greeted them affectionately. "Good health," he said, "my dear daughter, where did you disappear to for all these years?"

"Light, my dear father! I would have completely perished if it were not for this man. He freed me from a horrible inescapable death and brought me here to my native places."

"Thank you, good lad!" said the tsar. "For your good deed I must reward you. Take for yourself some gold and silver, and precious stones, as much as your soul may desire."

Martyn the widow's son answered: "Your royal highness! I need neither gold nor silver nor precious stones. If you wish to reward me, then give me that little ring from your royal hand, from your little finger. I am an unmarried man. I will look more often on that little ring and think about a bride and with that I will dispel my boredom." The tsar immediately took off the ring and gave it to Martyn. "Keep it for your good health, but watch out: don't tell anyone about the ring or you will find yourself in a great deal of trouble."

Martyn the widow's son thanked the tsar, took the ring and a little money for the road, and set off back along the same route he had previously walked. Whether near or far, whether quickly or shortly, he returned to his homeland. He sought out his old mother and together they began living and prospering without any trouble or sadness. Martynka felt like getting married. He approached his mother and sent her off as his matchmaker. "Go to the tsar himself," he said, "and arrange a marriage for me with the beautiful princess."

"Oh, my son, you should cut down the tree by yourself; it will turn out better," she said. "Otherwise, what will he think? Why should I go to the king? It's obvious. He will get angry and order that both you and me be punished."

"Never mind, mother, in fact if I send you, you can go bravely. Whatever the tsar's answer, just tell me, but don't come home without an answer."

So the old woman got ready and wound her way toward the royal palace. She came to the courtyard and straight to the parade staircase and strode up without any sort of pass. The sentries stopped her: "Halt, you old witch! Where are the devils taking you? Here even generals do not dare to walk without a pass. . . ."

"Oh, you so-and-sos," the old woman shouted, "I have come to the king on a good deed. I wish to court his daughter the princess for my son and you are detaining me here by the hems of my skirt." She raised such a racket that lord have mercy! The king heard the shouts, looked out the window, and ordered that the old woman be admitted to him.

So she came right into the royal chamber, prayed at the icons, and bowed to the king. "What would you say, old woman?" asked the king.

"I have come to your grace, to speak to you in no anger. I have a merchant, you have the goods. The merchant is my son Martynka, a very bright young man. The goods—that is your daughter, the beautiful princess. Will you not marry her to my Martynka? They would make a fine pair."

"Have you gone out of your mind?" the king shouted at her.

"Not in the least, your royal highness! Please just give me your answer."

So the king at that very moment called together all his lord ministers and they began to deliberate and calculate as to what answer to give to the old woman. And this is what they determined: let Martynka build a most luxurious palace in one complete day with a crystal bridge from that palace to the king's and along both sides of the bridge there were to grow trees with gold and silver apples and various birds were to sing in the trees and let him also construct a five-cupola cathedral where they should receive the wreath, where the wedding would be celebrated. If the old woman's son can do all this, then the princess should be married to him. It would mean that he's really wise. But if he cannot, then let his and his mother's heads be lopped off for their transgressions. And with this reply they let the old woman go. She walked along home, swaying from side to side, overflowing with bitter tears. She saw Martynka: "Well," she said, "I told you, my son, not to undertake anything needless, but you would have it your way. And so now both our poor old heads are lost. Tomorrow we are to be executed."

"That's enough, mother, we shall remain among the living! Pray to God and lie down to rest. The morning, as you will see, is wiser than the evening."

At exactly midnight Martynka got up from his bed, went out into the vast courtyard, and moved the ring from one hand to the other. Immediately twelve young men appeared before him, all just alike, hair for hair and voice for voice. "What do you require, Martyn the widow's son?"

"This is what: make me before dawn in this very place a most luxurious palace and from this palace to the king's there is to be a crystal bridge and along both sides of the bridge trees with gold and silver apples will grow and in the trees various birds will sing, and also build a five-cupola cathedral where one can receive the wreath, where one can celebrate a wedding."

And the twelve young men answered, "All will be ready by tomorrow." They rushed about in various places, they brought together workmen from all sides, and carpenters, and they set to work. Everything went very well and the deed was done and Martynka woke up the next morning not in his simple hut but in high-class, expensive rooms. He went out onto a high porch and looked and everything was ready: the palace and the cathedral and the crystal bridge and the trees with the gold and silver apples. And at that very time the king came out on his balcony, gazed through his telescope and was astonished: everything had been done to his order! He called the beautiful princess to him and ordered her to prepare to be married. "Well," he said, "I never thought, I never guessed, that I would give you to a peasant's son in marriage, but there is no way to avoid that now."

So while the princess was washing and drying herself and being dressed in her finest raiment, Martyn the widow's son went out into the wide courtyard and moved the ring from one hand to the other and suddenly the twelve young men appeared as if they had sprung up from the ground. "What do you wish, what do you require?"

"Now, brothers, clothe me in a boyar's kaftan and prepare a painted carriage and six horses."

"It will be ready immediately." Martynka did not have time to blink three times before they brought him the kaftan. He put on the kaftan and it fit him perfectly, as if it were tailor measured. He glanced around. The carriage stood at the approach and marvelous horses were hitched to it, one set of reins was silver and the other gold. He sat in the carriage and drove up to the cathedral. There they were already summoning them for the liturgy, and an innumerable host had gathered. Right after the groom the bride rode up with her nannies and mamas and the king with his ministers. They stood through the liturgy and then, just as is proper, Martyn the widow's son took the beautiful princess by the hand and took the oaths with her. The king gave a rich dowry for his daughter and he rewarded his son-in-law with a high rank and gave a feast for the entire world.

The young folk lived for a month, two, and even three. Regardless of the day Martynka built new palaces and laid out new orchards. But the princess was much bothered in her heart that she had been married not to a tsarevich or a prince but to the simple peasant. She began thinking about how to remove him from this earth. She turned out to be such a vixen as you've never seen. She followed her husband about in all things, she waited on him in every manner, and sought out his wisdom and advice. Martynka grew stronger, and he said nothing.

Once he was visiting at the king's for some reason, and he drank a glass or two. Then he returned home and lay down to rest. The princess came up to him and began kissing and caressing him and flattering him with tender words and she so buttered him up that Martynka told her about his wonderworking ring. "Fine," the princess thought, "Now I'll deal with you!" When he had fallen into a deep sleep, the princess grabbed him by the hand and took the ring off his little finger. Then she went out into the wide courtyard and tossed the ring from hand to hand. Immediately the twelve young men appeared before her. "What do you wish, what do you require, beautiful princess?"

"Listen, you lads, I don't want any palace, or cathedral or crystal bridge here by tomorrow morning. Let there be just that old hut as before. Let my husband remain once more in poverty and take me beyond the thrice-nine lands to the thrice-ten tsardom, to the kingdom of the mice. I no longer can live here in this shame!"

"We are pleased to attempt this, all will be fulfilled!" At that moment she was caught up by a wind and carried away into the thrice-ten tsardom, to the kingdom of the mice.

In the morning the king woke up and went out onto his balcony to look with his telescope and there was no palace with crystal bridge, nor five-cupola cathedral, just an old hut stood there. "What could this mean?" thought the king. "Where has it all gone?"

Without hesitating, he sent his adjutant to investigate on the spot, to find out what had happened. The adjutant galloped on his horse, looked over everything, and came back. He reported to his majesty: "Your highness! Where the richest palace stood, there now stands an old hut, as before, and in that hut your son-in-law and his mother are living, but there is no sign of the beautiful princess and no one knows where she is now to be found."

The king summoned a large council and ordered them to try his son-in-law as to why he had succumbed to wizardry and destroyed the beautiful princess. They sentenced Martynka to sit in a high stone pillar and be given nothing to eat or drink. Let him starve to death. So the stone masons came and they raised up the pillar and walled Martynka in tightly. They left only a little window for light. So he sat there, the poor thing, imprisoned with nothing to eat or drink for a day, a second, and a third, with tears pouring down his cheeks.

Now the dog Zhurka found out about this misfortune and she ran to the hut. And the tomcat Vaska was lying there on the stove, purring, and then she [Zhurka] started cursing him: "Oh, you useless villain Vaska! All you know how to do is lie there on the stove and stretch yourself out. You don't even know that our master is imprisoned in a stone pillar. You have obviously forgotten an old favor, how he paid a hundred rubles to free you from death. If it were not for him, you fiend, the worms would long ago have devoured you. Get up, immediately! We have to help him with all our strength."

The tomcat Vaska leapt down from the stove and together with Zhurka ran off to search for their master. The cat ran up to the pillar, clawed its way up to the top, and crawled in through the window. "Good health, master! Are you alive?"

"I am scarcely alive," answered Martynka, "I am completely worn out without any food. I have to perish by starving to death."

"Wait, don't grieve. We shall feed you and give you something to drink," said Vaska and he jumped out the window and climbed back down to the ground. "Well, brother Zhurka, you see, our master is dying there of starvation. How can we think up some clever way of helping him?"

"You are a fool, Vaska, you can't even think something up. Let's go to the town. As soon as we meet a baker with his tray, I'll quickly get between his legs and knock the tray off his head. You watch out, don't hesitate, but grab the buns and rolls and take them off to our master."

So fine. They went out onto the main street and there they approached a peasant with a tray of breads. Zhurka rushed at his legs and the peasant tripped. He dropped the tray and spilled all the bread, and then he ran off to one side in his fright. He was frightened that perhaps the dog was rabid, and that would be a real misfortune. So the tomcat Vaska snatched a bun and carried it to Martynka. He gave him one and then ran back for another. He gave him a second and then ran back for a third. In just such a manner they frightened a peasant carrying sour cabbage soup and for their master they also obtained more than just a single bottle. . . .

After that the tomcat Vaska and the dog Zhurka decided to go to the thrice-ten tsardom, to the mice's kingdom, to fetch back that wonderworking ring. It was a long road, and much time would pass. . . . They brought Martynka some dried biscuits, some buns, and all sorts of other things to last him a whole year and they said, "Now see here, master, you eat and drink and keep a close eye out so that these supplies last you until our return." They took their leave and set off on the road and way.

Whether it was near or far, quick or short, they came to the deep blue sea. Zhurka said to the tomcat Vaska, "I hope I can swim to the other side, but what do you think about it?"

Vaska answered, "I'm no good at swimming, I'll surely drown."

"Well, climb on my back." So Vaska got on the dog's back and dug his claws into his fur so he wouldn't fall off, and they started swimming over the sea. They got to the other side and came to the thrice-ten tsardom, to the mice's kingdom. And in that country you won't see a single human soul. But there are so many mice that you can't count them all. Wherever you poke something, a flock of them will be scurrying about! Zhurka said to Vaska, "Well, brother, get to hunting! Start squishing and squashing these mice, and I'll rake them up and put them in a pile."

Vaska was used to this sort of hunting. He set out to deal with the mice in his own way. Whichever one he caught, that one was dead! Zhurka could hardly keep them piled up and in a week he had a huge stack of them. A great sadness lay over the whole tsardom. The mouse tsar saw that there was a great deficit in his population because so many of his subjects had been subjected to cruel death. He crawled out of his burrow and appeared before Zhurka and Vaska: "I bow down to you, oh mighty warriors! Have pity over my little nation, do not destroy us to the last. Tell me, what is it that you require? What ever I have power to do, I will do it for you."

Zhurka answered him, "In your country there stands a palace and in that palace there lives a beautiful princess. She carried a wonderworking ring away from our master. If you do not obtain that ring for us, you will perish yourself, and all your tsardom will be destroyed. We shall lay everything waste!"

"Wait," said the mouse tsar. "I will gather my subjects and ask them."

So he gathered the mice immediately, both large and small, and he started asking them whether any of them would undertake to make his way into the palace to the princess and obtain the wonderworking ring. One little mouse spoke up, "I often frequent that palace. In the daytime the princess wears that ring on her little finger, but at night when she is going to sleep she puts it in her mouth."

"Well, try to get it. If you perform this service, I shall reward you in a royal way." The little mouse waited for night, then he made his way into the palace and climbed quietly into the bedroom where he saw that the princess was soundly asleep. He climbed up onto her bed, stuck his little tail into the princess's nostril and started tickling her. She sneezed and the ring flew out of her mouth and fell onto the carpet. The little mouse jumped off the bed, grabbed the ring in his teeth and carried it to his tsar. The mouse tsar gave the ring to the all-powerful warriors, the tomcat Vaska and the dog Zhurka. They thanked the tsar for it and began discussing the matter between themselves. Who would be able to take better care of the ring? The tomcat Vaska said, "Give it to me; I won't lose it for anything."

"Very well," said Zhurka, "but see that you guard it with your life!" So the cat put the ring in his mouth and they set off on the return journey.

They came up to the deep blue sea. Vaska jumped up onto Zhurka's back and he started swimming across the sea. He swam for an hour, he swam for another, when suddenly out of nowhere a black raven flew up, landed next to Vaska, and started pecking him in the head. The poor cat didn't know what to do, how to defend himself from the enemy. If he put his paws into him, which would be best, he'd be toppled into the sea and go straight to the bottom. If he were to bare his teeth to the raven, he would probably drop the ring. It was a real misfortune! He endured it for a long time, but finally he came to the end of his strength. The raven had pecked his ferocious head until it bled. Vaska got mad and started defending himself with his teeth—and he dropped the ring into the deep blue sea. The black raven rose up and flew away into the dark woods.

Zhurka, as soon as he had swum out onto the shore, immediately asked about the ring. Vaska stood there with his head hanging low. "Forgive me," he said, "I am guilty, brother, I dropped the ring into the sea."

Zhurka pounced on him: "Oh, you damned blockhead! Fortunate is your god that I didn't know this earlier. I'd have torn you up and drowned you in the sea! And now what are we going to take before our master? You go directly into that water and either you get the ring or perish!"

"What good will that do if I perish? It would be better to be clever. Just as we caught the mice before, this time we can hunt crabs and perhaps it will be our good fortune for them to help us find the ring."

Zhurka agreed. They started walking about on the seashore and they killed crabs and put them in a big heap. They got a really big pile! Just then an enormous crab crawled out of the sea wanting to take a walk in the fresh air. Zhurka and Vaska immediately pounced on him and pestered him from all sides. "Don't kill me, oh mighty warriors, I am tsar of all the crabs. Whatever you order, that I will do."

"We have dropped a ring in the sea. Seek it out and fetch it, if you wish mercy. Otherwise we shall destroy your kingdom utterly."

The crab tsar that very minute summoned all his subjects and began asking them about the ring. One little crab spoke up: "I know," he said, "where it is located. When that ring fell into the sea, the sturgeon fish seized it and swallowed it before my very eyes."

So all the crabs rushed off into the sea to search for the sturgeon fish, and they trapped her, poor thing, and began pinching her with their claws. They chased her and chased her and simply gave her no rest even for a second. The fish went here and there, twisting and twisting, and finally she jumped out onto the shore. The crab tsar crawled out of the water and said to the tomcat Vaska and the dog Zhurka: "Here you are, oh mighty warriors! The sturgeon fish! Torture her mercilessly. She has swallowed your ring."

Zhurka rushed at the sturgeon and began eating at her from the tail. "Now we shall eat our fill." And that rascally tomcat knew where the ring ought to be and he set about the sturgeon's belly. He gnawed a hole, pulled out the guts and quickly came upon the ring. He grabbed the ring in his teeth and— what did God give him legs for!? He ran with all his might and he had this thought in mind: "I shall run to the master, give him the ring, and brag that I managed the whole thing myself. The master will love me and reward me more than Zhurka."

At that very moment Zhurka finished eating as much as she wanted. She looked around—where was Vaska? And she guessed what her friend had in mind: she wanted to pander to the master by means of a lie. "You are lying, you good-for-nothing Vaska! I shall catch you and tear you into tiny bits." Zhurka set off chasing the cat. Whether it was a long time or a short time, she caught up with Vaska and threatened him with an impending catastrophe. Vaska saw a birch tree in the steppe and scrambled up it and sat in the very tip-top. "Very good," said Zhurka, "you won't sit the rest of your life in that tree, some time you'll want to climb down. But I won't move a step away from here." The tomcat Vaska sat there in the birch tree for three days and for three days Zhurka stood guard over him, not taking her eyes off him. They both got really hungry and agreed to make peace.

They made their peace and set off together to their master. They ran up to the pillar, Vaska jumped up through the little window and asked "Are you alive, master?"

"Good health, Vaska! I had already thought that you wouldn't come back. I've been sitting here three days without any bread."

The tomcat gave him the magic ring. Martynka waited until it was pitch dark at midnight and then he shifted the ring from hand to hand, and suddenly the twelve young men appeared before him. "What do you wish, what do you require?"

"Lads, put my former palace back, and the crystal bridge and the five-cupola cathedral, and bring my unfaithful wife here, and have all this ready by morning."

No sooner said than done. In the morning the king woke up, went out on his balcony, and looked through his telescope. Where the little hut had stood, a tall palace had been built, and from that palace to the king's a crystal bridge stretched, and on both sides of the bridge trees with gold and silver apples were growing. The king ordered up a carriage and set off to find out whether everything was just as it had been before or was he just imagining it. Martynka met him at the gates, took him by his white hands, and led him into his decorated chambers. "So and thus, this is what the princess did to me," he reported to the king. The king ordered that she be executed. At the king's word they seized the unfaithful wife, tied her to the tail of a wild stallion, and sent them into the open steppe. The stallion flew like an arrow and scattered her white body among the ravines and the steep valleys. And Martynka is still alive, and chewing his bread.

A–T 560

316. The Devil's Gratitude

There lived this old woman and she had a son, Andrei, and Andrei said, "Why, mama, do I just live and exist? Shouldn't I go out and search for an occupation?"

She said to him, "What is this, my child, where will you find any work?" But Andrei went off to look for work, and he walked for a while and he came up to a lake, but he didn't quite get to the lake because a little devil was hanging there on a lime tree.

The little devil said to Andrei, "Let me loose and I will do much good for you." So Andrei knocked the little devil down and they went off together toward the lake. The little devil said to Andrei, "My papa will try to stuff you with money, but don't take any money; ask for a ring." So they went up to the lake and the devil came out of the lake and was going to give him some money as a reward, but Andrei asked for the ring. So the devil gave the ring to Andrei. He gave the ring to Andrei and Andrei went off with the ring and said to himself, "What is there about this ring?"

On the ring there were ten little screws, like pins. Andrei unscrewed one of them and three young men came out of the ring. Then he unscrewed four more and there were twelve men in all. He ordered the young men to make a stone wall across the road. And they laid down the stone wall. A cart was coming. The drovers asked, "Who made this wall?"

And they began to plead with Andrei to take the wall away. "How much will you pay for each horse? Wouldn't a half ruble be about right?"

"Be so kind, take it, only just take the wall away." So he ordered the young men to take the wall apart, and the drovers went on. He collected the money and thought: "Why should I go home with just this money?" And Andrei went off to earn some more money. He came into the town. The merchants were putting up a bridge. Andrei contracted for the job. As soon as it was night, he put his young men to work and by morning all was ready and he asked for payment. A merchant rode over it about ten times to test it and he gave Andrei a hundred thousand. Andrei had gotten a lot of money together and he set off home.

He came home and appeared to his mother. "Living alone is so boring," he said. So his mother went off to the deacon's to inquire about a bride.

The old woman came and the deacon asked her, "Why have you come, granny?"

"I am on a good mission, courtship. I have the groom and you have the bride."

"Well, granny, there's no denying it. I would give her to you, but you have such a poor house."

The old woman went back home. "Well, Andreiushko, how are we to come to grips with such a man? He says our house is poor."

"What's to be done, mama, lie down and sleep."

In the night Andrei opened six of the little screw tops and let out the young men, and in that one night they built him a house. The next evening Andrei sent his mother to arrange the marriage. The granny came. "What do you need, granny?"

"I am on a good mission, courtship. I have the groom and you have the bride."

"There's no denying it. Why should I not give her to you? But the path from here to your house is muddy. Let there be a stone bridge from my house to yours." In the night the young men put up the stone bridge.

In the evening he sent the old woman out to arrange the marriage again. The old woman came and the deacon asked her, "Why have you come, granny?"

"I am on a good mission, courtship. I have the groom and you have the bride."

"There's no denying that. Why should I not give her to you, but the way to the church is muddy. Let there be a bridge from my house to the very doors and from your house to the other doors."

Andrei set his young men to do it and in the night they built these bridges. On the fourth evening Andrei sent his mother to arrange the marriage once more. The granny came and the deacon asked her, "Why have you come, granny?"

"I am on a good mission, courtship. I have the groom and you have the bride."

"There's no denying that. Why should I not give her to you, but we need three pairs of raven-black horses and their carriages."

The old woman went home. "Oh, Andrei, how are we to deal with such a man? He needs three pairs of raven-black horses with carriages."

"What should we do, mama? Lie down and sleep." In the night Andrei turned six screws and let out the young men. In the night they bought the horses at a bazaar.

In the evening she went off once more to arrange the marriage. She came and the deacon asked her, "Why have you come, granny?"

"I am on a good mission, courtship. I have the groom and you have the bride."

"Very good, granny, come to me at the palace." So they came and they feasted, they came and they were married. I visited the son-in-law. I was there and I drank vodka and beer.

A–T 560*

317. The Little Giant

There once lived and dwelt a peasant. And he had just a single son. The mother and father were already old. Suddenly an ancient old man came to them, when the father had already died. "Good health to you! I've come to spend the night."

"Dear traveler! But we live very poorly. There's nothing to feed you."

"That's quite all right."

In the morning he arose, ate a little something, and said, "My son-in-law's mother! Let your son come roaming with me!" The lad was clever—he was a peasant's son!

"Mama, I'll go roaming with the old man!"

So off they went toward the town, and they passed through the town, and there lay a huge stone. The old man moved the stone to one side and beneath the stone was a hole into the earth. It was a huge hole. He said to the boy, "Climb down into that hole and bring me what I order you to bring." The boy cried, but he climbed down into the hole; the old man put him on a rope and let him down, and he said, "There on your right hand is a door. Don't go through that door. There's another one next to it, and don't go through that one either. Then there's a third one. Go in there." He opened the third door and went in. It was empty, but there was an old icon lamp burning. He took that and went on. He came to the hole and said, "Uncle†, lift me up."

"First give me the lamp," he said.

"No, you lift me up first." So they quarreled and quarreled and they fought and fought, and then the old man kicked the stone over the hole. So the boy sat there and cried. "There's nothing to eat here. I miss my mama."

---

†By uncle, the narrator probably means the tsarevich's mentor. In ancient Russia a high-born son was often brought up by his mother's brother.

He wandered through the underworld. He went in the first door and there lay some women face down. That terrified him. He went in the next door and there lay some men face down. He saw that one had a golden ring, which he removed. He began polishing the lamp and suddenly out jumped the Little Giant. "What do you need, peasant lad?"

And he said, "Nothing." So he went away, but then he thought better of it and he rubbed the lamp again. "What do you need, peasant lad?"

"What's your name?"

"Little Giant."

"Little Giant, take me back up on earth."

"Get on!"

He got on him and they flew back like a well-tempered arrow. He quickly threw him. Then the boy returned home and hung up the lamp, but he said nothing to his mother. She asked him, "Where have you been?"

"I was walking for a long time with the old man."

They lived but they lived poorly. Times were tough, there was no grain, their clothing was worn out, there was nothing to eat. "Well, mama, I'll go out and earn a little money."

"Go, but don't thieve." So he went and swung his lamp. Out jumped Little Giant.

"What do you need, peasant lad?"

"Go and bring me a jewel stone in a hen's egg." He brought it immediately and so the lad went to the bazaar and was tossing the egg from hand to hand.

A merchant came up to him and looked at it. "How much do you want for that?"

"A hundred rubles." So he bought a lot of bread and his mama was pleased.

"Where did you get the money?"

"Oh, I met this peasant and I started crying, so he gave me the money." The second time he also sold a jewel in an egg. For two hundred rubles. Vaska took the money, bought some bread, a sarafan for his mother, and a coat for himself.

"Where did you get all this money, Vaska."

"I found this nice man, and he gave it all to me."

So they lived and lived on, and they ate all the bread. Vaska rubbed the lamp and out jumped Little Giant. "What do you need, peasant's son?"

"What I need is for you to go and bring me a precious jewel." So then he sold the stone to a merchant. He bought some grain, he bought all that was needed, and he came home already very rich. "Well, mama, I've got every-thing," he said. So he started growing older.

And in that tsardom there was this tsar, and he had a daughter. She was Beautiful Martha. And she said, "Papa, choose a husband for me in the town who is richer than all the rest, either a merchant or a general."

Very well. So they set up the parade grounds and they all brought their capital. Some brought millions, others thousands, and some brought goods. And the tsar was supposed to evaluate it all. They brought in all these enormous piles. And Vaska went along to have a look. His mother said, "Now, Vaska, look and don't thieve. There are so many goods there."

"No, I'll just look." But in the evening he rubbed his lamp and out jumped Little Giant.

"What do you need, peasant's son?"

"You go and bring to this one place a pile of precious stones." The Little Giant went and brought a huge pile of stones, enough to fill a display table. Vaska concealed them, and then stood nearby. But the merchants had seen. "Heh, you rogue! Have you brought a load of manure?"

"Probably," he said. Then the tsar came to evaluate all the piles, thousands, and goods. And Vaska opened his pile, and the tsar said, "This pile is beyond value."

Then all the merchants, all the millionaires, and all the generals looked at Vaska; they were amazed at this peasant's son. "Well," said the tsar, "come and court my daughter."

So then all the piles of goods were taken away, and Vaska hid his in a room. The next day they drank and ate their fill, they drank much tea and said, "Mama, let us go court the tsar's daughter."

"What are you thinking? He will have us executed!"

"They'll do no such thing. If the thin man goes courting, he'll lay down a good path for the plump man." Then he called Little Giant and ordered him to arrange carriages, and horses, and a coat, and for his mama a fine shawl. And then he said, "Mama, get ready. I have your clothing prepared for you, and the horses are waiting." So she got ready. He gave her a plate with precious stones on it. "Give this to the tsar."

So the old woman took the present, and the horses flew. And folks watched, "Oh, my lord! What horses!"

So then the tsar came out on the parade porch and the old woman took the present and gave it to him. "Here, your majesty, the groom sends this to you." So the tsar received the old woman and put out all kinds of drinks and wines, and he gave her much to drink and he fed her, and he said, "Come back tomorrow. My daughter requests a day to think about it."

So then the old woman set off a little tipsy, and her head was spinning, and she was humming a little song. Vaska met her. "So, the tsar didn't execute you?!"

"No, Vaska, he got me a little drunk. I'm tipsy."

In the morning he rubbed the lamp and obtained even better horses and carriages, and she went off to the tsar.

"So that groom is a rich man!" Then the tsar began treating the old woman at the oaken tables with every sort of thing.

"Well," she said, "your royal highness, I have come for the final word."

The tsar asked the tsarevna, "A week," she said, "and during that time he is to build two palaces, and from one palace to the other there is to be a crystal bridge."

The tsar said, "So, granny, it's not on yet, but there's a task to be done."

So she came home and said, "Now they've put this task on you, to build two palaces in a week, and from one palace to the other palace there's to be a crystal bridge."

So he went and rubbed his lamp, and out jumped Little Giant. "What will please you, peasant's son?"

"Now, Little Giant, I will give you this task, and if you can't manage it, then I will never see the tsarevna."

"What is it?"

"To build two palaces, and from one palace to the other there's to be a crystal bridge."

"All right, but that, Vasilii the Peasant's Son, is a task."

A day passed, two days, three days, and the week was drawing to a close. Then Little Giant gave a shout on Saturday. By morning everything was ready, and the groom was living in his new home. And now Beautiful Martha was to marry that peasant's son! And Vaska said, "Go, mama, for the final answer. Everything's in order. The house is fine, and there's plenty of bread."

So mama went flying off to the tsar, and once more he was most hospitable. "I've done my riding back and forth, and now I've come for your final answer," she said.

Then Beautiful Martha came out and handed her some gifts for her future husband. It was clothing, clothing for the wedding rituals. "Since we are going to be married, let him put these on."

So Vaska met his mother. "She sent me clothes?"

"Yes, silk ones, to be worn at the wedding."

And so they began getting ready for the wedding, both the bride's family and the groom's. Vaska gathered his friends, acquaintances, and matchmakers. And the tsarevna and peasant's son were married. The tsar put on a suitable feast and they then began living together. He hung the lamp up in his room, but he didn't warn his wife about it. Once he said, "I am going into the forest hunting."

"Go, Vaska."

He went away for a long time. An ancient old man was walking through the town, crying out, "Mistresses, maidens, newlyweds! Don't you have old icon lamps to exchange for new ones?" And she took the old lamp and said, "Here, grandfather, I'll change this lamp."

So he got hold of the lamp. He rubbed it and out jumped Little Giant. "What do you need?"

"Take this palace with this woman and put them in a deserted place such that no bird will fly by, nor beast run by, nor anyone go by it at all."

When Vaska came home, there was nobody there. The tsar was grieving. "Oh, you son of a bitch! Where have you sent my daughter?"

He was sad, he was in despair, and he set off again for the forest, weeping. He walked and walked, in sorrow. Then he noticed a ring on his finger. He knelt down on the ground and a stone happened to be in the ring, and he rubbed it and out jumped a tiny Little Giant. "What do you need, peasant's son?"

"Tell me where my mother and wife are, and where my palace is."

"Oh Vasilii the Peasant's Son, they are far, far away, beyond the thrice-nine land, beyond the thrice-nine seas, in the middle of the earth, where no bird will fly by, nor beast run by. And your lamp is in a cellar behind twelve doors, behind twelve locks."

"Can you not get me there?" And off they flew. He flew and flew and then he grew tired. He rested and then flew on. They managed to get inside the house. His mother was overjoyed. They embraced and she wept and wept. Then she said, "The wizard will come and devour you."

"Where does he keep the lamp?" He banged on the door, but nothing happened. He rubbed his ring and out popped the tiny Little Giant.

"What do you need?"

"Get me the lamp." The tiny Little Giant yanked off the doors and got the lamp. He rubbed the lamp and out jumped Little Giant. He said, "What do you need, peasant's son?"

"Take me back to my own tsardom." It was difficult but tiny Little Giant and big Little Giant flew there. They flew and flew and the wizard was right after them. Then tiny Little Giant shouted, "Fly faster, fly faster."

So they flew to the borders and there the wizard couldn't do anything more. And the palace stood in its old place. So the tsar came and said, "What is this? Have you been joking?"

"I am sorry, your royal highness. I wasn't joking—it was my wife."

"How is that?" So then he told him everything.

"Can that be true?"

"It can be."

"Well, let's argue about that." So they argued, and it was left without an outcome.

A–T 561

318. How the Old Man Gavrila Was Rejuvenated

There lived and dwelt this old man, Gavrila. His old woman had died. And he decided, "I'll go into the tsar's service." So he came to the palace and said, "Let me in to the tsar."

The courtiers reported this to the tsar. He came into the royal palaces. "Good health, your highness. I have come to serve."

"Ha, ha," laughed the tsar. "Go on with you! You are old. You're seventy years old. Oh, alright. Here's some money. Come back in three days, and they will dress you like a soldier and you can take your post."

In three days the old man came back. "At your service, your majesty!"

So they gave him some shoes, and they dressed him, and they shaved him. And the old man became a soldier. Then they posted him to a place where three roads come together to make one. And this place was haunted. Every night they put soldiers there and every night they disappeared. So they ordered the old man to stand watch beneath a dark spruce and let no one pass.

At midnight five persons came along with an enormous coffin. "Guard the coffin, Gavrila, and don't doze."

A little time passed, and then suddenly the coffin rose up on one end! The old man wasn't timid. He struck the coffin with his rifle butt, and it broke open. He struck a match and saw the tsar! "Oh, dear, I've killed our tsar! Tomorrow there'll be a court case over it!"

But instead he heard a voice from underneath the earth, "Dig me out. I'll be of use to you!" So he forgot about the coffin and he dug and dug until he saw a stone plinth. He pulled it out and beneath it was a woman, a most beautiful woman. She fluttered her wings and flew away. Nothing remained, neither coffin nor woman. And it would soon be daybreak.

In the morning the tsar went out on his balcony and looked with his binoculars: the old man was still standing there beneath the spruce. The tsar was astonished. Every night the soldiers had disappeared, but this one had remained alive. They brought the old man to the tsar. "But your majesty, I killed you!"

"How so?"

"Five men came along at midnight, carting this coffin, and they ordered me to watch over it. But then the coffin raised up on end, and I bashed it with my rifle butt. And you were lying there in the coffin. So it follows that I killed you."

"But that wasn't me. That was a cannibal. He took on my appearance and every night he ate my sentries. Now you may have three days rest for your service. Think about it and choose what you would like. I will reward you with enough until your very death."

"Oh your majesty, give me a document that will permit me to be driven from town to town free of fee as long as I live."

The tsar wrote out such a document for him in gold letters and the old man set off for another town. In a restaurant there some swindlers robbed him. In the morning he saw that they had quite literally taken every stitch that he had. He had neither documents nor the bag they had been in. He found a little money in a pocket and set off. He had a little drink to drown his woes and thought, "I'll go through the woods, the deep fir woods!"

He walked and he walked. He walked over one hill, then a second, and from a third he went down onto a meadow. There stood a three-story house. The first story was bronze, the second was silver, and the third was gold. He entered the house. On the first story he found a candle, which he lit. Two young men came flying to him.

"What do you wish?"

But he didn't think he needed anything at the moment, only he felt like some supper. He put out the candle and the young men disappeared. Suddenly the old man saw a table set with many different foods. He had his supper and lay down to sleep. In the morning he went into the capital, taking the candle. He got to about two hundred meters from the tsar's palace when he lit the candle. Again the young men came flying to him. "What do you wish?"

He ordered them to build a crystal house for all to see, for the tsar to envy. He lived in this crystal house, he swung on swings, he feasted. The tsar had a beautiful daughter about seventeen years of age. The old man wanted to marry her. Once in the middle of the night he lit the candle. The young men came flying to him. "What do you wish?"

"Bring me the tsar's daughter together with her bed."

He spent the whole night with her and early in the morning the young men carried her back into the palace. So it was on the second and third nights. But the tsar found out that his daughter was missing at night, and on the fourth night he ordered tied to her bed seventy-five pounds of peas in a bag with a little hole. The young men were carrying her off to the old man and the peas went dribbling out, making a trail as it were. The old man got up earlier than the tsar, looked out the window, and noted that the tsar had resorted to sly tricks. He lit the candle and the young men came flying. "What do you wish?"

"Spread peas over the whole town up to the knee."

So the people happily collected the peas, and the tsar was amazed and thought, "Can my daughter have been all over the town?" Then he guessed that these were tricks of the old man who lived in the crystal house and who possessed some magical powers. He went with several courtiers to the old man. "Good health, old man. Don't torment my daughter any more. If you want to marry her, do so."

Gavrila agreed, but she didn't want to live with such an old man. Before the wedding, she got him drunk and found out how he had managed to spirit her out of the palace in the first instance. He babbled about it, and when he was asleep, the tsar's daughter lit the candle. The two young men came flying up. "What do you wish?"

"Carry him out of here, onto the dung heap."

The young men took hold of him and carried him away. The tsarevna went back to her father, taking the candle with her.

In the morning the old man woke up. Instead of a pillow beneath his head there was dung. "So, the good-for-nothing has done this to me." He set off through the forest, a fir forest, and once more he came to the clearing where the house stood. He found nothing on the first floor, but on the second he saw a staff. The point of it was bronze, the shaft was silver, and the end was gold. He took it, turned it over, and at that instant a cavalry appeared before him. It occurred to him that he could go to war with his father-in-law. What a fine idea! So Gavrila moved his troops against the tsar. The tsar saw that his town was surrounded. He ran here and there. "Fathers, what is to be done?" He said to his daughter, "You good-for-nothing! This is your doing! Fall before his knees and beg forgiveness."

There was nothing to do. She took her candle and went to the old man. "Gavrila, I made a little mistake. Call off your cavalry!"

"No, let the tsar come and bow down to my feet."

So the tsar came, and he bowed down. And with that they made their peace. They put on the wedding and for three years they lived happily. But the old husband bored the tsarevna. She decided to get rid of him. She got him drunk again and asked him, "Gavrila, where did you get your army?"

The old man told her about the magic staff and soon fell asleep. The tsarevna lit the lamp and when the two young men had appeared, she belted her husband up, tucked a loaf of bread in his shirt, and ordered the young men to carry him off to the dung heap. And that's what they did.

The old man woke up in the dung and immediately he understood everything. Once more he set off through the forest, the fir wood. He went through one mountain, and then another. He descended down into a valley and there he saw a three-story house. The first two floors were completely empty but on the third, the gold one, he saw a woman in a coffin, that very same woman whom he had rescued from beneath the plinth. She was so beautiful that the old man said, "If you were alive, I would better have married you than the tsarevna."

She responded, "If I were alive, you still would not have married me. But do not come here anymore, or else you will meet your end. Hide behind the stove and watch to see what happens."

So the old man hid himself. At midnight steps were clearly heard and he heard the coffin opening. Scrunch! Scrunch!—It was her bones speaking. In the morning he saw that the coffin was empty. Someone had devoured the woman!

So he set off wherever his nose would take him. He walked and walked and then he saw another meadow. A creek ran through it. Three apple trees were growing there. On the first were the most beautiful apples. On the second the apples were not quite so fine. On the third they were worm-eaten. The old man picked a beautiful apple—and fur immediately grew on two of his fingers. He ate one of the apples that was not quite so fine—and horns grew out of his head, so heavy that he could scarcely raise his head up. He ate a wormy apple and turned into a seventeen-year-old youth, so handsome that when he looked at himself in the stream, he fell into a faint from astonishment. He quickly came to his senses. Then he braided three baskets and picked some apples from each tree. After that he set off for the capital.

The tsar's daughter saw the handsome seller and sent a servant to buy some apples. The lad sold her the apples and said, "Let the tsarevna first eat the most beautiful apples, and then those not quite so nice. But don't let anybody look at her all this time." He said this and disappeared.

During the night the tsarevna began eating apples. She didn't see the fur on her, but the horns were heavy, and when she felt them, she shouted out. The tsar came running in, took fright, and asked her, "What? Is it Satan that has come among us?"

"No, it's I, papa," she said. Then a maid came running in and told the tsar about the apples. In the morning the tsar gathered the best doctors and they decided to saw off the horns. But the horns got no smaller, and a lot of blood flowed.

Meanwhile, the young man was strolling around the town, and he met the main doctor. He asked him what had happened at the palace and the doctor explained that the tsarevna had grown horns and that they no longer fit in the room. "I can cure her," the young man said.

So they set off for the tsar. Gavrila ordered them to heat up the bathhouse and he brought three branches from a cherry tree. When the bathhouse was hot, he brought the tsarevna there and whipped her with the cherry branches until all the fur came off her. As he beat her, he muttered, "Give me my candle, give me my staff." When all the fur had flown off, he gave her a wormy apple. Then she became a seventeen-year-old maid, more beautiful than she had been before.

The tsar saw them embracing and rejoiced. The young man said that he was the old man Gavrila rejuvenated. So once more they put on a wedding, and the tsar appointed Gavrila his prime minister. They began living happily and they prospered. And even now they are living well.

A–T 562

319. The Horse, the Tablecloth, and the Horn

There lived, there was an old woman whose son was a fool. One day the fool found three peas, went out beyond the village and planted them there. When the peas came up, he began to guard them. One day he came to the vines and saw that a crane was sitting in them and pecking at them. The fool crawled up and caught the crane. "Oh!" he said. "I'll kill you!"

And the crane said to him: "No, don't hurt me. I'll give you a present."

"Hand it over!" said the fool, and the crane gave him a horse, saying: "If you want money, say to the horse: 'Whoa' and when you get enough money, say 'giddap!'"

So the fool took the horse, started to climb on it, and said: "Whoa!" The horse dissolved into silver. The fool burst into laughter, then said: "Giddap" and the silver turned into the horse. The fool said goodbye to the crane and took the horse home. He brought it into the yard and right into the hut to his mother. He brought it home and gave his mother a strict order: "Mother! Don't say 'whoa!' Say 'giddap!'" and he left straight-away to go to the peas.

His mother was lost in thought for a long time. "Why did he tell me such words? What if I say 'whoa?'" And she said it. Well, the horse dissolved into silver. The old woman's eyes lit up. She quickly began to collect the money into her box, and when she had enough, she said: "Giddap."

In the meantime the fool found the crane among the vines again, caught it, and threatened it with death. But the crane said: "Don't hurt me. I'll give you a present," and it gave him a tablecloth. "When you want to eat, say: 'Unfold' and when you have eaten, say: 'Fold up.'"

The fool tried it right away. He said: "Unfold," and the tablecloth unfolded. He ate and drank his fill and said: "Fold up," and the tablecloth folded up. He took it and carried it home. "Look, Mother. Don't say to the tablecloth 'Unfold,' but say 'Fold up.'" He himself went back to the vines. The mother did the same with the tablecloth as with the horse. She said "Unfold," and started to make merry, to eat and drink everything that was on the tablecloth. Then she said "Fold up," and the tablecloth folded up.

The fool again caught the crane in the peas and it gave him a horn as a gift. As the crane took to the air, it said: "Fool, say 'from the horn.'" To his misfortune the fool said those very words and suddenly from the horn there jumped two young men with clubs who started to beat the fool, and they beat him so that he, poor thing, was knocked off his feet. The crane yelled from above; "Into the horn" and the young men hid themselves.

The fool went to his mother and said "Mother! Don't say 'from the horn' but say 'into the horn.'" Just as soon as the fool had left for the neighbors, his mother locked the door on the latch and said "from the horn." Right away out of the horn the two young men jumped and started to beat the old woman. She screamed with all her might.

The fool heard the cries and came running as fast as his feet would carry him. He got there but the door was latched. He yelled "Into the horn! Into the horn!" The old woman came to after the blows and unlatched the door. The fool came in and said "Well, Mother! I told you not to say that."

The fool decided to throw a banquet and started calling the gentry and the boyars. They had only just arrived and seated themselves when the fool brought the horse into the hut and said "Whoa, good horse!" The horse dissolved into silver. The guests were amazed and started to steal the money and hide it into their pockets. The fool said "Giddap!" and the horse appeared again, only without its tail. The fool then saw that it was time to feed the guests and took out the tablecloth. He said: "Unfold!" Suddenly the tablecloth unfolded and on it a great many dishes and drinks had been placed. The guest began to drink, carouse, and make merry. When all had had their fill, the idiot said, "Fold up!" and the tablecloth folded up.

The guests started to yawn and mockingly said: "Show us something else, fool!"

"Alright," said the fool. "For you it can be arranged." And he brought out the horn. The guests yelled out right away: "From the horn!" Out of nowhere came the two young men with clubs. They started hitting them with all their might and beat them to the point that the guests were forced to give back the stolen money and they themselves scattered. And the fool and his mother, the horse, tablecloth, and horn lived happily ever after.

(Translated by Nina Palmin)

A–T 563

320. A Tale About an Old Man and His Son, a Crane

In a certain village there lived and dwelt an old man with his wife, who constantly berated and scolded her husband. Even in his advanced years he wandered in the forest and caught whatever sort of bird there happened to be there. The old man was fed up with the daily complaints and scoldings of the old woman and so one day, having arisen earlier than usual, he set off for the forest, where he lay down snares for catching birds. Then he hid himself behind a bush. With his good fortune in a very short time a crane was snared. The old man jumped out from behind the bush with unutterable joy and went up closer to the snares. He said to himself, "Well, glory to God! Now the old woman will not berate me. I will bring the crane to her and we shall kill it, boil and roast it, and eat together."

The crane, hearing this, spoke out to the old man in a human voice: "Esteemed old man! Do not take me home and kill me but let me out of the snare and give me freedom. You shall be a father to me and I shall be your son. When your old woman gets angry at you for anything and scolds, come to me." Then pointing to a glade he said, "This is my dwelling place. I always inhabit this place."

For a long time the old man was deeply preoccupied, thinking that this crane was deceiving him. He did not want to be deprived of his booty. Finally, after much begging by the crane, he agreed to placate him and let him out of the snare. He said, "Listen, son, be true to your word." The crane, on the other hand, affirmed with his oath that he would never break his given word and that he would not only call the old man his father but would never leave him in need. In such a manner the old man, not hesitating in the steppe at all, returned to his house from which he had come and said to his old woman: "Well, wife, today I caught a crane."

"Very good, father!" she answered in light spirits. "Why ever should you sit at home! You should go out more to bring in a little something, then all will be right in the household. Now then, where is that crane?" she asked.

"I let it go again," said the old man. "He called me father and swore an oath that he would never leave me."

These words so irritated the old woman that she cursed the old man mercilessly and finally going beyond the bounds of all civility she grabbed a poker and began to jab the old man all the while repeating, "Go on, you old sod, get out of this house and away from me, go live with your son, the crane."

Thus she chased him out of the courtyard. The poor old man walked by the path and road, pouring out bitter tears, and finally he reached the meadow where his son, the crane, roamed. Seeing his father, he ran up to him in great haste and courteously asked him, "Are you still in good health, father?"

"Not really," said the old man, lowering his eyes. "The old woman drove me out like the devil with a poker and beat me out of the yard, telling me to go live with my son, the crane." The crane took great pity at the misfortune of the old man. He then took his father into a hut, fed him and gave him a drink. Having entertained his father in such a manner, he sent him away from his house in a good state, gave him a sack as a present with the instructions that if he needed anything, he should just shout "two from the sack" and when all was satisfied, he would say "two into the sack." Then he told him to go straight home to his old woman, not stopping in anywhere on the way.

The old man, having thanked his son, the crane, set off by the path and round and he walked a good time through the open steppe. Then it occurred to him to find out what was in the sack. In the middle of the open steppe he suddenly shouted out, "two from the sack!" Suddenly there jumped out two lads, and there in the midst of the steppe they set up a solid oaken table, spread out ironed tablecloths, placed on them sweet meats and intoxicating drinks. The old man, seeing the sack in action, was amazed and being some-what impassioned by the drinks, he determined to drop into his godmother's, who lived along the road and whom he had never visited previously. As soon as he came to his godmother's house, and she had received him not so very warmly, she began to ask him where he had been and how he had thought to visit her. "I was at the house of my son, the crane," said the old man, "who presented me with this sack."

"So what sort of sack is it?" asked the godmother.

"Ha, ha, ha," said the old man, "sit down at the table and you will see straight-away." As soon as the godmother and the old man had sat down, he suddenly shouted in a loud voice, "two from the sack." Immediately there jumped out two lads, who spread ironed cloths on the table, and placed sweet meats and intoxicating drinks there.

Noting these things, the godmother desired impatiently to acquire this sack for herself and she suddenly said to her godson very kindly: "My dear-est little godson, I think you must be very tired from the road. Should I not heat the bathhouse for you?"

"Not a bad idea, godmother," said the little old man. Immediately the bath was prepared. And when he had gone in to wash himself, the godmother sewed up a sack just like his own and hung it on the wall. She carried the real one to her chest and locked it up firmly. Later, when the old man had steamed and washed himself in the bath, he came out of it, thanked his godmother for the hospitality and friendship, and put the false sack on his shoulder. He hurried off to his old woman with joy, reasoning to himself that she would no longer scold him or beat him.

With these thoughts he came up to his own courtyard and as soon as he had gone into the entrance hall, he shouted, "Old woman! Come meet me!"

"What is this, you old sod?" she said with feeling.

"Don't scold, old woman, I was at my son's, the crane's, and he presented me with this very valuable present and I hope you won't jab at me the rest of my life." And then he said to her, "Sit down at the table, I shall feed you and give something to drink." And so the old woman sat down at the table at the near corner and the old man sat alongside her, and not knowing that his sack had been exchanged for the other he shouted out, "two from the sack!" as before. But nothing happened. He shouted once, then twice and even more but not knowing what had happened to his own sack, he guessed that his little godmother had switched with him and, saying nothing, he got up from the table and left.

The old woman decided that the old man was laughing at her and so she began scolding him and finally she grabbed the poker and began treating him with it. "Go to your son, the crane, you old dog, but don't come back to me," she said. Just as before she chased him out of the courtyard.

The old man, weeping bitter tears, went through the field and in a little time came to his son, the crane, who greeted him not quite so kindly and asked, "Are you still in good health, little father?"

"Not really, my son, not really in good health. The old woman beat me and chased me out of the courtyard again!" Then he told his son in detail about it all, how he had dropped in to his godmother's and seated in her bathhouse, and how she had substituted a bag for his. The crane was somewhat amazed at his father and bawled him out for not heeding his words and for dropping in on his godmother rather than going straight home to his old woman. After all this he led his father into the hut, fed him and gave him drink, and presented him with yet another sack with which he was advised to operate the same as before. Then he told him that until he got home he was not to call anyone from the sack nor stop off anyplace, but go directly to his old woman. The old man thanked his son, the crane, and promised to follow all his instructions. But as he went further into the open steppe, he could no longer endure the burning curiosity and he shouted out "two from the sack." Immediately two youths jumped out, stretched out the old man, and began to thrash him, all the while repeating: "Heed your son, the crane." The old man, feeling the sharp pain, was just able to say through his teeth "two into the sack." Suddenly the two youths disappeared. Arising, he went on further and wishing to revenge himself on his godmother for exchanging sacks, he went straight to her.

The godmother, seeing the old man, greeted him extraordinarily warmly, and asked him where he had been. "At my son's, the crane's," answered the old man. "He gave me yet another sack." The godmother, saying nothing at all, told him to steam and wash in the bath. "Very good, my dear little godmother," the old man answered.

He had scarcely managed to leave the parlor when his godmother, wishing to satisfy her curiosity as to what was contained in the sack, sat down at the table and shouted "two from the sack." Immediately out jumped two youths who stretched her out on the floor and began to lash her, intoning, "Give the old man's sack back!" The godmother's children, seeing their mother so severely punished, ran to the old man in the bathhouse at once and the eldest daughter asked him to leave the bathhouse at once and forbid the youths to lash their mother further.

Having heard these things, the old man said, "Wait, my friend, I still haven't washed my head!" A little while later, in ran the second daughter and asked him the same as her mother was getting worse. "In good time, my friend, I still haven't washed my head." Finally the third daughter ran in and said that her mother was really dying. "Very well," he said, "I've already combed my head, now I'll come out." Then going into the entrance hall he said "two into the sack." And the youths suddenly disappeared. Meanwhile with great effort the godmother got up, went to her closet, fetched out the sack, and gave it to the old man. The old man took both sacks together, parted from the godmother, and went with great joy to his own house.

Arriving home, he said as he had before, "Old woman, receive me!"

The old woman started jabbing at him. "Why are you raging here, you old dog?" Finally he forced the old woman to sit at the oaken table and he sat alongside her and suddenly shouted "two from the sack." Immediately out jumped the two youths and laid the pressed tablecloth out, placed on it the sweet meats and intoxicating drinks, and the old woman was extremely overjoyed. Meanwhile, the old man got up from the table and put that other bag in the closet and hung the second one in its place. Then he went out.

The old woman thought that the same sack was hanging there and shouted "two from the sack." Immediately out jumped the two youths, stretched out the old woman on the floor and began to lash her, saying, "don't scold the old man, don't beat the old man, live with him in harmony." Then the old man came into the parlor and the old woman asked him to have mercy on her, and she promised never again to quarrel with him. Suddenly the old man shouted "two into the sack." Immediately the two youths went away. After that the old man and old woman began to live and dwell well, and they began to prosper.

A–T 564

321. About the Birch Tree

There lived and dwelt an old man with his old woman. They were very poor. Once the old man got some flour somewhere and brought it to the old woman. She started making a pie. But there was no firewood. "Old man, you'll have to go into the forest. There's no firewood and we'll need to heat the oven.

So the old man got ready and went into the forest. He chose a fine birch, brought his axe, and was about to chop it down. But the birch began weeping and pleading with the old man. "Don't chop me down, have pity on the children! See how many children I have. I have to raise them. And if I perish, then what will become of my children?"

Well, the old man heeded the voice and he spared the birch. He went on. He came to an aspen. He was about to chop down the aspen but the aspen also begged him, and he spared the aspen, too. He came to a juniper and the juniper started weeping and pleading with its own voice. So he spared the juniper. Then he came to a fir, but the fir wept more than the others. "Look, just see how many little children I have, and you want to kill me? Who will raise the children?"

So he saw that things weren't quite the way they should be. He went up to an oak, but the oak also pleaded. Then he took off his cap and started scratching his head. "What am I to do? I can't go home without some firewood. The old woman will eat me alive and chase me out of the house. What am I to do?" He stood there, thinking.

Suddenly there appeared an old gray-haired man who came up to him and asked him, "Well, papa, what are you thinking so deeply about?"

"Well, why wouldn't I stand here thinking? My old woman sent me to cut some firewood, but no matter which tree I approach, every one asks in its own voice for me not to cut it. What else can I do? I'm just thinking about how to get home without angering the old woman."

Then the old man answered, "It's a good thing, papa, that you spared my children. Here is a golden rod. If the old woman gets after you, tell the rod. And if you need anything, come to an anthill, walk around it three times, wave the golden rod, and ask for whatever you need. All will be done as you ask. Only don't ask for something that can't be done, that the rod can't fulfill."

So he went home and the old woman attacked him. He thought a little and then whispered to the rod. And then birch rods leapt out and they let the old woman have it. They kept on until the old man said, "That's enough, rod!" (The old man in the forest had taught him how to call it and how to stop it.)

Then he went to an anthill, walked around it three times, waved his rod, and ordered firewood. He came home and a whole cart full of firewood was standing there. So the old woman, rejoicing, made the pies.

Their shed and their hut were in poor shape, so he decided to test the rod. He went to the anthill and walked around it three times, waved his rod, and asked it to build a new shed. He came home, and it was already standing there, new. "So the old man didn't deceive me, he told the truth." And then he went and asked for a hut, and he came home and the new hut was standing there. All ready.

So that's how he lived with the old woman and the children. But he didn't tell anybody about it. He did it all himself.

When he was dying, he passed the rod on to his sons, showing them how to use it. And he told them not to ask for the impossible, for something the rod couldn't perform.

The sons lived their lives well, too. And they passed the rod on to their sons, who also used it. In the end it came down to the last grandson. He was greedy. Everything was too little for him. Whatever he asked the rod, the rod always gave him. But he wanted to be a boyar. The rod even did that for him, made him a boyar, which other folk envied. He lived for a while, but that seemed too little for him. "Let me ask it to make me a god." He went to the anthill, walked around it three times, waved the rod, and asked that the rod make him a god." But at that moment the rod burst into flames, threw itself at him, and burned him up.

In the village they noted that someone was missing. Where had he gone? They saw where he had gone, but they didn't see him return. They went into the forest. The anthill had burned up, and other grandsons said, "That's what a greedy person he was! He asked for the impossible."

A–T 564*

322. The Magic Millstone

There lived and dwelt two brothers. One was poor, the other was rich. Once the rich one butchered a pig. Just then the poor one came visiting and asked for a piece of meat. The rich one got angry and said to him, "Go to the devil. He will give you some."

So the poor brother set off. He was walking through the forest when he met some woodcutters. He asked them, "Do you know where the devil lives?"

They answered, "Go along this path and you will find a swamp. Shout for the devil there." So the poor brother set off.

He got to the swamp and shouted for the devil. An ancient old devil came crawling out of the swamp. "What's going on? Why did you call me?"

So then the poor brother told him everything and asked for his help. The devil dove into the swamp. Some time passed and he [appeared] carrying some kind of stone. "Here is an old millstone. But it isn't an ordinary millstone: it's magic. Whatever you ask of it, it will give you."

The devil told the poor brother the magic spell. The poor man was overjoyed. He thanked the devil and ran off home.

A marvelous life began for him. Oats filled his granary bins. There was plenty of grain. Once the grooms of the rich brother rode by the house of the poor brother and they noted that the poor brother's horse was eating oats. They told the rich brother about this. He got interested in the matter and went to visit. "Where did you get oats?" the rich brother asked.

The poor brother was a simple candid man, and he told him everything. The rich brother asked him to loan him the magic millstone for just one evening. The poor man gave it to him.

The rich man went out in a boat fishing. He caught masses of fish but he had nothing to salt them with. So he asked the millstone for some salt. The millstone began grinding and it ground the whole boat full. Salt started going over the sides of the boat, but he couldn't stop the millstone because he didn't know the magic spell.

So the boat sank together with the rich brother. But the millstone kept on grinding salt and it is grinding even now. And that is why the water in the sea is salty.

A–T 565

323. How the Beggar Paid for His Overnight Lodging

There once lived a poor peasant. But he was very good. Alongside him lived a miserly, rich landlord. Once a beggar knocked at the door of the rich man and asked to spend the night. The rich man chased him away. Then the beggar knocked on the door of the poor man. The poor peasant fed him, gave him a drink, and gave him a bed. The next morning in gratitude the beggar gave the peasant a little trunk. The peasant opened it and saw a little mill in it. He turned it by the handle and coins poured out of the mill. The peasant began to live beyond his fondest dreams. He even became richer than the rich landlord.

The landlord once asked the peasant how he had obtained his wealth. The peasant was guileless and told him everything. Oh, how the rich man was furious with himself! But there was nothing to be done. Then on another night the beggar again knocked on his door. The rich man let him in to spend the night. On the next day neither daybreak nor morning star had appeared when the landlord woke up. He saw a large trunk, but the beggar was no longer there. The rich man opened the trunk and three-headed serpents came out of it and threw themselves on him and tore him into pieces.

A–T 565*

324. The Magic Tablecloth

There lived an old man and an old woman. And they hadn't a crust of bread. The old man said, "Old woman, go off somewhere, perhaps somebody will give you something." So the old woman got ready and off she went.

The old woman walked, she walked along a path through the steppe and she saw a little table standing there. She thought: "Let me sit beneath that table; it's not just standing there for nothing. Something is going to be on it."

So she crawled under the table and sat there. Suddenly three doves flew up and spread out a tablecloth. One dove said, "Wettit!" The second dove said, "Thicken!" The third dove said, "Sufficient!" As soon as each had pronounced his words, a complete meal appeared: shchi and kasha.†The doves ate their fill and flew away, and the tablecloth remained on the table.

The old woman noted the three words, crawled out from under the table, folded up the tablecloth and went off to her home.

She walked for a day and got hungry, and she wanted to try the tablecloth. She spread it out in the steppe and said "Wettit! Thicken! Sufficient!" As soon as she had said this, a complete meal appeared. The old woman ate her fill and thought, "Now I shall have enough."

She came home and the old man asked her, "Did you find anything, old woman?"

She answered him, "I was walking through the steppe—I met nobody—I was walking through a deep forest, and I was frightened, so I turned and quickly came home. And thus I met no one."

A day passed and then the second finished. The third began and the old man noticed that she had become happier, that she was getting ready to go away somewhere, but that he was famished. "Let me just look after her," thought the old man, "for some reason she's started singing a fine little song."

He went to the old woman and said, "Old woman, you stay here and I'll go strip some bast. I need to soak some."

He said this and then he pretended to go away but he hid behind the door

---

†Cf. The well-known proverb, "Shchi and kasha are our food."

and peeked through a crack. He saw the old woman spread out a tablecloth and start eating. The old man listened and he heard just one word: "Wettit!" The old man watched the old woman hide the tablecloth and as soon as she had gone, he took the tablecloth, spread it out, and said, "Wettit!" The water started pouring out and he didn't know what to do. The old man got frightened and started repeating over and over "Wettit! Wettit! Wettit!" By now the water had gone right up to his throat so he got up on the stove and shouted "Wettit! Wettit! Wettit!" The water came up to the stove, so he climbed up into the loft and still he cried "Wettit! Wettit! Wettit"

Just then the old woman came and opened the door and she saw that the hut was completely full of water. She shouted "Thicken!" With the water kasha started cooking. But she had forgotten the third word! The old man lay in the loft in the kasha and his path to the old woman was cut off. So the old man and old woman ate kasha for three years. The old man cleared a path from the loft and the old woman from the entrance hall.

A–T 565A*

325. Bronze Brow

There lived this tsar in his tsardom, a lord in his country, and he was married to a beautiful woman, and in the first year the tsaritsa gave birth to a son. The midwife carried the royal son to the bathhouse, then back, and she said to the tsar, "You've a strong son and he'll be agile, but there's one bit of misfortune: on his head there's this inscription that he'll kill his father." The tsar was saddened by this, and he pitied his son, his very own child, and he decided that while he was young, they ought to live together, and then later they would see what would happen to him.

The son grew up and the tsar assigned a man to him to watch over him carefully, but he watched, too, and so did the tsaritsa. Once the boy was walking in the garden with his uncle and suddenly he saw a man with a bronze brow and tin belly sitting beneath a bush. The tsarevich ran to his father and told him about the man with the bronze brow and tin belly in the garden. The tsar ordered his soldiers to cordon off the garden and catch whomever was to be found there. So they surrounded the garden and presented that person to the tsar, and he really did have a bronze brow and tin belly. The tsar ordered them to put him in the fortress. Some time passed and the tsar let it be known in his and in foreign countries that whoever would like to view a man with a bronze brow and tin belly should come for three days and he would appoint the time.

The royal son was learning to shoot from a bow and every day he went with his uncle to the garden and shot, and so he became proficient. He would shoot at whatever he liked and the arrow would go right to the target. The wall of the fortress where Bronze Brow was sitting was right next to the garden.

Once the tsarevich let fly an arrow and it flew in the window where Bronze Brow was sitting. The tsarevich went off to look for his arrow and the arrow was lying next to the wall. The tsarevich picked up his favorite arrow and looked it over to see whether it had been dulled. He saw something written on the arrow: "Let me out and you will receive whatever you want." The tsarevich guessed that Bronze Brow had written this and in the night he agreed with his uncle to let Bronze Brow out of the fortress. Later the tsars and many people gathered together, but Bronze Brow was not in the fortress. The tsar sternly ordered them to find out how Bronze Brow could have gotten out of the fortress, and when he found out that the tsarevich and his uncle had let him loose, the tsar ordered the uncle put into the fortress and he ordered them to take the tsarevich into a foreign land under strictest watch and not let him return to his tsardom.

So the uncle sat in the fortress and the tsarevich was off wherever his nose might take him. He was bored and so he made a horn and learned to play. He came into a city and stopped at an old man's, and the old man was a herder. He herded the royal livestock for a small fee, and so he hired himself out to the old man. He would go into the forest with him and play on his horn. The old herder played well, but his assistant played still better. And in a short amount of time he began playing such that people would come running to hear him, and the royal daughter asked the tsar for the assistant to come and always take the livestock out, and she and her mother would sit and listen to his playing.

But then the old herder died and the tsarevich took over his place. He drove the horses out into the forest for the first time and he thought, "So this is what I've become, a herder! Somewhere out there is Bronze Brow and he should assist me and tell me what to do." He drove the horses into the forest and noticed that for some reason the horses were shaking their heads. "What can be the matter with the horses?" thought the tsarevich, but he couldn't explain what was the matter with them. He grazed the horses and thought about Bronze Brow.

And then one day when he was playing on his horn especially ardently, all the horses lay down to rest, and when he drove them home at night, he saw a marvelous marvel: all the horses had grown silver manes. Everyone was astonished, and the tsar fell to thinking, "What does all this mean? What sort of man is this herder of mine?"

So then the tsar ordered the herder to herd the cows. "You have fattened up the horses really splendidly, now herd the cows," said the tsar, and he ordered a double salary for the herder. The herder herded the cows, but all the while he kept thinking about Bronze Brow. The cows got fatter and fatter and then one evening he noticed that the cows were growing bronze hooves and horns. When he brought the cows with their bronze hooves and horns in once, everyone was amazed.

So then the tsar ordered him to herd the swine and he ordered a triple salary for him. "Now they've ordered me to herd swine," thought the tsarevich. "What will come next?" He remembered Bronze Brow. He herded the swine and once when he brought them back in, it was a real wonder: there was a tiny pearl on each pig's bristles and the bristles themselves were gold. Everyone was amazed and the tsar got to thinking. He summoned the herder and asked him, "What sort of person are you?"

The herder said to him, "I am the son of a tsar, but my father chased me out of his tsardom because I let Bronze Brow out of the fortress."

"I know," said the tsar. The tsar told his wife and daughter, and saw that the daughter really loved the herder. He suggested to her that she marry him in order to test him better, and she agreed with joy. The tsar saw that the whole business was bad, and in secret from his wife and daughter, he ordered the herder taken abroad under the strictest surveillance so that he would not escape. They took the herder abroad but then when he had crossed the border the horses, cows, and pigs became ordinary ones again. In the evening when the herders brought them in, the tsar was saddened, and he told his daughter and wife that he had exiled the herder abroad because he was the son of a tsar and his father would declare war on him if he kept him at their court.

So the tsarevich set off further. The road led through a forest. He walked and walked through the forest and he saw a huge house. He went into the house, but there was nobody there. Night came and at midnight he heard someone coming. The tsarevich was frightened, but there was nothing he could do. In came a little demon. "Aha," he said, "a youth to a youth has come. Very well."

The tsarevich recalled Bronze Brow and suddenly sensed that he had something in his pocket. He felt around and realized that it was something like a snuffbox. He took it out of his pocket and it really was a snuffbox full of tobacco. The little demon looked at the snuffbox and said, "What's that?"

"It's tobacco," said the tsarevich.

"I've never tried it."

"Well, sniff some." The demon sniffed and started to sneeze. "Fine stuff, now let's play cards. We'll play three hands and if I win, then you give me that snuffbox, but if you win, then I'll give you whatever you want." And he offered him many wonderful things, but the tsarevich agreed to take only a purse that had nothing in it until you opened it and then it was full of gold. You could give away as much gold as you liked, but there would always be some in the purse.

The demon dealt the cards. They played once and the tsarevich lost. He also lost the second hand. The third time the demon dealt the cards and the tsarevich recalled Bronze Brow and asked him to aid him. The demon led, the tsarevich covered, a second, a third time and the tsarevich covered. Then the tsarevich led clubs and the demon couldn't cover the clubs so the tsarevich beat the demon and received the purse. He let the demon have another sniff of tobacco and the demon left.

So the tsarevich went on further and he saw a city. He went into the market and bought some things, giving gold from his purse, but the gold never diminished. So he lived in this city and played cards with the merchants and the lords, and finally he got to playing with the tsar. The tsar was fond of playing cards, and his daughter often played too. Finally it got to the point where the tsarevich and royal daughter played cards every day and every day the tsarevich lost. The tsarevna began noticing where so much money was coming from and she thought that he most likely had an inexhaustible little purse. So once she gave the tsarevich a sleeping potion and then took the purse and the tsarevich was left with nothing. When the daughter told the tsar that she had possession of the purse, the tsar ordered the tsarevich exiled from his tsardom under surveillance.

So they sent him away, they took him to the border, and the tsarevich went on. "So," thought the tsarevich, "this good young man is left with nothing. Now what shall I do? Assist me, Bronze Brow, to get out of this misfortune so that I can live somewhere and not fall into error." He went on ahead and he came to a sea and on the shores of the sea were some apple trees growing and on the apple trees the apples were ripe. He picked several apples. He ate one apple and grew a horn, but he didn't notice it. He ate another and another horn grew. He ate a third and noticed that something was moving at his feet. He grabbed at it and felt that he had a tail. He wanted to wipe his eyes with his hand and he put his hand on the horn. He felt it and in fact there were horns on his head. The tsarevich was frightened and he recalled Bronze Brow but the horns and tail remained. He walked and walked along the shore of the sea and then he set off further. Several days passed. He gazed at himself in the water and saw the horns on himself. Finally he walked to a certain place where there was a thicket of thorns and among the bushes grew some little trees on which were some little red fruits with the appearance of apples. He picked one of the fruits and thought, "Well, these horns and tail grew from apples. Maybe from these fruits something else will grow and then I can walk around like a real marvel. Probably that's what's necessary." He ate one fruit and felt—no horn. He ate another and the other was gone. He ate a third and the tail fell off. He looked at himself in the water and saw that the horns were in fact gone. The tsarevich rejoiced. He picked a lot of the fruits and thought, "I'll eat some more and maybe it will be even better." So he ate one fruit and looked at himself in the water. He didn't recognize himself, he had become so handsome such that you couldn't describe him in a tale or depict him with a pen. "Well, then, I'll make my way back. I've become another person and they won't recognize me."

He set off back and picked some apples and then set off further. He came to the border and they didn't detain him. He made his way to the tsar's palace and stopped there, selling apples like a trader. Two servant girls ran out of the palace to buy some and he sold them each a single fruit. The servant girls ate them and praised them, and the trader went on further. The two servant girls ate the apples and became beautiful young women. They discussed it between themselves and then went to the royal daughter, who didn't recognize them. When they told her what had happened, the tsarevna gave them some money and ordered them to buy some more apples. One of the servants caught up to the tsarevich and asked the trader to sell them three apples, which is what the tsarevna had requested. The tsarevich took the money and gave her three apples. The servant girl brought the three apples, the tsarevna went away into her own room, and she ate all three of them. Then she went to look at herself in a mirror, something trailing along behind her. She looked in the mirror and also saw that horns had grown on her forehead. The tsarevna gasped and immediately sent for the trader. He came and she asked him to cure her. The trader remained in the palace into the night, and the tsarevna strictly forbade the servant girls to tell anyone what had happened, that she had these horns and so forth.

When everyone had gone to bed, the trader took a mallet and struck each horn, which was painful for the tsarevna. She endured it—anything to get out of her misfortune. Then the trader gave her a fruit, which she ate, and one horn fell off. He gave her another fruit and the other horn fell off. "Well, now, tsarevna, you had better make a deal with me and then tomorrow night your tail will fall off."

"What can I give you?"

"I love gold, you can make a deal with me with gold." So the tsarevna got the purse and started giving him gold, but the trader saw that it was his purse and he asked for the purse until the next night because he had no place to put all the gold. The tsarevna didn't want to agree to this but then she finally thought that he wouldn't learn of the magic with the purse so she gave it to him, only asking him to return it.

The trader went away and left the town that very night, carrying the purse with him, and he left the tsarevna with the tail. He went to that city where he had herded stock for the tsar, sat down beside the palace, and sold apples. The tsarevna came out and bought a fruit, ate it, and became a beautiful maiden. She invited him into the palace where he told them everything, where he had been after he had been banished from the tsardom, and what had happened with him. He stayed on, living in the palace and at the request of the tsarevna the tsar made him manager of the palace. This manager did not spare the gold and won over all. The tsar died and they chose the manager to be tsar in his place. And he and the tsarevna were married and began ruling the tsardom, and there was no one richer than he was.

A–T 566

326. About Ivan, a Peasant's Son

In a certain tsardom, in a certain land, and in fact in the very land we live in, there lived a tsar called Kartauz, who wore a watermelon with a pickle on the end, and he turned out to be a handsome young man.

There lived and dwelt a peasant and his wife, and a son was born to them. And then off went the peasant to obtain the services of a godfather. He went up to one neighbor and said, "Come and be a godfather. We have just had a son."

Now that peasant's mare had just given birth to a foal. And he said, "I'll come and be a godfather, and I'll bring my little foal to the christening as an offering."

And so they were baptized and they all became friends, and they called their son Ivan. The neighbor gave the peasant three coins and said, "When your son is grown up and going off somewhere, let him use these coins to buy the first thing he encounters."

This Ivan grew not by the days but by the hours; not by the hours but by the minutes. And the little mare grew, too. Then once Ivanushka set off and met this boy, and the boy was carrying a hen. "Buy my hen," he said.

"Is it expensive?"

"Three coins."

Ivanushka thought and thought about it. That's all the money he had, just the three coins. "Very well," he said, "My godfather ordered that the first thing I met I was to buy. I'll buy that little hen."

The little hen laid golden eggs. Every day a golden egg. Each day and every day a golden egg. And then with these eggs they got rich and quickly became very prosperous. They sold the gold from the eggs (and you know how expensive gold is!). Father traveled everywhere buying up goods, and they opened shops everywhere. But his mother fell in love with his friend. And this friend asked his mother, "How is it? Formerly you were very poor but now you have somehow become very rich."

She said, "We have this little hen and every day it lays a golden egg. Each day and every day a golden egg."

"Bring this little hen to me and show her to me."

So she brought her and he raised her left wing, and beneath it was written "Whoever eats this wing will become a warrior, and whoever eats the right wing will become the tsar." So then the friend said to Ivanushka's mother, "If you want to be friends with me, kill this little hen and roast her."

At that very time Ivanushka ran home from school to his little mare. The mare was standing there, neither eating nor drinking. "What's the matter, little mare, that you neither eat nor drink? Do you sense some misfortune about to happen, either to you or to me?"

"Not to you and not to me," the horse said. "But Ivanushka, your mother has slaughtered your little hen and roasted her, and she has put her in the oven. You run there without being seen and tear off the wings and eat them."

So he ran and took the chicken out of the oven, tore off the wings, and then put the little hen back in the oven. In the evening his mother's friend came to visit. His mother heated up the samovar and brought him the little hen. He took a fork and turned and turned the hen, and then he said, "Where are the wings?"

"Probably Vania ate them."

"If Vania ate those wings, then you must kill him for me and roast his heart."

Vania ran from the classroom to his little mare. The mare was once more standing there and neither eating nor drinking. "Why, my little mare, are you not eating or drinking? Do you sense some misfortune for me or for you?"

"Not for me, but for you, Ivanushka. Your mother has heated up the samovar for you, but she has added poison to it. Don't drink any tea. Poor it out the window without being seen."

So he came home and his mother had the samovar boiling. She said, "Why are you so late today, Ivanushka? The samovar has been ready for a long time already."

"I stopped along the way; that's why I am late," he said. She poured him a glass of tea. He sat down next to the window, took the glass, and added a sugar lump. His mother took her eyes off him for a minute and he took the glass and poured the tea out the window. A dog came running up and grabbed the sugar lump. It died right there beneath the window.

He wouldn't drink any more. She said, "Go on, Ivanushka, and drink. That was so little, wasn't it?"

"No, I've had enough," he said.

She thought and thought. What should she do now? She went to an old woman who was an enchantress. "I've come to you, granny, to find out how I can get rid of my son."

"Heat up the bath when he comes home from school. Then don't give him clean underwear but send him to the bathhouse and bring the underwear to me."

Once more Ivanushka ran out of the classroom and straight to his little mare. The little mare once more was standing there neither eating nor drinking. "What's the matter with you, little mare, that you neither eat nor drink. Do you sense some misfortune either for you or for me?"

"For you, Ivanushka. Your mama has heated up the bathhouse for you, but she won't give you clean linens. She'll bring them later. You go to the bathhouse, but don't undress. Wait for your underclothing. When she brings it, take it and throw it at the pile of stones, and get out of there."

He came home and his mother said, "Why have you been so long, Ivanushka? The bath has been ready for a long time. Go and wash; I won't give you your linens right now; I'll bring them later."

So he went to the bathhouse and waited to see whether his mother would soon bring his clean underwear. When she brought it, he threw it at the pile of stones, threw out the water, and ran away. And the bathhouse fell apart right down to the last logs. The old woman enchantress perished there in the bathhouse.

So Vania was alive and the old woman was dead. His mother thought and thought: what more could she do? The old woman had formerly had a husband who was a wizard. "I'll go to that old man and see what he will say."

So she went to see the old man. He was lying on the stove. "So because of your son my old lady has gone. Here's how to get rid of that son, though. You first have to get rid of the little mare. When your husband comes home today, you pretend to be sick, pretend you are ill, and that all the technicians and doctors have come but you are no better. All the doctors say that you have to kill the mare and take out the mare's heart, and only after massaging you with it will you be cured."

Her husband didn't pity the little mare; he only pitied his wife. So he sharpened his knives and got everything in order to kill the little mare.

Ivanushka ran from school to his little mare. The little mare was once more standing there, neither eating nor drinking. "What is it, little mare, that you are neither eating nor drinking? Do you sense some misfortune for you or for me?"

"It is for me, Ivanushka. Your father has come home and your mother is pretending to be ill such that all the technicians and doctors have seen her and she is no better. The doctors all say that they must kill the little mare and massage her with the mare's heart. Then she will be cured. You must not leave your father's side. Wherever he goes, you go, too. He will come to kill me and lead me out of the stanchion and then you say, 'Papa, for seven years I have fed her and watered her, and I have never once ridden her around town. Let me just this once go riding on her.' "

His father did not stand in his way. "Go riding," he said.

So the boy got on his little mare and set off riding about the town. He rode around once, twice, and then on the third time his cap flew off. "Papa, give me my cap!" His papa gave him his cap, and he waved with it, and farewell! Off they rode!

They rode and rode until they came into another tsardom. As they rode into it, the little mare said, "I'm really exhausted now, Ivanushka. I'll rest here in this meadow and you go to that tsar and hire on as a worker, but keep me informed."

So Ivanushka went to the tsar. He came to the court and said, "Servants, please inquire of the tsar whether he doesn't need a worker." So the servants came to the tsar and asked him. Now his gardener had been setting out plants in the gardens for three years but to no avail.

"Can he perhaps be a gardener and plant my gardens? If he can, then let him come."

"Why not? Of course, I can." And so they gave him his own little room. "Live in this little hut and help our gardener."

That night he went to tell everything to the little mare. "The tsar's gardener has been planting these gardens for three years but nothing has come of it." So the mare and Ivanushka went to the gardens and tore everything up completely that first night. In the morning the gardener arose and looked out the window. Everything was completely torn up. He was so frightened that he went to the tsar.

The tsar said, "That's fine." So the second night they put everything in order. They planted all the beds, and even the apple trees were in blossom. Everything was alive, all in an instant!

The gardener looked out the window again and everything was done in the gardens, everything was beautiful: even the apples and everything. And he was frightened and ran to the tsar.

"Little Father Tsar, everything in the gardens is beautifully done, even the apples—everything."

The tsar said, "That's just fine."

The tsar had three daughters, and the eldest daughter said to him, "Papa, I'm going to go pick some apples."

"Go and pick some," he said. "But I don't know whom you should ask about them."

"What do you mean, 'whom should I ask?' I'll just go and do it."

So she went and was about to pick some apples when Know-Nothing ran up to her, pinched her, and then she ran away.

The second daughter said, "Papa, I'm going to go pick some apples."

"Go and pick some," he said. "But I don't know whom you should ask about them."

"What do you mean, 'whom should I ask'? I'll just go and do it."

So off she went and she was about to pick an apple when Know-Nothing came running up, pinched her, and then she ran away.

The third one said, "Papa, I'm going to go pick some apples."

"Go and pick some," he said. "But I don't know whom you should ask about them."

So she went into the garden, raised her apron and curtsied, and then she said, "My dear little Know-Nothing. Pick me some apples!" He filled her apron full of apples, and then she came and teased her sisters. "So Know-Nothing gave these to me, but he didn't give any to you."

Then there came an order to the tsar that he should give over his eldest daughter to be devoured by a monster. The tsar had three workers: one hauled water, one hauled hay, and the other hauled wood. He said, "Whoever saves my daughter shall be married to her."

The worker who hauled wood said, "I will preserve her."

So they tried arming themselves, and they tried preparing the daughter for devouring, but nothing went right and they weren't armed. The tsar came and said, "Summon Know-Nothing. Perhaps he'll be better equipped."

So Know-Nothing came running in. He grabbed a shock of hay, tied it around, and then put it in a carriage. "Cart it off!" he said.

The worker who hauled wood took her and left her beside the sea. Then he went off up the hillside and hid behind a bush.

But then Ivanushka came running to his little mare and said, "An order has come to the tsar that he must take his eldest daughter off to be devoured by a monster. How can she be saved?"

The mare said, "Climb in my right ear and out the left." So he climbed in the right ear and out the left, and he became a warrior. And she gave him a sword. And then he set off. He came to the sea where the girl was sitting by the shore, crying.

"Well, maiden, whom are you waiting for as you sit here?"

"I've been brought her to be devoured by the three-headed monster."

"And where is your defender?"

"My defender is up the hill there, hiding behind a bush." So they sat there talking and all of a sudden the sea became violent and the heads poked up out of it. But he swung his sword and immediately all three heads were lopped off. Then he went back to his little mare and climbed in her right ear and out the left ear and became once more who he had been—Know-Nothing.

And her defender, the hauler of wood, took the girl home. And the tsar rejoiced that he had saved the girl.

The next day they had to take the middle girl to be devoured by a six-headed monster. Again they tried to arm themselves, but they couldn't do anything. The tsar came out and said, "Summon Know-Nothing. Perhaps he'll be better equipped." They ran after Know-Nothing and he came running. He took a shock of hay, tied it around and then put it in a carriage. "Cart it off!" he said.

The water hauler had agreed to defend the maiden. So again they came to the sea. And the defender hid up the hillside behind a bush. And so Ivanushka came running to his mare and said, "An order has come to the tsar that he must take his middle daughter off to be devoured by a monster. How can she be saved?"

The mare said, "Climb in my right ear and out the left." So he climbed in the right ear and out the left ear and he became a warrior. And she gave him a sword. So then he set off. He came to the sea where the maiden was sitting, crying.

"Well, maiden, whom are you waiting for as you sit here?"

"I've been brought here to be devoured by a six-headed monster."

"And where is your defender?"

"My defender is up the hillside behind a bush." So he sat talking with the girl, and then suddenly the sea became violent and the monster rose up. He waved his sword, and the six heads went flying off. Then he went back to his little mare, climbed in the right ear and out the left, and he became what he had been.

The third night the youngest maiden was to be taken to a nine-headed monster to be devoured. So again they prepared the youngest maiden for devouring but they couldn't get it right. So finally the tsar went out and said, "Summon Know-Nothing. Perhaps he will be better equipped."

They ran after Know-Nothing and he came running. Once more he put the straw out, then tied it, and put it in the cart. "Cart them off," he said.

This time it was the hauler of straw who took her. He carted her away and she sat down by the sea while he went up the hillside and hid behind a bush. And then Ivanushka came running to his mare and said, "How can she be saved?" (There had been an order.)

And the mare said, "Climb in my right ear and out my left ear."

So he climbed in the right ear and out the left ear, and he became a warrior. And then she gave him a sword and off he went. He came to the sea where the maiden was sitting, crying.

"Whom are you waiting for, miss, as you sit here?" he asked.

"I have been brought here to be devoured by a nine-headed monster."

"And where is your defender?"

"My defender is up the hillside here, behind a bush."

Ivanushka leaned over and put his head on her knee. "If I fall asleep, wake me up; prick me with a needle and I'll wake up."

Suddenly the sea became violent and the monster appeared out of it. Ivan was asleep. The girl pricked him and pricked him, but she could not awaken him! She started crying and her tears fell on his face, and this awakened him.

The monster said, "Let's become blood brothers!"

Ivan swung with his sword and eight heads went flying off, but the ninth flew into his hands and he tried to finish it off. Blood was flowing as he swung again and the ninth head went flying off.

The girl was wearing a ribbon in her hair from her name-day celebration. She took the ribbon and unplaited it, and then she tied up his hand with it. And off he went. He didn't go to his mare this time, but straight to his little hut.

Then the defender (the hauler of hay) took the maiden back to the tsar. And the tsar was really happy. So Ivanushka climbed up onto the stove in his warrior's dress and went into a deep sleep as only warriors do, for three full days and nights.

And the tsar was arranging for the wedding, because that is what he had said. And the wedding was going on and they were all feasting, but Know-Nothing wasn't there. The tsar said, "Go and wake him up." He sent his eldest daughter. She tried and tried but she couldn't wake him up. The second one also tried and tried but she couldn't wake him.

The third one tried and tried, but then she turned him over and saw her ribbon on his hand. She came and said, "Papa, we have to extend the wedding for three full days."

The three days passed and the youngest daughter went to wake up Know-Nothing. She tried and tried, and she woke him up. "Come on," she said. "We are playing out the wedding.†So they went together and went into the room where the young folk were sitting at the tables. When they went in, the other young brides left their grooms and ran and threw their arms around his neck. Then they said, "Those who are seated at the table are not our defenders. This is our defender who has just appeared. The tsar was furious with his workers and ordered his servants shot for their deceit.

Then the tsar said to Ivanushka, "Well, Know-Nothing, take whichever one of my daughters you wish!" So he took the youngest one, and he and she

---

†To play out the wedding—an important indication of the total ritual nature of the three days.

celebrated their wedding. And they lived and prospered, and then the tsar became really ancient and said, "I am really ancient! You sit on my throne and rule the tsardom." (And he did and he's still ruling somewhere.)

A–T 567

327. Twelve Lads out of a Snuffbox

A soldier had served out his term. That service had been difficult—twenty-five years. He walked and walked along the high road and the byroad, and he thought to himself, "Oh, I am a soldier, such a soldier, and a fool. I've served so many years, and I've never looked the tsar in the eye. I'll go and have a look."

So on he walked but then he got off the track. He wandered for a day, then for a second day in the forest. A little black dog came up to him. He took off his rifle and was getting ready to kill that little dog. He was going to kill that little dog when suddenly it was no more: it simply melted away. So he set off following the little dog's tracks and he came up to a little hut. He went into the little hut and climbed under the stove grate to sleep. He listened and then an old woman with her old man and daughter came in. The daughter began feeding her elders their supper. When she had finished feeding them, the old ones lay down to sleep, while the daughter cleared away the dishes and then she crawled up on the stove ledge to sleep herself. But then she heard someone snoring beneath the stove! She saw the soldier sleeping there.

"Hey you, tramp, climb out of there!" The soldier climbed out from underneath the stove and sat down at the table. The girl brought him a carafe of vodka, something to eat, and she was hospitable to the soldier. When the soldier had eaten enough, the girl said, "Climb up on the stove ledge to sleep." So he climbed up on the stove ledge and the girl cleared away the dishes after the soldier.

When she had cleared them away, she went up to the soldier on the ledge. The soldier thought, "She's crazy. The old ones will get up and they'll kill me."

But that's how they slept until daybreak. The old woman woke them; she tried to wake up the daughter but she couldn't. Then she jumped down by herself. "Oh, old man, God has given us a son-in-law!" Then they brewed some tea, had something to eat, and they woke the young folk to drink their tea. "Get up!"

"Now, my dear young one! You won't get away from us. You will stay here in this hut, sweep everything, tidy everything, and we three shall go out hunting."

So their son remained there. He said goodbye, but in his mind he was thinking, "What will I do here? I'll go after them."

He turned it over in his mind, took his rifle, and set off through the forest. He wandered around for a whole day. He couldn't manage to find his way out, he couldn't manage to get away. Whatever he did, he came back to the hut.

They came back from the hunt. He hadn't swept anything, he hadn't cleaned anything, and he hadn't cooked anything for supper. "What have you been doing here, my dear? Perhaps you have been wandering through the forest all day? But weren't you told that you'll never get away from us? Your first misstep will be forgiven, but if you do it again tomorrow, we will punish you severely."

He was forced to sweep and clean the next day, and he prepared supper, but then he set off wandering. "Somehow I'll still manage to get away." But he still couldn't get away, and they came back.

"Darling, you went wandering again. Tomorrow you come hunting. You're poor at domestic chores."

In the morning they got up. "Now you go to a certain lake, and there you'll see a rake. Take the rake and fish in the lake with it. Whatever you grab hold of, put it on the lakeshore, and then make it into a big pile."

So he set off, but then he met that same little dog. "Wait, I won't kill you; instead, I'll pet you," he thought to himself. So then he petted the little dog, and the little dog led him out onto the road, and they swept the thing from their minds, they forgot all about it. And he and the little dog set off.

The little dog brought him to a huge house in the forest—enormous—and it led him through the gates. It opened doors, stuck its nose in, and closed the door itself. But he didn't know where he was, in a hut or just where. He couldn't feel any walls; he couldn't feel anything; it was completely dark. Then in the darkness something spoke to him in a soft, human voice: "Come a little more to the left and you'll bump against a table." So the soldier obeyed, and he went a little to the left, and he felt the table, and once more the voice spoke to him. "In that table there's a little box in which are matches and candles."

The soldier lit a fire, warmed a candle, as it was a wax candle, and then he looked around. It was a vast barn, rather typical: no windows, nothing at all, and in the middle of the barn there hung a dry, stitched-up skin, and from this skin the voice was coming out. "So, now then, soldier, save yourself and save me too. There are going to be three terrifying nights here for you. If you can endure them and save me, you will be a very fortunate person. Here is a gospel book for you. Draw a circle and sit in that circle by the table, and read the gospel. But watch out: they will try to distract you. Don't look back. That distraction will be a ghost!"

So the soldier started reading, while outside it was already dark. The first thing that appeared was the old man and old woman in whose hut he had been living. "Why did you leave us? Come back to us. You married our daughter!"

Then the tsar came second. "So you wanted to look upon my face. Well, now, good health to you, brother."

But no matter how they struggled with him—either with kindness or terror—they couldn't do anything. The cock crowed and they all went away. Then the voice came once more from the skin, "Now sleep, soldier; no one will touch you now."

And then he could see legs up to the knees coming out of the skin. Then, sooner to say, the second night fell, and it was more terrifying. They pulled him, they fawned over him, they tried to distract him in every way, but they could not distract this soldier. The cocks crowed, and the soldier remained alive. Once more from the skin: "Sleep now," and he could see a girl coming out of the skin as far as her chest.

So then the third night came, and they burned his hair, and they shoved him around on a stool about the barn. But he sat there—he was a strong soldier—and they couldn't distract him at all. Finally the cock crowed.

"Lie down and rest, soldier." And the girl came out of the skin. When it got light and the soldier had rested, they carefully left the barn.

"So now, soldier, what can I give you to thank you for this service? You could go to my father and he would thank you. What makes me rich also brings joy. And I have these two promised napkins. I'll give the better one of them to you, and I'll keep the one that's not so fine. Whenever you need anything, just spread your napkin, and you shall have it!"

So then they parted, and the soldier thanked her, and he set off. And the girl went her way and the soldier went his way. And the soldier left the town, but then he didn't have any more patience, so he spread the napkin. "Let's eat!" So the napkin spread itself—and a tsar wouldn't have eaten such food. He was very happy, and satisfied, and he ate a little, and then the napkin folded itself up. "Well," he thought happily, "now I have it all."

He walked on for a while, then he sat down and ate some more. He walked on until he met a gentleman riding on a chestnut horse. "Bread and salt, your grace."

"You are welcome!" They sat down and ate a little. "Now then, soldier, sell me that napkin."

"What do you mean? Not for anything!" But someone whispered in the soldier's ear, "Don't sell it; trade it. We shall be of further use to you."

"So, soldier, I'll trade you a snuffbox for it."

So the soldier traded it for a snuffbox and on he went. "I'll just take a look at it." He opened it, and out jumped twelve young men. "What would please you?"

"I just traded my napkin to that gentleman."

"Are you going to feed us? That scoundrel nearly starved us. If you feed us, we will serve you with faith and truth."

"Of course, I will. Whatever I have to eat, I will give to you, too."

"All right. He starved us, the scoundrel, in that snuffbox. Let's catch up to him and take it away."

So they ran and caught up to their former master. Then they took away the napkin and they took away his horse, and they gave him one in the back of the head to boot. "We are taking your horse away, master, so that you will have to walk on foot."

The soldier spread out the napkin. "Sit down, good fellows, and eat!"

"Here's a proper master! Here's a proper master! Look what he gives us to eat. And that scoundrel just completely starved us. We will serve you with faith and truth."

When they had eaten, he folded the napkin and put it and the snuffbox in his pocket, and then he rode to Petersburg and went straight to the tsar himself. There the sentries reported that "this simple soldier wants to see you, little father tsar."

The tsar ordered them to let him in. "What do you require of me?"

"Well, little father tsar, I served you for twenty-five years and now, halfway home, I returned here so that I could look at your face."

"You shouldn't have bothered to come here when you were halfway home. What interest do you have in my person?"

"Why should I have no interest when I spent my entire youth in your service?"

So then the tsar asked him, "So now, do you want to go to your birthplace or are you going to live here?"

"Everywhere is fine with me, little father tsar."

Then the tsar said, "Feed the soldier."

"Little father tsar, let me first treat you."

The tsar thought. How can this be? The soldier is standing here with empty hands. What is he going to treat me to? "Well, sit down then when you are told to."

"Little father tsar, you couldn't feed me with my people."

"Why not? I feed all my regiments but I couldn't feed you with your people? Why, are you quarreling with me?"

"Yes, I am." And so there ensued some shouting and a quarrel.

"Alright. How big a household do you have?"

"I have twelve workers, and I am the thirteenth."

The tsar started laughing. "I feed a regiment, but I can't feed thirteen men?!"

The soldier insisted that he was right. "All right, little father tsar, let us bet on it."

So they took wagers. If the tsar won, then off with the soldier's head and his men would be given over to the tsar, or if the tsar should lose, he would give half his tsardom to the soldier.

"Well then, when should we have this dinner for the two of us?"

"I am ready today, little father tsar. Aren't you?"

The tsar thought, "What a fool!" But they decided to go to the soldier's, and they gave three days to the tsar to prepare provisions, butcher, get everything in. And they decided to have the dinner on an island. At the appointed hour the soldier came. "Well, little father tsar, you are welcome to dinner with your troops."

The tsar gathered all his troops, his regiments, and they formed up in order, and he led them to the soldier. The soldier asked for his napkin, and then he spread it out over the whole island. The tsar was terrified, there was so much of everything. And every man had the same to eat as the tsar himself. No one was shorted, all had the same. And they all ate and drank their fill. The dinner put on by the soldier went on for two full days. And all were satisfied, and they all thanked the soldier, and then they were to go the next day to the tsar.

The tsar was on the square and they were bringing in loaves, they were cooking, and baking, and carts were going everywhere. The tsar sent a messenger for the soldier. The messenger told the soldier who came with his twelve young men from the snuffbox. They went together, and when they got there, they sat down to dinner. They shouted, "Pour it out!" then "Add some more," or "Give us still more." None of them ate enough, and they shouted, "We are still hungry!"

The tsar started taking supplies from the margraves, the princes—they brought in everything and nothing remained for their soldiers. But they were still hungry. They came, shouted, hacked. It was no use. They tsar had lost. He signed the papers just as had been agreed.

A–T 569

328. The Wondrous Hares

There was once this herder. As he walked around, he sang songs. And there was in that place a landowner. He knew sorcerer's enchantments. He became irate with that herder. Why should he sing songs, why was he so happy?

So he went to him once. "Herder, come and herd for me."

"I will."

"The condition is that if you take care of my livestock, I'll give you a hundred rubles. But if you don't take care of them, I'll cut out three strips from your back and you can go to hell without any pay."

"Very well," he said.

So then the landowner gave him a hundred hares. "Drive them into the forest to feed, but they must all be at home by this evening. If you don't care for every one, then I'll cut out three strips from your back and you can go to hell without any pay."

"Very well," he said, "but don't start cursing me before time, your highness." So he drove the hares into the forest. And they all ran away in different directions, wherever they wanted. You could see their tails bobbing along. But he just lay down and fell asleep. There was a whistling through his nose. Oh, that son of a gun!

Well, evening came. He woke up, sat up, took out his fife, and started to sing:

> *Hares, oh you hares!*
> *You've munched enough,*
> *You've gobbled too much!*
> *Now come here!*

And all the hares came running out. He gathered them together and drove them home. The landowner looked at it and turned black. "How did you manage that, you trash? Well, go and sleep and tomorrow there'll be another task."

In the morning he gave him two hundred hares. "If you bring them all back, you'll live, but if you lose even one, it'll be a strip from your back and you'll be off without pay."

He drove out the hares but the landowner called in his wife. "That herder is going to drive us into ruin. He always brings back all the hares. And he keeps on singing songs. Go to him and buy a hare."

She dressed and fixed herself nicely. She put on her very best dress. And then she rode out to him in the forest. She rode up to him but he was asleep, and there was a whistling through his nose. "Good health to you, young man" she said. "What are you doing here?"

"I herd hares, my beauty!"

"Couldn't you possibly sell me just one hare? Such curiosities are of great interest for us in the city."

"You see, my lady, these are not for sale. They are in my trust."

"And what sort of trust is upon them?"

"Agree, my beauty, to sleep with me."

She was a young woman and she saw that the herder was handsome, but her husband was strict. Yet he had ordered her to do anything to obtain the hare. So she agreed. And so they delighted in each other. Then he said, "Mistress, you are so sweet and you require this hare, for our pleasure." And he gave her the hare. She was happy and stuck the hare in her bosom. And he lay down and went to sleep (he'd gotten steamed up with that sweet woman!). Evening came and he took out his fife and sang:

> *Hares, oh you hares!*
> *You've munched enough,*
> *You've gobbled too much!*
> *Now come here!*

And they all came running. And the one he had given her also leapt away and came too. Well, the herder set off home. The master, that is, the land-owner, was standing in the gate, counting the hares. All the hares were there to be seen. What could be done?

So in the morning he gave the herder three hundred hares. Once the herder had gone, he immediately called his daughter. "Now, Masha, you go into the forest and get a hare however you like."

The mistress got dressed and set out. She walked and walked until she came to the forest. There the herder was sleeping, whistling through his nose. She said, "Well, young man, are you the one in charge here?"

"I'm herding the hares, mistress."

"Would you let me look at just one hare?"

"Why not? With money everything is possible."

"How much money do you need?"

"These aren't for coin, they are in trust."

"What sort of trust is that?"

"If you want to see, pull up your dress to the knee."

She pulled it up. He whistled and a hare came running up. "Oh, what a beautiful little thing. Could I take it into my arms?"

"If you want to take it in your hands, pull up your dress to your belly button."

She was ashamed, but there was nothing else to be done: she was afraid of her papa so she raised it to her belly button and said, "Couldn't I just hold it completely?"

"Well, if you want to hold it completely, then raise your dress up to your breasts." She was conscience struck but there was nothing else to be done. She raised it to her breasts and there between her breasts was this birthmark. He saw it. But he didn't force himself upon her, no, he let her go very politely. And she went away.

Evening fell and he took out his fife and sang:

> *Hares, oh you hares!*
> *You've munched enough,*
> *You've gobbled too much!*
> *Now come here!*

And all the hares came running, even the one that was in her arms—he just hopped out. So he herded all the hares home. The landowner stood in the gates, counting, but all were there. He was offended and even got angry. In the morning he gave him five hundred hares.

"If you bring them all back, take your wages, but if you don't, you'll give me a strip off your back."

Once he had gone away, the landowner changed his clothing, put on somebody else's hair, took a decrepit old mare, and rode off for the forest. When he got there, the herder was sleeping. He woke him up. "Are you in charge here?"

"I'm herding the hares."

"Won't you sell me a hare?"

"What will you give me?"

"I'll give you a thousand rubles."

"No, I won't sell one."

"What do you want then?"

"Kiss your mare under her tail and I'll give you one."

Well, there was nothing to be done. Even though he was the landowner and it was disgraceful for him to do it, he regretted having to pay this worker his wages even more. So he turned the mare's tail aside and kissed her in the ass. He got bespattered by horseshit all over. So the herder gave him a hare. He rode away, completely satisfied. But the herder played on his fife and all the hares turned up. He drove them in and the landlord had turned utterly white. He said, "The first time you were lacking one."

"When? When your wife and I . . ."

"Alright, alright. The second time you were lacking . . ."

"When your daughter lifted her dress and . . ."

"Alright, alright. And the third time . . ."

"When you gave the mare . . ."

"Alright," he said, "You son of a bitch! Take your wages."

So the herder deceived the landlord. And he sang even more than before. He became very cheerful.

A–T 570

329. The Golden Pig

There lived and dwelt this tsar. Not far from this tsar there lived another tsar. Between their capitals lived a beast who was half man and half bear. Once the first tsar sent the other tsar a letter and a basket of pies with his servant. The servant set off but on the way the beast jumped out and started chasing him. The servant started throwing the pies down and the beast started eating them. When the servant got to the palace, the beast shouted at him in a human voice, "Stop!" The servant stopped. The beast came up to him and said, "Show me where the priest's barns and house are." The servant showed him. Then the beast said, "When you set off back home, pass by these barns and whistle; I will be in the barn and will have turned myself into a golden pig." The servant went off to the tsar and the beast went into the priest's barn and became a golden pig.

Then the priest's two daughters came into the barn. The oldest one said, "What a fine pig that is lying over there." And she grabbed hold of it, but she got stuck to it. And then the second daughter, when she stretched out to help her sister, got stuck to it, too. They were both stuck there. They started shouting. The priest's wife came and grabbed them, but she got stuck, too. Finally the priest came and tried to drag them away, but he got stuck too.

The servant was walking by and he whistled. The pig set off and all the priest's household went with the pig to the other city along after the servant. Along the way a devil jumped out of a lake and grabbed hold of them but he also got stuck. Then the priest started saying prayers, but that didn't help.

They saw a peasant grinding grain. The peasant said, "Let me cut off the devil's heels." He came running and started hitting at the devil's heels, but he got stuck to the pig, too. Finally they got to the other palace. That tsar had a daughter who was so grumpy that she never laughed. The pig said to the tsar, "Go and lead your daughter out here. If I amuse her, you can give me three thousand silver rubles." The tsar went after her. The pig turned into the beast and said, "Now, here are the priest's daughters, the priest's wife, and the priest, but what is the devil doing here?" The tsarevna laughed and the tsar handed over the promised money. The beast divided it among the daughters, the priest's wife, the priest, and the peasant, and then he set them free.

A–T 571

330. The Wooden Eagle

In certain tsardom, but not in our land, there lived and dwelt a tsar, and this tsar had a son. At his court the tsar also had a goldsmith and a joiner. Now once these two quarreled, and then various other court officials, just as the ministers, got involved in the quarrel. They heard about it and asked, "What are they quarreling about?"

So they summoned the goldsmith and the joiner to appear before the tsar. They said, "We are quarreling over who can make a certain thing better. The goldsmith says he can make it better, but the joiner says that he can."

And the tsar said, "I'll give you a month for your work, and then whoever brings me the better thing I'll pardon, but the other I'll execute."

So the goldsmith went to his wife and started to work, and the joiner also started in. The goldsmith bought a bucket of wine and sent it to the joiner with a friend so that his friend could find out what the joiner was doing. The friend came there and said, "Let me see, please, what you are making."

"If I won't let my own wife know, I won't let you know either." And twice the friend came, but to no avail. A month passed, and it was time for them to carry their work to the tsar. The goldsmith came and said, "Bring a cask of water." So they brought in a cask of water and he released a golden duck with a duckling in it, and they started swimming around and diving.

The tsar was most pleased. "That's very good; I wonder what that carpenter can do." The carpenter came in and said, "I'll show you. Just come outside." So they went outside and he untied his sack and took a wooden eagle out of it. He took the eagle, sat down on it, and then he flew away. The tsar looked and looked as it flew high and then out of sight. He came back down to earth, and the tsar said that this was very good indeed and that he should do as he pleased with the goldsmith. The goldsmith in his fine clothing and watch got down on his knees before the joiner and begged for forgiveness. The joiner said, "I don't know what the tsar wants."

And the tsar said, "As you wish."

So the joiner said, "If you won't quarrel anymore, I'll forgive you."

So the tsar took the wooden eagle into his palace, and his son was soon asking to be taught how to fly. After some time the tsar allowed it, and the joiner began teaching him to fly, and he soon learned and was flying alone. He flew and flew, for two days at a time he flew. The tsar became angry and locked up the wooden eagle in his study. Then he gave the key to this old man. Once the old man went out and forgot to take the key. The tsarevich went into the study, took the eagle, and flew away. He flew for a day, then two, three, and four, but then because he was so hungry he forgot how to direct it, and the eagle landed on the sea. There were some ships there who pulled them in and brought them to his father.

Once more his father hid the eagle. They all lived there for some time. The tsarevich read newspapers and in one he read that in a certain forest in a palace there lived a beautiful maiden. So he took the eagle and flew off. He flew to that palace and right in a window, and there he saw the maiden. She was asleep. At her head were two gold candlesticks and at her feet two silver candlesticks. He waited. When she woke up, they became acquainted. "What is your name?"

"My name is Ivan Tsarevich." And so they became friends. Dinner came. The tsarevna took him and locked him in a cupboard. Then she ordered two places set. The two places were set with all the dishes of food. Then she said to a servant, "Go now, you are no longer needed." She immediately opened the cupboard and let Ivan Tsarevich out. They dined together.

So the month passed and the tsarevna told her nanny. Ivan Tsarevich started going out everywhere, and he was very happy. And the tsar, his father, was also in love with this tsarevna. His jester saw that somebody was visiting the tsarevna and so he told the tsar. Ivan Tsarevich's father was angry, and he ordered them to catch the person. They caught him and brought him in. The tsar ordered a detachment of soldiers to conduct him to the gallows. Then he said, "Permit me first to get dressed." So he went and put on all his ribbons, and his royal regalia, and he came into the main room where they were waiting for him. The soldiers came in and he said, "Now take me and lead me to the gallows. Why aren't you leading me?" So they took him and led him to the gallows. His mother the tsaritsa came and recognized him, and did not permit them to execute him. And they all began to live and dwell and prosper.

A–T 575

331. The Esaul and His Sister

In a certain village there lived a father and he had three sons. Two were married, but the third was a bachelor and a fool. There was also a daughter.

Since this father sensed the approaching end to his life, he desired to bless his children with his estate while still alive. So he summoned all three and bequeathed the two older sons everything. The youngest son stood there and said, "And what's for me, father?"

"Oh, my dear son, I forgot all about you!"

But since there was nothing left at all, he blessed him with just the old bathhouse and his sister.

Soon after that the father died, and the brothers dispatched their youngest brother Ivan and his sister to the bathhouse and they gave them nothing at all—neither bread nor money. So then the sister said, "How shall we live, little brother?"

And he answered her, "Just as soon as I have strength and health, then I will only need to a cable or rope and I'll go into the forest. There I will cut down some oaks and then I will make sleigh runners."

"And how will you bring them back here?"

"I will carry them on myself."

Then in orderly fashion he remade the stove in the bathhouse. He temporarily borrowed a little flour from a neighbor and also got a cable rope, took his axe, and went off into the forest and cut down so many oaks that even a horse couldn't carry them. He tied them up with his rope, swung them onto his shoulder, and started off carrying them. At home he steamed them and fashioned them, curved them, and carried them to the nearest bazaar to sell. And that continued for some time and soon he already had some money. When his brothers found out that he was living well, they came to him and said, "Since the death of our father you have collected some money, and now you should share it with us."

But since his bank was quite small, his money was lying in a pot and it was a pot filled with gold. Then Ivan said to his brothers, "If you require money, take some. I'll earn some more." And so he went back again even further into the dark and dreamy woods and he suddenly stumbled upon a fancy house. He went into the house and thirty bandits attacked him there. When Ivan saw that they were attacking him for no good reason, he struck at each one and soon they were just a wet spot. He killed them all. But one esaul, seeing the danger, stood on his knees before him and begged him, "Don't kill me!"

"I wouldn't have killed anyone if you hadn't attacked me. Why should I kill you if you haven't done me any harm?"

The esaul said to him, "You can have this house now, and everything that's in it—gold and silver and all these riches—because I am the only one left and now I shall be your faithful servant."

Then Ivan went home and said to his sister, "Now we shall go live in our country house. That's enough of living in the bathhouse."

When they came to the fancy house, they found there lots of various fine clothes, and they dressed themselves properly, and besides that, they found many weapons, so that they would not require any more of anything after that.

And so having lived there a year or two, Ivan started to go hunting. Suddenly his sister became acquainted with this esaul. When they were acquainted, her brother began to bother them, so she and the esaul began thinking about how to kill him. The esaul said to her, "Let's play cards with him. If he beats you, then let him tie your hands together with a handkerchief, and you will have to tear the handkerchief off. But if you beat him, then we'll bring a horsehair rope. If he can't break it, then we'll remove his head with the saber. Otherwise, there's no way to defeat him: he's very powerful."

When he returned from the hunt and had eaten, the sister brought out a deck of cards and said, "Let's play."

And he said, "I don't know anything about playing cards." The esaul explained everything about cards to them and taught them to play. Then the brother and sister sat down to play and the esaul watched them. At first Ivan beat his sister, and so he tied her hands behind her with the kerchief. His sister, no matter how she tried, could not break the kerchief. So he untied her hands and they started playing again.

The second time the sister won the game and tied his hands behind him with a strong horsehair rope and said, "Well, brother, try your mighty hero's strength now!" And so her brother just shrugged his shoulders and the rope broke. So they started playing again, that is, for the third time. And again the sister won and they tied his hands behind him even tighter but he still broke the rope. The next day, as usual, he once more went out to hunt. They caught sight of him when he was returning from the hunt.

"How can we destroy him so that he won't bother us anymore?"she said.

Then the esaul said to her, "This time you pretend to be ill and say to him, 'When I was sleeping, I had this dream. Sixty versts from here there stands an enormous house with a very fine garden attached to it. And in that garden there is a white apple tree. If I could eat some of those apples, I would certainly recover.'"

The next morning when he came in, his sister was lying in bed, completely pretending to be scarcely alive. Ivan asked her, "What is the matter, sister? What has happened?"

"Oh, brother, probably I won't survive, I'll die. But last night I had a wondrous dream. About sixty versts from here toward the east there stands a gorgeous house and around that house there is a very fine garden. And in that garden there is a tree—a white apple tree. If I could eat some of those apples, I would certainly recover."

"So that is what's the matter! I'll just have to go get some, sister." And he took a basket and set off in search of that house. And after several hours he turned up in that garden. When he had picked the apples and filled the basket, he wanted to leave, but then he thought, "They will think I am a thief. I'll have to go and pay for these." So he went up to the house and there were sixty robbers in it. And as soon as the ataman of that gang saw him, he sent ten young men against him. Ivan immediately understood what was going on and with one stroke he killed several men. And then he killed every last one of them.

And when he had killed them all, he started looking over the rooms and suddenly he saw a beautiful maiden sitting behind a wrought-iron door. She had tears in her eyes and asked him, "Spare me, do not kill me, I am not a robber."

He said to her, "Why should I kill an innocent person? I would not have touched them if they had not attacked me. I came for some apples because my sister lies near death, and I wanted to pay some money for the apples. But then they rushed at me, trying to kill me." Then Ivan freed the beautiful maiden and said to her, "If you wish, come with me and you can live with my sister; it will be better for her."

And so he started to lead her back, but she couldn't keep up with him and soon started to lag behind because Ivan walked very quickly. So he took her and put her on his shoulders and carried her like a child.

When his sister and the esaul saw them, they were very surprised that he was still alive and well, and besides that he was bringing some maiden. Then he gave her a white apple, she ate it and recovered. And Ivan started going out hunting again.

But the beautiful maiden started noticing that his sister and the esaul were lovers. And one time she overheard a conversation about their wanting to kill Ivan. And this is how: once more to play cards and tie his hands with the very thickest horsehair rope.

When he returned from the hunt, they ate, and then they proposed a game of cards again. And this tsarevna, somehow unnoticed, got hold of the saber and observed their game. When his sister beat Ivan, she and the esaul dragged out the heavy horsehair rope together and tied his hands firmly behind him. And his sister said to him, "Now, brother, test your strength."

He started testing it, but the rope wouldn't break. Then he said to her, "Untie me, sister, I can't break this rope." But she quickly darted behind the door and the esaul put a saber into her hands and she was just about to cut off his head when the beautiful maiden in one blow struck off her own head, and her weapon went flying out of her hands. Then Ivan understood what was going on and he jerked at the rope and it broke. Then he cut her corpse up into little bits and he also killed the esaul.

And that beautiful maiden said to him, "It is too dangerous for us to live here. It's like in the dark forests with robbers everywhere. Take me back to my parents, for I am a tsar's daughter. This is how I ended up here—once when the entire royal suite was out hunting, I had a very fast horse, and I spied a deer and rushed off after it and I rode so far away from my retinue that I fell into the hands of these robbers. And my parents didn't know where to find me. But because you have saved me, I give my oath that I will marry you if only I am pleasing to you." And as a sign of his agreement she shook his hand firmly and kissed him ardently, and Ivan answered this ardent kiss an innumerable number of times.

Then Ivan took the beautiful maiden by the hands and placed an enormous pile of gold in a large sack, enough to fill three carts. And he came with this gold to his own village and he shared the gold with all the village. And besides what he had divided up, they came from other villages, and he didn't slight them, he gave them a share, too. And he said to his brothers, "If you wish, go into that dark forest, and there stands a fine house, and much money remains there, and clothing and weapons too. But I am going to the capital city, accompanying this beautiful maiden."

His brothers thanked him, and, moreover, all the people wished long years of good health, life, and happiness for such a generous act.

So when they came to the capital city and appeared before the tsar, the tsar and tsaritsa were so delighted at the sight of their daughter, that she turned out to be alive and healthy and unharmed. They thought that fierce beasts had torn her to bits. She said to her parents, "If it had not been for this kind man, in fact I should never have returned alive. I was in the hands of sixty robbers who held me as a criminal, imprisoned. And Ivan got there entirely by accident. Because he possesses an uncommon strength, a hero's strength, he killed all these good-for-nothing robbers and spared my life and so presented me to you, my dear parents. And I have given him an oath that for this rescue I will marry him and be his faithful wife." Then the tsar and tsaritsa agreed and gave them their parental blessing and they were married.

After several years when Ivan had been well educated in writing, and the tsar was already old, he handed the throne over to Ivan and Ivan accepted it. After the coronation he became very generous and no matter what sort of complaints came to him, he would satisfy them and he always rewarded the poor. Then he wrote his brothers and invited them to come visit him. When the brothers arrived and began to live just as well, Ivan gave a feast for the whole world. And I was there, drank wine and beer, and it flowed through my whiskers, but none got into my mouth.

A–T 576

332. Olesha Popovich

In this one village there lived a widowed priest. After the priest's wife died, there was left a little girl. And consequently she grew into maturity, but because she was around her father all the time, she became very accustomed to him. And at the same time he used her, and the daughter became pregnant. When she sensed this, it made her very much ashamed and she refused to go out on her own, hoping that people wouldn't notice her. And so at a certain time when the priest had gone away about the parish, she decided to run away and hide. And she wandered for a long time, she went through many towns and many villages and finally she came to a deep and dense forest. And then she ran out of all her food supplies. And then suddenly she came up to a landlord's house and she decided to ask for some alms to nourish her, and, perhaps, they might take her into the kitchen as a servant. She went into the house to ask for some alms to nourish her. The landlord's wife gave alms to her and paid some special attention to her. "Perhaps you would like to hire on here as a servant?"

"Why not, I would be glad. It would be better than to go on wandering throughout the whole, wide world. But I don't know whether you will take me because I am pregnant and soon I should give birth."

But the landlord's wife said to her, "Since we have no children, your child will not bother us at all, and, on the contrary, we shall consider him as one of our own." So she stayed with them. And after a little while she had a child to whom she gave the name of Olesha, and he was surnamed Popovich, the priest's son.

And she lived there for a long time. Olesha also grew up completely but he didn't know that the kitchen maid was his mother. He thought that the landlord and landlady were his mother and father. Then suddenly rumors started going around that a priest was going throughout the forest searching for his daughter. But since she was really angry with her father and did not wish to meet face to face with him again, she decided to leave the place and abandon the landlord's rooms. So she called Olesha and said, "The landlord and landlady are not your father and mother. I am your mother." And she told him everything in detail, that he and she had the same father, a priest, who was going about searching for her. But because he had disgraced her and she had given birth to Olesha, she no longer wanted to meet up with him and she would leave the landlord's household. "If you wish, you can come with me, but if not, you may remain here."

But Olesha said, "Since you are my mother, how could I leave you and abandon you?" So they explained to the landlord and the landlord's wife that "we are not going to live with you anymore, for this reason." The landlord and his wife understood this and gave them supplies for their journey. Olesha also filled a canvas bag of water. And they set off by no known route, nor by a road, wherever their eyes should take them. And they walked for a long time through the deep forest and they ran out of food supplies and not a drop of water was left. From fatigue and hunger and thirst they could go no further.

And the mother lay down on the ground and said to Olesha Popovich, "My son, you climb up in that very high tree and see whether there isn't some dwelling around here."

When Olesha had climbed up in the tree, he saw a river not far away and a splendid house. He said to his mother, "Not far away from here is a river and on that river there stands a very fine house. You rest here and I'll try to go there and beg for some bread and I'll take some water and bring it to you." So he set off in the direction of that house. And having gone on a little while, he encountered a thorn-covered path and on that path he found a belt and on the belt was written, "Whoever belts up with this belt shall be the strongest one in the world." In a flash he had put on the belt. And when he was buckled up, he felt this enormous strength, and he went up to the thick tree and took it and ripped it out by its roots and thought to himself, "This means that the belt doesn't lie."

He soon came up to the river. At the river there stood a gristmill. He came up to the little hut by the gristmill and said to the miller, "Sell me some grain because my mother is dying of hunger, and if you won't sell it, then give it to me." But the miller refused him and gave him nothing. So Olesha Popovich said, "If you won't give me anything, then I'll tip your mill into the water."

The miller laughed and said, "Go ahead and tip it in!" So Olesha took the mill by one corner and dumped it into the mill pond. Then he suddenly saw not far away a very fine house and he headed for it. "Maybe there somebody will sell me some grain."

When he went into this house, there were a hundred robbers there, sitting around a barrel and drinking wine from scoops. As soon as the headman saw him, he sent ten men to meet him. They wanted to kill him, but Olesha turned right around and struck them one at a time and each flew off, but he killed several right away. And he slaughtered them all, right to the last one. There remained only the guard who had kept the headman's entrance. And he got on his knees before Olesha Popovich and started begging for mercy. "If you will spare my life, I will serve you to the grave and never do you any sort of wrong."

Then Olesha said to him, "First of all, give me some grain." And so he showed him, of course, all the food supplies. And he took several loaves of bread and filled a bag full of water and went off to his mother. He gave his mother something to drink first, and then he gave her a piece of the bread. When his mother had eaten a little, he took her in his hands and carried her to this elegant house. And in this robbers' house there was much of everything—of gold and silver and precious stones and all kinds of precious clothes, both outerwear and underwear, and there were huge supplies of foodstuffs. And so it was that they had enough to live on without running out. But Olesha was bored sitting about with nothing to do and so he took up hunting. An esaul guarded Olesha and his mother at this time. And his mother fell in love with this esaul and the esaul was very happy about this. But Olesha Popovich began to interfere. His mother said, "You kill Olesha Popovich."

"I cannot kill Olesha Popovich because I gave him an oath that I would never do him any wrong, but if you want to destroy him, about a hundred twenty versts from here to the southeast is another robbers' house and in it are three hundred men and besides that there is a very fierce bear, and there'd be no saving him there. Send him there. Pretend to be ill and say, 'I really feel like some pears. If I were to eat them, I would surely recover.' And he will ask, 'Where can I get them?' and then I will tell him."

So when he came back from hunting, his mother pretended to be ill and took to her bed and lay there scarcely conscious. And she asked him, "Oh my dear little son, get me some pears! As soon as I eat them I will surely recover." Now around their house was a garden but there were no pears.

Then Olesha Popovich asked, "Where am I to get these pears? All around here there is just this dark, dense, impenetrable forest."

Then the robber said to him, "I know that about a hundred twenty versts to the southeast of here there is a house, and about this house is a very fine orchard. And in this orchard there are pears. If it wouldn't be too difficult for you, go there and bring a large pear back for your mother."

So Olesha set off and when he entered the garden, he picked some of these pears, as many as were required, and was about to return back when suddenly he thought: "Perhaps they will take me for a thief here. I should probably go and make known to the landlord why I have entered his garden and taken his pears." No sooner had he entered the house than the robbers fell upon him, desiring to kill him. But Olesha Popovich dealt with all of them instantaneously. Just one of them ran away and told the headman. Then the headman sent a second gang to kill this good-for-nothing. But he also dealt with the second gang. The headman, having waited for some time, saw that not one of his comrades had returned, got up and together with all his robbers went to meet him. But he slaughtered them all. Then the ataman, the headman, saw his disaster and whistled at his bear. And at that very moment he was killed by Olesha Popovich. But the terrible, enraged beast with its gaping maw spread its sharp claws and went toward Olesha Popovich. Then, seeing such a hero, and rather than tearing him to bits, the bear began to fawn over him like a dog. He stroked her and scratched her back.

The bear lay down on the grand parade porch and Olesha Popovich went to look at the robbers' rooms. When he went into the house, while examining it, he found in one room a beautiful tsarevna, who with bitter tears began begging him not to kill her. He answered her, "I am no robber, but I do defend my own life, and then all these armed men wanted to chop me into little pieces, which is why I killed them all."

And then he freed this tsarevna. She said to him, "For this great deed of yours I shall give you my oath that I shall marry you." And as a sign of this she gave him an engagement ring from her very own hand.

Olesha Popovich said, "Why all this for me? Let's divide it all half and half." He took the ring and broke it in two. He gave half to her and kept the other half for himself.

But then she begged him, "Come with me and we'll go right away to my parents and there we can be married."

But he said to her, "I can't right now because my mother is near death and

I have to hurry to her as quickly as possible. But I shall lead you out onto the main highway and there you will be able to manage for yourself." When they had left the robbers' house, the bear refused to stay behind and went along with them. When they had gone out onto the main road, they suddenly noticed a troika tearing along in the direction of the capital city. Olesha Popovich stopped the troika and asked that they take the beautiful girl to the capital city and the driver and passengers agreed. So he quickly said farewell to the tsarevna and set off for his mother. As he approached the house, it was already dark. He locked up the bear in a cellar, saying nothing to anyone, not to his mother nor to the robber. And then he started bringing her good food. When his mother had eaten the pears, she got well, but she didn't know how to kill him, so she decided to do it at night when he was in deepest sleep.

When Olesha was sleeping most soundly, she quietly went into his bedroom with a dagger in her hand. The end of his belt was hanging over his bed and some words were written on the belt. His mother took an interest in it. "What sort of belt is it, I've never seen it before." She pulled the belt out from under Olesha and read that whoever should wear that belt would immediately feel in himself an incredible strength. So then she decided not to kill Olesha but to torture him. With her dagger she dug out both of his eyes. And she called the robber whom she harnessed to his legs and they dragged him down the stairs with his head bouncing on each stair, all three stories. They didn't want his head to splinter apart all at once. But the robber, having given his oath to Olesha that he would do no harm to him, as soon as he got out of Olesha's mother's eyes, took him by the hands and carefully carried him out of the rooms and to the river and laid him down beneath a rowboat. But Olesha groaned so loudly from the pain they had inflicted on him that the bear heard the groans in the cellar. She smashed down the door and came running to Olesha Popovich and licked the blood from his face and also the wounds on his eyes, and she got him on top of her back and rushed off with Olesha to the capital city, and she was just short of the city when she put him down on the main road. And she herself lay down behind a bush to make sure that nobody harmed him.

When the tsarevna had come home, she took several hospitals under her patronage in honor of her having been saved and she gave an order: "If anyone brings an unfortunate one here, let him be paid twenty-five rubles." And she often visited these hospitals.

Olesha Popovich didn't have to lie long on the main road when along came a cart going into the city and they immediately saw the unfortunate man. And two of them began to quarrel among themselves. One said, "I saw him first." But in fact he had seen him from the lead horse. He took and laid Olesha in the cart very carefully and brought him into the royal hospital.

When they had staunched the flow a little from Olesha's eyes, he came to his senses and began thinking. "What a piece of luck it was that a princess once promised to marry me and now what am I good for without any eyes? Not only a princess but even a pauper wouldn't marry me." And he recollected the piece of the ring that he had in his pocket and he found it and threw it onto the hospital floor.

When the charwomen began sweeping the floor, they found the half of the ring and gave it to the nurses. The nurses immediately understood that this was a ring from the royal family. So one fine day that very tsarevna came to look at the patients in the hospital. And the nurses gave her the half of the ring. "Probably it is yours."

She said, "Yes, this ring is in fact mine." But she thought that she had lost it. When she went back to the palace, she looked and there she had the second half of the ring and she immediately guessed that somewhere near there Olesha Popovich was lying. Perhaps right in the hospital. She went right back to that hospital and started asking who had lost the ring. And one charwoman said they had taken it, that "I took it from a certain ward, from the floor." When she went into that ward, she began asking.

When Olesha Popovich heard this, he said, "I threw it."

"And why did you throw such a valuable thing away?"

"Once it was very dear and valuable to me, but it is no longer of any use to me at all. A tsarevna gave me this ring when I was healthy, but then my evil mother dug out my eyes and left me near death, and I am no longer fit for marriage. So even if I were healthy, could a tsarevna possible marry me, a simple man? Besides all that, I am blind. So that is why I threw it away."

The tsarevna said to him, "It's me, the tsarevna, you're talking with, and I shall never agree with you nor shall I violate the oath we gave."

"But if it is you, then do something to heal my eyes, at least so that the blood doesn't keep running out of them." Then the tsarevna summoned the very best doctors who soon healed his wounds and he got better. When he had recovered, the tsarevna took him by the hand and led him to her parents and asked them to give their blessing and marry them.

The tsar and tsaritsa did not agree for a long time. "Why should you marry such a poor fellow, despite the fact that he saved you? If he had eyes, then maybe you could marry him. We have wealth enough but he is a blind cripple! Don't ruin yourself, don't disgrace us!"

But their daughter begged them so persuasively saying that "I cannot violate an oath once given, and I love him even if he is now blind." Then the tsar quietly married them and sent them to a suburban estate where they lived.

Once Olesha had an extraordinary dream. "If you, Olesha, will go out for thirty morning stars and wash in the morning dew, your eyes and sight will be returned to you again."

When he awoke, he told this to the tsarevna. "Alright then, Olesha, I shall lead you out for the morning star and the morning dew."

When Olesha went out for the last time to wash in the morning dew, his eyes appeared as if they had never been hurt. Then he said to the tsarevna, "Let's go, I wish first of all to take revenge on my mother, then we shall start living."

When they had gone a little way from the estate, they suddenly heard this explosion. They turned around and their house had been raised up into the sky and shaken into tiny bits. Then Olesha Popovich said to his tsarevna, "Do you see, it's not just my mother who is evil; your parents are no better than she. If we hadn't gone outside, we would have been crumbled into tiny pieces."

The tsarevna said, "We shall perhaps manage to take revenge on my parents, too."

Then they approached the robbers' house and Olesha said to his tsarevna, "You go and hire out to my mother as a servant girl. Say that 'I am from foreign parts, I ran away from my parents,' and she will probably take you. And I will be here, not far away. You can carry food to me. But somehow try to get that belt from her. As soon as you get it, run quickly and shout for me."

He remained and she went into the house. When she had gone in, she said "Mistress, will you not take me to be a servant girl since I have left my parents for the reason that I was bored with loafing about. I shall work for you for bread alone." Olesha Popovich's mother agreed to it. So she started preparing food for them and heating their quarters. And she noticed the belt on her, the one he had talked about. And then once she went and didn't heat up the stove so that her bedroom became cold.

Then the mistress gave her a bawling-out: "Why did you heat the rooms today so badly, I was frozen as I slept."

"I do apologize, mistress, tomorrow I will heat them more." And so the next time she heated the rooms so much that it was like a bathhouse. Then the mistress took off her clothes, but still she could not sleep.

The tsarevna came into her room precisely at twelve o'clock, but the mistress said to her, "Why have you come in here at the wrong time?"

"I have come here, mistress, at the wrong time to take your slippers because at the right time I forgot to take your slippers."

"Well, take them and get out." The tsarevna cleaned the slippers and started listening at the door to see whether the mistress slept. When the heat in the bedroom had passed, the mistress fell into a deep sleep. She quietly went up and started looking to see where the belt was, it was beneath her side. And although the belt was unbuckled and had nearly slipped off the end, when she grabbed the belt and pulled on it firmly the mistress immediately woke up. With all her might she ran away out of the house with that belt to Olesha Popovich. And the mistress was after her. As soon as she had run out, she shouted, "Quickly, Olesha, come here, I have the belt." Olesha immediately jumped up and ran to meet her, and he grabbed the belt and belted it on. When he had managed to belt himself with it, his mother came running up. And with one blow he crushed her like a cracker. Then he went into the house and the robber met them and said, "Forgive me, I am not guilty of anything. Your mother was responsible for it all. She seduced me and asked me to kill you. But I, as you know, didn't do that to you."

Olesha forgave him and said, "I forgive you and present this house to you with all its riches." And then they went to the tsar and tsaritsa to take revenge on them for their attempt on their life. When they had come to the palace, Olesha Popovich killed the tsar and tsaritsa and all their courtiers and mounted the throne himself and chose simple assistants, as he himself was, and he made an effort to offend no one at all. On the contrary, he began helping all the poor and unfortunate, as did the tsarevna. And in honor of their having been saved and their accomplishments, they put on a feast for the entire world. And I was there, drank beer and wine, and it flowed through my moustaches, but none got into my mouth.

A–T 590

333. The Hired Man

There lived this priest with his wife. He took this hired man to help him out, and they agreed that if the priest should send the hired man away, then he would have to pay him double, but if the hired man went away himself, then he would get no payment at all. So the hired man lived with the priest for a month and then two. Summer came and the priest sent him out to the meadow to shear the sheep.

So then the hired man bought two poods of frankincense, went out into the meadow, lit it, and began praying to God. Suddenly he heard a voice, "Hired man, what are you praying for?"

The hired man said, "I am praying for the lord to send me a fife such that when I start playing it, everyone all around will start dancing." He had not finished saying all this when the fife flew down from heaven and fell near him. The hired man took the fife and started playing on it and suddenly all the sheep started dancing. The hired man played and played and the sheep kept on dancing. The hired man stopped playing and the sheep stopped dancing. The hired man did it once more and once more after that. The priest noticed that the sheep were losing weight and he thought he would look and see what the hired man did with them in the field.

In the morning the hired man drove the sheep out and the priest sat in among them and went along too. The hired man pretended he didn't notice and he tried to drive the sheep but they wouldn't go, they just wouldn't, so he lashed them with the knout, trying all the while to come closer and closer to the priest's head. The hired hand drove the sheep into the field, took out his fife and started playing on it and the sheep started dancing and the priest jumped up from the midst of them and started dancing while squatting. The poor priest was tormented. Sweat poured off him and still the hired man played. The priest started begging the hired man to stop playing, but he paid no attention. Finally he stopped playing, the priest jumped out of the flock and went off toward home, running as fast as he could.

He came running in and told his wife, "Wife, our hired man has this fife! He starts playing it and everything starts dancing!"

The priest's wife scolded the priest for being a fool and dancing so deliberately. "Now, then, when he comes in from the field, I will ask him to play."

So the priest asked his wife, "Put me in a box, tie it up in the attic beyond the crossbeam, so I won't hear anything." And that is what the priest's wife did. Evening came and the hired man drove the sheep back from the field. The priest's wife asked him to play on the fife.

The hired man took out his fife and started playing. It was just like a holiday. The priest's wife was mixing up some pastries just then and her hands were all covered with dough and so when she started dancing, she moved the dough from one hand to another. The priest heard it on the roof, but it was tight for him in the box. He banged his head against the roof, tore himself down from the crossbeam together with the box, banged himself hard, knocked his head against the ceiling, and jumped out of the box. Then he started dancing, squatting up in the attic. The priest's wife got tired of dancing and the dough bounced out of her hands, but the hired man kept on playing. He finally stopped playing and went outside. The priest's wife was rolling around on the floor, oohing from exhaustion. The priest came down from the attic. He couldn't get his breath, he was so tired. He went down onto the floor and they rested there until dawn.

In the morning they started counseling each other about what to do with the hired man. The priest had this mill in the swamp that had not been used to grind anything for about thirty years. Some devils had moved into it and they wouldn't let anybody pass by nor would they let anyone in. The priest thought of sending him to this mill to collect the quitrents from the devils. "Then, you see, they will strangle him." The hired man got up and the priest ordered him to go to the mill. The hired man protested but there was nothing he could do and so he asked for a horse. The priest didn't mind parting with the horse and gave it to him. The hired man hitched up the horse to a cart and rode off.

The hired man rode and rode and came to the mill. He cut the rope from the bridle and wove the two ends of it together, then he sat down on the bank [of the swamp] and waited for the devils, twiddling the rope in his hands. Suddenly a young devil jumped out of the swamp and said to the hired man, "What are you doing here?"

The hired man said to him, "Give me the rents for all the years that you have been living here! Otherwise, as surely as I have braided this rope without a beginning and without an end, I will pull you all out of this swamp."

The little devil was amazed as he had never seen such a rope before. "Show me your rope," he said. The hired man handed him the rope and the little devil took it into his hands, twiddled it around and was astonished: there was no beginning and there was no end! He gave it back. "Wait and I'll tell our grandfather." He twitched his tail and jumped into the water. The hired man remained alone on the bank. He sat and sat and became bored, so he started cursing the devils for taking so long to come with the money.

Suddenly the little devil crawled out of the water and croaked, dragging something. The hired man was overjoyed, thinking that he was bringing about twenty poods with him. The little devil crawled out of the water, dragging with him an iron rod of about thirty poods. He said to the hired man, "Grandfather sent you this rod: whoever of us can throw it higher will be judged right."

"Go on, throw it!" The devil threw the rod straight up so that it was scarcely visible and then it flew back down, crashing noisily against the earth, and the earth shuddered. The hired man grabbed the rod, but he didn't lift it. He somehow rested it on his knee and looked upward. The devil asked him, "What are you looking at? Throw it!"

The hired man said, "Wait. Let that cloud come over. I'll throw it up on the cloud and it will stay there." The little devil took fright. The rod was his grandfather's favorite. He had been strictly forbidden to lose it or else they wouldn't let him back into the swamp hole. The little devil grabbed the rod and dashed back into the water.

He wasn't there long before he came out again and said, "Grandfather has ordered that whichever of us can outwrestle the other will be judged right."

The hired man laughed and said to the devil, "How will you ever manage to defeat me? My grandfather is a hundred years old and you couldn't even defeat him." The devil started asking him to show him this grandfather because that little devil was really very strong. With one arm he had defeated the very strongest warrior. The hired man led the devil to a bear's lair and told him to enter into it and take a look. The devil climbed into the bear's den and began enticing the bear to come out and fight him. The bear got angry, came out of his den, grabbed the devil around the middle, and began breaking him up. He broke all his bones. The devil screamed and screamed that this grandfather bear had done enough, that he should let him go. But the grandfather bear wouldn't listen, he just went on breaking him up. He bent him into the shape of a ram's horn. The little devil finally tore loose out of the bear's paws and quickly went into the water.

Once more the hired man sat on the bank, waiting for the little devil. He didn't wait long. Soon the little devil came out again and said to the hired man, "Grandfather has ordered that whichever of us can outrace the other with be judged right."

The hired man let out a laugh and said to the devil, "How can you ever outrace me? I have a nephew not yet seven weeks old and he can outrace you." The devil asked him to show him this nephew, because the devil was speedy himself: he could even outrun the magic self-running boots.†The hired man led the devil to a hare's burrow and whistled. Out popped a hare and took off running. The devil shouted, "Wait, wait up! Let's start out even!" The hare wouldn't listen and kept on running. The devil dove back into the water.

The hired man sat down on the bank again and waited to see how things would end. The little devil popped out again and said, "Grandfather has ordered that whichever of us can whistle louder will be judged right." The devil whistled mightily. When he had sat with Il´ia Muromets, he had knocked people off their feet for a hundred versts around.

The hired man took offense. "What, are you making fun of me?" The little devil took fright." This is the last time; we are not going to bother with this anymore." The hired man ordered the devil to whistle. The devil whistled so mightily that it scattered the leaves from the trees and only with effort could the hired man stand on his own feet. It was now time for the hired man to whistle. The hired man suspected that there was no way he could whistle like that. He said to the devil, "I have pity for you. You won't withstand my whistle. You had better sit down on that little mound, close your eyes, and stop up your ears; it will be easier for you. The devil sat down on the mound, closed his eyes, stopped up his ears, and waited for the hired man to whistle. The hired man went up to his cart, took out a wooden cudgel, and did it whistle right over that devil's ear! The sparks flew out of his eyes. The devil somersaulted back into the swamp hole, the hired man sat down on the bank and waited for the devil to come out to him.

He didn't wait long. The little devil came out of the water and asked him how much money he needed for the ransom. The hired man said, "I don't need much—just fill this hat with gold."

The devil cracked his tail, jumped into the water and laughed to himself: "What a fool this hired man is! He has tried and tried all this only to get a hat

---

†"Sapogi-samokhody" are self-propelled boots akin to flying carpets, and the like.

full of gold. I wouldn't have taken a whole barrel in his place." The hired man went a little ways off from the bank, dug a deep pit and made the hole at the top a little narrow, then he knocked a hole in the bottom of his hat and put it over the pit. Dusk was falling. Here came the devil dragging a big bag of gold, which he thought would be too much. He poured and poured, but it wasn't enough! He ran after another bag, but that wasn't enough either. He poured five bags out, but it was still too little. The water tsar, the vodianoi, lit into him because he had taken so much money, but there was nothing to be done—he had to live up to the agreement. The little devil dragged three more bags and finally filled the hat. Only after the little devil had gone back into the water did the hired man fill up his cart with the gold and what was left he covered over with earth and then he went off to the master.

At that time the priest was in a field. He saw the hired man coming from a long way off. The hired man came home and the priest and his wife were overjoyed that he had brought so much gold. So the priest ordered the hired man to pour out all the gold in the barn and then stay there and guard it. The hired man sat there, he watched over the gold, and he didn't leave the barn. The next day someone came and called the priest away for a memorial service. The priest was pleased with the summons, and as he was going he said to the hired man, "Listen, hired man, I am going to a memorial service. You watch the door and don't go away anywhere or else someone will carry off the gold." The priest went away. Suddenly the hired man remembered that he had not told the priest that he would have to divide the gold with him fifty-fifty. So he took the door off its hinges and went off along the street, looking at it. He came to the house where the priest was at the memorial service, never taking his eyes off the door. The priest saw the hired man, jumped up from the table, and started cursing him.

The hired hand said to him, "But you ordered me to watch the door, and I have done that." They went home to see whether the gold was all together in the barn and they took it away.

In this tsardom, in the one where the priest lived, there was a tsar and this tsar had a beautiful daughter and the tsar sent out notice throughout the entire tsardom that the one who could state what sort of mark this daughter had on her body should become her husband. The hired man heard and asked the priest to let him go to the tsar. The priest let him. The hired man knew what sort of mark the tsarevna had. Once she had been walking in a field and the hired man had been playing his fife and the sheep were all dancing and the tsarevna had asked him for a pair of little lambs to amuse her with their dancing. The hired man had agreed to give her the pair of sheep with the condition that she tell him about the birthmark on her body. She told him that in her armpit there grew a golden hair.

That day when the tsar had ordered everyone to gather and guess, a whole lot of ministers, princes, generals, and the hired man among them all came to the palace. He was unwashed and uncombed as he sat on a golden chair. The tsar began going around asking them, but no one knew what the princess's mark was. Next to the hired man sat a general. The tsar came to the hired man and asked, "Why have you come here to the royal places, you crude peasant!"

The hired man answered, "I know what kind of mark the tsarevna has!"

"What kind?"

"She has a golden hair growing in her armpit."

The general blurted out, "She has a golden hair growing in her armpit." The general didn't know—he just said it after the hired man. The tsar fell to thinking: to whom should I marry her? They had both spoken together. He order a council called. The council decided that they should both sleep with her with the tsarevna in the middle and in the morning she would be facing the one whom she should marry.

So they gave them various things to eat and fruits, and they also treated the ministers and the princes, and the generals, and they treated the hired man too. The hired man ate nothing but he took a handful of raisins and a damson plum and put them in his pocket, and he filled his pocket up. Then when supper came, the hired man again ate nothing but the general didn't stint himself and really shoveled it away. After supper they led the tsarevna, the general, and the hired man away to bed and the tsarevna was in the middle. In the morning the tsar came into their room and saw that the tsarevna had turned her face to the hired man. He thought that she had preferred the hired man and so he married them and refused the general. The hired man and his young wife began to live and prosper. He dug up his gold that he had received from the devils at the mill and afterward he became the tsar and began ruling his own tsardom.

A–T 592

334. The Healing Apple

There lived this little peasant, he lived and did not complain, he just worked as he should. He plowed and sowed and reaped and tended his garden. He fed his wife, raised his sons, and taught them wisdom and wit. But he got no pleasure from the fact that there were three fine lads in the tower and all those ripe apples in the green garden. The peasant himself lived righteously and had taught his sons to do the same but the sons had taken their father's teaching differently. . . . The youngest had taken all his father's words to heart and observed them religiously. But the older ones let them go in the right ear and out the left. The little peasant had planted an apple tree in the garden for each of his sons and he had taught the sons to guard the apple trees, to grow them and admire the sweet apples. Neither of the older sons grew apples like those grown by the youngest brother: his were tasty, sweet, aromatic, and with bright red spots just like the dawn. So now, my dear friends, those apples were growing and the young lads were shooting up. As the trees grew, so did the lads.

The older ones went out to work willingly but to their elders they were unfriendly. The youngest didn't put a hand to the work, but he had a kind soul, he was lovable. He esteemed the elders, he was sociable with his equals and he amused the young ones. So the little peasant lived and rejoiced in his youngest son and there is simply nothing to be said about the mother. But not everything on earth is joy, sometimes bitter misfortune can quickly approach. The old folks say that misfortune strolls not in the forest but among people. . . . And so this misfortune peeked in at two households in this tsardom: at the household of the tsar and at the household of the peasant, and it peeked in at the same exact moment, and at the same exact time. . . . At the peasant's household misfortune carried off his wife and laid her to sleep in the moist earth. And at the little father tsar's household misfortune chained his only daughter, the incomparable beauty, the brightest of all, to her bed tightly and firmly. . . . She lay there, the darling, moving neither her little arm nor her leg, she didn't even move a finger. But nothing seemed to hurt, yet the beautiful maiden couldn't move anything at all. Where had her strength gone? Where were all her powers?

So his majesty the tsar gathered together all the doctors from throughout the whole, wide world, and distributed much gold treasure to them without even counting just so that they could raise up his child. But it didn't help her, the darling, and she turned pale, just as pale as the pillowcase underneath her little head. So then the tsar thought of summoning all the elders and grand people, the wise men, from the entire tsardom, to ask their advice, to obtain their wisdom. And so all the elders and the ancient women began to stream toward the tsar's court, all bent over as if they had become rooted in the earth, some hunched as if by a harness shaft-bow, still others doubled over, going along as if they were carrying more than a single century on their shoulders. They all gathered together in the tsar's chambers. And the tsar and lord came out to greet them. They bowed low to the waist, and he bowed to them even lower still. And the tsar said to these ancient people: "Oh, you old people, you wise people! You have lived much, you have lived through much on earth, you have seen much misery and misfortune, but have you seen anything more bitter than mine? My child has been lying here for nearly a half year. She moves neither arm nor leg, nor even her finger. Will you not look at her and tell me how she can be saved from this fierce illness?"

And so the old people moved into the tsarevna's bedroom. They looked at the maiden, they mumbled, they shook their heads, but they couldn't think of a thing. Finally an ancient old crone stepped out. Her face was just like a baked apple, her head was sunk into her shoulders, her nose could whisper with her beard, but the old woman's eyes were bright and penetrating, and they bore into you like an awl. They could see right to the bottom of the soul. The old crone went up to the tsarevna, bent low over the sweet young thing, chewed at something with her toothless mouth and then said to the tsar: "There is a cure for this fierce disease, little father and tsar, but it is not in liquids nor in ointments. It is a sweet ripe apple. But this apple must have been nurtured by a fine hand, ripened by the purest of hearts and that pure heart will have deceived no one at all, never thought evil thoughts of anyone, nor an impure thought ever befogged the mind. If such a heart can be found and if it can ripen a sweet apple, that will be a healing apple. If the tsarevna and little mother should eat this apple, she will get up on her frisky little feet, but if it cannot be found, prepare the grave for the dear child."

The tsar bowed very low to the old crone, desiring to reward her with some gold, to feed and give her drink in the palace, to have her sleep on a couch covered with sable skins, but the old woman refused it all: "I have lived without a cent, and I have never feared a soul sleeping on my stove, and that is where I want to die. You go on ruling and make it so that in your tsardom fewer tears are shed." And then the old woman wound her way back to her unheated hut.

So now, you dear friends of mine, royal messengers flew to all ends of the mighty tsardom; the messengers shouted out the decree according to the royal order: "Oh, all you good people, bring the healing apple to the tsar, to his royal daughter in order to heal her. And if an old man brings it, he shall live at the tsar's in a chamber of joy, eat and drink sweet things, sleep in a soft bed, cover himself up with sable skins. If a beautiful maiden brings it, she shall be the tsar's second daughter. The tsar will clothe her in brocade, velvet, and pearls, and give her in marriage to any tsarevich. And if a fine lad brings that apple, the tsar will give him this coveted treasure, his beloved daughter, and all the tsardom as a dowry."

So all the people began streaming toward his majesty's chambers with their apples. The old men went along, thinking of a bite and of the warmth; the beautiful maidens of the royal finery, of enormous round pearls and of tsareviches; the fine lads of a bogatyr's delights, they had little thoughts of jolly feasts, but of the ailing tsarevna no one had the slightest care. . . . And so they all trampled a path from the royal threshold to his majesty's throne—

all the people went along with their apples. But none of this helped the tsarevna. And her parent and little father wept tears, his eyes were never dry, and those bitter tears ran from his bright eyes through his gray beard, from his gray beard onto his velvet kaftan, and from his kaftan onto the fine-planed floor. . . . The floorboards haven't been dry near the royal throne for a long, long time. That's how easy it is for a parent's heart to look upon a sick child!—but it was no better for the little dove, the tsarevna. She was already preparing herself to die.

Then rumor of the healing apple finally reached the three brothers whose apples were growing in their parents' orchard. When the older ones heard of it, they turned on each other like wolves. "There's no way the princess will recover from that apple of yours. The tsardom will be mine." They could scarcely await the ripening of the apples. But when the youngest heard of the fierce illness, his heart burned with great pity. He thought of her lying there, the poor thing, unable to move, and his soul was scarcely alive.

"Grow, grow healing apple so that she can rise up, the little swan, and stroll in the garden, pick flowers in the open steppe, listen to the twittering little birds in the dense forest." And it grew and he observed that little apple as it was covered with leaves from the high heat, as it would appear in the mornings in the sunlight.

The oldest brother could not wait for his apple to ripen, he became impatient and he picked the one that was largest of all and set off for the tsar's. When he had gone just out of the village, a little old man met him. Our young man didn't look at the old grandpa, he didn't tip his cap, didn't bow his head. And the old man spoke a kind word to him: "Greetings, my child! Where are you going, my child, and what is that you are carrying in that basket?"

And the youth replied to the grandfather: "I am going just wherever my eyes lead me, and some frogs are sitting in this basket."

"Frogs!" said the old man, "well, if you say frogs, let them be frogs!"

And he went on his way. And the young man went to the tsar, thinking about his apple and the tsardom, pondering his riches. So he came before the tsar and he was terrified of looking at him. "Well, show us your apple," said the tsar to the young man.

The young man opened up his basket and frogs began hopping and jumping out. There were big ones and fat ones, they went plopping and flopping around, and they scattered throughout all the corners of the chamber. The tsar saw it all and he was furious. He ordered them to execute the fool. As for the fool, he himself didn't know what had happened to him. He stood there, dropped his basket, let hang his arms, his eyes bulging out. He really looked like the fool.

"Oh, you loyal servants," shouted the tsar, "chase that fool away and throw that filth away!" The royal servants came running and they chased the fool away, about a verst, and they treated him to a few strokes from the rod. And they somehow caught all the frogs and threw them out the window. The oldest brother came home as dark as a storm cloud.

And the middle son rejoiced. He picked an apple, put it in a basket, and set out at a run for the royal palace. When he was just outside the village, he met the same little old man. And this young man and his older brother were like two berries from the same bush. The middle brother didn't look at the old man, he didn't tip his hat, he didn't bow his head. But the old man had a kind word for him: "Greetings, my child! Where are you going, my child? And what are you carrying in that basket?"

And the young man said in answer: "I am going wherever my eyes lead me and in my basket there are worms."

"Worms?" said the little old man, "well, if you say worms, let them be worms!" and he went on along his way.

So the young man went along, thinking of his apple, and he thought a little thought of the tsardom . . . and they led him in to the tsar. "Show me your apple!" said his majesty.

So the young man opened his basket and worms started crawling out, and they crawled and crawled. There were long ones and fat ones, some rolled up in little balls, some twisting and turning. And they spread out all over the entire floor of the reception room just like a red carpet.

The tsar was furious and he ordered the fool executed. As for the fool, he himself didn't know what had happened to him. He stood there, he dropped his basket, his arms hung down, his eyes bulging, just like a fool.

"Oh, you loyal servants," shouted the tsar, "Chase this fool away and get rid of this filth." So the tsar's servants came running. They chased away the fool, and they accompanied him for about two versts with rods, and they gathered worms right up until evening, crawling around the floor on all fours. And the middle brother returned home with nothing.

And then the youngest son's apple ripened—juicy, with a blush, and really fragrant. People stopped beyond the picket fence to wonder at the scent. The youngest brother took a little basket, spread one of his mother's cloths, and covered the apple with one end. He put on a clean shirt, tied a silk belt around him, put some new bast lapti on his feet and a cap made by his mother on his head. He combed his russet curls and set off. . . . On the outskirts of the village he met the same little old man. Our youth was first to bow to the old man, he took off his hat, and bowed: "Greetings, grandfather, peace to you."

The old man smiled. "Greetings, my dear child! And where are you going, my child, and where are you carrying your basket?"

"Oh, grandfather, I'm going, well, I don't know how to say where I am going, I'm not sure these quick legs will carry me to the tsar himself."

"Somehow you'll get there, my child, the tsar's a man just like you and me. . . . And what is in the basket?"

"Just an apple."

"What's that for?"

"Oh, grandfather, is it possible that you don't know anything at all?"

So then the young man told the old man about the tsarevna's fierce disease and about how it was ordained that she be cured by an apple. "Well, if God wills it, she will be cured," said the old man and set off along his own road.

The young man came to the tsar's chambers. They reported to the tsar that somebody else had come with an apple. The tsar ordered him brought in. The young man came into the tsar's room, carrying the apple with the aroma of the apple preceding him announcing its own arrival. The tsar started, he had never smelled anything like it.

"Show me your apple!" The young man bowed, uncovered the apple, and the apple aroma filled all the royal chambers. The tsar looked and there on the handcloth was this juicy, blushing apple, just asking to pop into a mouth. The tsar's heart shuddered in his breast. "Let us go, young man, let us go and take your apple to my sick child."

The tsarevna by now rarely even opened her eyes. She was breathing faintly so that only one skilled would know she was alive. The tsar and young man came in, carrying the apple for the tsarevna and the apple aroma ran ahead of them, announcing its arrival. They went up to the bedroom and stood at the threshold as the apple aroma swirled beyond the threshold. And then at that very time the tsarevna sighed as she sensed the apple fragrance. She sensed it and tried to rise up. She rose up and sat there! She sat there, not having moved for nearly a year. The tsar opened the door. He stopped on the threshold. He couldn't believe his eyes. There sat his beautiful child! As the tsarevna sat there, they put the lid on the coffin. Her cheeks had been whiter than linen, and they were sunken in. Her nose had become sharp, her eyes had occupied her whole face. The tsarevna stretched out her white arms for the apple and her arms were as thin as splinters, they were all dried up, and her fingers were like matches.

"An apple," said the tsarevna, "give me the apple." And in the young man's heart such pity burned, like life, and he knew he would spare nothing if only the tsarevna would recover. He took the apple out of the basket and put it in her hands, but she could scarcely hold it. Her little arms were shaking. But then the tsarevna took hold of the apple and she raised it up to her parched lips and kissed it. And her lips crimsoned like cherries. And the tsar stood there, pressing his hands to his breast.

"Oh, my dear, dear child!" he said, with tears rolling and rolling down, but this time not from woe; this time they rolled down from joy. The tsarevna took a bite and her cheeks turned crimson like the scarlet dawn. She ate a second bite, and she was like a ripe apple, she bit off a third and let her little legs down from the bed.

"Now, father, I want to get dressed." And then the nannies and mummies came running with sarafans, and with kokoshniks and fine little Moroccan leather boots.† And they gave her a necklace of precious pearls, rings with precious stones, they dressed the tsarevna as she finished eating the apple. And when she had finished it, she said, "Father, I am healthy now, ready to go dancing."

"I'll be the one to dance, my darling little child, I'll dance at your wedding, for you are a bride who has been well courted!"

"And who has courted me, my own father?"

"Here is your promised one." And he pointed to the young man. But it had never entered the head of the young man that he would marry the tsarevna. He stood there blushing like the scarlet dawn. He rumpled his hat in his hands, and what was he to do? He didn't know whether to stand there or run or just sink through the very earth. The tsarevna looked at him and he seemed quite fine to her. She took him by his white hand and led him up to her father and tsar.

"He is very pleasing to me, dear father and parent. I shall marry him of my own free will."

And so the youngest brother was married to the beautiful tsarevna and so they lived happily, so happily that people made up tales about them. And this tale has been made up and has come right down to you and me.

A–T 610

335. Riazantsev and Miliutin

There were these two merchants, Riazantsev and Miliutin. They lived window to window, so they were neighbors. They had no children, neither the one nor the other. Riazantsev gave a dinner and all the generals came and the merchants. And they made a note that if one of them had a son and the other had a daughter, they were agreed to give them in marriage only to each other. And all added their signatures to this—the generals and the merchants. It only remained for the tsar to sign. The tsar demanded that they all appear

---

†Moroccan leather boots reflect the notion that new footwear was to be worn at the wedding.

before him to undertake royal commissions in particular cities. His majesty and all of them agreed to the contract and finally put their signatures to it and then the tsar looked through their paper. "There is no way I can put my signature to this business! If the first one born is clever and the second is a fool, it simply won't work! I will sign this paper and keep it with myself. If you have clever children, both of you, then I will be able to officiate at the marriage.

So they got the royal missions ready and set off to their particular cities. And when they came home, their wives, both the one and the other, had gotten pregnant (it was as if the wind had blown them up). After a certain time a son was born to Riazantsev and a daughter to Miliutin. The priest gave Riazantsev's child the name of Vaniusha and to Miliutin's he gave the name Katia. And everyone was happy after this. And so they were—well, the one wouldn't drink tea without the other. They went everywhere together.

Vaniusha grew up to about the age of ten and his father decided to go to some particular cities trading. He loaded twelve ships with goods, took on some hired men—ship pilots and clerks—and they came to England and spread out their goods to trade in an English city. And they traded there for about six years. One Sunday he sat down with the clerks to take tea. First he said to the clerks, "I, master clerks, am thinking of appearing in my city of Petersburg and leaving England."

In answer the clerks said to him, "We are amazed that you have endured this for so long. A son and daughter at home and for six years you have been living here."

So they packed all their goods into their ships and set off home. They went out into the sea on their ships, but the ships were calmed. And no matter how they tried, the ships would not go anywhere. And they struggled for three full days in the same spot. And on the fourth day Riazantsev went out onto the deck and shouted at the water that "if some thief has taken hold of our ships, we will pay him what it takes, only stop holding us up!"

From out of the water something shouted in a human voice, "We don't need any gold, nor silver, nor do we need your goods. We need Riazantsev in the water himself. That is why we are holding up these ships." Riazantsev answered them three times and they repeated three times to him that "we don't need anything except you! You yourself in the water."

Riazantsev went into his office and composed a paper. "Whoever has been living on a hundred rubles, if he gets my goods home to my wife will receive two hundred rubles." He doubled the wage of every man. He gave it to the main clerk. Then he got ready in his white shirt and undershorts. (Never mind that he was preparing for death.) So he came outside and took his leave of all the people and of the whole wide world. And then he fell into the sea.

The ships at once were loosed from the hooks that held them and set off on their journeys. Riazantsev stayed in the water, he struggled like a swan and didn't drown. His main clerk took a telescope and said, "If I go back with the ship [for him], the ship will once more be snared. Better that one head die than all of us perish."

Riazantsev went out of his senses, he became utterly confused, and then he suddenly turned up near an island. Riazantsev came out onto the shore and praised God, "Glory unto God! I didn't drown!" (He had come out on the dry shore.) He took off his trousers and shirt, rung them out and hung them up in the sun. The shirt dried quickly and so did his undershorts. He put both the shirt and undershorts on and set off along the edge of the beach. He needed to find some food. He had nothing with him. Riazantsev came upon a path.

So he set off along this path and he came up to a fine house. It was a stone house and two-storied. He walked through all the rooms on the ground floor, but he didn't see a single soul, nor was there so much as a crust of bread. So he went up to the upper story and in the first room he saw a portrait fixed to the wall. It was a maid. He went up to the portrait and read what was stated: that Riazantsev was to marry this maid, in this very house. "If you don't take me," Riazantsev read on the portrait, "then we will kill you here, we will never let you out of this house!"

So he went into the next room. In the next room there was an even better portrait of an even better maid. This maid stated the same thing: "If you won't take her, then take me! And if you won't take us, then we'll kill you!"

Then he went into the third room. And in the third room was a portrait even better, of his wife. "Riazantsev," it said, "we shall take pity. If you can't take these, then take this one," the third, they meant.

To this Riazantsev said, "Can it be that the Lord will bring me to marry a second time? Oh, well, I talk away with the portraits and I really want to eat but there's no one here to ask." Suddenly a table appeared and on the table a samovar, a decanter and vodka, and then lots of both roasted and steamed foods. He drank his fill, ate his fill, all the while praying to God, and then the table was cleared away, I don't know by whom. And all this really amazed him. Then he saw a couch and he lay down to sleep on it and he fell soundly asleep.

In the night he heard little bells tinkling—the brides were coming to him. And there appeared a candle and chair before Riazantsev. And then three maids came up to him. The maiden in the first portrait went up to him and said, "Riazantsev, take me!" (She kissed and caressed him.) "Here there are far greater riches than you have."

"Get away from me. Am I really supposed to get married for a second time? You are not beautiful, you are ugly. My wife is much cleaner than you are!"

So the maid in the second portrait came up, kissed and caressed him, and persuaded him: "Riazantsev, you are not yet bored by the whole, wide world! Take me as your wife. And if you won't, then we shall finish you off here." But Riazantsev wouldn't have her either.

So the maid of the third portrait came up, kissed and caressed him, and with tears she pleaded with him: "Listen, Riazantsev, you are not yet bored with the whole, wide world. I am no worse-looking than your wife, if not better. You will have a good life here, peaceful."

In answer Riazantsev said to her, "Leave me until tomorrow. I got sick at sea, I lost my senses. But tomorrow I'll surely take one of you."

In the morning the sun rose and at dawn Riazantsev got up and paced the rooms. Riazantsev needed to bathe and dry himself but he couldn't find any water and there was no one to ask for any. Then a hand towel appeared on the wall and a washing basin. So he washed, prayed to God, and said, "Yesterday I ate very well. Now who will feed me today?" Immediately a table materialized, and on the table were a samovar and a decanter of vodka, and somebody carried out roasted and steamed things for him. He could eat what he pleased! So he drank his fill, ate his fill, and moved away from the table. And while he prayed to God, somebody cleared the table, but I don't know who. "Even if I don't see any people," he said, "they feed me well. I shall go through the rooms: whichever room most charms me is the one I'll live in."

So he went into the first room. The room was decently furnished, but there were chips all over the floor. He took a broom and started sweeping (he would keep house for himself). And then he saw among the chips a Jack of Spades. And out of the Jack of Spades there emerged three desperate men and they said, "Good health to you, Riazantsev!"

So Riazantsev said to that: "Brothers, this is the first time I've seen any people here!" So then these lads said to him, "We aren't people, we are spirits. Whatever you desire we shall perform. And if you will not send us anywhere, then we will kill you yourself."

So Riazantsev said this: "Brothers, you wouldn't deliver me back to Petersburg, would you?"

"And why not? Go out on the deck, tie your eyes with a white kerchief, and in an hour you will be there!" So Riazantsev went out onto the deck and sat there for about an hour. And the hour passed and it was time to open his eyes. So he opened his eyes and saw that he was no longer on the deck but near Petersburg. He turned up in a glade (they hadn't had time to drag him into town).

So then Riazantsev gave praise to God: "Even if I don't live long now, I am still at home."

He had only just gone out onto the highway when suddenly his great friend Miliutin came riding toward him. The coachman recognized him and told Miliutin that his great friend was walking toward them disheveled, in just his shirt. Miliutin ordered the coachman to stop the horses and he greeted him. The coachman stopped the horses. "Greetings, my lord and good friend Riazantsev! What is this I see? Has some misfortune befallen you?" (Because he was all ragged and torn.)

Riazantsev told Miliutin, "If you perhaps can believe it, I'll tell what has happened to me. I was going along over the waves and I saw many strange things. But then I sent my ships off over the seas and I set off by the overland coach." (He fibbed a little as he was telling it, he started misleading him.) "It was the last station. And then the horses reared up, they were obviously young ones, and they started beating us out of the way. They completely broke up the carriage and they killed the coachman. I," he said, "somehow flew out of there, I got myself out of it and it was easier to get out in just my shirt and barefoot—all my clothes I threw off."

"You won't have such an easy time of showing yourself to your wife. Even though I was off on business, sit down with me. You can get dressed in the stalls." Miliutin turned back and took him into the city.

In his own market stalls he dressed in his merchant's clothes and then he appeared before his wife. His wife shouted to her servants to put the samovar on in a hurry and they dragged out all sorts of foods and began to treat him as a guest. She waited on him too and asked him, "Oh, my dearest, even though I knew you, my heart was not in its place, for you appeared as naked as a falcon!"

To this Riazantsev said to his wife, "My dear, after I left here, I traveled over the seas and saw many wondrous things. Now my ships are sailing over the seas and I have come by the overland coach."

So then his wife said to him, "If your ships don't come, my dearest one, then in any case we will have something to live on, it is enough that you are alive!"

And so they lived on until their ships came up to the wharf. The clerk demanded that Riazantsev receive the goods. Riazantsev harnessed his horse, sat his son and wife [in the coach], and appeared at the wharf. Then he greeted all of the crew by name, he honored each by his patronymic, "Thank you, you have delivered to me both the goods and my treasury."

They handed over a letter to Riazantsev's wife, which said, "we do not recognize him as our master; it is not the master but some unclean spirit that has attached himself to you. We have a letter from the master." And they handed her the letter.

She looked at it and said, "Why did you explain everything untruthfully?"

He said to her: "It is no business of yours how I got here. I am your master. If I am an unclean spirit, then say a prayer and the unclean spirit should disappear from you. (I am not going to tell you how I got here. That's no business of yours.) Whoever lived for a hundred rubles will get three hundred, and I'll add another hundred to that. I'll triple the price for every man. Only unload the ships, the goods! After that, feast for three days (at my expense), only don't make it a habit. And then after three days come to me and we'll reckon up!" And so on the fourth day he paid them all off and some would have to seek other work, while some others were to remain in his service.

So then Riazantsev went down to his glass factory and he poured himself a glass chest. Then at the bazaar he bought some cotton wadding and he took the Jack of Hearts and wrapped it in the cotton and locked it in the chest. He locked the chest in a chest of drawers, and threw the key in the sea so that no one could get into it. "There's no point to my dealing with an unclean spirit; I have money enough of my own."

After that the unclean spirits began to torment Riazantsev. He lay down sick and died soon after. And after that business they started tormenting Riazantsev's wife. She got really sick and they soon finished her off. Now it would please them to torture the young boy. Just let him start trading with his father's capital! But Vaniushka's business went well.

It wasn't long after that all three of the spirits came to him one noon. They greeted him and he greeted them too. "What would you like to buy from me?" he said.

"We have not come to buy but to invite you to pay us a visit."

"And where are you asking me to go visiting?"

"We are asking you to come with us to a tavern (first of all)."

"I won't go into a tavern."

"But we are not going into the tavern for any bad reasons. There is a special room there where all the merchants (traders) gather and generals even frequent it. (It's called the Merchant's House.) And there you can ask in which cities it is possible to buy goods cheapest."

"But should I take any money with me?"

"No, you don't need any money. We will entertain you with our own." So Vaniusha agreed to go with them. He locked up his stalls and went off to the tavern.

They got to the tavern and the spirits told the serving boy to "bring us all sorts of wines, and roasted and steamed dishes, and all sorts of dessert." Since he had never drunk any strong drink in his life, Vaniusha soon drank too much and he got drunk. They tricked him saying that there were generals there and that the merchants were all sitting there. They said to him, "Now, Vaniusha, you can take counsel with them all. We have not brought you here for any bad reasons." (In fact there was nobody there.) Vaniusha was completely drunk. He lay down and just lay there. And so the spirits went away, saying to the serving boy, "Don't move him. Watch over him and in the morning we will come and pay for everything."

The next morning early the spirits came and the serving boy came running: "What do you require?"

"We need the same room! Bring us all sorts of wines and each and every dessert." They woke up Vaniusha. "Vaniusha, you shouldn't do that. You saw last night that fine people were sitting here. You need to talk a little bit and then go home!" They sobered Vaniusha up a little, said goodbye to all and left. And Vaniusha went home. He went home, drank lots of tea, and then went to his stalls to trade.

"Yesterday I was in a tavern. A soldier there had a little money, and what a Fraulein he had picked up (a wench)! If I were to take a thousand or two, then I'd find a first-rate woman for myself. If I have to wait for them, the scoundrels, I wouldn't ask for a woman in their presence" (it would be embarrassing, he said). So he went to the tavern. "What would you like?" It was the serving boy speaking.

"I need a woman. Bring me a Fraulein and every sort of dessert, too." So twenty maidens came out and he was to choose any one. Whichever one pleased him, he could choose! So he chose a very attractive woman, young, and he sat her down opposite him and began to treat her to wine. But the girl didn't drink much wine, she supplied him with the wine. (They know what to do: he came in with money—the game's to hook him.) She got him completely drunk, took his money from him, and then ordered the serving boy to throw him out of the tavern.

Some policemen came along and saw Vaniusha Riazantsev. They started to wake him up and Vaniusha woke up. "What do you want?"

"Get up, we will take you down to the station so you don't hang around in the night air." Vaniusha said, "Take me home and tomorrow come to my stalls; I'll settle up with you then." In the morning he drank his fill of tea and set off to his stall to trade. The policemen came, he gave them all sorts of goods and some money. "Just don't embarrass me, don't say that I was in the tavern."

So then he took quite a little money: "I won't take her, I'll take a different one! Won't it be better with a different one?"

So Vaniusha went into the tavern. "What do you need?"

"Give me a room, all sorts of wines and some snacks! And I need a fine Fraulein." So a girl with a pretty face came to him and sat down opposite him. "My darling," he said, "We shall spend today together and make love." But though she drank no wine herself, she gave more and more to him. She got him quite drunk. She got his money away from him and ordered the serving boy to drag him out beyond the tavern yard. The same policemen led him home once more, for some money. In the morning he woke up early, drank his fill of tea, and set off to his stall to trade. They wouldn't let him enter the tavern any more so he started hanging out with coarse women and frequenting dives. He squandered all his money and started selling off his goods. He went so far as to squander his whole household, and he had nothing to live on.

Miliutin went to the tsar with a complaint against him, saying "I will not give my daughter to him."

And the tsar said, "I will ask him about it tomorrow. Why didn't you tell me about this earlier? I would have put a watch on him." In the evening Vaniushka came in drunk. With him there was a retired soldier also named Ivan. "Why, Vaniusha, have you become such a drunk, become so dissolute? You should at least have gotten an education."

So the old man, the soldier, started instructing him. "I have my father's money, about a hundred or hundred and a half. I'll give it to you, or would you trade for it? Take some spice cakes or nuts."

The soldier gave him one and a half hundred rubles and he set off around the whorehouses where he blew it all. Then, of course, he got up in the morning and arrived drunk and there was nothing to drink to sober up on.

"Heh, Uncle Ivan, bring that couch to the bazaar and buy half a fifth of vodka! And they'll give you a drop more and you can buy a little fish for some soup!"

"Oh, you, Vania the Fool! I've saved away a hundred fifty rubles for my funeral. My father's money is all in trust, but you've drunk all yours up."

To all this Vaniusha merely said, "For all these rooms there'll be enough to bury us and all." (We have a fine house, so to say.)

So Uncle Ivan dragged the couch off to the bazaar to sell it. "When it's sold, I'll go through all the rooms to see what other good things there are to sell."

So he came to the chest of drawers. "Oh, if I only had the strength to drag out this chest of drawers! I would shout out 'heh, brothers, pour me a quarter! I'd buy a round for everyone!' " In the chest of drawers he saw the chest. But nowhere was there a key. He didn't value the glass at all, so he smashed it with his fist and got the chest. "Now this is one proper little chest. If it's sold to a fancier, they'll give me a half a fifth for it. But perhaps my father locked some gold up in it? My father was a man of means." He threw the chest against the floor. The chest broke and in it there turned out to be some cotton wool. "Oh," he said, "before trading on my father's capital, I could have wiped my ass with this cotton." He spread the cotton out and saw in it the Jack of Hearts.

The three spirits came out of the Jack of Hearts, three men. "Good health to you, Vaniusha."

"And where have you come from, brothers?"

They said, "We tortured your father and then your mother and we've got you to such a state that you've got nothing left. If you can control us, then do so. If you cannot, then we will finish you off! . . . Go to that room you've been living in. There is a lot of merchant's clothing lying there on the table. About a hundred fifty rubles' worth."

"Even if I had this little samovar, two golden cups, some sugar and tea, and a bottle of vodka to drink, I still will not drink any more wine," he said.

The uncle [waiter] came, brought a bottle of wine and a little fish for him. "Oh Vaniusha, do you still have some money?"

"Can it be that I have drunk my way through it all? Why, you and I couldn't get through all that money in a lifetime!"

"Here, then Vaniusha, give me a hundred fifty rubles, my own money."

"Take all five hundred. I won't regret it!" And he counted out a hundred fifty rubles for himself. "Here, uncle, don't live with me anymore; go to the kitchen! And when I call you for dinner, then come in."

The spirits left. "We shall teach you, Vaniusha."

"Go on and teach me!"

The spirits said that "a soldier sent by the tsar will come for you and will demand that you go to the tsar to give advice. Watch out, he will try to force you to get married, but you say, 'it's not time for me to get married yet; I still haven't taken account of all my father's capital.'" (He was taking account of it alright!)

The soldier [came and] then went away, after he [Vaniusha] had promised to appear. He gave the soldier a hundred rubles for his expenses. The soldier came to the tsar and explained to him that "he isn't drunk; he gave me a hundred rubles for boots, for my expenses."

And so he spent the rest of the day until evening and then he said, "I ought to go in style better than the tsar himself." (He started talking brazenly.) "They should deliver me a troika of horses and a coachman."

And the troika of horses came running up with a coachman, and the coach was entirely of gold and the harness shaft-bow was gilded. He rode through the town and many people ran out of their homes and looked at him: who was this knight riding by? Runners were sent to the tsar: "Some sort of knight is coming to visit. How do you command us to receive him?"

"Let him ride into our courtyard, receive him by the hand, lead him into my hall, and sit him next to me!"

The tsar asked him: "What is your family? What kingdom are you from?" (He thought he was some prince.)

"Your royal highness! Don't laugh at me! I am Ivan Vasil'evich Riazantsev's son, at your command! What do you desire to ask me?"

"So now, Ivan Vasil´ich, are you literate?"

"I am literate!"

"I have my father's notes, would it be at all convenient for you to look through them?"

"Yes, your royal highness, show them to me and I'll look at them." So they gave him the notes. He looked through them and said, "Our fathers did a good job."

The tsar then said to him: "Ivan Vasil´ich, it's time for you to get married."

"Your royal highness, it is not time for me to get married."

"And why is it not time?"

"It is not time because I still have not gone through, accounted for, all my father's capital."

To this the tsar said, "The earth is filled by rumor. I have heard that with your father's money you have filled the taverns, and the dives, and given to the whores."

Riazantsev said, "Your royal highness, if you wish to know me, undertake to build a cathedral somewhere, and then tomorrow send for our brothers [for their contributions], for the merchants, then you will come to know me."

For this the tsar praised him. "Now go home and tomorrow I will send a general for the merchants."

So he went home and said, "Spirits, tonight you must bring me about thirty thousand and everything in my home must be furnished, in a word, really well! There must be two chairs of gold and two gilded goblets so that I'll have what I need to entertain the general." In the morning Vaniusha got up and everything was ready. The carpets were spread on the floor and all was decorated with precious stones, the walls were all lacquered and everything was shining like a mirror. There were two chairs of gold, and two gilded goblets and they'd brought about thirty thousand to him.

In the morning the general came to him. And he had the samovar all ready for that general. The general came in—he was afraid to stand on the floor, it was so beautifully decorated. He and Riazantsev greeted each other. Riazantsev invited him to drink tea. But he wouldn't sit down to take tea: "In every house I have to sit down to tea—I've had enough of it! I've come on account of yesterday's agreement. What can you pledge for the new cathedral?"

Riazantsev said, "Are you writing down, your worship, who pledges what? Give me your notations, I'll look through them." And some from generosity had given ten, others five, or even a hundred, but his father-in-law Miliutin had pledged only one silver ruble. He said to the general, "Give me your advice, general. My father-in-law, Miliutin, considers me to be a drunkard, yet he has pledged only a single silver ruble. I only have one-quarter of a kopeck to subscribe. I cannot pledge anything. Better the tsar should summon me for advice tomorrow. But I'll give you a hundred for boots, for your expenses." The general came back and said that "all have pledged, but Riazantsev didn't pledge even a quarter of a kopeck, yet he gave me a hundred for boots. Oh yes, we are to call him to a meeting tomorrow."

The next morning there arrived at Riazantsev's these Ukrainians (sent by the spirits) on twelve harnessed oxen and all in state livery. The soldier Ivan went out and then ran to Vaniusha and told him about these Ukrainians. Vaniusha said, "Go, uncle, and tell them that there's no time to feed the oxen here; they should rather go to the unloading depot (where they are practiced at unloading things, I mean)."

So the Ukrainians rode for St. Petersburg to the tsar's palace. Then the general saw them and said, "They're going with state property goodness knows where, but their livery is ours."

"Good." The tsar ordered him to ask them what they were carrying and where. So the general rode up and asked them.

"We are carrying gold!" the Ukrainians answered. He didn't believe it so he asked another.

"We are carrying gold to the palace for the tsar." He asked a third. The third jumped down and struck him with his whip: "How dare you come out at us with that force?"

The general went to the tsar with a complaint, saying, "those fools coming here are no fools. I asked one of them and he told me. I asked another and he cursed me, and the third with his whip."

To this the tsar said, "They beat you, but not enough. They are coming with no convoy at all and you go approaching them with great force. You should have asked the first and then come right back. Greet them! If they've no deceit with them, then say 'thank you.'"

The tsar could wait no longer. He went out to look at the gold himself. No matter which barrel he opened, there was good gold. The tsar said, "Who is all this gold from? Why has it been sent here?"

"This gold was sent here by Riazantsev the merchant for the cathedral, twelve barrels."

Then the tsar said, "So, he is no fool. Look, general, you get on your little horse and bring him here for a talk."

So the general quickly got on his little horse and appeared at the house of Riazantsev the merchant. He can to Riazantsev and asked him to come immediately to the tsar for a talk. Riazantsev said, "I'll be right after you, but I won't ride on your little horse." Riazantsev said to his spirits, "Fit me out even better than the tsar and get me the same carriage with a coachman!" The carriage came running up, he got in that carriage and appeared before the tsar.

The tsar ordered that he be met in the same manner, led into the hall and
sat next to him. The tsar said to him, "Listen, Ivan Vasil'ich, it's time for you
to get married!"

Ivan Vasil'ich said, "I won't take her [I won't have a wedding], I'll put
my signature to that!" (Miliutin was trying to marry off this daughter to the
general.) "Wherever she wants to go, let her, if my father-in-law considers
me a drunkard." And he signed his name to it.

The tsar said to him, "I shall give you a rank" (which represented a
lot of gold)."

"And what rank will you give me?"

"I shall give you the rank of general, you shall serve me as a general."

"No, I cannot accept the rank of general, that would cause difficulties for
me. . . . I would never get through all my father's capital. It would be better
if I gave you a thousand rubles a day for the army: I don't know anything
about military service. You probably think that this money, these twelve barrels of gold are it, but my father's stores are filled with bronze to the very
top, in a whole lifetime I'll never spend it all."

"Anyway, I'll give you a rank for this."

"What rank?"

"I'll give you the rank of governor of the town. You shall be governor of
the town and every day you shall come to the meetings of the Synod and we
shall dine at the same table." He agreed to that. The tsar ordered a lace front
for him and appointed him governor of the town and he ordered a sentry box
built so that a guard could be posted near his house (so that watch-soldiers
could stand there day and night).

"Spirits, is it possible that I shall never ever marry?"

The spirits said to him, "Here are three things for you. With these three
things deceive your promised bride."

Evening came and since they lived window to window, he hung some
gold earrings (above the window). The young girl saw the earrings: "I'll go
and bargain for them. Tomorrow I'll be with the general at a party and look
very pretty." She went to the window. "Oh, my promised groom, Ivan Vasil'ich
the governor. Aren't those little earrings of yours for sale? Sell them to me!"

"They're not for sale. But come into my room and kiss me tenderly. Then
I'll give them to you as a present!" So she kissed him, took the earrings, and
went into her own rooms. She put them on her ears and saw that they were
very fine.

Then he hung out some gold beads. "I'll go and trade for them. Tomorrow
I'll be sitting with the governor at a party and look very pretty. So she came:
"Oh, my promised groom, Ivan Vasil'evich the governor! Won't you sell me
those gold beads?"

"They're not for sale, they're already promised. But come into my room, kiss me tenderly, and I shall give them to you as a present." So she kissed him tenderly and took the beads. Then she went home, put the gold beads on herself, and looked in the mirror: she thought she looked very pretty.

So after that he hung out a gold ring. She came: "Oh, my promised groom, Ivan Vasil'evich the governor, isn't that ring of yours for sale?"

"Come into my room. You and I were born the same hour and minute, but now they intend to marry you to a general, to an old man, and you will give your honor to this old man! Better to give it to me!" She agreed and gave it to him. "Listen, that maiden's thing of yours, take off that petticoat and I'll give you a fresh one, one of mama's. Then tomorrow I'll heat up the range and burn it." Afterward she went off home.

In the morning Miliutin set off to invite the tsar to a party that evening. The tsar said, "If the governor permits me, I'll come. Let him send me a note. I am not obligated to go out in the evening. Will the governor find fault with me for it?" (The tsar was trying to dodge the responsibility for deciding.) Miliutin came home and said to his wife, "It's just the person we don't want, but the tsar has ordered him invited." Then Miliutin set off to invite him.

He came into his rooms, but was afraid to cross the floor. His son-in-law already had the samovar ready. He and the governor exchanged greetings and he said, "I want you to come to us to a party, and the tsar has ordered you to give him a note ordering him to come to the party."

"Am I greater than the tsar? Let the tsar send me a note himself, ordering me to come, and then I'll be ready to go. I am not greater than the tsar!" (It's obvious you can't put one past him in a hurry either!) For the second time Miliutin went to invite the tsar to his house for a party. Then the tsar wrote a note: "Let the governor get ready for the party," and he ordered him to give him the note. Miliutin came and handed it over. "Now I shall be ready to visit you."

Evening came. "Spirits, get me the gold carriage and troika of horses with the coachman. And all around the house let there be lanterns and sentries on guard." In the evening the tsar came to Miliutin's. As he was driving up to the house, Riazantsev drove up too. They both got out of their carriages, they exchanged greetings with the tsar, they took each other's hands, and went into Miliutin's hall.

There were chairs and places for everyone, only there was no governor's chair. Everyone sat down at his place, but the governor had to remain standing. The tsar saw the mistake and took the very chair he had been sitting on and gave it to the governor. Then they gave the tsar another one.

They started passing around the vodka and treating all to various desserts. The merchants boasted of their money and goods, as they do at feasts, and the generals just bragged about their money. (If you drink enough, you'll start in boasting.) Everyone was bragging like mad. To this the tsar said, "Now, governor, you and I will finally have to do some boasting. You go on, governor, and start the boasting; you're a little younger than I am."

The governor said, "I've nothing to boast of! My business is young, I haven't been about all these foreign cities, I've seen nothing, I've nothing to boast of!"

Then Miliutin's wife jumped up and said, "Your royal highness! He has been lots of times to taverns and to dives and with whores. This is what he has to boast of!"

This embarrassed the tsar. "Nobody asked you, stick to old women's business, keep quiet! At least he donated twelve barrels of gold for the cathedral and you gave only a single silver ruble. He outdid you all."

But anyway, you have to boast. "Yes," he said, "I do have something to boast of. It's something worth hearing. When you chose me to be governor, you wanted me to go about with a coachman. We went out of town to a certain stockade. A dark red fox was running alongside this stockade. I had my father's fine pistol. When I fired it, it knocked the fox off its feet. But when I ran up to it, it jumped up and ran away. I loaded it a second time. We rode on. Another dark red fox came running by. When I fired, it knocked the fox off its feet. (I hit it, I mean.) When I ran up to it, wanting to grab it by the ears, it ran away, this one too.

"A third time I loaded. We rode on further. Again we encountered a fox, a third time. When I fired, it knocked the fox off its feet and it didn't even wriggle. Then what did I do? I took off the skin, so the flesh could still run away."

Everyone clapped and said, "He's lying!" (They didn't believe him.)

"Now I could show you in practice how it was, with the skin and the flesh!"

"It would be fine if you could show us, then we might more easily believe you." At that moment he took out the petticoat, and it was the saint's day petticoat of Miliutin's daughter. "So then, with my father's pistol I shot her. See, a bit flew off!"

Then the tsar grasped the whole business. He ordered the general to leave and the governor sat with Miliutin's daughter. "As you knew how to take the maiden's honor, then she should be your bride." So the general left and he went over to her at the table. Her mother and father were not very quickly happy about it, but there was nothing they could do.

In the morning they were married and they had a great feast.

A–T 611*

336. About Ivan the Russian Merchant

There was once this merchant. He had a son, Ivan. This merchant had trade connections with other merchants. Once they agreed among themselves where they would go to procure their goods. And a merchant neighbor had a daughter and they wanted to marry her off to Ivan.

But once in a dream an old man appeared to Ivan and said, "Marry a poor girl; there'll be no advantage to taking a rich one."

Ivan woke up in the morning and told his father, but that didn't please his father at all, and he was even more determined to marry Ivan off. Ivan decided to set himself up as a junk dealer and go out looking for a bride of his own taste.

He wandered for a long time throughout the world, but he couldn't find anyone. Then once he went into a village and in a house on the outskirts there lived a girl named Marusia. He asked to spend the night there and he was attracted to Marusia.

Ivan unharnessed his horses and the woman put on the samovar. They ate something, they drank, and Ivan courted Marusia. She agreed to be his wife. Within two weeks they held the wedding.

Ivan didn't want to live in the house. There was nothing to do but go to work. He set himself up as a foreman on a building site. After a few months he had to go enlist people to work in order to fulfill the procurement plan. He went away and the very next day a regiment of soldiers came into the village, and the commander asked to be billeted in Marusia's house.

She took a liking to the commander and after three days and three nights Marusia went away to Moscow with the commander. There they took an apartment and lived quite happily. Ivan came home and saw that Marusia was gone. He took stock and then set out to find her. He walked for three months and three days. Once in the forest he met an old man who said to him, "You are looking for your death, but I'll help you."

When he had said this, he gave him a kerchief and a little vial and taught him what to do with them. Ivan went on further and met a soldier from the regiment whose commander was the one with whom Marusia had gone away. The soldier told Ivan everything. "Let's exchange clothes," Ivan said to the soldier. "I'll go to your unit and make short work of them all."

So they exchanged clothes and Ivan went to the unit and lived in the barracks where the soldier had lived. He worked there and did all that was required of him.

Once Marusia had a dream that her husband, Ivan, was serving there. She told it to the commander. The commander didn't believe it but Marusia insisted. "Form up all the soldiers, and I'll recognize Ivan."

So the commander ordered all the soldiers to appear in ranks and Marusia recognized Ivan. The commander looked at him and said to Marusia, "That soldier has been serving here a long time, for three years. I know him."

But Marusia kept insisting she was right and she proposed to the commander, "Say that you are going away, but hide under the cot. Then put Ivan on watch around this house."

That's what the commander did: he slid under the cot and put Ivan on watch at the gates. Ivan stood on guard. And Marusia cleared away the table, put out the samovar, and invited Ivan in to her. He felt that something wasn't right. He called a soldier and gave him the kerchief and vial, and said, "I sense that I am going to my death. If something happens to me, pour a little water on me from this vial and wipe me with this kerchief." Then he went into the house to Marusia. Ivan ate a little, drank some tea, and talked about himself.

The commander listened and listened, came out from under the cot, aimed his pistol at Ivan, arrested him, and put him in the guardhouse. A military tribunal sentenced him to be shot.

They shot Ivan and buried him in the steppe, and they put guards beside his grave. But Ivan's comrades thought about how to help him. And then once they got those guards drunk such that they went into a deep sleep.

The soldier dug up Ivan out of the grave, sprinkled him with the water out of the vial, wiped him with the kerchief, and Ivanushka came back to life. Then Ivanushka went away to wander throughout the world. He bought himself a rifle and a dog, and he went into the forest. There he dug himself a dugout and lived there in the forest. To his dugout he nailed a sign: "Here lives a famous doctor."

At that time the tsar's daughter fell ill and no one could cure her. Once the royal servants were hunting in the forest and they saw the sign on the dugout. They decided to drop in to Ivanushka's to spend the night and find out everything about how he cured people. Ivan listened to them and decided to undertake this wild scheme—he would try to cure the tsarevna and take half the tsardom for it.

The guests spent the night with Ivan and in the morning they set off for Moscow to report everything to the tsar. The tsar heard them and sent for Ivan. They brought Ivan before the tsar. Then he went to take a look at the tsarevna. He examined her and promised to cure her.

So he went into the tsarevna in her room, splashed a little water on her from his vial, wiped her with his kerchief, and everything was in order. The tsarevna began getting well and soon had completely recovered.

The tsar asked the tsarevna about rewarding the doctor and she wished to get married to him. Ivan decided to marry her, too. Three days later they had the wedding, and the tsar gave him half the tsardom. The young newlyweds lived there for a week, then a second, but Ivan was bored with nothing to do. He asked to be made commander of all the forces. The tsar gave the order, just as Ivan wished it. Ivan served for a month, then a second, and in the third he decided to go inspect all the forces.

Once he was riding across the steppe and he saw some guards standing there. Ivan asked them, "Why are you standing here, what are you guarding?"

They answered him, "A soldier is buried here. Somebody they shot. The commander has ordered that we guard his grave. He is laughing at us."

Ivan went to the commander and asked him, "Can it be as I have heard, that dead people come to life and come out of the grave? I order you to open the grave."

They went and opened it, but there was nobody in it. Ivan said to the commander, "Why are you tormenting them, making them guard over this empty ground?" The commander of the unit thought about it deeply. Then Ivan ordered him to summon his wife. And Marusia recognized Ivan in the supreme commander. She fell at Ivan's feet and begged his forgiveness. But Ivan wouldn't forgive either one of them.

"Summon a tribunal and shoot them both," Ivan ordered, "because they have tormented people."

They were shot and buried in a single grave. And Ivan made his friends—those who had saved his life—commanding officers. And since then everything has been fine everywhere.

A–T 612

337. The Two Brothers

In Maksimovka there lived two brothers. The older one was rich, but the other one, the younger one, was poor. Poverty is poverty, and the poor one had a heap of children as well. The rich one had a wife. And they lived prosperously. Once when he was hungry, the poor brother went to his older brother for some grain, or to take a loan until fall. He came and his brother wasn't there, he had gone into the town to make some purchases. Only his wife was at home. "So it is," said the poor brother, "I came to my brother to borrow a little grain."

The rich brother's wife began to shout at him: "Go to the devil's mother, that's grain enough for you!" So the poor brother went away with nothing.

He came home and his wife asked him, "Well, did you bring some grain?"

"Of course not," he said, "my brother wasn't at home and his wife sent me to the devil's mother."

"Well," said his mistress, "Go and look for her, perhaps you will find the devil's mother." The peasant thought and thought about it and then he set off to look for the devil's wife.

He walked and walked through the forest and then he saw a little hut. He went in and saw an old man sitting there and he was rummaging about in some lapti. "God help you, grandfather, will you let me in to spend the night?"

"Why, of course," said the old man, "you may stay here. There's a place to sleep." The peasant stayed. They started talking over supper—how, what, and where.

"So, it's like this," said the poor man. "I am going to look for the devil's mother. You don't know where she lives, do you?"

"I don't know," said the old man, "but my brother lives here in the forest and he knows. Go straight on along this road and you will find his hut."

The peasant slept through the night and in the morning when it was barely light he set off to the other old man. He walked the whole day and toward evening he came upon a very poor little hut and in it a very old little old man. "What do you need, my good fellow?"

"Well, such and so, and I am looking for the devil's mother. I was at your brother's and he told me that you know where she lives."

"Of course, I know where she lives. You go along this road and you will come to a crossroads and wait there. She will come. But set off right away. By morning you should somehow be able to reach her."

Even though the peasant was tired, there was nothing to be done and so he set off. Toward morning, it is true, he came to the crossroads, and he sat down to wait. Then he saw some old woman coming along and she asked him, "Where are you going, little peasant?"

"I am going to look for the devil's mother."

"And what do you need of the devil's mother?"

"Well, you see, I have this rich brother. I went to him and asked for some grain, but he wasn't home, and his wife said to me, 'Go to the devil's mother!' So I set out to look for her."

"Well, my little peasant, I am that very devil's mother. Go along, not far from here is Maiorov's Mill. There you will find an upturned boat. You will get there in the evening. Lie down and listen all night, and watch out that you don't go to sleep." The peasant ran off to the mill, got there and lay down.

In the night the peasant sensed that someone had come to the boat and sat down. Afterward, two more came. One asked the other, "Well, what have you done today?"

"Oh, I did a great deal," he said, "I fixed one rich man. In one place I took some money, a whole trunk full, and hid it somewhere else, and no one will ever find it because you have to dig for it with a cock's leg and not a shovel."

"That's good," said his friends. "Well, what did you do?" they asked the second one.

"I also did a good deed. I let the water out from the miller's dam and he will never fill the pond up again, no matter how much effort he puts into it, because you can only fill up the pond with an aspen branch, and he won't guess that."

"That is also very good," said the devils.

"And I," said the very oldest of the devils, "I spoiled a merchant's daughter such that no one will ever be able to cure her. And this is the only way to cure her: at the priest's altar there is a small stand and underneath that stand is the communion loaf on which a frog sits. If you ask the priest for some of the communion loaf and three times he gives you a piece, then she will be healed. Now who would guess that?" The devils finished their conversation and went away.

The peasant climbed out from beneath the boat and went home to his wife. "Well, wife," he said, "let's hitch up the horse and go after some money. You only need to catch a chicken. Then we'll butcher it."

"What for?"

"You'll find out." So the peasant cut the leg off a chicken, harnessed his horse, and he and his wife set out after some money. When they had ridden out of the village, the peasant began digging up the earth with the cock's leg and he soon struck the trunk full of money and off they went home.

"Just a minute," the peasant said, "I'll get some flour." So he went to the well. He saw that at the dam about fifty people were trying to dam up the pond with manure and trees, but the business was going nowhere. "God help you!" said the peasant, "what are you doing?"

"Well," said the miller, "we have been trying to dam up the pond for two days but we can't do it and we are exhausted."

"Let me dam up the pond for you," said the peasant, "but I need only five workers and five carts, and I will do everything."

"Oh, go on with you! We've got five men working to dam it and can't manage it."

"Let me, it's my business."

"Very well, dam it up," said the miller, "but if you make it worse, I shall take you to court."

So the peasant detailed five carts to the forest after aspen branches and he sent the fifty men off. They soon brought the aspen branches back and immediately dammed up the pond. The mill started going.

"Well," said the miller, "for this I shall reward you with grain." He hitched up ten carts, loaded them with flour and said, "Take this for yourself, peasant." So now the peasant also had grain.

So then he went off to the merchant's shop to buy some goods. The merchant was complaining that, well, you see, his daughter was withering away and no healer was able to cure her. It was obvious, she would die.

"What will you give me if I cure her?"

"What, are you joking? How can you cure her if not a single doctor can?"

"I will cure her," the peasant said brazenly. "What will you give me?"

"I would give you all the goods in the shop and a thousand rubles more."

"Very well. Go to the priest and ask him for the communion loaf that is lying beneath the little altar stand—the one with the frog on it."

The merchant went to the priest. The priest said that there was no such communion loaf there and that he wouldn't go to the church. So the merchant hung his head and came back to the peasant all sad. "Whatever," he said, "the priest won't give it to me."

"You give him a hundred rubles and he'll find it."

So that is what the merchant did and he brought the communion loaf to the peasant. The peasant cut the loaf into three pieces and gave the merchant's daughter one that evening. In the morning he came and asked, "Well, how is your health, merchant's daughter?"

"It's better," she said.

The peasant gave her another chunk. In the evening he came and she was still better. He gave her the third chunk and in the morning the merchant's daughter was already completely recovered. So the merchant gave the peasant what he had promised and now the poor peasant had become richer than his brother.

But his brother found out that his brother was now the richer and sent his wife to find out how he had become so wealthy. The peasant told her everything, just as it had been. His brother's wife became envious because the poor brother had become richer by following her advice. She decided to find the devil's mother. Whether she searched a long time I do not know, but she did find her. The devil's mother sent her beneath that very same boat.

The woman lay down and waited. The devils came flying up and said, "By some miracle, last time somebody apparently overheard us. All our deeds were disclosed. Is someone perhaps listening underneath the boat? Well, let's just have a look!" They raised up the boat and saw the woman lying there. "Aha!" said the devils, "this is who has been overhearing us," and they drowned her in the river. In that very pond the peasant had dammed up.

A–T 613

338. The Everlasting Piece

A soldier was leaving the service. He walked all day until evening. Night came. The soldier climbed up into a tall oak. Soon he saw an old man beneath the oak with hair as white as the moon and a big white beard. The old man went up to the oak where the soldier was sitting and sounded a horn. Out jumped twelve wolves. The old man took a loaf from his bag, divided it into thirteen parts, and gave one piece to each wolf. The remaining piece he gave to the soldier. The soldier took the piece of bread and began eating it greedily. But however much he ate, the piece was not diminished. At dawn the old man once more sounded his horn and the wolves ran away. The soldier climbed down from the oak and walked on. Soon he came to a village and he asked a rich peasant to spend the night. The soldier went into the hut, sat down at the table, and decided to eat after his journey. He took out the piece of bread and ate. The peasant saw that the piece was not diminished. "Soldier, sell me that piece," said the peasant.

"I won't sell it," answered the soldier, "it's an everlasting piece; with it I'll never be in want; I'll always be full."

The peasant began questioning the soldier as to where he had acquired the everlasting piece, and the soldier told him. Having spent the night, the soldier left.

Then that evening the rich peasant went into the forest, climbed up into the oak, and waited for the old man. Soon the old man came, went up to the oak, and sounded his horn. The twelve wolves came running. The old man drew a loaf out of his bag, divided it into eleven parts, and gave them to the wolves. For one wolf there was no bread. The old man pointed at the peasant with his finger. The wolf leapt into the oak and tore up the rich peasant.

A–T 613D*

339. The Louse's Skin

There lived a tsar and tsaritsa. They had one daughter. One splendid time he sat down next to her and began to search on her head. And he found a louse on her head. He put the louse in a tank and for three years he reared the louse and he grew it up on a cow. And then he killed the louse and took the skin off it and tacked it to the wall. Then he drove all from old to young before him and said, "To the one who finds out whose skin this is I'll give my daughter." Well, the daughter was on display! (The daughter was like mine, she was beautiful.) But no one could guess. Why, who would guess that it was a louse's skin?

The daughter pleased one young, handsome and good lad, and she liked him, too. How could she let him know!? But he was far away from her. Near her there stood an old man, old, really old. And she said to the old man very quietly, "Old man, whisper to that handsome man standing there that it's a louse's skin."

The old man kept standing a while and he thought, "Shall I pass it on or not?" And then he said to the tsar himself, "Lord Tsar, you're witless, it's a louse's skin!"

"Well," the tsar said, "you've guessed it, my daughter is yours, take her away!" The daughter really didn't want to go, but her father's word had been given and she was given to the old man.

And so they played out the wedding and they crossed the river in a boat, the daughter and the old man, going home. He sat on one gunnel and she on the other. Because she didn't love him, she shoved and pushed against the side and he went into the river.

Off he went and he drowned. But he had made it so that a voice would come from her stomach. Whatever she said would be repeated immediately afterward. She crossed to the other side of the river, went out onto the shore and said, "Oh, how beautiful the grass is!" And the same thing came out of her stomach, "Oh, how beautiful the grass is!" She went on. She went and came to some large fields. She said, "Oh, what big fields!" And in her belly it was repeated: "Oh, what big fields!" She went into a village and went up to the tsar's palace. They asked her, "Where are you from?" She said nothing but made signs to say, "Take me on as a servant girl." So she lived there for three years and said not a thing. Now this tsar, he had a son, Tsarevich Ivan. And he was ready to get married. He liked her and she liked him but because she was dumb, he didn't take her and began courting another girl.

So she started to work in the kitchen for the wedding. For a royal wedding you need lots of everything. So she cooked up a kettle of fatted meat and said to herself, "Oh, how tasty!" And from her belly came the echo, "Oh, how tasty!" She said to him, "It's tasty, come out and try it!" He came out like a little child, a little man, and sat on the edge of the table to taste it, but she shoved him off the edge into the soup, and he fell in and was cooked. And in the kitchen she began saying everything, and no one spoke from her belly again.

And so Ivan Tsarevich got the wedding party together. They summoned all the guests to come. And the servant girl carried the various dishes to and from the table. And the young couple sat at the table, Tsarevich Ivan and his bride. And the servant girl said, "Please eat, all you guests!" Ivan Tsarevich turned his eyes to her, three years she had lived there and not spoken, and now she was serving the guests. He thought to himself, "What is this? If she had spoken earlier, I would long since have married her," he mused.

And then for a long time he lived with her—the one whom he had married. But then he drove her away and married the servant girl and began living with her. And she was already a tsarevna, so they lived together and were happy, Ivan Tsarevich, the tsar's son and the tsarevna, a tsar's daughter. But she had drowned her old man!

A–T 621

340. The Snake Groom

A certain prince put a flea in a bread yeast batter and waited until it had grown to weigh about a kilogram. And the flea grew to about a kilogram. Then they skinned the flea and summoned some guests. Whoever could guess what kind of meat they had would marry the prince's daughter.

One said it was raven's flesh, but a dispute broke out and others said it was not. A third also couldn't guess and so they all departed.

In the morning the daughter went out for a walk and she met a friend on the bridge. The friend asked her, "Didn't they find a groom for you last night?"

"No."

"Why not?"

"No one could guess what kind of meat it was."

"And what kind was it?"

"It was flea meat."

At that very time a snake was sitting under the bridge, listening. But it wasn't really a snake, it was a cursed man. He climbed into the palace to the prince and told him what kind of meat it was.

So the prince gave him his daughter in marriage. She started to get ready for the wedding, to say farewell to all. She ran to her horse. "My dear horse, I am so sorry to leave you."

The horse answered her, "Take a comb with you."

She ran to the pigs and began crying, and she said, "Pigs, oh my pigs, I am so sorry to leave you." And they gave her a pair of brushes.

She ran to the bulls. And they gave her a horn. The snake took her and led her into the forest. They rode for a long time. Finally they came up to his burrow. The snake opened the doors and said, "Crawl in!"

"No, you crawl in first."

They quarreled for a long time and finally the snake crawled in. He had just managed to do this when she slammed the doors shut and ran away.

His brothers chased after her. She looked around and they were already close. Then she remembered the presents. She threw down the comb and so many horses appeared that they trampled all the snakes. Again she ran. And again they were chasing her. She threw down a brush. And there appeared many pigs. They started eating the snakes. Again she ran. Again they chased her. And she threw the horn. And there were many bulls. They butted all the snakes. She ran away and started living with her very own father.

A–T 621*

341. About Ivanushka

There lived and dwelt this widow and she had this son Ivanushka. They lived poorly and the mother fed her son with her own labors. And then when he was about twenty years old, he stated to his mother, "Mother, I am going to go out looking for some work for myself." His mother let him go and he went off looking for work. Ivanushka walked and walked and then he saw a priest standing there. "Well friend, my friend, you wouldn't be needing a hired man, would you?"

"What do you mean, I wouldn't need one? Of course, I need a hired man."

"Then take me on and I'll work for you."

"But how much will you be wanting from me for a year?"

"I won't take a lot, for a year just two whacks to the forehead."

The priest laughed and thought, "What a fool! This will be cheap labor. I can rely on that. And I've got a worker for sure." So he led the hired man home. And they went into his house and the priest said to his wife, "Well, my dear, I've found this hired man for you."

The priest's wife said, "Well, my dear hired man, run and fetch some water."

Ivanushka took a bucket and set off and then he brought them some water. The priest said, "He's a fine worker, quite a lad."

Time passed. The rye began to ripen. When it had ripened, they cut it and stacked it. Some more time passed and the priest said to Ivanushka, "Good worker, go to the threshing floor now and start the thrashing. So Ivanushka got ready, took a little bundle of bread, and set off. He came to the threshing floor, put down his bundle, and went off into the nearby forest, cut two oaks, tied them end to end, and quickly thrashed the whole stack. He dragged the straw off to someplace else, and winnowed the rye. Then he went back to the little father, the priest. He went up to him and said, "Well, my dear little father, I've thrashed it all."

The priest found that difficult to believe. He got the carts ready. "Well, hired man, let's go."

So they rode off to the threshing floor, where the priest was amazed by the oak flail, even frightened. So they loaded the grain onto the carts and brought it in and stored it in the sheds. Then the priest started thinking, "Things are bad here." He went to the next-door neighbors and told them about Ivanushka's work and asked them, "What should I do now?"

His neighbors said to him, "Well, good little father, send him into the woods for some oak and there a bear will gobble him up and he won't come back." That cheered the priest up a little. He went home and said, "Well, my dear worker, will you go wherever I send you?"

"I will, little father."

So the priest's wife got a little bread for him and Ivanushka got ready and set off toward the forest. He got there and tied his horse to a bush, and then he started pulling up oaks. A bear came up to him and pawed him on his chest with his paws. Ivanushka gave him a whack on his forehead. The bear sat down and let out a roar. Ivanushka said, "If you're going to yell, I'll whack you again. Now help me pull up this oak."

So the bear and Ivanushka put their shoulders to it and pulled it out by the roots. Then they loaded it onto the cart. Ivanushka hitched the bear up to his horse and they moved off. He came to the yard and he shouted, "Oh, little father, open the gates. Let's deal with this oak." The priest went out and sat down in his fright.

He said, "Bring it in and deal with it, and I'll go and tell them to get something ready for you to eat." He went into the hut and said to his wife, "Oh, my dear, now what are we to do? The hired man has come back, and with a bear, too."

So Ivanushka dealt with the oak, fed and watered the horse and bear, and the bear he put in a separate place. He went into the house, ate his dinner, and lay down to rest. And the priest went to his nearby neighbors and told them about Ivanushka. The neighbors all began giving the priest advice as to how to get ride of Ivanushka once and for all.

"Send him off to a far away and dark forest and he'll go and never come back. In the forest it's dark and there are lots of bears there and as soon as they see a human they'll rip him to bits."

So this made the priest a little bit happier. He came home and said, "Well, hired man, will you go anywhere I send you?"

"I will, little father."

"Then go to a far away, dark forest. I need a dry oak."

"Alright, I'll do it."

So Ivanushka got ready and rode away. He rode and rode until he rode to the dark forest. He tied up his horse and went off to choose a dry oak. He found the dry oak and started pulling it out. A bear came up to him and gave him a bear hug. Ivanushka gave him a whack and the bear started roaring. Ivanushka said, "If you shout, I'll strike you again. Give me some help."

So he and the bear set to and soon pulled the oak out by its roots. They loaded it onto the cart and Ivanushka harnessed the bear and horse to the cart and rode off. He rode and rode and finally rode up to the priest's yard where he shouted, "Heh, little father! Open the gates!"

The priest came out and started. What was this! He had come riding in on another bear. Now what was the priest to do? He said, "Well, my dear Ivanushka! You take care of things and I'll order them to get dinner ready for you." The priest went into the house and said to his wife, "Now what are we to do, my dear? He's come in on another bear. Get some dinner ready for him and I'll go around to the neighbors for a chat, to get their advice as to how to get out of this mess."

Ivanushka finished his work, put his horse in the stables, the bear in with the other bear, and then he went into the house, ate, and lay down to rest. The neighbors gave the priest their advice. "Send him beyond the several rivers and lakes, dear friend, and there on the river is a mill and devils work the mill there in the water. You send him there. He'll go and never come back. And that's the way to be rid of him."

This made the priest a little happier. He came and said to his hired man, "Dear hired man, I'll send you to just one more place and you'll go there for me. I heard that beyond several rivers and lakes there's a mill and they say that this mill grinds very fine flour. Load up a cart of rye and go over there and get it ground for us."

Ivanushka loaded up the cart and set off. He rode for a day, he rode for a second, and finally he got there. He looked and saw these devils fooling around in the water. He rode up closer and one little devil popped out of the water at him. Ivanushka gave him a whack on the forehead and he went back into the water with a cry. Then another little devil popped out and Ivanushka gave him a whack, too, and that one flew off. The devils saw that things were bad! They asked Ivanushka, "What do you need, young man?"

"I need some rye ground really finely."

"Well give it to us, we'll grind it."

So they took the sacks from the cart and dragged them into the water. After a while they dragged the flour back. Ivanushka loaded up the sacks and set off back. He got to a little bridge and a little devil leapt out of the water and frightened his horse. She shied to one side and broke the rear axle. Ivanushka caught the little devil, shook him up, and said, "Because of you that axle is broken. Now you are going to push the cart along the entire way. If you stop, I'll kill you."

The little devil saw that there was no way out. He took hold of the axle and they set off and the dust rose from them in a column. Ivanushka got to the priest's gates and shouted, "Dear little father, open the gates! I've brought the flour."

The priest went out and saw how he'd got there and he was even more timid. "What can I do now? And his work contract is almost up."

Ivanushka dragged in the sacks, put his horse in the stables, and the little devil in with the bears. Then he went into the house to eat. The priest went around out of his mind and didn't know what to do, how to save himself from this hired hand. Once more he went to his neighbors and they tried to talk him into this and that. They advised him: "We've heard, dear friend, that in this certain tsardom there's a very strong fighter and he defeats all. Send your hired man there. Give him some money for the road so that he'll be happy and he won't come back from there."

Well, the priest was happier now. He went home and said, "Dear Ivanushka, my fine hired man! I want to send you to this place—not for work but to have fun. I've heard that in this certain tsardom there's this fighter and he wants to defeat you. Go over there and fight him. I'd like to know whether you can defeat him."

Well, there was nothing for Ivanushka to do, he'd just have to go. He started to get ready. He drove out the light carriage and started hitching up his team. He put the little devil in the middle and the bears at either side, at post. Then he set off. He rode through the street and not only dust but rocks flew to all sides, banging against the windows and doors. From sheer fright people took refuge in their huts.

Ivanushka arrived at that tsardom where the fighter lived. He went up to the fighter and greeted him. The fighter asked him, "Well, young man, why have you come here?"

"I've come to fight with you. They say you're ready to take me on!"

"So it's you, is it. I've been getting ready for you for a long time. Shall we box or shall we wrestle?"

Ivanushka said, "Let's fight with blows."

"What? Are you mocking me?"

"Why should I mock you? We'll first go at it with blows and then we'll see. Let's go out there to that lookout tower. That looks like a good spot."

The fighter went up onto the tower first and Ivanushka came after him. They started drawing lots to see who would go first. The fighter won. He whacked Ivanushka in the forehead, but Ivanushka didn't even flinch.

Then it was Ivanushka's turn to go. When Ivanushka gave him his whack, the fighter turned and crashed down from the tower. And he refused to fight any further—Ivanushka had defeated him.

Ivanushka climbed down from the tower, harnessed the little devil and the bears, and set off on the journey back home. Already as he was riding along, rumors got to the priest that he had defeated the fighter. The priest was dejected. "What was to be done? What was to be done? Where can we escape to?" And he and his wife began getting together some provisions for the road because they had decided to flee. He'd have to pay off Ivanushka in just three days. They got ready what they needed, stuffed it in some bags, and put them down on the stove.

So then in Ivanushka came and they fed him and he lay down to rest. The priest and his wife said, "Dear Ivanushka, for some reason our chimney has started to smoke. Would you clean it?"

"Alright, I'll clean it in the evening."

It started to get dark. The priest and his wife went out somewhere and Ivanushka emptied everything from one of their bags into another. Then he climbed into the bag and tied himself in. The priest and his wife came back and saw that there was nobody in the house and they thought that the hired man was cleaning the chimney. They took the bags, flung them over their shoulders and set off. They walked and walked and they said, "When our hired man has cleaned the chimney, we'll already be far away and he won't catch up to us."

They wanted to sit down and take a rest. But Ivanushka in the bag shouted, "I see you, I see you!"

"Oh, my friend, we've gone far away, but he still can see us from the roof. We'll have to go still further."

They walked and they walked, and they were completely tired. "Let's rest."

But he shouted, "I see you, I see you."

"Oh, how far he can see!"

They wanted to go on further but they were completely out of strength. The priest sat down. He couldn't go on. "Well, my love, let's have a bite to eat and then go on."

He untied the bag, the one that Ivanushka was in. Ivanushka came out of the bag and gave them a whack and they were no more. They flew off God knows where.

So Ivanushka went back to the priest's house, brought his mama there, and started living and prospering and looking around for a bride.

A–T 650A

342. Ivanko the Bear's Son

In a certain village there lived and dwelt a wealthy peasant and his wife. Once the wife went into the woods after the milk mushroom, got lost, and stumbled into a bear's den. The bear kept her with him, and after some time, a long time or a short time, he had a son with her: down to the waist he was like a man but below the waist he was a bear. His mother called him Ivanko the Bearlet. Years went by, and when Ivan grew up he wanted to go away with his mother and live with the people in the village; they waited until the bear went to an apiary, got ready, and ran away. They ran and ran until they managed to get to the place. The peasant saw his wife and rejoiced—he had long since ceased to hope that she would somehow return home. And then he looked at the son and asked, "And what sort of monster is this?" His wife told him everything, how it had all taken place, how she had lived in his den with the bear and borne him a son: up to the belt a human but from the belt up a bear.

"Well, Ivan Bearson," the peasant said, "go out in back and slaughter a sheep; we've got to prepare a meal for you."

"And which should I slaughter?"

"Oh, the one that stares at you." So Ivanko Bearson took a knife and set out for the backyard and he shouted at all the sheep and all of them stared directly at him. So Bearson immediately went and slaughtered the lot, took off their skins and went to ask where to store the meat and skins.

"What?" roared the peasant at him, "I commanded you to slaughter just one sheep and you've butchered them all!"

"No, father, you ordered me to slaughter the one that stared at me; I went into the backyard and they each and every one stared at me; they just gazed away at me!"

"Oh, you're a bright one! Go on and take all the meat and the skins into the shed and keep watch by the door of the shed all night so that thieves don't steal it or dogs eat it up!"

"Very well, I'll stand watch."

It was as if on purpose that a storm gathered that very night and a heavy rain fell. Ivanko Bearson broke down the door to the shed, carried it off to the bathhouse and stayed there the rest of the night. It was a dark night, and thieves were about. The shed was open and there was no guard, so why not take what you want? In the morning the peasant woke up and went to have a look to see whether all was well. As it were, nothing remained. Some of it the dogs had eaten, or the thieves had carted away. So he started looking for his watchman and found him in the bathhouse, and he started cursing him more than ever before.

"Oh, father! What am I guilty of?" said Ivanko Bearson, "You yourself ordered me to stand watch at the door and I stood watch by the door. Here it is! No thieves stole it nor did any dogs eat it."

"What's to be done with such a fool?" the peasant thought, "if he lives another couple of months, I'll be ruined. How can I get him off my hands?" So he set to thinking. The next day he sent Ivanko Bearson to a lake to weave a rope of sand. In that lake were a lot of unclean spirits—let the devils drag him into their pools!

So Ivanko Bearson set off for the lake and he sat down on the shore and started weaving a rope out of sand. Suddenly a baby devil popped up out of the water. "What are you doing, Bearson?"

"What? Oh, I'm weaving a rope, I'm going to rumple up the lake and scrunch up you devils—because you're living in our pools and you don't pay any taxes!"

"Wait a minute, little Bearson! I'll just run and tell grandfather." And with that one word he dove into the water. In about five minutes he popped up again: "Grandfather said that if you can outrace me, he'll pay the taxes, but if I outrace you, he has commanded me to drag you into our pool."

"Oh, you're a fast one! Well, where are you going to outrace me?" says Ivanko Bearson. "I have a grandson (!), he was just born yesterday, and even he can outrace you! Wouldn't you rather go against him?"

"And where is this grandson?"

"Why he's over there lying beneath that fallen tree," the Bearson answered as he shouted to the hare: "Hey, Hare, don't blow it now!" And the hare tore off like a flash into the steppe and in an instant disappeared from view. The little devil was after him, but where had he gone? He was already half a verst behind. "Now if you like," Bearson said to him, "let's you and me run; only this time, brother, with the condition that if you fall behind, I'll beat you to death!"

"What?!" said the little devil, and he dove into the pool.

A little while later he jumped out of the water again and brought out grandfather's cast-iron crutch. "Grandfather said that if you can throw this crutch higher than I can, he'll pay the taxes."

"Well, you throw it first."

The little devil threw the crutch so high that it was scarcely visible. It flew back to the ground with a terrible roar and went halfway into the earth. "Now you throw it."

Bearson put a hand on the crutch but he couldn't move it. "Wait," he said, "that little cloud will come up soon and I'll throw it up on it."

"Oh, no! How would grandfather be without his crutch?" said the imp and he grabbed that devil's club and threw it back into the water.

A little bit later he popped up again: "Grandfather said that if you can carry this horse around the lake one more time than I can, he'll pay his taxes. If not, you go into the pool."

"That's a fine thing, off you go!" The little devil flung the horse on his back and dragged it around the lake; he carried it around about ten times and then the cursed thing got tired—sweat was pouring off his snout!

"Well, now it's my turn," said Ivanko Bearson, he got on the horse and rode it around the lake, and he rode it and rode it until the horse fell.

"Hey, brother, what is this then?" he asks the little devil. "Well," the unclean one says, "you've carried more than I by far, and between your legs as well! I couldn't carry the horse even once that way. How much tax do we have to pay?"

"This is how much: fill my hat with gold and work a year for me as a servant, and that will be enough for me."

So the little devil ran off for the gold and Ivan Bearson cut a hole in his hat and placed it over a deep pit. The little devil carried and carried gold and poured and poured it into the hat. He worked a full day and only toward the end did he fill the hat up. Ivanko Bearson got a cart, loaded it with the money, and drove the little devil home hitched to the cart. "Get rich old man, here's a servant for you and much gold, too."

A–T 650A + 1006* + 1009 + 1045 + 1072 + 1063 + 1082 + 1130

343. The Warriors

There lived and dwelt a priest and he served in a church. Once he went outside to take a shit. Along came a little goat and butted him in the ass. The priest jumped up, grabbed the goat by the horns, and threw him into the churchyard. Then he ran into his house without pulling up his trousers and shouted, "Oh my ass! Oh my ass! I'm feeling really great! I grabbed that kid-goat and threw him into the churchyard. Wife! Bake some breads for a journey. I'm feeling really strong and I'll go to war." So his wife baked some bread for his journey, packed a bag, which the priest took and then he set off.

He came to a river where a peasant was standing in the water, waving his beard in the water and catching fish with his mouth. The priest said, "Good health, peasant."

He replied, "Good health, priest."

"Carry me across the river."

"How should I carry you? Pleshko the warrior was just walking by, and he took my wife away from me. He said to let no one else pass."

"Let me pass. I'll catch up to Pleshko, kill him, and bring back your wife."

So the peasant stood up and let the priest grab hold of his beard. Then he took the priest over the river and the priest asked him, "What's your name?"

"My name is Usynka the warrior."

So the priest went off along the road and he came up to a peasant standing in the road, braiding a barricade. There was no way to pass him other than to take apart the barricade and make a gate. "Let me go through, peasant."

"How can I let you through? Pleshko the warrior passed by here and took away my wife, and he ordered that no one should pass."

"Let me pass and I'll kill Pleshko the warrior and bring back your wife." The peasant moved the barricade aside, the priest passed through, and asked, "What is your name?"

"My name is Elinka the warrior," he said.

So the priest ran along the road and right up to where a peasant was standing, holding two mountains in his hands, and he was squeezing them. There was no way to pass unless he would move them apart and make a gate. "Let me pass, peasant!"

"No, I can't let you pass. Pleshko the warrior passed by here and took my wife away from me. And he ordered that no one should pass."

"Let me pass and I'll catch up to Pleshko and kill him, then I'll bring back your wife." So the peasant moved his hands apart and the priest passed through. He asked, "What is your name?"

And the peasant answered, "I am called Gorynka the warrior."

So then the priest ran on ahead and he caught up with Pleshko the warrior on the road. Pleshko was lying there asleep, and he had been playing around with Usynka's wife. Elinka's wife was standing at his feet, swatting mosquitoes, and Gorynka's wife was swatting mosquitoes at his head. The priest ran into the forest and found a pole of an appropriate size and then he came back and hit Pleshko on the head. Pleshko the warrior shouted, "You are doing a poor job of swatting mosquitoes, wife!"

So the priest had second thoughts about it. He ran back into the forest and brought back a larger pole, thinking, "That must have hurt him." He hit him alongside the head again. Pleshko said, "Those must be Russian mosquitoes biting me now."

He got up on his legs. The priest ran away in front of him. Pleshko came along behind him. The priest came to a hut and by the hut a lame old man was cutting wood. "Grandfather, hide me from Pleshko the warrior somewhere."

"Where shall I hide you?" The old man untied his sash and let his trousers down over his ass. "Here, climb in here and sit down." So in went the priest and he sat there while the old man went on cutting wood to heat his stove with.

Just then up came Pleshko the warrior and he asked, "Well, old man, have you seen that priest?"

"No, I haven't seen him." Pleshko the warrior started beating the old man and the old man lost his temper. He threw Pleshko onto the ground and kicked him with his lame leg. That killed Pleshko. Then he went into his hut and lit the stove. Then he lowered his trousers and let the priest out of his asshole. He sat him down beside him and asked him, "Where are you going?"

"I used to live at home and I served in the church. Then I went outside to shit and this goat came and butted me in the ass. I jumped up onto my feet, took the goat, and threw him into the churchyard. Then I thought, 'I have all this strength!' So I set off to go to war."

"All right, priest, listen as I tell you this tale: We were seven brothers and we went out into the steppe to go to war. A threatening dark stormcloud came upon us and we had no place to hide. Then we found this dry bone, a human skull. So we all went inside it, all seven brothers, and we sat down to play cards. A warrior came up and struck the skull with his whip. He said, 'I defeated you forty years ago and you still lie there without rotting.' He raised up the skull on his whip higher than the forest standing there and it fell to the earth and broke apart. My six brothers were all killed and my leg was crippled."

The old man fed the priest with bread and salt and showed him the way home. "Go back now and serve and pray in your old place, and don't use your strength to go to war." So the priest went home and brought the three wives with him. He left Gorynka's with him, then Elinka's with him, and he left Usynka's with him. He came home and lived and dwelt, and he prospered, making profit, and he is living even today.

A–T 650B

344. Little Boy Green

This took place in the city in Kiev at the prince's, at Vladimir's, where he was holding a feast. It was a most honorable feast and it was a joyful feast. All at the feast drank too much and all at the feast ate too much and all at the feast did begin boasting. The foolish man boasted of his good wife, the wise man boasted of his golden treasure, but there sat Little Boy Green, and he boasted of his fine horse. So then Prince Vladimir spoke, "If you have such a horse, I will assign you a task. You are to ride far, far away through the open steppes, to the meadows along the seas, and bring me from there a man who knows the tsar's thought, the ruler's thought."

So everyone went home from the happy feast to their own homes, but the little boy went home with his reckless head hung lower than his mighty shoulders. His mother and father met him and spoke these words to him, "Oh, our dear child, our beloved child, everyone has come away from the feast happy but you are walking along unhappy, with your head hung low."

And he spoke such words to them as these: "How am I supposed to be happy, mother and father, when the tsar has put upon me a very heavy, a very difficult task? He has ordered me to ride far, far away through the open steppes, to the meadows along the seas, and bring from there a man who knows the tsar's thought, the ruler's thought."

He saddled and bridled his good horse and rode off, did Little Boy Green. He rode one full day, then another, and finally a third. His horse became tired and wanted to eat, but they came upon a great military force, a defeated army. So many men had been killed that a black raven could not encircle them in a full day, nor could a fine young man ride round them on his horse. He went among the troops and found one living person, and he asked that living person, "Who fought this army and slaughtered it?"

"It was Ivan, the Russian warrior."

"And why did he fight and kill?"

"He fought that army and destroyed it because he needs to get married in our king's land and he would take the king's daughter by force because she will not marry him and her father won't give her away. So he came for her and beat that army." So the boy went away from that army and he rode a full day, then a second day, and finally a third, and he came upon a great military force, a defeated army. A black raven could not encircle them in a full day, nor could a fine young man ride round them on his horse—so many had been killed!

Once more he found a single living man and he asked that living person, "Who has defeated this army and killed everybody?" The living person said that it was Ivan the Russian warrior who had defeated the army and killed everybody. "And why did he fight and kill everyone?"

"He fought and killed everyone because he has to take our king's beautiful daughter by force because she won't go of her own free will and her father won't give her away."

So then Little Boy Green rode on for a full day, then a second, finally a third. He rode upon a great army, a vast force that had been defeated, and in the steppe he saw a white canvas tent standing there, and there was a pillar next to the tent, and there was a gold ring by the pillar with a fine horse attached, and a white banner unfurled. The horse had been given spring wheat. Little Boy Green got down from his good horse and let it go to the feed bag, and it pushed away Ivan the warrior's horse and the little boy's horse munched the spring wheat and Ivan the Russian warrior's horse had to wander over the green meadows nibbling the green grass.

The little boy went into the white tent and in the white tent Ivan the Russian warrior was sleeping a warrior's sleep. Little Boy Green saw a white oak barrel with some strong drink, with vodka, and in the barrel a gold goblet was floating upside down and there was an inscription on it: "This goblet is one and a half buckets." He decanted the first goblet and drank to the strong drink. He decanted a second goblet and drank to health, then he decanted a third and drank to foolishness. And now the little child was drunk, and he smashed up that white oak barrel with the strong drink, with the vodka, and he smashed the golden goblet and then he ruined the white oak tables with their various sweet dishes and more drinks, and he smashed the icon of the Savior, and he extinguished the candles of fine wax, and then he tumbled off to sleep.

Then Ivan the Russian warrior woke up and he was absolutely amazed: "What sort of idiot has ridden up here? He's let his horse in to my horse's fodder, opened up my white oak barrel with strong drink in it, smashed my golden goblet, ruined the white oak tables with the various sweet dishes and more drinks. He smashed the icons of the Savior and extinguished the fine wax candles." And he raised his sharp sword and got ready to cut off his reckless head, thinking that "It's the same thing to kill someone sleeping as the dead. He won't get out of my hands in any case."

But just then Little Boy Green woke up and sat on the bed. "Oh, Ivan the Russian warrior, I am now your guest. Give me something to drink!"

In response Ivan said to him, "You are not worth my wasting my drink on."

"How can that be? I am your guest!"

"You are no more a guest here than a bone from the open steppe. You're just worth nothing to a warrior."

And in reply he spoke these words, "You may be a warrior in your tent, but you are a useless hound in the steppe." So now Ivan saw that an unforeseen misfortune had arrived at his white tent. He took a goblet and ladled some water and then he took it to the little boy to drink. And when they had both drunk, the two warriors went into the open steppe to test each other's strength.

Little Boy Green set off at a fair pace and Ivan the Russian warrior at a full gallop, and they rode apart about a verst, and then they rode at each other and struck each other, but they didn't wound each other seriously, and so they rode apart two versts and rode at each other and struck each other again, but they didn't wound each other seriously. So the third time they rode three versts apart and then they came at each other, and Little Boy Green knocked the Russian warrior right out of his saddle and his horse pinned Ivan the Russian warrior down by his armor. So then Little Boy Green spoke these words, "God aided me to pin Ivan the Russian warrior with this dull lance." So then he asked him, "Which do you want, death or life?"

"Oh, little boy, formerly we had no quarrel with you and in the future there shall be none." Then Little Boy Green got down from his horse and took Ivan the Russian warrior by his white hands and raised him up on his shaky legs, kissed him on his sugary lips, and they called each other brothers. Little Boy Green was called the big brother, and Ivan the Russian warrior was the little brother, and then they rode to the white canvas tent, and there they began drinking and eating and making merry.

So Ivan the Russian warrior went to the king to get married and he invited his brother Little Boy Green to go along, and the king received them as good folk and they spent whole days feasting. Then Ivan the Russian warrior got married at the court of that king and Little Boy Green asked the king, "Would you happen to know someone who knows the thoughts of the tsar, his royal thoughts?"

The king found such a person beneath the red banner, and this person knew the tsar's thoughts. So then Little Boy Green took this person with him and conducted him to Prince Vladimir.

Then Prince Vladimir said, "You have served me in a great task and earned my friendship. For that friendship you will now take some towns and suburbs, and various districts." He did not stint himself the towns or suburbs or various districts.

And Prince Vladimir had a beautiful daughter, a princess, and so he said to Vladimir, "Give her to me in marriage, and then at your very end, give me your position!"

So then Prince Vladimir agreed to give his daughter to Little Boy Green and at his death his kingdom to his son-in-law.

A–T 650B*

345. Il′ia Muromets

There lived and dwelt this peasant, and he had twelve sons and twelve daughters. One of them, Il′ia Muromets, didn't have the use of his legs. His father took him off into the forest to this little hut, and there he prayed to God for twelve years. Once in the summertime an old man came to him. The old man exchanged greetings with him and said, "Il′ia Muromets, you wouldn't have something to drink, would you?"

"I have a little beer that my father brought me. But I can't use my legs so perhaps you'll go and get it yourself."

The little old man said, "Just as good folk walk, so can you get up and go!" Then Il′ia Muromets got up, took his birch bucket, and went and brought the bucket full of beer. The old man drank a little and then he said, "Il′ia

Muromets, now you drink the rest of the beer in this birch bucket." And he drank it up.

Then he explained to the old man that "I feel within me an immeasurable force. It's as if a pillar went from the earth to heaven and there was a ring in the pillar and I would take the ring and turn everything."

"Now, bring me some more beer, Iliushinka." So he brought another birch bucket of beer. The little old man drank and then gave the rest to Il'ia Muromets. "Drink what's left, Iliushinka."

So he drank it and he said, "Now I feel I have only one-third of my former strength. I have very little strength."

"That's enough for you, that will be enough against the common folk," he said. "That will do." Then the old man took his leave and he was no more to be seen.

Il'ia Muromets collected a few things together and set off home on foot. He got home and his mother was very glad to see him. His father was out in the field and there was no one else at home. Il'ia Muromets said, "Parent, bake some crackers and pancakes, and I'll take them out to father as a little gift." So his mother baked some crackers and pancakes and he took them out to the fields.

He came there and some of his brothers recognized him. "It's our brother, Il'ia Muromets, coming there."

And he shouted, "Father, brothers, come and eat. I have hot pancakes to eat." And so they threw down their axes and came together. They greeted him and then they all began eating. When they had eaten, Il'ia Muromets said to them, "Lie down, father and brothers, and sleep. I'll cut a little of the wood for you." So the brothers all offered him their axes, and he said, "All right, brothers, just lie down and sleep. I'll take the one I most like the look of."

Il'ia Muromets was just like a weed. He tore out all the brush. When he had torn something out, he threw it into the River Neva. He wanted to dam up the River Neva, but the river just ran in some other direction. (He couldn't dam it up.) No matter how much forest there was there, he uprooted it all and threw it in the river. He came to their camp, "That's enough sleep, father!" So they got up and began moving. They hitched up the horses and went home.

So they came home and he said, "Father, let me go into the steppe, the vast plain, to have a look at people, to show myself off." And so he came to the public square and he saw many people there. He said, "Do you have a wrestler here?"

One came out of the crowd. "Let's fight." And first they made a bargain that neither would lodge a complaint as a result of what happened. And so they took up the fight, and Il′ia Muromets lifted him up, shook him, and threw him on the ground, and the guts spilled out, out of that person. Then he took another and tossed him and killed that one, too. "A weak people!" he said. "There's no point in just killing them."

So he went home and sat on the rampart. And his neighbor was a merchant. He told the merchant of his adventures and the merchant was astonished. "I should have such a person in my shop!" he said. "No one dare to do any thieving then." So Il′ia Muromets agreed to be one of his shop clerks and he was hired on for forty chervontsy. and his family would go to the merchant to dine. It was expensive for the merchant. "Well, we'll give it a try and see what happens," he agreed. So he brought him into the shop and told him at what price he was to sell various things. And so he began trading and the trading went well for him.

The merchant went to the fair and Il′ia Muromets was left behind to mind the shop. When he came back, all the goods had been sold. Il′ia Muromets said, "Mr. Merchant, please take all your money and deliver fresh goods to the shop."

The merchant was amazed at this business. "I've been trading here for thirty years, and I never sold as much as you sold in one week!" But Il′ia Muromets no longer would agree to sit in the shop and sell: "Better for me to go wandering over the whole, wide world," he said.

So he went to the market in search of a warrior's horse for himself. No matter how much he went around the market, every time he put his hand on a horse it would buckle under. Then as he was wandering through the town, he met a priest, and this priest had a mite-infested colt. But that colt could stand up under his hand. "Father, come and buy me that little colt from the priest. Whatever he asks, give it to him!"

So his father went to the priest and traded for the colt, and the priest was asking a hundred rubles. That seemed much too much for the old man and he came back home without the colt.

Then Il′ia Muromets said, "Why didn't you buy him for me, father?"

"It's too expensive. He's asking a hundred rubles."

"If he's asking two hundred rubles, then give him two hundred rubles. Don't begrudge that. Buy me the colt!" So he went a second time, and the priest asked for two hundred rubles, and the old man gave him the two hundred. Somehow he brought it back to the yard, put the colt in a shed, and looked after him day and night, feeding him. Then in two months he sensed his strength and he leapt out of the shed and overturned the well. So Il′ia Muromets quickly caught his horse and tied it up. Then he went to the market and bought himself a warrior's saddle and bridle.

Then he said goodbye to his father, saddled and mounted his horse, and set off. He lived at a distance of about a hundred versts from the tsar. He had been at home at matins, but he desired to be at the tsar's for the liturgy. How

should he go? The direct way was where Solovei the Nightingale Robber†
sat in twelve oaks. But Solovei the Robber let no one pass, neither mounted
nor afoot, nor did he let anyone come closer than twelve versts to him. Then
he would whistle, and a horse would die and a man might perish. Formerly
there had been this great noise, but they had abandoned that because now no
one rode that way, although Il´ia Muromets was daring to do so. He rode up
close to Solovei the Robber and Solovei the Robber whistled. His horse fell
on its knees. So he took his war club and beat it on the hips, "So, you grass
nose bag, are you submitting to the enemy? I may be a straw bag but I will
not give in." So the horse jumped up and started running with more spirit.

He rode up close to Solovei the Robber, and Solovei the Robber whistled as
loudly as he could. Again his horse collapsed and fell on its knees. "Oh, you
grass nose bag, do you believe in the devil? I may be a straw bag but I don't
believe in the devil." And he beat him on his hips. Then the horse jumped up
and ran on with even more spirit. And then Solovei the Robber saw that he was
pursuing him and he whistled his most evil whistle. Then his horse didn't even
look but flew straight at the oaks. When he had come up to the oaks, Il´ia drew
his bow and with a maple arrow he knocked Solovei out of the oaks. He tied
him to his stirrups and set off for the tsar.

Il´ia Muromets rode by Solovei's daughters. The daughters saw him and
said, "Papa's bringing us a gift." Solovei the Robber responded that "they
are bringing your father all trussed up. You had better make a fine meal for Il´ia
Muromets or he will not spare me." Quickly they hung a heavy board over the
gates saying, "we will invite him to be our guest and then drop this on him and
crush him." But Il´ia Muromets heard their words and said, "I have no time to
dine with you; I must hurry on to the great feast of the liturgy."

So he rode right up to a monastery and he let his horse into the churchyard
as he himself went into God's temple. They were completing the liturgy and
all the people were leaving. And some warriors were leaving, too, and they
saw that his horse was in the house of God, in the churchyard, which was
pretty irregular! "How can you possibly bring your horse into the church
precincts? I'll take you and shake you up until you're dead!" Il´ia Muromets
was angered by these words and he took his hundred-pood mace and struck
that warrior, who flew into tiny bits.

Then another of them said, "Do you know, brother? I want to see whether
we are equal in strength."

And then Il´ia Muromets said that "we can come together in the steppe
and pay no attention to our kinship so let's first test our strength and then be
brothers. We can then call each other true brothers." So they rode apart for a

---

†Nightingale translates the Russian *solovei*, but it has been pointed out that it is an
anagram of the Slavic god Volos (English: wealth), god of animal husbandry, wisdom, and poetry.

verst and then they struck each other and they hit each other with their maces but neither could overcome the other. So they called each other brothers because they were of equal strength with each other.

The tsar gave a ball. They were passing goblets around—one, two, and three—and some of them began to boast. The merchants boasted of their money, the warriors of their armies. And Il´ia Muromets boasted of the fact that he had taken the direct way and knocked Solovei the Robber out of the oaks. But no one believed him and it was reported to the tsar that Il´ia Muromets had been boasting about Solovei the Robber. So they said, "Let him drag him in here and we'll have a look and see who this nightingale, Solovei the Robber, really is." So they dragged Solovei the Robber in and everybody had to have a look. The tsar said, "Well, Il´ia Muromets, can you make him whistle?"

Il´ia Muromets said very carefully, "Your royal majesty, I can make him whistle but don't blame me for the consequences. Some folk are so weak that they'll perish." The tsar ordered him to make Solovei whistle quietly.

So then he took the tsar under his right wing and the tsaritsa under his left and he shouted to Solovei the Robber to whistle has quietly as possible. But Solovei whistled with all his might and many folk, many of the simple folk, were knocked down as if with boiling water and killed. So then Il´ia Muromets took Solovei the Robber and flung him on the ground and smashed him into tiny bits (because he had broken the rules there when he killed so many folk). The tsar thanked him, and there was no investigation made for his involvement in the death of all those folk.

So then he set off further on his journey and he met up with Egor Zlatogor. This Egor Zlatogor tossed mountains from one hand to the other. He was even stronger than Il´ia Muromets. Now Il´ia Muromets hit Egor's horse and it jumped, and Egor Zlatogor couldn't turn around enough to see what had made his horse jump. So Il´ia Muromets struck Egor's horse a second time, and the horse leapt even further ahead. Finally he saw Il´ia Muromets and said, "Il´ia Muromets, you are teasing my horse!"

So Egor Zlatogor put Il´ia Muromets and his horse in his pocket, but his horse began stumbling. Egor said to his horse, "Why, my little horse, are you stumbling? Are you getting old?"

The horse answered that "You put a warrior no less than yourself in your pocket. No wonder it's difficult for me, no wonder I stumble." So he let him out of his pocket and the two of them rode along together.

"So now, Il´ia Muromets, let's go visit my parent," said Egor Zlatogor. But then they met an old woman, and the old woman was walking along with her basket.

As she was approaching them, her basket seemed to leap out of her hands, and she put it down on the ground. Then she said, "My lord warriors, take my basket. My back hurts and I can't bend over any more." So Egor Zlatogor told Il´ia Muromets to take the basket. He rode up to it and tried to lift it with his foot, but he couldn't do anything. He jumped down from his horse and tried to lift it up, but he could only move it a little bit—he certainly couldn't get it off the ground. He couldn't really budge it at all.

Finally Egor Zlatogor sat there laughing. "Oh, Iliusha, you can't even help the old woman with her basket!" So he got down from his horse and grabbed the basket, but he couldn't move it all. Then Egor Zlatogor got back on his horse and said to the old woman, "Raise it up as you know best; we can't do it."

So then the old woman said, "You shits! You call yourselves warriors but you shits can't even lift an old woman's basket." So she took her basket and went off. And they rode on.

Soon they came to Egor's home. And Egor Zlatogor told Il´ia Muromets to put his mace down in the fire. When you greet him, don't offer him your hand. Give him your mace; otherwise he'll cripple your hand. My father is completely blind; he can't see a thing." So they came and Il´ia Muromets threw his war mace in the fire and Egor Zlatogor greeted his father.

Then his parent said, "You have a friend with you, don't you, Egorushko?"

"I have brought my blood brother, Il´ia Muromets."

"Il´ia Muromets, give me your right hand and let's get acquainted." Il´ia Muromets grabbed his war mace and gave it to the old man instead of his hand. The old man squeezed it, and from both ends juices ran. Then the old blind man said, "You've some strength, Il´ia Muromets, not quite that of Egorushko, but strong anyway."

They ate dinner and then they rode further. They came up to the River Neva and in this deserted place they heard this noise, this crackling. "What could that be? We'd better go back." But they went to the deserted place and there was nothing there but this coffin, and in the coffin there was nothing at all. Egor Zlatogor said, "Well, Iliushinka, don't you think this coffin could be for one of us? Lie down in it and let's see whether it fits." So Il´ia Muromets lay down in the coffin, but it was too long and too wide for him. So he got out of it and Egor Zlatogor lay down in it and it was just as if he'd been poured into it. "All right, Iliushinka, put the lid down and let see how it goes!" Il´ia Muromets closed the lid, and it was just as if he had been poured into it. "Now you can open it!"

Il´ia Muromets tried to open it, but he couldn't. He said to Egor Zlatogor, "I can't tear it off with my hands."

"Strike it with your mace and bash it apart."

So he hit the coffin and an iron hoop appeared on it. He hit it a second time and there appeared a second. He hit it a third time, and a third hoop came. "Do you know, Egor Zlatogor, you are doomed to be in this coffin forever. There's nothing to be done with three iron hoops holding you in."

"Make a hole just below my adam's apple and I'll give you my strength." So Il'ia Muromets used his mace to make a hole. And then Egor Zlatogor said, "Look, Il'ia Muromets, while white liquid is coming out, drink it; but if yellow comes out, don't drink that!"

So he drank and he felt this immeasurable strength in himself. Then the yellow liquid started coming and he stopped drinking. "That will be enough of this strength in me, Zlatogor!"

"Take my mace and test it. Strike that oak and see whether it flies into pieces." So he struck it and the oak flew into little chips everywhere.

So then Iliushinka said farewell to Egor Zlatogor. He rode a little way away and then sat on his horse, turned to stone. He couldn't walk—the Lord wouldn't let him. And Egor Zlatogor turned to stone in his coffin. Nowadays there are no more warriors and those two are turned to stone not far from the River Neva.

A–T 650C*

346. About Alyosha Popovich

In Rostov City there used to live this priest. And a daughter was born to the priest, and they never let her out anywhere; they kept her at home; they protected her. But then she grew up and folks started noticing her. The girls came and tried to entice her to go out walking with them. So they enticed her and then they all went away for this walk. And some Tatars surrounded her and took her away to the Tatars' Home. After that a son was born, Alyosha, and he grew not by the years, not by the weeks, but by the ribs! He was that healthy. And he asked to be let out, but his father wouldn't let him go out: he'd had this daughter and she had gotten lost. "Let me out or not, I'll go out for a walk anyway. It would be better to let me go with good will." So they let Alyosha go out. And when he was in the steppe, he saw Ekim Ivanovich, a warrior. Ekim Ivanovich had once seen some flies on a threshing floor and swatted them. "With one swing we killed fifty-five men," he said, and they became sworn brothers. So once they went to Alyosha's house to visit his father. They said, "We are going with some gifts to such and such a ruler in order to fight."

They rode and rode, near or far, low or high, in the open steppe. They pitched their tent and fed their horses, and began to rest themselves, but a pilgrim came to them. "Where are you going, young men?"

"We are going to such and such a king to serve him, and you have to take presents to this king." In this steppe there lies the warrior Invincible, and it's a full sazhen measured between his shoulders. So now Alyosha was afraid, but the pilgrim said, "Take my clothes." And that pilgrim had a cap that weighed three poods.

So Alyosha went along, and he came up to that warrior, Invincible. He was so frightened that he was seized with a passion, and every hair stood on end and he pretended to be deaf. He shouted, "Have you seen the priest's son Alyosha?"

The other one said, "Come closer, I can't hear." He was getting ready himself to trample him. Again he shouted, "Have you seen the priest's son Alyosha?" And then he came right up to his ear and then struck him with his dagger, and his head rolled away. He took this head, tied it to his stirrup and rode off to the pilgrim and Ekim Ivanovich. Well, then they caught sight of that head by the stirrup and thought that Alyosha had been killed. They took their horses, saddled them, and rode back. But his horse was spirited and he tried to catch up. As he was catching up, whether near or far, he, that is, Ekim Ivanovich, struck Alyosha with his dagger. And Alyosha fell.

Then Ekim Ivanovich jumped onto his chest and saw Alyosha's cross. "Oh, my brother Alyosha!" And he started bringing him to his senses and he brought him round. Then he said, "Tie that head to your stirrup and ride to that ruler."

They rode and rode until they got to that ruler. The ruler was giving a feast, a ball (it was a small crowd from those parts). They wouldn't let them in to the ruler but they kept on asking, saying that some warriors had come but they weren't being let in. So they were playing patty cake! The ruler himself came out to them and said, "Why are you behaving so brazenly?"

"We've been playing this silly game, patty cake."

Then the ruler decided that they weren't such simple people. So he invited them and sat them down at the table to feast. And then they hastened and they brought Tugarin in on a red cloth and sat him at the table. They brought a goose and they also brought bread. The landlord's wife so hurried that she cut her hand off. He took the bread and swallowed it in a single gulp, and then the goose like any beast.

And Alyosha Popovich said, "We had this really, really old cow and she went into the threshing barn and ate our lead measuring cup and that finished her off. I predict the same fate for you." Then his eyes filled up with blood. And Tugarin went and stabbed Alyosha with a dagger and Ekim Ivanovich grabbed him: "This is not the place to squabble—go into the open steppe to fight."

"That was no dueler who struck me, that was like Invincible in the open steppe, like fighting with him." And Alyosha said, "I struck off his head. Permit me to bring it and show it to you." But the other turned into a coward. They brought it to him on a platter and showed it to him. And then they said, "Let's go into the steppe to fight!" So they rode away. And Ekim Ivanovich came to be the observer, maybe even to collect up Alyosha's bones. So they rode. When that warrior shouted, leaves would fall from the oak and the earth shook. So they came close to the place, and they had to fight.

Then Alyosha said, "And why do you have so many folk behind you today?" He turned around and Alyosha sliced off his head—he deceived him.

So then they rode back to that ruler. The ruler was grateful, but he was afraid of him—he'd have to feed him. They were afraid of Alyosha. Alyosha courted there, and the girls went out onto a raft to bathe and he managed to mix up their rings. The very girl who lived in the room and was never let out, she had already been courted. "Whatever you say," he said, "I'll steal you away." But then this ruler had two brothers. They both rode up, sat down at the table and were received as guests. So they were received, and they sat there, and some there boasted of this and that. Some had many soldiers, some a young wife, some a treasure of gold. But the brothers sat there and boasted of nothing. "Heh, you, why don't you boast?"

"We don't have a young wife, nor a treasure of gold. We have only a sister, unlike all others, and today is her wedding day."

So Alyosha said, "I love her," he said. Then one brother stabbed him with a dagger so that he wouldn't go on bragging. But Ekim Ivanovich grabbed him: "This is not the place to squabble—go into the open steppe to fight." So he and the brothers rode toward it. He stopped the brothers and with a kerchief he knocked open the window. "Windows, swing on your hinges and let Alyosha in!" The brothers started talking, whispering, but she was unconscious. So Alyosha came out and locked the doors.

He took her away to get married. Alyosha was married. And his sister in the Tatar house pleaded, "Won't Alyosha be coming soon?" But the Tatars married her off. And she didn't want it.

Alyosha rode and rode, thinking about her. "I have a sister in the Tatar house." He turned up at the Tatar house but they wouldn't let him in. They locked everything, locked it up. He shouted, "Give me back my sister and nothing will happen to you." Somehow they had to give her back and Ekim Ivanovich admired her so that he fell in love, and he couldn't live without her and he'd have to take her. They had called each other brothers and now he was married. And they went to his father, each with a wife, and Alyosha went to that tsar and he left Ekim Ivanovich as if he were his son.

A–T 650D*

347. Vasilii Buslavich

Buslav lived ninety years, and then having lived, he died. And he left his dear young wife, Vanilfa Timofeevna, and he left his young son, Vasilii Buslavich. And so this son Vasilii Buslavich began playing with the other small children. He would rip an arm off one or break open the head of another. So Vanilfa Timofeevna handed her dear son over to the old man, the Old Pilgrim, to be taught, to read among the pages, and he learned not how to read among the pages but how to fly like a falcon.

Once the old man Old Pilgrim had this feast and council, and he didn't invite his favorite, young Vasilii Buslavich. But Vasilii Buslavich came to this feast and council, and he seized the guests in the front corner, yanked them from their benches, and conducted them to new quarters with his black elm club. The ancient Old Pilgrim was furious with him, with his favorite, and he said, "Don't flog, young flogger! You are not to drink water from the Ob, nor drive folks out of the town. If you [don't] drink the waters of the Ob or drive folk out of town, here's five hundred rubles."

So then our Vasilii Buslavich came home to his mother and said, "Oh, my dear mother! I boasted in my young years and have quarreled with the elder Old Pilgrim." His mother got him dead drunk and put him away in a dark dungeon.

But now people gathered to fight with him, and he slept on and on in the dark dungeon. He knew nothing of it. A woman was going for water and she shouted at him through a window, "Why are you sleeping, Vasilii Buslavich, why, don't you know what's going on? I've been going for water, and as I went, I struck so many people with my yoke!"

Vasilii Buslavich, hearing these words, knocked down the stone wall of his dark dungeon and went out to fight the forces. And the elder Old Pilgrim pleaded with him, "Heh, you, Vasilii Buslavich! Calm your ardent heart; rest your warrior's shoulders. I promised you five hundred but now I'll give you a full thousand!"

So Vasilii Buslavich cooled off and went to his mother. "Oh, my dear mother, today I spilled much blood and killed many people!"

So his mother became angry with him, and she made him a ship, and she put men on that ship and then sent it out to sea. She said that he was to go wherever he liked, and then she waved her hand. So Vasilii Buslavich sailed to green pastures. There lay a sea spout, all around as far as one could see. He walked around it and then he kicked it, and it spoke to him, "Vasilii Buslavich! Don't kick me, or you'll be here yourself." Then later the workers joked among themselves and jumped through that sea spout. All of them jumped across it and he went last, but he got caught up by the toes on his right foot, and there he perished.

A–T 650E*

348. Dunai Ivanovich

In the glorious city, in the city of Kiev, there was a grand feast given by the kind Prince Vladimir. And at this feast there was a host of guests. Princes and boyars, trading merchants and warriors, peasants and town dwellers. He seated them all at oaken tables, on pine benches, and on these tables were sweet meats and strong drinks. And Prince Vladimir himself went about at this feast, and he questioned his guests, and he offered them the bread and salt of hospitality. And then he spoke these words, "Oh, you invited guests of mine, all seated at most honorable places. You are all cheerful, you are all married. I am the only one among you who goes about unmarried, a bachelor. Where am I to get a bride who is tall, beautiful, with strong bones, and cheerful, and also hospitable, and hardworking, and intelligent, with an elegant walk and well spoken? There would be someone for me to spend my long life with, to think thoughts with, and you would all have someone to bow to!"

Everyone at the feast fell silent and they all began to ponder—some knew of this and some knew of that. Then one glorious and mighty warrior, Dunai Ivanovich, stood up from behind that oaken table and he spoke these words: "Oh, Prince Vladimir Beautiful Sun, I know this. In brave Lithuania the king there has two daughters. Neither of them has been given in marriage; neither of them has been courted. The older daughter rides out into the steppe, she rides a warrior's horse; the second daughter is Evprakseiushka and she manages the household and embroiders with silks. She is tall in height and beautiful of countenance, and she has a strong frame, and she is also intelligent. She would be someone you could spend your long life with and think thoughts with."

Prince Vladimir, the ruler of Kiev, spoke these words: "Oh, you Dunai Ivanovich. Go to brave Lithuania to that king. Take with you trusted servants and gold treasure, and court this younger daughter Evprakseiushka. If he will give her, take her; if not, then bring her back by force."

"I don't need any brave army, Prince Vladimir; nor do I need any gold treasure. Just give me as a comrade the good young man, that brave warrior Dobrynia Nikitich. We will court Evpraksinia, and if they won't give her to us, we'll take her by force."

So Prince Vladimir summoned Dobrynia Nikitich, they mounted their fine horses, and rode off to brave Lithuania. And when they were mounting their fine horses you could see them, but you couldn't see them riding! They rode across the open steppes, through drowsy forests, and before the rising of the red sun they had ridden into brave Lithuania, to the king's courtyard, to his very window.

And Dunai Ivanovich spoke, "Oh, you Dobrynia Nikitich! Herd the horses, stand next to the window and watch, and I'll go into the king's chambers. If it's necessary, I'll call you."

So Dunai Ivanovich went in to the Lithuanian king, who recognized him. "Well, Dunai Ivanovich, where are you going, where is your route taking you, and why have you honored us with a visit? Have you come to take a look at us, or show yourself off? Or perhaps you have come to serve us in faith and truth?" (They say that's how it was once upon a time when he was there in Lithuania.)

"I have come to do a good deed: to court your youngest daughter Evpraksinia for our glorious prince Vladimir."

These words of Dunai displeased the king of Lithuania. "You have come here not of your own accord, but for that shiftless one. Putting the rear wheels in front won't make the cart move. Oh, you Tatars, take Dunai, tie his hands behind him, and lead him into the cellar. Let him sit in the cellar and be our guest."

Dunai Ivanovich stood up, leaned on the oaken tables, and the tables scattered. The dishes with the food clattered, the strong wines spilled out. The servants led him away into the deep cellar, and then they covered it over with fine golden sand. Those Tatars then went into the king's chambers. "Oh, you brave king, eat and drink, and know no misfortune. We have in the courtyard an incomparable lad. In one hand he has the horses' reins and in the other hand the Sorochinsk billyclub. He flies about the courtyard, swinging this rough club. He has killed Tatars to the last one; he hasn't left a one for seed."

Then the king understood, and he ordered them to release Dunai Ivanovich. So they opened the heavy portcullis and they let him out. They saddled their good horses, took Princess Evpraksinia, and set off for the glorious city of Kiev, back to Prince Vladimir.

They rode from dawn until evening. Then dark night overtook them on the way. They spread out their white tent and stopped to spend the night. At their feet they tethered their good horses, and at their heads were lances for long-distance flight. In one hand they took their sharp swords, and by their sides they put the steel daggers. They slept well; they saw nothing in their dreams. In the morning they arose, saddled their horses, and rode further, toward the capital city of Kiev.

Then they saw ahead of them an enormous Tatar horde, all mounted on warhorses. Each horse sank into the ground up to its fetlock, and it threw rocks behind it for two full versts.

And Dunai Ivanovich spoke, "Dobrynia Nikitich, you go on toward the city of Kiev, and I'll go out to meet these Tatars."

When he had met with the Tatars, he fought a duel with one of them, and he knocked him out of his saddle. That Tatar fell onto Mother Moist Earth just like a sheaf of oats. He pressed a stone onto the Tatar's chest and said, "Now tell me, Tatar, what is your clan and which is your tribe?"

And the Tatar answered him, "If I were on your chest, I would not ask what your tribe and clan were. I would slit open your chest and take out your heart and liver."

Dunai ripped off the cloak from that Tatar's chest, and saw that these were women's breasts. And Dunai asked, "Who are you then (for he felt guilty because he was a warrior and had been fighting with a woman).

And she answered, "Oh, Dunai Ivanovich, can it be that you don't recognize me? Have we not ridden through the same steppe, have we not sat at the same table, have we not drunk from the same goblet?"

And then Dunaiushka recognized her. "Oh, Princess Anastasia, forgive me that I thought you were a Tatar, that I insulted you, a beautiful maiden, that I stepped with my foot upon your white breast. Ride with me to Kiev for we have had enough of this roaming the steppes and it is time for us to accept the gold crowns of marriage."

So they rode into the capital city of Kiev to Prince Vladimir, who was at that time getting married to the youngest daughter. So the youngest daughter was getting married to Prince Vladimir, and the oldest daughter was getting ready for her wedding. A very happy feast was taking place. And the feast went on for five full days. And there was a great host of guests. There were merchants gathered there, and boyars, and peasants. They sat at oaken tables, on fir benches. And on the tables were many foods, and strong drinks. And they all drank too much and boasted. The merchants boasted of their gold treasure, and the mighty warriors of the warhorses and the war deeds.

The wise ones praised their father and their mother—the foolish praised a young wife. And Dunai Ivanovich praised his courage. "Who," he said, "is better than me? I married myself, and I presented Prince Vladimir with his wife. There is no one more daring, no one braver."

Then Nastasia said, "Oh, Dunai Ivanovich, don't boast in vain. Alyosha Popovich is more daring than you, and Dobrynia Nikitich is smarter than you. And I can shoot better than you."

Dunai did not like these words. "Now, then, Dunai, let's go into the untamed steppe. We shall test our strengths, we shall shoot the arrows from the bow."

So they rode out into the untamed steppe. Nastasiushka pulled back her bow with a steel arrow and it struck a dagger in its scabbard and cut it right in half. Just a glance with the eye or weighing it in the scales—precisely in half.

Then Dunai shot, but he undershot it. He shot again, and overshot it. The third time he hit it, but it didn't stick. This did not please Dunaiushka. So he became angry and he grabbed Nastasia. He threw her onto the moist earth, drew his dagger and was ready to cut open her white breasts. But she pleaded with him, "Dunai Ivanovich, don't touch me, don't destroy me. I am carry-ing a child for three months in my womb. There is no such other. His legs up to his knees are silver, his arms from his wrists to his elbows are of pure gold. He already has a pigtail, and on its ends are silver stars. On the crown of his head the bright sun shines, and in one arm is a tempered arrow, and in the other a long-distance lance. Better you whip me or bury me up to my breasts in the earth."

But Dunai Ivanovich did not heed her and he cut open her white body. In truth, there turned out to be this indescribable baby: his legs to the knees were silver, his little hands from the wrists to the elbows were pure gold, he had a pigtail, and on its ends were bright stars, and on the crown of his head the bright sun was shining, and in one hand was a tempered arm, and in the other a long-distance lance.

When Dunai saw the child, he immediately killed himself. And where his head fell, there flows the Dunai or Danube River (perhaps that's true). And where Nastasia's head fell, there is the River Anastas´ia.

That is all the tale about Dunai Ivanovich. The pre-tale will be tomorrow after dinner, when we've eaten white bread.

A–T 650F*

349. Diuk Stepanovich

In the village of Gracharovo† there lived Ivan Grigor´evich and his old woman. They had seventy-five years each. Ivan Grigor´evich and the old woman gave birth to a son and they gave him the name Il´ia. He survived the first six weeks. He could move neither hand nor foot. For three more years Il´ia lived, he could only sit—he still had no control of his hands or feet. The father and mother had given birth to a son who could only sit. Il´ia Muromets reached thirty-three years. As he had been a sitter, so was he a sitter even now.

One time the father and mother were putting in the harvest, but Il´ia was at home, sitting on the stove. Two pilgrims came to Il´ia. They asked for a little homebrew from Il´ia.

Il´ia said, "Now, monks, you go into the cellar and drink it!"

But the pilgrims said, "Get up and go after the brew, Il´ia!

---

†In the byliny this is usually Karachaevo, said to be in the province of Murom.

Il′ia said to the pilgrims, "For thirty-three years I haven't been able to walk, I cannot move a hand or leg."

Again the pilgrims said, "Get up, Il′ia!"

Il′ia moved his leg and arm, and got up immediately. He took the keys and a bucket, and ran down into the cellar with joy. He brought the brew. The grandfathers said, "Drink some yourself, Il′ia!" Il′ia drank. "Bring another, Il′ia." Il′ia drank two more buckets. Then the grandfathers said, "Drink another!" Il′ia drank another. "Now run for a third time." So Il′ia brought the third round. "Drink grandfathers," Il′ia said.

The pilgrims said, "You drink the third." Il′ia drank the third.

"Well, Il′ia, can you feel a lot of strength in you now?" the pilgrims asked him.

Il′ia answered them, "I can turn the whole wild world over now: the heavens and the earth. If I could only grab hold of it all. If there were, for instance, a pillar between heaven and earth, with a ring on it."

The pilgrims talked something over between themselves. "Il′ia, bring a fourth bucket of brew." Il′ia brought it. "Drink some, grandfathers!"

"You drink it yourself, Il′ia!" And Il′ia drank the fourth. "Well, Il′ia, has a lot of strength been added, or taken away?"

Il′ia said, "Half of it's been taken away." So then the grandfathers spoke to Il′ia Muromets: "Do combat with all. Your death will never come in battle. You will die your own death. Save Rus! Only don't go into combat, Il′ia, with Sviatogor."

Then Il′ia said, "And where shall I get a warhorse?"

Then the pilgrims said, "Go to your parents and tell them you will learn about the steppe. Then leave your parents and go and you'll fall asleep. When you get up, an old man will lead you a gray colt, and you buy it from him. In the morning and evening let him roll in the dew and for three months feed him on spring wheat. After three months your horse will be ready and able to carry you. Your name is Il′ia Muromets. We have given you the strength to save Rus. The horde and the nomads have battered it (the horde means the Tatars)," said the pilgrims.

Il′ia said farewell to the pilgrims and then out of joy he took a barrel of brew and as much baked bread as there was, put it all in a sack, and set out for his parents. But he didn't know the way. On his journey he came across a forest and a river. He couldn't get across. Il′ia lowered the bread and barrel to the ground and started in pulling out oaks, throwing them over the river, and making a bridge. Then he set off over this bridge to his parents' house. He got there. His parents were very glad to see him. He had brought them some food, enough for two weeks, he had thought to himself. Then

Il'ia set off back home. He walked and walked, then he sat down on the road and fell asleep between two rows of rye. His parents arrived back home. They didn't know where to find Il'ia but he was asleep in the field. Il'ia woke up. Just as the pilgrims had foretold it, it occurred: before him there stood an old man with a colt. Il'ia bought the little gray colt from the old man for himself and started feeding it. And in the morning and the evening the little colt rolled about in the dew. After three months Il'ia was even riding the colt and the colt with Il'ia on its back could jump over an oak or over the house.

Then Il'ia asked his parents to let him go out and save Rus. His father would let him, but his mother said "no." "Oh my son, you will leave orphans and widows if you go out to kill people."

He said, "Mama, I won't kill people without cause. I will only kill those who give no peace to us, to our Russia."

So Il'ia put on his bast boots and his armor, and he made himself a bow and arrows, and a sword, and a lance, and a shield. He set out for the capital city from the village of Gracharovo. Il'ia rode and he saw the city in captivity, Chernigov city was besieged by the Tatars. Il'ia let fly an arrow. The invisible arrow made a street through the Tatars. Il'ia came galloping up. He swung his sword and there was a street, and he let loose his lance and there was a lane. He killed them all to the last one— just count them. He left just the khan to tell the tale: that in Russia there was such a warrior as Il'ia Muromets.

The commandant of the city invited Il'ia to remain forever in the city. Il'ia said to the commandant, "I am not going to save just this one city, I'm going to save all Rus."

Then the commandant said to Il'ia Muromets, "Don't take the middle road through the forest; that's where Nightingale the Robber is roosting and he's been perched there for forty-three years. He slays folks with his whistle. There's no way through. Be careful he doesn't kill you, Il'ia."

So then Il'ia decided to ride that way and see what sort of a bird this was. He rode into the forest. And he saw Nightingale the Robber's nest on twelve oaks. And Nightingale (Solovei) caught sight of Il'ia. Solovei whistled as loud as he could in order to kill the warrior with the whistle. And from the whistle Il'ia's horse stumbled and Il'ia was frightened by that whistle and he spurred his horse with his spurs.

"Didn't you hear the squawk of some old gull? Aren't you ashamed?" Il'ia said to his horse.

Then Il'ia drew his bow and let fly an arrow, and it hit Solovei right in his right eye. It knocked Nightingale right out of his nest onto the ground.

"Now, Nightingale, whistle!"

Solovei pleaded to Il'ia: "Let me go free, Il'ia. Don't kill me!" Il'ia said nothing. He took Solovei and tied him to his stirrups. Then he got on his horse and rode on.

Solovei the Robber had a seven-story house. And in it there lived his three sons-in-law, three daughters, and his wife. The oldest daughter said, "Papa's bringing someone in tied to his stirrups. And the second one said the same, but the third daughter said, "No, you didn't guess that right. Papa's tied to the stirrups!"

Seven men surrounded Il'ia. They attacked. Solovei the Nightingale Robber shouted, "Go away! If I couldn't deal with him, why should you try? Ask Il'ia to let me go of his own free will."

But Il'ia just kept riding along. An old woman excitedly tried to strike Il'ia with an iron rod, but Il'ia just leaned to one side and she ended up striking the old man, old Solovei, and Il'ia got off free.

Il'ia arrived in the capital city and rode into the prince's court. He tied his horse to the hitching post and went into the palace. There the boyars were feasting and the lords and the warriors of Prince Vladimir.

Il'ia exchanged greetings with the prince. He bowed separately to the tsarevna. The tsarevna recognized Il'ia, saw that a good warrior had arrived, but Prince Vladimir asked Il'ia, "What is your clan?"

Il'ia answered, "I am from the village of Gracharovo, and they call me Il'ia Muromets."

"Why have you come here?" the prince said.

Il'ia spoke straight out: "To save Russia."

Prince Vladimir poured a bucket of wine and gave it to Il'ia to drink. Il'ia drank it in a single gulp and that was that.

The prince said, "Well, you have plenty of strength. Sit down with my warriors and feast with them."

So Il'ia sat down. He felt out of place. He touched them with his leg and all the warriors went tumbling over on their sides, from his leg alone. Alyosha Popovich, an arrogant braggart, grabbed his sword and wanted to chop off Il'ia's head. But Il'ia didn't let him. He grabbed the sword from Alyosha, raised it up and then thrust it through the table up to its hilt.

"Well, Alekha," Il'ia said, "now you pull it out." But Aleksei didn't have the strength to pull it out. "So, braggart, you don't have the strength to kill Il'ia!"

And then Alyosha Popovich said, "Prince Vladimir, ask him whether he by chance came by the middle way."

The prince asked him and Il'ia answered, "I have Solovei tied to my stirrup."

Everyone immediately ran out into the courtyard to take a look at Nightingale. Vladimir went up to Solovei. "Well, Solovei, now whistle!"

Solovei said, "Stand off a little way. I am no servant of yours. I submit only to Il′ia."

The prince turned to Il′ia, "Force him to whistle."

Il′ia ordered Solovei to whistle half like a serpent and half like the nightingale. He blew himself up to the maximum and whistled enough to kill even Il′ia. When he whistled, chimneys fell down from houses and the glass in the windows was broken. Regardless of how many people there were in the town, all fell down dead. Only the three were left alive: Il′ia, his horse, and Solovei. Il′ia forbade Solovei to whistle like that again.

When the prince came to his senses after the nightingale's whistle, he ordered Solovei arrested. "I've never, ever seen such a bird."

Il′ia rode out of town, dug a deep pit, untied Solovei from his stirrup, chopped him into little bits, threw them into the pit, and filled it in. Then he rolled a big stone on top and returned to the palace.

From among the twelve warriors Il′ia chose two warriors and the three swore brotherhood. Il′ia was the eldest brother, then Andron the middle brother, and Anton, the third. They swore to live in friendship and never betray each other. The rest of the warriors were of no use to Il′ia. In all lands they found out that in Russia there was this Il′ia Muromets, and therefore it was peaceful in Russia. Il′ia lived a year in the capital and all was quiet. Then he returned home to the village of Gracharovo after that year. He buried his father and mother and remained at home to work.

Then Il′ia rode out into the steppe on his warhorse. He rode along the dusty road. An old man was riding right at Il′ia. The old man had an iron staff. And this iron staff weighed twenty-five poods.

Il′ia asked him, "Where are you from, old man, and where are you going?"

The old man replied, "From Tatar captivity. I was a captive."

Then Il′ia asked the old man, "How did you manage, how did you get out of captivity?"

And the old man answered, "The Tatars sent a wave of us toward the capital city of Kiev, and I fled out of captivity. The khan himself lives with the Russian princess, and Prince Vladimir is of no account at all. Where Il′ia is I've no idea," the old man said. "The Tatars have surrounded the city without Il′ia."

Il′ia said to the old man, "I am that very Il′ia."

Then the old man said, "You've got to go to the rescue of Prince Vladimir."

So Il′ia took the old man's staff of twenty-five poods and was about to set off on foot for Kiev. He gave the old man his horse. "Live in my house until I come back from Kiev," he said.

Il′ia got dressed in his shabby clothes and made himself into a pilgrim. Then he went to Kiev, and the city was surrounded by the horde.† People asked him, "Where are you from?"

Il′ia said, "I am from the village of Gracharovo."

And then the horde said, "Did you see Il′ia there?"

"Yes, I saw him," said Il′ia.

"What's he like?" the horde asked Il′ia.

"Oh, just like me," he said.

He let the horde know right away. The khan demanded that the pilgrim come to his house. Il′ia came to his house. Prince Vladimir was sitting in the entranceway. He recognized Il′ia and spoke to him, "Why did you come here, pilgrim, without permission?" So the prince had recognized Il′ia and the khan heard this and went out of the house into the entranceway in order not to alarm the old man.

The khan spoke, "Tell me, pilgrim, what is Il′ia like?"

Il′ia answered, "Like me."

"What sort of warrior is that! I'm a real warrior."

Then the khan asked the pilgrim, "And does Il′ia eat a lot of bread?"

And Il′ia answered, "Three pretzels a day."

"That isn't even breaking straw." Then the khan said, "I eat more than that, old man."

Il′ia said, "How much?"

"I can drink two buckets of wine at a time and eat at one sitting two poods of pretzels and two poods of meat."

So then Il′ia said, "A rich peasant had a cow, and she ate and ate, and she burst. That's what you'll do."

The khan grabbed his lance and was about to kill Il′ia, but Il′ia abruptly turned and the khan missed completely. So Il′ia gave it to the khan with his rod, and the khan didn't even shout out. Il′ia took the khan's sword and went out into the open air, to survey the horde. He killed them all to the last one and freed the capital from the khan.

"It was good enough for me just to kill the khan; I don't need the rest of this stuff."

But you won't find anymore such insignificant warriors. There's just Il′ia. Well, Il′ia took a rest as was his right and then set out again to his village of Gracharovo for his horse. Il′ia collected the horse and all his other equipment. He couldn't stay at home. Il′ia came back to Kiev. He gathered all his

---

†The various divisions of the Tatar–Mongolian empire were called "hordes." They remained an important factor in Muscovite political life through the sixteenth century.

warriors together. Once more when everyone found out that Il'ia was living in Kiev, it became more peaceful. They feasted and caroused.

Then Il'ia set off to visit the warrior Sviatogor beyond the mountains, to take a look at Sviatogor. Then Il'ia came to Sviatogor in the mountains. He tied up his horse near the foot of the mountains and then Il'ia climbed up the mountain to Sviatogor. Sviatogor was asleep on the mountain. No way could Il'ia wake him up. Il'ia struck him with all his might, he hit him with his fist with all his might, and he awoke him. Sviatogor woke up.

"Whose that throwing pebbles?" said Sviatogor. "Whose flipping stones?"

Then Il'ia Muromets said, "Sviatogor, I have come to take a look at you."

Sviatogor got up. By the side of Sviatogor Il'ia was just a twig. Il'ia started questioning Sviatogor, "Why aren't you saving Rus?"

"Because Mother Moist Earth can't hold me up."

Sviatogor and Il'ia became sworn brothers, and Sviatogor was the elder brother and Il'ia the younger. Sviatogor began telling Il'ia about himself.

"Whenever I go out through the villages, everyone laughs at me. 'What sort of warrior is he?' they say. 'Ha! Ha! Ha!' Then, Il'ia, I went on and I encountered a letter pouch with two arms. For three days I tried to raise up that pouch. I didn't get it halfway up before I sank away into the earth, and since then I haven't gone riding there but have lain here in these mountains."

"What kind of horse do you have?" Il'ia asked him.

"He's out wandering in the steppe."

"And what color is he?"

"He himself is raven black, with a white mane, and his tail is also white."

Then Sviatogor and Il'ia went out wandering through the mountains. Suddenly there appeared a coffin. And it was an enormous coffin. "Il'ia, measure that coffin and see whether it fits you." Il'ia measured himself in it and then got out. "Well, brother, I rolled around in it like a ball. Now then, brother Sviatogor, you measure yourself in it."

Brother Sviatogor lay down in the coffin and said, "Well, brother Il'ia, it fits me perfectly," and then he started expiring, he began dying. "Oh, brother Il'ia, I am dying. Ride over to my father Samson and tell him that his son Sviatogor has died."

Then he let out his spirit and died. And then he closed the top. Il'ia grasped the lid with his sword and there appeared an iron hoop. Il'ia stepped back from Sviatogor and commended him to eternal peace. "So be it, that is your fate, Sviatogor: you became acquainted with Il'ia and then you died," said Il'ia.

Il'ia rode off to his father, to Samson. And then he came to Samson's, of course. And Il'ia said, "Your son Sviatogor has died in the mountains. Why did you not save Rus, Samson?"

"I do not save Rus because Prince Vladimir considers me good for nothing. He despises warriors from the commoners. He loves merchants, lords from among the offspring of priests. For that reason I gave an oath never to go to war," said Samson.

Once more Il´ia returned to the capital city. While there was peace in Rus, Il´ia lay down in a tent next to a river. He slept for a week and then for another. At that time Diuk Stepanovich came riding from another tsardom to take a look at Il´ia. Diuk Stepanovich came right up to Il´ia, to the tent, and Diuk Stepanovich woke Il´ia up.

Il´ia got up. "Why have you come here, Diuk Stepanovich?" Il´ia asked Diuk Stepanovich.

"Just to take a look at you," he replied.

"And where are you going from here?"

"To Prince Vladimir," he said to Il´ia.

"Alright, but don't you boast to the prince at his court or else Alyosha the boaster will cut off your head." And he also said, "Such a penalty, Diuk Stepanovich, I won't let them take off your head."

Again Il´ia fell asleep and Diuk Stepanovich appeared at the court. Alyosha Popovich began following him around. He was trying to catch him out.

Diuk Stepanovich and the prince went to the church. From the palace to the church apple trees stood in the courtyard. Diuk Stepanovich said to Vladimir, "I have had the way up to the church paved with stones so you won't get your feet dirty, and there are two rows of apple trees."

Alyoshka the boaster spoke out against Diuk Stepanovich. "Tsar Vladimir, don't talk with this man. This man came here, dressed himself up, as if he'd just robbed somebody."

And so they fell to quarreling, with everything they were worth.

Alyosha Popovich had started the quarrel and he proposed that they ride out for twelve full days on various horses: in the morning and in the evening. And they should have differing clothing. And then see whom would wear out whom and what. And whoever was worn out would lose his head.

Diuk Stepanovich wanted to ride over to his tsardom for his clothes, but Alyosha Popovich wouldn't allow that. So Diuk Stepanovich sat down and wrote a letter to his mother. "Send me twelve suits of clothes." So then he sent that letter in a letter pouch; he tied it to a saddle and sent the horse off alone.

The horse came running into the yard and neighed with a whining voice. His mother recognized it. "Very likely, Diuk Stepanovich, my son, has been killed." His mother ran up to the horse and spied the letter pouch. In it was a letter. "Send Diuk Stepanovich twelve suits of clothes." His mother tied them on his horse and the horse raced back to the capital city of Kiev.

Alyosha Popovich and Diuk Stepanovich were on different horses to see which would outrace the other and wear him out. Alyosha Popovich rode out on his various horses, but Diuk Stepanovich went on just one. In the morning and in the evening Diuk Stepanovich's stallion would roll in the dew and change its hair color. Finally Diuk Stepanovich knocked Alyosha Popovich down with his clothes and horse. Alyoshka was unsettled by this act.

"So now let's see who can get across the river Dnepr and back," he said.

Diuk Stepanovich rode up to the river with Alyosha Popovich. Just then Il´ia Muromets arose. "No matter what happens, I won't let you take Diuk Stepanovich's head."

So then Diuk Stepanovich rode back from the river Dnepr and on his horse he leapt over that river Dnepr. It was Alyosha's turn to jump. Alyosha jumped into the river—into the middle of it with everything he had, including his horse.

After that Prince Vladimir had this feast. For some reason they didn't invite Il´ia to the feast. So Il´ia took his bow and an arrow. (The prince had some gold ornaments on his palace.) Il´ia summoned the barefooted, pulled back his bow-string and knocked two gold ornaments off the building. The barefooted ones picked up the gold. They bought some wine together with Il´ia Muromets and sat down in the flea market.

Prince Vladimir found about this, how his home had been shaken by the arrows. He himself couldn't summon Il´ia, so he sent his older brother Andron after him.

Andron came and said, "Brother Il´ia, come into the house, the prince summons you."

Il´ia didn't refuse. "I'll come but only if my brethren comes. I'll come with my brothers."

The prince ordered him to come with his brethren. When Il´ia entered the house together with his brethren, Prince Vladimir sat Il´ia down at a table with the other warriors. "No," said Il´ia, "Give me a separate table with my brethren."

The feast was ended and all were dispersing. Il´ia headed for his tent once more to sleep, still vexed. His brothers dispersed. Diuk Stepanovich rode away. Prince Vladimir presented presents to all, but he forgot about Il´ia.

The princess said, "Prince, what are you doing? Why do you not remember Il´ia before all the others?"

Prince Vladimir and Andron sent a Tatar fur coat, a sable coat, to Il´ia as a gift. Andron brought it to him. Il´ia took the fur coat, tore it into two halves, and threw it aside. "Just as I tore up the Tatars, I'll tear up a Tatar fur coat."

So then they reported Il´ia to Prince Vladimir: "He's dissatisfied with the gift."

Vladimir ordered his warriors to bring Vladimir in alive, put him in a cellar, in a dungeon, and put him to death by starvation.

The warriors went to Il´ia. He was asleep. How should they bring him in? The warriors deliberated and brought some ropes and hawsers. They tied his hands, and legs and then they woke him up. Il´ia woke up. In an instant the hawsers and ropes on his hands and legs just popped off and the warriors all ran, got on their horses, and headed for home.

Il´ia went to Vladimir by himself. Vladimir locked him in the cellar to kill him without drink or food. Il´ia read books there in that cellar. That very night the princess tunneled through to him and brought him every day some food and some water, but the prince knew nothing of it. After a certain time the horde approached the city, the capital. A Tatar warrior jumped over the house on his horse and called out to the prince to declare war on him. The prince became timid. "I've killed Il´ia, having neither fed him nor given him anything to drink, and all the rest have gone to their homes. What am I to do now?" The prince ran into the house to the princess. "Princess, now what are we supposed to do? I've killed Il´ia."

The princess said to the prince, "Il´ia is alive. I've been feeding him, prince. Il´ia's in that cellar." The prince went to him. "Il´ia, forgive me."

Il´ia said, "Prince Vladimir, let's get out of here right away. There's no time to ask forgiveness."

So Il´ia mounted up his horse and set off for the horde. Il´ia came and asked the khan for two weeks' respite—to call up the other warriors.

The khan came to the capital and gave the prince a letter. "We have one warrior. If you can't find a single warrior to go against him, we will devastate all Russia.

Il´ia took on the task, aided by the two brothers, Andron and Anton. They made a barrier on the way through which the enemy warrior would have to pass. The three of them began to guard it. They would seize the enemy warrior as he rode through. You couldn't see the sun for the dust. He was riding up to the barrier. Anton was at the ready. The warrior laughed heartily and Anton's horse's feet buckled under him. Anton said, "Oh lord, give my horse his feet so we can get away to Il´ia."

"Brother, no way will I fight with him." So Andron rode off. The foreign warrior laughed even more loudly. And the horse's legs buckled under him.

He said, "Oh lord, give my horse his feet so we can get away to Il´ia." And he rode to Il´ia, too. It was time for Il´ia to ride out himself. He set off like a whirlwind. He turned as black as night. His moustache and his eyebrows came completely together. Il´ia flew at the warrior. They struck each other. Only the handles of their swords survived. They struck with their lances and their horses' girth straps flew off. So then they came to fight on foot in hand-to-hand combat.

Il'ia swung with his fist, twirled round and fell onto the ground. The foreign warrior threw himself onto him, reached into his pocket for his knife to stab Il'ia. Il'ia recalled the pilgrims. They had told him, "you shall never die in battle." So he thought, "It appears that I am to die from the pagan knife of this foreigner anyway." But suddenly Il'ia's strength was renewed. Il'ia staggered to his feet, the warrior flew off him like a ball. Il'ia swung with his fist again and struck the warrior. And only droplets remained of him. He took his head and spiked it and put it on the barricade.

Once more there was a celebration at Prince Vladimir's. But Il'ia had heard of one more thing, that he should ride toward a mountain, at the base of which were some doors and inside were much gold and silver. Il'ia didn't need the money but he wanted to go out of interest.

So Il'ia rode out and there he saw a letter on the wall. "If you go to the right, you will be killed."

So Il'ia went to the right. He went deep into the forest. There in the forest some bandits were sitting. Il'ia killed every last one of them. He came back, tore the letter down, and hung up another, "Il'ia was there, he killed the bandits. You can ride freely."

So then Il'ia set off down the middle way where he was to be married. Il'ia rode up to a house. All around the house was a fence, but no one was to be seen. Il'ia stuck his hand into the door. The door flew off its hinges. A beautiful young lady came out onto the porch. "Il'ia, come inside the house." Il'ia went in and she sat him down at the table. "Here, eat a little of this and then lie down on the divan and later I'll come to you."

Il'ia said, "I have had enough to eat; I want nothing at all. Let's go to bed instead." But she didn't say a thing to him. Il'ia grabbed the young lady and threw her onto the bed, but she shouted out something into the cellar.

Il'ia immediately understood it all. He got out of the house, found the iron doors in the cellar, knocked the doors off their hinges, and ran into the cellar, where he found a witch. Beneath the bed she had some iron shackles.

Il'ia Muromets chopped her in two. Many young men had "gotten married" to her, and they were all dead, all had fallen into the cellar. Il'ia burned down the accursed place and rode away.

Il'ia rode up to the mountain. Again there was a door leading into the mountain. There stood a little boy, Vania, and he was guarding the castle.

"So, Il'ia, all these riches are yours. Take what you wish," said the little boy.

Il'ia refused. All the riches went to his brethren.

In Rus all was quiet and peaceful. Il'ia Muromets lived on seven years after the war and then died. And then he was seventeen years old (!).

A–T 650G*

350. (The Merchant's Son)

In a certain town the bridge had collapsed, and a merchant who lived in the town decided to build the bridge with his own money. Everybody accepted this with great pleasure since they knew the merchant would not stint his money on the construction. Soon the bridge was finished. The merchant sent his workman to find out whether people would praise him for it. The workman went, sat down beneath the bridge and listened. Many people passed over it, and they all praised the merchant. But then two pilgrims passed by, and one of them said, "This is a good man and he deserves praise, but he is to have even greater riches: he shall be given a son, and whatever he asks of God, it shall be given to him." The workman heard it all, came home, and told the merchant that everybody was praising him. But he said nothing of the two pilgrims.

The merchant went off to a fair, and while he was gone his wife gave birth to a son. The workman stole the child and carried him off to a village to raise him up. When he came back, he went around to all the neighbors and told them that his mistress had given birth to a boy and then eaten him in an attack of some disease. The child's mother lost all her senses when she asked, "Where's my child?" and they responded that she had eaten it. The police were notified and they wrote the merchant that he ought to drop everything and return home immediately. But he didn't particularly hurry, and therefore when he did arrive home, his wife wasn't there, having been locked in a tower until the case should be resolved.

About four years passed and then the workman took the child away from the village and started educating him. When the boy already understood everything, the workman led him into the garden and said to him, "Tell God to give you money." The heavens opened and at the feet of the boy there shone a heap of gold. Soon the workman grew very rich and married, but his wife gave him no peace and kept asking him where his wealth was from. At first he deceived her, but with her feminine curiosity the wife kept on asking and he told her everything. To prove it he promised to lead her into the garden. The boy heard this and set about punishing them. Once they went into the garden and told him to ask for some money, but the boy thought to himself, "Oh Lord, turn them into hounds!" Having thought that, he set off for the town in which he had been born. The dogs ran along after him. On the square there was a crowd of people. From someone in the crowd he learned that they were going to execute a woman who had eaten her child at its birth. He shouted out that they should let him go forward. The astonished people looked at him, but he paid no attention. Finally he got up to the scaffold and said in a loud voice, "Do you all believe that this woman could eat her own child?"

Then he ordered them to bring fire and he gave it to his dogs, saying, "Lick this!" Then he said, "But they can't lick fire, and neither can a mother eat her own child." And so he told it all in detail, who the dogs were, how he had led them into the garden, and he asked then that God make them into people again. They freed his mother, and then cut off the workman's head. His wife was put in a prison tower for a while.

A–T 652

351. The Seven Simeons

There lived and dwelt an old man with his old woman in the middle of the steppe. The hour came: the peasant gave his soul up to God, but the old woman a little later gave birth to seven identical boys, each one to go by the name of Simeon. So they grew and they grew, each just like the other, in face and in stature, and every morning all seven would go out to plow. It happened once that a tsar was riding through that area and from the road he saw that far away they were plowing the earth there in the steppe not as indentured laborers—there were so many people—and it was clear to him that in that area over there indentured labor was not the norm. So the tsar sent his groom to find out who the people were who were plowing there, of what family and status, whether they belonged to a landlord or to the tsar, whether they had permanent residence or whether they were hired.

So the groom came to them and asked, "What sort of folk are you, of what family and occupation?"

They answered him, "We are just such people, our mother gave birth to all of us seven Simeons. And we are plowing the land of our father and grandfather."

Returning, the groom told the tsar everything he had heard. The tsar was astonished: "I have never, ever heard of such a miracle!" he said, and right then he sent someone to tell the seven identical Simeons that he was waiting for them in his tower for their services and errands.

All seven of them got together and came to the royal chambers and stood in a row. "Well," said the tsar, "now answer me: what skills are you each capable of, which trade does each of you practice?"

The eldest stepped up. "I can forge an iron pillar about twenty sazhens high."

"And I," said the second, "can plant it in the ground."

"And I," said the third, "can climb up it and see all around far, far away, what is going on all over the whole world."

"And I," said the fourth, "can put together a ship that travels over the sea or over dry land."

The fifth one said, "I can trade various goods in many foreign lands."

"And I," said the sixth, "can dive into the sea with the ship, its people and goods, and swim beneath the water and then surface again where I need to."

"And I am a thief," said the seventh. "I can steal wherever I choose or whatever I admire."

"I cannot tolerate such a skill in my land, my tsardom," the tsar answered the last Simeon angrily, "and I'll give you just three days to clear out of my land, go wherever you like, but the other six Simeons I hereby order to remain here." The seventh Simeon grieved, having heard these royal words. He didn't know how he would live or what he was to do. At that time there was a beautiful tsarevna whom the tsar much adored. She lived beyond the mountains, beyond the seas, and there was no way he could acquire her to get married. The boyars and the royal voevodas thought that the thief, as he said he was, might be of use, and perhaps he would be capable of kidnapping the marvelous tsarevna, so they began trying to convince the tsar to keep the thief Simeon for a period. The tsar though about it and ordered him left at court.

So the next day the tsar summoned all his boyars and his voevodas and all the people. He ordered the seven Simeons to demonstrate their trades. The oldest Simeon, not hesitating at all, forged an iron pillar of twenty sazhens in height. And the tsar ordered his own people to plant the iron pillar in the ground but no matter how hard the people struggled, they couldn't plant it. So then the tsar ordered the second Simeon to plant the iron pillar in the ground. Then the third Simeon climbed up this pillar, sat down on the very top and began looking far far around, to see what and how everything was going on throughout the whole, wide world: and he saw the deep blue seas and ships dimly visible on them like spots, and he saw villages, and towns and a host of people; but he didn't see that marvelous tsarevna whom the tsar was so in love with. So he looked still harder at all aspects and suddenly he spied something: at the window in a far-off palace there sat the beautiful tsarevna, with crimson cheeks and white face and fine skin, and it was clear that marrow simply flowed through her bones (!).

"Do you see her?" the tsar shouted to him.

"I see her."

"Well, climb down quickly and fetch the tsarevna as quickly as you know how, and then bring her here regardless of anything else."

So the seven Simeons came together and they hewed together a boat, loaded it with every sort of good and with gifts, and all together they set out to sail over the seas to fetch the tsarevna beyond the dusky mountains and beyond the deep blue seas. They rode and they rode beneath heaven and earth and they tied up at a harbor of an unknown island. And the thief Simeon went off the boat with his Siberian tomcat and he walked over the island, but he begged his comrades and brothers not to disembark until he came back. He walked over the island and came to a town and in the square in front of the tsarevna's chambers he cavorted with that trained tomcat, the Siberian one. He ordered the tom to fetch things, to leap through a noose, to perform all sorts of foreign, German tricks.

At that very time the tsarevna was sitting at her window and she caught sight of this unknown beast, the likes of which she had never seen, nor had such in all her born days ever been raised there. She immediately sent her servant girl to find out what sort of beast it was and whether it was for sale. The thief Simeon listened to the beautiful maid, the tsarevna's servant girl, and he said, "My beast is a Siberian tomcat. As for sale, I wouldn't sell him for any money, but if he ever falls deeply in love with someone, I will give him to that person, I'll present him."

That's what the servant girl said to her tsarevna, and the tsarevna once more sent her sweet young thing to Simeon the thief: "Your beast has fallen deeply in love, so they say."

So Simeon went to the tsarevna's chambers and brought her as a gift his Siberian tomcat. He asked only that in exchange he be allowed to stay in her chambers for three days and partake of some royal hospitality, and then he added, "Shall I not teach you, beautiful tsarevna, how to play with and amuse yourself with this unknown creature, with the Siberian tomcat?" The tsarevna allowed it and the thief Simeon remained to spend the time in the royal palace.

News went throughout the chambers that the tsarevna had brought in this amazing unknown beast; everybody gathered together, the tsar and tsaritsa, and the tsareviches and the tsarevnas, and the boyars, and the voevodas, and all looked at it and admired it, why, they couldn't admire this playful beast, this learned tomcat, enough! They all wanted to acquire one for themselves and they asked the tsarevna, but the tsarevna didn't pay attention to any of them, nor would she give anyone her Siberian tomcat, she just stroked his silky coat, and played with him day and night, and she ordered that Simeon eat and drink as much as he wished so that everything was pleasant for him. Simeon thanked her for the hospitality, for her cordial welcome, and for her kindness, but on the third day he asked the tsarevna to permit him to return to his ship, to look at how things were going there and at the various beasts, seen and unseen, known and unknown, that he had brought with him.

The tsarevna begged permission of her father the tsar and in the evening with her servant girls and nannies she set off to look at Simeon's ship and the beasts seen and unseen, known and unknown. They came. Simeon the least was waiting on the shore and he asked the tsarevna not to get angry, but leave the servant girls and nannies on the land, while she would make the trip to the boat. "There are many beasts there, varied and beautiful. Whichever one you take a fancy after will be yours! But we can't present all those who fall in love with them—the nannies and servants—we can't give all of them beasts." The tsarevna agreed and she ordered her nannies and servant girls to wait for her on the shore and she followed Simeon onto the boat to see the wondrous wonders, the miraculous beasts. But when she had come on board, the ship set sail, and started going over the deep blue sea.

The tsar waited and waited for the tsarevna. The nannies and servant girls came back, crying, and told him of their misfortune. And the tsar became enraged and ordered a chase to be organized. They outfitted a ship, crowded people onto it, and the royal ship set off after the tsarevna's. It was scarcely visible in the distance—the seven Simeons' ship didn't know that the royal ship was flying after it, not just sailing. Now it was already close! When the seven Simeons saw that their pursuers were already close by, even catching up, they dove under the water together with the ship and the princess. For a long time they swam beneath the water and they surfaced again only when they were close to their native land. The royal boat in pursuit sailed for three days and three nights but it found nothing, and with that it returned.

So the seven Simeons came home with the beautiful maiden, they looked and there on the shore were as many people as there are peas, a really big number. The tsar himself was waiting at the harbor and with great joy he greeted his guests from over the seas, the seven Simeons and the beautiful tsarevna. When they had all disembarked onto the shore, the people began to shout and make noise. The tsar kissed the tsarevna on her sugary lips and led her into his white stone chambers where he seated them at oaken tables, with ironed tablecloths, and he treated them to all sorts of mead drinks and sweetmeats and soon they played out the wedding with his sweetheart, the tsarevna, and everyone was happy and there was a big feast for the entire baptized world. And he gave the seven Simeons their freedom throughout the tsardom, his country, to live and dwell freely, to trade without tariff, to possess lands granted by him without fear of forfeit. He showered all sorts of favors on them and sent them home with treasure for their livelihood.

I had this little old nag with wax shoulders and a pea-vine halter. I looked and I saw that the peasant's barn was afire, so I tied up my nag and went to water the barn. While I was watering the barn, my old nag melted and ravens pecked the peas out of the halter. So I traded her for a brick and was left with nothing. I had this cap, but near the gates I tripped; I bruised my knee, and now it hurts. And with that the tale's at an end.

A–T 653 + 1880

352. The Seven Semeons

There lived and dwelt this merchant. And he had seven sons. The seven sons were seven Semeons. Voice for voice, hair for hair alike, they were all of one womb. The merchant called them together and said, "I am getting old. Who will feed you? Go out and learn from the world."

So off they went. For a year they were gone, then for seven. After that they had learned everything.

Now, once the tsar was going through the town and he saw these seven bogatyrs walking around, these seven Semeons, voice for voice, hair for hair alike, seven all of one womb. And he said, "Where are you from?"

And they said, "We are a merchant's sons, seven Semeons all of one womb who have wandered over the earth for seven years learning."

"And what have you learned?"

The first said, "In seven minutes I can build an iron pillar from the earth to the sky, twenty sazhens."

The second said, "And I can climb up that pillar, look in all four directions and see what is going on."

The third said, "And I can shoot from my bow and hit a fly right in the eye."

The fourth said, "What my brother can shoot at a hundred versts, I can catch in flight."

The tsar was amazed at all this. "And you," he said, "what can you do?"

The sixth said, "I can go bang-bang and build a boat."

And the seventh said, "And whatever you require, I can steal."

At that the tsar turned red and he summoned his senators and his commanders and he ordered each to show his skill. So the first Semeon grabbed a fifteen-pood hammer and forged a pillar of twenty sazhens. The tsar ordered the commanders and senators to lift the pillar. They struggled and struggled, they broke into a sweat, but they couldn't raise the pillar. So the second Semeon set the pillar on one palm and breathed. He breathed and climbed up it. He climbed up to heaven itself and covered his eyes with his palm. Then he looked out in all directions. The tsar shouted, "What do you see?"

And he said, "I see that little father priest is squashing a louse with his knife."

"And what else?"

"I see some ships sailing on the ocean sea."

"And what else?"

"I see in another tsardom Elena the Most Beautiful weaving a carpet next to the window."

"What is she like?" pleaded the tsar.

"She is such a beauty as you've never seen. There is a moon below her braid, and on every little hair there is a pearl."

So here the tsar turned red and he ordered him to bring Elena to him, or else he would remove all their heads from their shoulders. The first Semeon said, "If you wish, your royal highness, you can order us to obtain for you a forest, lumber, and all sorts of materials most cheaply." The tsar ordered them to do so. So they took some of every sort of material from the shops and they also bought a cat, a singing and purring cat.

One Semeon took the boards and bang-bang he made a ship. Everything was loaded on board, they laid in candies and snacks, and they put the cat in a cage. And they set off. A fierce northerner got up and they were away. For three days they sailed until they came to the other tsardom.

The second Semeon looked: "I see her, I see Elena the Most Beautiful walking on the shore with her girlfriends, she is leading a procession." Then the youngest brother went out onto the shore, sat down and began playing his fife. And the cat—the songster and purrer—began singing songs and dancing with his paw. Ta-ta, ta-ta, just like that!

Elena the Most Beautiful said, "Sell me that kitten."

And he said, "That cat of ours is half a miracle. On board the ship we've got all kinds of miracles. Come on board and visit us."

So they all went onto the ship. And he said, "We have a narrow passageway, we have to go one at a time."

So she went first. He went after her, and then they took the gangway up and her girlfriends were left behind. They called her into a cabin and began showing her all their goods, trying to impress her. Meanwhile, they sailed away. She looked and looked and then she looked out the window and there was water all around. She went out onto the deck and cried out, "You have taken me away from my girlfriends, from my dear mother!"

And then she threw herself onto the floor and flew off as a gray duck. So one of them grabbed his bow and shot at her. She would have fallen into the water and perished, but the fourth grabbed her. So once again she became Elena the Most Beautiful. And she broke into tears.

And they said, "Don't cry, we are not bandits. We are taking you to become the wife of the Russian tsar."

So they brought her to the tsar. He was walking along the shore, waiting for the boat. And his commanders and senators were all there. The music had started playing and the bells had begun ringing. The wedding was played out ever so beautifully.

I was there, I drank mead and beer, but my mouth is crooked and it has a hole besides!

A–T 653

353. About a Tsar

There lived this tsar and tsaritsa and they had three sons. One was called Vasilii, the next was Semen, and the third was Ivan. There was also this stepdaughter, not one of their own, called Maria. And they all loved her. So they all grew, and they grew up and they all became men. They wanted to get married. So they all went to their father with this desire to get married, and they all wanted to get married to Maria. Their father thought about it. To whom should she be married? He thought about it from all sides, he even tried fortunetelling. All the courtiers helped him by reading in all the old books, but they could not decide. The father said, "Each of you go into your own town and there buy a present for Maria. Whoever buys the best present will be the one she marries."

So he gave them each an entourage and they rode off to their point of departure. There they agreed that whoever came back first would wait for the others.

So they rode up to each other, embraced, and said farewell. And the first brother, Vasilii, went his own way. He rode and rode and finally rode into a city where he took an apartment and started to live. He went to the bazaar to look for some sort of gift to buy in order to fulfill the task. He was walking along when he chanced to meet this man.

"Where are you going, good man?" he asked.

"Where are you going?"

"Do you not have some object to sell?"

"Yes, here is a flying carpet, buy this!"

"How much does it cost?"

"A thousand rubles." He bought it and set off for his apartment where he lived a month, rested, strolled around a little, and then he set off to the appointment place to wait for his brothers.

Now let's talk about Semen. He set off to seek his fortune. He rode and rode and he rode and there on a high hill stood a city. He rode into this city and took rooms with a certain old lady. This old woman had two daughters. He bought them earrings, he brought them rings. All the people around were amazed that such a guest had come. So he visited here, he drank there, and then he set off to find a purchase according to his instructions. He walked along and he met a man. "Buy this one thing of me!"

"Show me what it is!" And the man took out a telescope.

Semen asked, "How much does it cost?"

"Two thousand," the man answered.

"Why is it so expensive?"

"Because you can see in it whatever it is that you want to see."

Semen took the telescope and the very first thing he did was look to see where Maria was. Maria was sitting with her friends, all happy and cheerful. He looked and smiled, and he paid the money for the telescope. Then he went to his apartment, lived there two weeks and then went to the appointed place from which he and his brothers had parted.

And now about Ivan. Ivan had also set out and he came to the same town. He visited there, looked around and then set out to search for a purchase according to the assignment. He met this man. The man said, "Buy this one thing of me."

"What is it?"

"It's an apple."

"And how much does your apple cost?"

"Three thousand rubles."

"Why do you ask so much money for such an apple?"

"Because this is a special apple. If a person is near death, he can be cured. Just give it to him to sniff and he will be cured, he will recover from his illness."

So he bought it and paid the money and then he lived for a while in the town and then he rode off. He came to his brothers. They were already waiting for him. His brothers greeted him and then they began looking to see what kind of purchases each had made. Semen took his telescope and right away looked at Maria. Suddenly they saw that Maria was lying very ill, that she was near death. Then the brothers sat on the flying carpet and flew home; leaving their entourages behind, they flew alone.

They flew home and with the apple. They gave it to Maria to smell and she immediately began to get better and then she recovered completely. Once more their father didn't know how to proceed. If it hadn't been for the telescope, she would have died. If it hadn't been for the flying carpet, she would have died. If it hadn't been for the apple, she would have died. So they looked and looked and then their father said, "Each of you take a self-shooting arrow and shoot it. Whose arrow lands furthest will marry Maria."

Vasilii shot and his arrow landed, then Semen shot and his arrow landed further away. Finally Ivan shot and they couldn't find his arrow. They searched and searched, but they couldn't find it. So Maria was married to Semen, the middle brother.

Greatly annoyed, Vasilii went into a monastery, couldn't live there, and got sick. But Ivan went off to search for his arrow. He set off as he couldn't believe it was lost. So he walked and walked and walked and he saw a mountain with a shining white top and crevasse in it. And there in the crevasse his arrow was stuck, in the stone mountain. So he went up and let himself down into the crack and he turned out to be in an underworld tsardom. He was walking along and there were rooms everywhere, and everywhere people, and he walked and walked and he found the tsaritsa of the underground tsardom and he stayed there to live. He lived and lived there and then after about two months he became homesick for his own home. The tsaritsa, his hostess, said to him, "Why are you unhappy, Ivan Tsarevich? Why do you hang your unruly head so low?"

"I have this desire to see my father," he said.

"Then go there!" she said.

She gave him a ring, which he put on his finger, and he turned up at his father's palace. They saw each other, rejoiced, and his father began asking him questions. "How have you been, Ivan Tsarevich?"

"I've been living in an underworld tsardom where my wife is the tsaritsa of the underworld tsardom."

All the ministers began to envy him and said, "Give him a task: let him bring a tent, fold it so that it goes in his pocket, then unfold it so that it covers an entire army."

Ivan Tsarevich went home unhappy, with his unruly head hanging low. "What has saddened you, Ivan Tsarevich?"

"My father has given me this task."

"Oh," she said, "take this tent and carry it to your father."

So he took his father the tent and his father was utterly amazed, it was so wondrous. All the courtiers once more raged at him. "That task was no task. Somewhere there is a firebird in a golden cage. Give him the task of fetching it here."

So his father gave him that task. And again he came home. The tsaritsa asked him, "Why are you so unhappy, Ivan Tsarevich? Why do you hang down your unruly head? What has saddened you?"

He said, "My father has give me this service, to obtain a firebird in the golden cage."

"For that I will give you my gray wolf. Sit on him and ride to such and such a tsardom. There some harps will be laid out. You must leap across them, not disturbing any of them, and take the firebird in the golden cage."

So then he came and jumped on the wolf and began loping backward. He disturbed a harp and all the harps began to sing and the bells began to tinkle and they grabbed Ivan. They threw him in a dungeon. He lay there until morning and in the morning that tsar said, "Bring out that thief and show me who he is." They met. "What do you want the firebird for?"

"My father has ordered me to obtain it."

"Go to the Lion lake and get me a pitcher of water to make me young again and then I will give her to you, this bird."

So Ivan got on the gray wolf again and the gray wolf said to him, "Be a little more careful: when we come, fetch the water quickly." On the road the wolf met a flock of sheep and he slaughtered a sheep. "Here," he said, "when we get there, I'll throw hunks of sheep and the lions will throw themselves on them and you will fetch the water at that same time and then jump on me quickly."

When they got to the lake, he did just that. The wolf threw the meat and Ivan Tsarevich got the water, and jumped on the gray wolf so that the lions couldn't grab him. So he came to that tsar with the water, the tsar washed and became young. (If only he had brought me a pitcher of it so that my back wouldn't hurt so!) So then the tsar gave him the golden cage with the firebird, embraced him and said, "We shall be friends forever!"

Ivan Tsarevich came to his father, bringing the firebird. He presented the firebird to his father. His father was delighted. The firebird lit up the entire courtyard. His father thanked him and yet the courtiers again were outraged. They said, "Give him this task: we have heard that there is a dwarf as big as a thumbnail with a beard as long as a forearm, and he carries an iron rod on his shoulders that weighs thirty poods. Such a little fellow but so quick."

So again his fathered gave him the task of obtaining this little dwarf. Ivan Tsarevich again came home unhappy, his unruly head was hanging. "Why are you so concerned, Ivan Tsarevich? asked the tsaritsa.

"My father has given me the task of finding this little dwarf as big as a thumbnail with a beard as long as a forearm, who carries a thirty-pood iron rod on his shoulder."

The tsaritsa said, "That is not a difficult task. That dwarf is my own brother." She took and struck a fire, let off some smoke and suddenly the dwarf appeared, roaring like a beast.

"What do you need from me?" he asked. She entrusted the dwarf to Ivan Tsarevich and he led the little monster to his father. When he led the dwarf to his father, the dwarf roared, "What do you need from me?" And then the courtiers shrank from fear in their places. He made one swing with his rod and killed half of them at once. The others ran away from there. Then his father let his son go free. He came home to his father and from that time they have lived and been happy.

A–T 653A

354. Light of the Moon

There lived and dwelt a tsar. He had three sons. The tsar summoned them and said, "Each of you let fly a tempered arrow. You are to take a bride from the household of the yard where your arrow lands."

The first son's arrow landed in a boyar's yard, and the second son's in a merchant's yard. Ivan the Warrior set off after his tempered arrow and his fate and found a little old woman. Her bones were scarcely held together. Ivan the Warrior took a look at her and spat, then he turned and went away.

He walked and walked, and he walked deep into a swamp and soon was up to his ears in slime. "Oh," he thought to himself, "I'd have been better off to marry that old hag than to perish here in this swamp."

No sooner had he thought it than he was clean and dry. He went to the old woman and she said to him, "Call me your God-given bride, your beloved."

And he said, "Light of the Moon, Light of the Moon, my dearest."

And she said, "Don't be sad, Ivan the Warrior, until the tables pass by, I'll be an old woman, but afterward we shall see what God grants."

Ivan the Warrior led her to the tsar who said, "Present her with some gold and silver, with some pure pearls and let her depart."

But she said, "Wherever the arrow flies, there lies your fate, there is your wife."

And she would not depart. The people rejoiced in the first bride, they admired the second one, but they laughed at Ivan the Warrior.

Then after the wedding, he woke up in the night and there beside him was a beautiful woman such as has never been seen. And so every day she was as the little old woman but at night she was the beautiful woman. And Ivan the Warrior loved her so much, he caressed her so much, and he was vexed only that no one else could see her beauty.

Once the tsar ordered the brides to sew him a shirt over one night. The young brides watched the old woman to see how she would sew. But she knew how to trick them. She took a strip of coarse linen and tore it to shreds. "Winds, little winds, carry my shreds to the city, to my father, and there he has a shirt without seams, without stitches, it's like molded. Have it here by morning."

In the morning the young brides took their shirts to the tsar. The tsar took the first and said, "Oh, this is not satisfactory." And then the second: "And this is no better." The great man took the third and shook his head: "Now this is a shirt! What a beautiful thing it is!"

So then the next day the tsar said that the brides were to weave a carpet overnight. And the oldest brides said to the youngest maid, "Go, Chernavushka, and watch to see how the old woman weaves."

Then the old woman tore up her yarn and threw the pieces out the window. "Winds, little winds, take those pieces to the city to my father. He has a carpet that is neither sewn nor woven but nonetheless beautifully decorated."

The maid told this to the older brides who tore up their yarn and scattered it to the wind. But the yarn just lay beneath the window. So then they sent some boys and girls to collect the pieces and out of the ripped up yarn they made carpets. The great man took the carpets and shook his head. "These two won't even do for the kitchen, but the third carpet isn't a carpet—it's a thing of beauty."

So then the tsar ordered them to bake bread. The brides sent their maid Chernavka to the old woman and she said to her maid, "Bring some cold water and bring some unsifted flour." She mixed it, kneaded it, and placed it in a cold oven, and then she closed the oven tightly. "Bake, my bread, white as snow, and soft and crumbly and tasty!"

A little later she opened the fastener on the oven and took out the bread. The bread had baked as white as snow, and soft and crumbly and tasty. The maiden Chernavka told them everything and the brides said, "Husbands, bring us some cold water and some unsifted flour."

So they took it and let it rise and they put it in a cold oven. When they went to take it out, it had flowed all over the oven and they couldn't get it together. It was sticky and tough, and they couldn't think how to get rid of it. They summoned some house decorators and then set to work on the bread. And it was milled by the one and browned by the other.

So the great one accepted the bread, but he shook his head. "The first loaf and the second one too, to the backyard, for the pigs. But the third loaf is simply a beauty."

So then the two older brothers were already ready to exchange both their beauties for the old woman. So the tsar called a feast for the whole world and he invited the two brides. And they again sent their maid Chernavka. "Go, maid Chernavka, and see how she is getting ready."

The girl obeyed them and the old woman said, "Ivan Tsarevich, I shall go in a golden carriage, with black horses, and a golden harness."

And so the others repeated it. Then her carriage drove up for her and they helped her dress and led her out and she looked magnificent! The others waited and waited but there were no carriages and no horses. So they finally got in a droshky† and set off. But they came late!

Well, everyone sat down to feast. What she couldn't finish eating she put in her sleeve, and what she couldn't finish drinking she poured in her sleeve. So the others did just the same—they stuffed what they couldn't eat in their sleeves and poured in what they didn't drink. And so they ate and drank and then the tsar led them into his garden. And what a fine garden it was! So the old woman said, "My father's garden is a hundred times better."

And then the young brides said, "Upstart."

So then she took hold of one sleeve and shook it, and rivers flowed out, and ships; and then the other sleeve, and out came forests and little birds singly sweetly! And then she began dancing. The old woman danced heavily but her gestures were beautiful. So then the others set to dancing, but when they shook their sleeves with their faces smugly turned toward the ceiling, they

---

†An open, four-wheeled, horse-drawn carriage.

splashed everything and bespattered all. The tsar banished them from his sight. And after that feast and after that dance she would have become that beautiful woman, but Ivan the Warrior could not contain himself, he could not endure to await the night when she would become the beautiful woman (and for that reason she would remove a ring from her finger), so he took the ring and flung it into the sea. And she became angry, she was very vexed with him.

"Oh, Ivan the Warrior, after this feast and after this dance I would have become a beautiful woman, but you could not wait and now you must seek me in the thrice-nine tsardom, in the thrice-ten land." And she disappeared.

He wept and wept but then he set off seeking her. He had neither a coin nor a crust of bread. He walked and walked and finally he came to Baba Yaga's. "Good health to you, Ivan the Warrior, where are you aiming for, and are you going of your own free will or are you forced?"

So then Ivan the Warrior told her everything. "In my great sadness," he said, "I am going not of my free will to seek out my wife, Light of the Moon."

"But why should you seek her when she will fly here as a serpent and then you must hold her fast and not let her go, for she will try to burn everything with fire."

So he lay down underneath the bed. He grabbed her and she tried to burn everything with fire, and then he couldn't hold her anymore and she flew away. He started weeping and Baba Yaga said to him, "If you yourself are bad, no help from God's to be had!"

And so he set off further. He walked and walked and he came to a second Baba Yaga. She gave him a drink and fed him. "Well," she said, "Light of the Moon will soon fly here, so hold her tightly."

He had just lain down beneath the bed when up she flew as a serpent. He grabbed her, she spit some fire at him, and he let her go. Then she flew away. "Well," said Baba Yaga, "If you yourself are bad, no help from God's to be had!" Go to my eldest brother. He's very clever and perhaps he will be able to help you."

Then Ivan the Warrior started crying and he set off. He walked and he walked until he came to an old man. The old man questioned him and sat him down to eat several barrels of straw and several barrels of sour milk and then he sent him off to sleep for twelve months. After twelve months he woke him up saying, "Get up and have breakfast!"

So Ivan the Warrior got up and the old man gave him seven barrels of food to eat and then he sent him off to sleep for six months. After six months he woke him up: "Get up, Ivan the Warrior, and eat your dinner!"

He gave him three barrels to eat and sent him back to sleep for three months. After three months he woke him up and led him into the steppe. With his left hand he threw a mace high into the sky, and Ivan the Warrior caught it with his right. So then the old man gave him a counselor and some drops. So Ivan the Warrior set off again. He walked and walked and he walked up to the sea. And the sea was threatening. The counselor said to him, "Ivan the Warrior, pour out the drops."

He poured them out and suddenly a little boat came sailing toward him. He boarded it, crossed over the sea, and went on. He walked quickly. There he found a magic castle. And the birds all around shouted, "Ivan the Warrior, don't climb up that mountain, don't enter that castle, don't touch the wizard, but stay here with us. You will have everything except your wife, Light of the Moon."

"No, I need Light of the Moon!"

So he went up to the mountain and he climbed it, never glancing at his counselor. But then a wind blew him down off the mountain. He glanced at his counselor, took his sword, and started fighting with the wind. There was a shout. He had struck every sort of evil spirit. He fought and fought and then the evil wizard came flying at him. He flew at Ivan the Warrior, grabbed him in his claws and carried him off into the heavens. But Ivan the Warrior reached up to his throat and cut off his head with his sword. Ivan the Warrior fell onto the earth like a feather, but the wizard came down like a bag of bones.

"You may go, all you free birds. I am releasing you, I am freeing you. I have killed the evil spirit and freed you all. I have burned his bones and scattered the ashes."

So then he destroyed the castle and its marble halls, and he found his wife, not as an old woman but as the beautiful woman. And they set off home. They went as far as the sea, but how should they cross it? "We don't have an axe, we don't have a club."

But the counselor said, "Pour out some more drops." He poured the drops, a boat came up, they boarded it, and flew across the sea.

The tsar was already longing for them at home and he rejoiced when he saw Ivan the Warrior. "And who is this, this beautiful woman?"

"This is my wife, Light of the Moon."

A–T 654

355. A Tale About a Merchant

There lived and dwelt this merchant. He had several shops, and he had three sons. He educated them, gave them all the same education. He married two of them off, but the other, young, remained unmarried. The merchant gave them each a portion of his estate, to each he gave ten thousand, and he said, "I've now given you the main part. Now go out and earn what you want yourselves."

The two married sons went together and acquired a fishing business, but the third one, the unmarried one, set off to seek his fortune. He went away from home.

He walked and walked until night fell. He looked and saw in front of him a hut, and in it a light was burning. He went up to a little window and asked to be let in to spend the night. There lived an old man and an old woman. They let him in. He told them that his father was a merchant who had given him ten thousand rubles and that he had decided to go and seek his fortune.

The old man and the old woman advised him first of all to learn to play cards. "Then you will receive a diploma for that. Later study to be a captain, and afterward a full general."

So the merchant's son first learned to play cards, and then he became a captain, and he even studied enough to become a full general. After that he wanted to celebrate and to treat the entire town. He got some food and some wines, and he began treating all. But he himself never drank any wine at all. Everyone was having a good time, everyone was full of joy, and they were regaling him with wine.

So he drank and he got drunk, and he drank some more and then he passed out. Then some bandits robbed him. They took his shoes and they took all his money from him, and they gave him just an old sweater.

Where should he go? So he went home to his father. When he got there, his father had a watchman. His father came out but he didn't recognize his son. He ordered his watchman to put him in a dark cellar. "I never had such a son as this man," he said.

So they put him in this cellar, and then his father received a shipment of goods from America. Shortly the merchant who had brought the goods came to his father and said that the ship's entire crew had perished. He asked him to hire a new crew.

"We'll find one, we'll hire," said the merchant. "I have here a fine young man; he claims to be my son. I'll give him to you for your crew. And here's a package for you to give the master and mistress. Let them send this young man to work in a factory."

The ship traveled for a long time and then stopped in a certain town. The captain got off to go for a stroll. He saw that on shore a card game was going on. Three men were playing. The captain went up to them and said, "I want to play cards with you." They agreed. He sat down and lost all his money. He even lost the ship.

He came back to the ship despondent, and the merchant's son asked him, "Why are you unhappy, Captain?" The captain told him of his woe. "That's no woe. Give me your clothes. I'll go and play with them and get back all the money you lost."

The captain took everything off and the merchant's son got dressed, and put on his shoes—all his clothes—and set off for the town. He sat down to play cards with them and won everything. He got back all the money. He thought and thought about what to do, and then he decided not to go back onto the ship.

So he went into a shop and bought himself some fine clothes. Where should he go now? He thought and thought, and then he decided anyway to go back onto the ship, to be honest to the very end.

He came onto the ship, wearing the new clothes. He saw the captain and said, "However much money you lost, captain, I'll return to you. The rest of the money is mine."

He bought some food, some wines, and he began to treat the entire company. When they had all had too much to drink, the merchant's son went into the captain's cabin and took the letter that his father had written for the mistress. He unsealed it, read it, and wrote another letter saying, "As soon as you come to the harbor, marry this young man to your daughter." He sealed the letter, signed it, and placed it back on the table.

They sailed on for a long time. Suddenly they encountered a misfortune. Their ship got caught in such a maelstrom that they couldn't get out of it. Nobody could do anything at all. The merchant's son saw that things were bad, so he asked them to let him out of the brig, where they had locked him up, and give him the command of the ship. They agreed to this.

According to his instructions they prepared the cannons and shot them all into the maelstrom. The ship was thrown back by a half-kilometer but they got out of the maelstrom. They sailed on further.

They soon came into the harbor, in America. The mother and daughter were waiting at the docks. The captain gave the letter to the mistress. She was delighted and soon undertook to put on a wedding. The mistress married them, signed over a shop to her son-in-law, then all her shops, and they lived very happily.

The mistress's daughter had some wondrous name that you can't pronounce, not in our language, and therefore the merchant's son called her simply "my little wife."

The father-in-law was very important. He walked never looking from side to side, just like someone not quite a general should. And he thought that in the whole world there was no one more noble than he. And the merchant's son was a full general, but he didn't say a word about it.

Once he was going about town and he encountered his father-in-law. He saw him and quickly put on his epaulettes. The father-in-law didn't notice his son-in-law the full general, and didn't give him the required honor.

The son-in-law called him over and gave him a reprimand, and then he sent him to the lockup. He returned home, quietly undressed, and said nothing to anybody about it. He just said to his wife that her father had been locked up. Her mother came running in tears, and the son-in-law said, "They've taken papa, and you see it was because he considered himself number one in the town. I'll have to go and get him released."

The merchant's son put on his uniform of the full general and set off to see to the release of his father-in-law. He came and opened the doors, and the father-in-law saw him and was ready to run. Then the merchant's son came back and ordered his wife to summon her parents to dinner. They came and her father was frightened at the sight of a full general. He shouted, "Oh, I've come to the wrong place. Oh, this isn't the right place."

The son-in-law laughed and explained everything, how it had all happened, and then he said, "I don't need anything of yours at all. My wife and I will go away to my parents, and you can give me some goods to trade there."

The father-in-law agreed to do this. They took all the wealth with them and set off to his father, to the town where his father lived. He took over some shops and started trading, receiving goods to sell from abroad, from America. And they sent him all kinds of goods to sell.

His father saw that this new merchant had come and that he was trading better than he was. He didn't want to have anything to do with him. But then he did want to have a deal whereby they would trade together. But the young merchant didn't want to have anything to do with it. He traded just for himself and he got richer and richer, and the old man was being ruined more and more. He received no goods to sell.

So did the son pay back his father for not letting him in his house and causing him to wander throughout the world.

The young folk lived well, becoming richer and richer, and his father was completely ruined. That's all there is to say. That's all the tale. You've all heard enough.

A–T 654B*

356. The Three Engineers

Three engineers were walking along. They were having a conversation. One said, "I can cut out an eye, put it on a plate, and go without it. And later I can put it back in and it will see for me."

The second said, "I can cut out my heart, put it on a plate, walk around for a while, then put it back in, and it will work for me."

The third said, "I can cut off my arm, put it on the plate, walk around for a while without it, then reattach it and it will work."

So they did just what they had said. One cut out his eye, the second his heart, and the third his arm. They ordered a guard to watch over everything so that the cat wouldn't eat it. But the cat got into it and ate it all up.

The eyeless engineer caught the cat, cut out one of its eyes, and put it in. The engineer without the heart caught a pig, cut out her heart, and put it in himself. And the handless engineer caught a thief, cut off his arm, and attached it to himself.

They met again on the road and they had a conversation. The first said, "One of my eyes sleeps during the day and at night it looks for mice."

The second said, "I walk and walk and keep on trying to crawl into the garbage pit."

The third said, "I walk around and one of my arms keeps trying to find its way into other men's pockets."

A–T 660

357. Sleight of Hand

There was once this ship sailing and they had to tie up the ship to the shore. When they had tied it up, there was this ringing of bells everywhere, just like at Easter. "You are free to go now, men! Enjoy yourselves!" And they released them—the sailors, of course.

One of the sailors went to this German inn to dine. When he asked them to let him dine, they fed him. "What are you, feeding pigs out of a washtub?"

The waiter said, "If you want it, eat it; if not, don't. The master has ordered that you pay for it anyway." He gave him five rubles. Then the waiter brought him the change and he said, "The waiter and the buffet server can keep that for tea."

So then he wandered around for a whole week, and every time he paid for something, he refused to take the change. He always gave it away for a tip, for vodka. They began to like him and they welcomed him everywhere.

The German collected his money and went to do some shopping. When he had made his purchases, he handed over gold. The merchant said, "Why are you giving me this money? These are soldier's buttons! Just look!" He looked, and it was true. He rushed off home. He came back, wanting to take back the tips from the waiter and buffet server. It started a fight.

The affair spread. A document was sent to the governor. The governor summoned the sailor before him, "Listen, sailor, you had better admit to what you were doing."

"But I don't know anything about it."

"Admit it."

"Right now I can't admit to anything. Wait a while. For some reason the alarm bells are sounding everywhere."

"What do you mean, the alarm bells are sounding?"

They went running off and there were flames from top to bottom! It was impossible to go down the stairs. He ran back in. "Where are we to go next?"

"Quick, grab your papers and out the window!" But they were high up and it was impossible to jump. He grabbed hold of a feather bed and flung it out of the window. "Jump! Save yourself, and I'll save myself."

So the governor jumped out the window, but it turned out he was only jumping from the table onto the floor. He jumped up and then he shouted, "Sentry, sentry! Where is that man?" He was standing behind the door. "Shout for him to come here immediately.—So, sailor, here are two hundred rubles. Go now, and don't tell anyone about this (that he'd jumped from the table to the floor)." Of course, everyone found out about it and they made fun of him.

So they handed the affair over to a general. The general summoned him and shouted at him. "I'll tear your skin right off you!"

"Wait just a little bit. You and I are not to shout anymore."

"Why not?"

"There's a terrible spring flood."

"And why are there terrible floods?"

They went to have a look, and from floor to ceiling there was water rushing such that they couldn't get outside. They rushed to the third floor. The water had already come up to the third floor. They went into the attic and then out onto the roof, onto the gables. There was water there, too. So they climbed up onto the chimney.

Then, just when they were about to drown, along came a little boat, sailing right toward them. There were no oars in the boat, but it would take them somewhere—God only knows where. Then they came out onto dry land. The sailor said to the general, "Now God only knows where we have been brought—into some foreign lands. We won't be able to understand a thing here."

So off they went. Not far away there was a little village. They entered it but they couldn't understand anything anyone said. They didn't know anything, neither the one of them nor the other. So the sailor said, "They will probably hire us to herd cows."

"Where should we go? We'll have to take the job." So they were hired. The sailor became a herder and the general was his assistant.

So they herded all summer long. And they had been engaged for twenty-five rubles. When they had received these twenty-five rubles, they went out into a meadow to divide them. The sailor took fifteen rubles and gave the general ten. "Why did you give me just ten and take fifteen for yourself?" asked the general.

"I am the herder and you are my assistant. You used to be a general but now you are my assistant. I am your senior." The general agreed and took his ten rubles.

Then he said, "Whoever can get me back home can have these ten rubles."

So the sailor said, "Will that really happen?"

"I promise in body and soul." So then it turns out that they were sitting in the sailor's room and counting out the money. The general jumped up and shouted, "Just a moment! What sort of spring flood was that anyway?"

"Just a normal spring flood."

"Where? My children went off for a walk. Where are my children now?"

"They haven't come back from their walk. They're still out walking."

The sailor said, "Let's count out the money." So the general gave the sailor ten rubles.

"Now go with God," he said, "and if that German mug of yours comes around again, I'll be after you."

A–T 664A*

358. The Trickster

A certain soldier served twenty-five years in the service and after the twenty-five years he received retirement. For twenty-five years he had served, but never once did he look the tsar in the eye. He received his retirement papers and set off home. He was leaving the city and he thought to himself, "What a fool of a soldier I am! For twenty-five years I have served, but I've never seen the tsar! The home folk will ask me when I get home about the tsar and what will I tell them?"

So he took and turned and set off back into the city. He went straight to the royal court. A sentry stopped him, "Where are you going, countryman?"

"Well, countryman, I am going to see the tsar. I served for twenty-five years, but I have never looked the tsar in the eye. Be so kind as to report this to him." The tsar's attendants reported to him. The tsar ordered them to summon the soldier in person.

The soldier came face to face with the tsar and paid his respects to him. The tsar said, "Good health, countryman!"

"I wish you good health, your royal highness!"

"What do you need?"

"Just to see your face. I served for twenty-five years but never looked you in the face."

The tsar brought a chair over and sat him down on it and then he said, "Sit a little here on this chair, soldier, so that the devils don't singe you!" He sat down and the tsar said, "Well, soldier, I'll riddle you a riddle." So the tsar set the soldier this riddle: "How great is the whole world?"

"Not very great, your royal highness, not very great at all. In twenty-five hours the sun goes all around it."

The tsar said, "That is true, soldier, and now here is another riddle for you. How far is it from the earth to heaven?"

"Not very far, your royal highness. It's not very far from earth to heaven because if there's a clap up there, we hear it down here."

"That is true. And now here is a third riddle for you. How deep is the sea?" The soldier said, "Oh, your royal highness, that is not known. I had a grandfather of seventy years. He went away to that other world and now he is not here."

"That is true, soldier," said the tsar. The tsar took out twenty-five rubles as a reward for the soldier.

The soldier took them and went straight to the tavern. He caroused for an entire day and night and he spent ten golden rubles. "Now then," said the soldier to the tavern keeper, "here's the next to the last banknote for you. I'm off to get some gold for you." He went to the bazaar and there he bought a red carrot for three kopecks. He made ten gold pieces [from the carrot], brought them and handed them over. "Permit me, my lord!" He took the gold and gave the fourth banknote back to the soldier. And he put the gold in a little wooden box. Oh, how that miser tavern keeper wanted to gaze upon that gold! He grabbed them and they were nothing but rounds of carrot! He took the soldier by the scruff of the neck and dragged him off to face the tsar. He put the carrot slices in his pocket. He came before the tsar and pronounced a complaint against the soldier, saying that the soldier had wasted ten gold pieces and given him ten carrot rounds in payment. The soldier said, "Your royal highness, order him to show with what I settled my bill." The tavern keeper drew out of his pocket—finely minted gold! "Now you see, your royal highness, how I settled up with him."

"Young man and soldier, sit down here and talk with me. You, tavern keeper, can be off." The tsar said to the soldier, "Now then, soldier, show me a trick, but an easy one."

"I can, your royal highness. Sit down there on the couch, then look and tell me what time it is!"

"The beginning of the first!" Suddenly the door burst open and the room was filled with water. The tsar was up to his neck in water on the couch! The tsar broke into a run in an attempt to get out of the house. But in the courtyard he had to swim for it. His house was a three-storied one and there were stairs on all the floors. He managed to get there [to the top], but the flood waters covered all the dark forests. He sat on a roof finial and took a sip of water. A boat suddenly appeared before him. He popped into the boat. A wind came up and he was carried away God only knows where. The waters began to subside. They subsided and it became dry. The tsar was left on the dry land, but he didn't know where. And he really wanted to eat something. An old woman was coming along with some buns. "Come over here, old woman, and sell me a bun for three kopecks!"

She came up to him, she brought them up to him. "Oh, your royal highness, these buns are really hard, but if you will hold this tray, I'll bring you some soft ones."

So the tsar held the tray and a local soldier came up to him, by the name of Borisov, and he said, "What are you holding there?"

"These are buns."

"Hmm, let me have a look." He looked, and they were human skulls. The soldier grabbed him and put him into custody. They brought him to the court. He was to appear at the circuit court the next day. They sentenced him to a year in jail, then ninety corporal punishments, followed by eternal exile and hard labor.

"Oh," said the tsar, "That soldier! What has he done to me?!" So at the appointed time they drove up to the jail and they sat him back to front and brought him up to the gallows. They took off his clothes and tied him to a mare, then the executioner came up, took a double-tailed knout, snapped it and cracked it, and said "Once!" And the tsar shouted with all his strength "Oh, holy fathers!"

The tsar's attendants stood at the gates, frightened, and they ran into the reception room and there sat the soldier on the chair and the tsar on the couch. "Well, thank you, soldier. You played a good joke on me."

The soldier said to him, "Look, your royal highness, and tell me what time it was when we sat down." The tsar thought about a year had passed but it was just an hour. He wrote something out in his own hand. For the joke he gave him a wolf's ticket,† so that no one should take him in.

The soldier took it and set off. He came to a village where a bunch of people was gathered. And the soldier said, "Peace to you who are gathered here. Let me in to spend the night."

One old man said, "Come to my place. But do you perhaps know how to tell tales?"

"I can tell them, grandfather."

---

† A half-year reprieve given to those sentenced to eternal exile.

"Well, then, tell them!"

"But should I tell them to you alone? Don't you have a family?"

"There are two sons and two brides."

"That is just fine. When they come to your hut, all of them will hear." So they all gathered in the hut. They sat down and had supper and then the grandfather and the soldier lay down in the loft. The grandfather said, "Well, soldier, tell us a story."

"But the brides are sitting here and I tell tales with lots of swear words."

The old man shouted, "Brides, quickly, go to sleep!" The brides made up their beds and lay down to sleep. "Alright, soldier, now tell the story!"

"But what should I tell you. Just look at us! You are a bear and I am also a bear."

The old man felt himself. "In fact I am a bear and the soldier is also a bear."

"There's no point to your and my lying here in the loft," said the soldier. "We'll have to run away into the forest. But watch out, grandfather, if we run away into the forest, hunters may kill us. If they kill you, grandfather, then I'll do a somersault over you, and if they kill me, then you do one over me. And we'll both be alive."

They ran into the forest. Some hunters appeared and, bang at the soldier and they killed him. The old man stood in the forest and looked. "What should I do?" thought the old man. "He told me to turn a somersault." He flipped over him and banged onto the floor, and he shouted with the loudest voice: "Oh, fathers, I'm killed!"

The brides lit the light and raised him up from the floor. He thought he was in the forest but he had just toppled out of the loft and was all banged up. The old man got up and said, "Chase that villain out of here! He nearly killed me!" The soldier got up and went away, who knows where, and the old man is even now just dying.

A–T 664B*

359. The Prankster (two variants)

(A) In a certain village a soldier stopped in a hut to spend the night. In the hut were some maids and they were spinning at their wheels. The soldier was a prankster. He felt like amusing himself with the maids. So he drew a bottle with some sort of liquid out of his knapsack, uncapped it, and out of nowhere water started coming and there was soon a full yard on the floor. The maids all leapt onto the benches, but the water was after them, coming ever higher and higher. The maids let out a hue and cry as they were frightened that they would all drown, while the soldier rolled around laughing at them.

The girls saw that the soldier was no ordinary person but a prankster, and they started begging, they pleaded with him to let the water go out the door. So the soldier decided to please the maids. He went up to the door, opened it, and it was as if there had never been any water there. Immediately all the frightened maids took off running to their own houses. And the master saw that the soldier was a very knowing man so he treated him well before bedtime so that he wouldn't pull any more pranks in his hut.

(B) A soldier stopped one night in a village to spend the night in a very rich house. He was tired from the journey and asked for some supper. The master and mistress were stingy and wouldn't give him anything. Bitterness overcame the soldier. So he decided to play a prank on them. "It cannot be that you have nothing," he said, "I smell porridge and cabbage soup in the stove."

"Of course not, there's nothing," said the mistress, "have a look yourself."

"Show me," said the soldier. So the mistress went to unlatch the oven door and the soldier pulled some powder out of his backpack and went after her. The mistress unlatched the latch and the soldier saw that in fact in one corner there stood both porridge and cabbage soup. His heart tightened and then he threw that powder in there. And out of nowhere there appeared water! The water just poured out of the stove onto the floor. The master and mistress went onto the benches and the water went after them, the master and mistress went onto the stove and the water came up there too. The master and mistress saw that the soldier was no ordinary man and began asking his mercy against the water. The soldier then said, "So what did you think? That I wanted to drown you? Why, I simply can't pay attention to that. Why are you so timid? I was just thinking of making some supper for me. In just a moment some ducks will come flying—that's why I let so much water loose." And then out of nowhere a brace of wild ducks came flying up and started swimming in the space beneath the stove. The soldier said to the master, "Catch them under the stove and cut off their heads!" He cut off their heads. And the soldier said, "So now, fix supper. Now we don't need all that water." And he opened the door and in an instant all the water went away. The master looked at the dead ducks and where the ducks' heads had been lying, he had cut off his boots' uppers. The master saw that you just couldn't play jokes on the soldier and he started cursing the mistress for not having given the soldier something to eat. So the mistress climbed down from the stove and went to work and they did treat the soldier fine, like a dear guest. That's what it is to refuse strangers—such strange folk are everywhere.

A–T 664C*

360. The Prankster

A soldier was playing pranks on the folks. He asserted that he could climb through a tree. He lay a log down and as everyone watched he started climbing. But instead of climbing through that tree, he climbed behind it. The people were standing on one side and he was climbing on the other. A peasant came riding by on his way to town with some hay. So he was riding along and he saw how the prankster was tricking the people. He drew up even with the folk and said, "Orthodox Christians! Just look there. He's climbed on the back of the tree and not through it." The soldier decided he had been offended. He got up from behind the tree and said, "Peasant, oh peasant! Just look how that hay on your cart has caught fire!" The peasant looked and the hay really had caught fire. Then that peasant really did move around to put it out. And the people were rolling around with laughter because the prankster had put one over on the peasant.

So the peasant spread the hay out and the prankster said to him, "Peasant, oh peasant! Your wagon tongue is burning!" So the peasant started chopping the wagon tongue off. He chopped up the wagon tongue and then the prankster said to him, "Peasant, oh peasant! Your horse's collar and shaft bow have caught fire." So the peasant started chopping the harness tugs and the horse was out of the collar and away! "Enough already!" said the trickster. "Look, peasant, there's no fire to be seen, the hay never thought of burning, it's just scattered everywhere. You destroyed your horse collar and tugs for nothing." The peasant started howling at the prankster because he had tricked him. "Next time be more clever!" the prankster said to him. "When you see someone who knows what he is doing, be quiet if you want to be all in one piece." And so the peasant lost a whole cartload of hay, his cart, and collar all for nothing on account of his tongue, and he rode back home on his horse with empty hands.

A–T 664C**

361. The Prankster

A certain tsar had this prankster. The tsar was very stingy, he was greedy for gold. Once he summoned the prankster to him and said, "Make it so that all my table service—the cups, and spoons and glasses—all are gold." The prankster gave his word and did it. The next time the tsar called this same prankster to him and said, "Make it so that all my chairs, tables, and cupboards are gold!" The prankster gave his word and did it. A third time the tsar summoned him and said, "Now make it so that everything formal in my home is gold—all the clothing, and everything—so that I won't be able to see anything but gold."

The trickster said, "Oh, your majesty, you're ordering me to do something that isn't right."

"That's not your business," said the tsar, "you do as you're told!" So the prankster did everything according to the royal decree and then he went away. The tsar looked: everything everywhere was all gold. There wasn't even a speck of dust in the house that wasn't gold. He sat, admiring it all. And then he felt like having a drink. He summoned a servant and ordered him to bring him a drink. The servant brought it: a gold decanter, and a gold glass. The tsar looked and just couldn't look enough. But then he was pouring some water out of the decanter, but instead of water it was this gold liquid. The tsar was hesitant about taking a drink at first, but he really wanted something. So he drank a little glass full and as soon as he had drunk it, the gold started rolling around in his stomach and some sort of pain came. He immediately sent for the prankster. When the prankster came, the tsar had already died. That's what human greed leads to.

A–T 664D*

362. The Volunteer Soldier

In a certain village there lived a peasant, and he had three sons. They had all been born in the same year—they were triplets—and on the night when they appeared on earth, their father heard a voice that told him when the children grew up, each of them was to be occupied at his own business, for which God would bless them, and they could find out about this at the well beyond the village.

The children grew up and their father said to them, "Well, children, now you have grown up. It is time for you to begin a trade in something. For the next three nights each one of you go in turn to the well that is beyond the village and there you will learn everything."

So on the first night the eldest brother set out, and he stood beside the well, and at midnight an angel flew up and asked him, "What do you want to do in your life, oh servant of God?" The angel waited a long time for the answer but the youth was silent. "Then be a trader, that is what you have been destined to do since birth," said the angel and flew away. The youth came home and told his father what had happened.

On the second night the second brother went to the well. At midnight the angel flew up and pronounced him to be a tiller of the soil. On the third night the third brother set off. At midnight the angel came flying and asked, "What do you want to do in your life?"

The youth said, "I want to serve Father Tsar, I want to become a soldier."

"God will bless you in this service as you serve in faith and truth. And because you knew what to choose, throw yourself upon the earth."

The youth threw himself upon the earth and became a deer, and then he ran, the youth ran as a deer, and he strained himself with all his might and came to the well. "You were a deer, now, youth, be a lynx," said the angel. And the youth turned into a lynx. He ran for a while and was tired. The angel said, "The youth was a lynx, now let the youth be a falcon." The youth became a falcon. He flew and flew, and he grew tired, and then he threw himself upon the earth and became a youth again. "Now whenever you need to be something, throw yourself upon the earth and you can be a deer, a lynx, or a falcon," said the angel and flew away. The youth came home and said to his father, "I've decided to become a soldier and an angel has blessed this."

"Oh, my child, that is a bad decision, but it's too late to do anything about it. Probably, it is as God wishes it."

There was a general draft and the youth volunteered to go into the army. Just then there was a war and he immediately found himself in it. The war was a success, the tsar defeated the enemy and they concluded peace. The tsar and his army had gone far away from their tsardom, and when all the tsars gathered for a council, all were in their crowns but one. Our tsar was the only one without a crown. He had forgotten his crown at home and they wouldn't let him into the council without his crown. They gave him nine days to get a crown, although he and his army had been marching into the foreign land for a full year. Anyway, he asked of his army whether anyone could obtain the crown for him.

Morning came, then the day, and then evening fell. In the evening the soldier came to the tsar and said, "Your imperial highness, I can obtain your crown in nine days."

The tsar was overjoyed and said, "If you obtain it, I will marry my daughter to you and you will be tsar after me." So the tsar wrote a letter to his daughter and the soldier set off. He went into the steppe, threw himself against the earth, and became a deer. He began running. When he was tired, he became a lynx, and then a falcon, and in three days he had flown to his own tsardom.

He gave the letter to the tsar's daughter and she gave him the crown. In three days he was back again at the tsar's and he gave him the crown. Everyone was amazed and came to look at the soldier. The tsar concluded the peace and ordered them to conduct the soldier to his tsardom with honors and he appointed three generals to accompany him. The generals set off conducting the soldier but they became bored. It seemed beneath them to serve this simple soldier, so they decided to kill him.

The soldier heard the generals' conversation about their desire to kill him where there was a lake near the road. They drove up to the lake and the three generals looked at each other. One of them said to the soldier, "Go and bring up some water from the lake. You are still a soldier and we are generals." So the soldier got ready to get out of the carriage and go for the water, but one of the generals got a rifle. The soldier threw himself from the carriage onto the ground, became a deer, and headed for the lake. He ran to the lake and heard them shooting at him, so he threw himself into the lake, but as soon as he hit the water, he turned into a youth again. To his misfortune, at the lakeshore the grandson of the water spirit was swimming, and he grabbed the soldier and carried him away into the depths. The generals looked and looked at the lake. They saw that there was no deer, but the soldier didn't come out of the water either.

They decided to ride on. As they rode, they agreed to marry the son of one of the generals to the tsar's daughter, and when he was married, to divide the tsardom in three parts.

So the grandson brought the soldier to his grandfather: "Grandfather, I caught this Russian man and I've brought him to you. What should we do with him?"

"Let him go around with you and learn from him. He knows a lot."

So the soldier and grandson started going around together. The grandson showed him everything and the soldier said, "In Russia we have things even more amazing. Watch and I'll turn into a deer." He threw himself against the earth and became a deer. They walked around for a while and then he turned himself back into the soldier.

The grandson went up to him and said, "Teach me how, teach me to do that!"

"Such learning isn't given for nothing," said the soldier. "Throw yourself on the earth."

The grandson threw himself down but he didn't turn into a deer. "You're a good for nothing! You can't even throw yourself on the earth. Here then." The soldier took him in his hands and beat him with his head against the earth, and the boy squealed and howled, and he clobbered him, and he cuffed him here and there, but nothing happened at all. "You just can't do it," said the soldier, "tomorrow you'll see something else and maybe you'll be able to do that." So the next day they set off again, and the soldier turned into a lynx, and they walked for a while and then he turned back into the soldier. The grandson really wanted to become a lynx but nothing happened even though the soldier struck, ripped, clobbered him, and cuffed him about, but the boy didn't ask the soldier to turn himself into the falcon there. The soldier said, "Let's go to this certain place and perhaps you'll be able to do it there." So they went out to the shore and the soldier became a falcon and in an instant he pecked out the grandson's eyes and flew away.

The soldier flew away from the lake and back to his own tsardom. He flew into the town at the very moment the tsar's daughter was getting married to the general's son, and the feast had been announced for the next day, and everybody who wanted to come was invited to be the tsar's guest.

The soldier dressed himself as a beggar and also went to the feast, and he sat with the beggars. The tsarevna and her groom were strolling about and she went up to a table and asked, "You haven't heard how a soldier could have obtained that crown so quickly, have you?"

Nobody answered a thing. Then one beggar stood up and said, "I never saw him and I never heard anything about him, but in times past I could do that. I would turn into a deer and run, and then into a lynx and run, and then into a falcon and fly."

"Can you still do that?" asked the tsarevna.

"I can," said the soldier. So the soldier went outside and turned into a deer, then into a lynx, and finally into a falcon, and the folk there were amazed.

So the tsarevna said to her father, "Here, father, he has been found." So from a most honorable little feast to a true celebration! They were married, the soldier prospered, and afterward was tsar, and not a single other tsar dared go to war with him.

A–T 665

363. How Grandfather Sold the Stallions

The old man was away at work. And the old man didn't know that his wife had been left pregnant. Without him, without the old man, she gave birth. Then the old man set off home, but he didn't know that a son had been born to him.

He was walking home. It was the hot season. He suddenly wanted a drink. He had just started drinking, when a devil grabbed him by the beard and pulled. And he pulled. He said, "Let me go," and the devil said, "No, I won't let you go unless you give me what you don't know you have at home." The old man said, "Take it!"

So then he came home. And his wife had given birth to this boy. He thought to himself, "I'll have to give the devil this boy."

Then one night the devil appeared to the old man in a dream. "Bring me the boy, and if you don't bring him on the third night, I'll come myself and I'll make you pay for it."

So then the old man said to his wife, "You see, it's like this, I'll have to give up the boy." The mother cried, but he led him off.

He led and led him, and there stood a fine building. He passed through some doors, but there was no one there. He passed through others, but there was no one there. He passed through a third set of doors and there sat a fat devil. He started chuckling.

"So the old man is true to his word and has brought him!" Then the old man started crying and he went home and he left the boy there.

"Come after a year and if you can recognize your son, then I'll give him back to you."

So the year passed. The boy lived through the year and his father came to see what had happened. He opened a door and out ran a boy and said, "They are going to let us all out as doves. All will come out, but I will come out alone, dragging one wing."

"Let's go," said the devil, and if you recognize him, then your son will be yours. They were all coming out quietly, and he came along, dragging his little wing. And the devil said, "You two are clever, but I am more clever still. Come again after two years, then I'll give him to you."

Two years were up. For the second time he came after two years to see what had happened. His mother had packed up some supplies. The boy ran out. "They are going to let us out as bulls. All will go quietly, but when I go, I will switch my tail."

Then they let them out. All went quietly, but his own switched his tail and the devil said, "He is clever, he is becoming more clever than I. Well, for the third time, after three years you will come, old man, and if you recognize him, then you can take him."

He came for the third time and the boy ran out and said, "They are going to let us out as stallions. All will go quietly, but I will toss my head."

The devil said, "Well, let's go, old man, I will let them out." So the old man went and they let out the stallions, and all went quietly except one tossed his head. The old man shouted, "That one is mine! The one over there who tossed his head." So he led his son home but the devil paved the path with red-hot bricks: he wanted to burn them up. They went and they went and they came to a river.

"My son, how are we going to get across that river?" He quickly put the old man on his shoulders and swam straight across. They set off home. The old woman rejoiced as he brought their son in.

Then the son said, "Do you know, now I will become a well-fed bull. And you will take me to the bazaar and sell me. Whatever you do, don't give my halter to the person who buys me. If you give away my halter, you will lose me."

So he became a bull. And that very same devil appeared. "Well, old man, will you sell the bull?"

"I'll sell him."

"How much are you asking?" Whatever the old man asked he was paid. The devil took hold of the halter, as did the old man.

The old man said: "I won't give you the halter." The old man tore it away. He went home. The boy was running along in front of him.

Time passed. He said, "Do you know, now I will become a stallion. Whatever else, don't give my halter to whomever buys me."

So he led him to the bazaar and that same devil came along. "Old man, are you selling that stallion?"

"I am selling him."

"How much are you asking?" Whatever the old man asked, the devil paid. They yanked and yanked, and the devil yanked away the halter. The old man came home in tears and said, "I sold my son, that's it, he is no more. That evil one yanked the halter away from me."

The old woman shouted and cursed him: "How could you let go that halter?"

So the devil brought that stallion to his place. He stuck him in a bag and walled him in so that the boy had no way out. What was to be done? He became a cockroach. Gnaw, gnaw, he gnawed right through the wall and the boy went away and now the old man sells stallions.

A–T 667

364. Serpent Teaches a Herder the Language of the Birds

A certain herder was herding. There in the field he lit a bonfire. And in that bonfire there sat a serpent. The serpent began asking him: "Herder, pull me out of the fire."

"I'm afraid you'll bite me."

"Don't be afraid, you hold out a stick and I'll wind myself around it." The herder held out a stick and the serpent slithered up onto his shoulder and said, "I won't bite you. Take me to my father and he will pay you, only don't take it in money. Instead ask him to teach you to understand the language of the birds, which is what dogs and other beasts speak.

The herder took the serpent to his father and the father agreed. "Only don't tell anybody, only you can know, or else it's death." So he taught the herder to understand what all the beasts say.

The herder returned again to his herd and lay down beside the bonfire. In a tree there were two magpies cackling: "If only that herder knew where the gold is. It's lying right under that black ram over there."

The herder heard this, ran, and dug, and indeed he found a pot of gold. He brought it home and from day to day began to live better and richer. But his wife was curious. She kept on asking him, "How is it, why are we becoming richer and richer?" The herder took strength, but finally decided to tell her and then die. He dug a pit in the yard, lay down in it, and called his wife.

But just at that time a cock and a dog were in the yard. The dog said, "So our master has decided to die."

And the cock said, "Our master's a fool. I've got so many wives! And I am in control of them all, but the old man here can't control even one." The herder lay in the pit and heard them talking. Then he got angry, jumped out of the pit, and let his wife have it with a stick. And he never told her anything about his secret.

A–T 670

365. (The Wizard Okh and His Pupil)

There lived this old man and this old woman. The old man had this only son, Ivan. The old woman wasn't his mother. They had no more bread to eat. The old woman whined, "Old man, I don't care where, but you've got to send off your son. He's not needed."

The old man put on his belt and led him into the forest. He walked through the forest, he walked until he tripped on a stump and fell. "Okh," he said, "I fell."

Suddenly out of nowhere Okh appeared. "Where are you off to, old man? Where are you taking your son?"

"Into the forest, to leave him. We've nothing to eat at home."

"Give me your son. I'll teach him for three years."

"How much will you give me?"

"A hundred rubles."

"Son, live there for three years for a hundred rubles."

So Okh took him. He gave the old man a hundred rubles in coin. That was for bread for the old man. Then he said, "Come back in three years and I'll give you the rest."

So the old man went away. Three years passed. The money was all spent and there was nothing to eat. The old man set off. He saw two girls on the river in the forest, washing their clothes. "Where are you going, old man?"

"I've given my son to Okh and now the three years are up. It's time to take him away."

"He'll show you some sort of documents. If you know how to choose the right ones, you can take him; if not, he won't give him up."

"What can I do? How do I know?"

"Here's how: he'll bring out twelve doves and your son will be one. The one who drags his right wing a little lower than the other will be your son. Then he'll let loose twelve colts. Your son will come to the trough and a swarm of flies will be around him. Choose him."

So he went to the same place where he fell again, he tripped. "Okh," he said, "I've fallen." Out of nowhere Okh appeared again.

"Where are you going, old man?"

"I'm going to Okh. I gave him my son to be a worker."

"If you can choose him, I'll give him to you. If not, I won't give him to you." This was an obstacle for the old man. They went and he let loose twelve doves. "Which is your son?"

The old man looked and looked. Then he saw this one dove dragging its right wing lower than the left.

"It should be that one," he said.

"Someone is telling you this. How are you choosing, with your own mind or with somebody else's?"

"It may be poor, but it's mine."

He led him away to the yard. There he let loose twelve colts. "Which is your son?" The old man looked and looked. They all went to the trough to munch some oats. One of them had flies around his ears and he was unable to eat because he was shaking his head so much.

"That one's my son, my very own."

"And how did you recognize him? With your own mind or did other people teach you?"

"It may be poor, but it's mine," the old man kept on repeating.

"Well, can I take him now?"

"Wait. I'll give you dinner." He fed them dinner.

"Now can I take him?"

"No, I won't give him over to you yet. I still need to cook him in the kettle." He laid a fire, put the kettle on it, grabbed the boy, and threw him in it. He jumped out unharmed. He threw him in a second time, and the boy came out unharmed.

"Isn't that enough?"

"No, once more. But you already know better than I what will be." But in fact he didn't throw him in again.

The old man led his son home through the forest. A raven croaked, sitting on a birch. The old man asked his son, "You lived at Okh's. Perhaps you know why the raven is croaking?"

He started testing him. "I'd tell you, but you'd get angry."

"No, I won't get angry."

"Here's what it is: I am to rule, to become tsar, and you will wash my feet and drink the rinse water."

The old man didn't even look around. "I'll sell you again!" he said.

He went on a little further and met three hunters. They had two dogs, although each of them should have had a dog. The son saw the hunters. "There, father, I will turn myself into a dog. You can put a leash on me and lead me. Sell me to the hunters. Ask three hundred rubles."

The old man put him on a rope and led him off. The hunters said, "Where are you taking that dog, old man?"

"To sell him."

"Sell him to us."

"Buy him." They started haggling. "Three hundred rubles."

"Is he a good hunter?"

"Good."

The son had told the old man to sell him without the leash. "Sell me, but don't give up the leash." So they gave three hundred rubles for him.

"But I won't give you the rope. I need that."

"All right. If he's a good as you say, we will lead him just with a necktie." So they led the dog away, tying him with their own leash. Then they caught sight of a fallow deer. The other two dogs rushed at it, but the third sat there on the road. The deer tried to get away into the forest but the dog wouldn't let it by and grabbed it. The hunters caught it and then praised the dog. "A fine dog, that was a cheap purchase for such a dog."

So they went to another place and the dog rushed into the woods. It ran away. When it had disappeared, it turned back into a young man and went off home to the old man.

Soon they had eaten through all the money again. The old woman whined, "Go and sell our son."

The old man put him on a rope, because he had turned into a horse. He said, "Sell me as a horse but don't sell the halter." He became a golden-maned and golden-footed horse. "Don't take too little for me either. Ask for gold up to your knee."

He led him to the market. Merchants came up but they didn't have enough gold. Then two hunters were found and they bought him for their artel. They bought him, hitched him to a sleigh, and rode around. "This is a fine little horse; you just have to encourage him a little." They rode and rode. Then he pulled up, turned back into a young man, and left them there on the sleigh.

He went to the old man again. He lived there a year, then a second. They went through all the money again. The old woman whined that they had to sell him again. He turned into a horse even finer than the first. "Don't give him the harness."

The old man mumbled, "I will be tsar and you will drink the rinse water. Fine. This time I'll sell you with your halter."

He led him to the bazaar once more. Buyers came around and asked about him, but the price was too high. He wanted gold piled up to the chest. Not a single buyer could be found. Then along came Okh, who had taught the boy, and he turned out to be the buyer. He said, "I'll take him, but you'll have to give me the halter, too."

The old man thought, "He has angered me so that I'll sell him together with that halter." That Okh bought him, mounted him, and drove him off. He came home, all in a lather. Okh stretched out his legs up to a high crossbar and then went off to sleep.

Okh had a sister who took pity on him. "He wants a drink," she said. She led him off to the river to drink. He came to the river and then pulled deeper and deeper into it. He got far away and then he turned himself into a bird and flew away.

Okh looked for him but he was not to be found. He turned himself into an eagle and flew after him. He flew up to him, he almost caught him, but then he went into the sea and turned himself into a ruff. So Okh turned himself into a pike. The ruff found a stone with a hole in it, and he jammed himself into it. The pike stirred up the waters. "No," he said, "that pike is sharp, but he won't eat the ruff tail first!"

So Okh turned back into an eagle and flew home. And a general's cook went to fetch water and brought up the ruff in a bucket of water. She carried the water along in her bucket and he turned himself into a ring. She took the ring and put it on her finger. She had it on her finger and in the daytime she wore the ring but at night she slept with the young man: he had become a handsome young man.

Okh found out about it. A general had a large house, which he occupied by himself. And Okh came to rent part of the house from him. The general said, "I have no money."

"I'll work for you cheaply. Give me your cook's ring."

"I'll buy her three, all gold, and she'll hand it over." So they started asking her.

"I won't give it to you," she said. "It's something I found."

"If you won't give it up, they'll use force. Throw me on the floor and I will fall apart as poppy seeds," said the young man.

So they tried taking it off her and she threw it on the floor and he was transformed into poppy seeds.

Then Okh turned into a cock. The cock picked up a couple of seeds from the floor, and he turned into an eagle. He grabbed the cock, dragged it off, and killed it in the steppe.

So then Ivan the old man's son went back to his father again. He lived there about a year, or two, and then his stepmother started complaining again. "Go and sell your son! Sell him as a young man this time."

He led him through the town. "Where are you going, old man?"

"To sell my son."

They met some sailors. He was very handsome. "I'm selling my son. How much will you give me?"

"Three hundred rubles." He sold him. They took him and sent off to some other tsardom with goods to trade.

They came and tied up at the shore. They put out the flags. The tsar sent his servants to invite them. The royal servants came and saw Ivan the old man's son. He was really handsome. They looked around and forgot to ask why they had come. The tsar himself came and saw Ivan the old man's son. "Give him to me! I'll give you however much you want, just give him to me."

"No, the three of us bought him, and there's no way we could sell him."

"If you won't sell him, I won't let you in. Or you can trade, trade everything without cost."

So they took and gave him away for nothing. And then he was called Ivan Darokupets, Ivan Bought for Nothing.

The tsar took him back to the court and immediately gave him the title of general. Then he also had this daughter. So he married them and gave him all the tsardom. They had a wedding, and a very happy feast.

They say that the young mistress gives out gifts. And his father was a pauper. He heard about it and came for a gift, right into the room where the young tsar was with the young tsaritsa. "I need a place to live," he said. He needed a place to spend the night. The tsar was getting ready to go to bed. He washed his feet and the servants forgot to take away the basin. They gave the old man a place to sleep on the stove. In the night he needed something to drink. He walked around but couldn't find anything "Well," he said, "royal feet aren't poison. I'll drink this." And he drank his fill.

His son recognized him. In the morning he got up and said, "Well, father, I told you that you'd get angry, but that I'd be ruler of a tsardom and you would drink the rinse water from my feet. That's exactly what happened." Then he took his father in to live with him.

A–T 671

366. The Dreams

There lived and dwelt a peasant with his wife and children. One night he dreamed this dream, that beneath the stove in the hut lay this big bear. In the morning he told the dream to his wife. She said, "Ah, master, I had the very same dream."

And the children said, "Oh, father, we had the very same dream, too."

The peasant fell to thinking, "It can't be an accident that we all dreamed the same dream. It's a prophetic dream! But what does it mean? Is it for bad or for good?"

He thought and thought, and then he decided to go to the wizard Ason, who alone in all the tsardom interpreted dreams. He was riding to the village, and on the way he met a boy. "Uncle, let me hitch a ride!"

"Get along with you! No way am I taking you!"

"Uncle, let me hitch. I'll tell you something very special. You see, I know where you're going. You are going to Ason to have him interpret your dream."

The peasant was astonished. "Oh my goodness," he said, "what a clever boy you are! Get in the cart." He put the boy in the cart, and drove him around the village. Then he drove him to the outskirts and let him down.

"Thank you, uncle," said the boy. "Look here now, Ason will try to buy your dream, but don't sell it cheaply; take a hundred thousand at least! And if he asks who gave you that information, you be silent. Don't say anything about me."

So the peasant came to Ason. "Well, you see, one night I had this dream that there was this enormous bear lying beneath the stove. Figure out what this dream means for me."

The wizard rushed to look at his books. He looked something up and shook for joy. "Listen, peasant, sell me that dream!"

"Oh, why not sell it?!"

"What will I have to give for it?"

"Give me a hundred thousand."

"Oh, you son-of-a-bitch!" Ason shouted at the peasant and stamped his feet. "What's there for me in your dream—a lot of greed? I want to aid you in your poverty, but you, fool, have put such a price on it."

"Whatever, but I won't take a kopeck less." They argued and argued; they swore and swore; but the wizard saw that there was nothing to be done: he couldn't out-argue the peasant, and the price really wasn't out of line. Even if he had to pay a hundred thousand, there'd still be another hundred thousand profit. He loaded up two big carts of money for the peasant, and the next morning went to the village with four carts. He broke down the stove, and there was gold and silver everywhere. He could scarcely carry it away in four. He started getting ready to go, and said to his host, "Listen, peasant, tell me who instructed you to ask just so much for selling that dream? You never would have guessed that yourself."

"No, brother, I'm not going to tell you."

"Tell me, and I'll add in another five thousand."

The peasant was immediately seduced by the money and he betrayed the boy. Then they said their farewells, and the wizard set off home. The peasant was now rich and started living like it, like a merchant.

The next day Ason got ready, just like a landowner he harnessed his horses, sat down in the carriage, and rode right to the courtyard of the boy's parents. He rode up and said, "Could I rest here a little?"

"Why not? Rest!"

He went into the hut, and there were some conversations: "Whose boy is that sleeping there?"

"That's my son," said the old man.

"Listen, old man, I've taken a liking to that boy. I see that you are living in poverty here, and I have gold and all sorts of property—whatever your heart desires—but God didn't give me any children. Give me the boy; I'll be a father to him; I'll introduce him in society; and you and your old woman I'll reward with money and grain."

The old man and the old woman fretted and fretted about it, then they agreed. They sold their son for five thousand. Ason took the sleeping boy, put him in a cart, and drove off to his hut. They got home and the boy woke up: where was he?

"Why are your eyes popping out? Why, you know why I brought you here!"

"How should I not know?" said the boy. "In order that I should sleep with your young wife later on!"

"No, brother, you haven't guessed it," said the wizard. He smiled wickedly and shouted, "call the cook in!"

The cook came in. He whispered to him in his ear, "Take this boy, kill him, remove his heart, fry it, and bring it to me."

The cook led the boy into the kitchen, got a big knife, and proceeded to sharpen it on a stone. "What's that for? You intend to kill me."

"You're quite right!"

"Listen, brother, take pity on me; let me go free. God will reward you."

"I would let you go, but my master is clever; he'd find out."

"Don't be afraid; he won't find out. Outside you have this pregnant sow. Go and ask your master how many piglets she will farrow. He won't guess it."

The cook went to Ason and asked him about the sow. He returned and said, "the master says that there will be twelve piglets."

"Well, he didn't guess right. Your sow has already farrowed, and she delivered thirteen."

The cook ran out to check it: there were precisely thirteen.

"You are absolutely right," he said to the boy.

"So now let me go free. Kill the thirteenth piglet, take out its heart, fry it, and take it to your master."

So that's what the cook did. He brought the piglet's heart, but as soon as he had crossed over the threshold, he dropped the platter. A dog grabbed and ate that heart.

"Oh, the hound take it!" said the wizard. Then the boy went out onto the highway and in a long time or a short time he came to the capital city. He stopped near the traders' booths to admire some foreign luxury goods. A merchant saw him and hired him on as a supply clerk. After that time the merchant's trade expanded greatly. Buyers crowded into the shop. There was simply no keeping them out. They could hardly manage to collect all the money.

Time passed, and the boy grew and grew until he had grown up and become such a fine young man, and so handsome that you can't tell of him in a tale or describe him with a pen. Then one day Ason's young wife came to the traders' booths to shop. She went into the richest shop, and saw the young clerk, and immediately fell in love with him. She selected a whole pile of all sorts of goods, and said, "Listen, my good young man! I don't have any money with me. Take it upon yourself to come after the money and spend the evening with me in my house. I live such and such. . . ."

"My pleasure, madam."

In the evening he went to her after the money. She seized him by his white hands and led him into her bedroom. There she started kissing him and pressing him to her breast. She lay him down in her soft bed beside her.

"Now," she said, "move closer to me. We'll be warmer."

So they made love, and afterward began visiting each other, whiling away the nights together. About a year had passed; then the tsar of that land dreamed a dream. In his palace there stood a precious gold goblet, but the cusp of the goblet was broken. The tsar got up in the morning and wondered what that dream could mean. He sent forth the wizard, Ason. "Well, Ason, figure out my dream." The wizard rushed to look at his books. He searched and searched, but he found nothing. He couldn't figure out the tsar's dream. The tsar got angry and gave him three days. "If you don't guess it, I'll order you executed."

Three days passed. They brought Ason out onto the square and hanged him on the gallows. Then the tsar sent orders throughout the land: whoever could interpret his dream would receive half his tsardom. The young clerk heard about this, appeared before the tsar late one evening, and said, "Your Highness, I can interpret your dream."

"Interpret it then! If you tell me the truth, I'll reward you with half the tsardom. If you lie, then it's my sword, and your head from your shoulders."

He said, "Your Highness has three daughters. Tell me which of the three do you love most? Which do you give most to?"

"All three are dear to me," answered the tsar. "But I love and favor the youngest most of all. There's no one dearer on earth."

"Let's go into her bedroom then; there's the answer to your dream."

They went into the tsarevna's bedroom. They looked: the door was locked. The tsar knocked. "Open up, daughter!"

"Oh, father, I've already gone to bed."

"Never mind, open up."

"But I'm not dressed."

"Open up, or I'll order them to break down the door." The daughter opened the door. The tsar and the clerk went into the bedroom. The tsarevna was just in a night shift, and so was her nanny. The clerk ran up to the nanny and turned back her shift. "Just look, your Highness." The tsar looked, and there between the nanny's legs lay this enormous cock! "That very night, your Highness, when you dreamed that the lip of your precious goblet was broken, this 'nanny' broke your daughter's cherry."

The tsar gave the clerk half his tsardom; he punished his daughter; he executed the nanny; and he ordered all that had taken place be kept a secret. No one else was to be told a thing.

The clerk became tsar and married Ason's widow. He got rich and lived and dwelt well, becoming prosperous. He knew no misfortune.

A–T 671E* + 875D

367. A Cunning Gentleman

A gentleman was riding along a road once with his coachman, and the gentleman was one of those cunning ones. He saw a snake on the road, took it, ordered some water poured into a pot, started a fire and threw the snake into the water. From this he boiled up the first snake soup. Then he threw the hot water on the grass and the grass was as if burned up! A second time he boiled it and again he poured it out and the grass turned pale. He boiled it a third time and left it to cool, instructing the coachman not to touch it. But the coachman thought, "Why did the gentleman forbid me to touch it? Let me just try it!" He sipped about three spoonfuls and became frightened: all around him he heard the grasses start to talk, and the flowers and the trees. Every grass blade muttered about his own thing, "What sort of miracle is this?"

They rode off through the forest and he listened to some grass standing on a knoll as it bowed and said, "And I, I am from the last sheaf, I am from the last sheaf."† It seemed funny to him and he started laughing.

The gentleman asked: "Did you eat some of that soup?"

"No, sir!"

"Then why are you laughing?"

"Just because, sir."

"But don't you remember the name of that grass, something like wormwood?"

"Chernobylnik, sir." As soon as he said "Chernobylnik," all was changed by some unseen hand and it was again quiet in the forest and not a tree, not a blade of grass, said a word.

A–T 672D*

368. Emelian the Fool

It was in a certain village: there lived a peasant and he had three sons, and two were clever but the third was a fool whom they called Emelia. And so as their father lived for a long time, he came into deep old age, and he called his sons to him and said to them:

"Dear children! I sense that you will not live long with me. I am going to leave you the house and livestock, which you are to divide into equal portions; and I am also leaving you one hundred rubles each." After that their father soon died, and the children, burying him honorably, lived happily.

But then Emelian's brothers decided to go into town to do some trade with that three hundred rubles their father had willed them and they said to the fool Emelian: "Listen, fool, we are going into town and we'll take your hundred rubles with us and we'll do some trading and then we'll divide the profits in half and buy you a red kaftan, a red cap, and some red boots. But you stay home here. And if our wives ask you to do anything, because they're your sisters-in-law (you see they were married), you do it." The fool, wanting to get the promised red kaftan, red cap, and red boots, answered his brothers that he would do whatever they desired. After that the brothers set off for town and the fool stayed at home and lived with his sisters-in-law.

Well then, after a little time, one day when it was wintertime and there was a heavy frost, the sisters-in-law told him to go fetch some water. But the fool, who was lying on the stove, said, "Why don't you do it?"

---

†The last sheaf was thought to have magical qualities.

The sisters-in-law shouted at him: "What do you mean, fool, 'why don't we do it?' Can't you see there's a heavy frost and a man should go at such a time?" But he said, "I'm too lazy." The sisters-in-law shouted at him again: "What do you mean, lazy? You'll want to eat and if there's no water, then nothing can be cooked." And they added: "Very well, we'll tell our husbands when they come and even if they've bought you that red kaftan and everything, they shouldn't give you anything," which, when the fool heard it, and really desiring the red kaftan and cap, he was forced to go, he got off the stove, began to put his boots on and get dressed. And when he was completely dressed, he took some buckets and an axe with him and set off for the river, because their village was set right alongside the river, and when he got to the river, he started to cut an ice hole, and he cut an extremely large one. And then he filled the buckets with water and set them on the ice and stood there alongside the ice hole, looking in the water.

At that very moment the fool saw an enormous pike swimming in the ice hole, and Emelia, no matter how stupid he was, wanted to catch that pike and so he started creeping up on it, and he came up right close and suddenly grabbed it with his hand and pulled it out of the water and then he stuffed it inside his shirt and was ready to go home. But the pike said to him, "What are you doing, fool? Why did you catch me?"

"What do you mean?" he said. "I'll take you home and tell my sisters-in-law to cook you."

"No, fool, don't take me home; let me back in the water and I will make you a rich man for it." But the fool didn't believe the pike and got ready to go home. The pike, seeing that the fool wouldn't let him go, said, "Listen, fool, let me back in the water; I will do this for you: whatever you desire, I shall fulfill your desire."

The fool, hearing this, was overjoyed, for he was extraordinarily lazy, and he thought to himself: "If the pike will do whatever I want, then all will be perfect, and I won't have to work anymore." He said to the pike: "I will let you go only if you do what you promise," to which the pike replied, "First you let me back into the water, and then I'll fulfill my promise. But the fool said to the pike that it had to fulfill the promise first and then he would let it go.

So the pike, seeing that he didn't want to let it go into the water, said, "If you want me to tell you how to do what you don't feel like doing, then first you have to tell me what it is." The fool told her, "I want these buckets of water to go up the hill (their village was on a hill) and I don't want the water to splash out."

The pike immediately said to him, "Nothing will splash out at all! Only remember the words that I'm about to tell you. And these are the words: "By order of the pike, and by my request, march, buckets, right up that hill."

The fool repeated after her: "By order of the pike, and by my request, march, buckets, right up that hill." And the buckets together with the shoulder yoke set off up the hill all by themselves. When he saw this, Emelia was really astonished. Then he spoke to the pike, "Will it always be like this?"

And the pike answered him, "All will be just as you wish; only don't ever forget the words I've told you." So then he released the pike into the water and set off after his buckets.

His neighbors, when they saw him, were amazed and talked among themselves: "What is that fool doing? Those buckets of water are walking along by themselves, and he is just walking along after them." But Emelia didn't say a word to any of them. He just came home. The buckets went into the hut and stood on a bench, and the fool climbed up onto the stove.

After a little while his sisters-in-law spoke to him again. "Emelia, why are you lying there? You should go and chop some wood."

But the fool said, "Yes, and you?"

"What do you mean, us?" his sisters-in-law shouted at him. "It's winter now and if you don't go chop some wood, you are going to be cold."

"I'm too lazy," said the fool.

"Why are you so lazy?" the sisters-in-law asked him. "You won't freeze!" And they added, "If you don't go chop some wood, we'll tell our husbands not to give you the red kaftan or the red cap or the red boots."

Because the fool wanted to get the red kaftan, red cap, and the red boots, he was obliged to chop some wood, but since he was lazy and didn't want to get down from the stove, he said very, very quietly, while lying on the stove, the following words: "By order of the pike, and by my request, you, axe, go and chop up some wood, and then you, wood, come into the hut and lay yourself by the stove." The axe out of nowhere jumped out into the courtyard and started chopping. And then the wood came into the hut and laid itself down by the stove. When they saw this, the sisters-in-law were greatly astonished at Emelian's cleverness. And so every day whenever they ordered the fool to chop some wood, the axe would chop it up.

And so he lived with these sisters-in-law for some time, but then the sisters-in-law said to him, "Emelia, we are out of wood. Go into the woods and cut some down."

The fool said to them, "And why don't you do it?"

"What do you mean, why should we?" answered the sisters-in-law. "The woods are far away and it's winter and we'd get cold going into the woods for wood."

But the fool said to them, "I'm too lazy."

"Why are you lazy?" said the sisters-in-law. "You'll be cold if you don't, and we'll tell your brothers, our husbands, if you don't go, and we won't let them give anything to you, neither the red kaftan, nor the red cap, nor the red boots." The fool, desiring the red kaftan, the red cap, and the red boots, was forced to go into the woods for wood. Arising, he got down off the stove, put on his boots and dressed.

When he had dressed, he went outside and pulled the sleigh out from under the side porch, took a rope and axe with him, got in the sleigh, and told his sisters-in-law to open the gates. His sisters-in-law saw that he was proposing to go in the sleigh but without any horses because the fool hadn't bothered to harness the horses yet. They said to him, "Emelia, you're a fool for sitting in the sleigh before you've harnessed the horses!" But he said that he didn't need any horses and would they just open the gates.

The sisters-in-law opened the gates and the fool, sitting there in the sleigh, said, "By order of the pike, and by my request, sleigh, set off for the forest." With these words the sleigh immediately left the courtyard, which greatly astonished all the peasants living in that village, seeing Emelia riding in a sleigh without any horses, and so quickly to boot. Even if there had been a pair of horses harnessed up, they would not have gone any faster than Emelian was going. So then Emelia had to get to the forest by going through the town and so he started through this town but he didn't know what he ought to shout so that people wouldn't be crushed by the sleigh, so he rode along without shouting for people to get out of the way and therefore he crushed a whole lot of people. They chased after him but they couldn't catch up to him at all.

So then Emelia left the town and came to the woods, and then he stopped, climbed out of the sleigh and said, "By order of the pike, and by my request, axe, chop some wood, and you, logs, lay yourselves in the sleigh and be tied up by the rope!" The moment the fool said the words, the axe started chopping the wood, and the logs arranged themselves in the sleigh and were tied with the rope. When he had cut all the wood he needed, he ordered his axe to cut a club. When the axe had cut it, he got into the cart and said, "Well, now, by order of the pike, and by my request, go home now, sleigh, go home by yourself." Off the sleigh set, very quickly, too, and he approached the town where he had crushed so many people. They were waiting for him there, hoping to catch him. He rode into the town and they caught him and started dragging him out of the sleigh. They were beating him, too. Noticing that they were dragging him out of the sleigh and beating him, the fool quietly said these words: "By order of the pike, and by my request, club, break their arms and legs!" The club immediately jumped up and started beating all of them. So then all the folk started running away and the fool drove out of the city for home, and the club finished beating them all and then rolled along after him. And so Emelia came home and climbed back onto the stove.

After that he left the town and they began talking about what had been going on—not so much that he had crushed a whole host of people as that he could ride on a sleigh without horses. Little by little these conversations got to the king himself. When the king heard it, he really wanted to see him and he sent an officer together with several soldiers to search him out. The officer sent by the king rode out of town quickly and happened on the road the fool had taken into the forest. And when the officer rode into the village where Emelia lived, he called the mayor and said to him, "I have been sent by the king to fetch your fool and take him before the king."

The mayor immediately pointed to the courtyard where Emelia lived and the officer went up to the hut and asked, "Where's the fool?"

And there he was lying on the stove, and he answered, "What's it to you?"

"What do you mean? Get dressed quickly. I will take you to the king."

But Emelia said, "What business have I there?" The officer got angry with him for his rude words and slapped him on the cheek. The fool, thinking they were going to beat him, said very quietly, "By order of the pike, and by my request, club, break all their arms and legs." Immediately the club jumped up and beat them, and it beat them all up, the officer and the soldiers. The officer was forced to ride back. He rode into the town and it was reported to the king that the fool had beaten them all. So this time the king chose a wise man and sent him off to bring back the fool if at all possible— even if by deceit.

The king's messenger set off and came to the village where Emelia lived, and then he summoned the mayor and said to him, "I've been sent by the king for your fool, to bring him in. Call before me all those who live with him." So the mayor immediately ran and brought back the sisters-in-law. The king's messenger asked them, "What does the fool like?"

And the sisters-in-law answered, "Esteemed sir, what does the fool like? If you ask him persistently about something, he will refuse once, a second time, but on the third time he'll do it. But he doesn't like it if someone acts coarsely toward him."

So the king's messenger let them go, ordering them not to tell Emelia that he had summoned them before him. And then he bought some raisins, some prunes, and some grapes, and then he set off to see the fool. He came into the hut, went up to the stove, and said, "Why are you lying on the stove, Emelia?" and then he gave him the raisins, prunes, and grapes, and he asked him, "Emelia, come to the king with me, I will take you there."

But the fool said, "I'm warm here," for he really didn't like anything except warmth.

Then the king's messenger began begging him, "Please, Emelia, let's go! It will be really fine for you there."

But the fool said, "I'm too lazy." And then the king's messenger begged him, "Please! Let's go. The king has ordered a red kaftan, a red cap, and red boots made for you."

When the fool heard that a red kaftan was ordered sewn for him if he should go, he said, "Let's go. You go first and I'll come along behind you."

The king's messenger continued pestering him. He walked a little way off from him and asked the sisters-in-law very quietly, "Will the fool deceive me?" But they assured him that he wouldn't be deceived.

So then the messenger rode back and the fool lay there on the stove and said, "Oh, how I don't want to go to see the king! But I'll have to." So then he said, "By order of the pike, by my request, let's go, stove, right into town." So then the hut shook and the stove left the hut and then the courtyard. And the stove went so quickly that you couldn't catch up to it. On the road he caught up with the messenger who had been sent to fetch him and they rode into the palace together.

When the king found out that the fool had come, he and his ministers went out to look at him, and when he saw that Emelia had arrived on a stove, he didn't say a word. Then the king asked him, "Why did you crush so many people when you went into the forest after wood?"

Then Emelia said, "I'm guilty, am I? Why didn't they move to the side?" Just at that moment the king's daughter went up to the window and looked at the fool, and Emelia unexpectedly looked up at the same window through which she was looking, and when the fool saw that she was extremely beautiful, he said very quietly, "By order of the pike, and by my request, let that beautiful girl fall in love with me!" He had no sooner said these words than the king's daughter looked at him and fell in love. And after this the fool said, "Now then, by order of the pike, and by my request, go home now, stove!" And then the stove set off home, and when it got there, it went back to its usual place.

For some time after that Emelia lived very comfortably. But in the town, at the king's, things were developing very differently, for on account of the fool's words the king's daughter had fallen in love and she was asking her father to marry her off to the fool! The king was extremely angry with the fool but he didn't know how to deal with him. Just then his ministers proposed to the king that he send that same officer after Emelia who hadn't known how to get hold of him earlier. Following their advice he ordered the officer to appear before him on account of his failure. When the officer appeared, the king said to him, "Listen, my friend, I sent you after that fool before, but you didn't bring him in. For your failure I am sending you a second time and you will bring him here unfailingly. If you bring him back, you will be rewarded; but if you don't bring him back, you will be punished."

The officer listened carefully to the king and then quickly set off after the fool. As he came into the village, he once more summoned the mayor and said to him, "Here is some money. Buy everything you need and then invite Emelia to come to dine tomorrow. Then while he is dining, get him stone drunk such that he falls asleep."

The mayor knew that he had come from the king and thus he was forced to obey him. He bought everything and invited the fool. When Emelia said he would come, the officer looked forward to it with great pleasure. The next day the fool came. The mayor gave him a lot to drink and got him stone drunk, such that Emelia went to sleep. The officer, noting that he was asleep, immediately bound him and ordered a kibitka.† When they brought it, he had Emelia put in it and then he himself sat down in it and he took the fool to the city. When he drove up to the city, he went straight-away to the king's court. The ministers reported his arrival to the king. As soon as the king heard of the arrival, he ordered them to bring a large barrel with iron staves, and this barrel was readied and brought to the king. He inspected it and then ordered his daughter and the fool put in the barrel and the barrel tarred up. When this had been done, the king ordered the barrel released into the sea in his presence. And according to his order, they released it and the king returned to the city.

The barrel released into the sea floated for several hours, and all that time the fool slept. When he woke up, he saw that it was dark and he asked himself, "Where am I?" because he thought that he was alone.

The princess said to him, "Emelia, you are in a barrel, and I've been put in here with you."

"And who are you?" the fool asked.

"I am the king's daughter," she answered, and then she told him why she had been put in the barrel with him.

Afterward she asked him to free her from the barrel. But he said, "I'm warm in here!"

"Oh, please," the princess said, "take pity on my tears; save me and yourself from this barrel!"

"Why should I?" Emelia said, "I'm too lazy!"

The princess once more started asking him, "Oh, please, Emelia, save me from this barrel and don't let me die."

The fool, touched by her request and tears, said to her, "Very well, I will do that for you." After this he said very quietly, "By order of the pike, and by my request, oh sea, throw this barrel in which we're sitting out onto the shore, on a dry place, not too far from our own country. And you, barrel, in that dry place, fall apart."

---

†A small covered wagon, usually with two wheels.

The fool had scarcely managed to finish saying these words when the sea became agitated and at that moment it cast the barrel out onto the shore—in a dry place—and the barrel itself disintegrated. Emelia got up and went with the princess about the place where they had been tossed up, and the fool noted that they were on a really splendid island on which there were many, many trees with all kinds of fruits. The princess was overjoyed when she saw all this and that they were on this really splendid island, but then she said to him, "Emelia, how are we going to live? There isn't even a lean-to here."

But the fool said, "You want too much!"

"Oh, please, Emelia, order them to put up some kind of little house so that we'll have a place to take shelter when it rains." The princess knew he could do anything if he wanted to. But the fool said, "I'm too lazy." Again she asked him and he was touched by her request and obliged to do it for her. He went to one side and said, "By order of the pike, and by my request, build in the middle of this island a palace grander than the king's and with a crystal bridge from my palace to that of the king. And let there be in my palace people of various ranks." He had hardly managed to speak these words and at that very moment there appeared an enormous palace and the crystal bridge. The fool and the princess went into the palace and saw that all the rooms were very richly furnished and that there were many people, including servants and pages, who awaited the orders of the fool. The fool, seeing that all the people were normal people and he alone was unattractive and a fool, wanted to make himself better, and therefore he said, "By order of the pike, and by my request, make me handsome without compare and extremely intelligent." He had scarcely managed to speak these words when at that very moment he became handsome and also intelligent, and all were amazed.

After that, Emelia sent one of his servants to the king, inviting him and all his ministers to be guests. Emelia's messenger went to the king over the crystal bridge that the fool had made. When he arrived at the court, the ministers brought him before the king and Emelia's messenger said, "Merciful sovereign! I am sent by my lord with obedience to invite you to dine with him."

The king asked, "Who is this lord of yours?"

But the messenger answered him, "I cannot say anything about him to you (for the fool had ordered him not to say anything about who he was). Nothing is known of my lord. But when you dine with him, then he will tell you about himself." Most curious to know who had invited him, the king said to the messenger that he would come without fail. When the messenger had gone away, the king immediately set out after him with all his ministers. Returning back, the messenger said that the king would unfailingly come, and he had no sooner said it than the king arrived at the fool's crystal bridge with the princes.

Then when the king came riding up to the palace, Emelia went out to meet him, and he welcomed him with his white hands,† kissed his sweet lips, and cordially led him into his white-stoned palace where he sat him down at the oaken tables with ironed tablecloths and with their sweet foods and honeyed drinks. At table the king and his ministers drank, ate, and enjoyed themselves. And when they got up from the table and sat down in their places, the fool spoke to the king, "Merciful sovereign! Do you recognize me, do you know who I am?" And because Emelia was in very expensive clothing, and besides he now had a very handsome face, it wasn't possible to recognize him and therefore the king said that he didn't know him. But the fool said, "Do you remember, merciful sovereign, how a fool came to visit you in your palace on a stove and you sealed him and your own daughter up in a barrel and set them off to sea? Now recognize me! I am that very same Emelia." The king saw him before him and was very frightened, such that he didn't know what to do. But the fool went after his daughter then and led her before the king.

When the king saw his daughter, he rejoiced and said to Emelia, "I am guilty before you and therefore I will marry my daughter to you." When the fool heard this, he obediently thanked the king, and since Emelia had everything ready for the marriage, they celebrated it that very day with great ceremony. And on the next day the fool put on a splendid feast for all the ministers, and for all the common folk casks of various drinks were out. And when the merrymaking had ended, the king gave him his kingdom, but the fool didn't want it. After that the king went to his own kingdom, but the fool remained in his palace and lived very happily.

A–T 675

369. The Self-covering Hat

So an old man had gone out riding one day after firewood. He crawled under his cart, lay down, and was just lying there. Along came twelve thieves. And they opened a cellar not far away from him. And when they were opening the door, they said: "Self-covering Hat, Open!" And the door opened. All of them went inside and said, "Self-covering Hat, Close!" The thieves went inside, collected their wealth, and again set off to rob.

"Well," thought the old man, "Whatever is this? I'll have to test it myself." So the old man said: "Self-covering Hat, Open!" And the door opened. He went in. There he saw much gold. He carried out a lot of gold and put it

---

†That is, he wore no gloves.

on his cart and rode away. And he said: "Self-covering Hat, Close!" The door closed and he went home.

In the village there lived a rich peasant. He saw that the poor one suddenly had become rich, so he went to him and asked: "Where did you get so much money?"

The poor man answered: "There's a cellar in the woods. Go up to it and say, 'Self-covering Hat, Open!' And the door will open."

The rich man listened no more and ran into the woods, oh, if only the door would open for him! He ran into the woods and found the cellar. He said, "Self-covering Hat, Open!" And the door opened. He went into the cellar, said nothing, the door just took itself and closed. The rich man rushed around and began collecting precious stones. In another bag he saw gold and began to let it run through his fingers. He wanted to go out, but the door didn't open. In his greed he forgot what to say. He said some sort of words to the door. Suddenly he heard: "Self-covering Hat, Open!"

And the door opened. And in came the twelve thieves. The head man said, "There's who stole our gold!" They took this rich man and killed him. So the rich man got no money, nor gold on account of his greed.

A–T 676

370. (In the Underwater Tsardom)

There lived and dwelt a merchant. He went overseas to trade, to another country. He sailed and sailed, but his ship was becalmed. What was needed? The ship had stalled, it wouldn't go at all. There came an answer from out there: "Hand over the ship's master." (Into the sea, it was demanded.)

There was nothing to be done, the master of the ship would have to go there. He had waterproof safety clothes (!). He said goodbye to everybody on the ship but there was nothing else to be done, he had to go. He descended into the sea. He arrived, and the sea lord was fighting with the sea mistress.

"What do you require?" he asked. "What do you require of me?"

"What in Rus is more necessary and precious—gold or tempered steel?"

The sea mistress said: "Gold is most precious of all in Rus."

But the sea lord said: "Tempered steel is dearest." And so they quarreled.

He decided that he would have to speak in favor of the sea lord. "You can buy everything for gold, but the peasant can live without it," he said. "But tempered steel is more precious for the peasant because he cannot live without it." Alright, he had judged it, he had committed the sin.

He got back on his ship, sat down, and went off again. He arrived and traded—whether for a long time or a short one—and then started back. He came to the same place, and the ship stopped.

"Hand over the master of the ship here," the voice resounded from there. Well, so the master had to go. "Give us that which you don't know you have at home."

He thought and thought, but couldn't remember what he didn't know he had at home. "What I don't know I won't be sorry for."

He made a note, and signed it, that "what I don't know I have, I'll give up." So off he went. But he didn't know his wife was pregnant. (Apparently, he had been traveling a long time.) When he arrived home, his wife had given birth to a daughter. "That is who I didn't know and pledged to the sea lord."

The daughter had been born, Anastasia of the Golden Hair. Time passed, the daughter grew, they knew nothing, but he kept thinking: "But she's pledged to the sea lord." Little by little Nastasia attained twenty years of age.

Suddenly he looked up—the sea lord and mistress were coming! "Alright," they said, "hand over what was pledged. Give us your daughter."

There was nothing to be done. But she unexpectedly still wasn't ready, they'd have to come another time. Well, they agreed, and went off for another time. Now this Anastasia had a golden-haired goat that she called Brother. That day came when the sea lord and mistress were to come to court her and the goat said: "Well, Nastasia of the Golden Hair, lie down in the sleigh!" She lay down in the sleigh, he covered her up with a rug and drove off.

The little goat ran and they said: "Where are you running, little goat, where are you running, young one?"

"Into the world to feed the stock."

"What's that knocking, tinkling on the sleigh?" they asked.

"It's the golden bridle," he said. "Is Nastasia of the Golden Hair at home?"

"She's at home, strolling through her chambers, combing her russet curls, waiting for you to visit."

They arrived and were told: "She was just now home, yes, she was strolling through her chambers, she combed her hair and was waiting for you." They searched and searched but could not find her, so they went away.

After something like a long time there was a knocking, a tinkling, again the sea lord and mistress were coming. The little goat said to Nastasia the Golden Haired: "Lie down in the sleigh!"

She lay down in the sleigh, he covered her with a rug, and started pulling it away. Again they chanced to meet the sea lord and mistress: "Where are you going, little goat, where are you going, young one?"

"Into the world to feed the stock."

"But what is that knocking, tinkling, in the sleigh?"

"A golden bridle!" And up he jumped and off he ran.

"Is Nastasia of the Golden Hair at home?"

"Yes," he said, "she's strolling through her chambers, combing her golden curls, and waiting for you."

They arrived. "Where is Nastasia of the Golden Hair." They looked everywhere for her, but she was nowhere there. "But she was just now in her chambers, where did she get to?" They searched and searched but they could not find her.

"Well," they said, "since you have deceived us, do not go close to water, or else we'll grab you away from the dry land." The little goat ran home, and he began to live and thrive.

They lived and thrived and then a merchant began to court Nastasia, and then she got married to this merchant. This merchant managed a large trade over the deep blue sea. He had a servant girl who lived with her daughter in the back room. He went away and this servant went and did this: she tied a stone to Nastasia of the Golden Hair and dragged her off and threw her into a frog's pond. She put her daughter into Nastasia's dresses as best she could. She began turning her around, but the slippers didn't fit. She took and chiseled her daughter's feet. The merchant was coming home. He is displeased with his wife, she's not the same. They lived either a long or a short time.

She said, "Husband, kill the little goat. I'm carrying a son. I need the meat."

"Well, let's," he said.

But the little goat said: "Let me go, master, for a stroll, to drink some spring water and nibble the green grass." He went to the pond.

"Oh, Nastasia of the Golden Hair!" he said, "the pots are boiling, they're sharpening their knives, they want to cut my body."

And she answered there: "And the frogs are sucking at my body!"

She and the little goat started weeping. "Well, forgive me, farewell" he said, "Nastasia of the Golden Hair! They will butcher me!"

So the little goat came home. The master noticed—he had gone for a stroll but come home so dejected. And she kept repeating: "Kill the little goat, I'm carrying a son, I want some meat."

So on the next day the little goat was to be killed, but again he asked: "Master, let me go to walk around for just one day!" So again he let him go for the day. He released the little goat but went after him. Where did the little goat go?

The goat went to the pond and wept: "Oh Nastasia of the Golden Hair! Baba Yaga says: 'kill the goat, I am carrying a son,' she says, 'I want some meat!'" And he wept.

"And frogs are sucking at my body!" And now he (the master) heard it! He immediately took a little net, pulled out Nastasia, and they went home, mother and daughter—he killed them both, and Nastasia and he began to live the good life.

A–T 677 + 313A + 450

371. Sadko

This old man had three sons in all. One of these came and said, "Father, I am going to Moscow to work as a stone mason." He got his equipment together, got dressed, and set off. He walked and walked along the road, and no one knows whether it was far or near that he walked.

Then there was a river that ran over the road and over the river was a bridge, and on the bridge sat a maiden. "Well, young man, where are you going?" she asked. "Won't you take a letter to my brother? My brother is engaged in trade in Moscow."

"Maybe," he said. Then she let herself down and she jumped into the water and afterward she brought him the letter. Then she got out of the water and told him, "Now my brother is trading and note this: give him the letter with the left half up."

So he went to Moscow and sought out her brother in the market. He looked carefully all around one whole day and then another, and even a third day but he didn't dare approach him. He knew who he was but he wouldn't go up to him. Finally he noticed him (the brother did) and he said to him, "Well, young man, you don't buy, you don't sell, you just wander around."

"There's this letter that's been sent but I'm not sure that it's for you." He gave him the letter. When he had read the address, he said, "It's a letter for me."

So he read the letter and then he said, "This is a letter from my sister. A peasant is building a mill opposite her house and there's a lot of smoke coming out of the chimney. What do I owe you for bringing me this letter?"

"You don't owe me anything," he said.

"Go and hire some net makers." And he gave him some money. "Go and make fishnets." He went, hired them, and made a net. "If there isn't enough money, come back to me," her brother said. So then he ran out of money and went back to him. And he gave him some more money. "Now hire some fishermen," he said to him. "But if you run out of money, come back to me. Fish and you'll catch some wood chips. Keep them nearby in a pile, and if you catch rubbish, put that in another pile. But if you run out of money, come back to me."

So he started fishing, and he put the wood chips in one pile, and the rubbish in another pile, and kept on fishing until he caught nothing more and he had this big pile. So he went back to the maiden's brother because again he had no more money. Again her brother gave him money. "Now build two large warehouses and in one put the wood chips and in the other the rubbish. Then don't enter them, for six weeks do not enter either warehouse."

After six weeks he came to him, and her brother said, "Now open the warehouses." They opened the warehouses and in one was gold, and in the other there was silver. So he took it and in three days in Novgorod he bought everything, all the goods there were. Then he loaded all these goods onto twelve ships and they set off to sea.

When they had sailed to the middle of the sea, all the ships suddenly stopped. Sadko himself was required on the bottom of the sea! So he said, "Give me a board, one made of linden, and give me my well-strung gusli." So he descended on that board, and the ships all went on ahead. He ended up on the bottom of the sea, but he didn't know how he got there.

There stood a big palace and he was met there by somebody saying: "Here comes Sadko, the richest merchant."

Then the tsar came out and met him, and he put on a ball, and he said to Sadko, "Sadko, rich merchant, play on your well-strung gusli."

So he played for three days, and the tsar began to dance. But then a voice came down from the heavens and spoke to the tsar, "It is time to become quiet. Three hundred ships have been sunk, and there's no counting the little boats."

So then the tsar was so happy that he said, "Whatever you need, I'll reward you with it, and whichever maiden you wish to marry you may take."

There was this one maiden dressed in dark blue who said to him, "Take me, I am of a Christian family, ask for me." So he pointed to her and said, "I'll take that one." The tsar was quite happy for him to take her if he could select her. He lined up thirty maidens and said, "Choose her."

She had told him, "The first time you approach me, you will see a fly flying around me. The second time I'll be changing slippers, and the third time I'll wave a kerchief, and then you'll know."

So then he was to marry her, this maiden. And the tsar gave him six fine horses, and these carried them away to where his ships were, and there they were married, and got back all he had lost, and then Sadko the richest merchant went back to trading.

A–T 677*

372. The Fiddler in Hell

There lived and dwelt a peasant who had three sons. He lived richly, he collected two pots full of money and one of them he buried in the threshing barn, the other beneath the gates. Then this peasant died, not having told anybody about the money. Once there was a festival in the village and a fiddler was walking about when he suddenly fell right through the ground. He fell through the earth and found himself in hell right at the very spot where the rich peasant was being tormented. "Good health to you, my friend," said the fiddler.

The peasant answered him, "Bad luck to you for falling into this place. This is hell, and I am sitting here in hell."

"So, uncle, what did you do to get yourself here?"

"I'm here on account of my money. I had a whole lot of money, I gave nothing to beggars, and I buried two pots full in the ground. And now I'm being tormented, beaten with sticks, torn with claws."

"Could that happen to me? Maybe they're going to torment me too!"

"Go and sit behind the chimney for three years without eating, and you'll remain whole."

So the fiddler hid himself behind the chimney, but then the devils came and started beating the rich merchant and repeating, "This is for you, money-bags! You got masses and masses of money, but you didn't know how to hide it very well; you buried it where it's hard to watch over it. People are always riding over it at those gates and the horses' hooves pound our heads, while in the threshing barn we're always being thrashed with those flails."

As soon as the devils had gone away, the peasant said to the fiddler: "If you get out of here, tell my children to take the money. One pot is buried by the gates and the other beneath the threshing floor, and make sure they give it to the poor."

Just then a horde of devils came running in and they asked the rich peasant, "Why does this place stink of Russians here?"

The peasant said, "It's because you've been wandering about Russia and you picked up the scent there."

"What nonsense!" They started searching and they found the fiddler and shouted "Ho, ho, ho! There's a fiddler here!"

They dragged him from the stove and made him play on the fiddle. He played for three years, although it seemed like only three days to him. He was exhausted and said, "How amazing! Sometimes I've been playing and I've broken all my strings in one evening, but now I've been playing for three days and they are still good. Blessed be the Lord!" No sooner had he spoken when all the strings burst. "Well, brothers," said the fiddler, "see for yourself. The strings have broken and I've nothing to play on."

"Wait," said one of the unclean ones. "I've two bunches of strings and I'll bring them to you." He ran and got them. The fiddler took the strings, stretched them out, and once more said, "Blessed be the Lord!" and both bunches burst. "No, brothers, your strings are of no use to me. I have my own at home. If you let me, I'll go get them."

But the devils wouldn't release him. "You're not getting away," they said.

"If you don't believe it, then send someone from among you to accompany me." So the devils chose one of their own and sent him with the fiddler.

The fiddler came to the village. In a distant hut he heard a wedding being celebrated. "Let's go to the wedding!"

"Alright, let's."

So they went into the hut and there they recognized the fiddler and asked him, "Where have you spent these past three years, brother?"

"I've been in the other world."

They sat for awhile, they walked about for a while, and then the devil called the fiddler. "It's time to go."

But the fiddler said, "Wait just a little while. Let me play my fiddle a bit, to amuse the young folk." So they all sat there until the cocks crowed and then the devil disappeared and the fiddler told the rich peasant's sons, "Your father orders you to take the money. There is one pot buried next to the gates and one in the threshing barn. And you are to give all this money to the beggars." So they dug up both pots and gave the money away to the beggarly brotherhood, but the more they gave away, the more there was.

So then they took the pots to the crossroads. Whoever passed by could take as much money as he could grasp in his hand, but still there was no diminishing of the money. They sent a petition to the ruler reporting that in a certain town there was this twisting road about fifty versts long, but if it were straightened, it would be about five versts. The ruler gave orders to build a straight bridge. So they built the straight bridge of five versts and with that they used up both pots of money.

At that time some maiden gave birth to a son and abandoned him in his infancy. For three years this little boy neither ate nor drank, but the angel of God always walked beside him. Then the little boy came to the bridge and said, "Oh, what a fine bridge. Let God grant the kingdom of heaven to the one whose money built this bridge." The Lord heard this prayer and ordered his angels to let the rich peasant out of the inferno of Hell.

A–T 677** + 761A*

373. The Devils' Guest

Are there devils nowadays or no? I was little and my brother was older than I by twenty years, and this is what he told us. He wasn't very big and he and grandfather had gone to Arkhangelsk [for a visit]. They were walking about the city and the old man met someone acquainted with our grandfather. One eye was beaten out, or crooked. Well, our brother wasn't very big and it was really interesting to him.

"Why, grandfather, does he have one crooked eye?"

And grandfather told him: "This is why he as one crooked eye. He used to be an accordion player when he was young, but he also went out, caroused, drank with his friends, and one of them became attached to him. "Let's go together to the dance." He invited the accordion player, and the musician agreed to go with him. So then, his friend drove him there to the fine rooms, fine vistas, to what seemed like rich folk, and everyone was dancing with his partner. So he sat on a chair and began to play and the dances ended. Then one young gentle lady slapped him with her tail, she whacked him with the train of her dress in his eye. As he was bemoaning his eye, he wiped it, and with that he eye he saw—no people, only devils with horns and with tails, and they weren't sitting in a room but in a swamp on tussocks. When he closed that eye and didn't look with it, then there were just people, playing and dancing. But with the sore eye they were devils! It was so horrible for him that he asked his friend, "Please take me back home," he said, "I don't feel well."

At first he demurred, but finally he agreed. So he sat him in a cart, a troika of horses hitched to it, and he set off. And he, the accordion player, wanted to see what he was riding in, and somehow he looked with his injured eye. It was no cart but a fir tree and he was sitting in the fir tree and instead of horses there were three men harnessed, sinners, and in the fir tree a devil with horns and a tail [sat] in the top and whipped these people, and they snorted, poor things. So he brought the man to his own house as indicated. Then with his healthy eye he looked to see where he was and they parted for the time. Then when he went to the market and with that bad eye he could see the filth. And they were stealing and thieving and knocking things over and spilling them just to make people quarrel. He saw his old friend, "Good health, friend!"

His old friend started, as if burnt. "How did you see me?"

He said simply, "Once upon a time I was with you and a woman struck me with the train of her dress right in the eye, and ever since then I have been able to see you, to see you and see what you are doing." The other one waved his arms and hit him in the eye and he couldn't see and the eye fell out.

At that point I fainted and they took me away," he said to the old man, our grandfather. They took him away then and healed his eye but it remained crooked. So grandfather told this to my brother Grigorii, and after his military service Grigorii told it to me, he was already big but I was still a young girl.

A—T 677**

374. When the Old Woman Was a Midwife

An old woman had lived to old age, but she had never been midwife to anybody and she had always wanted to be. She went into the woods for mushrooms (or cloudberries or something) and she saw a female frog. The frog was lying on the road and how fat she was!

"You," the old woman said, "are about to give birth, so let me be midwife!" and she laughed. So the granny was asleep and in the night there was a rapping at the door. "Who's that?"

"You said you would be midwife, so I've come to call you out." So she got up and went with him. He took her there and a child was born. The bathhouse was heated and they went off to the bathhouse.

And this woman said, "Do not wash yourself with the water." They entered the bathhouse. There was neither tub nor basin. He said, "I'll bring one right away."

So he brought the leavening trough in. She looked at it: the leavening trough was somebody else's. She took it and knocked the dried crust off it. So once more, they all washed, but she had nothing to put on. He said, "I'll run and bring you something." She saw that it was the sarafan-pinafore of her daughter-in-law. She tore a swatch out of the sarafan, and she took notice of it. She didn't wash. Then they went home. He started to give her drinks and feed her, and then he put her to bed. But his wife wouldn't let her sleep ("I am Russian," she said).

"If you are going to sleep, then cross yourself and recite a prayer." So she got ready to sleep and she said a prayer.

She rolled onto the featherbed and turned up on the trunk of a big tree, at the top, near the river itself. Some fishermen were going by and she started shouting, "Get me down!"

They got her down. "Where have you come from?" She said, "I'll tell you later." So later she told them.

She came home and the same leavening trough was there, with the handles broken off. She looked at the sarafan and a piece was torn out. And so it went until the holiday. Nobody knew anything more about it.

She went into a shop to buy something and that devil was stealing candies and cakes behind the counter. She said to the shop assistant, "That man there is stealing."

But the assistant said, "There is nobody there."

So the devil came up to her and asked her, "Do you see me?" She said that she did. "And with which eye?"

"With the right one." So he poked out her right eye and the old woman became blind.

A–T 677***

375. Lipuniushka

There lived this old man with his old woman and they had no children at all. And so he said, "How can this be, old woman? We have no children." So the old woman spun some cotton and put it in a little table.

Then the old man rode out to plow the field and the old woman started baking pancakes. "How can this be," she said, "I haven't got anybody to take the old man his breakfast." And then a little son crawled out of the cotton. "Oh Lord Jesus Christ! Where have you come from, my little son?"

"Why Mother, you spun the cotton and put it in the little table and I hatched out of there. Let me take some pancakes to father, Mother!"

"But will you be able to carry them?"

"I'll carry them, Mother, I'll carry them!" So she tied up a little bundle of pancakes, he took it, and off he went.

He went along, he carried the breakfast, and he made a noise, he shouted, "Father, oh father! Lift me over this hummock!"

The old man was astonished, and thought, "Where did this little son of mine come from? There was no son, and then all of a sudden there is one." So then he said, "Where have you, my little son, come from?"

"Well, you see," he said, "Mother spun some cotton and put it in a little table and from that I was hatched out. Father, I have brought you your breakfast. Sit down and eat it and I will plow."

"How will you plow, my child? You don't have the strength."

"Never mind, it won't be difficult for me," he said. So the old man sat down and ate his breakfast and the boy plowed and sang songs behind the plow.

Some nobles were riding by and they sent a man off. "Man! Go and find out what sort of wild thing that is! The horse plows, but no human is to be seen there."

So the man came up and asked, "How is that, man, does your horse walk and plow alone?"

"No," he said, "there's a little boy plowing there."

The man came back and said, "Well, how is it that we can't see anything?"

"You can't see him because he is so small."

So a landlord went up to the old man to trade with him for the little boy. "Old man, sell me the boy."

"No," he said, "I cannot sell this boy, he is the only one I have." And this boy quietly said, "Father, sell me. I will soon get away from him." So the old man said to the landlord, "Landowner, what will you give me for him?"

"Take a hundred rubles."

"Very good." So the landlord gave him the money and he took the boy, wrapped him in a kerchief, and placed him in a pocket. And the landlord came riding home. "Mistress, do you know what joy I have brought?"

"What is it, what is it? What joy?" She was herself overjoyed as she helped the landlord undress. He reached in his pocket, grabbed hold, but the boy wasn't there: he had gotten away. The landlord said, "Look at the joke he has played, the . . . has gotten away."

A–T 700

376. The Snow Maiden

There lived and dwelt this peasant Ivan and he had a wife Maria, but they didn't have any children. Ivan and Maria lived in love and harmony; and so they grew old but they still didn't have any children. They were greatly saddened by this and only looking at the children of other folks brought them any comfort. But there was nothing to be done! So, apparently, that was what the Lord had allotted them. Everything on earth happens not by our will but by the Lord's design.

Then once when winter had come and much new snow had fallen up to the knee, all the little children went outside to play and our old folks sat up next to the window to watch them. The children ran, they raced about, and they started making a snow woman† out of the snow. Ivan and Maria watched silently, deep in thought. Suddenly Ivan started laughing and said, "They should come over here, wife, and make a snow woman for us."

A cheerful moment apparently also struck Maria at that same time. "Well," she said, "let's go and have some fun in our old age. Only why do you need to make a snow woman? Neither of us needs that. Instead, we'd better make a child out of snow, since God didn't give us a live one."

"That's right, that's right . . . ," said Ivan, and he took his hat and went off into the garden with the old woman.

And in fact they did start in making a doll out of snow. They put the body together with the arms, then the legs, and on top they put a little round heap of snow and smoothed a head out of it.

"God help you!" said someone, walking by.

"Thank you, we are most grateful!" answered Ivan. "God's help is always good in anything," he added.

"And what are you making there?"

"Well, you see," answered Ivan. "A snow maiden," Maria said, laughing.

And they sculpted a little nose and beard (!) and then two little pits on the

---

†The figure made from snow is invariably a "snow woman" in Russian.

face, and just as Ivan had finished sketching a mouth, a warm breath of air came out of it! Ivan quickly raised a hand and looked as the little pits on the face began bulging out and out of them little blue eyes began peering, and then the raspberry lips started smiling. "Oh my gosh," said Ivan, "is this some sort of a ghost?" And he crossed himself. But the doll bowed her head to him, as if she were alive, and began moving her arms and legs in the snow, just like a newborn infant in diapers.

"Oh, Ivan, Ivan!" Maria shouted, shivering from delight. "The Lord has given us a child," and she rushed to embrace Snow Maiden and then all the snow tumbled off Snow Maiden like the shell from an egg, and in Maria's arms there was a real, live girl. "Oh you are my very dear Snow Maiden!" the old woman exclaimed, hugging her long-desired and unexpected child, and they all ran into the hut. After seeing such a miracle Ivan came to his senses with great difficulty, but Maria was wild with joy.

Now, Snow Maiden grew not by the days but by the hours, and each day was better than the last. Ivan and Maria could not have been more over-joyed with her. And everything about the house was joyful. The girls from the village were constantly in and out, they amused themselves and always selected granny's daughter to play, just like a doll, and they talked with her, they sang her songs, they played all sorts of games, and they taught her to do all the things they did. And Snow Maiden was very clever. She took note of everything and took everything in. And over that winter she became just like a maiden of very nearly thirteen years, and she under-stood everything, and she could talk about everything, and with such a sweet voice, that they all listened, spellbound. And she was so kind, so obedient, and so outgoing to all. And she was as white as snow, her eyes were like forget-me-nots, her blond hair came down to her waist, but she didn't have any red on her cheeks, as if she didn't have any real blood in her body. . . . Despite this she was most attractive and pretty as a picture. And when she would ever start playing, she was so considerate and pleas-ant that the heart was overjoyed. People just couldn't admire Snow Maiden enough.

The old woman Maria could find no fault with her. "Ivan," she said to her husband, "God has given us this joy for our old age! And my heartsick sadness has passed!"

But Ivan said, "It is a thanksgiving to the Lord! Here joy is not eternal, nor is sadness without end. . . ."

Winter passed. The spring sun began playing about in the heavens and it started warming the earth. In the melted spots the grass began to show green, and the lark began to sing. The beautiful maidens began to gather in the processions through the villages, singing:

Beautiful Spring!
How did you come here?
How did you arrive?
On the plow, on the harrow!

But the Snow Maiden became somehow bored. "What is the matter with you, my child?" Maria said so often to her, drawing her close. "You are not ill, are you? You are so unhappy, so out of sorts, has some evil man cast a spell on you?"

But the Snow Maiden would always answer, "Never mind, granny, I am healthy. . . ."

Then one day the spring with those beautiful days drove away the last snow. Gardens and meadows burst into bloom, the nightingale started singing, as did the other birds, and everything in God's world became more alive and more cheerful. And Snow Maiden, the dear, began to pine away even more and more. She avoided her girlfriends and kept hiding from the sun in the shade, just like a lily of the valley beneath a tree. She only liked it splashing in the icy spring beneath the green willow tree. Snow Maiden stayed in the shade and cold, or even better, the frequent showers. In a shower or in twilight she would become happier. And then once a big gray cloud moved over them and spattered them with big hailstones. Snow Maiden was as overjoyed by this as another would have been by precious pearls. When the sun once more began to bake and the hail had turned into water, Snow Maiden broke into tears over it, as if she herself would begin weeping liking a sister weeps for her very own brother.

Then the end of spring came and St. John's Day arrived.† The village girls gathered for their walk to the groves and they dropped in to take Snow Maiden with them. They went up to granny Maria. "Let her, let Snow Maiden come with us!"

Maria was afraid to let her go and Snow Maiden did not want to go, but there was just no way of talking them out of it. Besides, Maria thought, it would be good for her Snow Maiden to get out and enjoy herself. So she dressed her, kissed her and said, "Now go, my child, have a good time with your girlfriends! And you, girls, see that you look after my Snow Maiden. She's my heart's own joy, as you know."

"Good, good!" they all shouted happily, and they grabbed Snow Maiden and went off in a bunch to the grove.

There they wove wreaths for themselves, braiding in bunches of flowers,

---

†23 June, Midsummer. An important holiday in rural Russia. The village girls went to birch groves to cut a birch tree to decorate in the village.

and they sang their sad and glad songs. Snow Maiden would not be parted from them.

When the sun was going down, the girls made a bonfire from grasses and brush, lit it and got in a long line one behind the other in their wreaths. They placed Snow Maiden at the end of the line. "Look," they said, "when we start running, you come running behind us, and don't fall behind." So drawing out their long Midsummer song, they leapt through the fire.

Suddenly behind them there was a great noise and pitiful groaning. "Oh, ah . . . !" They looked around in fright, but there was no one there. They looked at each other and saw that Snow Maiden wasn't there. "She is probably hiding, the naughty thing," they said, and they ran off to look for her. But nowhere could they find her. They shouted, called out, but there was no response at all. "Where could she have got to?" the girls said. "It is obvious that she ran home," they said and went back into the village. But Snow Maiden wasn't there either.

They looked for her all the next day, and they looked for her the third. They covered the entire grove—bush by bush, sapling by sapling—but Snow Maiden was still not there, any trace of her was lost.

For a long time Ivan and Maria were bitter and they wept for their Snow Maiden. Every day for a long time the poor old woman went into the thickets to look for her, and she always called out for her just like a hapless cuckoo.

"Ai, ai, little Snow Maiden! Oh, Oh, my little dove!"

Frequently it seemed to her that she heard Snow Maiden's voice calling back to her: "Oh . . ." but there was no sign of Snow Maiden.

What had happened to Snow Maiden? Had a fierce beast carried her off into the deep forest, or a cruel bird carried her off to the deep blue sea? When Snow Maiden ran off after her girlfriends and leapt into the fire, she had suddenly been carried upward by a light breath of air, wrapped in a thin little cloud . . . and she flew up into the ethereal heights.

A–T 703*

377. The Armless Maiden

In a certain tsardom, not in our country, there lived a rich merchant; and he had two children, a son and a daughter. Both the father and the mother died. The brother said to his sister, "Come, sister, let's leave this town. I'll open a shop and we'll start trading, and I'll rent some lodgings for you, and that's how we'll live." So then they set off for another province, and they came to that province, and the brother registered himself, and rented a shop with fine goods. The brother decided to get married, and so he got married. He took a sorceress as his wife.

The brother got ready to start trading in his shop, and he ordered his sister, "Sister, you look after the house." His wife found what he ordered his sister to do offensive. To get back at him she broke up all the furniture, and when he returned, she was waiting for him. She met him and said, "See what kind of sister you have, she has broken up all the furniture in the pantry!"

"Oh well," he answered, "that happens from time to time."

So then the next day he set off for the shop, and he said goodbye to his wife and sister, and he said to his sister, "Sister, please look after the house as best you can."

So then his wife watched for a time when her husband wasn't there and she went into the stables and cut off the head of his favorite horse with his saber. She stood on the porch and waited for him. "Look what sort of sister you have," she said. "She's cut off the head of your favorite horse!"

"Let the dogs eat what's for dogs!" her husband answered.

On the third day her husband went once more to the shop. He said goodbye and spoke to his sister, "Please look after the mistress so that she doesn't hurt herself or the baby, if she should happen to give birth to one." When she gave birth to a baby, she cut off its head. Then she sat there and wept over the baby.

So then in came the husband. "Oh, what a sister you have! I hardly had managed to give birth to the child, when she came and cut off its head with a saber." The husband said nothing; he burst into tears and left them immediately.

Night came. At precisely midnight he got up and said, "Dear sister! Get ready. You and I are going to liturgy."

"But brother, my dear," she said, "I don't think there's any holiday now."

"No, sister, there is a holiday. Let's go."

"It's early," she said, "too early to be going, brother."

"It's just like you young maidens, to take time over getting ready. Hurry and get dressed," he said. So his dear sister began getting ready. But she couldn't get ready because her hands fell off. Her brother came and said, "Faster, sister, get dressed faster."

"But it's still early, brother!"

"No, sister, its not early—it's time."

Finally the sister was ready. They sat down in the carriage and rode off to liturgy. Whether they rode for a long time or short, they came to a forest. The sister said, "What forest is this?" He answered, "This is a hedge around the church." Their carriage got caught up in some brush. The brother said, "Get out, sister, and untangle the carriage."

"Oh brother, my dear, I can't, I'll soil my dress."

"But, sister, I'll buy you a new dress, better than that one."

So she got out of the carriage and started untangling it, but her brother chopped off her arms at the elbow, whipped up each of his horses and rode away from her.

So the sister was left there, weeping tears, and then she set out through the forest. But no matter how much she walked, whether for a long time or a short time, she walked about the forest, she got all scratched up but could find no sign that would lead her out of the forest. Then there was this little path that went out and led her out of the forest, after several years. So then she got out of this forest and came to a trading town and she went up to the window of the richest merchant to beg for alms. This merchant had a son, an only son, and the apple of his father's eye, and he fell in love with the beggar girl. He said, "Papa and mama, marry me!"

"And to whom should we marry you?"

"To that beggar girl."

"Oh, my friend, can it be than in this city of merchants there are no fine daughters?"

"Marry me to her! And if you won't marry me to her, I'll do something to myself," he said. So though they were ashamed of their favorite son, they gathered all the merchants together, and the clergy, and they asked them to judge: should he be married to the beggar girl or not? Then the priests said, "It appears that it is his fate, that it is God's will that he marry the beggar girl."

So then they lived together for a year, and then another, and then he set off for another province where her brother, you see, was still sitting in his shop. As he was saying farewell, he asked, "Papa and mama, do not abandon my wife! When she is giving birth, write me the news immediately, at that very instant." As soon as their son had left, after two or three months his wife gave birth to a child up to its elbows all gold and both sides studded with many stars, while on his forehead was a crescent moon and opposite his heart a beautiful sun. When the grandparents looked at the child, they were delighted and set out to write their dear son about it immediately. They sent an old man with this express note.

But the sorceress daughter-in-law found out about it and called in the old man. "Come here, old man, and rest."

"No, I have no time, they are sending me in haste."

"Oh, come, old man, rest and dine."

So she sat him down to eat, and took his letter pouch away, took out the note, read it, tore it into tiny bits, and wrote another saying that "Your wife gave birth, and it was half dog and half bear, which she conceived living in the forest with the beasts."

Then the old man went to the merchant's son and gave him the letter. He read it and burst into tears. Then he wrote a letter saying not to touch anything until he returned home. "I'll come and find out what sort of child has been born."

So then the sorceress called the old man in again. "Come and sit and rest," she said. So he came in and again she enchanted him, took the note away from him, read it, tore it up, and wrote another saying that when the letter was received, she was to be chased away from the court.

The old man delivered the letter, the father and mother read it and grieved. "Why is it that he has brought us this loss? We married him off, and then, apparently, he no longer needs this wife!" They weren't so sorry for the wife as they were for the infant. They blessed both her and the infant, tied it to its mother's breast, and sent them from the courtyard.

So she set off, weeping bitter tears, and she walked for a long time or a short time through the steppe. There was no forest, nor was there a village. Then she came up to a hollow, and she felt like having something to drink. She glanced to the right and there was a well. So even though she wanted something to drink, she was afraid to bend over for fear of dropping the infant. But then it seemed to her that water was somehow closer to her. She bent over and the child fell out of its wrapping and into the well. She walked around the well and cried. How should she get the child out of the well? An old man came up and said, "Why are you crying, maid?"

"Why should I not cry? I bent over the well to get a drink of water and my infant fell into it."

"Go, bend over, and take him out."

"No, little father, I have no arms—just these stumps."

"Go, bend over, and take the infant!" So she went up to the well, stretched out her arms, and the lord favored her—her whole arms appeared. She bent over, got her child, and began praying to God in all four directions.

When she had prayed to God, she set off and came to the court where her brother and husband were, and she begged to spend the night. Her husband said, "Brother, let that beggar woman in. Beggar women can tell folktales and preambles to folktales, and they can also utter some real truths."

Then the bride said, "We have no place for her to sleep; it's already tight here."

"No, brother, let her in, please. I love how beggar women tell tales and stories more than anything else." So they let her in. She sat down on the stove with her infant.

Her husband said, "Well, my dear, tell us a little tale now, at least tell us a yarn."

She said, "I don't know how to tell tales or stories, but I do know how to tell the truth. Listen," she said, "and I'll tell you some truth, ladies and gentlemen." And she began to talk. 'In a certain tsardom, but not in our country, there lived a rich merchant and he had two children, a son and a daughter. The father and mother both died. The brother said to his sister, 'let's leave this town, sister.' And so they came to another province. The brother got himself situated. He rented a shop with fine goods. Then it occurred to him to get married. He got married, he married a sorceress. . . ."

At this point the brother's wife blurted out, "This bitch has just come here to bore us!"

But her husband said, "Go on, go on, little mother. I just love stories like this one."

"So then the brother got ready to trade in his shop and he said to his sister, 'Sister, you look after things at home!' And his wife was offended that he gave such an order to his sister. And in her anger she broke up all the furniture. . . ."

And when she had told how he had taken her to liturgy, then chopped off her arms, and how she had given birth, how her brother's wife had summoned the old man, the sorceress again shouted out, "Now she's talking plain gibberish!"

But her husband said, "Brother, make your wife be quiet. This is really a fine story!" So then she went on talking and told how her husband had written that they should keep the child until he arrived home.

Here her brother's wife shouted out, "What nonsense she prates!" Then she told how she had come to this house, and her brother's wife again shouted, "See how the bitch babbles on!" Then her husband said, "Brother, tell her to shut up. Why does she keep interrupting?" So then she told them how they had let her into the hut and how she had told them the true story. She pointed to them and said, "You are my husband, you are my brother, and you are my sister-in-law."

Then her husband jumped up to her on the stove and said, "Oh, my friend, show me the child. Is it true what my father and mother wrote?" They took the baby and took off the blankets and underclothes—and the whole room lit up! "It's true, it's the truth what you've told in the story. This is my wife and this is my son—golden up to his elbow, with stars scattered on his sides, a crescent moon on his forehead, and opposite his heart a beautiful sun."

Then her brother took his very best mare out of the stables, tied his wife to her tail, and let her loose in the steppe. She galloped away and returned with just one braid. The rest of her was scattered in the steppe. Then they harnessed a troika of horses and set off home to his father and mother, and they began living and prospering. I was there and drank mead and wine and it flowed through my moustache and none got into my mouth.

A–T 706

378. Ivan Tsarevich and Maria the Yellow Flower

In a certain tsardom, in a certain land, there lived and dwelt a tsar. He had been married but was now widowed. He set off to seek a bride for himself. He came to one tsardom and there were three sisters, the daughters of a tsar. The oldest of them said to him, "If you take me, I will clothe all your army with a single thread." The middle one spoke: "I will feed all your army with a single crumb." Then the littlest daughter spoke: "And if you take me, tsar, I will bear you a son and a daughter such as have never been seen on earth before. On the forehead will be a sun, on the crown a crescent moon, and all throughout their hair will be stars."

The tsar said, "For me that will be best because my army is already clothed and fed." The older sisters said, "Well, take her. She will give birth to pups for you." The tsar took the youngest sister, went back to his own tsardom, and was married to her.

He lived for some time with his young wife and the wife became pregnant. Then the tsar went off to war. "Well, dear wife! If God grant it, give birth safely and send me a letter. Here is where I shall be stationed with my army."

So then some time after that she gave birth to a son and daughter as she had promised and with just those markings. She immediately wrote him a letter and summoned a trusty servant. "Listen servant, here is a letter for you. Take it to this certain place, to the tsar, but whatever happens to you on the road, don't stop off anywhere." The servant saddled his horse, got all ready, took the letter and put it in a pouch, locked his pouch, put the key in his pocket, set off, and for quite some time he rode along just fine.

Suddenly it started to rain and there was mud everywhere. Then there was a severe frost. All his clothing was soaked through from the rain and then with the frost he was so frozen that he couldn't ride on further. In the distance he saw a light. He rode up to this light. He saw a house standing there. Two girls came out of the house. "Greetings! Where are you going?"

"I am going somewhere."

"Stop over and spend the night. Where can you go in such weather?" He was very happy; he cared for his horse and went into the house. They immediately gave him tea to drink and gave him something to eat. He lay down to sleep. Now these two girls were the tsaritsa's sisters. When he had fallen asleep, they took the letter out of his pouch and read it. Then they wrote another in their own manner: "Forgive me, my dear husband, for having promised to bear you a son and a daughter. What happened I don't know, but they're not humans nor kittens nor dogs." They sealed it and put it back in the pouch.

The servant got up in the morning and saw that his pouch was still hanging as before. "Glory to God that no one touched it," he said. He saddled his horse, thanked them and set off on his journey.

So then he came to the place where the tsar was standing with his army. He immediately gave the tsar the letter. The tsar didn't read it but put it in his pocket and said to the servant, "Go into the camp and come to me in the evening." In the evening he came to the tsar. The tsar had forgotten about the letter. He took the letter right away and read it, and then he fell to thinking. The servant said, "Oh, your majesty! What children God has given to you!"

"What are they like?"

"I've lived so many years and traveled so much, but such as these I've never seen."

"Did you perhaps stop off somewhere on the way here?"

"I'm guilty, your majesty. I stopped at some house or other."

The tsar guessed that it was his wife's sisters, and he wrote a letter. "Whatever children they are, keep them safe until I return." Then he sent the servant off and ordered him not to stop off anywhere.

So the servant was riding along and the same thing happened to him on the road. Rain and frost. And once more he rode up to that house. The two girls met him and got him to spend the night. And once more he cared for his horse, came into the house, and they gave him tea to drink and they gave him supper and put him to sleep. When he had fallen asleep, they again took the letter from his pouch, rewrote it so that "before my return neither my wife nor those children are to be in my tsardom. Whoever keeps them will be severely punished." They sealed the letter and put it back in his pouch.

In the morning the servant got up and looked: his pouch was hanging in the same place. "Glory to God," he said. "No one has touched my pouch." He got all ready, thanked them, and set off.

He came to his own tsardom and handed over the letter. They read it and were astonished. "What is this?"

The tsaritsa began asking about it. "Listen, servant, did you stop off somewhere?"

"I am guilty, I stopped off." The tsaritsa gathered all the ministers and began taking counsel with them as to what to do. The ministers all counseled her to remain in the palace but to hand over the children to a certain old woman in the town for safekeeping. And that is what they did. She remained there, and they handed the children over to the old woman so as to keep them safe.

The war ended and the tsar was coming back. Suddenly the same thing happened with him as with the servant. Rain and frost. He saw the house standing there. So he stopped by this house and in the house were his wife's two sisters. "Well, so what, tsar?" they said. "We warned you that she would give birth to puppies and not children."

"So what is to be done? That seems to be my fate."

And the middle sister said, "It would be better for you to marry me and chase the other one away." So the tsar married the second sister and they rode away. The tsar came into his own tsardom, went into the palace, and his wife met him. He caught sight of her, drew his sword, and was ready to cut off her head.

She fell on her knees and begged forgiveness. "I am not guilty," she said. "As I promised, I have had the children."

The second wife said, "No, look at those pups in the cradle." The tsar looked and saw some sort of monsters there. He got angry and ordered her chased away so that she would no longer be in his tsardom.

But the children were being kept by the old woman. The old woman found out that the tsar had chased away his first wife and that there was a rumor about that whoever was keeping the children would be severely punished. She went to the bazaar and bought a plain barrel. Then she knocked out the bottom. She made a bed in the barrel and put the children in it. Then she sealed it tightly and sent it out to sea. The children floated for some time and neared an island. On this island there lived a hermit who had been saving his soul for thirty years and had not only not seen a barrel—he hadn't even see a bird fly overhead. Then he caught sight of the barrel and two candles were burning on it. He went down to the shore and took the barrel, and he started to put out the candles, but the candles would not be put out! So he broke open the barrel and took the two children out of it, and he took them to his cell and admired them. He lay down to sleep and thought, "What am I going to feed these children with?" In the morning he got up and saw that on the table was a pot of kasha, and there was also a loaf lying there. No matter how much he fed the children, neither the bread nor the kasha were diminished. And so for several years he raised the children, until they were ten. "Well, my dear children, let's go and I'll show you where you can get off this island from."

As they were going through the steppe, he showed them things and then they came to a thicket. They went through the thicket and he broke the bushes for them. "Here's where the road will be, go along this way." And then he led them out onto the main road. "Now did you see where you've been walking?"

"We saw."

"Then turn back!" So they went back to the cell and lived there for some time. Then one time the hermit lay down in a coffin and the coffin rose up and flew off no one knows where.

They were left alone and they lived there for some time, but they became bored and so they went out along that same road that the hermit had shown them. They came out onto the main road. It was already night and they had no place to go. They crossed the main road and lay down to sleep. Suddenly in the night some coachmen (it was a large wagon train) were riding along and they saw some sort of light. "That's either another goods train that was going along and has stopped or it's some bandits." They rode up closer and went to look. What could it be? When the children heard their conversation, they woke up and put on their caps.

The peasants soon found them and took them in. One said, "I don't have a son so I'll take the boy to be with my children." Another said, "I don't have a daughter, so I'll take the daughter in."

The oldest of them said, "No, you can't take them. They are obviously important children. Let's take them and bring them into the town. We'll let them go in the town wherever they want." So that's what they did.

They brought them into the town and let them go. And they walked through the royal precincts and wondered, "Where should we go now? They won't let us into the big house so let's go into a small one." They went into this hut and prayed to God. An old woman was sitting there. "Good health to you, granny!"

"Good health, children!" The old woman began questioning them: who they were, and where they had come from.

"But we really don't know ourselves. We only know that we lived on an island and our papa flew away. Then we set off to find a refuge."

Then this Cossack servant came in, the husband of the old woman, and he asked, "Whose children are these?"

"They say they don't know themselves where they are from. Speak with them. Perhaps they would stay here as our children."

This servant spent some time with them and then he went away. The old woman asked them, "Why should you children wander from here to there? You had better stay and live with us." So they stayed on living there. And the boy helped out, tidying the courtyard and cleaning, and the girl in the hut.

They lived there for some time very happily, until they were already seventeen years old. But then the servant, the old man, died. And the headman came to the house and said, "Your father is dead; don't you want to take his place?"

And the boy said, "With pleasure."

"Then come tomorrow to the inspection." The tsar himself was at the inspection. The tsar was taken by the boy and didn't so much take in the inspection as he did look at the boy. And every day the tsar would admire him.

His stepmother, the sorceress, found out that he was alive. There was no way she herself could bring harm to him so she sought out another sorceress. She found an old woman and said, "Take whatever you want, only bring down that Cossack and his sister."

The old woman said, "I have these two objects. If they can destroy them, fine, but otherwise there's nothing to be done." So once the Cossack was riding home and this old woman came up to him and said, "Well, young Cossack, how handsome you are, and your sister is so fine, but your hut is awful. You need to construct a new one."

"That would be fine," he said, "but I've no means to do it."

Then she said, "In this certain place mountains rub right up against mountains and they're grinding sand. Go over there and take some of this sand, and then scatter it around your hut and yard, and everything will be as new." She took her leave and departed. The Cossack and his sister thought about it. It would be useful to go over there. So he went to the inspection and asked the tsar for permission to go for some time. The tsar dismissed him, he saddled his horse, and rode away.

He rode along the roadway and he saw an old woman walking toward him. "Good health, to you, Ivan Tsarevich," she said to him.

"Phooey, you old woman! What kind of Ivan Tsarevich am I? I'm a Cossack and nothing more." Then he rode on and then he said, "Why did I have to insult that old woman?" He turned back and asked the old woman for forgiveness.

"Now then, little father and Ivan Tsarevich, you should not insult old folks. Where are you going?"

"I am going to this certain place where one mountain rubs against another because I need to get some sand."

"So that's your business! But you need to drop in to my place first." So he went to her place. And there she gave him something to drink, and something to eat, and then she hid him.

Suddenly her son came flying in, a six-headed serpent. "Phooey, mama!" he said. "Why does it stink of a Russian here?"

"You, my friend, have been flying about Rus and you've picked up that Russian odor."

Then a nine-headed serpent came flying in. "Phooey, mama!" he said, "Why does it stink of a Russian here?"

"You, my friend, have been flying about Rus and you've picked up that Russian odor." Then the third son, a nine-headed serpent came flying in. "Phooey, mama!" he said. "Why does it stink of a Russian here?"

"You, my friend, have been flying about Rus and you've picked up that Russian odor."

"Give us our dinner."

So they started eating dinner and she said, "What would you do with him if I had a Russian here?"

"Nothing," they said. So then she right away opened the door and led out Ivan Tsarevich and they all shouted at one, "Good health to you, Ivan Tsarevich! Have you still far to go?"

"To such and such a place where one mountain rubs against another, grinding sand." They all went right away into the black smithy and ordered three iron shafts. As soon as they were ready, they all of them rode away to that place.

As they approached the mountains, they looked: it was precisely so! One mountain was rubbing against another, grinding sand. They threw one shaft and it was completely buried in it. They threw the second and it, too, was buried. Then they threw the third and it was buried. Finally the sand started coming from the other end. "Well," they said, "take as much as you want." They all said farewell to him and they said, "If you go out riding again, drop by to see us without fail. And there are those who want to destroy you."

He took some sand and set off home. When he got there, he spread the sand around the hut and around the yard, and then he lay down to sleep. In the morning he got up and found himself no longer in the previous hut, but in a palace. He looked, and the courtyard was outstanding. The tsar was passing through these royal precincts and saw the house. He asked, "Whose is this house?"

They told him, "It's the house of some Cossack." The tsar was very pleased that his favorite Cossack had such a house.

But then that old woman sorceress came to him again and she said, "Well, young Cossack, you've built your house. Now you ought to get married."

"It would be fine to get married, but there's no bride around."

"Ah, but there is a bride," she said. "Beyond the thrice-ten land, in the thrice-ten tsardom, there is Tsaritsa Maria the Yellow Flower."

"But how can I get married to a tsaritsa? I'm just a Cossack!"

"She will marry you. She's waiting for you. She's had many suitors."

When the old woman had finished speaking, she left. He talked it over with his sister. He said, "You often are unwell, and I need to get married."

His sister said, "Well, so what? Good luck!" Then he once more went to the tsar and asked his permission to be absent for a time. The tsar permitted it. He said farewell to his sister and rode away.

He came back to those serpents. They met him. "Are you going far away, Ivan Tsarevich?"

"To this certain tsardom to court Maria the Yellow Flower."

"Listen, Ivan Tsarevich, when you come to her tsardom, you will see many stone statues. Those are her suitors. And if you don't say the right thing, you will be turned to stone. When you come to her, don't be afraid, but go right into the palace. She will be sitting there, sewing, and she won't look at you. You say, 'Good health, Maria the Yellow Flower. I am your groom.' She will wave her kerchief and you will be turned to stone up to your knees. Say it a second time: 'Good health, Maria the Yellow Flower. I am your groom.' Again she will wave her kerchief and you will be turned to stone up to your elbow. Then for the third time say 'Good health, Maria the Yellow Flower. I am your groom.' Then you must say that you are Ivan Tsarevich or you will be turned to stone." He said goodbye to the serpents and rode off.

So then he came to this tsardom and he saw really a lot of stone statues, and he got frightened. He went into the palace and he saw her. She was sewing. He said, "Good health, Maria the Yellow Flower! I am your groom." She waved her kerchief and he was turned to stone up to his knee. Then he spoke again, "Good health, Maria the Yellow Flower! I am your groom." Again she waved her kerchief, and he was turned to stone up to his elbow. A third time he said, "Good health, Maria the Yellow Flower! I am your groom, Ivan Tsarevich!"

She suddenly raised her head. "Oh," she said, "Why didn't you tell me before that you were Ivan Tsarevich." Then she made him entirely alive. "Where should we get married?" she said, "in my tsardom or in yours?"

"I'd rather lead you back to my tsardom," he said. She immediately tied her tsardom up in her kerchief and she rode off to his tsardom.

So they were coming back and his sister was so happy, and she met them. The bride said to the groom, "Go to the shops and buy this and that: they'll let you have it all without money." He bought everything and they brought it back. When he had come back, she said to him, "Now go to the tsar and ask the tsar and tsaritsa to the wedding. When you come to the tsar, the tsaritsa will bring you some wine, but don't drink it. A little dog will be leaping around about you, and pour it out for the little dog, as if it were an accident. When you set off, you will see an old woman who will meet with you first. Get out of the carriage and kiss her hand." So he rode along and he saw an old woman walking. He stopped in from of her, got down on his knees, and kissed her hand. The old woman started crying. "Oh, my God, what has happened to me? I used to ride in carriages, not like this one but in royal ones, and now a handsome young man has kissed an old woman, an old woman's hand!"

This Cossack then came to the tsar and invited the tsar to the wedding. The tsar was very pleased, "I will come with pleasure."

"Permit me please to invite your spouse as well."

She came out and brought him a glass of wine. "Very well," she said, "we'll come, but please drink this."

He said, "I don't drink wine of any sort."

"Never mind, drink it!"

He took it and then apparently by mistake he poured it onto the dog, and the dog immediately died. The tsar got angry with the tsaritsa, but said, "Oh well, we'll come."

So then they were married. The tsar came and they were all seated at the table. Then Maria the Yellow Flower was brought a basin and in the basin was a golden branch and on the branch were three little birds. Suddenly one of the little birds disappeared. And Maria the Yellow Flower said, "Listen, tsar! Didn't you see that I had three little birds?"

"Yes, I saw them."

"Just look how they are crying!" The tsar looked and indeed they were crying. "Somebody here among our guests stole the third one." The tsar took offense and began looking to see who had the little bird. They searched everyone but they didn't find the bird anywhere. Then they started searching the tsaritsa and the bird was in her pocket. The tsar was so angry that he slapped her on the cheek.

So Maria the Yellow Flower asked, "Listen, tsar. Are you married for the first time or the second?"

"I am married a second time."

"And where is your first wife?"

"I don't know what the point is in talking about such trifles."

"No, I am very desirous of knowing. What children were born of your first wife?"

"They were pups," he said.

"No, I've heard, tsar, that your wife gave birth to children just as she had promised."

"But that cannot be."

"Are you desirous of seeing your children?"

"I would look at them with great pleasure if in fact they were like the ones my wife promised me." She took the cap off her husband's head, and then from her husband's sister. The tsar took one look and rejoiced.

"And do you desire to see your first wife?"

He said, "I would look at her with pleasure and take her back to me and live with her." Maria the Yellow Flower ordered a carriage readied and she went to a certain house to bring a woman back without further ado. They came to that house. She wouldn't leave. They forced her into the carriage and brought her back. The tsar saw her and rejoiced and then he ordered his second wife tied to a horse's tail and scattered through the steppe. And with the first wife he lived and prospered.

A–T 707

379. A Tale About an Invisible Cap, a Self-hewing Axe, a Self-laying Tablecloth, and Tsarevich Amafus

In the Glubdubrid or Deep Oak tsardom there ruled a ruler by the name of Farafontii Esaulovich with his spouse, Efrosinia Seluianovna. For quite some time they lived happily and without care. Finally, to their great joy, a son was born to them, to whom they gave the name Amafus. On the occasion of this joy Tsar Farafontii organized a great feast and lifted many tariffs and taxes. But not a year had passed after the birth of Tsarevich Amafus when Efrosinia Seluianovna was slandered before Tsar Farafontii, although she was blameless. The tsar, in great anger, having believed the slanderers, wanted to kill his spouse and son, but well-wishing courtiers persuaded him and advised him to imprison them in a barrel and send them out to sea. The tsar, relenting a little, agreed to this, and thus they put Efrosinia Seluianovna and her son Amafus in the barrel, into which every sort of supply had been placed, and it was released into the sea. Floating around for quite a long time in the sea Tsaritsa Efrosinia and her son had no hope at all of being saved from death. Tsarevich Amafus grew not by days, nor by the hour but in a short time he grew so much that he lay hunched over in the barrel. At one time he began to say to his mother the following: "Mama, permit me to stretch myself out in this barrel."

"Amicable son," his mother answered him, "How is it possible to do that? If you stretch yourself out and both ends of the barrel pop out, then we shall inescapably perish in the depths of the sea."

"Oh, Matushka, isn't it all the same for us to die from hunger, because all our food has run out, or drown in the sea? But anyhow, I have a presentiment that we will be saved from death."

"If you have decided, amicable Amafus, then do as you please. I agree to everything."

After this Amafus stretched out so forcibly that he broke out both the barrel's ends. On this account Efrosinia fell unconscious, she imagined that she had already completely perished, and that she was already found on the bottom of the sea. When she came to, she was astonished to see that she was lying on the shore of the sea and that standing next to her was Amafus. "Oh, my son! amiable son! We are saved! We are rescued! O happiness! O well-being! But tell me then how it happened?"

"I don't know myself, mama," answered Amafus, "how it is that we are now on the shore of the sea; I just stretched out and both ends popped out of the barrel. Then I got up and saw that we were on the shore."

Efrosinia and Amafus set off along the shore and saw that they were on an uninhabited island. A new sadness! A new tedium! What would they eat? What would they be fed by? Without wasting any time, Amafus went into a wood, leaving his mother on the shore. "I'll go, mama, I'll look for something for food and you stay here meanwhile and rest." Having gone a little way away from his mother and having ventured into a thick forest, Amafus heard an unusual noise and shout. Being curious, and moreover, daring and not timid, he set off in the direction from where the shout had come. He had gone off only a little when he caught sight of two wood spirits (*leshie*) fighting between themselves. Next to them lay a cap, a tablecloth, and an axe.

Amafus went up to them and separated them, and asked them after the reason for their quarrels, to which they answered as follows: "In this wood we found the objects that you see beside us on the ground. Although from their appearance they contain within themselves nothing particular, their characteristics are invaluable. In the first place, this cap, it is called the Invisible Cap. If anyone puts it on, then there is no way that person can be seen. In the second place, this tablecloth is called a "Self-laying Tablecloth," and it has the characteristic that whoever has it has only to spread it out and wish for whatever sort of food or fine delicacies—tea, coffee, chocolate, and things similar—and in one minute they will appear. The third object consists of this axe which is called the "Self-hewing Axe," and whatever you could think to build—a house, a palace, a ship, or the like—you have only to wish and hurl it out of your hands, and then in a minute all that you desire will appear in its very best form. And we are conducting this quarrel, gracious sire," the wood spirits continued, "because each of us wants to own these objects. The tenth day has already passed since we began quarreling, but neither of us has defeated the other."

Amafus, seeing these things and being astonished at their quality, desired to acquire them for himself. He thought a little and then said the following to the two who were quarreling: "Would you desire me to resolve your dispute?"

"Oh, gracious lord," the wood spirits answered Amafus, "You will most sensibly oblige us if you will give us counsel by which means we should cease our dispute."

"Listen then," Amafus said to them, "do you see far away over there that tall coconut tree? That will be the goal. You must run from here to it, and whoever of you two runs up to it sooner shall own these things, and I shall stay here, in the first place to guard the cap, the tablecloth, and the axe, and in the second place in order to be a witness to your contest and the end of the dispute." The wood spirits heeded Amafus's advice and took it; they drew themselves up even and threw themselves with all their strength into running to the spot indicated. They had scarcely got any distance at all from Amafus when he, without any hesitation, put the invisible cap on his head, put the self-laying tablecloth under his arm, and with it the self-hewing axe, and then he stopped over there to see what would take place between the two wood spirits. Returning and seeing neither Amafus nor the invisible cap nor the self-laying tablecloth nor the self-hewing axe, they were amazed and then they came into a great rage, but a little time later they laughed with all their strength and said, "That's a fine lad! He deceived us artfully, we wish you happiness in possessing our things!"

When they had said these words, they ran away and soon disappeared from the eyes of the amazed Amafus. Amafus was beside himself with joy, having obtained these valuable gifts, in the first place because having been cast together with his mother by fate onto this unknown and uninhabited island, they could have been deprived of life by hunger but now having the self-laying tablecloth, there was no reason to fear death from hunger. In the second place, wandering through the woods of the island they could have been made the prey of wild beasts, they could have suffered want and cold, and endured all the changes of air, but now that they had the self-hewing axe, they could live in a splendid house. And the invisible cap? And that object will with time become useful.

With the exit of the wood spirits Amafus quickly rushed to his mother. When he came to that place where he had left her, what did he see? Efrosinia lay senseless on the sand, while beside her stood a terrible lion. He had opened wide his mouth and was preparing to tear her apart with his claws. Who would not shudder at such a spectacle? But Amafus, without losing presence of mind, readied his self-hewing axe: "As total and actual master I order you this minute to cut off the head of this terrible beast." He did not finish uttering these words when the self-hewing axe threw itself at the lion, and at that same time the lion's head already lay beside the unconscious Efrosinia. Amafus, seeing this, rushed to help his mother. He held her tightly in his embrace, washed her with his tears, and with much weeping exclaimed, "Matushka, dear Mother! Open your eyes. You are still alive, you are saved, rescued from death."

A little while later she opened her eyes and in a weak, halting, and scarcely audible voice pronounced these words, "Dear Son, I am dying. Fear, weakness, and hunger have taken my strength away; accept my bless . . . ." She did not finish these words before she again closed her eyes. Amafus was beside himself. He poured forth tears, wrung his hands, and raised up his eyes to heaven. When he was in this position, he suddenly heard the following words:

> Oh dear Amafus! Give your Mother some wine!
> It will give her strength, and revive her!
> Now she lies senseless from hunger.
> Spread out the tablecloth, there you'll see all,
> [And it will revive her.]

When this unfamiliar voice had finished, Amafus came to his senses, rushed to the self-laying tablecloth and having spread it out, he said, "Self-laying tablecloth, give me, a good lad, something to eat and drink." In a minute there appeared on the tablecloth every sort of food and various wines. Amafus took a bottle of the best grape wine and poured it into a goblet, and with great effort he poured several drops into the mouth of the senseless Efrosinia.

About two minutes later she opened her eyes and began to come to her senses. "What kind-hearted creature is reviving me?" she asked in a weak voice. "Oh, if there were only about two more drops." When he heard this Amafus poured some more wine into the goblet and poured it into her mouth. After this she completely regained her senses. When she had come to, she saw Amafus kneeling beside her and holding up her head. "My son! Amiable Amafus! I am still alive! I still have the pleasure of holding you to my breast. What most kind spirit has returned life to me? Oh, my amiable Amafus!" she continued. "Although man is life-loving, is there anyone on earth more unfortunate than I? My life is one long chain of sorrows and evils. But despite all this I am very happy that life has been returned to me! I am beside myself from rapture that I can press you to my maternal breasts."

"Mama," said Amafus, "I beg you, fortify yourself, eat a little something."

"Where did you get such food?" the astonished Efrosinia asked him. "Who killed this terrible lion? Tell me, for I understand nothing." Then Amafus told her everything in detail that had happened to him. When he had finished his narration, Efrosinia and Amafus sat down to eat.

Having fortified themselves with food, they began to think by which means they should make themselves comfortable and choose for themselves a safe refuge. Having walked for a considerable time about the island, they found a splendid meadow on the shores of the sea and from one side there was an immeasurable stretch of water, and from the other high mountains covered with green vegetation. Efrosinia and Amafus decided to settle down in this place. Taking the self-hewing axe into his hands, Amafus said, "As total master and commander I order you to make a wooden house, the most peaceful and beautiful." As soon as Amafus had uttered these words, the self-hewing axe began to go about the wood cutting down trees, and then building the house from them. In five hours it had hewn the most splendid and rather large and quiet house. It also made tables and chairs. In this way when everything had been built, Amafus and his mother settled in the house hewn by the self-hewing axe.

For some time they lived happily and securely, but Amafus began to notice a major change in his mother. He often found her burdened by great pondering, sometimes he saw her pouring forth tears and releasing heavy sighs. He was very disturbed and wanted to know the reason for it. Once when they were sitting together, Amafus started a conversation about his homeland. "Do not open old wounds with these bitter recollections," Efrosinia answered him. "Alas, there is no hope for us ever to see the place of our birth. We are exiled from it and our fate is to drag out our poor life on this distant and unknown island. Oh husband, you are cruel and unjust but even at this time still amiable and dear to my heart! You will find out my innocence, but it is already late, and immeasurable seas separate us from each other. God, defender of innocence and exposer of slanderers and evildoers, sooner or later will give to each his own." She finished these words and fell into deep thought.

So Amafus learned the reason for her bitterness and her tears. A little later they heard an unusual noise. Amafus hurried outdoors to see what was happening and when he had gone down to the shore, he saw a ship standing at anchor near the very island that he and his mother were inhabiting. He ran to his mother in great haste: "Mama! Mama!' he shouted from afar, "A ship! A ship!"

"Where? Where, my amiable son?"

"It has come to our island!" Efrosinia ran straight-away out of the house and with alacrity went with Amafus down to the shore.

They had still not reached the shore when they saw people coming toward them. Such amazement from the one side and exhilaration from the other! Those coming from the ship were amazed to see people on the uninhabited island, and Efrosinia and Amafus were excited to have a hope of returning to an inhabited land. After an extended silence Amafus first began to ask those arriving on the island what sort of people they were, from which country, where they were going, where they had been, and for what reason they had stopped at this island. "We are subjects of the Kolkhid tsardom, by trade we are merchants, we were going home with various goods but because of a storm we were a long time at sea and have docked at this island solely in order to supply ourselves with fresh water and whatever provisions of food so as not to die of hunger, because our food has now been almost exhausted.

After these words they began to ask Amafus and Efrosinia who they were. But Efrosinia preferred to be silent about their origins and told them that she was a poor widow with her son, abandoned on this island by a single ship that left them there already about twelve years ago. On finishing this, Amafus asked them into his house, to which they agreed. As they approached it, they were struck with amazement on seeing this most beautiful house on such an island where besides Efrosinia and Amafus no other person lived. When the Kolkhid merchants went into the house, Amafus unfurled the self-laying tablecloth and treated them in the very best fashion.

The merchants' amazement grew greater hour by hour. After dinner Efrosinia asked them from where they were returning to their homeland.

"We are sailing," they answered "from the Deep Oak tsardom with which we conduct a large trade."

"What!?" exclaimed Efrosinia. "You are returning from the Deep Oak tsardom? Oh, that country is the place of my birth. Permit us to ask whether Tsar Farafontii Esaulovich is still alive?"

"Glory be to God!" the merchants replied, "but when we were returning from there, we were witnesses to an extraordinary spectacle. If it pleases you, we will relate it with pleasure."

"Do me the favor and tell me, "Efrosinia said to them.

"More than twenty years ago," one of the merchants began, "Tsar Farafontii, having received denunciations from several courtiers, grew angry with his spouse and put her in a barrel together with their infant son and sent them off to sea. It is even now unknown whether she is a alive or dead, or whether she was saved, or whether she perished in the depths of the sea. Since that time the tsar has lived alone and has entered into marriage with no one. But finally he has decided to marry after twenty-two years have passed. We happened to go to the Deep Oak tsardom at the very time Tsar Farafontii wanted to be married. He had only just gone into the church when there was a terrible clap of thunder, the heaven was covered with storm clouds and he heard the following words, 'Farafontii, cease! You have a wife, the virtuous and unhappy Efrosinia. She is alive, the Spirit, protector of the unfortunate, has saved her and her son from death and she is innocent. Punish those who slandered her and after some time she will appear herself before you. Farewell.' When these words were finished, there was once again a clap of thunder and the heavens cleared. Tsar Farafontii, when he had recovered, ordered the accusers of the tsaritsa to be executed immediately and then in greatest sorrow he returned to the palace. After that we set off on our way."

With that the Kolkhid merchants finished. "That's true!" shouted Efrosinia. "Sooner or later virtue triumphs and innocence turns out in all its splendor." When the merchants of Kolkhid were ready to go on to Kolkhid, they offered Efrosinia and Amafus a place on their ship, which they accepted with the greatest pleasure and in this manner after a twenty-year stay on the uninhabited island, they left it and set off for the Kolkhid tsardom. They soon arrived there. But no sooner had Efrosinia sailed into the Kolkhid harbor than they heard that in Gunigrad, the Kolkhid capital, the greatest misfortune had taken place: a thousand homes had fallen victim to flames from a fire. Amafus heard this and then said that in one night he could rebuild all the burnt-out homes.

They immediately put him and Efrosinia in a fine carriage and brought them to Gunigrad and presented them to the Kolkhid tsar, Anemon. "I have heard," Anemon said, "that you can rebuild all the burnt-out houses in one night. If you were to do this, my gratitude would be incomparable."

"Permit me, most gracious sovereign! If the work begins this very night, then tomorrow, as soon as you arise, you will see all the houses ready."

"Good, good, my amiable friend," Tsar Anemon replied.

After this Efrosinia asked Anemon to hear her in private. When he had agreed to do this, and they were alone, Efrosinia said to him, "Sovereign, you see before you the unhappy tsaritsa of Deep Oak."

"What?" Anemon exclaimed. "Efrosinia! Famous and unfortunate lady! Oh, I am so happy that I have the pleasure to receive such a famous guest. By what means were you saved from death and do you come to my country?" Here Efrosinia told him everything in detail. At the end of the narration Anemon led Efrosinia to his daughter. When they arrived, he said, "Selanira"—for so they called Anemon's daughter—I have brought you a famous guest, the unfortunate Deep Oak Tsaritsa Efrosinia. I shall leave her with you and hope you will make all possible efforts to make her stay here pleasant." Then he left. He ordered rooms alongside his own for the use of Amafus.

Only when night had fallen did Amafus take his axe in his hands and say to it, "I order you to rebuild tonight all the houses burned out in this city before sunrise." When he had uttered these words, he flung the axe out of his hands and went to sleep. In a minute the axe set off to go through the woods and cut trees and in the one night all the burnt-out houses were rebuilt in the very best manner.

The next day in the morning Tsar Anemon saw that the houses were all rebuilt, and he was not a little amazed. He called Amafus to him and said, "With the utmost feeling I thank you, most amiable Amafus, for your kindness. Your service for me and for my subjects is invaluable." While he was talking in this fashion, Selanira walked into her father's room to wish him good morning. When she saw Amafus, who was a most splendid man in full youth, she reddened and lowered her eyes to the ground. A heretofore unknown feeling came over her soul and the image of Amafus was irrevocably etched on her heart. And Amafus, for his part, saw Selanira and felt an unfamiliar fluttering and confusion. In a single moment with unbreakable bonds love united two hearts hitherto inexperienced in love. Amafus left Anemon and Selanira and went into his own rooms, but even there the image of the lovely Selanira followed him, she occupied all his thoughts, filled his soul and erected in his heart an indelible movement that could be destroyed by death alone.

Soon the rumor was spread that the Almanzar emperor Gadarik was coming with his great naval forces against the Kolkhid tsardom, but Tsar Anemon's fleet was very small and he became greatly afraid when he heard it. He didn't know what steps to resolve to take. When he found himself overcome by fear, Amafus came to him and said, "Fear nothing. I shall take everything on myself and bring Gadarik here alive; only give me one small sloop."

Anemon jumped up from his place and embraced him saying, "My dear Amafus! The hand of my daughter shall be your reward if you manage these things." This was enough for Amafus. Quickly he took his self-hewing axe, put on his invisible cap, and went to the shore. He untied a small sloop and set out into the open sea. When he had moved off a little, he saw the Almanzar fleet, so he immediately took his self-hewing axe and said, "I order you to chop up this fleet immediately!" No sooner had he finished these words than the axe set off to go among the ships and chop them up. But Amafus, unseen by all, sailed peacefully around the sinking ships and looked to see on which one Emperor Gadarik was located. Finally, having noted the ship, he approached it. He saw Gadarik. He noticed him on account of his excellent clothing and the crown glistening on his head. Finally, the turn came of that ship, too.

As soon as the self-hewing axe had struck at his boat, Gadarik threw himself into the water. Amafus, right alongside him, grabbed him out of the water and put him on the sloop where he lay unconscious almost until his arrival in Gunigrad. "Where am I?" he shouted.

"In Gunigrad," Amafus answered him.

"What?! I am in the hands of my enemy, Anemon? Oh most unmerciful gods!"

Amafus took Gadarik by the arms and led him off the sloop onto the shore where Tsar Anemon and a host of people were already expecting him. "I thank you, oh most magnificent Amafus, for this service, performed for me by you. The reward promised you by me is at your command. If you wish to receive it, then do so. If you do not wish it, then I do not know with what I can thank you."

"Oh, most gracious sovereign!" Amafus exclaimed, falling onto his knees. "If I dare hope . . ."

"Get up, get up, amiable Amafus. I know that you love my Selanira, but she is also not insensitive to your passion. Fellow citizens and people, my most amiable subjects!" Anemon continued, raising his voice. "Congratulate me on a son-in-law, and my daughter with a groom!" Instantaneously, thousands of voices exclaimed, "Long live Amafus and Selanira!"

Then turning to Gadarik, Anemon said to him, "Take part in our joy. I receive you not as an enemy but as a friend." After this they all set off for the palace.

Immediately a runner was sent to Deep Oak tsardom to Tsar Farafontii to invite him to Tsar Anemon's tsardom on the occasion of the marriage of his daughter to the famous tsarevich. A little later Tsar Farafontii himself arrived. Efrosinia, when she caught sight of Farafontii in the distance, could not refrain from tears. She noticed on his face some sort of gloomy pensivity and heavy sadness. When Anemon welcomed Tsar Farafontii, he presented Amafus and Selanira to him. At the sight of Amafus Farafontii felt some certain feeling and tears poured from his eyes. "Oh how happy you are!" he said to Anemon, "and I am so unhappy, soulless, and cruel. . . ."

"No, you are not unhappy!" Efrosinia exclaimed.

Farafontii looked at her and, shaking all over, he fell senseless onto the floor. When he regained consciousness, he threw himself at Efrosinia's feet and said, "Unhappy and dear spouse! Forgive your cruel husband. I implore you at your feet."

"Rise up, oh amiable husband, I forgive you. Embrace your son, for this is Amafus, our son," Efrosinia said.

"Father . . . !" Amafus exclaimed and threw himself into the embrace of the rapt Farafontii.

When the raptures had subsided, Tsar Anemon ordered them to prepared for the nuptial celebrations. And in this manner did Farafontii and Anemon unite the hands of their children. After this Farafontii and Efrosinia set off for their tsardom and Amafus stayed in the tsardom of Kolkhid. After a certain time had passed, Tsar Anemon died and passed on the crown to his son-in-law Amafus who with his amiable wife Selanira lived to a great age; and he was a good husband, child-loving father, and glorious sovereign.

A–T 707 + 518

380. Barmynka the King

There were these two kings: King Elisei and King Barmynka. King Barmynka had huge herds of every sort of horned animal. His wife was already old.

Elisei had daughters. They sat and spun, each before her own window. Barmynka walked by. He went up to the window of the eldest. She said, "If Barmynka were to marry me, I would feed the entire world by myself." And he didn't take that daughter.

He went up to the window of the middle daughter. She said, "If King Barmynka were to make me his wife, I would spin the whole world with just threads."

And the third said, "If King Barmynka made me his spouse, I would bring him twelve sons in one belly."

Now that's what he liked. He took her to be his wife and they were married. And his old wife remained at the court. He just fed her, but he didn't live with her.

They lived together a year and then the young wife got pregnant and it came time for her to give birth. They wanted to call the granny. But the old wife knew how to act as midwife herself. "Why call a granny?" she said. "I can do everything."

So they took them to the bakehouse. Then she started giving birth. And God gave them first a son. Out of spite the old woman, and this is why the king had got rid of her, she picked him up high and threw him onto the floor. Then she turned him into a bird. She was a magician. He turned into a cuckoo and flew away into the forest. God brought another. And she raised that one up and threw him onto the floor. And so on; all eleven sons turned into cuckoos and flew away. But the twelfth she raised up and turned into a dog.

Then she herself went off to tell King Barmynka. "Instead of twelve sons for the king she gave birth to just a single dog." He didn't believe this and sent a servant. She came back and he didn't believe her. A second servant told him also, but he didn't believe it. He went to see for himself. He saw the puppy and then he ordered a barrel with iron bands made. In it he put the pup and its mother. Then he let them out to sea along with some food. They did make a little hole in the bucket so that they wouldn't die in it.

The pup grew day by day, and then he said, "Well, mama, where are we?"

She told him how she had given birth to twelve sons, but the magician had changed all of them into cuckoos except him. He said, "If God only would give his blessing to have this barrel float top side up." And the barrel no longer swayed because they were standing on the bottom. "That would be a good thing, my son," said his mother. And so the barrel bobbed along. "We are floating top up, it seems."

"Well, if God would bless us, he would blow this barrel onto the shore. Then, perhaps, some folk would come along and find us." They heard how the barrel stopped bobbing. "That means God has brought it onto the shore."

He lived through another day and added to his wisdom. And he said, "Mama, if God sent a cast-iron ram, he would butt it on the bottom and break the bottom out." And out of nowhere there appeared a cast-iron ram and bashed the barrel and knocked out the bottom.

So mama and the pup crawled out of the barrel. And there were huge meadows all around. And they feasted on wild berries of all sorts and sweet herbs. The pup might have been a pup but his memory worked like a human's.

"Let's go, mama, and find some possessions," he said. And his mother said, "You will go away and abandon me, and I'll be bored here alone."

So later his mother blessed the pup, just asking him not to leave her. He said, "I will only heed what is heard on earth, and I will not abandon you."

So he was walking along the water. A ship was sailing out there. Barge haulers were pulling it along the shore. The pup saw them and ran to his mother. He said, "Look what I've seen on earth. People are walking along and they are pulling a great big ship. We, too, need to build a house."

"And how should we build a house? Perhaps if you were a man, but you are just a pup."

"We shall pray to God, mama." Night fell and the pup lay down to rest with his mother. They woke up and looked. There was a palace with a grand parade porch facing the sea. Mama was overjoyed and said, "God granted us just what you asked for." So they lived there.

Then for a second time the haulers came along. He called them and they were amazed. No matter how many times they had come through these places before, they had never seen anything like the palace that was there now. They ate and left various fruits and so on. And they asked them always to drop in when they were passing.

The pup started begging to go with the haulers. His mother was afraid but she blessed him. He tagged along and went off with the ship. In the evening when they had come home, they made some dumplings and put them on the table in a big wooden basin. There were many people. The pup sat down on a low bench and listened to what they had to say about his mother's and his palace. The boats and their goods belonged to King Barmynka. The haulers said to King Barmynka, "What a striking palace they have built there, finer than yours."

"Who lives there?"

"This one beautiful woman and a pup who speaks like a human."

The old wife heard this and understood who it was, and she said, "That's a miracle! In the steppe there is a golden bull and on one horn there is a bathhouse, and on the other a lake of milk. If you want to bathe in the bath-house, you have to bathe in milk."

The pup stirred the dumplings with his tail and wiped everyone's lips. Then he ran home and said to his mother, "Here's another miracle I know: we've got to get it."

"Don't go, my son, we are living well as it is."

"No, I'll go," he said.

He set off and soon found the bull. He said, "By God's will and my father's blessing, this bull must come to us." And he led him off and right into the court just opposite the window.

Once again the haulers came. They heated up the bathhouse for them, bathed them, and then they went into the milk lake. And the pup said, "Well, mama, I'll go with them."

"Enough of that!" she said.

"No, I'm going!"

Once more they went to the city with their boats and again they went to the bakehouse where they feed the workers. For the second time the haulers spoke to the king. "There was this other miracle there. Beneath the window stood a golden bull. On one of his horns was a bathhouse and on the other a river of milk."

"And who obtains these things?"

"Probably the pup."

The old wife spoke, "There is this garden and in it is an apple tree. The leaves are the size of your palm and the apples are gold. Birds sit in it and sing songs. One bird crawls up the tree and tells tales; as it crawls down the tree it spins stories. What a miracle that is!"

The little pup heard this and asked his mother to let him go again. She said, "What are you doing? If only you were a human. How will you get it?" He went off anyway.

He found the garden and said, "Lord help me move this tree!" And it went along in front of him and he along behind it. And the pup brought the tree home and put it in front of the window, alongside the bull. And his mother rejoiced.

Then for the third time the ship came and they stopped to dine, to take supper, and they were interested in this new miracle. They steamed in the bathhouse and made the bird sing and tell tales. Then they went home. They came back to King Barmynka and told him everything. And once again the pup went into the room among them. It was there that the king always fed his workers with dumplings. They said, "Such miracles! New ones. They steam you in the bath, and the bird tells tales, and the garden has just grown there."

The old wife said, "That's a miracle, but I know something that is really a miracle. In this one place in the dark forest there are eleven brothers, all with the same face and of equal beauty. One is a carpenter, one a musician, one a cabinetmaker."

The pup came out from under the table, wagged his tail and wiped everyone's lips. Then the pup ran home and said, "Now here's a miracle. In the dark forest there are eleven brothers and from your stories those are your sons. I will go and fetch them here. They can work here because I am unable to."

"Don't go, my son, you'll perish." But he went.

And there was a little hut on cock's legs, and it could turn around, but no one could go into it. "Don't turn, little hut. Stand with your rear to the forest and your front to me." He went in and saw his brothers. "Let's go and feed our mother. You live like lords here. I can't work for her alone." So his brothers took their tools and their music and set off.

They came into the hut and greeted their parent. "We shall live here," they said. "And we shall take in travelers."

For the fourth time a ship came. The brothers went out to meet it. They stopped the ship. Once more the haulers washed in the bathhouse, and they were told tales, and they played their instruments, and the little dog danced from joy for having brought the brothers home.

Then the pup said, "I'll go. Perhaps I'll hear something else."

"Don't go," said the mother.

"No, I'll go. And if I perish, in any case my brothers will be here to feed you."

So he hitched on the ship again and set off. And the haulers once more told everything to King Barmynka. "Such a miracle has taken place there! Now there are eleven brothers from one mother and father, and their faces are all identical."

The old wife said, "Well, King Barmynka, it's bad for you. Gather an army and march against them or they'll kill you," she said.

So the king gathered an army and set off for war. But the pup crawled out from under the table, wagged his tail and wiped everyone's lips: the king's, his wife's, and all the haulers. He went home and told them about the war. "What will we do?" Then the pup said, "We'll go out and stop the whole army. We won't raise our caps and we won't fire a shot. First we'll take the king into our hands."

The king was riding in front in a carriage. Behind him was the six-hundred-man force. They stopped before they had gone a verst. The pup was following along after them. "Well," he said, "Greet the guests! Take all your musical instruments, the violin, the balalaika, and I'll go out in front and dance." The king saw them, came closer, and became interested. They called him over to them. They all went into the hut where they had prepared all kinds of food and drinks. Then they heated up the bathhouse, washed him in the milk lake, plucked some golden apples, and gave them to him on a plate. He asked them, "You have traveled to many different towns—tell me, perhaps you know of some miracles?"

They said, "We don't know of any."

But their mother was lying on the stove. They asked him to ask their mother. And she said, "What tales can I tell? I got married and gave birth to twelve sons. But the old wife turned them all into cuckoos. I'll tell you a tale about myself. It's a tale I know well." And so she told him everything. "And now we live here, thanks to God."

So King Barmynka heard everything and when the queen had finished her story, the king said, "Are you my wife?"

"Truly. And here are our eleven sons and the twelfth pup. She did all this." So the king took his wife and all the sons to his home.

And they tied the old wife to a stallion's tail and sent him into the steppe, and that tore her into bits.

A—T 707A*

381. Prince Bova

In a certain tsardom the ruler's wife was widowed. The ruler had died and she had been left just with the heir. His name was Prince Bova. She fell in love with the ruler of another tsardom. That ruler said to her, "Depose and kill your son, and I shall love you. But if you won't depose him, I won't!"

She took her son and put him in a dark dungeon, and then locked him up with a padlock before going off with her lover for a walk in the garden. Her son looking out the window saw her and said, "Who is that walking there? Some merchant or traveler? And why does my mother want to starve me to death?"

Then his mother went to the cook and said, "Take some snake fat and bake a fine wheat pie. When he eats it, he'll quickly die." So the cooks baked it and gave it to a nanny who had always looked after him. "Take it to him," she was told.

The nanny took pity on him. She cut off a chunk of bread and went to him. She opened the door and he saw that she was bringing him something to eat, but crying tears at the same time. He answered her, "My dear nanny, why are you crying? Is it that you pity me?"

"It's not just that I pity you. I've looked after you these seventeen years. Your father is no more, and your mother wishes to kill you. She's put snake fat in the pie. Eat some of this black, rye bread instead; you'll be healthier."

So he broke off a piece of the rye bread, ate it, and cried. "Oh, my dear mama, what is she doing with me?"

"She is not really your mother, she's an evil serpent."

"Dear nanny, please don't close the door behind you."

"Your mother is an evil woman, and she will pursue me. I'll have no life left from her."

Then he said, "I'll go out into God's world and I'll never forget you." All the bridges had been taken out so that there would be no way for him to escape. His mother had been afraid he would get away. Then he leapt out of the dark dungeon and shouted, "Raise all the bridges!" So they raised all the bridges, and he ran over them. He ran up to the sea and shouted, "Hello, you seamen! Take me to the other side!" They took him and put him on a ship.

His mother caught on, but he was no longer there. She immediately gave chase and they came running up to the sea. His mother made a great noise, "Oh, you seamen, give me back my son!" They said to her, "We'll give him back. We ate bread without him! To which he said, 'Go on, try giving me back and I'll throw you all into the water.' So we took him to the other side."

They took him over to their side and went off with their goods to trade, and they took him with them. The tsar sent a man to buy some goods. That man stayed there three full days. No matter how much he looked at those goods, he couldn't take his eyes off the boy. The little one played the gusli so well.

He sent a nanny. "Nanny, go and see why my man hasn't moved." The nanny stood there for six full days—not so much looking at the goods as looking at the boy: he played the gusli really well. Then he sent his daughter. "Go, my daughter, and find out why they haven't moved." So the daughter went and she spent nine full days there. She really liked him—and how well he played the gusli.

The ruler got angry. "Why is it they don't come? I'll go myself!" So he came. "Why haven't you come back?"

"Well," he said, "They have fine goods but the lad is even better—he plays the gusli really well."

"Well, if you like him so much, we'll take him." So they took the boy and put him in charge of herding the horses.

The ruler's daughter watched him from the window. He was really very pleasing to her. "Oh, my dear papa, what sort of person have you put there herding horses? Better order him to serve me my food."

"If you are so fond of him, my darling, take him."

So he brought her food to her, and she asked him, "Lad, tell me, what family were you born into?"

"I am of simple birth."

"No," she said, "I can see that you are not of simple birth."

"But I am of simple birth."

"Then what is your name?"

"My name is Angusei!"

Again she responded, "No, I see that you are not of simple birth. You are the son of a lord, or a merchant, or a prince."

The next time he brought her food, she fell on her knees before him and wept, "Tell me, Angusei, what is your birth?"

"I told you that I am of humble birth. My mother washed linens and that was how she fed me." So again he brought her some food and she fell on her knees before him and said, "Tell me, Angusei, what is your birth?"

"Why do you need to know this about me?"

"Because I've fallen in love with you, and if you tell me what sort of family you were born into, I'll marry you!"

So he started telling her: "I am not of simple birth; I am of princely origins. My name is Prince Bova."

So she immediately kissed him on the lips. "Let you be my betrothed!" And then she ran to her father. "Well, papa, he's not of simple birth but a prince. His name is Prince Bova. I am going to marry him."

Her father was glad that she would be getting married and so they soon were.

Then the tsar gave him a horse. This horse had been standing for twelve years in a room behind twelve iron doors with twelve steel chains. You couldn't look him in the eye, let alone ride him. The tsar gave him the key. He opened one door and the horse knocked down all the other eleven. He was pretty strong! The horse leapt out, reared up on its hind legs, and tried to devour him. "Wait, you useless nag! Who should ride on you besides us, true warriors!?" He saddled that black warhorse and got into the saddle. Then he rode up to the porch and said farewell to his mistress. "Well, farewell, my darling. I'm going away, I'm going roaming!"

At his father-in-law's there was an old man at court who had been guarding the palace for fifty years so that no bird should fly through it, nor any beast run through it. He rode through it and the old man didn't notice. He was asleep. So Bova took his nogaika† and he struck the old man. "Well, you old fool, don't you get enough sleep lying down?"

He looked at him. "What do you want? Not a single beast has run through here, nor a single bird flown through here, and you stand there insulting me." The old man was really angry with him. He took two vials of herbs. One contained sleeping herbs and the other aging. And Prince Bova didn't know, he didn't see that the old man was carrying the vials.

He said, "Well, grandfather, give me something to drink."

The old man gave it to him with spite. "Here, drink this!" He drank the sleeping potion and fell asleep. Then the old man wrote a letter out of spite. "When you wake up, young man, go visit such and such a tsar." And to that tsar he wrote a letter: "This bandit is the one who killed your son."

He woke up and thought, "Where shall I go?" He looked and there was this letter tucked behind his belt. He read the letter. "Oh, I have to go visit such and such a tsar." So he came to visit that tsar, and Bova gave him the letter.

"So," said the tsar, "the bandit has come who killed my favorite son." He put him in a dark prison.

He had a daughter. "Papa, why did you put such a person in prison? At least he ought to prepare our food for us."

"Well, darling, if you like him so much, then let him prepare it." So he brought food to her. "Accept our faith!" she said.

"How could I possibly enter into the Latin faith?"

She immediately went and fell on her knees before the tsar. "Papa, I am guilty. He says that he remembers all evil things and that he will not accept our faith." So the tsar ordered them to hang Prince Bova, and they attached

---

†Nogaika, also nagaika. A short Tatar whip used to drive men or wolves away from riders and their horses.

twelve men to guard him. But he threw all twelve over, tore out of captivity, and ran away.

Not far away he came to his palace. There were beggars there. His wife was preparing dinner for them in his memory. He had been gone five years already. He heard them mentioning him. He took the vial of aging herbs, washed, and became old. Then he came in, threw all the beggar women off his porch, and went in to his wife. "Grant me alms not for myself but on account of Prince Bova," he said.

She dropped a plate and said, "Nannies and mummies, offer food to the beggars!" Then she led him into another room and questioned him. "How do you know him?"

"I walked with him right up to this courtyard." She didn't believe that and insisted that he tell her the truth. "What more is there to say? I am Prince Bova!"

"But you are an old man. You are joking. I would know you, but you are so old." He went into another room, washed with some other herbs, and became a handsome young man. He went up to her and she said, "My darling, where have you come from?" Then she ordered them to drive all the beggars away, and they began living and prospering, and enjoying their life.

A–T 707B*

382. About the Warrior Guak and the Maiden Polkan Polkanichna

All this took place in a certain village, like the one where we live our peasant's way of life. There lived this old man and this old woman. His wife hadn't given birth in forty years. And suddenly a son was born to them. They thought and thought about a name for him, and they decided to call him Guak. He grew so quickly that you couldn't tell it in words, and when he had grown to be sixteen years of age, he felt in himself an enormous strength, and he began asking his father and mother for their blessing so that he might ride into town.

His parents grieved bitterly, but there was nothing to be done, and they let him go. He set off for town. And there, in the town, a certain landowner had a warrior whose name was Polkan Polkanich. No one could defeat him, and he had already overcome many other warriors.

Guak heard that in Moscow there lived a very powerful warrior who could defeat all other warriors, and he rode off to Moscow. A blacksmith lived on the road to Moscow. Guak dropped in to visit him and he asked him to forge a sword for him weighing a hundred poods. The blacksmith forged the sword of a hundred poods for him. Guak raised it and said, "This is a sword for my strength!"

He took the sword and rode to Moscow to a certain rich landowner. When he got there, he said, "I heard that a very strong warrior lives here. I want to fight him."

"Well, go ahead and fight, but you will have to make a wager with the master of that warrior. If you are victorious, I will pay you, but if you don't win, you will have to pay for everything."

So they went to where the warrior lived and they agreed to bet a thousand rubles from either side.

In the morning the warriors went out into the steppe. One of them had a lance, the other a sword. They mounted their horses, rode into the steppe, and began fighting. Polkan Polkanich tried to strike Guak with his lance but it missed, and Guak struck Polkan Polkanich with his sword and knocked him out of his saddle. The two landowners came running up and looked at Polkan Polkanych, but they didn't know what to do. And Guak said to them, "You have to uncover Polkan Polkanich's chest and perhaps he'll come to life."

When they bared his chest, they saw that he was a maiden. The wind, a light zephyr, began to blow, and she got up and said, "Well, Guak, never mind how many warriors I had met, none of them had been able to conquer me. You turn out to be stronger than I. Marry me. I live abroad, and my father is a very rich landowner."

She said this and drew an address out of her pocket, where to go, her kerchief, and her ring. And she entrusted them all to him, and then she herself disappeared; she rode away across the border.

Guak went to the landowner, and they drank a few shots, they celebrated. The landowner gave him his half of the money, and Guak went home to his father, and gave the money to him. His father was overjoyed. He and his old wife had lived in poverty. Right away they bought a horse and a cow, and his father began living like a proper peasant. Guak lived at home and said, "I have given you all my money, and now I am going away, where I want to go." And he set off on foot to look for his bride. He walked a whole day, three whole days, and even twelve whole days. He had to go through the forest. He went deep into the taiga and came to a crystal house standing there with crystal gates.

Guak went up to it and saw that watchmen were standing at both sides of the gates, and along both sides of the courtyard were boulevards. He went up to a watchman, but he wouldn't let Guak in and shouted, "Don't come within twenty meters, or I'll shoot!"

Guak sat down on some logs and just sat there. Suddenly he saw a young lady approaching the gates, and the watchmen treated her with respect. She was an enchantress. She opened the gates and went up to Guak and said, "Guak, wherever you are going, you won't get there."

"Why?" said Guak.

"Because you don't eat right. Come and be my guest."

So he went with her. She led him into a room where everything was crystal and you could eat whatever you wanted. Guak looked and thought, "What is going on here? Here is this crystal house in the very deepest forest."

She entertained him well and said, "Wherever you are going, you won't get there. You had better marry me. You won't have to work, and you can drink, eat, and do what you wish."

Guak thought and thought about it, and then he decided, "I already gave my word to another."

And so he went on; he went abroad. And to get there you have to go over the sea. So he went up to the docks and asked the captain whether the next ship would soon be coming. The captain answered, "The ship will be coming in ten hours and then it will go abroad."

The ship came, and Guak set off abroad to his fiancée. But then just as soon as the ship had moved off, after it had gone about fifty kilometers, the enchantress sent a terrible storm and the ship had to turn back to the docks, all bashed up. Guak went off the steamer and asked the captain, "Will the steamer be repaired soon?"

The captain answered, "Not for at least three full days."

So Guak decided to wait. In the captain's hut there hung a rifle. So Guak said, "Comrade captain, give me your rifle and I'll leave you my documents, my passport. I'll go hunting in the forest."

So the captain gave him the rifle. He walked and walked through the forest and he came to some caves. He entered the caves and climbed down into a cavern, and there he saw a hut. He opened the first door but there was nothing there. He opened the second door but there was nothing there either. He opened the third, and there sat an old man chained in twelve chains. He asked him, "Well, grandfather, have you been sitting here long?"

"I, my benefactor, have been sitting here these twenty-five years. An enchantress chained me here, the one who sent the storm against you. And you would have ended up here if you hadn't gotten away from her, from that young lady. I know where you are going but you won't get there if you don't follow my advice. She will send another storm against you. Help me, and I will help you."

Guak thought about it. "What's to be done?" And he decided. "I will help you, grandfather," said Guak.

He raised his sword and struck it against the chains, and they all snapped.

He let the old man free and the old man said to him, "You have helped me, and now I will help you. Take that kerchief and your fiancée's ring, and place them on the bow of the ship and then go to your fiancée."

The old man said this and disappeared God knows where. And Guak set off for the docks. He came to the captain, gave him his rifle, and took back his documents. In three days the ship had been repaired. He did just as the old man had told him: he placed the kerchief and ring in the bow of the ship and set off over the sea to his fiancée.

He got to the middle of the sea and a storm arose, but the steamer kept going on and on. And the steamer got to the town where the fiancée was living.

Guak came to the docks, had a bite to eat, and began looking for her. His fiancée was already waiting for him, standing on her balcony. She saw him from the balcony, ran up to him, threw her arms around his neck, and led him to her father.

The landlord welcomed him with great honor and began entertaining him. And Guak stayed there, living in the house of the landlord. He lived there for two weeks and then the landlord said, "It's time to go to the priest to get married (in former times they had religion, you see). But before you go to get married, you need to go to a village seven kilometers from here where there is a twelve-headed crocodile. It is devouring all our stock. When you have defeated it, then you can go get married. And if you defeat the crocodile, I will grant you half my estate. Then you will live as you should."

Guak fell to thinking: how can this be? He took a horse from the landlord, saddled it, took his sword, and rode off.

He came to the crocodile. It jumped out at him and spread open all its twelve reptile heads. Guak struck it so hard that six heads were immediately sliced off. He struck it again, and three more heads flew off, and he had just begun striking the others when the enchantress flew up at him and began burning him with fire. Everything he had on was burning: his shirt, his boots—even his horse was on fire. What could he do? "Oh, if you could only help me now, old man!" thought Guak.

And the old man appeared. And they defeated the crocodile. They burned the crocodile's heads, and they brought its corpse to the landowner. Everybody gathered round to look: the workers, the servants, the peasants. They decided to reward Guak.

"Well," said the landowner, "let's go get married!"

They had only just got to the church when the enchantress blew up a whirlwind, and it carried the bride away. The whole wedding was ruined. The landowner put up some ads: "Look for my daughter!"

The wedding party dispersed. Everybody sat around and was sad. Guak went and sat down on a bench, and he, too, was miserable. "What should I do now? I'm not needed here," he thought. "I'll have to leave here now that my bride is gone."

He grieved and grieved, and then at midnight the old man came up to him and said, "Why are you grieving?" Guak told him of his misfortune. "That is no misfortune," said the old man. "The misfortune is still to come. Saddle your horse and drive him toward an oak. Whip him around the oak and tie him there while you go into a swamp, into a quagmire. There's a path there. Go along that path. Go straight and you will come to some caves. Open the first door, and you will see nothing. Open the second door, and you will also see nothing. Open the third door, and you will see your bride, but she will be dead. Take this little bag with the living water, sprinkle her with it, and here is a kerchief—wipe her with it, and then quickly carry her away from there."

So Guak set off and he did everything the old man had ordered him to do. With his bride he ran to the oak tree, and she woke up and said, "How long I have slept!"

"You would have slept still longer if it had not been for that kind old man. Quickly get up on my horse."

They mounted the horse and set off to her father's. When they arrived, her father rejoiced, and they soon were ready for the wedding. They went to the church, and the old man appeared and said; "Sprinkle your bride, put the kerchief on her, and then get married. The enchantress won't be able to do anything about it." They had just gone into the church when a storm came up, but they stood there as if rooted. All the others fell down to the ground, but they remained standing.

The priest married them, and then the landowner put on a wedding such as no one had ever seen. And they all remembered especially the little old man who had done such a good deed.

A–T 707C*

383. The Beast-Son

There lived and dwelt this peasant and his wife. They had just a single daughter. The mother died and the stepmother hated this stepdaughter. And yet the stepdaughter was very fine.

So the stepmother sheared all the hair from all the beasts, from the mice, the dogs, the hares, the foxes, the horses, the cows, simply from all of them. And she dried it and then she made some coffee from it and she had her stepdaughter drink this coffee. And from that she began to swell up.

So the [stepmother] said to the father, "Take her off into the forest; she is soon going to have a child. (You see it used to be considered a great shame if a maiden was carrying a child.) Make a coffer with iron staves on the ends, put some drinks and food in it, and carry it off to the forest."

The father made the coffer with the iron staves and took her off into the forest. Then she ate the food and drinks, started crying and lay down in the coffer, and suddenly she gave birth to a child. She touched it with her hand and in places it was sticky and in others it was soft, and she didn't know what the child looked like, it was dark in the coffer.

So the child grew and said, "Where are we, mama?"

"We are in a coffer." He strained with his head at one end of the coffer and with his feet at the other and he knocked out the bottom (he had gotten strong in there). And he went out into the world, but he closed the coffer up again so that his mother wouldn't see that he was such a monster, so that she wouldn't be frightened, and then he climbed up on a high tree trunk and looked about: there all over the earth were something like balls rolling around and like a city. Then he got back down from the tree trunk and went to his mother and said, "Mama, mama, what is that rolling around over the earth like balls and like a city?"

And she said, "That is our city and the balls rolling around are riders on their horses."

And he said, "Mama, I am going to run into the city."

"Why ever for? You don't need to do that!" she said.

"No, I'm going to run over there."

And so he ran into the city. And all who met him were terrified—what sort of monster could this be? Then he ran into a shop and he took everything he needed and all were afraid. Then he ran into another and poured lots of drinks into a tub, hoisted it on his shoulders and carried it to his mother.

Well then, the whole populace gathered together and they wanted to shoot him the next day. So he carried the tub to his mother and she said, "Now if you go there another day, bring things back on plates; you see you put it all here, and it should be some sweet and some bitter and some tasting of fish, but this just isn't right."

"All right, mother, I'll bring it all on plates." The next day he got up really early and ran away. They started shooting at him. They shot at him, but he hopped away from the bullets, and they just didn't know what more to do.

Then he spoke to them in a human tongue so that he was like a human being only with a skin put on. "Don't shoot me, don't touch me! I'll do no harm to anybody, but if you touch me, I'll turn your whole city upside down."

So then he went among the shops and he selected things on plates and he carried them off to his mother. And he started visiting that town and they no longer feared him.

He didn't taunt anybody and he didn't touch anybody. He would go into a shop, and whatever he needed for his mother, he would take; he would take things, eat them himself and no one would take anything from him.

Thus they lived for a while. He heard that the tsar was intending to get married. He ran to the tsar and said, "Marry my mother, or else I will turn the whole city upside down." Well the tsar didn't know what to do. Take her and they would think she was like the monster, but not to take her was impossible. They said, "Bring your mother!"

And he said, "I won't bring her until it's time to go to the wreath. I will bring her to the wreath in the church. My mother," he said, "must have a wedding dress."

"Well," they said, "go and take the measurements for whatever dress and slippers."

So he came back and he said, "Mama, I've been arranging your wedding with the tsar, I need to take the measurements for your dress and slippers.

So she measured everything on herself and he set off for the tsar, dragging these measurements. They looked at the measurements and then measured them again and everywhere they tested the measurements, they were just like on a human. And the tsar became more cheerful. So they prepared the dress and the slippers and they brought the dress to the mother and the mother dressed up and readied for the wedding.

He went to that tall tree with the roots and he attached himself to it and shouted, "All you sea creatures, and lake creatures, and forest folk, whoever you are and wherever—some in the air, in the waters, and forest, come here!"

And all the beasts came flying together and each of them strove to grasp hold of the roots, and they sat on their "carriage" and they dragged it out of the forest. They dragged it toward the church and all the people were terrified, and all the beasts threw off their straps and then they all ran away.

His mother was still closed in, but he said that until they had brought a circle of silt, they would not show their faces, but he said to one man that as soon as they had brought the circle of silt, he would chop off the head of the beast.

So they brought the circle of silt, and they uncovered the face, and it turned out to be such a beautiful maiden as can't be told of in a tale or drawn with a pen. So then the tsar was even happier. So now that they had brought the circle of silt, they chopped off the head of the beast. But it turned out to be not his head, a sheepskin fell off and the monster turned out to be such a handsome lad as can't be told of in a tale or drawn with a pen.

So they lived there and the tsar started asking them, "Where are you from and what kind of kin do you have? How did you manage to get into the forest?

She said, "I had this father and stepmother, the stepmother gave me this drink and I started swelling up. She then ordered my father to lead me off into the forest to some sort of coffer. And there I gave birth to a son, but such a monster."

And the tsar said, "Where are they, your relatives? We shall search for them." So they brought them in and she completely forgave her stepmother and took them to the tsar and they lived there as one family until old age. And she was so kind of heart, she forgave her stepmother who had sent her off to her death.

A–T 708

384. The Magic Mirror

In a certain kingdom, in a certain land there lived, there was a widower-merchant. He had a son, a daughter, and also a brother. . . . At a certain time this merchant prepared to go to foreign lands, to buy up various goods, and he took with him his son but left the daughter at home. He called on his brother and said to him: "I entrust to you, my dearest brother, all my house and household and especially I ask you—look carefully after my daughter, teach her to read and write, but don't permit her to be spoiled!" After that the merchant said goodbye to his brother and daughter and set off on his journey.

But the merchant's daughter was at such an age and of such indescribable beauty that, search the whole world, another similar you could not find! An unclean thought came into the head of her uncle that gave him no peace neither day nor night and he began to implore the beautiful maiden: "Either you commit sin with me," he said, "or you are not for this earth: I shall kill myself and I shall kill you, too!"

Once the maiden somehow went to the baths, her uncle behind her. Just at the door she grabbed a basin full of boiling water and poured it over him, from head to foot. For three weeks he hung on, hardly got well. A terrible hatred gnawed at his heart and he began to think: how should he pay back this mockery? He thought and thought, then set about to write his brother a letter: "Your daughter is engaged in bad things, she's frequenting the wrong houses, she doesn't stay home at night and will not listen to me."

The merchant received this letter, read it, and got really angry. He said to his son: "Well there's your sister! She's disgraced the whole household! I do not wish to forgive her. Go back this very minute. Cut up the good-for-nothing into tiny bits and on this knife bring back her very heart! Let good people not laugh at our family, our clan!"

The son took the sharp knife and set off for home. He came to his native town on the sly, saying nothing to anyone, and began to inquire here and there about how the merchant's daughter was getting along. Everyone unanimously praised her, they couldn't praise her enough. She was quiet and modest and knew God, and paid attention to good people. After having found out everything, he went to his sister. She was overjoyed and threw herself at him, embraced him, and kissed him. "O my dear brother, how has the Lord brought you here? How's it with our dear father?"

"Oh, my dear sister, don't be so quick to rejoice. My arrival is for no good. Our father has sent me here. He has commanded that I chop up your white body into tiny bits, take out your heart and bring it to him on this knife."

The sister started crying. "Oh my God," she says, "what is this unkindness for?"

"This is what it's for!" answers the brother and he told her about her uncle's letter.

"Oh, brother, I am not guilty of anything!" The merchant's son heard her out, what and how everything had happened, and then he said, "Do not weep, sister! I myself know that you are blameless and even though father ordered me not to accept any justifications, nonetheless I cannot punish you. Better you get ready and leave your father's house and be off to wherever your eyes take you. God will not abandon you!" The merchant's daughter did not think about it long, but she got ready for the journey, took her farewell of her brother, and set off—to where she herself did not know. And then her brother killed the household dog, took out its heart, attached it to his sharp knife and took it to his father. He gave him the dog's heart: "So here," he said, "in accordance with your parental orders I have punished my sister," and her father answered, "So much for her, a dog's death for a dog."

Whether for a long time or a short time, the beautiful maiden wandered throughout the whole wide world and finally she found herself in a thick, dreamy forest: the heavens were scarcely to be seen behind the high trees. She began strolling about in this forest and accidentally came out onto a broad meadow; on that meadow there was a white stone palace, and around the palace was an iron grating. "Let me just go into this palace," thought the girl, "not all people are bad, probably there'll be nothing to fear." She went into the rooms, but in the rooms there was not a human soul.

She was about to turn back when suddenly two mighty warriors galloped into the courtyard, came into the palace, caught sight of the girl and said, "Greetings, Beautiful Maiden!"

"Greetings, Honorable Knights."

"Well, now, brother," said one warrior to the other, "we were saddened that we had no one to look after us and God has sent us a sister!" The warriors left the merchant's daughter to live with them, and they called her their very own sister, and they gave her keys and made her mistress over the entire house. Then they drew their sharp sabers and touched each other in the chest and made the following agreement: "If either of us dares to impose himself on this sister, he shall be cut to pieces without mercy with this saber."

So this beautiful maiden lived with the two warriors, and her father bought up all sorts of foreign goods, returned home, and a little later married a second wife. This merchant's wife was of indescribable beauty and she had a magic mirror: look in the mirror and you could instantly find out where what was taking place.

Once the warriors had readied themselves to go hunting and they said to their sister: "Look that you don't let anyone in until our return." They said their farewells and rode away.

At that same moment the merchant's wife looked in the mirror, admired her beauty and said, "There is no one more beautiful than I in the whole world!"

But the mirror replied, "You are beautiful, there's no argument about that. But you have a stepdaughter who lives with two warriors in the deep forest, and she is more beautiful."

These were no pleasing words for the stepmother. She immediately summoned an evil old woman to her. "Well," she said, "here is a ring; go into the deep forest, and in that forest is a white stone palace and in that palace lives my stepdaughter. Bow to her and give her this ring. Tell her that her brother has sent it to her as a keepsake!" The old woman took the ring and set off whither she had been sent. She came to the white stone palace, the beautiful maiden saw her and came running out—she so very much wanted to ask for some news from her family. "Greetings, Grandmother! How has the Lord brought you here? Are they all alive and well?"

"They are alive and chewing their bread! Your brother has asked me to inquire after your health and has sent you this ring as a present. So, enjoy!" The maiden was so happy, so very happy I can't even tell you. She brought the old woman into the rooms, treated her to every sort of tidbit and drink, and then instructed her to bow low to her brother. After an hour the old woman wound her way back, and the girl began admiring her ring and she thought of putting it on her finger. She put it on and at that very instant fell dead.

The two warriors returned, came into the rooms, but their sister did not meet them. What could this be? They looked into her bedroom. She lay there dead, without saying a word. The warriors grieved: what had been more beautiful than anything else was thus suddenly and unexpectedly taken by death! "We shall have to dress her in new clothes and put her in a coffin," they said. They started undressing her and then one of them noticed the ring on the hand of the beautiful maiden. "Should we perhaps bury her with that ring? Better I'll take it off and keep it in her memory." As soon as he had removed the ring, the beautiful maiden immediately opened her eyes, gasped and came alive. "What happened with you, sister? Did someone perhaps come to visit?" the warriors asked.

"A familiar old woman came to visit from my family and brought me a ring."

"Oh, how disobedient you are! It was not without reason that we instructed you not to let anybody into the house without us. See that you don't do it another time."

After a little time the merchant's wife again looked in her mirror and saw that her stepdaughter was once again alive and beautiful. She called in the old woman, gave her a ribbon, and said, "Go to the white stone palace where my stepdaughter lives and give her this little gift. Tell her that her brother has sent it!" So again the old woman came to the beautiful maiden. The girl was overjoyed, tied the ribbon around her neck and at that very moment fell dead onto the bed.

The warriors returned from the hunt and saw that their sister was lying there dead, then they started dressing her in new clothing and as soon as they had removed the ribbon, she opened her eyes, gasped and came alive. "What is the matter with you, sister? Or was that old woman here again?"

"Yes," she said, "The old woman came from my family and brought me a ribbon."

"Oh, you are too much! Why, we begged you—don't receive anyone unless we are here!"

"Forgive me, dear brothers! I couldn't stand it, I so much wanted to hear some news from home."

A few days passed and then the merchant's wife again looked in the mirror. Again her stepdaughter was alive. She summoned the old woman. "Well," she said, "Here's a hair! Go to my stepdaughter, and this time you kill her!"

The old woman waited for the right time when the warriors had gone off hunting, then she went to the white stone palace. The beautiful maiden saw her through the window and couldn't stand it: she leapt out to her. "Greetings, Grandmother! How is God treating you?"

"Oh, so far I am alive, my darling! Well, I've been wandering around the world and made my way here to inquire after you." The beautiful maiden brought her into the room, treated her to every sort of tidbit and drink and asked about her relatives, and instructed her to bow to her brother.

"Very well," said the old woman, "I shall give him your regards. And now, my darling, is there no one here to look around on your head? Let me take a look!"

"Go ahead and look, Grandmother!" So she began searching the head of the beautiful maiden and braided into her plaits the magic hair. As soon as she had woven the hair in, the maiden immediately died. The old woman laughed wickedly and went away quickly so that no one would find her there, no one would see her.

The warriors came home, they came into the rooms, their sister lay there dead. They looked and searched for a long time to see whether she had something unfamiliar on her, but they could see nothing! So they made a crystal coffin—such a marvelous one it was that you can't imagine it, or even guess about it, just tell about it in a tale, and they put her very best dress on the merchant's daughter, as if she were a bride ready for the wreath, and then they placed her in the crystal coffin. They placed the coffin in the middle of a large room and above it they raised a canopy of red velvet with clusters of diamonds and with golden fringe and they hung twelve lamps on twelve crystal columns over it. After that the warriors dissolved in bitter tears, they were overcome by great sadness. "Why should we live on this wide earth?" they said, "Let's go and determine our fate." They embraced, said goodbye to each other and went out on a high balcony, held each other's hands and leapt down. They struck the sharp rocks and ended their lives.

Many, many years passed. And then it happened that a certain tsarevich was out hunting. He rode into the dense forest, sent his dogs off in all directions, got separated from the other hunters and rode along a certain, overgrown path. He rode and rode, and then suddenly before him there was this glen and in the glen stood a white stone palace. The tsarevich got down from his horse and went up the staircase. He began examining all the rooms; everywhere there was lavish warrior's equipment, but there was no trace of an owner's hand. Everything had long since been abandoned, let go to the wind! In one room there stood a crystal coffin and in that coffin lay a dead maiden of indescribable beauty. A rose spot was on her cheeks, on her lips a smile, just as if she were alive and sleeping.

The tsarevich went up and looked at the maiden and he was fixed to that spot as if some unseen force held him. He stood from morning until late in the evening, he could not remove his eyes, anxiety filled his heart. The maiden's beauty had transfixed him, it was awesome, unseen, such as one could never hope to find on earth. But his hunters were long since looking for him, and they had galloped around the forest, blowing on their horns and calling out to him, but the tsarevich stood next to the crystal coffin, hearing nothing. The sun set, darkness thickened, and only then did he come to his senses. He kissed the dead maiden and rode back. "Oh, your highness, where have you been?" asked the hunters.

"I chased after a beast and got a bit lost." The next day—it was barely light, the tsarevich got ready for hunting. He galloped into the forest, separated himself from the hunters and rode along the same path to the white stone palace. Once more he stood the whole day long beside the crystal coffin, not taking his eyes off the dead beauty. Only late at night did he again head home. On the third day and the fourth day it was the same, and so a whole week passed.

"What has happened with our tsarevich?" asked the hunters. "Brothers, let's follow him so that no harm will come to him."

So the tsarevich rode off hunting. He released his dogs into the forest, separated himself from this suite and set off for the white stone palace. The hunters were right after him, they rode out into the glen, came to the palace and went into the palace where the crystal coffin was standing. In the coffin lay the dead maiden, and in front of the maiden the tsarevich was standing. "Well, your highness, it was not for nothing that you have been out and about in the forest for a whole week. Now we will not be able to get away from here until evening." They surrounded the crystal coffin, looked at the maiden, admired her beauty and then stood there in the same spot from morning until late in the evening.

When it was completely dark, the tsarevich turned to his hunters: "Brothers, do a great service for me and take this coffin with the dead maiden and carry it home and place it in my bedroom. And quietly, do you hear, do it secretly, so that no one may know, no one find out. I will reward you in every way, with much gold treasure, such as no one has ever rewarded anyone before."

"It is your choice to reward us, but we, tsarevich, are happy to serve you," the hunters said, and they raised up the coffin, carried it out into the yard, placed it on their horses and took it to the royal palace. Then they brought it in and placed it in the tsarevich's bedroom.

From that very day the tsarevich ceased even thinking about hunting. He sat by himself at home, never going out of his room, always admiring the maiden. "What has come over our son?" thought the tsaritsa. "Why, he's been sitting at home for ever such a long time, he never leaves his room, and lets no one in. Such sadness and longing has come over him, as if some sort of sickness had overcome him. I'll go in and look upon him." The tsaritsa went in to his bedroom and saw the crystal coffin. What could it mean? She asked and questioned and then immediately gave the order to bury the maiden, according to custom, in Mother Moist Earth.

The tsarevich began weeping, he went into the garden and plucked several magic flowers. He brought them and began combing out the russet trusses of the dead beauty and then was going to arrange the flowers on her head. Suddenly the magic hair fell out of her plait—the beautiful maiden opened her eyes, gasped, raised herself out of the crystal coffin and said, "Oh, how long I've been sleeping!"

The tsarevich was speechless with joy. He took her by the hand and led her to his father, then his mother. "God has given her to me," he said. "I cannot live without her for a single minute. Permit me, my dear own father, and you, my dear own mother, allow us to marry."

"Marry, my son! We shall not go against God and such beauty you'll never find in the world." There is no reason for tsars to have to wait: that very day there was a handsome feast and fine little wedding!

So the tsarevich was married to the merchant's daughter and he was living with her, there was no end to his joy. Some time passed and then she decided to go to her own land, to visit her father and brother. The tsarevich was not against this and so he asked permission of his father. "Very well," said the tsar, "Go, my dear children! You, tsarevich, go the roundabout way by dry land, inspecting with this opportunity all our lands and examining our rule. But let your wife go by ship the direct route." So they prepared a ship for sailing, equipped the sailors, appointed the commanding general. The tsarevna got on the ship and it went off to the open sea, and the tsarevich set off over dry land.

The commanding general, seeing the beautiful tsarevna, envied her beauty and he began flattering her. "What is there to fear," he thought, "now she is in my hands? Whatever I want to do, I'll do." "Make love to me," he said to the tsarevna, "and if you won't make love to me, I'll throw you into the sea."

The tsarevna turned away, she gave him no answer, she was only overflowing in tears. A certain young sailor overheard the general's words, went up to the tsarevna in the evening and said, "Do not cry, tsarevna! Dress in my clothes, and I'll put on yours. Then you go up on deck and I'll stay here in the cabin. Let the general throw me into the sea, I'm not afraid. I'll manage somehow, I'll swim to the wharf. It's good for me that land is so near." So they exchanged clothes. The tsarevna went up on deck and the sailor lay down on her bed. In the night the commanding general appeared in her cabin, grabbed the sailor and threw him into the sea. The sailor started swimming and by morning had reached the shore. The ship came into the harbor and the sailors began disembarking. The tsarevna also disembarked, rushed to the market, bought herself a cook's dress, turned herself out as a cook and hired on to her very own father to serve in his kitchen.

A little later the tsarevich came to the merchant's. "Greetings," he says, "Father! Receive your son-in-law, you see, I am married to your daughter. But where is she? Hasn't she come yet?" And then the commanding general appeared with a report. "Well it was this and that, your highness! There was an accident. The tsarevna was standing on the deck, a storm came up, we started rocking, her head started spinning, you couldn't wink before the tsarevna had been thrown into the sea and drowned!" The tsarevich grieved and wept, for you can't bring her back from the bottom of the sea: it was obvious that this was her fate. The tsarevich stayed for some time with his father-in-law and then ordered his suite to prepare for departure. The merchant gave a huge feast in farewell. All the merchants, and the boyars, and all his relatives gathered at his house. And his brother was there, and that evil old woman, and the commanding general.

They drank and they ate, and they took it easy. One of the guests said, "Listen, Honored Guests! Just to drink and drink is to get no good from it. Better that we all tell tales!"

"Very well, very well!" they shouted from all sides. "Who will begin?" This one didn't know how to, that one wasn't very good at it, and the third one had lost his memory in the wine! What now? The merchant's steward called out, "We have a new young man in the kitchen who's traveled much in foreign lands, seen all sorts of extraordinary things, and is a master at telling tales. Call him out!"

The merchant summoned the young cook. "Entertain my guests," he said.

The young cook and tsarevna answered him: "What shall I tell you, a tale or a story from real life?"

"A story from real life!"

"Then a story from real life it will be but with one condition: if anyone interrupts me, then it's a bop on the head for him."

So they agreed to everything. And the tsarevna began to tell everything that had happened to her. "So then, this merchant had a daughter. The merchant went abroad and entrusted his very own brother to look after this young maiden. The uncle was struck by her beauty and would not give her a moment's rest. . . ."

Then the uncle heard that she was talking about him and he said, "Oh, my good gentlemen, this is not true!"

"So, it's not true in your opinion? Then here's a bop for you in the head."

After that the story turned to her stepmother, how she had questioned her magic mirror, and then to the evil old woman who had come to the white stone palace of the warriors, and the old woman and the stepmother shouted out in one voice, "What nonsense all this is! This could never be." So the tsarevna gave them a bop in the head with her soup ladle and started telling about lying in the crystal coffin, how the tsarevich found her, brought her back to life and married her and how she had gone to visit her father.

The general noted that affairs were going badly and he begged of the tsarevna: "Permit me to go home, for some reason my head has started to ache!"

"Never mind, sit a bit longer!"

So the tsarevna started telling about the general, and he simply couldn't take it any longer: "All this is untrue!" he said. The tsarevna bopped him on the head with her ladle and threw off her cook's clothes and revealed herself to the tsarevich: "I am not a young cook, I am your married wife!" The tsarevich was overjoyed, the merchant also. They rushed to embrace and kiss her. And then they started judgment proceedings. The wicked old woman together with the uncle were shot on the city gates; the sorceress stepmother was tied to a stallion's tail, the stallion ran into the open steppe, and scattered all her bones among the bushes, in the ravines; the tsarevich sent the general into forced labor and placed the sailor in his position, the one who had saved the tsarevna from misfortune. And since that time the tsarevich, his wife, and the merchant have lived together—for a long time and happily.

A–T 709 + 883A

385. The God-Daughter of the Mother of God

There lived and dwelt this peasant and he was so poor that all he possessed was a trunk, and that was empty. What should he do now? He kept thinking about it. There was nothing to eat, and he had nothing to buy anything with! Probably he would have to sell his very own daughter, but who could possibly need her? He had just been thinking about this when suddenly the Most Pure Virgin came into his hut and said, "Good health, peasant. Sell me your daughter."

"How amazing!" thought the peasant. "I haven't even said a word and yet it is all known to her! Why not sell her?" he said. "Buy her. She's yours."

So the peasant took the money and handed over his daughter. The Most Holy Mother of God led her to her high chambers and said, "Remain here and live in peace. If you are bored, here is a key. Open any door and go in for a stroll. You'll find pleasure there." The girl opened a door and went into a very large garden. There was every sort of flower and tree in it. She stayed a whole month there, but she just couldn't admire it enough, she never grew tired of strolling about there.

Much time passed and the Most Holy Virgin gave her another key. "If you are bored, open this door and admire God's creation." The little girl opened the other door and saw there a great host of various birds as if gathered there from the entire world. She could have admired them forever without growing tired and she could have listened to their sweet singing without growing tired of it. Again much time passed, and the Most Holy Virgin gave her a third key. "If you are bored, go through this door and admire God's creation." She opened the third door and saw there a great number of various beasts. All the beasts were gentle and beautiful. She started playing with them, watching their leaps and jumps for a long time. Afterward the Most

Holy Mother of God gave her all the keys and said, "I permit you to go everywhere and see everything, except in there where there is the brass lock hanging on the door."

The little girl started thinking to herself, "What can that be? I can go anywhere and look at everything except there where that brass lock is hanging. I'll just take a little peek in there." She had no more than barely opened the door when a flame shot out of it and she hardly managed to run to one side.

"Where were you and what did you see?" asked the Most Holy Virgin.

"I wasn't anywhere and I didn't see anything," the little girl answered.

"If you don't admit it, I will make you deaf and dumb."

"I wasn't anywhere and I didn't see anything," the little girl repeated. So the Most Holy Virgin made her deaf and dumb, and led her into the dark and dense forest.

So she wandered for a long time in the forest. She became tired and exhausted, and she climbed into a hollow tree to rest. At the time the tsar's son was hunting there, and he came across the hollow and saw the little girl. He was very attracted to her beauty and asked her who she was and how she had come to be there. But no matter how much he asked her, she uttered not a word. Then the tsarevich ordered his people to take her with them and he brought her to the palace. The girl grew up and fell deeply in love with the tsarevich. He wanted to marry her and he told his parents, but they said to him, "Dearest son, we do not wish to take your freedom from you but this is our advice. What is this desire of yours to marry someone dumb? You would be better to marry a tsarevna or a princess."

But the tsarevich so relentlessly insisted that there was nothing else to do, and his mother and father gave their parental and eternal blessing. The tsar had no time to brew the beer or make the vodka before there was a happy little wedding. They celebrated and lived in joy. Precisely after a year a young son was born to them and on that very night, as soon as everyone was soundly asleep, the Most Pure Virgin came and woke up the tsarevich's wife. She said, "You may use your tongue, only admit to what you saw in that chamber where the brass lock was hanging."

"I saw nothing."

So the Most Pure Virgin once more made her dumb and deaf, and she took away the child. In the morning the tsarevich asked about his son. The mummies and the nannies were in an uproar. They searched and searched, they thought and thought, but they found nothing. The tsar and tsaritsa began saying that his wife was an evil witch and that she had destroyed their dear child. She ought to be executed, they said. The tsarevich pleaded with his parents with tears and they took pity on him and forgave their daughter-in-law. After a year she gave birth to another son, and once more the Most Pure

Virgin came in the night and carried that second child away, too. After another year a third son was born to the tsarevich, but the same thing happened. Then the tsar became very irate and ordered the tsarevich's wife executed with a horrible punishment. They led her out to be executed. All was ready: the axe and the block! At that very moment the Most Pure Mother of God appeared with the three fine little boys, and she said, "Admit what you saw in that chamber with the brass lock on the door." So finally the tsarevich's wife admitted it, and the Most Pure Virgin pardoned the sinner, granted her the use of her tongue and ears, and gave her back the children. After that the tsarevich and his wife lived and lived well, and they prospered, and when his father died, he became tsar and he governed his people long and charitably.

A–T 710

386. How the Cock Took Away the Tsar's Money

There lived an old man, he had no old woman. He lived and every day he went fishing. His fate was bound up in the sea: if he caught a fish, he was satisfied, if he didn't catch one, he'd go to bed hungry. This old man had nothing but a cock. Now next door there lived a lonely grandmother. And she had a hen. So once the old man came to her: "Neighbor, give me just one egg!"

"Take one, old man, my hen has just laid it." So she gave him an egg. The old man went home, cooked it, and ate it. The next day the old man had no catch and he went back to the grandmother. "Neighbor, give me an egg!" The grandmother gave him an egg. He went home, cooked it, and ate it. On the third day he again caught nothing in the sea. So he came to the grandmother and asked her: "Neighbor, rescue me! Give me an egg!"

"Oh, old man! You keep on asking, you catch no fish. Your back doesn't ache, I gave you one egg, I gave you a second, will you take a third? I won't give it to you! Go home and chop off your useless cock's leg. He'll bring you an egg!"

The old man thought carefully: "If I chop off the cock's leg, he'll bring me an egg; otherwise I feed him and there's no profit from him at all."

He went home, caught the cock and was just about to chop off its leg when the cock hopped and skipped from the old man. He ran and ran and so he got away. One day passed and the cock was not at home, then a second and a third. On the fourth, the old man went to the old woman: "So, old one! You taught me to cut a leg off my cock so it would bring eggs to me, but he has completely disappeared! Three days he hasn't been home."

But the cock was walking down the road, just walking along. He walked and walked and then he met up with a jackal. The jackal asked: "Cock, where are you going?"

He answered: "I'm going to fight a war against the tsar and take away from the tsar half his kingdom and his money."

The jackal said, "I'll go with you."

"Come on."

So they walked and walked along the road and the jackal said, "I'm exhausted, cock."

"Well then, crawl into (!) me." The jackal crawled into the cock and sat there, while the cock walked on.

He walked and walked and then he met up with a wolf. The wolf asked him "Cock, where are you going?"

The cock answered, "I'm going to fight a war against the tsar and take away from that tsar half his kingdom and his money."

The wolf said, "With that tongue, cock, you could clean up a Turk!"

"If you don't believe it, then don't come," answered the cock.

The wolf thought and thought and then stated: "Cock, for such a cause, I'll join with you."

"Come on."

So they went down the road. They walked and walked and the wolf grew tired. "Cock, I'm exhausted."

"Well, if you're exhausted, climb into me." In the wolf climbed and he sat there, and the cock walked on.

He walked and walked and some bees came flying toward him. They saw the cock and asked: "Cock, where are you going?"

"I'm going to fight a war against the tsar and take away from the tsar half his kingdom and his money."

The bees began to discuss it: "And we'll fly with you for such a cause."

"Come on, come fly with me!"

So the cock walked on and the bees flew behind him. They flew and they flew and they stated: "Cock, oh cock, we're exhausted from this flying!"

"Then crawl into me." So the bees crawled into the cock and sat there, but the cock, you know, he just walked on.

He walked and walked until he came to a stream. The stream was large and he couldn't walk across it, nor could he fly across. He became sad. He paced and paced on the bank and thought: "What should I do now?" He thought and thought, then turned his asshole to the stream and said, "Water, oh water, come into me!" So the water went into the cock. The stream dried up and the cock went on further. He came to the outpost where the tsar was living. He went up to the tsar's house, climbed onto the wattle lattice and shouted:

> *Cock-a-doodle-do, cock-a-doodle-do!*
> *I, the cock, have come to fight the tsar!*
> *On my shoulder I'm carrying my saber,*
> *I'll take away the tsar's treasure!*

And from within the cock the wolf and jackal made a noise: "The tsar has no money! The tsar has no money, the tsar has no money!"

The tsar heard these words and was taken aback at the wonder: "What is this that I have no money! Put that cock, servants, with my hens in the chicken house! Let them peck him!"

So the tsar's servants ran and caught the cock and put him in with the hens for the night. They put him in with the hens and went away themselves. Then the cock stated: "Well, now, jackal, climb out and slaughter the royal hens!" The jackal climbed out and slaughtered all the hens. In the morning the servants came, opened the hen house and the cock jumped out, sat down on the wattle lattice and shouted:

> *Cock-a-doodle-do, cock-a-doodle-do!*
> *I, the cock, have come to fight the tsar!*
> *On my shoulder I'm carrying my saber,*
> *I'll take away the tsar's treasure!*

And then the wolf made a noise from within the cock: "The tsar has no money! The tsar has no money! The tsar has no money!"

The tsar heard these words and was taken aback by the marvel. So he gave his servants an order: "Catch that damned cock and put him down on the floor with the cattle. Let them trample him."

So the servants went, caught the cock, and put him with the cattle for the night. The cock sat on the floor and stated: "Well now, wolf, climb out and slaughter the royal livestock or else the cows and bulls will crush me."

Out climbed the wolf and he slaughtered all the royal livestock. In the morning the royal servants came and all the royal livestock were slaughtered. The cock jumped from the floor, sat on the wattle lattice and crowed:

> *Cock-a-doodle-do, cock-a-doodle-do!*
> *I, the cock, have come to fight the tsar!*
> *On my shoulder I'm carrying my saber,*
> *I'll take away the tsar's treasure!*

And from within the cock the bees made a noise: "The tsar has no money, the tsar has no money, the tsar has no money." For a whole day the cock shouted away.

The tsar was angered and he gave his servants an order: "Catch that cock, put him in the oven, and let him roast!"

The servants came and heated up the oven; they caught the cock, put him in the oven, and closed it. The cock sat in the oven and stated: "Water, water! Pour out over the oven!" The water poured over the oven. In the morning the royal servants opened the latch, the cock jumped out, and in the oven only water remained.

The servants ran to the tsar and reported to him: "We didn't even get the latch opened and the cock jumped out. In the oven just water remained."

The cock perched on the wattle lattice and shouted out to himself:

> Cock-a-doodle-do, cock-a-doodle-do!
> I, the cock, have come to fight the tsar!
> On my shoulder I'm carrying my saber,
> I'll take away the tsar's treasure!

And from within the bees made a noise: "The tsar has no money! The tsar has no money! The tsar has no money!" The tsar listened and listened and grew angry at the cock: "What is this, I have no money?! Catch that cock and bring him here to me in my chambers."

The servants ran and they caught the cock, and brought him to the tsar in his chambers. The tsar had devised a way to offend the cock. So he stated: "Put that cock in my trousers!"

So the cock perched in the tsar's trousers and stated: "Bees, bees! Fly out and sting Tsar Yerokha!" Out flew the bees and began to sting the tsar. They stung Yerokha so much that he swelled up. The tsar's trousers fell off him and that cock flew out!

In the morning the servants came and opened the doors to the palace, and the bees flew away as the cock jumped outside. So the cock jumped outside and perched on the wattle lattice and then he shouted:

> Cock-a-doodle-do, cock-a-doodle-do!
> I, the cock, have come to fight the tsar!
> On my shoulder I'm carrying my saber,
> I'll take away the tsar's treasure!

And then the wolf and jackal ran around the royal hut and made this noise: "The tsar has no money, the tsar has no money, the tsar has no money." All day long they shouted, then another, and then a third.

On the third day the tsar stated to his servants: "Catch him, that damned thing, put him in a trunk full of money and let him see whether I have money or no."

The servants caught the cock, placed him in the trunk full of money, and the cock took and pecked all the gold sovereigns. In the morning the servants came, opened the trunk, and the cock flew out, but there was no money in the trunk. They went to the tsar and reported to him: "Oh, Father Tsar! There is no money in the trunk!"

"How so, no money?"

"Just isn't," the servants stated.

But the cock perched on the wattle lattice and shouted:

> *Cock-a-doodle-do, cock-a-doodle-do!*
> *Tsar Yerokha has no money!*
> *Tsar Yerokha has no money!*

The cock shouted and then ran home to the grandfather, the wolf and jackal ran into the woods, and the bees flew away to the steppe. When the cock got home, he shouted:

> *Old man, old man, old man!*
> *Open the gates wide!*
> *Lay down new carpets!*
> *Receive the cock, I've brought some money!*

The old man heard the cock, opened the gates and spread out new carpets. The cock sat on a carpet and poured out all the sovereigns. The old man went off to the neighbor woman's and praised him: "That cock of mine has brought me a whole pile of money."

The old woman ran to the old man's to look at the money. She saw a heap of money and began to ask for some. The old man gave her two sovereigns. The next day she came back and asked: "Old man, give me a coin!" And on that next day the old man gave her two sovereigns.

On the third day she also came to ask: "Old man, give me a coin."

"And how many times did you give me an egg?"

"Twice," answered the old woman.

"And I have twice given money to you, but now I won't. Go chop off your hen's leg and she will also bring you some money."

The stupid old woman went home and chopped off her hen's leg. And the hen wriggled and shuddered, wriggled and shuddered, and died. The woman was left without a hen and the old man lived on with his cock. They began to live and prosper and accumulate wealth.

I was there with them, mead beer I drank, little cakes I ate. They lived well, received their guests politely. Whoever dropped by would be fed and offered a drink.

A–T 715A*

387. About a Doctor and the Devil

There was once this physician, I mean, he was a doctor. And he knew everything, everything, everything! His wife had left him. He had no children. So he sat in his study and talked to himself. "Well, they say the devil really exists. But what does the devil know? Nothing. Let him exist. I am a physician, that is, I am a surgeon. I know everything a man has inside him."

He was sitting there, deliberating at his desk. He was even smoking a cigar. The transom was open. And through the transom a snowflake flew onto the desk. It turned out to be a devil with hooves. On his feet were hooves!

"Greetings, doctor!"

"Greetings, devil!"

"Why do you sit here repeating to yourself that you know everything and that I, the devil, know nothing?"

"But of course, I am a physician, you see. A famous surgeon. I know everything about a man. When I do an operation, I know everything to do inside there."

"Oh, you are a fool! You know, do you? But do you know where a man's conscience is?" the devil asked him.

He thought about it. "Perhaps I don't know that."

"Aha! Do you want me to show you?"

"I do."

So then the devil took out the doctor's conscience and showed it to him on his hand. It was some sort of liquidy stuff, a little like brains. Tiny. So he showed it to the doctor.

"And the mind of a man? What's it like? And where are his thoughts?"

"I don't know, devil."

So he removed the doctor's thoughts. The doctor became an utter idiot, with cold ears even. He couldn't comprehend anything. He sat there in his chair and he knew absolutely nothing. So the devil took that doctor and put him into a rattle, the sort they buy for children, and then he shook it around the table.

"Now see what a fine thing has become of you! I'll give you to the children. Let the children play with what was you, and you'll be no more. No more the physician who claims the devil knows nothing. Oh, all right, I'll take pity on you." So he poked the doctor's thoughts back into him, he returned them. And the doctor came to life a little. "Now then, doctor, I'll give you this liquid that I took out of you, your conscience." He put it back. Everything was normal. The doctor and the devil sat and conversed.

"You are right, devil. You know more, you, sir, know much more than I do."

"That's right. Don't ever forget that the devil knows. The devil knows much more than you do. And don't forget it: I'll be right here if you do." And once more he became a snowflake, and the devil flew away.

After that the doctor believed that devils really do know more. And that's it. The tale's at an end.

A–T 716**

388. A Pre-tale

> *Urka, yes Urka!*
> *Urka flew out onto the street.*
> *Urka, yes Urka!*
> *He sat down on the picket fence.*
> *Urka, yes Urka!*
> *Here come rich guests!*
> *Urka, yes Urka!*
> *Sing, Urka, a song!*
> *Urka, yes Urka!*
> *Yes, my father killed me.*
> *Urka, yes Urka!*
> *My stepmother ordered it.*
> *Urka, yes Urka!*
> *My sister ate none of my flesh.*
> *Urka, yes Urka!*
> *She walked about the outskirts of town,*
> *Urka, yes Urka!*
> *Collecting up the bones.*
> *Urka, yes Urka!*
> *She placed them on the windowsill,*
> *Urka, yes Urka!*
> *And watered them with fresh milk.*
> *Urka, yes Urka!*

A–T 720

389. Twelve Mikitas

A father had three sons. So he built a new house and said, "As we are moving into this new house, we need to spend a night in it." The oldest son spent the night in the house and then he came to tell his father what he had dreamed. The second son spent the night and then came to tell his father what he had dreamed. The third night the youngest son went. He spent the night, then came to his father, but he didn't tell him his dream. His father and mother ceased loving him for that reason and everybody hated him.

A passing peasant stopped in to them and said, "Well, that's probably not your own son. Sell him to me."

"He's our own, alright, but we don't need him. You take him."

So he went off with the peasant. "Well, Mikita,† what sort of dream did you actually see?"

"I wouldn't tell my own father, nor my mother, and I certainly won't tell you." So he no longer had any liking for the boy, and as they went down the road, he beat him.

They met a landowner. "Why are you beating him?"

"Because he spent the night in a new house and he won't tell his dream."

"Give him to me."

"Take him!" And he did.

"So, Mikita, come with me now." They rode for a long time, and the landowner kept trying: "Tell me, Mikita, what did you dream?" But Mikita wouldn't say, so the landowner disliked him and started beating him and striking him.

On the way they met the tsar's family. "Why are you beating your servant, landowner, what for?"

"Because he spent the night in a new house, but he won't tell the dream he had."

"Give him to me!" So he went home. "Well, Mikita, tell me, what dream did you see?"

"There's no way that I can tell it." So they put him in prison and every day they gave him a pound of bread and the same of water.

The tsar organized a ball. He summoned his ministers and brought out three stallions. "Guess the age of each." No one could guess their ages.

So they let the young man out of prison. The young man said, "Forge me a shepherd's staff of seven poods." So they forged it and he took the staff and hit one of the stallions on the forehead. When he had been hit, the stallion fell to the ground. "That one's a yearling." He hit the second one twice and

---

†A peasant form of Nikita, from the Greek Nicetas.

down it went. "That one's two years old." He hit the third one three times. "That one is three years old." He had guessed them all. Then they put him back in the prison.

After that the great ruler went off to various lands to get married. He left only his sister behind. She waited for her brother a year, a second, and a third. But there was no news from her brother. She grieved and she was given this advice: to summon Mikita. "So," she said, "Our lord went away and for three years there has been no news of him, Mikita."

"Permit me, but I must gather another eleven Mikitas alike in both voice and hair, just like me. I will then set sail in a light ship and sail away to search for the tsar."

So they gathered another eleven Mikitas for him who were alike in voice and hair, and he set sail. He soon caught up with him, and as he landed, "What is it, Mikita?"

"Your sister is lonesome for you."

They came up to the shore. The bride's father had twelve daughters, absolutely identical, you couldn't tell them apart. But Mikita said, "Your highness, recognize them, don't make any mistakes. They are there in those apartments where the raven will perch."

The father came out and said to the tsar, "Recognize the one who is your bride. Which room is she in?" He stood and stood, and he looked and looked.

Suddenly the raven appeared out of nowhere and perched on a particular room. "My bride lives in that room."

The father said, "Well, come tomorrow and find your bride; I'll bring them all out for you to see."

So Mikita came up. The tsar asked him, "How am I to recognize my bride?"

"Don't be sad," he said, "pray to the Savior and go to bed." They all got up in the morning. He said to the tsar, "Your bride will be the one on whose face a fly alights and she wipes it away with a kerchief."

The father brought out all his daughters, all just alike. He looked and he looked. Suddenly out of nowhere the fly appeared. "That's my bride," he said.

Her father said, "If that's your bride, then we have to sew a coat for her before the wedding. I shall sew one half and you the other."

Mikita approached once more. The tsar said, "He orders us to sew a coat; he will sew one half and I the other. I don't know how to solve this!"

"Never mind! Pray to the Savior and go to sleep." Then he put on the self-walking boots, the invisible cap. Whichever material the father buys is the one he'll cut, too. The father gave the material to the tailors, while Mikita sat there and sewed, but no one could see him. Both halves of the coat were done exactly the same. He gave it to his tsar. The tsar brought it to his father-in-law. They put them together and they matched exactly, precisely.

"Do you use your magical wisdom to do these things?"

"Our own!"

"Well," he said, "she needs some slippers for the wedding. You make one of them and I'll make the other."

The tsar came and told Mikita. "Pray to the Savior and go to sleep." And he put on his invisible cap and the self-walking boots. Whichever leather the father-in-law bought, he cut the same. They were sewn on the same last and in the morning he brought it to his tsar. "Your highness! Take it!"

He took it to her father. "Very good. Now, let's get ready for the wedding."

They were getting ready for the wedding. Mikita said, "If you want to be alive, don't go to the feast but directly from the church onto the ship."

So they were married. His father-in-law summoned all the guests to the palace. But the tsar said, "No, I beg you, come to us on the ship."

They feasted and then got ready to go to bed. She was intending to smother him. She started to roll over onto him and he shouted, "Mikita, Mikita!" Mikita came running and broke three iron rods on her.

The next day she got up and asked, "Who is that Mikita of yours?"
"Ask him yourself."

So she shouted, "Mikita!" And all twelve Mikitas came running in, exactly alike, hair for hair and voice for voice. The next night she decided to strangle him. But Mikita came running, and broke three steel rods over her. And so she became submissive and they set sail for home.

So the great lord came to his home and Mikita set off to the wall. "Mikita, you are not worthy of being here," he said. "You are worthy of half the tsardom!" So he married Mikita to his sister and gave him half the tsardom. And then Mikita's father came to visit him. Servants washed his feet, and they left the dirty water from Mikita's feet. In the night his father wanted something to drink and so he drank the water from that basin. In the morning they all got up and Mikita said to him, "The dream I had was that they would wash my feet and you would have to drink the dirty water."

A–T 725

390. A Tale About Osip

There lived this father and this mother, and they had four sons with them. The very youngest of them was called Osip. The three oldest brothers took care of the herd, but the father and mother loved the littlest one and didn't make him work.

Once the father and mother went away to a bazaar, and they ordered Osip to carry dinner to his brothers. So Osip carried the dinner, but his brothers butchered a sheep, smeared his clothes with blood, wrapped Osip in the sheep skin, and threw him into a deep, empty well. "Let him die of hunger." And then they told their father and mother that wolves had eaten Osip, and they showed his clothing all in blood. His mother and father grieved over their favorite son.

Some carters were bringing their goods from the bazaar. They were carting onions. They stopped at the well to water their horses and they heard a child crying. They fetched the bundle from the well and took it with them. The drivers went to a different country and there they sold Osip to a Muslim tsar. Much time passed. Osip grew up, wise and intelligent. And he knew how to interpret dreams. Because he was so clever, he was thrown into prison, together with two friends. And once they had these dreams. In the morning they told them to each other, and Osip interpreted them. To one of the friends he predicted release from prison; a second he said was to hang; and he said that he would remain sitting in prison. And that is just what happened.

Time went on. Once the tsar had a dream. He dreamed of seven plump cows and seven scrawny cows. The seven scrawny cows devoured the plump ones, but they became no plumper. Learned wise men came from all over to the tsar, but none of them could interpret the dream. And then a certain man came to them and said that Osip sitting in the prison could interpret the dream. So the tsar ordered his servant to lead out Osip. Osip came and interpreted the dream, saying that for seven years the earth would bear nothing and there would be famine. And the tsar then ordered them to build barns and save grain. And he appointed Osip to distribute the grain to all the starving.

And a great famine took place in other lands. Osip's own brothers came from their land after grain. Osip recognized them, but they didn't know him because so much time had passed. But Osip didn't let them know that he knew them. He sold them two cartloads of grain, but with the money they paid he threw in the wheat in their carts. The brothers departed, and Osip sat down and wept and said, "Oh, father, dear Jacob, your sons and my brothers have sold me into a foreign land, into a foreign country, to serve a pagan and most evil tsar."

His brothers came a second time for grain. Osip sold them three cartloads, and tossed into one of the wheat carts a gold scoop with which the grain had been measured. And then he said that they had stolen it. His brothers wept and said that they hadn't taken it. They sought out a guard to help them find the scoop, and they found it in the wheat. Then Osip said, "Leave the youngest of you as hostage."

And his brothers said, "How can we leave him if the youngest of us long ago disappeared and our parents are still weeping for him? If we leave yet another behind, they will die from grief." And then Osip told them who he was and the brothers started weeping and begging his forgiveness. And Osip forgave them. And they all went home to their parents and lived peacefully and happily.

Something like that. The bad is always forgotten, but the good remains.

A–T 725*

391. The Golden Axe

There lived two brothers, one poor and the other rich. Once the poor brother went into the forest to chop wood. He was chopping right next to a stream. And suddenly his axe fell into the water. The peasant sat down next to the stream and burst out into tears. Suddenly an old man with a white beard appeared.

"What has happened?" he asked.

The peasant told him of his grief. The little old man went into the water and pulled a golden axe out of it. He asked, "Is this your axe?"

The peasant replied, "No, it isn't mine."

Then the little old man pulled out an iron axe and gave it to the peasant. The peasant was overjoyed and asked, "How can I thank you? I am ashamed to invite you to be a guest, for I've nothing to treat you to."

The little old man just laughed. "You don't have to thank me. Just go home; your wife is waiting for you." And he disappeared, just as he had appeared.

So the peasant came home and he couldn't believe his eyes: in place of his old hut there was a fine, new house. The old lady, his old wife was full of joy. And dinner was on the table.

The peasant began to get richer than his brother. And the brother asked how he had managed to acquire all this. The peasant told him everything, but he didn't tell him about the golden axe.

The rich peasant went to the stream, threw his iron axe in it, and let out a howl heard throughout the whole forest. That same little old man appeared, gave him the golden axe, and asked, "Is this your axe?"

The rich man immediately shouted, "It's mine! It's mine! Give it here!"

The old man gave him the axe and disappeared without saying a word. The rich man ran home. He ran and ran, and the forest became darker and darker. Night fell. The rich man realized that he had gotten lost. He lay down beneath a tree and decided, "Morning is wiser than the evening." He woke up near his house, and beneath his head lay his iron axe.

A–T 729

392. Two Fates

There lived and dwelt this peasant, and he fathered two sons and died. The brothers decided to get married. The older one took a poor bride, but the younger one a rich one. They lived together and wouldn't be parted. But then their wives began quarreling and squabbling. One of them said, "I am married to the older brother. I should have first place."

But the other said, "No, I have first place because I'm richer than you are." The brothers took a hard look at this and saw that their wives could not get along. They divided their father's estate equally and parted. It wasn't even a year before children were born to the older brother, but the prosperity of the estate got worse and worse. It got so bad that he was completely ruined. While there were bread and money, he looked at the children and rejoiced, but when he became poor, he didn't even like the children. He set off to his younger brother. "Help me in my poverty!"

But his brother rebuked him sharply: "Live as best you can; I have my own children to raise."

So a little later the poor brother went to visit the rich one once more. "Loan me a horse, just for one day," he asked. "I've no way to plow!"

"Go into the field and take it for just one day, but look out that you don't ruin it!" So the poor man went into the field and saw some people plowing with his brother's horses. "Wait," he shouted, "Tell me, who are you?"

"Why do you ask?"

"Because these are my brother's horses."

"But can't you see," one of the plowmen answered, "that I am your brother's Fortune. He drinks, carouses, knows nothing at all, and we work for him."

"And what has happened to my Fortune?"

"Your Fortune is over there, lying beneath that bush in a red shirt and it does nothing, neither in the daytime nor at night, except sleep!"

"Fine," the peasant thought. "I'll get you!"

He set off and he cut a thick stick. He stole up to his Fortune and whacked him in the side with all his strength. His Fortune woke up and asked, "Why are you hitting me?"

"I haven't started beating you yet! These good folk are plowing the earth and you are sleeping without stirring."

"But maybe you want me to plow for you? Don't even think of it!"

"What is this?! Are you just going to lie there beneath that bush? And then I'll just have to go and die of starvation."

"Oh well, if you want me to help you, then quit trying to be a peasant and take up trade. I'm not accustomed to your kind of work but I know all kinds of merchant activities."

"Then I'll start a business! But how can I get to doing that? I have nothing to eat, let alone anything to put into a business."

"Well, at least you can take that old sarafan from your wife and sell it, and with that money you can buy a new one, and then sell it. And I will help you. I won't go so far as a step away from you!"

"Good!"

In the morning the poor man said to his wife, "Well, wife, get ready! We are going to town."

"What ever for?"

"I want to register as a townsman, I'm going to start a business."

"Have you gone out of your mind? There's nothing to feed the children and you would make your way in town?"

"It's none of your business. Pack up all our possessions, collect the children, and let's go." So they got ready. They prayed to God, and locked up their hut tightly and then they heard someone crying bitterly in the hut. The master asked, "Who's crying in there?"

"It's me, Misery!"

"And what are you crying about?"

"Why should I not cry? You are going away and abandoning me here."

"No, dear friend. I'll take you with us, I won't leave you here. Wife!" he said, "empty the baggage out of that trunk." His wife emptied the trunk. "Well then, Misery, climb into the trunk." Misery climbed into the trunk and he locked him in with three locks. Then he buried the trunk in the ground and said, "Go to hell, cursed one! I don't want anything to do with you in this lifetime."

So now the poor man and his wife and children came into the town, rented quarters for themselves, and started a business. He took his wife's old sarafan, carried it to the bazaar and sold it for a ruble. With this money he bought a new sarafan and sold it for two rubles. And so with such fortunate trade where he would sell each new sarafan at twice its cost he became rich in a very short time and became a registered merchant. His younger brother heard about this and came to visit him. He asked him, "Tell me, perhaps, how you are so clever, to become rich from having been poor?"

"Oh, it was simple," said the merchant. "I locked my Misery in a trunk and buried him in the earth."

"In which place?"

"In the village, in the old yard." The younger brother was nearly in tears because of his envy. He rode off immediately to the village and dug up the trunk. Then he let Misery out. "Go back to my brother," he said. "Ruin him down to his last threads."

"No, I'd rather attach myself to you. I'm not going back to him. You are a good man; you've let me back onto the earth. He's an evildoer to hide me away in the earth." After a little time the envious brother was ruined and from a rich peasant he became a naked pauper.

A–T 735 +735A

393. Two Brothers

There lived two brothers. One lived well, the other was poor. This poor brother went to his rich brother on a holiday and said, "You should give me some vodka, brother, or a little brew."

But the rich brother responded to the poor one, "Go drink as much as you like from the vats."

So the poor brother went up to the vats and drank some water, and then he went home, where he started singing songs. He would sing a word, and then after him someone would draw it out. He asked, "Who's that singing after me?"

And the answer came, "It's me!"

"And who are you?"

"I am your Need."

"So what are you doing here with me?"

"I go everywhere with you."

"But when I get home, I'm going to die."

"And I'm going to die with you."

So he came home, and he made his coffin, the one he was going to die in, and then he said, "Heh, Need, I'm going to get in and die now."

So Need said, "I'll also die."

He got in the coffin but Need was in there first. And when she had lain down, he hammered the lid shut and carried the coffin with Need in it to the cemetery. He didn't lie down to die; he fooled Need, and after that he began to live really well. And so then his brother came to see him and he said, "How is it, brother, that you were poor and now you are living well?"

"Don't you remember after you treated me when I was your guest on the holiday? I set off home and started to sing songs. And I heard someone singing after me, and so I said, 'Who's singing?' And an answer came, 'Your Need.' So I came home and put together a coffin, and then I told Need that I was going to die. Need said she was going to die, too. I let her climb into the coffin first, then I hammered it shut, and carried it to the cemetery."

So then the rich brother spoke and he was envious of the brother who had been poor but was now living well. So he set off and went and dug up his brother's Need, because his brother had told him where his Need was buried. And he said, "Rise up, Need! Rise up!" She was still just alive, and then he said, "Go back to your master."

She said, "I won't go to him; I'd rather be with you." And so he became poor, but the other was rich who had earlier been poor.

A–T 735A

394. The Two Brothers and the Cock

There lived and dwelt two brothers and one was poor and the other rich. The rich one had a big house and much livestock. The poor one had a hut for a house and it was falling down, and he had a heap of children.

So once the poor man went to his brother to ask for a loan of grain, but his brother wouldn't even listen to him and chased him away. The poor man despaired. He was walking next to a forest, thinking a bitter thought: how to feed his children. Then suddenly out of the forest came an old man, and in his hands he held a cock.

"What are you thinking about?" the old man asked.

The poor man told him all his woe and the old man listened. Then he gave him the cock. But the poor man wouldn't take it. He said, "My children are starving to death! What do I need your cock for?"

"Take him," said the old man. "He will be useful to you."

So the poor man took the cock. Now once the cock was strolling through the grass near the forest, scratching in the dirt with his feet, and he uncovered a treasure. It turned out to be a pot of money. Then the cock with the bright red comb began to crow and flap his wings and stamp his feet. The poor man heard the cock crowing and thought, "Probably some sly fox has carried off my cock. I'd better go and have a look." So he ran to the cock who was flapping his wings and pointing out the treasure. The poor man saw the money and didn't believe his eyes. He brought the treasure home, and built himself a fine house, and he raised livestock, and he took even better care of the cock than before.

Then the rich one found out about it and he became envious. He ran to the poor man to find out all about it, and the poor man told him everything. "Give me your cock," he begged.

The poor man didn't feel like giving up the cock, but his brother kept insisting: "Give it to me, give it to me."

Suddenly the cock spoke up in a human voice, "Give me to him; I'll return to you." So he agreed to give the cock to the rich brother.

So the rich man was overjoyed to have the cock. He carried him home and let him loose in his yard, and then he watched him, waiting to see when he would call him to a treasure.

He waited for a day, then a second, and then he became angry with the cock. The third day came and the cock crowed. That's what the rich man had been waiting for. He ran to the cock and grabbed hold of the pot, but he couldn't lift it up, it was so heavy. He barely managed with it. Then he opened it and out jumped a witch!

"Phoo! How fine it is to be free!" she said. The witch was pleased to be out of that pot, so pleased that she immediately loosed a plague on the cattle. The cattle started to die and it completely ruined the peasant.

The peasant thought and thought as to how to rescue himself from the witch. Then he decided to make an iron barrel with a heavy lid. Afterward he went to the witch.

"Witch, oh witch! You've been sleeping long enough. Let's go play by the stove."

The witch was very pleased to play. They started hiding. First it was the rich peasant's turn to hide, but the witch soon found him. She said, "You won't find me in an eternity! I'll hide so well."

He answered, "Wherever you hide, you bony thing, don't crawl into that barrel over there."

So she crawled into the barrel and he slammed on the lid and threw it in a swift river. Then the rich brother took the cock and carried him back to his poor brother. He was overjoyed to see his cock. He was also kind. He gave half of all his wealth to his brother, and they lived prosperously.

Finally the old man came and got his cock so that he'd cause no more grief. And that's the end of this tale.

A–T 735A*

395. The Best Friends

There lived in a certain village two brothers—one rich, and the other poor. So the rich one went to town and sold wheat, but the poor one's children wandered through the world begging and fed him in his hut.

One day the rich brother arrived from the city and said to his poor brother, "Oh, brother, the price for wheat is good in town now, and it's good for other crops as well. Go and harvest your crops and we'll go to town!" The poor man had a really poor little horse, but the rich man's was fine. The poor man plowed up the soil on the land he had cleared but he harvested only about

five measures there. The rich man sent off his cart loaded such that his ho[...]
could scarcely move it.

So they set off down the road. The rich one went ahead and the po[...]
behind, and because the rich man's horse was so much better than th[...]
man's, he soon left the poor man behind. They approached a mountai[...]
rich man struck his horse with his whip and quickly rose up the mou[...]
But the poor man only got halfway up the mountain and his horse cou[...]
no further. He took some hay out of the sleigh, put it out for his hor[...]
cause it was evening already), and he himself went off to break o[...]
limbs in order to lay a fire.

So he set off through the forest and he got separated from his hor[...]
he went deep into the forest, and he couldn't find his way out. He clim[...]
in a tree to see whether he could see where he was, to see whether he[...]
see a light in any direction. In one direction he did barely notice a little l[...]
and so he set off in that direction. He came out unto a large meadow and s[...]
a huge house standing there, bigger than he had ever seen before. So he ca[...]
up to the house but there was no one in it and he really felt like something[...]
eat. In one room he saw on a table all kinds of wines and a lot of different kin[...]
of food. He was about to sit down at the table when he heard a voice (the fore[...]
spirit's wife) from another room. "Don't sit down, my good young man, or it'll
be too bad for you. My husband will come and kill you."

"Where should I go?"

"Go? Why, just crawl under the stove."

So the poor man climbed under the stove, and just then she started having
birth pains, and she started shouting out, did this peasant's wife. The peasant
came and took the child and immediately baptized him. Then she sat the
poor man at the table and was a proper hostess to him. He ate so much that
his sides puffed out, and drank so much wine that he got drunk. Then he
crawled back under the stove and sat there.

He heard something knocking at the door, and in came the woman's husband. "You have somebody here, some Russian, don't you?"

"No, there's nobody."

"Well, let's eat now."

So they sat down to eat. "You don't know what happened here," she said.

"What happened to you?"

"If it hadn't been for a good man, I might not be alive now."

"What did this good man do for you?"

"What indeed! He helped me baptize the baby and helped deliver it. So
now he's our close friend."

"Where is he now?"

"He's sitting there beneath the stove."

Well, friend, come out! Once you're our new friend, come out and we'll
and eat as we ought."

the peasant came out from under the stove and sat down at the table
his new friend. And they drank and caroused. And the poor man said
at the table, "I am so well fed and have drunk so much at your table,
my children and wife are sitting at home in hunger."

Don't go on about it, my friend, I'll have a bag of rye flour tossed off
that will suffice until you get home."

the poor brother was a guest there for two days. And he said to his
"It's time, friend, for me to go to town."

it, my friend, and I'll give you Serko." So he hitched Serko up for his
and loaded a cart full of wheat, and his hostess wrapped up some travel
sions for him in a tablecloth. "This should be enough for you, friend,
you get back home." So he took the provisions and sat on the cart. And
his friend said to him, "If you have any misfortune, my friend, just think
out me, and I'll know about it. So now, friend, go with God, but keep a tight
ld of the cart. As you ride by that hill where your horse is standing, your
orse will still have a lot of hay. But when you go down that hill, hold back a
ittle on account of your brother's wreck. He was riding that way and had a
wreck. His cart tipped over and he was pinned down by the cart."

So the poor brother was sitting in the cart and he didn't even have to drive
the horse. She knew where to go without his help. "Well, friend," he said,
"Farewell." And he waved his cap. Serko set off, and the snow flew out
behind the sleigh runners of the cart. And the poor man sat in the cart alive,
but nervous that Serko would somehow kill him. And he rode past that hill
where his horse had been left, and he saw that the horse had a lot of hay. So
much that the horse couldn't even be seen. So then he started descending the
hill and he saw his brother lying beneath his cart. He went by and released
him, and righted his cart. Then his brother came out and set off behind his
poor brother.

It got to be evening, and the rich brother indicated to his poor brother that
he would stay overnight with the priest because he couldn't keep up.

So the poor man rode up to the priest's, tied Serko up in the courtyard, and
crawled onto the stove. He ate what he wanted and just lay there. He looked,
and his brother was coming. When he had arrived, they took his horse away
to be cared for, and they invited the rich brother in to drink tea, although the
poor brother had not been invited. And then the priest's daughter lost her
gold earring, and they talked about that, and the priest said, "You don't know
where my daughter's gold earring could be, do you?"

"No, I don't know, but my poor brother probably knows."

"And where is he?"

"On top of the stove."

So they summoned the poor brother. "You don't know, do you, where my daughter's earrings are?"

"I know," he said.

"Where are they, then?"

"Give me three hundred rubles and I'll tell you where they are." The priest gave him the three hundred rubles. And he said, "Go into the bathhouse and you'll find them behind the fireplace stones." So they went there, and in fact the earrings were behind the fireplace stones.

The rich brother envied his poor brother on account of the three hundred rubles he had received from the priest. "I'll go out into the courtyard and pile some stones into his cart, and then we'll see how he can get his Serko to move!" So he piled on stone after stone, until the cart was full. "Now," he said, "he won't move an inch." And then he went back into the hut.

The rich peasant set off ahead of his poor brother. The poor brother was still lying on the stove. "Go ahead, brother, I'll catch you up." The rich one set out ahead and the poor brother had breakfast, hitched up his Serko, and set off after his brother. He soon caught up to his brother, and his brother thought, "Why doesn't he sense that his cart is filled up with stones?" Evening came. The rich brother said to his poor brother, "Now you go on ahead of me. My horse is worse than yours and I won't be able to keep up."

So the poor brother went on ahead and the rich man lagged behind. And then he came to a rich man's house where he could spend the night. He let his Serko into the yard, and then he went into the hut and lay down on the stove. Two or so hours later the rich brother arrived, and he also put his horse in the yard. Then he came into the hut, and they invited him to sit down to tea. While they were drinking tea, they talked among themselves, and the rich man said he had lost a gold ring and didn't know where to find it. "Perhaps one of you knows where I ought to look for this ring?"

"Somebody here knows, the one lying on the stove. He's my poor brother, and he knows."

So they invited him to drink tea, too, and then the rich master asked him, "Do you know, perhaps, where my gold ring might be?"

"I know," he said. "Give me two hundred rubles and I'll tell you where your ring is." So he gave him two hundred rubles and told him that there was a plank in the corner of the main room, and beneath it was the ring. "Go and lift that plank in the corner of the main room and you'll find your ring." Sure enough, he went, turned up the plank, and there he found the ring.

So they spent the night there, and in the morning they set off for the town. The poor man was behind his rich brother and thus he didn't know where his rich brother would be stopping. So they came into the town and stopped next to each other, and then they uncovered their carts. And people came to buy the wheat. They went up to the rich brother and looked, but his wheat was poor. They looked at the wheat of the poor brother and it was fine indeed. They started taking his wheat. And soon the poor brother had sold all his wheat, and there on the bottom of the cart instead of the stones were large blocks of sugar. So he sold all the sugar, too, and collected an entire bag of money for it. Then he covered his cart and sat down in it. His rich brother didn't sell a single grain, so he took his full cart home, but the poor man set off with good receipts.

So now the poor peasant had only to wave his hat for Serko to trot off, and he was stronger than the wind and quickly brought him back to his friend. His friend asked him, "Well, did you sell your wheat?"

"I sold it all," he said.

"And now do you have enough money?"

"I have enough, my friend, for now."

"Then sit down after your trip and dine with me. And we'll drink a drop as well." So they sat down together at the table, and the poor brother said, "I like it here, but my children are hungry at home."

"Don't worry about it, my friend. We tossed off two bundles for them; they'll have enough until you get back home."

So he spent two days with his friend. "Well, friend, now I need to get ready to go home." His friend led him into the cellar, and he measured out three bins of money for him: three bags of gold, and three bags of silver, and three bags of bronze. He carried them out and put them in the cart, and said, "Here's some money for you, and I am making Serko a gift to you. If something goes wrong with Serko, bring him back and I'll give you another."

So they said farewell, and he got in the cart, whistled, and Serko trotted off at such a pace that he couldn't keep his hat on his head. He rode past that mountain where he had left his horse. She was still standing in the hay and he couldn't even see her. He dug her out, tied her to the back of the cart, and set off home. He let Serko into his yard, and the children came running to greet their father. "Papa, now we have lots of bread, and we won't have to cry anymore."

He went into the hallway and saw four bushels of flour stored there. And in the hut itself there was freshly baked bread on every bench. And then he put the money he had brought from his new friend in the barn.

Soon his rich brother came to visit. "I think I'll go see whether my brother sold all of his wheat."

So he came to visit his brother. His brother was angry with him. "So how are your profits?" he asked his rich brother.

"Poor," said his brother, "I had to bring all my grain back. Nobody wanted so much as a fistful. And how did you do?"

"I sold everything with ease. By the way, brother, loan me your measuring cups."

"What do you have to measure?"

"Oh, I brought home a little grain." So the rich man greased the bottom of his measure with wax, and gave it to the poor brother. He measured out four measures of gold, and then four measures of silver, and then five measures of bronze. And thus the poor brother became rich, and the rich brother became poor.

A–T 735A**

396. About Two Brothers and a Swallow

There were these two brothers. One of them was rich and the other was poor, and with children. The poor man worked for his brother. The poor man's house was old. Somehow a swallow flew in and wove a nest beneath the bed. And the master saw it and left it, and even watched as the swallow flew in and out and out and in again. She laid some eggs and hatched out some children. Then he noticed that one of her legs was being eaten by worms. So he treated her, putting some medicine on it. And he cured it.

Spring came, and he said, "I need to dig up the garden and plant the potatoes." He dug and looked, and there was the swallow with six of her children. They threw him three seeds and he planted them. They quickly grew up and produced some big watermelons.

"Well," he said, "Thanks to God. One of them is ripe so we'll cut it open now." He took a knife and cut and cut, but it was as hard as oak. He took a handsaw and sawed and sawed—and finally he sawed it in two. Out of that watermelon jumped some dwarfs with saws and axes, and by nightfall they had built a whole house with all the furnishings.

The rich brother soon found out about it, and he came flying over. He looked and the house was already standing there. "How did you do that so quickly?" he asked.

The poor brother told him about the swallow. The rich man rode home, caught the swallow, cut off its leg, made a nest, and treated it.

By this time the poor man had another watermelon ready. He cut it open and out jumped the dwarfs. They built a barn. Then the third melon got ripe. He started sawing it with the saw and out jumped all kinds of animals—pigs, cows, geese, chickens—a full barn. The rich man came flying over, and he was envious.

"Give me the saw," he said, "I have one melon that's ready." So he took the saw and he sawed and sawed. He sawed and sawed until he had sawed through the melon, and out jumped mice and into his barn! It was a big barn, like on a collective farm. The rich man had been ready to grind his flour, but now the mice turned it all to chaff.

He sawed the second melon. He sawed and sawed and out jumped swindlers and started taking all his property. The rich brother ran away in fright. In the morning he and his wife came back to their house but there was nothing there.

He sawed the third, and flames leapt out, a fire covered all his face, and everything burned up. Only ashes remained.

A–T 735A****

397. Two Brothers

There lived two brothers, one of them poor and the other rich. The rich one built a new home and to the housewarming summoned all the rich folk, and the merchants, but he didn't invite his brother. The poor brother thought that even though he hadn't been invited, the rich man was his brother and it would be awkward of him not to go to the housewarming and congratulate him. So he ordered his wife to bake a pie and he set off for his brother's with some bread and salt. When his brother caught sight of him in his new home, he became angry and cursed him to the devil. The poor brother started crying and left the house, and then his wife scolded him saying that he had gone without an invitation and should have stayed at home. They were walking along when they met an old man, a little St. Nicholas the Wonderworker. And he said to the poor man, "Let's go. I'll take you to another housewarming." And his wife tagged along with them. He led them to a river and to a deep pool and then he ordered him to throw himself in without crossing himself, together with the bread and salt. "They will treat you," he said to him, "to all sorts of delicacies and drinks, but don't drink or eat anything, just throw it all over your right shoulder. And don't sleep at night or accept any gold or silver, but just ask for a little gray lamb. That little lamb is a cursed boy. So the poor brother did just as the little old man told him. He threw himself into the water without crossing himself and he turned up at a feast where he didn't eat or drink but threw everything over his right shoulder. After the feast they tried to get him to go to sleep, but he wouldn't sleep but just kept on thinking about what would happen next. In the morning they began offering him gold and silver for the bread and salt, but he didn't take it; he just asked for the little gray lamb that was lying on the hay in the corner. For a long time they wouldn't give it to him, but finally they did. The poor brother took it and went out onto the shore as if over a bridge. He looked up and there stood the little old man holding a colt by the reins, a colt as solid as if it had just been washed with milk. The little old man said to the poor brother, "Give me the little lamb and I'll give you this little colt." The poor brother agreed to the exchange and handed over the little lamb, and then he took the colt. He led it home and his wife said, "Where are we going to keep such a colt? Someone will steal him from the yard." So they put him in a lean-to. And they led their horse in there but he wouldn't go any further than just his front feet. The wife began dragging him back out and then she hit him on his ass and he fell apart and turned to pure gold. All night long they carried away that gold and filled all their trunks with it.

With the money the poor man built a fine house and he had a housewarming. He invited all the poor folk and migrant workers, and he didn't forget his rich brother either. The latter was truly amazed that his poor brother had money enough to build a fine new house and put on such a housewarming, even if it was the thing to do. He began questioning his brother, who wouldn't tell him, but his wife, the rich man's sister-in-law, couldn't stand it and blabbered it all. The rich brother decided to get some more money himself. He baked a pie and went to that same deep pool with the bread and salt, crossed himself, threw himself into the pool, and there he drowned.

A–T 735*****

398. Grishania the Wretch

There lived these three brothers, and two were rich but the third was poor Grishania. One brother was the military governor, the voevoda. And the second brother was a merchant. These two were always gone on some business or other. But Grishania the wretch lived at home, plowed the land, fed his horse, and tended some sort of livestock.

Spring came. Grishania the wretch got ready to plow his strip. He hitched his horse to the plow, drove out into the field and plowed. Suddenly his horse stopped. She just stopped and wouldn't move from the spot. Grishania struggled and struggled with her, but there was nothing to be done. He broke out into a sweat and so did the horse. Then Grishania thought, "What is this? What is the reason for this? Oh well, I'll just clean off my little plow."

He turned the plow over and saw the reason for the misfortune: a little devil had attached himself to the share and that wouldn't let the little horse go. Grishania saw what the matter was and immediately caught the little devil and said to him, "So, you little devil, you! What are you doing? You have been tormenting my horse and giving me stomach cramps, too."

The little devil was frightened and said, "Let me go and I'll heal your stomach, and I'll show you something else as well. Go and pull up that root and eat it, and your stomach will get better right away."

So Grishania pulled up the root and ate it, and truly his stomach stopped aching right away. Then the little devil said to him, "Bring me a sheaf of old rye and I'll make you a lot of soldiers."

Grishania brought him a sheaf of old rye and the devil took it apart, and what happened? The whole field was filled with soldiers. Grishania looked at them and asked the devil, "Now how is one supposed to get them from this field, get them out of here?"

The devil said, "Will you let me go?"

"I'll let you go, but tell me how to get rid of them."

The little devil tied up the sheaf and not a single soldier remained in the field. Grishania the wretch let the little devil go. "Go, then, and live."

So he finished plowing his little strip and returned home. He lived at home for some time and then he needed some lumber to make repairs to his house. Grishania hitched up his horse and set off for the woods. He got to the woods, selected a tree that would meet his needs, and started sawing. He sawed down the tree and felled it on its side. The tree was down, but not entirely. Grishania the wretch struggled and struggled, but there was nothing more he could do—he couldn't get the tree down right onto the ground.

"Well," thought Grishania, "Let me cut off the branches." So he cut off the branches and saw that same little devil sitting on a branch. It was he who wouldn't let the tree fall cleanly to the ground. Grishania the wretch caught the little devil and cursed him, "Why are you interfering in my business? What has brought you here?"

The little devil was frightened and begged Grishania to let him go. Grishania asked him, "And if I let you go, what will you do for me?"

The little devil said, "You take some leaves from these trees and I'll do something."

So Grishania collected some leaves and the little devil turned the leaves into money. Grishania took the money, let the little devil go, and set off home. He got home and with the money he built himself a home. People found out that Grishania could make soldiers and money. His brother, the voevoda, heard it, too, and he came to Grishania the wretch and said, "I've heard, brother, that you can make soldiers."

"Yes, brother, I can."

"Then make some for me, Grishania."

So Grishania took several sheaves of old rye, untied them, and all the field was filled with soldiers. Grishania's brother, the voevoda, took them away and for a full month fought with them until they were all dead.

Then Grishania's other brother, the merchant, came to Grishania and said, "They say, brother, that you can make money."

"I can."

"Then make some for me."

So Grishania said to him, "Go into the forest and collect the leaves from the trees." The merchant brother went into the forest with three carts and brought back the leaves. Grishania immediately turned the leaves into money and the merchant brother went away.

He traded and traded, but soon all the money was gone.

More or less a lot of time passed and the voevoda brother came to Grishania. "Make me some more soldiers."

Grishania said, "No, brother, I can't make any more soldiers for you because you just destroy them. You kill the guilty and the innocent alike." So he wouldn't do it and his brother the voevoda went back home.

That one went away and the merchant brother came to Grishania and said, "Well, brother, make me some more money."

But Grishania said, "No, brother, I'm not going to make you any more money because you rob the poor, the lame, and the orphans, and you cheat them too.

There was nothing for the merchant brother to say to that, so he turned his horse around and went back.

And Grishania the wretch got married and lived and prospered.

A–T 735G*

399. The Tsar's Daughter

Alright, very well, this is how we'll tell it. So then, in a certain tsardom, in a certain country, and in fact in that very one in which we are living, there lived a tsarevna. And she was cursed. And finally the time came for her to go free, only someone had to rescue her, but no one knew about her or how to rescue her. There was this one village lad who loved to sleep all the time in the threshing barn where they thresh. He was constant—he'd have dinner and then go there and when he'd lie down to sleep, she'd appear to him and say:

"Rescue me and I will be your wife. And when you rescue me, we'll have everything. We will live well."

"But how am I to rescue you?"

"You choose how yourself. I won't tell you how to rescue me."

He saw that she was a very pretty girl. But he kept silent. And he often went to the threshing floor in the afternoon, but in the afternoon he never saw anyone, only at night time. And then he started telling his mother:

"Well now, mother, there is this thing that happens."

"What, my son?"

"Well, this girl comes to me every night in the threshing barn and every night she talks with me and says that I must rescue her. I asked her, 'How should I rescue you?' and she said to me 'Choose for yourself.' "

So then the mother spoke: "Now then, my son, certainly the unclean spirit is tempting you, so you don't go to that threshing barn to sleep anymore, my son. Perhaps she'll leave you alone."

"But Mother, I'm already quite used to her. I don't have any fear of her at all."

So then the mother says to him: "You'll have to tell the priest."

So they told the priest, and the priest said: "It's difficult to rescue such a girl, I myself can't think how to do it."

So then a rumor got about and people found out that the unclean spirit was visiting so-and-so. They even started avoiding him on account of his acquaintance with the unclean spirit. But no one really knew anything. So he told this old man. And the old man was a magician. And he said to him: "You come here to me for two nights and I will look in the Book and tell you whether you can rescue her or not."

So he came. The first night they sat and he read and read the Book and he looked and he told him something (just like I'm sitting here with Novikov: I tell everything and he writes, but whether it's true or false, that no one can tell). In the morning he said to him: "Now go home, my dear friend, and tomorrow come here again. And as you are coming here, wear your shirt back to front."

And that's what he did, and he set off to that magician's. The magician took the book and opened it up and started reading further, and then he read to where he needed to and he said to him: "Yes, young man, great fortune is coming to you. She is a tsar's daughter and she was cursed for a period of three years, and now she's twenty years old. If somebody rescues her this year, when she's twenty, then she will live if, but if they don't, then she will have to be there for another twenty years. So that's why she's taken to visiting you. Now then, we'll read this Book until dawn and perhaps the Book will show us how to rescue her."

So they read the Book and the old man showed him: "It's simple to rescue her. Only when you are rescuing her, you mustn't be frightened, because if you're frightened, then you'll never see her again except after twenty years. Now go to that priest and take his cross with the heavy chain and go off to the threshing barn to sleep. When she comes to you and lies down to sleep with you, throw the chain onto her. And then she'll struggle to get away from you. In the first instance she'll turn into a frog. But don't be frightened, just hold onto her. Then she'll turn into a snake. But don't get frightened and just hold her tighter. And finally she'll start showering fire on you. But you just hold her and don't get frightened, she won't burn you. And then she'll take you by the throat, to strangle you, but don't you get frightened, she won't strangle you. And when the cock crows, she'll become a girl. And then she'll never go away from you. Then you can safely marry her and she will be a faithful wife to you."

When he came to the threshing barn, he lay down to sleep and she appeared and lay down next to him and she said to him: "Take what you brought and throw it away."

And he said to her: "I don't have anything."

"Well, if you don't, that's fine," she said.

Well, he didn't even have time to yawn. He sort of started to put his arms around her and then he threw the chain with the cross on her. And she immediately turned into this frog, but he grabbed her by the leg and held on tight. And she struggled, but she saw that there was no way she could get away. So she became a serpent and she tried to bite him, but she couldn't bend his arm to bite it. And she saw that there was no way she could get away, so she started sending flames out of her mouth to burn his hand, but the flames didn't reach his hand. And she saw that there was no way she could get away. She grabbed him by the neck and started choking him. And at this point things really did get a bit difficult for him, but he held on anyway, just as the magician had told him to. And at the time he didn't know how long he had been struggling with her because there were no cocks in the threshing barn. But anyway, one crowed in the village and she turned into what she had been earlier when she visited, a girl, only naked: she had neither shirt nor skirt. And she said to him: "Now go home and fetch some clothes for me. I'll get dressed and then we'll be off. Now that you have rescued me, you'll be my husband and I'll be your wife."

He ran home joyfully and he took some women's clothing from his mother, put it on her, and brought her home. But all his family was afraid. She said: "Don't be afraid of me!"

So they were married and they lived three years there. And they had two children. And the children grew not by the days but quite simply by the hours. And they had plenty of everything.

Once he was about to go to the city for three months on some sort of business. And as he was departing, she said to him: "Look, my dear! You can curse me, but don't call me a serpent!"

And so he set off for the city when the grain was ready to bring in. And he says, "Will you manage to bring it in alone?"

And she says to him: "It will all be brought in."

So he did his business and set off along the road. He comes to his field and the fields haven't been gathered, the rye is even trampled down. (She had taken the grain, but there was no place to put the straw so she had thrown the straw into the field.) Cattle were wandering all over and they had crushed the straw. And so he took pity on her because she had said that she'd get the grain in but she hadn't. And he said, "A serpent she was, and a serpent she is!"

He came home and she was lying on the table, coiled up like a jelly roll, but as a serpent. And when he came into the house, she said, "Well, my dear! You were told not to call me a serpent, but that's what you called me, and now I am a serpent. You thought that I hadn't gotten in your grain? Just you go to the storage bin and look in the bins and you'll see there the grain that you and your sons are going to be eating for five years. Now take me and carry me back where you got me, and then stay here with my children, your sons."

The peasant started crying: "I won't carry you back there. Even if you are a serpent, you will live with me!"

"No, my friend, it's too late. You will see me no more. I will see you, and I will see your and my children, but you won't see me."

There was nothing for him to do. He had to take that snake and carry it back to the place where he had got it. And when he had brought it and let it go, there was a great crackling in the threshing barn. And he didn't see where she went. He went home and stayed on living with his sons. And he lives there still. But he didn't remarry, and so he remained unmarried.

A–T 736

400. The Tsarevna Talan′

I heard this from some people, some old maids, some bitches. . . . In no certain tsardom, in our kingdom, in a level place, just like a tablecloth, in that very one where we live, there lived and dwelt a tsar with his wife, the two of them. They had no children. Then a daughter was born to them. They baptized her, and the godfather and godmother passed her around [in the church] and said that when the child grew up, she would be led around the bazaar and whipped with a knout. And the tsar said, "Can this be so? I will never let her out anywhere."

A tale is soon told, a deed is long in the doing. This girl came of age and she began asking her father to go out and about. "Papa, let me out to go for a stroll," she said, "with the mamas and with the nannies, and with the beautiful grown-up girls into the empty steppe to the steep bank, to the deep blue sea."

Her father let her go. The tsarevna set off with the mamas and the nannies and the beautiful grown-up girls into the empty steppe to the steep bank. And at that steep bank there stood a little sailboat. And the tsarevna went up onto the boat and a passing wind gusted. She was thrown into the deep blue sea. Everything went by, there was no one around. The tsar searched and searched, but there was no daughter, she was lost. And so then the tsarevna stepped out onto a steep bank. And there was a well on that bank. And at the well there was ever such a tall, tall tree. The maid climbed up into that tree and perched there. In this kingdom there was a Yega-baba (that's a bad word, isn't it?) and she had a daughter. She sent this daughter to the well.

"Go on you, you ugly thing, go get some water!"

So she came and started ladling out the water and in the well she saw this beautiful girl who was the tsarevna. She went to her mother and said, "Mama, why do you say I am so ugly? There's no one more beautiful than I in the whole world."

She jumped up: "What's that, what are you saying?"

"Let's go look in the well and you'll see what a beauty I am!"

So they went. They looked in the well and Yega-baba saw the beautiful girl. "Oh, you useless thing, why are you lying?" Then she looked up in the tree and saw the tsarevna. "Maid, climb down out of that bush!" Well, she climbed down and came over. "Now then, maid, you will live with me. What skills do you have? Do you perhaps know how to embroider a length of cloth?"

"Yes, I know how." She was indeed a master, no words can tell! She started embroidering and the old woman started selling it.

At that time the tsar sent out a clarion call: "Whoever can set pearls to my crown—let an old woman be a grandmother [to me]; an old man, let him be a grandfather; and middle-aged woman, an aunt; a middle-aged man an uncle; a man my age an adopted brother; a beautiful maiden a betrothed wife."

Just then Yega-baba heard this. "My daughter can set them," she said, and then she went home and said to the tsarevna: "Daughter, set to work on the tsar's crown."

So she set to work, and she laid all the supports out on the windowsill. She worked and she worked and she was nearing the end, there was just one more support brace on the sill that went just above the nose in the crown. A raven flew up and picked that support up in its beak and carried it off (it was shiny, you see). The time ran out. The crown was to be carried to the tsar in person, so Yega-baba carried it there and said: "It wasn't my daughter who sewed this, I have this adopted daughter."

"Bring her here, put her on trial." They ordered her to be led through the bazaar and whipped with the knout.

An old woman who lived on the edge of town with her old man turned up somehow and said: "Don't harm her white body, don't you defile her! Give her to me as a daughter, I don't have anyone at all." So they took and gave the tsarevna to her.

So now she was living pretty well. The daughter was fine, obedient. A little time went by, it was the old man's name day, his angel's day. "We are going, daughter, to holy liturgy, to pray to God, and you stay and bake and cook, prepare the food. When you've got it ready, set the table, carry out all the food, and go out onto the porch. Then bow to all four sides [and say]: "Grandfather's Talan′, come visit me for dinner, enjoy my hospitality, all sorts of drinks and dishes." And that's what she did. She went out and bowed:

> *Grandfather's Talan′,*
> *Come visit me for dinner,*
> *Enjoy my hospitality,*
> *All sorts of drinks and dishes!*

And so Talan′ came, and she was splendidly got up! So fine, really magnificent! She sat down at the table, she drank and she ate, and nothing was left. She poured out a pile of silver, gave her thanks, and left. And then grandfather and grandmother came from the liturgy and said: "Well, daughter, was that certain somebody here?"

"Talan′ was here, she drank and ate, nothing was left, and she poured out silver."

And so the next day was the old granny's name day. "Again, daughter, you bake and cook, and call Talan′." So she cooked and she baked and she set out the table, then she went out onto the porch and bowed:

> *Grandmother's Talan′,*
> *Come visit me for dinner,*
> *Enjoy my hospitality,*
> *All sorts of drinks and dishes!*

And Talan′ came, just as splendid, as beautiful, and she drank and ate and there was nothing left, and she thanked her and put down a pile of gold. Grandmother and grandfather came and again they asked and she told them everything.

"Well," they said, "Daughter, tomorrow it's your name day. You bake and cook and call your Talan.′ But don't let her go without paying you for the dinner, even if you have to ask her for something." So that's what she did. She went out onto the porch, and began to bow and call Talan′.

> *My very own Talan′, o bitter fate!*
> *Come visit me for dinner,*
> *Enjoy my hospitality,*
> *All sorts of drinks and dishes!*

Talan′ came all ragged, a complete mess, and ugly, and all shabby, and really horribly horrible. She sat down and began to gobble, and she gobbled everything up and she set off without thanking her. The daughter chased after her: "My very own Talan′, oh bitter fate, pay me for the dinner. You've drunk everything, eaten everything, give me at least a little something."

Talan′ crawled into a pit, but she grabbed her by her rags and held on. "Give me just a little something!"

She tore off a little bundle and threw it, then another, and she threw that, then a third she tore off. And she threw that. She collected all these bundles and set off. And she came home very sad. "What will grandmother and grandfather say to me?"

So then grandmother and grandfather came from the liturgy. "Well, so, daughter, was Talan′ here?"

"She was, all ragged, really ragged and ugly, horrible. And she ate everything I had."

"Did she give you anything?"

"She gave me just these three bundles of rags."

"Show us."

The daughter brought them. They untied the first bundle, and there was nothing; in the second, also nothing. But in the third were a golden eye and a golden hook. "Well, daughter, keep hold of those, they might be useful some time."

So once again there came a time and the tsar sent out a clarion call: he was sewing a kaftan, he was sewing some royal clothing for himself. But he didn't have another golden hook and eye. He had asked everywhere throughout the whole tsardom, but there wasn't a single one.

"Everyone brings up these pairs of hooks and eyes, but none of gold."

The grandparents said, "Go, daughter, and take yours to him, maybe it will do."

So she took it and showed it to him. Hers was just like his! So it matched very well. It was as if they had been made in the same mold. So right then he said, "You shall be my betrothed wife!"

There was a jolly feast after the wedding and they were married and began to live and prosper and acquire good things, and they put aside hard times. And they went out strolling and walking, they were walking around the garden. And suddenly a raven came flying up overhead and croaked: "Why is he croaking so?" asked the tsar.

She raised her hand up overhead. The raven flew over and spit the brace from the crown into her hand, and she said, "Once I was sewing your crown and a raven carried away this brace, and you ordered that I be taken through the bazaar and whipped with a knout."

And then they shot that witch Yega-baba at the gates.

A–T 737B*

COMMENTARIES TO TALES

279. A–T 500. Mitropol'skaia 43. Recorded from A.L. Gavrilova, fifty-five years old, 30 June 1967, in Veshintos Anikshchiaisk region, Lithuania (see A–T 812).

280. A–T 501. Rozhdestvenskaia 42. Told by A.K. Kalinina (see above under no. 57. Grimms' no. 14. Known as the "Three Old Women Helpers" in European tradition. This is the only example of the type recorded in Russian. There are two in Belarusian and six in Ukrainian.

281. A–T 502. Afanas'ev 123. Of unknown provenance. This is a very common tale in all branches of East Slavic. It has also been recorded throughout Europe and in North and South America. It is typologically related to the classical myths of Silenus and the biblical myth of Solomon and Asmodeus, but equally obvious are the ties to the old Norse Heimskringla and the Gesta Danorum of Saxo Grammaticus. In recent times the American Robert Bly has attempted to create a "masculine mythology" from the Grimms' version of this tale.

282. A–T 506B. Chernyshev 61. Told by Aleksandra Trofimovna Pankova, seventy-three years of age, married, illiterate. She and her aged husband lived their entire lives near Boldino, Pskov region. There are just five recordings of this tale type in Russian and two in Ukrainian. Recordings are also known in Swedish, Dutch, Danish, and Czech.

283. A–T 507B. Matveeva and Leonova 1993: 6. Recorded in Buriatia from eighty-six-year-old A.A. Khleskin in 1973. Khleskin was a well-known teller of tales. One fisherman said of him that "he would go out with the crew and tell them all sorts of tales. They would rake in the fish and feed themselves and drink, perhaps for a whole moon, as long as he'd tell tales. Young folk would gather to hear his tales." The beginning harks back to the legend of Nikolai Most Pleasing to God, a favorite Orthodox story of St. Nicholas, and especially to an icon dedicated to him. But there are also many similar East Slavic mythological motifs.

284. A–T 507C*. Tumilevich 1958, no. 6. Told by A.I. Zaitseva. This tale is related to the well-known story of how "Old Hospitality Is Soon Forgotten" but instead of featuring a man, a wolf, and a fox, the Cossack version has a man, a fish, and a serpent who intends to sting him. Unknown elsewhere in East Slavic.

285. A–T 508. Zelenin-Viatka 7. Known throughout the East Slavic world. This version was told by G.A. Verkhorubov, a thirty-eight-year-old peasant of Viatka province. He was extremely eloquent when he spoke Russian, despite never having been to school. By trade he was a carpenter and he was hired not only throughout Viatka but beyond as well.

286. A–T 508*. Onchukov 169. Told by Manuilo Petrov of Morskaia Masel'ga. Only two versions are known in East Slavic. Apparently not known elsewhere.

287. A–T 510A. Afanas'ev 292. Originally recorded in Shenkursk of Arkhangel'sk province. This version is closer to the internationally known Cinderella than 510B, which is not known outside of Europe.

288. A–T 510B. Onchukov 176. Told by Stepanida Maksimovna, village of Korel'skii Ostrov. This is a popular Russian tale. It is the English "Cap o' Rushes" and is related to the Cinderella cycle (see 510A above).

289. A–T 510B*. Kavkaz.XV$_3$, pp. 118–25, no. 13. Recorded by P. Semenov in the stanitsa of Sleptsovskaia, Vladikavkaz Okrug, Terekskaia Oblast. Unknown elsewhere in the East Slavic territory. Not listed in Thompson.

290. A–T 511 + 403. Afanas'ev 101. Recorded in the Arkhangel'sk province. A typical combination of types among the East Slavs, although it is not limited to them. The most ancient written version of this tale type is to be found in the *Mahabharata.*

291. A–T 513A. Khudiakov 107. From Kazan. Khudiakov noted that his narrator frequently lost track of his story but that it was nonetheless an honest folktale, similar in respects to Grimms' 134 (The Six Servants). This is a popular tale among all the East Slavs.

292. A–T 513B + 465. Mitropol'skaia 37. Recorded in 1969 in Ionavskii region, Lithuania, from F.E. Reinikov, seventy years of age. Known in Ukrainian and Russian, especially in the twentieth century. See also Grimms' 71. Common in Central Europe.

293. A–T 516. Khudiakov 110. From Orel province. In a note Khudiakov stated: "In a variant I heard in the town of Ishim, the petrified uncle stood in the hall, they took a penknife and sliced open the little finger (*mizinets*) of the child, and then with the blood they brought the uncle back to life." Perhaps this is just a coincidence that the slicing open or off of this finger was part of the initiation ceremony of East Slavic boys. The story is frequently

recorded throughout Russia and Ukraine. Grimms' 6 is a Western example of "Faithful John," as the type is known. It has been known in print since the *Pentamerone*.

294. A–T 516**. Khudiakov 62. From Riazan. Only two versions of this Russian variant are known.

295. A–T 517*. Bardin 204. Taken down by a part-time student of Chkalov Pedagogical Institute, M. K. Nikolaeva, from a worker, K.S. Khapugin, of the village of Kliuchi, Grachevski raion. Otherwise unknown in East Slavic SUS.

296. A–T 518 + 301A. Khudiakov 81. From Ol'ga Stepanovna Kotisheva, an elderly lady of Nizhnii Novgorod. Khudiakov found the mythological elements in the tale striking.

297. A–T 519. Afanas'ev 199. The first literary treatment of this plot in East Slavic belongs to Bishop Kirill of Turov in the twelfth century, but Afanas'ev pointed to striking textual coincidences between the Slavic folktales and the Old High German "Song of the Nibelungs." It is possible that the oral versions known from the nineteenth century have been influenced by the *lubki* texts, however. This particular text differs from most in the punishment meted out to Elena the Beautiful and the elevation of Nikita to the position of minister.

298. A–T 530. Afanas'ev 179. Recorded in Shadrinsk district of Perm province. Known throughout Europe, and carried to the Americas in English, French, and Spanish. Also known in Turkish, Caucasian, and various Indian languages.

299. A–T 530A. Afanas'ev 183. From Bobrov distict of Voronezh province and probably recorded by Afanas'ev himself. This version lacks the usual opening episode of the three brothers guarding their deceased father's grave. Known in Persian as well.

300. A–T 531. Mitropol'skaia 83. Told in 1970 in the village of Rimshe, Ignalinskii region by A.A. Skshidlovsk, fifty-nine years of age. A highly original combination of tale types. The text is dotted with polonisms. The tale is related to the "Little Humpbacked Horse" of Ershov and is extremely popular in all three branches of East Slavic. Dissemination limited to Eastern Europe, Greek, Turkey, and India.

301. A–T 532. Afanas'ev 295. Of unknown origins. This tale is outstanding for its rhythmic quality, a feature that crosses linguistic lines. The tale is common throughout Europe.

302. A–T 533. Karnaukhova 96. Told by Praskovia Dimitrievna Chornaia, sixty-two years of age, in the village of Shotova-Gora, Pinega. There are several recordings in Russian, one in Ukrainian, and none in Belarusian.

303. A–T 533**. Smirnov 214. Dorogobuzh uezd, Kokoshkanskaia volost'. Taken down from a fifty-year-old peasant, Ustin.

304. A–T 545B. Afanas'ev 163. Recorded in Senkusk district of Arkhangel'sk province, and reprinted by Afanas'ev from the journal *Moskvitianin* (1844, no. 1, pp. 122–24). The well-known type "Puss and Boots." Has been recorded on every continent. In many Russian versions of the tale the hero is a lazybones.

305. A–T 550. Azadovskii, *Verkhnelenskie skazki* 13. Despite the popularity of this tale among the reading public of the twentieth century, it is not a common tale, and its popularity likely derives from the versions of the early nineteenth-century poets, Iazykov and Zhukovskii, in themselves derived from the block-print, *lubki*. This variant was related to Azadovskii by N.O. Vinokurova, before 1915.

306. A–T 550. Shastina 74: 97–104. R.E. Shemetova, daughter of N.O. Vinokurova, here relates the same story as her mother (see previous tale and introduction).

307. A–T 551 + 300A. Balashov 27. Collected in 1964 from Iosif Fedorovich Kozhin, fifty-five years old, of Olenitsa. The earliest versions of this tale in Russian date to the eighteenth century. Common in Russian, less so in Ukrainian and Belarusian. Quite common throughout Western Europe.

308. A–T 552A + 302. Azadovskii, 30. Told by P.N. Bol'shedvorskaia, who lived on the Kulenga River.

309. A–T 552B. Zelenin-Viatka 19. Told by Grigorii Antonovich Verkhorubov of the Viatka province. Zelenin was intrigued by him, as he had no formal schooling and yet spoke an educated Russian.

310. A–T 553. Vasilenko 4. This is the only recording of this tale type in East Slavic.

311. A–T 554. Khudiakov 22. Khudiakov regarded this tale as the best told in his collection. It in fact contains elements of several tales. The basic tale is known as "The Grateful Animals" and it is very popular throughout the East Slavic world. It is widely known in Europe as well. It is "The White Snake" in the Grimms' collection.

312. A–T 555. Potiavin 24. Told in 1956 by N.I. Malyshev, born in 1907, of the Uren District, Gorkii. Such etiological tales are uncommon among the Slavs and may speak of their antiquity.

313. A–T 555*. Derunov 4. A unique rendering of a subtale type from the Poshekhonskii district near Yaroslavl, first published in 1869.

314. A–T 559. Afanas'ev 297. From Kursk province. Also 842C* ("An Honest Penny Doesn't Sink"). Common among the East Slavs and recorded throughout the world. Known in a written version since the old Norse Eddas.

315. A–T 560. Afanas'ev 191. From Novgorod province. An internationally known tale that may be derived from an ancient Sanskrit text. Widely

known in Tibetan and Mongolian, and in Western written versions from the *Pentameron* of Basile, dating from the seventeenth century.

316. A–T 560*. Onchukov 225. Recorded in 1900 in the Perm district. According to some authorities, the origins of this tale are to be sought in the East, either in India or in Tibet. It figures as tale no. 8 in the ancient Indian *Twenty-Five Tales of Vetala*. It first appeared in Western Europe in the *Pentameron* of Basile in the seventeenth century. It is very popular among the Slavs. There are more than fifty-five recordings in Russian, at least twenty-eight in Ukrainian, and twelve in Belarusian.

317. A–T 561. Karnaukhova 126. Told by Nikolai Vasil'evich Lokhnovskii, seventy-four years old. Blind and frail. A willing narrator, he apparently believed that everything he told had actually taken place. This is the Russian version of the well-known "Aladdin's Lamp," which is known throughout the East Slavic territory and generally throughout the European world.

318. A–T 562. Barag 1975: 24. Recorded in the Bashkir Autonomous Republic in 1967 from a professional hunter, Khabibullin Harif Khabibullovich, born in 1908. The tale represents a combination of three types (A–T 508 + 562 + 566). The narrator claimed to have first heard the story forty years earlier from a Russian named Gavrilo. This combination is unique.

319. A–T 563. Afanas'ev 186. From Lipets in Tambov province. Common all over the world.

320. A–T 564 (XVI c. 49) Originally published in *Starai pogudka*, 1794–95. In the nineteenth and twentieth century versions of this tale-type "Two from the Sack" is the main motif. The Thompson index refers to "Out, Boy, Out of the Sack!"

321. A–T 564*. Bakhtin-Shiriaeva 75. Told by A.V. Vorob'ev, seventy-one years old, originally from Vologda, but resident of Leningrad.

322. A–T 565. Mitropol'skaia 122. Recorded from D.I. Bezzubov, twenty-two years old, in 1972. This is an uncommon tale in East Slavic, with no recordings in Belarusian, only one in Ukrainian, and altogether three in Russian.

323. A–T 565*. Mitropol'skaia 105. From the Vilnius region. Told by M.V. Baliugin, sixty-eight years of age, in 1969. There are no other renderings of this subtype in East Slavic.

324. A–T 565A*. Sokolova, pp. 64–65. Recorded in Shatskii raion of Riazan in 1966 from Anna Stepanovna Bizenkova, born in 1882. Illiterate. There is but one other variant. Related to A–T 563.

325. A–T 566. Onchukov 150. One of the tales collected in the Olonetsk district by the teacher D. Georgievskii. Called simply "Horns," it is very common throughout the East Slavic tradition.

326. A–T 567. Pinega Tales 44. Told by D.I. Pashkova from the Pinega

region. She was born in 1900 and was illiterate in 1958 when the tale was recorded. She was a relative of the famed narrator and epic singer, Krivopolenova, from whom she probably heard this tale. The type is well known in both the Russian and Ukrainian traditions, and is also common in Europe. See Grimms' 60 and 122, for instance.

327. A–T 569. Azadovskii, *Verkhnelenskie skazki* 12. Told by N.O. Vinokurova. Common in East Slavic and throughout Northern Europe.

328. A–T 570. Karnaukhova 75. Told by Agrafena Efimovna Chernousova, fifty-four years of age. An outstanding narrator of tales, she claimed to know more than forty. Karnaukhova refused to record most of them on account of their erotic content. Although there are several Russian versions (including one in Afanas´ev's book of secret tales, 53, the tale is little known outside Russia. It is common in Western Europe.

329. A–T 571. Smirnov 333. Tobolsk, Surgut, 1890s. Known throughout the East Slavic world and found throughout all Europe and North America.

330. A–T 575. Khudiakov 80. From Nizhnii Novgorod province. It has been widely collected among the Russians. Under the rubric "The Prince's Wings" it is met in a number of Western European traditions as well.

331. A–T 576. Kovalev 17. As with most of the stories told by Kovalev, there is a distinctly social coloration to this tale. The following tale is a much better example of his art. There is only one other variant of this type recorded.

332. A–T 590. Kovalev 18. The hero of this tale (Olesha the Priest's Son) figures most prominently in the ancient historical epic songs, the *byliny.* This is the only Russian variant of this type.

333. A–T 592. Khudiakov 73. From Riazan district. Quite common throughout the East Slavic territory. Grimms' no. 110. Known throughout Europe.

334. A–T 610. Serova: 1925–19. Retold by Serova as part of an experiment in the early days of the Soviet Union to see to what degree folklore could be "popularized."

335. A–T 611*. Zelenin-Perm Tales 8. Told by A.D. Lomtev, who loved to tell the traditional tales in an updated form, giving the characters the names of people whom he knew or had heard of. Zelenin stated that he suspected Lomtev had added a great deal to this particular story, which is much more involved than other Russian versions, both of which are from Kareliia. This type is otherwise unknown in Russian. Thompson mistranslated the notation from Andreev's index. His "Map Produces Helpful Spirits" should read "Jack of Spades" (Pikovyi valet).

336. A–T 612. Sokolova, pp. 22–24. Recorded in 1967 from Fedor Grigorevich Kurletov, an illiterate born in 1902. This tale is recorded in Russian, Ukrainian, and Belarusian, and it is common in Western Europe.

337. A–T 613. *Skazki Saratovskoi oblasti*, 49–52. Recorded in 1922 in the village of Maksimovka, Viazov region, from an old man, Suchkov, sixty-six years of age.

338. A–T 613D*. Bardin 208 (Chkalov). Recorded from a certain Kalmykov in the village of Logachevka, Buzulukskii district. Only one other version known in East Slavic, and that from Siberia. Not recorded in Thompson.

339. A–T 621. Balashov 132. From Strel´na, 1962, Avdot´ia Petrovna Strelkova. Uncommon in Russian, where it is confined to the White Sea region. Grimms' 212, "The Hand with the Knife," provides a German analogue. Recorded throughout Europe.

340. A–T 621*. Mitropol´skaia 44. Recorded in 1967 in Kupishkskii district, Lithuania, from M.E. Demidov. Regarded as having extremely ancient antecedents. No other recordings known in East Slavic and Thompson has no record of the type.

341. A–T 650A. Anisimova 70–76.This tale from the Penza province was recorded in 1950. Compare to no. 7 above, from Viatka. Anisimova´s version provides evidence of anti-clerical attitudes characteristic of more recent wondertales.

342. A–T 650A + 1006* + 1009 + 1045 + 1072 + 1063 + 1082 + 1130. Afanas´ev 152. From Ufa province. So many types interwoven is very unusual.

343. A–T 650B. Onchukov 47. Told to Onchukov by the blind Aleksei Ivanovich Ditiatev in the Pustozersk region. He had been a hunter of sea mammals all his life and was still forced to do heavy labor at the age of seventy-one and despite the loss of his eyesight. One of two renditions known in Russian.

344. A–T 650B*. *Zhivaia starina* 1895: 424–26. A variant of the legend "Eruslan Lazarevich," common in Russian and Belarusian and somewhat known in Ukrainian.

345. A–T 650C*. Zelenin: Perm 16. A.D. Lomtev told this tale to Zelenin after 1908. Although there are more than fifty texts of "Il´ia Muromets" in collections of folktales, this is the only one from the Urals. This is odd in view of the fact that the first great collection of *byliny* by Kirsha Danilov (1800) was from the Urals and contained many texts relating the adventures of Russia's most popular epic hero. It is likely that Lomtev's ultimate source is to be found in the *lubki* editions of the nineteenth century.

346. A–T 650D*. Astakhova, *Byliny severa* II 198. Told by Dorofeevna Evfrosiniia Abbakova, Pinega, in 1927. Abbakova had originally heard the tale from her father-in-law, who lived on the Severnaia Dvina River.

347. A–T 650 E*. Afanas´ev 311. From Perm province. This is an example of Afanas´ev's editorial practices. He has combined two versions of

the same tale to "improve" it. The tale is another example of the heroic epic turned into a prose tale. The hero of the tale is closely associated with Novgorod of the pre-Mongol period (before 1240).

348. A–T 650F*. Korol'kova, pp. 38–43. Considered one of Korol'kova's better tales. This is a tale based on the old Russian heroic epics No other versions of this subtype are known.

349. A–T 650G*. *Tambovskii fol'klor* 1. There is one other version of this subtype known. This text is only partly about the hero, Diuk Stepanovich.

350. A–T 652. Smirnov 313. From Tobol'sk, 1892. Not uncommon in Russian. Thompson records nothing under this number.

351. A–T 653 + 1880. Afanas'ev 146. Taken down in Novotorzhok, Tver province. In general the type A–T 653 is well known throughout Europe, but not with this combination.

352. A–T 653. Karnaukhova 66. Karnaukhova's version was told on the Pinega by Efrosiniia Abbakovna Dorofeeva, sixty-three years of age. The story first appeared in Russian in 1818, and from there was taken by *lubki* to the masses of the public. But the telling by Dorofeeva has much more of a social cast to it than did its bookish predecessor. Well known in Russian but uncommon in Belarusian and Ukrainian. Grimms' 129. Well known through-out Europe and taken abroad from there.

353. A–T 653A. Balashov 87. Told by Marina Polikarpovna D'iachkova of Varzuga. Recorded in 1961. There is only one other recording of this tale in Russian, one in Belarusian, and none in Ukrainian. Rare in Europe.

354. A–T 654. Karnaukhova 65. Narrated by E.A. Dorofeeva (see no. 203).

355. A–T 654B*. Sokolova, pp. 88–91. Told by Anna Fedorvona Salianova, born in 1903, recorded in 1966. From Riazan.

356. A–T 660. *Skazki Saratovskoi oblasti*, 106–7. Recorded in 1935 from Fedia Rubivov of Khvalynski region, Saratov. Only one other telling of this type in known in Russian, and there are single examples in Ukrainian and Belarusian as well.

357. A–T 664A*. Zelenin-Perm 52. Told by S.K. Kiselev. Six recordings in Russian. Unknown elsewhere. In general, tales involving hypnosis are very common among all the Slavic peoples.

358. A–T 664B*. Sadovnikov 25. Told by the famous storyteller Abram Novopol'tsev. This strange tale of hypnosis is recorded elsewhere in Russia but not in Ukraine. Not recorded elsewhere.

359. A–T 664C*. Chudinskii 24 b, c. From Tver province. This is a unique rendering of the subtale type.

360. A–T 664C**. Chudinskii 24 a. From Tver province. This is a unique rendering of this tale type.

361. A–T 664D*. Chudinskii 24 d. From Tver province. This is a unique

rendering of this type. Nothing is known of the circumstances under which tales 359–61 were recorded.

362. A–T 665. Onchukov 156. A tale from the collection of the teacher, D. Georgievskii. Also known as "The Speedy Messenger." It is not frequently met in the East Slavic tales.

363. A–T 667. Mitropol'skaia 62. Told by N.M. Ivanovskaia, sixty-eight in 1963, from the village of Zarnishkes, Zarasaisk region, Lithuania. This tale type is better known in Belarusian and generally around the Baltic Sea.

364. A–T 670. Mitropol'skaia 55. Told by eighty-three-year-old E.A. Dymin in 1967 in the Anikshchiaiski region of Lithuania. This is rather different from Afanas'ev no. 158, although the individual episodes are similar. Here it is the serpent that is saved from the fire but in other East Slavic versions it is a bird or birds, or even animals. The tale type is especially common in Ukrainian but it is well known throughout the East Slavic territory. According to Thompson it is known throughout the Indo-European world, but is particularly common among the Slavs.

365. A–T 671. Zelenin-Viatka 30. Common, especially in the Russian North. Told by an old peasant, A.L. Perfilov, who enjoyed a reputation among his neighbors as a good *skazitel'* in the Viatka province. Recorded in each of the Slavic traditions and in some other European traditions bordering on the Slavic.

366. A–T 671E* + 875D. Afanas'ev, *Ne dlia pechati*, 134. This tale is common throughout the eastern branch of Indo-European—Armenian, Kurdish, Persian, various Indic languages, and Slavic. It is also known among Turkic-speaking peoples and in Finnish.

367. A–T 672D*. Sadovnikov 47. Told by Poluekhtov of Simbirsk. Known in all three branches of East Slavic, but this is the only Russian version. Unknown elsewhere.

368. A–T 675. Afanas'ev 165. From a *lubki* version. Common throughout the Eastern Slavic world.

369. A–T 676. Mitropol'skaia 118. Told by N.M. Ivanovskaia, sixty-eight in 1963, in the village of Zarnishkes, Zarasaisk region. This is a Russian version of "Ali Baba and the Forty Thieves," which is known throughout the East Slavic lands. Cf. Grimms' 142. Known throughout Europe.

370. A–T 677 + 313A + 450. *Pudozhskie skazki* 34. From the village of Staroe Sigovo, told by A.A. Portniagin, seventy-eight years of age. A rare combination of types and not otherwise recorded in the Pudoga region. The editor notes the strong tendency of the narrator to tell fantastic actions and phenomena in a realistic manner. Type 677 has been recorded in Russia, and infrequently in Ukraine and Belarus. Thompson lists no other recordings.

371. A–T 677*. Onchukov 90. Told by a peasant woman named Dmitrievna, thirty-five years old, who lived in the Petrozavodsk area. The

theme is that of an ancient Russian epic song of the same name. It originated in Novgorod, probably in pre-Mongol times. It is the subject of a colorful opera by Rimskii-Korsakov.

372. A–T 677** + 761A*. Afanas'ev 371. From Tver province. Related to the medieval Novgorod tale about the posadnik (mayor), Shchil.

373. A–T 677**. Balashov 118. A tale told by Irin'ia Andreevna Kozhina. All of her tales as recorded by Balashov feature the devil in some guise or other.

374. A–T 677***. Balashov 15. Recorded by T.I. Ornatskaia in 1964 from A.A. Moshnikova, sixty-eight years of age, who lived in Por'ia Guba. This is the only Russian version of the tale recorded. There are two versions in Belarusian and one in Ukrainian.

375. A–T 700. Khudiakov 55. A version of Tom Thumb, widely known in the East Slavic tradition. From the Riazan district.

376. A–T 703*. Skazki XIX c. 33. First published in Kiev in 1845 by M.A. Maksimovich. Maksimovich has added much to the story to make it more "literary." This is a common tale among Russians but it is less common among Ukrainians and Belarusians. Thompson lists only versions in Lithuanian and Serbian in addition to the Russian.

377. A–T 706. Afanas'ev 279. Recorded in Orlov province. A very common tale, known throughout Europe and apparently related to the tale of the maid with the chopped-off arms in the "Thousand and One Nights."

378. A–T 707. Khudiakov 63. A variant of the marvelous children type, widely known throughout Russia. The version given at 203 is the more familiar type in Western Europe.

379. A–T 707 + 518. Skazki XIX c. 1. Originally published in a lubok edition from which it made its way into many Russian versions, and influenced Pushkin as well.

380. A–T 707A*. *Skazki Saratovskoi oblasti* 1937: 111–16. One of three versions of the variant known throughout the East Slavic world. Recorded in 1920 from a shepherd, Savichev, then fifty years of age who was bilingual in Mordvinian and Russian.

381. A–T 707B*. Khudiakov 60. According to Khudiakov this is a tale that originated in Western Europe in the Renaissance as a literary tale and then in the later seventeenth century came to Russia, where it was known both in written and in lubok forms.

382. A–T 707C*. Sokolova, pp. 16–19. Told by Fedor Grigorevich Kurletov, an illiterate born in 1902. Recorded in 1967. The tale is very likely derived from a written source, but the collector (V.K. Sokolova) could not identify it.

383. A–T 708. Balashov 51. Recorded in 1957 from E.I. Sidorova of

Kuzomen. This is the only East Slavic recording attested but it is recorded in Europe.

384. A–T 709 + 883A. Afanas'ev 211. Traces of the merchant milieu in which this tale was apparently told remain.

385. A–T 710. Afanas'ev, *Legendy*, 63–165. From the collection of V.I. Dal'. One other Russian version exists, two Belarusian, and several Ukrainian texts. It is common throughout Europe.

386. A–T 715A*. Tumilevich 61: 3. Related by D.E. Belikova of Novo-Nekrasovskii khutor. The tale has Ukrainian and French analogues and three Russian analogues have been recorded.

387. A–T 716**. Bakhtin-Shiriaeva 71. From A.M. Komissarov, sixty-one years of age. Village of Zaovrazh'e, Volkhovskii raion (Leningrad), 1970. There are no other recordings.

388. A–T 720. Karnaukhova 127. Told by a blind and very old narrator, N.V. Lokhnovskii. This version is almost identical to that recorded in the Grimms' collection, 47, "The Juniper Tree." It is not otherwise recorded in Russian although there are versions in Belarusian and Ukrainian. Versions are known throughout Europe.

389. A–T 725. Khudiakov 87. Also known as "The Untold Dream." Not uncommon among the East Slavs. Well known in Irish, Danish, Flemish, and Hindi traditions.

390. A–T 725*. Kretov 54. Told by Anna Kirpasova, born in 1916, in 1968. Although motifs are borrowed from a number of sources, including the Old Testament, this original tale possesses its own logic.

391. A–T 729. Mitropol'skaia 106. From the village of Mitrofanovka, Vil'nius region. Told by M.V. Baliugin, sixty-eight in 1969. Related to tale type 735. Only one other recording of this tale type is known among the East Slavs. Known in Northern Europe, among the South Slavs and in French America.

392. A–T 735 + 735A. Afanas'ev 304. From the province of Novgorod. The type is common only among the East Slavs, although it has been recorded sporadically among their neighbors.

393. A–T 735A. Nikiforov 115. Nikiforov collected this tale from a fourteen-year-old boy, Ivan Emel'ianovich Kirin, of Chuchepaly, the Mezen. The 735 stories are all closely related and widely distributed among the East Slavs. These tales are not widely known outside the Baltic traditions and the West Slavic realms.

394. A–T 735A*. Sokolova, pp. 66–67. Told by Sofia Evdokimovna Bychkova, born in 1898, of the village of Kiritsy. Recorded in 1968. This is the only record of this tale.

395. A–T 735A**. Sokolovy 27. Told by Vasilii Vasil'evich Sharashov,

twenty-four years old and scarcely literate, from the village of Terekhova-Malakhova in the Belozersk district. This variant is unique in the East Slavic tradition.

396. A–T 735****. Mitropol'skaia 120. From the village of Rimkai, Ionav region. Told by A.F. Rodionova, eighty-five years old in 1964. Similar to a Polish tale recorded from west of here. This variant is rarely recorded in East Slavic territories.

397. A–T 735*****. Pereslavl-Zalesskii 7, pp. 90–91. Unique, according to SUS.

398. A–T 735G*. Anisimova 76–79. Recorded in the village of Malaia Izhmora, Zametchinskii region, Penza, in 1950. No other recordings attested.

399. A–T 736. Gospodarev 21. One of three Russian renditions. More common in Belarusian or Ukrainian. Known throughout Europe.

400. A–T 737B*. Ozarovskaia, Piatirech'e 27. Recorded in 1925 by Ozarovskaia of T.O. Kobeleva, seventy years old and blind, she loved telling stories to Ozarovskaia. Only Rozhdestvenskaia has another version of this tale in East Slavic. Versions are also known in Lithuanian and Serbo-Croatian.

BIBLIOGRAPHY

Short Citation	Source
Afanas'ev	Afanas'ev, A.N. *Narodnye russkie skazki.*, 3 vols. Ed. L.G. Barag and N.V. Novikow. Moscow, 1984.
Afanas'ev ne dlia pechati	Afanas'ev, A.N. *Zavetnye russkie skazki.* St. Petersburg, 1994.
Afanas'ev-Legendy	*Narodnye russkie legendy A.N. Afanas'eva.* Ed. V.S. Kuznetsova. Novosibirsk, 1990.
Anisimova	Anisimova, A.I., ed. *Pesni i skazki Penzenskoi oblasti.* Penza, 1953.
Astakhova	Astakhova, A.M. *Byliny severa.* Vol. II. Moscow and Leningrad, 1951.
Azadovskii	Azadovskii, M.K. *Verkhnelenskie skazki. Sbornik M.K. Azadovskogo.* Irkutsk, 1938.
Bakhtin-Shiriaeva	Bakhtin, V., and P. Shiriaeva, eds. *Skazki Leningradskoi oblasti.* Leningrad, 1976.
Balashov	Balashov, D.M., ed. *Skazki Terskogo berega Belogo moria.* Leningrad, 1970
Barag 1975	Barag, L.G., ed. *Skazki, legendy i predaniia Bashkirii.* Ufa, 1975.
Barag-Bashkiriia	Barag, L.G., ed. *Narodnye skazki, legendy, predaniia, i byli, zapisannye v Bashkirii na russkom iazyke.* Ufa, 1969.
Bardin	Bardin, A.V., ed. *Fol'klor Chkalovskoi oblasti.* Chkalov, 1940.
Blinova	Blinova, E.M., ed. *Skazy, pesni, chastushki.* Cheliabinsk, 1937.
Boi na mostu	Medvedev, Iu.M., ed. *Boi na Kalinovom mostu.* Leningrad, 1985.
Chernyshev	Chernyshev, V.I., ed. *Skazki Pushkinskikh mest.* Moscow and Leningrad, 1950.
Chudinskii	Chudinskii, E.A., comp. *Russkie narodnye skazki, pribautki, i pobasenki.* Moscow, 1864.
Derunov	Derunov, S. *Skazki Poshekhonskogo uezda. Trudy Yaroslavskogo gubernskog statisticheskogo komiteta, Vypusk 5.* Yaroslavl, 1869.
Gerasimov	Gerasimov, B. *Skazki, sobrannye v Zapadnykh predgor'iakh Altaia.* Zap. Semipalatinsk. otd. Russ. geograf. obshchestva, 1913. Part 7, pp. 1–87.
Gospodarev	*Skazki Filippa Pavlovicha Gospodareva*, ed. M.K. Azadovskii, (Commentaries by N.V. Novikov) Petrozavodsk, 1941.

Gurevich-Eliasova   Gurevich, A.V., and L.E. Eliasov. *Staryi fol'klor Pribaikal'ia*. Ulan-Ude, 1939.

Kalinnikov   Kalinnikov, I.F. *Sbornik skazok Orlovskoi gubernii*. [Orel, 1917?].

Karnaukhova   Karnaukhova, I.V., comp. *Skazki i predaniia severnogo kraia*. Moscow and Leningrad, 1934.

Kavkazskii sbornik   Semenov, P. "Skazki, zapisannye v stanitse Sleptsovskoi." *Sbornik materialov dlia opisaniia mestnostei i plemen Kavkaza*. Part 15. Tiflis and Makhachkala, 1893.

Khudiakov   *Velikorusskie skazki v zapisiakh I.A. Khudiakova*, ed. V.G. Bazanov and O.V. Alekseeva, Moscow and Leningrad, 1964.

Kitainik   Kitainik, M.G., ed. *Ural'skii fol'lor*. Sverdlovsk, 1949.

Komovskaia   Komovskaia, N.D., *Predaniia i skazki Gor'kovskoi oblasti*. Gor'kii, 1951.

Korguev   Nechaeva, A.N. *Skazki M.M. Korgueva*. Petrozavodsk, 1939.

Korol'kova   Pomerantseva, E.V., ed. *Russkie narodnye skazki A.N. Korol'kovoi*. Moscow, 1969.

Kovalev   Sokolov, Iu.M., ed. *Skazki I.F. Kovaleva*. Moscow, 1941.

Kozhemiakina   *Sibirskie skazki, zapisannye I.S. Korovkinym ot A.S. Kozhemiakinoi*. ed. N.A. Kargapolov, Novosibirsk, 1973.

Krasnozhenova   *Skazki Krasnoiarskogo kraia. Sbornik M.V. Krasnozhenovoi*. ed. M.K. Azadovskii and N.P. Andreev, Leningrad, 1937.

Kretov   Kretov, A.I., ed. *Narodnye skazki Voronezhskoi oblasti. Sovremennye zapisi*. Voronezh, 1977.

Kursk   Aristov, A., and M. Pavlov, eds. *Fol'klor. Chastushki, pesni, skazki, zapisannye v Kurskoi oblasti*. Kursk, 1939.

Lutovinova   Lutovinova, E.I., ed. *Russkie narodnye skazki o machekhe i padcheritse*. Novosibirsk, 1993.

Matveeva 1981   Matveeva, R.P., ed. *Russkie volshebnye skazki Sibiri*. Novosibirsk, 1981.

Matveeva and Leonova   Matveeva, R.P., and T.G. Leonova, eds. *Russkie skazki Sibiri i dal'nego vostoka: Volshebnye i o zhivotnykh*. Novosibirsk, 1993.

Mitropol'skaia   Mitropol'skaia, N.K., ed. *Russkii fol'klor v Litve*. Vilnius, 1975.

Nikiforov 1936   Nikiforov, A.I. "Pobeditel' zmeia." *Sovetskii fol'klor*, nos. 4–5. Moscow and Leningrad, 1936.

Nikiforov 1961   Nikiforov, A.I. *Severnorusskie skazki v zapisiakh A.I. Nikiforova*, Moscow and Leningrad, 1961.

Onchukov   Onchukov, N.E., ed. *Severnye skazki*. St. Petersburg, 1908, 2d ed. St. Petersburg, 1998

Otechestvennye zapiski   *Otvechestvennye zapiski*, 1857, CXIII, pp. 427–30. SPb 1839–1884.

Ozarovskaia   Ozarovskaia, O.E., ed. *Piatirechie*. Leningrad, 1931.

Pereslavl-Zalesskii   Smirnov, A.M., ed. *Etnograficheskie materialy po Pereslavl'-Zalesskomu uezdu Vladimirskoi gubernii*. Moscow 1922.

Pinega Tales   Simina, G.Ia., ed. *Pinezhskie skazki*. Arkhangel'sk, 1975

Pomerantseva   Pomerantseva, E.V., ed. *Russkie narodnye skazki*. Moscow, 1957.

Potiavin   Potiavin, V., ed. *Narodnaia poeziia Gor'kovskoi oblasti*. Gor'kii, 1960.

Pudozhskie skazki   Razumova, A.P., and T.I. Sen'kina. *Russkie narodnye skazki Pudozhskogo kraia*. Petrozavodsk, 1982.

Rozhdestvenskaia	Rozhdestvenskaia, N.I. *Skazy i skazki Belomor'ia i Pinezh'ia.* Arkhangel'sk, 1941.
Sadovnikov	Sadovnikov, D.N., ed. *Skazki i predaniia Samarskogo kraia.* Zapiski RGO. St. Petersburg, 1884.
Serova	Serova, M. *Sbornik russkikh skazok.* Leningrad, 1925.
Severnaia-Dvina	Mitrofanova, V.V., and L.V. Fedorova. *Narodnoe tvorchestvo Severnoi Dviny.* Arkhangel'sk, 1966.
Shastina	Shastina, E.I., ed. *Skazki Prilen'ia.* Irkutsk, 1974.
Smirnov	Smirnov, A.M., ed. *Sbornik velikorusskikh skazok arkhiva Russkogo geograficheskogo obshchestva.* Parts 1 and 2. Petrograd, 1917.
Sokolova	Sokolova, V.K., ed. *Skazki zemli Riazanskoi.* Riazan, 1970.
Sokolovy	Sokolov, B., and Iu. Sokolov. *Skazki i pesni Belozerskogo kraia.* Moscow, 1915.
Skazki Karelia	Razumova, A.P., and T.I. Sen'kina, eds. *Russkie narodnye skazki Karel'skogo Pomor'ia.* Petrozavodsk, 1979.
Tales of Saratov Region	Akimova, T.N., and P.D. Stepanov, eds. *Skazki Saratovskoi oblasti.* Saratov, 1937.
Tambov Tales	Sokolov, B.M., and E.V. Gofman, eds. *Tambovskii fol'klor.* Tambov, 1941.
Tumilevich 1945	Tumilevich, F.V., ed. *Skazki kazakov-nekrasovtsev.* Rostov on the Don, 1945.
Tumilevich 1958	Tumilevich, F.V., ed. *Russkie narodnye skazki kazakov-nekrasovtsev.* Rostov on the Don, 1958.
Tumilevich 1961	Tumilevich, F.V., ed. *Skazki i predaniia kazakov-nekrasovtsev.* Rostov on the Don, 1961.
Upper Lena Tales	Azadovskii, M.K. *Verkhnelenskie skazki. Sbornik M.K. Azadovskogo.* Irkutsk, 1938.
Vasilenko	Vasilenko, V.A., ed. *Skazki, poslovitsy, zagadki. Sbornik ustnogo narodnogo tvorchestva Omskoi oblasti.* Omsk, 1955.
Vladimir	Pomerantseva, E.V., ed. *Traditsionnyi fol'klor Vladimirskoi derevni.* Moscow, 1972.
XIX C. Tales	Novikov, N.V., comp. *Russkie skazki v zapisiakh i publikatsiiakh pervoi poloviny XIX veka.* Moscow and Leningrad, 1961.
XVI C. Tales	Novikov, N.V., comp. *Russkie skazki v rannikh zapisiakh i publikatsiiakh (XVI–XVIII vv).* Leningrad, 1971.
Zelenin-Perm (1997)	Zelenin, D.K., ed. *Velikorusskie skazki Permskoi gubernii.* St. Petersburg, 1997.
Zelenin-Perm (1991)	Zelenin, D.K., ed. *Velikorusskie skazki Permskoi gubernii.* Moscow, 1991.
Zelenin-Viatka	Zelenin, D.K., ed. *Velikorusskie skazki Viatskoi gubernii.* St. Petersburg, 1915.
Zhivaia starina	*Zhivaia starina.* (Russian Geographical Society). St. Petersburg, 1890–1916.

Jack V. Haney received bachelor's degrees in Russian language and literature from the University of Washington (1962) and Oxford University (1964), where he was a Rhodes Scholar. In 1970 he completed a D.Phil. in medieval Russian literature at Oxford with a dissertation on Maxim the Greek. He is professor of Slavic languages and literatures at the University of Washington, Seattle, where he teaches medieval Russian literature, Russian folklore, and the Russian language, and is chairman of the department.